The History of Bandon, and the Principal Towns in the West Riding of County Cork / by George Bennett ; with Two Chromo-Lithographic Illustrations

George Bennett

Faithfully Yours
George Bennett

THE

HISTORY OF BANDON,

AND THE

PRINCIPAL TOWNS IN THE WEST RIDING OF COUNTY CORK.

ENLARGED EDITION,
With Two Chromo-Lithographic Illustrations.

BY

GEORGE BENNETT, ESQ., B.L.

"The pleasant Bandon crowned with many a wood."
SPENSER.

CORK:
FRANCIS GUY, PRINTER AND PUBLISHER,
MUNSTER WORKS, 70, PATRICK STREET.

1869.

PREFACE.

THE history of a town, or of a locality, is often but the history of a nation in miniature. It frequently happens that the same passions, the same interests, the same aspirations, that are to be found in a small community, are to be found in a large one—indeed, this is generally the case where the same race occupies both. But when the two communities are peopled by different races—when the conqueror comes to take up his abode on the lands of the conquered—history is then very often but one protracted tale of the conqueror's difficulties; of the foes that stood arrayed against him on every side; of the circumstances that impeded his efforts to move forward; and of the hostility—often of the deadliest kind—that confronted him at every step.

Although some of the lands which our colonists rescued from the woods and the forests were almost worthless in the eyes of the former owners, and more of them, worse still, lying under stagnant waters, or were quagmires accessible only to the outlaw and the wolf, yet, when the settlers drained them, and when they were cultivated, then the original proprietor and his kern began to plot for their restoration; consequently the colonist, who had to labour hard to create a farm, had then to fight hard to keep it. The Saxon plantee in O'Mahony's country had to handle the arquebus as well as the mattock—he was as familar with powder and lead as he was with barley and seed oats. His Irish neighbours looked with longing eyes on the fruits of his toil. If they could but lay hands on his comfortable homestead—if they could but make their own of his cattle, and enjoy his cultivated fields —they could bask all day in the sun, and denounce the perfidious Saxon. But the Saxon, who won his fields and his home by dint of perseverance and hard work, had no idea of allowing others to possess them against his will. Hence the perpetual strife between the Saxon who had, and the Celt who had not; between the civilized Englishman, and the barbarous Irishman; between those who lived in cheerful homes, and who supplied their tables with beef and mutton, and those who dwelt in wretched cabins composed of wattles, plastered over with cow-dung and mud, and who lived on roots and whey.

Our Bandon colonists came over in the latter half of the reign of Queen Elizabeth, and they settled in a district escheated to the crown by the rebellion of a local chieftain. The country into which they had come had but little to recommend it. One who was alive at the time, and who subsequently became its possessor, describes the site of the new colony "as a meer waste bog and wood, serving for a retreat and harbour to woodkerns, rebels, thieves, and wolves." But, by the magic of their skill and industry, this was soon all changed. Not only did they alter the face of the country, but they built themselves a town, within whose walls they could shelter themselves in time of need, and they spread themselves about on every side for miles. They struck root in the earth; and now, like a brave old oak that stood many a gust of wind and many a storm; whose head oft bent beneath the force of the blast; whose ponderous limbs have creaked as they swayed to and fro; whose branches have beat many a time wildly in the air; whose leaves have fallen thick and heavy upon the glade—yet after the lapse of three centuries its heart is as sound as ever; it still puts forth its young shoots; it still blooms in all the pride of strength and maturity; and its vigorous grasp is still on the soil, and is as firm as of yore.

During the progress of our researches in connection with the colony whose history we have endeavoured to trace, we have noted much interesting matter connected with various other settlements in the west riding of this county; and as the plantees in those settlements had to undergo toils and dangers similiar to those of the Bandon colonists—and in some instances even greater, as they had no fortifications, or even an outwork, to stay the rush of the great wave that would fain engulf them—we have judged that the recital of their struggles too, to overcome and to save themselves from the common danger, would be acceptable to our readers. We are also actuated by another motive—that of essaying to preserve some of those old legends which garb with a deep interest the mouldering ruins of many an old keep, and some of those reminiscences—voices—which, as it were, speak to us from the grave, and tell us of the heroism of former days, and of scenes to many of which our age is happily a stranger.

To do this correctly; to relate any circumstance which we have thought may throw light on the social progress of our townsmen, their religious and political views, their passions; to describe the contests between our colonists and the natives in the great fight for supremacy; to narrate how at one time the former overwhelmed the latter, and floated uppermost, and at another time how they were nearly overwhelmed and sunk themselves; to portray the feelings and influences which actuated both the contending parties; to accomplish all this fairly and dispassionately, is the aim of the following pages.

HILL HOUSE, BANDON.
1869.

CONTENTS.

CHAPTER I.

CHAPTER II.

CHAPTER III.

CHAPTER IV.

CHAPTER V.

CHAPTER VI.

CHAPTER VII.

CHAPTER VIII.

CHAPTER IX.

CHAPTER X.

CHAPTER XI.

CHAPTER XII.

CHAPTER XIII.

CHAPTER XIV.

CHAPTER XV.

CHAPTER XVI.

CHAPTER XVII.

CHAPTER XVIII.

CHAPTER XIX.

CHAPTER XX.

CHAPTER XXI.

CHAPTER XXII.

CHAPTER XXIII.

CHAPTER XXIV.

CHAPTER XXV.

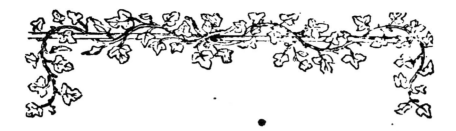

HISTORY OF BANDON,

AND OF THE

PRINCIPAL TOWNS IN THE WEST RIDING OF THE

COUNTY OF CORK.

CHAPTER I.

DEFEAT OVERTAKES THE DESMONDS—SOUTH MUNSTER A WASTE—QUEEN ELIZABETH RESOLVES TO COLONIZE IT WITH ENGLISH PROTESTANTS—THE O'MAHONYS OF CASTLE-MAHON—BEECHER'S PATENT—NAMES OF THE FIRST SETTLERS—THE SITE OF THE TOWN "A MERE WASTE BOG"—ALL THE ADJACENT LANDS RECLAIMED—THE RIVER BANDON.

THE rebellion of the great Earl of Desmond* was over. That great effort which the Geraldines had made to shake off the English yoke, ended as disastrously as many a previous struggle. For awhile the insurgents were victorious, and their hopes rose high with their success; but the tide turned on them, as it had often turned on them before, and those who rode out triumphantly on the ebb were overwhelmed with the flow.

So it was with the Red Earl. After carrying all before him for a time, defeat overtook him. His brother, Sir James, was captured,

---

* Gerald, the sixteenth Earl of Desmond, familiarly known as the Red Earl.

tried by court-martial, his body was quartered, and his head was set up over one of the gates of Cork. His brother, Sir John, after being stunned by a blow from a horseman's staff, had his head cut off and sent to Dublin. His body was sent to Cork, where it was hung up ignominiously by the heels on a gibbet at North-gate. And he himself—who upon one occasion narrowly escaped being taken prisoner by rushing out of his bed in his shirt, and hiding in the very depth of winter under the bank of a river, where he remained for some time up to his chin in the water—was hunted like a beast of prey across swamps and bogs, through woods, over hills and mountains, and was at last found in a lonely ruin in the wilds of Kerry.

"Spare me, I am the Earl of Desmond!" said an old man who lay stretched before the fire; but a blow from a sword had, ere he spoke, nearly cut off his arm, and life's purple current was flowing fast. Another blow, and the head which had brought such ruin upon himself, his kindred, and his associates, was soon to be seen a ghastly trophy on London Bridge.

The country, which was the theatre of this great devastating war for so many years, was a desert. There was not a fortress or a town, or a dwelling, or a stack of corn to which the Desmonds had come that they had not burned or destroyed, lest the English should possess it; and the English left not a house or a granary, or a habitation of any kind in their course that they did not demolish, lest the Geraldines should possess it. Thus it was that the vast tract of country which was the seat of war did not contain a fortified castle, nor a tenanted cabin, and had neither corn nor cattle. The greater portion of the population had starved to death, and the rest were starving. "All nearly were brought to such wretchedness," says Spenser, "as that any stony heart must rue the same. Out of every corner of the woodes and glynnes they came creeping forth upon their handes, for their legges could not bear them. They looked like anatomies of death; they spoke like ghosts, crying out of their grave; they did eat the dead carrions, happy when they could find them."

Into this wasted and almost dispeopled region Elizabeth resolved to introduce English colonies. By doing so she expected that, in a short time, the colonists would by their industry and skill turn waste lands into corn-fields and orchards, and occupy the pastures with sheep and cows. She expected that prosperity would soon reward their perseverance; and that South Munster, which had been for many years a heavy drain upon her exchequer, would for the future be a support to it; and that, should another outbreak occur, then she could reckon on the assistance of the colonists, and place unbounded confidence in their fidelity.

This was not the case with her Irish subjects. Although there were many among them upon whom she had conferred grants of land; whom she honoured and petted from time to time; yet she knew they only kept their oath of allegiance to her until they were strong enough to break it. What reliance could be placed in the people when their leaders laughed at their own protestations, and thought as little of breaking their oaths as they did of " drinking unstrained milk ?" How could she ever rely on the Desmonds again ? when Sir James of Desmond and his partizans knelt before the Lord-President, with hands uplifted, and with " countenances betraying their great sorrow ; with the eyes of my heart sore weeping," said Sir James, " and bewailing my most devilish life past. I acknowledge myself to have most wickedly rebelled against God, and most undutifully against my prince, and most unnaturally against my native country."

He was believed, and he was pardoned; and immediately after he set off for France, where he remained for two years soliciting help to invade the very country which he had used most "unnaturally," and to overpower the very sovereign against whom he had "rebelled most undutifully." Being unsuccessful with the French king, " who misliketh to deal in Irish matters," he proceeded to Spain ; where he was introduced to Phillip the Second, by whom he was furnished with letters of introduction to Gregory the Thirteenth. At Rome, Saunders and Allen,* two zealous priests, entered warmly into his designs; and they obtained from his Holiness a bull, addressed to the prelates and nobles of Ireland, exhorting them to join the penitent of Kilmallock ; and promising the same indulgences to any one that would kill a Protestant† in Ireland, as had been previously offered to any one that would kill a Turk.

---

* Allen was soon after killed in battle; and Saunders, who was subsequently raised to the dignity of Papal Legate, was found lying dead in a wood in Kerry, and his body half-eaten by wolves.

† A book appeared about this time: it was dedicated to Queen Elizabeth, and was entitled :— *The supplications of the blood of the English most lamentably murdered in Ireland, crying out of the earth for revenge.*

Sir John of Desmond, whose protestations of loyalty had imposed on the authorities, soon joined the force which Sir James had brought over under the auspices of Saunders and Allen, and signalled his hatred to those who treated him with so much tenderness by an act of the basest treachery. Entering Tralee at midnight, he found his particular friend, Henry Davels, asleep. Being aroused, Davels became alarmed at seeing men with drawn swords around his bed, but on recognizing his old acquaintance, Sir John, his fears forsook him, and he called out to him in his usual friendly tone :—

" What, son ! What's the matter ?"

" No more son—nor no more father," gruffly replied Sir John ; " but make thyself ready, for die thou shalt !"

Not only was poor Davels put to death, but also every one who was in the house when Sir John and his party entered it. Even the earl himself—(" who hath been before her Majesty ; whom her Highness liked well for his plainness ; and hath good hope of his truth and constance ") —detained in Dublin on his parole, going out one day under the pretence of hunting, showed his own estimate of his plighted word by trotting off to Desmond ; where he did not remain long until he rendered his English friends apprehensive for the safety of the country.

It is no wonder then that Elizabeth " should encourage and enable our loving subjects of good behaviour, and accoumpt, within our realme of England, to inhabit and re-people a great part of the province of Munster, which, through the late rebellion of the earl of Desmond and others his confederates, hath been utterlie wasted and unpeopled, and made desolate ; and that, as well by the attainders of the earl and his confederates, as by the forfeiture, escheat, and other lawful means, sundry lordships, manors, lands, tenements, and hereditaments within the province, are come into our hands ; and whereas, &c."

All these sundry lordships and tenements here referred to amounted in the aggregate to 547,628 acres ; and this large extent of country was expected in a few years to be inhabited by twenty thousand English people.

Elizabeth had set her heart upon the colonization of Munster. She sent Sir John Popham,* her Attorney-General, down to Somersetshire,

* Sir John Popham was descended from an ancient family that was formerly seated at Popham, in Hants. He was born in Somersetshire, in 1531. When about sixteen years old he entered Baliol College, Oxford ; and, upon obtaining his degree,

to coax the gentry in that district to send over the junior members of their families as undertakers, and caused letters to be written to people of distinction in every shire in England, with the same intent. To such as would come she offered estates in fee, at twopence and threepence an acre. Rent not to commence until the end of the third year, and even then a half-year's rent was to be accepted in lieu of a whole for three years more.† For every twelve thousand acres thus bestowed the undertaker was to plant eighty-six English Protestant‡ families upon the lands, and smaller or larger grants were to be peopled in the same ratio. He was to erect a suitable residence for each family. Three houses for freeholders,§ to each of whom was to be assigned three hundred acres at least, at the rate of sixteen feet and a-half to the lug or pole. Three houses for farmers, to each of whom was to be assigned four hundred acres of like measurement. Twenty-one for copyholders or other base tenures, to each of whom was to be assigned one hundred acres; and to the residue there was to be assigned fifty acres, twenty-five acres, or ten acres.

---

he became a law student in the Middle Temple. He was not at the bar many years before he enjoyed an extensive practice, and had attained to great eminence. In 1570 he was made sergeant-at-law. He was appointed to the office of solicitor-general, and subsequently to that of attorney-general; and in 1581 he was made Lord Chief-Justice of the Court of Queen's Bench. His "Reports and Cases" display considerable ability and great industry. In 1607 he died, leaving—besides seven daughters—one son, Sir Francis; who married Annie, daughter of John Dudley, by whom he had five sons and eight daughters. Amongst the sons were Alexander, one of Cromwell's lords, and Edward, one of the "sea generals" of the parliamentary fleet. Admiral Popham is described as a brave man, but violently attached to independence. He died of fever at Dover, in 1651, and was interred in St. John's Chapel, Westminster Abbey. At the restoration, his body was dragged out of his grave, at the same time as that of Mrs. Elizabeth Cromwell, the Lord Protector's mother, who had been buried with great state within the abbey walls. Mrs. Cromwell's remains were flung contemptuously into a hole dug before the doorway of one of prebendaries of St. Margaret's; but through some interest which the relatives of Admiral Popham's wife, Anne (daughter of William Carre), had with the government, his were given up to them, and his monument was permitted to remain where it was, but with the inscription reversed. The Bandon Pophams claim descent from the same parent stock as Sir John; and it is very probable that her Majesty's attorney-general, who endeavoured to persuade the gentry of his native shire to send some of their younger children over to this new colony, should also have induced some of his own kindred to do the same.

† Bogs and mountains were to pay no rent until improved, and were then only to be charged at the rate of a halfpenny an acre.

‡ The planters were to be English, and their heirs were to marry none but of English birth. The settlers were not to permit any of "the meer Irish" to be maintained in any of their families.

§ Every freeholder, from the year 1590, was bound to furnish a horse and armed horseman; and a copyholder, an armed footman. An undertaker for 12,000 acres had to supply three horsemen and six footmen.

The undertakers did not perform what they undertook. Most of them did not bring over the stipulated number of tenants. Many of them made leases and conveyances to the Irish, whom they were bound wholly to exclude. Some of them became absentees; and several abandoned their seigniories to their former possessors. In fine, it does not appear that a single one of the entire number of patentees complied with the conditions of his patent excepting Phane Beecher, the founder of the colony of Bandon-Bridge; who carried out the intentions of his patent with such fidelity, as to elicit from one of his contemporaries, who was engaged in an enterprise similar to his own, the following high testimonial to his integrity, and to his disinterestedness and success:—

"This Master Beecher," said he, "by means of his honest and plaine dealing, rather seeking to replenish his countrie with people, according to her Majesty's grant, than esteeming any great gain to himself, hath gotten more sufficient tennauntes into his saide countrie than any other two that doe attempte the like within the province of Munster. Soe wel doe oure countriemen esteem of his worde, that, of my own knowledge, a dossen gentlemen of good accompt have dealth with him for five hundreth acres apeace onely upon his report; none of which ever saweth same. But there is no hope of any more land to be had of him, for he hath already, to pleasure his countrie, straightned his demeasnes, which, I suppose, he would have done if he had had half the Desmond's land; so many are desirous to inhabbitte with him."*

If every other planter had executed the behests of his sovereign with the same honesty of purpose and assiduity as Master Beecher, South Munster would be to this day as loyal and devoted to the crown of England as any other portion of the British isles.

Among the confederates of the Earl of Desmond was Cnogher O'Mahony.† This young chieftain entered warmly into the earl's

---

* A brief description of Ireland, made in the year 1589, by Robert Payne.

† Cnogher O'Mahony, of Castle-Mahon, was of royal extraction. He was descended from Mathgamhain, who derived his descent through a long line of ancestors from Cas, brother to Nadfroch, son of Core, who was king of Munster; and who was himself descended from Olioll Olum, who was also a king of Munster, and who died A.D. 234. The O'Mahonys of Castle-Mahon were not a powerful sept. The utmost that they at any time were able to bring into the field were twenty-six horse—no gallow glasses—and one hundred and twenty kern. When the Lord-Deputy, Sir Henry Sidney, visited Cork in 1575, amongst those who came to pay their respects to him was O'Mahony, whom he represents as "a man of small force, although a proper countrie." They came into this neighbourhood from Carbery in 1460—according to the report of an Inquisition held in Cork in 1584—and possessed themselves of lands at that time the property of the crown, but previously the

designs, and lost both life and estate in his cause. His course was a brief one. At the early age of twenty-three, death overtook him in one of the many sanguinary engagements which took place between the Queen's troops and the rebels. But much injury may be inflicted upon an enemy, even in a short space of time, by an active and resolute leader; and it would seem that such a one was Cnogher O'Mahony, as not a single acre of the large inheritance he left behind him was ever restored to any of his kit or kin.

The forfeitures of O'Mahony included his residence at Castle-Mahon, and his lands—which lay for several miles on both sides of the river Bandon. The castle and a large portion of the lands, amounting in the aggregate to fourteen thousand acres, were conferred on Phane Beecher, son of Alderman Henry Beecher, of London.

The patent, which is dated September the 30th, 1588, grants to " Phane Beecher, of London, the Castle of O'Mahony (*alias* Mahown's Castle), and the moiety of all the lands and hereditaments therein— 14,000 acres—at the yearly rent of £66 13s. 4d." By the conditions of the patent, Beecher was bound " to erect, or cause to be erected, houses for fourscore and eleven—ninety-one families. One, the principal habitation for Henry Beecher; six others for freeholders, each of whom was to get three hundred acres of land, meadow, pasture, and wood; six more houses for farmers, to each of whom he was to assign four hundred acres of meadow, pasture, and wood; forty-two other houses

---

property of the Barry Oges, by whom they were forfeited in 1399. That they did " intrude" upon this portion of Kinalmeaky in 1460, is very probable; but there can be no doubt whatever but that the O'Mahonys owned this very country long before the Barrys ever set foot upon our shores. We know that the territories of the king of Rathleann, whose name was O'Mahony, were on both sides of the river Bandon. Even the very name of the barony itself, into which they are said to have illegally entered, Cineal-m-bece (the race of Bece), shows in what remote ages the O'Mahonys were connected with it; Bece being the name of one of their ancestors who lived there in the seventh century. O'Maghthamna, one of the O'Mahony kings, lived in Rathleann long prior to the English invasion. This royal residence— Rathleann—was on the banks of the river Bandon, and its site is said to have been occupied by a castle subsequently erected upon it by one of O'Maghthamna's descendants, and called Castle-Mahon (now Castle Bernard). We are convinced that Castle-Mahon does cover the site of this old rath; for what place is there throughout the entire domain of the O'Mahonys in Kinalmeaky where a representative of that royal line would be more likely to erect a stately residence—particularly as it was the only one of the kind they had in Kinalmeaky—than upon the very spot where his forefathers lived for several centuries; which was associated with their greatness and their glory, and where they exercised kingly authority, and wore the crown? It was in Rathleann, Saint Fin Bar—who flourished between A.D. 600 and 630, and who is universally known as the founder of the Cork Cathedral—was born.

for copyholders, each of whom was to be assigned one hundred acres of land similar to the former ; and, to each of the rest of the householders, lots consisting of fifty acres, twenty-five acres, and ten acres. If houses were not made before seven years, then commissioners may take portion where assignment was not completed, and retain same until the houses were erected. If patentee, his heirs, assigns, &c., do at any time hereafter make any alienation, conveyance, or estate of the premises, or any part thereof, to any person or persons being meer Irish, not descended of an original English ancestor of name or blood, and shall not redeem the same within one year next after such alienation, then it shall be lawful to and for us, our heirs and successors, to re-enter such part as shall be alienated, as if the Letters Patent had not been made."

The 14,000 acres bestowed "were lands of all sorts, and allotted for one whole seigniory for twelve thousand acres." The overplus of 2,000 acres being allowed by the commissioners in respect of the waste bogs, heath, and mountains. The lands to be held in fee-farm, "as of our castle of Carriggroghane."

This seigniory was on the southern banks of the river, and included the site of the southern portion of the town of Bandon, Castle-Mahon, and the adjacent lands; stretching as far to the west as the western boundaries of Farrinashishery. Whilst, on the eastern side, it was terminated by the Bridewell river, at that time known as the Little river.

Another portion of O'Mahony's country was bestowed on Sir Bernard Grenville. This was on the northern bank of the river, and extended from the little rivulet, adjoining which at present stands the Provincial Bank; and as far to the west as the stream which forms the eastern boundary of the village of Ballineen.

Beecher set to work with the energy of a man of business. He brought over many tenants to people some of his lands; and more of them he disposed of in convenient lots to those who undertook to perform certain obligations; just as we have seen land companies in our own day, who, having obtained from the government a grant of a tract of country in Australia or New Zealand, part with it in suitable lots, and on certain conditions, to those who are willing to leave the old country to try their fortune in a new.

Shipload after shipload of the colonists arrived in Kinsale harbour, where they landed, and made their way along a bridle-path. The bridle-path led from Kinsale to Roche's Castle, at Poulnalonge; thence along the northern bank of the river to Downdanial Castle; and from thence it continued its course still along the river's northern banks, until it reached a ford well-known in these days, the site of which may still be recognized by the rocks which appear above the surface of the water, a few yards to the west of the principal bridge of our town.

The country through which they passed was deeply wooded; and they struggled through it with more or less difficulty, until they reached Castle-Mahon. Many of the strangers had brought with them their wives and children, hazarding their all upon the venture; but more of them came alone, resolved on seeing and judging of the probabilities of getting on, before they left their peaceful homesteads in England for the swamps and the forests of a country where packs of wolves roamed about almost unmolested, and which a fierce and hardy native race claimed as their own.

Amongst those that settled here about this time—either being directly brought over by Beecher himself, or who procured lands from him and established little colonies of their own, or who came over to the infant settlement for purposes of trade and commerce—were the following :—

Abbott,	Clark,	Evans,	Greenway,	Jifford,
Alcock,	Christmas,	Ellwell,	Gardiner,	Joyce,
Adderly,	Carey,	Elliott,	Glenfoild,	Kerall,
Atkins,	Crofte,	Elms,	Giles,	Kito,
Austen,	Cox,	Flemming,	Grenville,	Kent,
Bernard,	Cotterall,	Fondwell,	Greatrakes,	Kingston,
Baldwin,	Clear,	Franck,	Grimstead,	Light,
Brayly,	Cooper,	Farre,	Hewitt,	Little,
Bennett,	Chipstow,	Flewollan,	Harvie,	Linscombe,
Birde,	Cable,	Fenton,	Holbedyr,	Law,
Beamish,	Cleather,	French,	Hodder,	Langford,
Brooke,	Churchill,	Franklin,	Howard,	Lapp,
Blacknell,	Cecill,	Fuller,	Hussey,	Lissone,
Burwood,	Dolbers,	Fryher,	Hitchcock,	Lambe,.
Berry,	Drake,	Frost,	Hill,	Lucas,
Booll,	Downes,	Grant,	Harris,	Lane,
Bramlet,	Dunkin,	Grimes,	Hales,	Lake,
Blofield,	Daunte,	Gamon,	Hammett,	Monoarke,
Coombes,	Davis,	Griffith,	Hardinge,	Moaks,
Corkwell,	Deane,	Green,	Jones,	Mowberry,
Chambers,	Dun,	Goodchild,	Jackson,	Meldon,
Cadlopp,	Dashwood,	Grimster,	Jumper,	Martyn,

Margets,	Rashleigh,	Scott,	Thompson,	Whaley,
Newce,	Radley,	Savage,	Taylor,	Wight,
Newman,	Rake,	Skinner,	Thomas,	Williams,
Nelson,	Richmond,	Skeuce,	Tobye,	Wheeler,
Osmond,	Spenser,	Shephard,	Tucker,	White,
Porter,	Symons,	Smith,	Travers,	Woodroffe,
Perrott,	Synoger,	Spratt,	Tanner,	Ware,
Poole,	Stanley,	Seymour,	Valley,	Warren,
Pitt,	Skipwith,	Sweete,	Vick,	Willobe,
Peyton,	Snookes,	Sugar,	Vane,	Watkins,
Preston,	Saunders,	Tickner,	Woolfe,	Wheatly,
Popham,	Skipwith,	Turner,	Wiseman,	Wade.

The country into which they had come did not lie in the track of communication between the towns already existing in the west of the county and its principal city. Should a traveller set out from Bantry, intent on reaching Cork, he should pass through a portion of O'Donovan's country, until he came to Ross. His route then lay through lands possessed by some sept of the Mac Carthys, until he arrived at Timoleague, from which place he journeyed through the territory of the Mac Carthy Reagh, to Kinsale. Upon leaving Kinsale, he made straight for Ballinahassig; and from thence over bare hills, and through an almost uninhabited district, until he approached the walls of Cork. The interior of the country—at least that region now occupied by the towns of Bandon, Clonakilty, and Dunmanway—was entirely unknown to the ordinary wayfarer. Indeed, so dreary and so insecure was the site upon which Bandon itself is built, that one who naturally took a great interest in the town's prosperity describes it as having been " a mere waste bog, serving as a retreat for woodkerns, rebels, thieves, and wolves." Whenever the Irish were worsted in a fight with the English at this side of Cork, they took to their heels in hot haste for this locality; well knowing that the latter were unable to pursue them " amongst the fastnesses of Kinalmeaky." And such was the unenviable pre-eminence those fastnesses had obtained for sheltering the worst kind of woodkern, and the meanest sort of rebel, that for many years—even after the colony had been firmly established—" You Kinalmeaky thieves"* was a term of bitter reproach, applied by an

---

* Even after the breaking out of the great rebellion of 1641, Lord Muskerry, who was one of the most conspicuous leaders in that great revolt, was so annoyed by the predatory propensities of many of his followers, that he executed several of them, " and sent some of the Kinalmeaky thieves to Bandon." The townspeople—who were unable to leave a head of cattle outside the walls, lest these nimble freebooters should make their own of it—understood the hint, and they hanged them forthwith.

English settler to those who ravaged his homestead, or drove away his cattle.

Although Kinalmeaky had its disadvantages, it had its advantages also. A beautiful stream, gushing from the bosom of Mount Owen, and swelled by tributary after tributary, wound its sinuous course among meadows—rich with the sweetest pastures, and rivalling the emerald in its hue. A grateful soil awaited the plough, ready to repay the husbandman for his skill and his toil; and there was no country better adapted for breeding horses, and for multiplying flocks and herds. A great deal of the rough land on the northern side of the river, and which is now occupied by an industrious and thriving tenantry, was at that time overspread with woods. It was the same on the southern side. Lands, which now annually produce oats and potatoes, were covered with timber for scores of miles. That there were many acres of green meadow along the green banks of the Green river,* and fertile lands in the glades and valleys, without a tree standing on them, is true; but the numerous woods thickly scattered throughout gave the entire scene the appearance of a vast forest.† And a vast forest it resembled in more aspects than one.

The devastating wars,‡ which had lately wasted the country of the O'Mahony and O'Crowley, had produced a solitude upon which no one intruded; unless when some half-naked savage, who was owned by a Mac Carthy or a Hurly, came through the thicket in quest of a wounded deer. And the silence—deep and grave—was unbroken, save when the wild pigeon cooed to its missing mate; or when the outlaw or the woodkern, brought to bay, shrieked for mercy from his pursuers.

About an English mile eastward of Castle-Mahon was a strip of flat land called Inis-fraoc (the heather inch). The Bandon river flowed in front of it. What is now known as the Bridewell river flowed in its

---

* One of the ancient names of the Bandon was the Glasslyn, or Green river.

† Writing of Kinalmeaky, in 1589, Mr. Payne says, " In this countrie is greate woodes ; the trees of wonderful length." " Twenty years past," writes Lord Cork (in 1606), " Bandon-Bridge was a great many woods."
" Around the Bandon of fair woods."
O'HERRIN.
" The pleasant Bandon crowned with many a wood."
SPENSER.

‡ Previous to the Desmond rebellion, some parts of this country were fairly inhabited; and it would appear from the tombstone of Willoughby Turner, who died in 1531, and was buried in the Roman Catholic graveyard at Ballymodan, that even some English adventurers were living in it many years previous to the earl's revolt.

rear, and on its eastern side ; and a stream of water formed its western
boundary.   Upon this strip of land, which is upwards of twenty-five
acres in extent, Beecher resolved to build the nucleus of a town.   For
this purpose it was admirably adapted.   The waters which surrounded
it could furnish mill-wheels with abundant water-power.   The same
waters could be rendered a defence against the enemy in time of danger.
And the proximity of the proposed settlement to Kinsale would give
the settlers facilities for exporting their grain, their hides, their wool,
and their cattle ; and returning with salt, iron, and other rough requirements of a young colony.

The plantees went to work with the energy and perseverance of their
race.   The heather-   arred in every direction with foundations.
Quarries of the best building stone were discovered in the neighbourhood,
and were speedily availed of.   The quivering ring of the axe, and the
crash of falling timber, were heard from morn till night.   The saw,
and the other carpenters' tools they had brought with them, were constantly in use in making doors and windows, and in shaping slabs for
roofs and floors.   The houses were constructed more with the design of
affording immediate shelter than of being either durable or ornamental.
A stone gable held the fire-place and flue ; so that when the flames
whisked up the chimney from the logs of wood that boiled the settler's
supper, or around which he and his friends sat and talked of their
prospects in the new country, they could do no injury.   All the rest of
the house was boards, laths, and plaster.   Streets sprang up on every side
of Inis-fraoc, and the dark green heather, which had often bent beneath
the foot of the fugitive kern or the wolf, was gone; and its place was
occupied by snug habitations, and an industrious people.*   One of the
principal streets faced the principal river.   Another faced the Bridewell river.   Midway, in the rear of these two, was the Main Street, now
known as the South Main Street.   Between these were several streets.
In fact, so numerous had they become, that before many years the settle-

---

* Increasing the worldly wealth of his people was not the only solicitude of Mr.
Beecher. " He took special care," says Mr. Payne, " that every inhabitor there should
have as much libertie as a freeholder in England.   He also had ordained for his
countrie a learned preacher, a free-schoole, and a good yearly stipend for the relieving
of mained souldiers, impotent and poore aged persons; and for perpetual continuance
he hath abated every of his tennauntes at least twopence rent for every acre for ever,
which others take ; and hath charged his owne demesnes with noe lesse ; soe that if a
few years be ended—if God blesses his proceedings—those partes will be more like a
civill citie in England than a rude countrie, as late it was in Ireland.

ment on the inch was officially recorded as "the town lately built on the southern side of the Bandon." Sir Bernard Granville was the patentee upon whose grant stands the northern side of the town of Bandon. He does not appear to have made any effort at direct colonization himself, as he leased some of his lands to John Richmond, and nearly all the rest to William Newce. Richmond assigned to the latter, and thus Newce became owner of most of the interests conveyed by Granville.

Captain Newce* was anxious to build a town like his thriving neighbours on the other side of the river; and, with that object in view, he selected a central plot on his estate, and resolved to perpetuate his connection with the new settlement by giving it his name. He was diverted from this design, however, by an incident which showed the fierce hatred entertained by the natives for the new comers. Whilst measuring the ground for the various tenements and thoroughfares which were to grace Newcestown, he put his foot on the end of the line:—"Here," said he, "will be the end of this street." A petty chieftain, who stood immediately behind him, heard the remark; and suddenly stooping down, drove his skein with great force through the outstretched foot, into the ground. "May you end there yourself, too!" said O'Crowley, as he escaped unharmed to the surrounding woods.†

This gross outrage, combined with fears least the supply of water there would be insufficient for manufacturing purposes, and that he need expect no protection or favour from the Irish, induced him to renounce his pet project,‡ and to adopt another; so that instead of erecting a town amongst the hills of Moragh, to rival the town lately built on the southern side of the river, he chose rather to join with it, by bringing his settlement to the river's northern side. He did so, and the ancient and loyal borough of Bandon-Bridge is the result.

The settlers on both sides of the river having now but one interest, and being, in fact, now members of the same colony, determined, before a habitation arose in Coildarac (the oak wood), on being united by a

---

* Subsequently Sir William Newce. Captain Newce commanded a company of foot, under Sir George Carew, at the seige of Kinsale.

† Newce, who is said to have been very kindly disposed to the Irish before this, from this out became their bitter enemy, and swore he would pursue them with fire and sword until the day of his death.

‡ A village was subsequently erected there, and called Newcestown. It is now a mere hamlet, consisting of only a few houses.

substantial bridge. Great heaps of stones were brought down to the water's edge ; all the masons that could be collected were set to work ; and the great artery, through which coursed the commercial intercourse and vitality of the settlement, was quickly completed. Running in a north-easterly direction from the northern end of Bridge Street to the opposite side of the river, the new bridge stood not many yards to the west of its present and more commodious successor. It consisted of six arches, and was built entirely of stone. Its parapets, however, were wooden railings, which were composed of intersecting rails joined to uprights, and surmounted by a hand-rail. Upon the hand-rail, where it was met by the uprights, were large round balls of wood. These were about six feet apart from each other ; and, combined with the trellis-work underneath, gave the whole structure a light and graceful appearance.

Newce granted long leases of the building ground, and at rents varying in amount from three and four-pence to six and eight-pence yearly, together with a fat hen at Shrovetide. The tenants were also bound " to do service unto the Courts Baron and Leet as often as they shall be holden for the manor of Coolfadda. To take their corn to the mill or mills of the same manor for the grinding thereof. To provide a man of the English nation, armed with a caliver, sufficiently furnished for the defence of the Fort of Coolfadda aforesaid ; and upon the death of the tenant, one half-year's rent was to be paid to the landlord in lieu of a herriott. In addition to the land assigned the leasee for the erection of his tenement, he was empowered to fell the timber that grew on it, and to fetch and carry away sufficient house-bote, hedge-bote, pale-bote, and fire-bote, without making any great waste or spoil ; provided the same should be spent and employed on the said demised premises, and not elsewhere." A special clause forbade any of the tenants from cutting or carrying away timber from the woods of Cool_ fadda ; they being reserved to the lord of the manor for his own use, or for any purpose of general utility he may deem desirable.

None of the " meer Irish " were allowed to live in the town, or even to reside within the bounds of the settlement. The great improvements which the colonists had been able to effect in a few years filled them with astonishment and hatred. Lands which they had themselves known for a great many years, and their forefathers had been acquainted with for centuries ; and which lands—like those who preceded them— they only valued for the four-footed game which lurked in their coverts, or for the wild duck or the widgeon who built their nests in their bogs or swam on their lakes—were now occupied by a town, from which stretched farm after farm; embracing within its boundaries—paddocks, where horses were bred—rich meadows, whose sweet pastures were fed on by cows, who produced the sweetest cream—comfortable dwelling-houses, from whose chimney-tops the smoke curled all the day long—and orchards, already bright with the bloom of the apple and the cherry.

That this happiness should be enjoyed—that this wealth, almost fabulous in the eyes of a hungry wretch who had never tasted a comfortable meal since he was born, should belong to the stranger, and produced from their own soil—made them curse the accursed Saxon the more; and long for the time to arrive when they should drive away the settlers, and possess themselves of their homesteads.

Bandon-Bridge was the name given to the new town by the English, but the Irish would not listen to it. · The town was there, no doubt, and so was the bridge; but then the country had belonged to the O'Mahonys from time out of mind, and they could not understand why a foreign people, who came from a foreign land and spoke a foreign tongue, should now call it theirs.* Drohid-Mahon (O'Mahon's-Bridge) was its name; and so long have they continued to so call it in remembrance of the old proprietors, the last of whom forfeited the site upon which it stands so far back as the reign of Elizabeth, that—despite history, geography, schools, banks, the post-office—it is not uncommon in the surrounding country, even yet, for a wayfarer, on his return from the fair or market at Bandon, to be asked—in the vernacular of former days—whether the prices of cattle or of pigs were high or low in Drohid-Mahon. Even the bog, from whence the inhabitants of Drohid-Mahon drew their turf when fire-bote was exhausted, bears the impress of its connection with the town—Mohn-Drohid (the turf of the bridge) being the name of an exhausted bog some few miles to the west of Bandon.

---

* Upon the death of Cnogher O'Mahony, Moil-mo-O'Maghon became chief of the O'Mahonys of Kinalmeaky. He attended as a freeholder at the general gaol delivery held in Cork, July 28, 1601, when he was arrested as one of those likely to succour the Spaniards upon their arrival in Ireland. He is described as "a man of turbulent spirit, discontented mind, and ill-affected to the English government." When Sir Richard Percy, on the 20th of the previous December, sent sixty men belonging to the Kinsale garrison into Kinalmeaky to make a prey "of all the cows in the same," Moil-mo-O'Maghon, Dermod Mac Carthy, and his brother Florence, attacked them with three hundred foot and some horse, "not doubting but to have cut all their throats." After a hard fight, which continued two hours, the Irish retreated, "not finding the defendants to be chickens."

The present name of our town is Bandon, the word bridge having gradually passed out of use for more than a century ; and as Bandon it is now universally known in commerce, in trade, in every-day life, and in every species of official correspondence and precedure, save one :— when the high-sheriff reads the writ which he has received from the Hanaper office, he invites the electors to send a member to parliament to represent the borough of Bandon-Bridge.

Bandon is so called from the river of the same name, and upon whose banks it is built. The river Bandon has a history which poetry and tradition would fain connect with a very remote period. It is stated that when Partholanus*—who is said to have come over from Migdonia, in Greece, and, according to an old writer, landed in Ireland upwards of twenty years before the grandfather of the founder of the kingdom of Israel was born—travelled through our green isle, he found that it was wild and uninhabited ; and that it contained only nine rivers and three lakes. Of the rivers two were in the county of Cork :—the Lagi or Lee, " which compasseth Cork with its divided flood;" and the Banna or Bandain, whose waters are described as flowing through the country lying between the Eille† and the Lagi. The Banna, Bandain, Bandon, or Ban, was also called the Glaslyn or Green river.‡ By all these names it was formerly known. In a great battle fought in the fourteenth century, between Miles de Courcy,§ Baron of Kinsale, and Florence Mac Carthy More, Mac Carthy was beaten, " and a multitude of his followers were driven into the river Bandon, where many of them were drowned." In the song of O'Heerin, who died in 1420, he says :—

> " Cuiel-m-Bece of the land of cattle,
> Around the Bandain of fair woods."

In 1544 permission was given by Henry the Eighth to Phillip Roche " to buylde a castell at Shepespool, neare unto the river Glaslyn." When the Spanish fleet arrived in Kinsale in 1601, " the place at which they put in was the harbour of Kinsale, at the mouth of the Green river of

---

* Partholanus is supposed to have been the great grandson of the great grandson of Noah, and is mentioned as having arrived in Ireland three hundred years after the flood.

† The Eille or Ilen flows through Skibbereen.

‡ Probably from the great abundance in it of that graceful bright green plant, the *renunculus aqua:ilis.*

§ Miles was the grandson of John De Courcy, Baron of Kinsale, who was slain with his brother Patrick, in the island of Inchydonny, A.D. 1295.

Bandon." And later—in the same century—"the river of Ban," we are told, separates the fort from the town of Kinsale; also that "the river of Ban doth run through the town of Bandon-Bridge."

The river, as we have before said, rises in Mount Owen;* and, rushing down its rugged sides, hides her young face among the water-lilies of Cullinaugh. Lingering there awhile, as if to catch a last look, or to bid eternal farewell to her mother mountain, she sets out on her long journey to the sea. Struggling through the thick sedge and the tall stout grass which besets her path, she hurries over a stony bed, skipping from boulder to boulder and from rock to rock, until she comes to the castle of the Togher. Loitering there awhile, on the skirt of the grassy lawn which oft felt the pressure of the foot of the thrice hospitable Teige O'Downy, and where her smooth waters oft mirrored the stalwart figure of that great mountain chief, she tardily moves along until she reaches the flat ground on which Dunmanway stands. The Kaal and another wide stream await her here, and pour their tributary waters into her fair bosom. Strengthened by these additions she proceeds; passing the walls of the dismantled keep where Randal Oge Hurly bid defiance to the Saxon, and sweeping by the sombre groves of Kilcaskin and the pine-covered hills of Manch, she arrives at Carrigmore. Here the Duvawain, springing from the classic region of "the steeple," and roaring down one of the rough valleys of Kennagh, co-mingles her dark waters with its own. Leaving Ballineen and Enniskeane behind her, she noiselessly approaches the ivy-clad trees and the time-worn front of "sweet Palace Anne."† From Palace Anne she flows on, past modest little country churches—past parsonages—country seats—past fields of corn—past grassy plains, echoing with the bleat of sheep and

---

* About half way up Mount Owen is a cave, anciently of considerable notoriety called Leabuig Dearmida (Dermod's bed). Tradition asserts that Diarmid O'Dyn, an Irish chieftain, held an important command amongst the Fenians, or old Irish militia, under the great original head centre, Finn Mac Cuil, himself. Whilst engaged in active service under Finn's orders, he had the misfortune to fall deeply in love with that officer's wife. The fair-haired grana reciprocated the tender feelings which glowed in Diarmid's breast; and turning her back upon the great militia captain, she fled to the Dunmanway mountains with O'Dyn; and in this very cave she spent the honeymoon, and resided some time in seclusion with her darling Diarmid. Dermod's bed appears at one time to have been much frequented by visitors, as its sides are literally covered with the names and initials of many of those who came to see where Diarmid and Finn Mac Cuil's faithless wife concealed themselves from the fury of that great Fenian.

† There is a song which records the amorous exploits of one of the former owners of this fine old residence. A line must suffice:—
"And he took her home in his flying coach to sweet Palace Anne."

the low of cattle, until she tarries beneath the bridge at Carhue. Standing on the crest of an adjoining hill, and looking as far to the west as towering Sheehy and the lofty mountains of Dunmanway will permit, our beautiful river may be seen gleaming in the sun like a belt of burnished silver, as she slowly winds her way with graceful ease over a carpet of the brightest green. From Carhue to the town on which she has bestowed her name, "the pleasant Bandon" is once more among fair woods. Her course now lies through a wide valley, where huge oaks stretch out their gigantic arms, and fling broad shadows over many an acre of velvet turf; probably some of those very oaks which the tourist, who visited this place when Elizabeth was still Queen of England, describes as trees of wonderful length. Herds of deer here bask on her verdant banks; and the waving willow dips the tips of its green tresses in her limpid stream. Flowing past that stately pile whose castellated walls enclose the site of the rude rath where St. Fin Bar* was born, she comes to Bandon. Refreshed by the waters of the Bride-well river, she again proceeds; and gliding by the riven walls of the mansion where Spenser's daughter dwelt, she flows into a wooded vale, and meets the Mugin at the Castle of Downdanial. Speeding past the ivyed bridge that spans that river's mouth, and touching the very feet of the old fortalice of Barry Oge, she sweeps down between high hills draped to their very summit with the foliage of the oak and the beech; and entering a deeply-timbered dell, where tall dark trees spread gloom on her waters, she hurries again into the light, and, bending low, kisses the wavelets which the old ocean hath sent up to welcome her to its home.

---

* Saint Fin Bar, the patron saint of the diocese of Cork, was the offspring of parents who left Connaught, and, after tedious wanderings, at length settled at Rath-leann; a residence over which a prince named Tygernach, one of the O'Mahonys, presided at the time. Amergen, St. Fin Bar's father, was a worker in iron or chief smith to Tygernach; and it was whilst in the employment of that prince at Rathleann that his son, the saint, was born.

CHAPTER II.

THE SPANIARDS IN KINSALE—OBSTINATE BATTLE ON THE BANKS OF THE BANDON, BETWEEN THE ENGLISH UNDER TAFFE AND THE IRISH UNDER THE POPE'S APOSTOLIC VICAR—THE IRISH DEFEATED AND THE VICAR KILLED—THE LETTERS PATENT GRANTED BY JAMES THE FIRST FOR HOLDING OUR FAIRS—CHRIST CHURCH, KILBROGAN, ITS CLERGY, CHARTERS, MONUMENTS, ETC.

OUR colonists did not remain very long in the enjoyment of undisturbed tranquility. The rebellious chieftains, 1601. who had been ardently awaiting the arrival of assistance from Spain, heard with exultation that a fleet consisting of forty-five ships, with three thousand five hundred Spanish veterans on board, had landed in Kinsale.* Scarcely had they set foot on the shore, when couriers were despatched in eager haste to O'Neil and O'Donnell to announce to them the glad tidings, and to urge them in the name of their church and their country to collect all their followers, and to march southward at once.

Red Hugh, overjoyed with the good news, and only too anxious to measure pikes with the Saxon again, hastily set out; and, after some difficulty, this "light-footed general" reached Innishannon, a village three miles eastward of Bandon.† There he was joined by seven hundred Spanish troops, who had arrived at Castlehaven, under Don Zuibar; by many of the Munster chiefs; and soon after by O'Neil.

After some delay they proceeded down the left bank of the river, and took up a position about a mile to the rear of the English camp. Here

---

* It was exactly two hundred and twenty-one years since the Spaniards were in Kinsale before; upon which occasion, A.D. 1380 (Richard the Second), they captured the town; but were subsequently driven out.

† He over-awed his enemies from the Boyne to the Bandon.—(See *The Four Masters*.)

they established themselves so effectually, as to cut off all supplies between the English and Cork. Thus Mountjoy, who was besieging Don Juan de Aquila in Kinsale, was himself besieged by O'Neil* and O'Donnell in his own trenches.

Under these circumstances the enemy thought that a combined night attack must prove a success; and they decided upon it without delay. The Spaniards were to sally from Kinsale, and attack the English front, at the same time that the Irish should set out from their camp and attack the English rear.

It happened that the night on which the great avenging blow was to be struck turned out a wild one. At one time the darkness was so thick that a soldier could scarcely recognize the comrade who stood shoulder to shoulder with him. At another time one could see the adjoining hills and valleys by the red light which the lightning flashed† on them for a moment; and then the darkness was greater than before. The superstitious mind of the Irish soldier was filled with ominous forebodings. Thousands of banshees, soaring on the swelling gale, muttered a doleful plaint as they swept over his head; and he heard it grow fainter and fainter in the distance. Anon returning, it increased; and gathering strength as it approached, the little fairies, swooping to the very earth, screamed it in his ears. When the wind howled, he heard angry voices speaking to him from the black clouds which madly sped past; and when it soughed, unseen singers, in a sweet and subdued tone, chanted a requiem for the dead.

Carew, who had been informed of everything, was ready. Accordingly, when the day broke, the Irish, who expected to fall upon a sleeping foe, found that the foe—already under arms, and drawn up in battle array—was anxiously awaiting them. They were disheartened before, but now they became downright cowardly, and began to retire in disorder. Mountjoy quickly perceived that now was his time. He immediately sent Carew back to Kinsale to deceive the Spaniards by a feint attack, whilst he himself boldly marched against the Irish army

---

* When O'Neil was on the line of march to Kinsale, and was passing Castle-More, he asked who lived there; and on being told it was an Englishman named Barrett, who, however, was a good Catholic, and whose forefathers had been living in Ireland for the previous four hundred years:—"No matter," exclaimed the chieftain, with an oath, "I hate the churl, as if he came but yesterday!"

† The watchmen set to watch, says Moryson, to their seeming did see lamps burning at the points of their staves or spears, in the midst of these lightning flashes.

with a small force, consisting of only twelve hundred foot and four hundred horse.

O'Neil's own column was the first to receive the shock. After a feeble resistance, they were broken and fled. A panic then seized O'Donnell's men; and soon after the entire Irish army, despite the vigorous exertions of Tyrrell Tyrconnell and Tyrone, were as powerless as a flock of sheep. The slaughter was great. Many Irish chieftains were killed. The bodies of twelve hundred Irish and Spanish soldiers lay dead upon the field,—hundreds more perished in the pursuit. All the arms and ammunition of the vanquished became the spoil of the conquerors. And thus ingloriously ended this combined effort of the Spanish and the Irish to wrest Ireland from under British sway.

There were many distinguished men of name, in the western parts of our county, who had joined with O'Neil and O'Donnell in the unsuccessful attempt to throw off the English yoke. These the commissioners determined to punish; and for that purpose they ordered Captains Flower and Bostocke, with twelve hundred foot and one hundred horse, to proceed to Carbery.

They set out, directing their course towards Ross and Bantry, and doing the enemy all the mischief they could, as they marched along. They burnt his corn-stacks—they pulled down his houses—they drove off his cattle; and finally they returned, bringing with them, amongst other trophies, the heads of thirty-seven notorious rebels, besides others of less note.

Captain Taffe also penetrated into the enemy's quarters in Carbery. His force consisted of forty of Wingfield's foot, some of the colonists* from Bandon-Bridge, and his own troop of horse. He, too, was pretty successful; and was on his way back with between two and three hundred cows and some horses, when the Mac Carthys, to whom the cattle had belonged, followed in pursuit, under the command of "that wicked and unnatural traitor, Donell O'Sullivan."†

Taffe was overtaken on the banks of the river Bandon; and instantly the Mac Carthys fell furiously on his infantry. This little body was unable to withstand the strength and the numbers of their opponents;

---

* The colonists were bound to furnish the authorities with mounted horsemen and footmen fully armed, in accordance with their tenures. These subsidies were sometimes called risings-out, and sometimes militia.

† Three hundred pounds was offered for the live body of Donell O'Sullivan, and two hundred pounds for his head.

and were on the point of giving way, when their commander arrived to
their relief with his horse. After killing a few of the enemy, the rest
gave way and fled.

It would seem that O'Sullivan was unable to rally his men after this;
for we find that, when next they advanced to the assault, they were led
by no less a personage than the Pope's apostolic vicar, Mac Eagan, bishop
of Ross. The Titular was undoubtedly a man of war as well as a man
of peace. He was most active in pursuading the chieftains in his
diocese to join O'Neil, and to aid the Spaniards in Kinsale; and was
at all times a bitter and uncompromising foe of the Sassenach. The
Sassenach consequently had no love for him. Mac Egan was " a
traitorous priest." He was " a Popish priest, and a most infamous
rebel." He never pardoned any Irishmen, says Cox,—though papists,—
that served the Queen; but as soon as they came before him he would
have them confessed, absolved, and executed.

Putting himself at their head, the apostolic vicar, with a drawn sword
in one hand and some of the emblems of his sacred calling in the other,
marched against the little band of heretics; who, flushed with their
recent success, stood together undauntedly. The fight was fierce and
obstinate. The Mac Carthys were assured by a faithful son of the
infallible church that they would be victorious; and they were not
apprehensive of danger befalling their holy leader—for how could a
sword or a pike, wielded by heretic hands, harm him?

On the other side, the colonists had now a chance of doing the
community an important service, by knocking this clerical agitator on
the head. With this intent they resolutely pressed on, bent on wounding *the invulnerable* prelate at the least; or killing him outright if they
could. The battle waged furiously. It was impossible to say on which
side victory would ultimately declare, until at length some of Taffe's
men forced their way to where the bishop stood. His lifeless body* soon
lay on the ground; and his followers, filled with terror and horror, fled,
utterly aghast. Some succeeded in making their escape to the neighbouring woods; others dragged themselves through bogs; but by far the
greater number endeavoured to cross the river, in which effort upwards
of a hundred of them lost their lives.

---

* His remains were carried off the field by O'Sullivan, and buried in the north-
western angle of the cloister of Timoleague Abbey; and a little cross was scored
in the overhanging wall, to mark the place of his interment.

When Elizabeth was dead, the pretensions and hopes of the
1604. Irish-priesthood received a new impulse and a new life. The
son of a Popish mother, if not openly affording them grounds to expect
the alleviation of their political grievances, at all events would not place
obstacles to the progress of their religion. Acting upon this supposition,
they began to repair and re-decorate the abbeys and religious houses
which had been erected and endowed by the piety of their forefathers;
and which they never ceased to look upon with feelings of veneration
and pride. Amongst those restored at this time was the Franciscan
Abbey of Timoleague, in our neighbourhood, and the Abbey of Kilcrea,
also belonging to the Franciscans.

Bandon had by this time attained so much strength and
1605. importance, that the inhabitants were anxious to settle its
future form of government. About this time great efforts were made
to induce the Irish to adopt English manners and customs, and to speak
in the English tongue. Even several years before, Sir John Perrott, the
Lord-Deputy, endeavoured to persuade the chieftains to wear trousers,
but he was unsuccessful. The wearing of such a garment—now an
indispensable article of dress in every civilized community—appeared
to them as an evidence of their subjugation. If they had their legs
in English trousers, they would hide their face in their Irish mantle,
for shame.

Instead, however, of the Irish adopting the costume and the customs of
the English, many of the English* imitated the Irish in these particulars.
They half shaved their heads; they twined their hair into culans; and
they wore the mantle, under which, we are told, " the outlaw covereth
himself from the wrath of heaven, from the offences of the earth, and
from the sight of men." The adoption of the dress and customs of
the Irish by English residents was not always a harmless piece of
policy on their part, as several of them were killed, being mistaken for
Irishmen.

Among all the languages of Europe, it is said the Irish alone retains
the original Cadmean alphabet of sixteen letters. These were not
added to even when the Christian missionaries adopted the Roman
letters; and it is remarkable that, notwithstanding the arrival of successive colonies here, each speaking in its own tongue, or in dialects of

---

* The English were forbidden to adopt Irish dress so far back as A.D. 1300, under
the penalty of being imprisoned, and degraded to the level of " the meer Irish."

the same tongue, yet the Celtic is living still—at least among the peasantry in the interior.

Its very great antiquity is undeniable. Speaking of it, an eminent historian says:—"The Irish nation are, by it, enabled to boast that they possess genuine history, several centuries more ancient than any other European nation possesses, in its present spoken language."

The Irish were very unwilling to give up their own tongue and adopt that of the Saxon. They disdained to strain their jaws by speaking English:—"What!" said O'Neil, "thinkest thou that it standeth with my honour to writhe my mouth in clattering English?"

Another chieftan showed a contempt for it still greater. Being told that a child of his had an impediment in his speech, he ordered that he should be sent into the Pale to learn English, as he believed that language to be fit for none other than stammerers. Neither would they allow a reproach to be cast upon the old vernacular, without defending it. When a gentleman, who had been in Rome, stated that he met with a woman there who could converse in any language, save the Irish. That, she was unable to speak, " as the devil was gravelled therewith." "No," said an Irishman, who stood by, " 'twas because it was so sacred and holy, that no damned fiend had the power to speak it!"

The English spoken in Ireland felt but slightly the influence of the great improvements effected in it in Elizabeth's reign. According to Sir William Petty, the English in use here, even in 1672, was neither English, Irish, Welsh, or Wexfordian. Before his time it was described as a mingle-mangle, or a gallimaufrie of both English or Irish. Stanihurst also stated it was the dregs of Chaucer English that were spoken here in his day. Thus, a spider was an atteroop—a lump of bread, a pucket—a dunghill, a mizen—a physician, a leech. Even the softer sex used to pronounce their words hard and broad, and, in dissyllables, used always place the accent on the last syllable—thus market was mar-ke-at; and so peevish, and sometimes so faint, was their utterance, that we are told they looked as if they were half sick, and ready to call for a posset. It is possible that, were it not for the forfeitures and slaughter caused by the great rebellion of " '41," and the subsequent uprisings in favour of James the Second, which also terminated in forfeitures and the expatriation of most of the Irish gentry, the Erse would be the prevailing tongue of most of our country towns and villages to this day.

1608.　Our town had by this time increased very considerably in size. The level portions on both banks of the river were entirely built over; and building lots on the rising ground on the northern side were anxiously sought after.

1610.　So pleased was James the First with the progress of the new colony, that he granted to Henry Beecher—Phane's successor—and his heirs for ever, the power of appointing a clerk to the market; of licensing tradesmen and artizans to pursue their vocations within the settlement; and a tenth of the salmon caught in that portion of the river Bandon bounding his grant. And, on the town "lately erected on the south side of the said river," he bestowed the privilege of a Saturday's market, and two annual fairs. Those fairs, which are now the oldest in our country, were established by Letters Patent, dated February 20th (7th James I.), and were to be held on the feast of St. Mark, and on that of St. Simon and St. Jude. The market to be held on "any day of the week," was also granted at the same time. The patent is as follows :—

"Letters of Patent of our lord James the King, granting to Henry Beecher, Esq., without fine, videlicit :—We do find and grant to Henry Beécher, Esq., his heirs and assigns, that he, his heirs and assigns for ever, will have and hold, and may be able to have and hold, one free market at the said town, lately erected on the south side of the said river of Bandon, near the bridge, in the county of Cork, on any day of the week; and also two fairs and markets annually for ever, at the said town, lately erected on the said river, near the bridge aforesaid. With a fair on the feast of St. Mark the Evangelist, and for one day next following; and also another fair on the feast of St. Simon and Jude the Apostle, and the day following, provided that neither of the said feasts fall on the Lord's Day. With a court of pie-powder, and all tolls, customs, &c., thereto incidental or belonging; and that the same be no injury to any neighbouring markets or fairs. Rendering twenty shillings current money of Ireland at the feast of the Passover, and St. Michael the Archangel, by equal portions, to be paid for ever."

On the 23rd of the next month, Sir Richard Boyle also obtained Letters Patent, March 23rd (7th James I.); and again on March 3rd (11th James I.), enabling him to hold two fairs and markets annually— one on the feast of the Ascension of our Lord, and the day following, and another on the 29th of September, and the day following; also a market, to be held on any day of the week—Wednesday—at Coolfadda, on the northern side of the town. A piece of waste land lying outside the walls, and now known as Gallow's Hill, was given by Beecher for the weekly market and the annual fair. The former has long since found its way into the town; but the latter, we need scarcely say, still occupies the old ground.

Christ Church, Kilbrogan, was built. It was erected on the site of a Danish fort, known at that time as Badger's Hill; and was the first edifice ever raised in Ireland for Protestant worship. It is true that the reformed faith was introduced into Ireland long before; and there were even Protestant prelates, wearing the mitre, in the neighbouring city of Cork for more than the previous seventy years: nevertheless, although Protestants did worship in Protestant churches in 1610, yet these churches were never built for that purpose; as it never entered —however remotely—into the thoughts of the founders or original donors, that a body of religionists would arise who could expel Irish priests from Irish sanctuaries, and laugh at the impotent rage of Rome.

At first the church consisted of a nave sixty feet long, by twenty-eight and a-half feet wide, and fifty feet high; and, at its western gable, of a steeple eighty feet in height, and containing two large windows, one above the other. The entrance door adjoined the steeple, and was twenty-five feet high and ten broad. Between it and the eastern gable— in which was a window of very considerable size, being no less forty-five feet high by twenty wide—were two windows, each thirty feet high by fifteen wide; and over the doorway itself was a smaller window, fifteen feet high by ten wide. In 1625* important additions were made near the entrance on the northern side, and the church itself considerably enlarged by the earl of Cork; and a stone with that date, and inscribed MEMENTO MORI, placed over a newly-erected porch adjoining the entrance. In changing the entrance to the southern side,† an effort was made to remove the stone which bore the date of the church's erection in 1610, from over the old doorway, in order to place it over the new. The attempt, however, was a failure—owing to awkwardness or accident, it was broken irretrievably; and the other stone (1625) was then thought of, and placed in the bed intended for the original.

---

* The earl of Cork became sole owner of the seigniory of Sir Bernard Granville, by deed dated September 20th, 1625. The seigniory includes most of the parish of Kilbrogan, and other lands.

† It is said that the reason the entrance was changed to the southern side was, that in troublesome times, the Irish used frequently plant themselves on the glen hill opposite, and fire at the congregation entering the church door.

Tradition asserts that the Puritans worshipped in this church, and also in that of Ballymodan, until the passing of the Act of Uniformity in 1663. We believe this to have been the case, as nearly all the plantees were Puritans; and even the few Episcopalians who were amongst them preferred making common cause with their English countrymen against the common enemy of both, rather than indulging in any disputations with them about vexed questions of doctrine and church discipline; and, therefore, they either joined with them,—which is highly probable,—or let them have everything their own way, undisturbed. Besides, the clergy—or at least that portion of them who pretended to any religion at all—were mostly puritanical in their views. There were many of them, who, although they refused Episcopal ordination, were yet allowed to enter into the possession of parish churches, and enjoy the livings. There were others who, not content with spurning the liturgy, went still further, and boldly proclaimed that they were Presbyterians; and there were some admitted to the ministry in the Calvanistic form. And yet there were bishops who conferred benefices upon them; and who deemed re-ordination in their case not only unnecessary, but even unlawful. In five years after Kilbrogan Church was built, and in the very diocese we live in, the ordinary complained that close upon a third of the resident clergy did not observe " the forme of common prayer prescribed in the common booke."

It should not be a matter of surprise that very many of the Protestant clergy of the Church of England should differ on many points with the Church herself. Those who respected the opinions of bishop Ridley, a martyr whose opinions remained unshaken in the midst of the flames which consumed him, were aware that, by his orders, the sacrament was administered upon plain tables, placed in the middle of the church. Another bishop looked upon clerical vestments as fit only to form a coat for a fool; and longed to see the day when they would be abolished. Archbishop Grindal was for a long time reluctant to accept a mitre, from the aversion he had to go through the ceremony of consecration; and another bishop thought that the very term itself should be repudiated, and that, in lieu of it, the chief rulers of the Reformed Church should be called superintendents. Tradition also asserts that, when the Act of Uniformity was enforced here, the Puritans left Kilbrogan Church in a body, and procured a minister for themselves. This statement is strongly supported by the fact, that it is about this period the name of a Presbyterian minister first appeared on the roll of clergymen of that persuasion, who have officiated in Bandon ever since.

The ancient name of the parish of Kilbrogan was Brochoyn, Bruchane, or Brochane. It was a fief of the See of Cloyne; and in the fourteenth century was held under the bishop of that diocese, by the Barrys. At an Inquisition held at Clenor, on Monday, the feast of St. Andrew the Apostle, in the fiftieth year of the reign of Edward the Third, A.D. 1377, before W. M., seneschal of the bishop of Cloyne, it was found that Nicholas Barry acknowledged that he held of the Lord-Bishop the manor of Kilbrogan, with all its appurtenances; the woods, meadows, and three carucates of land in the parish of Brochoyn, by service of homage, fealthy, wardship, relief, and socage at the castle of Kilma-cloyne; and by the service of sixteen and fourpence per annum, at the usual terms; and that he will do in all things as did Maurice Chapel.

On the tenth of January, 1481, William, bishop of Cloyne, visited the church of Brochane, and demanded a return of the manor of Kilbrogan from Sir James, son of Nicholas, son of Phillip James de Barry, lord of Brochane; and Sir James swore before M., rector and vicar of Brochane, Edmund Hoverd, and many others, that he would willingly comply with the will of the said bishop, William. The modern name of the parish is derived from Kiel-Brochane (the church of Brochane). In fact the parish was *sub invocatione Sancti Brocani*. Brogan, Brochane, or Brocanus, was no less a personage than the nephew of our great national saint—St. Patrick, and was also his secretary.[*] He was rendered famous by a prophecy of his, in which he foretold that the English would come to Ireland; and that their power would continue there as long as they would observe their own laws, but no longer.[†]

Richard Newman was vicar of Kilbrogan:—

1591.

"Preb. de Kilbrogan. Ab, graine et hosp, mor. sunt Rectores Vicarius ibm. Richs Newman."

Rory Flynn was also vicar of Kilbrogan, according to another visitation book of same date. Flynn was vicar of Inskenny in 1581; and vicar of Kilbonane, and rector of Knockavilly, in 1591.[‡]

---

[*] In the *Annals of the Four Masters*, A.D. 448, is an Irish poem, giving a list of the family and followers of St. Patrick; and among them is mentioned Brogan, the scribe of his school.

[†] *Canbrensis Eversus.*—Dr. O'Kelly.

[‡] For these particulars, as well as for nearly all those connected with the succeeding rectors and vicars of Kilbrogan, we are indebted to Dr. Brady's admirable work on *The Clerical Records of Cork, Cloyne, and Ross.*

1615.   In the royal visitation of this year, Robert Sutton appears as vicar :—

"Kilbrogan Vic. residens.   The master of Mourne Abbey and Grauy are rectores."

At this time Cormack Mac Donough Mac Carthy was in possession of Mourne Abbey; and Sir Garrett Alymer and Sir William Sarsfield were the patentees, and as such divided the revenues of Kilbrogan with Mac Carthy, the representative of Mourne Abbey.   Sutton was also vicar of Desertserges, and of Ballinadee.

1628.   September 28th.—Baptist Hassell was prebendary of Kilbrogan.

1632.   John Snary was prebendary and vicar.   He was installed March 31st, on Letters Patent dated March 2nd.   He was deaconed on the 23rd May, and priested on the 29th September, 1624, by John, bishop of Sodar and Man.   In 1634, the rectory of Kilbrogan was valued at £20 per annum, and the prebendary and vicarage at £37—in all £57 yearly.   Mr. Snary obtained a patent in 1635, uniting the rectory with the prebendary and vicarage; and as prebendary, rector, and vicar of Kilbrogan he appears subsequently.

1661.   Hugh Dunsterville, A.M., prebendary.   In 1663 he was also archdeacon of Cloyne.

1666.   John Easton, A.M., prebendary.   Also chancellor of Ross.

1669.   Richard Synge, prebendary.   In 1674 he became archdeacon of Cork.   He was also chancellor of Ross.   His daughter Thamer was buried in Kilbrogan, November 11th, 1711.

1674.   George Synge, prebendary and vicar of Kilbrogan, rector and vicar of Aghinagh, vicar of Aghabollig and Kiloolman, rector of Templetrine, and of Agiapallin, county of Meath.   He was son of the bishop of Cloyne.   In 1665, when sixteen years old, he entered Trinity College, Dublin.   In 1681 he married Mary, daughter of Thomas Hewytt, of Bandon-Bridge; and secondly, in 1687, Margaret Freke, of Templebryan, in Ross.   In his will, dated September, 1692, he desires to be buried near his first wife, in the chancel of Kilbrogan church.

1692.   Daniel Lord was prebendary, rector, and vicar, "per mortem Georgii Synge."   He was the son of Richard Lord, and was born in Dublin in 1657.   When only fourteen years of age he entered Trinity College; and subsequently graduated there as doctor of divinity.   His first appointment was to the curacy of Liscarroll.   In 1681 he

obtained the prebendary of Killaspugmullane. In 1682 he was rector
of Garryvoe, and the same year he was appointed to the rectory and
vicarage of Murragh and Desertserges ; and in 1683 rector of Killowen.
He was proctor cleri corcagen to Convocation in 1703. In his will,
dated November 25th, 1704, he is styled the Rev. Daniel Lord, D.D.,
minister in Bandon-Bridge. In this he directs that he should be buried
" in ye chancel of my own parish of Bandon-Bridge, as near the body
of my daughter Frances as may be." Dorcas, his widow, survived him
thirty years. She was buried in Kilbrogan on the 17th January, 1734.

1704.   Solomon Foley was prebendary, rector, and vicar of Kilbrogan;
rector and vicar of Murragh. In 1692 he was rector of Kilmeen,
vicar of Drinagh, and prebendary of Kilnaglory. In 1698 he was
rector of Ardnegihy and Killcully. His will was proved in March,
1738. In it he directed that he should be buried in the chancel of
Kilbrogan, near his deceased wife. Her name was Margaret. She
was buried in Kilbrogan, on the 28th March, 1731. His daughter,
Mrs. James Jackson, is also mentioned. This lady was probably the
wife of James Jackson, who was provost of Bandon in 1716, and again
in 1730-31. One of his curates, Robert Mac Clellan, priested in Cork
in 1737, married his daughter, Susannah ; and died in 1761.

It was during Mr. Foley's time that the bell, famed for its silvery
tone, and which summoned the parishioners to their parish church for
upwards of one hundred and twenty years, was cast. The casting was
performed by an Italian bell-founder, in the churchyard ; and during
the process several of the residents of Kilbrogan were present, and
threw in pieces of silver. It bore the following inscription :—

"EDWARD SPILLANE AND JAMES MOXLEY, S.N.,
CHURCH WARDENS, 1734."

Mr. Foley was buried in the chancel of Kilbrogan, on the 26th of
February, 1738. In addition to the children previously mentioned, he
had :—Jane, buried July 12th, 1708 ; Amy, buried September 26th,
1709 ; George, buried August 15th, 1710 ; Robert, buried April 30th,
1712 ; Solomon, buried April 22nd, 1725.

1738.   William Jackson, prebendary, rector, and vicar ; was also
rector of Agblish, and rector and vicar of Murragh—vacant
by Foley's death. In 1749, he was prebendary of Cahirlag, rector of
Little Island, and rector of Rathcany. In 1739, he was prebendary of
Templebryan, vicar of Templequinlan, rector of Templeomalus and

Kilnagross, in Ross; and in 1745 he was prebendary of the Holy Trinity, Cork. Mr. Jackson would seem to have been the son of James Jackson, who is supposed to have married the daughter of the preceding rector. He was born in 1713; and entered Trinity College, Dublin, when seventeen years of age. He was priested in Cork in 1737, for the curacy of Brinny; and the following year he married Mary Nash, of Brinny, to whom he bequeathed his property. He died in 1767.

1739.   William Robinson, A.M., succeeded, upon Jackson's resignation. He was also rector and vicar of Murragh; but was not in the possession of the one rectory of Aghlish, which—when vacated by Jackson—was bestowed upon Thomas Blennerhasset, and was not restored to Kilbrogan until 1746. Mr. Robinson was the son of the Rev. Thomas Robinson, of St. Nicholas, Lancashire. He married Anne Moorcroft; and by her he had a son, Thomas, who married Dorothy, daughter of Samuel Townsend, of Whitehall.

1746.   St. John Browne, L.L.D., was prebendary, rector, and vicar of Kilbrogan, rector and vicar of Murragh, rector of Killowen, chancellor of Ross, and rector of Innishannon and Leighmoney. He was a son of Edward Browne, "senatoris corcagiensis," and was a younger brother of Jemmett Browne, bishop of Cork. He entered college in 1729. He was ordained priest at Cork in 1736, and licensed to the curacy of Killowen, near Kinsale, in 1737. The next year he married Amelia St. George, of Kinsale; and had issue :—Rev. Thomas Adderly Browne, chancellor of Ross; Rev. St. John Browne, scholar Trinity College, Cambridge; and Sir St. George Sackville Browne, K.C.B., lieutenant-general in the army. Dr. Browne married secondly, in 1776, Mrs. Elizabeth Hodder; but it does not appear that there was any issue from this marriage. He died in 1796.

1796.   John Kenny, L.L.D., prebendary, rector, and vicar of Kilbrogan; also vicar of Kinneigh, and rector of Dunderrow. Dr. Kenny was for many years prebendary of St. Nicholas, Cork; and was also a vicar-choral and a vicar-general of Cork. He was deaconed on the 24th of May, 1761, and was priested the same year. He married Mary Herbert, of Muckross, and had :—Rev. Edward H. Kenny, rector of Kilmeen; Robert, who was a captain in the navy; Rev. Thomas Kenny, prebendary of Donoughmore; Rev. Arthur Kenny, F.T.C.D.; and a daughter Mary, who wrote *Letters on Prejudice*. Dr. Kenny died in 1814, and was buried in Ballymartle.

1815. Verney Lovett, D.D., was prebendary, rector, and vicar of the parish, and rector of Aghlish. He was the third son of Jonathan Lovett, of Liscombe, Bucks, and Kingswell, county Tipperary. He was a vicar-choral of Lismore from 1781 to 1825. He married Frances Mary, daughter of Henry Gervaise, archdeacon of Cashel; and had issue:—Jonathan Henry, ambassador and resident at the court of Persia; William, of the Royal navy; and Henry William, who, on the death of his uncle, Sir Jonathan Lovett, Bart., of Liscombe, inherited the estate of Saulsbury, in Buckinghamshire. Dr. Lovett, who was chaplain to his Royal Highness the Prince of Wales, left twenty pounds to the rector and churchwardens of Kilbrogan. He died in 1825, and was buried in Lismore. It is said that Dr. Lovett would have succeeded his brother, Sir Jonathan, in the possession of all the family estates, he being the next heir, were it not for his love of humour. It appears that the old baronet was both irritable and eccentric; and that our rector was as full of fun as his elder brother was of moroseness. One day he was amusing himself behind Sir Jonathan's chair, making hideous faces at him; and intimating, by his clenched fists and various movements of his legs and feet, the kind of treatment he thought Old Gouty deserved. Suddenly, Sir Jonathan turned round and caught the doctor in the fact. He never forgave him. This piece of innocent recreation cost the doctor an estate.

1818. Horatio Townsend Newman was prebendary, rector, and vicar, upon the resignation of Lovett. He married on the 10th of November, 1817, Charlotte Elizabeth, third daughter of the Right Honorable Denis Daly, of Dunsandle, county Galway. In 1842 he was appointed to the deanery of Cork. Mr. Newman was son of Adam Newman, of Dromore, county Cork. He entered Trinity College, Dublin, where he graduated as A.B., in 1803. On the 6th of July, 1806, he obtained deacon's orders, and was priested July 12th, 1807—both at Cloyne. In 1808 he was licensed to the curacy of St. Fin Bar's; and in 1818 he was appointed to Kilbrogan. In 1844 he published *A Brief View of Ecclesiastical History, from the earliest period to the present time.* He died, January 6th, 1864.

1842. Honorable Charles Broderick Bernard, M.A., Baliol College, Oxford, second son of James, earl of Bandon. He was born January 4th, 1811; ordained deacon June 28th, 1835, and priested September 11th, 1836—both at Cork. In 1835 he was curate of

Desertsorges.   From 1840 to 1842 he was vicar of Kilmocomoge, and in the latter year was appointed prebendary, rector, and vicar of Kilbrogan.   In 1843 he married the Honorable Jane Grace Freke, sister of George, seventh baron of Carbery; and had issue:—Percy Broderick, born September 17th, 1844 ; and James Boyle, born December 22nd, 1847, Mr. Bernard published many sermons and lectures, from time to time. Amongst the rest :—

A sermon preached in the cathedral church of St. Fin Bar, on Tuesday, June 23rd, 1840.

A sermon preached on Sunday, November 1st, 1846, being the last occasion on which divine service was performed within the old parish church of Ballymodan.

A sermon on the death of the Rev. Herbert P. Molesworth, curate of Kilbrogan, Bandon, preached in the parish church, July 4th, 1847.

Dagon and the Ark of God—A sermon on behalf of the Diocesan Church Education Society, 1851.

What is Truth ?—A sermon on behalf of the Society for Irish Church Missions to the Roman Catholics, preached in the parish church of St. Multose, Kinsale, 1854.

An address to the sunday-school teachers and scholars of Cork and its neighbourhood, delivered in Christ Church, December 5th, 1854.

An address to the parishioners of Kilbrogan, 1855.

A sermon preached at the consecration of Kinneigh Church, August 27th, 1856.

India.—A lecture delivered at the opening of the fifth session of the Bandon Young Men's Association, 1857.

Religious Activities, 1865.

In 1851 Mr. and Mrs. Bernard presented the churchwardens with a beautifully wrought silver cup and paten, for the use of the church. They are thus inscribed :—

> " CHRIST CHURCH,
> KILBROGAN, BANDON.
> THE GIFT OF
> HONᵉˡ. AND REVᵈ. C. B. BERNARD,
> RECTOR,
> AND HONᵉˡ. JANE GRACE,
> HIS WIFE."

Towards the close of 1866 Mr. Bernard was appointed bishop of Tuam, Killala, and Achonry; and on the 13th of January, 1867, was consecrated at Armagh by the Primate, assisted by the Right Rev. John Gregg, D.D., bishop of Cork, and the Right Rev. Hamilton Verschoyle, D.D., bishop of Kilmore.   The Honorable and Rev. William Conyngham Plunket, nephew of the late bishop of Tuam, preached the sermon, taking as

4

his text, Ezra iii. 13. Previous to his leaving Bandon for the scene of his new labours, Dr. Bernard was presented with several addresses and testimonials.

On Monday, December 31st, 1866, he was presented with an address and testimonial by a deputation from the Bandon Young Men's Association, consisting of Captain Wheeler, chairman of the Town Commissioners; George Bennett, churchwarden, Kilbrogan; R. N. Woulfe, church-warden, Ballymodan; Rev. J. Bleakely, Ballymodan; Rev. J. O'Sullivan, Kilbrogan; R. W. Doherty, Rev. W. Powell, and Thomas Hunter.

" The testimonial consisted of a massive inkstand of solid silver. The handles and bottle-stands are of exquisite workmanship; and running round the entire front is a deep fringe, in frosted silver. It looks extremely well; and is considered not only an appropriate, but a handsome present. In the centre of the plateau, on a raised shield, tastefully ornamented with chaste and elaborate devices, is the follow-ing:—'Presented to the Hon. and Rev. C. B. Bernard, D.D., by the Young Men's Association of the ancient and loyal borough of Bandon-Bridge.' "—*Cork Constitution*.

On Thursday, the 3rd of January, 1867, he was presented with an address and testimonial " by the parishioners of Kilbrogan, his fellow-townsmen of the ancient and loyal borough of Bandon-Bridge, and by numerous friends in its vicinity."

" The testimonial was a centre-piece, a candalabra, with straight lines. The superstructure, an exceedingly chaste design of oak branches and scroll-work, supported by a rich chased festooned pedestal, on which stand figures of religion, liberty, and hospitality; the whole surmounted by the figure of an angel, above the bowl. The altitude of the piece is four feet; the diameter of the plateau is seventeen inches. It has a bagot-chased edge, and contains festoons of flowers and scroll-work. As a piece of ornamental art, the candalabra is a master-piece of cunning workmanship."—*Ibid*.

On the 5th of January—Saturday—Dr. and Mrs. Bernard were each presented, by the teachers, students, and pupils of the Bandon Training Schools, with a handsome copy of Baxter's Polyglot Bible, in antique morocco, silver rimmed and clasped; with an inscription. Also with a suitable address.

"On the same day, the teachers of the Church Diocesan Education Society presented Dr. Bernard with an address and a testimonial, consisting of a clock of exquisite design and elaborate workmanship; having on its base, in front, a centre-piece, with an appropriate in-scription. And on the same occasion, the teachers and children of the Bandon Ragged Schools presented the Hon. Mrs. Bernard with a walnut ormolu case and blotter, of rare beauty."—*Ibid*.

On Tuesday, January 8th, he received an address and testimonial from "the Nobility, Gentry, and Laity of the County of Cork." The testimonial was composed of two centre-pieces, to match the candalabrum presented by the town of Bandon. On one is represented a shepherdess, bearing a pitcher, and surrounded by sheep; on the other a shepherd, carrying tenderly in his arms a lamb, and followed by his flock. The figures on each piece stand on a richly-chased tripod base, and are beautifully executed in frosted silver. An acanthus tree overshadows each group, on the clustering foliage of which rests the glass fruit bowl.

On the same date, the clergy of the united dioceses of Cork, Cloyne, and Ross presented their address and testimonial. The latter consisted of four corner-pieces, in perfect keeping with the centre-pieces previously mentioned. Above each bowl, which is supported by the leaves of an acanthus tree, surmounting a pedestal corresponding to the pattern of the great centre-piece, is the figure of an angel, in frosted silver.

On the same occasion, the general committee of the Cork, Cloyne, and Ross Diocesan Church Education Society presented an address and testimonial. The latter was one of Baxter's bibles, with gold rim, clasp, and plate; and on the same day he received an address from the clerical meeting at Bandon.

1867. January 13th.—Robert Gilbert Eccles, A.B., succeeded. R. G. Eccles, Trinity College, Dublin—son of John Eccles, Esq., of Ecclesville, county Tyrone—was born June 14th, 1826; obtained deacon's orders January 7th, 1850; priested December same year—both at Tuam. Was curate of Westport from 1850 to 1853; of Maguire's-bridge, from 1853 to 1862; of Shaseragh, from 1862 to 1865; of Clabby, from 1865 to 1866; and of Ballibay, from 1866 to 1867. In 1853 he married Nannie Elizabeth, daughter of Lieutenant-Colonel Dickson, of Hollybrook, county Fermanagh, and has numerous issue.

Amongst the virtues for which the rectors of Kilbrogan have been alway conspicuous, is charity. Although some of them may not have acted in strict accordance with the divine precepts which they preached from their pulpits, yet they all gave with an unsparing hand. It is told of one of them, that his glebe was the resort of a crowd of incurables, and to whom he regularly gave relief; but in such a manner as to leave the recipients under the impression they were only receiving their daily wages for their daily labour. A blind man might be seen scraping at a

4—2

gravel walk; a blind woman knitting stockings for a charity school; a lame man helping a lot of others like himself to mind cows; a cripple weeding, &c., &c.

One day a brother clergyman recommended a poor man to him for employment, who had not even the merit of being a Bandonian. "What can we put him to?" said our humane rector, looking along the walks, which were sprinkled with incurables, in every stage of helplessness. "Can he thatch?" "Oh, yes," replied the other, "I think he ought." "Well, then, suppose we put him to strip one of our summer houses; and then let him set to work, and thatch it." On the morrow, a little donkey-cart brought the labourer to his work; a ladder was placed for him against the house, and he was told to mount; but he couldn't—he had no legs!

The parish of Kilbrogan is five miles in length by three in breadth, and contains 7,255 acres. The glebe house, in which the rector resides, was built in 1813, at a cost of £2,861; and to it are attached thirty-two acres of glebe land, valued at two pounds per acre. The rent-charge derived from the parish amounts to £487 10s. 0d. The rector is also entitled to £39 2s. 0d. from the parish of Aglish. In 1860 the Protestant population was 1,038; and the same year, 223 Protestant children attended the schools. The charities of Kilbrogan derive their income from rents, and from interest-money arising from funds lodged in government securities. They are as follows :—

One hundred pounds, recovered by Dr. Browne. Interest to be distributed annually amongst the poor of Kilbrogan.

Fifty pounds sterling, which remained in the hands of Dr. Browne, received by him from the executors of his predecessor, Mr. Robinson. Two-thirds of the interest-money to be distributed annually amongst the poor of Kilbrogan; the other third to the poor of Murragh.

Two hundred pounds sterling, bequeathed by Walter Travers, Esq. Interest to be yearly distributed among ten poor housekeepers of Kilbrogan.

One pound, paid annually out of French's slip, city of Cork.

Five pounds per annum, left by Thomas Lisson to the poor of Kilbrogan, out of the lands of Droumillihy and Kilbegg.

One hundred pounds sterling, bequeathed by Dr. Browne. Interest to be paid to the poor of Kilbrogan.

One thousand pounds. Interest divided between the parishes of Kilbrogan and Ballymodan.—Conner's bequest.

Ten pounds per annum (Irish), left by Thomas Harrisson; chargeable on the lands of Baelgooley. Divided between Kilbrogan and Ballymodan.

Four hundred pounds, left by William Moxly. Interest thereof between Kilbrogan and Ballymodan.

Two hundred pounds, presented to the parish by the Hon. Mrs. William Smyth Bernard. The interest to be annually distributed among twelve poor widows, residents in Kilbrogan.

The following sums are not forthcoming :—

Five shillings, to be paid annually out of the holdings of John Hammet, in the town of Bandon.

One shilling, out of the holdings of George Wheeler, to be paid annually.

Thirty shillings, to be paid annually out of the holdings of Thomas Lisson, of Bandon-Bridge; being Langton's holdings.

Thirty shillings, to be paid by the provost of Bandon for the time being.

Two pounds, payable annually out of the holdings of the widow of the late George Conner.

Two pounds, payable annually out of the premises called Loves' holdings.

Thirty pounds, bequeathed by William Banfield, junior. Interest to be paid annually for the benefit of the poor of Kilbrogan.

On Sunday, March 16th, 1700-1, Bishop Downes admitted Mr. Christie and Mr. Mills to deacon's orders in the parish church, upon which occasion his lordship preached to a congregation of eight hundred people. During the time the French fleet lay in Bantry Bay, in 1796 and 1797, some artillery soldiers were barracked here; and several of the stones, upon which the cannoniers used to sharpen their side arms, may still be seen in the archway of the principal entrance, and in other parts of the sacred edifice. On the 26th of April, 1864, after an interval of one hundred and sixty-three years, another ordination was held here by Bishop Gregg; upon which occasion Mr. J. N. Woodroffe and Mr. Evers were ordained deacons, and the Rev. J. Hoare and Rev. Charles Crosale were priested.

The oldest monument to be found at present, either inside the church or in the adjoining graveyard, is a brass tablet to the memory of Richard Crofte, who was one of the original twelve burgesses of the Bandon corporation. Mr. Crofte was provost of the town in 1617, and also a captain in the town militia; and as such, was present at the great inspection held at Bandon by His Majesty's Commissioners, on the 30th of August, 1622. The brass, which is now affixed to the north wall of the chancel, contains the following inscription :—

"HIC. JACET CORPVS. RICHd. CROFTE VNVS. LIBER BURGENS HVJVS BURGI DE BANDON-BRIDGE, AC QUONDAM. PREPOSIT EJVSDEM QVI OBIIT. VIJmo DIE SEPTEMBRIS ANNO DOMINI ∞ 1629. POSVIT ANNA EJVS MESTISSIMA CONJVX."

On the south wall of the chancel, in Smith's time (1750), was an epitaph, surmounted by a coat of arms, to the memory of Edward Legard, lieutenant to Captain Robert Hyliard. He died January 6th, 1678 :—

> " From the rude world's campaigns, the much-admired
>   Legard! to this dark garrison's retired :
>   Legard! the daring soldier, whose loved name
>   Shall ever flourish in the book of fame!
>   Whose fair example might alone depaint
>   What 'tis to be a military saint!
>   True to his God, his prince, his friend, his word—
>   Rare ornaments—but fit to adorn the sword."

At present the chancel and nave contain monumental inscriptions to the memory of W. H. Stone, Jonathan Clerke, M.D., Rev. F. Spiller, Dean Newman, Captain Clerke, R.E., Rev. Herbert Molesworth, Rev. Robert Kenny, Rev. Thomas Kenny, Rev. Henry Gillman, Frederick Mayne, and Thomas Wright. In the churchyard, on the right of the principal entrance to the church itself, is a headstone to the memory of Eldad Holland, parish clerk,—

> " Whoe departed this life ye 29th day of 7 ber., 1722."

It was this Eldad Holland who paraphrased a portion of the Morning Service, to compliment William the Third. And, adjoining the window of the southern transept, a flat stone records the burial-place of Captain Nash, the celebrated Shane Dearg, or Red Jack :—

" Here lies the body of Captain John Nash, who departed this life 18th of February, in the 75th year of his age, and in the year of Our Lord 1725."*

Built against the east wall of the chancel (south end) is a monument, composed of an altar-tomb, faced with cut lime stone, and two ornamental pillars supporting a pediment, and enclosing a tablet affixed to the chancel wall, thus inscribed :—

" Here lie the remains of John Jones, Esq., formerly burgess and town clerk of this corporation, who died the 11th of August, 1743."

Close to the wall of the chancel is a flat stone, formerly erect, containing the following lines :—

---

* He was buried on the 20th. His wife, Abigail, was buried in Kilbrogan on the 22nd of September, 1722; and, perhaps, it was owing to this that Captain Nash was buried there also, and not to any fear on the part of his relatives that his remains would be exhumed by the country people.

> "Though Boreas's winds and Neptune's seas
>   Have tossed me to and fro,
> In spite of both, by God's decrees,
>   I harbour here below ;
> Where at an anchor I do ride
>   With many of our fleet ;
> But now again I hope to sail
>   Our Saviour, Christ, to meet."

Thomas French and family burying-place, 1782.

Over a vault, near to this, is an altar-tomb. On the slab :—

"Here lyeth the body of Mr. Thomas Harrisson, who departed this life in the year of our Lord 1674, and left to the poor of Kilbrogan ten pounds a year for ever."

On a small upright stone :—

"Here lyeth the body of J. P. Commarelli, who departed this life October 16th, 1789."

Underneath the inscription is a cross. Commarelli is said, by some, to have been the only Roman Catholic ever buried within the walls of this churchyard. Others assert that he was a Huguenot.

On an upright stone :—

> "Farewell, vain world, I've had enough of thee;
> And now I'm careless what you think of me !
> Thy smiles I court not, nor thy frowns I fear;
> My head's at rest—I now lie quiet here.
> What faults you see in me, be sure you shun,
> And look at home, enough there's to be done."

William Goodwin Atkins, departed this life the fourth of March, in the 52nd year of his age, 1797.

On a flat oblong slab, much worn :—

"Here lyeth the body of Stephen Duer, the only son of Stephen and Ann Duer, of ye Island of Antigua—1701."

On a headstone :—

"Here lies the body of George Ford *and family*, who departed this life December 12th, 1801, aged 55 years."

Adjoining the west wall :—

"Here lyeth ye body of Mrs. Rebecca Splaine, wife of Mr. James Splaine the elder, aged 83 years; *the weare* married 64 years and six months, and departed this life April 16th, 1782."*

---

* Within the recollections of some old people, who died during the last thirty years, there were Protestants also interred at St. Michael's burial-ground, in Kilbrogan parish; and tombstones are there yet to the memory of some buried there a

We are unable to state positively at what time the chancel and transepts were added; but it would seem that they were amongst the enlargements made by Lord Cork, when he became sole owner of the Kilbrogan side of the town, in 1625; and who claims to have enlarged and finished the two churches—Kilbrogan and Ballymodan—in this year. The chancel, at all events, was in existence in 1629; and it is highly probable the transepts also. Tradition says that they were built of stone brought from St. Michael's, an ancient building, which at that time occupied the site of the present Roman Catholic chapel at Kilbrogan.

In 1829, two hundred pounds were expended on the church by the Board of First Fruits; and prior to that, we have no doubt, various other sums from time to time. But it was reserved for a descendant of its first great benefactor, after an interval of over two hundred and thirty years, to enlarge and renew the old edifice; and thus render it more commodious and suitable for divine service than it was ever before. The church was lengthened by twelve feet. It was re-floored, roofed with dark oak, re-pewed, a rich stained-glass window placed in the chancel, a new organ placed in a new gallery at the western end of the nave, and a graceful tower and spire erected. The entire of these additions and improvements were effected at a cost of three thousand and thirty pounds. Of this sum the Ecclesiastical Commissioners granted twelve hundred and seven pounds; and the rest, amounting to eighteen hundred and twenty-three pounds, was raised by the untiring exertions of the late rector.

Although eighteen hundred and twenty-three pounds is at all times a formidable sum to be collected in a country town in the south of Ireland, by one individual; yet to those who remember the dire days of the famine years, when the owners of every tenement and every acre of land, in this part of the kingdom, trembled before the overwhelming responsibilities which met his gaze on every side, the task will appear still more arduous and more formidable.

---

long time since. In fact, before the erection of Kilbrogan church, it was there the original settlers used to bury their dead. The following are, we believe, the only two inscriptions remaining there now, or have been there lately:—

"Here lyeth the body of Anne Dyke, *alias* Harrisson, a virgin, formerly from Bristol."

"Here lyeth the body of Thomas Rice, a merchant from Bristol, who died A.D. 1639."

St. Michael's church was used as a place of Protestant worship by the first settlers. It was in good repair in 1615.

The church is approached from the North Main Street, by a flight of forty limestone steps. It is of the early English style of the thirteenth century, and consists of a nave seventy feet long by twenty-eight feet and a-half wide; a chancel, twenty-eight long by twenty-two broad; and two transepts (north and south), each sixteen feet long by twenty feet wide. In the entrance porch, on the left hand side, is the communion table used originally in the church. It contains a brass-plate with the following inscription :—

"Original communion table used in Christ Church, Kilbrogan, from the time of the building of the church, A.D. 1610 to A.D. 1862. Restored and preserved September, 1862."

The interior is lofty and imposing. A fine arch, of the early pointed style, separates the nave from the chancel; the open timbered roof is of varnished oak, and is supported by massive trusses, resting on corbels of Caen stone. The chancel window, which is divided into five lights by stone mullions, is filled with stained glass, emblazoned with brilliant colours. The other windows—two in the transepts and five in the nave— are lancet-shaped, and are divided into three lights by two stone mullions. The large window in the eastern end of the nave is also lancet-shaped, and is separated by four mullions (also of stone) into lights similar in number to those of the chancel. Of the tower, the base is square, and the upper portion octagon. It is surmounted by a spire, which, including the tower, is one hundred feet in height.

The memories of many successive generations render venerable the walls of this old historic pile. When the great rebellion raged in 1642, and when thousands of the enemy lay encamped in our neighbourhood, panting to extinguish our settlement by drenching it with the blood of the settlers, the church bell of Kilbrogan invited the people to the house of prayer as uninterruptedly as if all outside the church walls were in the enjoyment of peace and prosperity. When an Irish commander and an Irish garrison held our town for King James, it was the bell of old Kilbrogan gave the signal to the townsmen to rush on them and disarm them. When an Irish army surprised Bandon on a Sabbath noon, and when Irish soldiers and Irish pipers impiously interrupted divine service here, it was those old walls that then looked grave and sad. And when news of the great battle which the great Protestant king gained at the Boyne reached the ears of the Bandonians, it was those very walls that then looked bright and cheerful with the reflection of the bright and cheerful faces of those who looked up to heaven and thanked God.

1610.   In consequence of the number of " wandering travellers " roaming about the country at this time, orders were sent to Bandon-Bridge and other towns,—

" That no taverner, innkeeper, or ale-house-keeper, within the town or suburbs, shall receive or contynue any such wandering traveller in his house, without the lyke bringing or sending him, within three days, unto the said vice-president, or some one of the councell, to be further delt with ; all according to pollicy and justice."

1611.   The government were busy preparing bills for the approaching parliament. Amongst those was one for incorporating Bandon, Belfast, Enniskillen, &c. ; to encourage the making of linen cloth; the sowing of hemp and flax ; to restrain the inordinate haunting and tippling in inns, ale-houses, and other victualling-houses ; to prevent all persons from re-marriage until their former partners were dead ; to prevent a man having a wife from turning her away at pleasure.

1612.   Owing to the great quantity of timber growing on the banks of the Bandon river, they became a favourite place for smelting. The East-India Company* paid no less than seven thousand pounds for woods in the vicinity of Downdanial Castle. The ore was brought from various places, and taken in boats as far up the river as the water would allow. A great deal of what was smelted here was brought from the iron mines of Araglin, Saltibridge, and Ballinatray, by Lord Cork. Indeed, so extensively engaged was his lordship in mining operations, that at one time it was computed he had in his bloomeries no less than one thousand tons of bar-iron, twenty thousand tons of pig-iron (worth eighteen pounds a ton), and two hundred tons of rod-iron.

---

* Smith says the East-India Company built two new ships of five hundred tons here, and erected a dock for building more. It is not improbable that they built boats at Downdanial, and constructed a dock there to load them.

CHAPTER III.

THE CHARTER—THE FIRST PROVOST AND BURGESSES—"NO PAPIST INHABITANT"
TO DWELL WITHIN THE TOWN—THE PROVOST'S DAY—OUR TWO FIRST MEMBERS
OF PARLIAMENT—BALLYMODAN CHURCH, ITS CLERGY, CHARITIES, MONUMENTS, ETC.

HE Letters Patent incorporating Bandon bear date, Dublin, March 30th, "in the tenth yeare of oure reigne" (1613). "By these letters, all the inhabitants of said town and lands, for ever, shall, by means of these presents, be one body corporate and politic, in deed, fact, and name, by the name of the Portrief, Free-Burgesses, and Commonalty of the borough of Bandon-Bridge." They are addressed by James, "by the grace of God, of England, Scotland, France, and Ireland, defender of the Faith, &c.," to all to whom these Letters Patent shall come, and are as follows:—

"Know ye that we, as well by the humble petition of the inhabitants of the village of Bandon-Bridge, county of Cork, as also for the inhabiting and planting of these parts, within the said kingdom, depopulated and wasted, and by these presents, doth appoint the village or villages, houses, tenements, &c., on both sides of the water running under the bridge, to be one entire and free borough; and henceforth to be called the borough of Bandon-Bridge."

Then comes the appointment of a portrief and burgesses, all of whom are named. Power is then given to return two members to Parliament; to appoint a commonalty; to appoint a court of record; provision made in case provost should die, &c. The provost was empowered to hold a court of record for recovery of debt, trespass, contract and personal demands whatsoever, not exceeding five marks sterling, on every Thursday; to appoint a clerk of the market, who shall assize bread, ale, and beer, and who shall not charge more than fourpence

(Irish) for sealing (*i.e.* stamping) any barrel, peck, or other measure, or for sealing weights; jointly with the burgesses to make bye-laws; to have a guild mercatory; to choose proper officers, &c.   The first portrief or provost was Captain Sir William Newce, and the other burgesses were :—

Edward Beecher,	Christopher Lewis,
John Walley,	Stephen Skipwith,
Richard Richmond, *alias* Skipward,	Thomas Taylor,
Thomas Adderly,	William Walley,
Nicholas Blacknell,	William Cecill.*
Richard Crofte,	

Some of the very first enactments of the free burgesses were directed against Papists† and pigs.   Indeed, the Papists were treated even worse than the pigs.   A pig may feed and snooze away in his owner's backside until the fat shook on his ribs; but there was no one to place a trencher before a Papist, or to ask him, or even to permit him, to rest his weary limbs within the boundaries of the borough.   It was decreed "that no Papist inhabitant shall be suffered to dwell within the town."   There was also an ordinance "for the suppressing of hogs, swyne, and pigs openlye to passe and goe in the streets."   As "the proprietors of suche cattle, eyther out of some neglect or wilful contempte, have not redressed the saide unseemlinesse, ffor remedy thereof, it is decreed and established that henceforth, if, at any tyme, any hoggs, swyne, or pigs shall be found or observed to passe in the open streets of any parte of the borroughe, or shall be fedd, kept, or lodged nere unto the mansions or dwelling-houses of any of the inhabitants, but onelye in the farthest, remotest partes of the backsides of such as shalle keepe them."   Should any of these regulations be broken, the proprietor of the cattle had his

---

* The following is the bill of costs furnished to the corporation in connection with the Charter :—

	£	s.	d.		£	s.	d.
Paid the king's attorney-general	0	10	0	For copy of the king's letter,	0	15	8
Draft of warrant for attorney,	0	10	0	For entry of the king's letter,	1	15	8
For the order of reference to the				For report, ...	0	10	8
attorney-general, and entering				King's attorney-general, . .	3	10	0
thereof, ...	0	19	6	Attorney-general's clerk, . .	0	10	0
For report to the lord-lieutenant							
and council, ...	2	10	0		£13	7	2
Paid at the castle for two orders,	1	15	8				

† The act excluding the Roman Catholics was more a matter of policy than of prejudice.   The Irish were intensely hostile to the new settlers; and the latter thought it dangerous to leave them within the walls at night.   It was not the effect of whim or spleen, says the author of *Seasonable Advice*, but was a necessary support for the infant colony.

attention called thereunto; and if he did not "redress the mischief, then the saide hoggs, swyne, or pigs passing openlyc, or inwardly fedd, kepte, or lodged, shall be forfeited, and remayne to the use of the corporation, and bee disposed of as the provost or vice-provost for the tyme being shall think meete."

The corporation devoted a great deal of attention to sanitary purposes. They insisted that the streets should be kept clean; that the water-courses should not be converted into open sewers; "and, because sundrye other nuisances are daylie used and committed by the inhabitants residing within the libertie of this borroughe, as well by directing soyle in the open streets there, as also in the water-courses, or small streams of water, now made and provided for their necessarye uses of household, which the passage in the saide street bye that means, and want of due riddance of the same, doe become most fowle and loathsome; and the saide water also no lesse putrifiyed and unwholesome. Therefore, &c., it is hereby ordered and decreed that if any of the saide inhabitants shall be convycted for any of the lyke nuysance or other whatsoever annoyances, either abroade or within theire several backsydes or dwel-lings, and shall not reforme same upon warning given, shall forfeite, severally and respectively, the sum of ivs. iivd. sterling for each nuis-ance or annoyance so by hym done." In case the transgressor had no goods or chattels, he was "to be restrayned in the marshalsye of the saide borroughe; there to remayne without boyle or mainprise, according to the will and pleasure of the provost or vice-provost aforesayde."

The streets the authorities had resolved to keep clear as well as clean. There was a bye-law against the abuses of dogs; and no one but a free-man was permitted to buy or sell calves in the street, under a penalty of three shillings and fourpence for each offence. The houses in the streets were also looked after. No freeman was allowed to receive into his dwelling, under a penalty of forty shillings, any lodger, without first acquainting the provost; and landlords themselves were not permitted, under any circumstances, to let a house or a tenement to either a strumpet or a vagabond. Destitute people, who are to be found in almost every community, were not wanting in this; neither was their destitution overlooked or forgotten. The corporation were not half a dozen years in being, when a fund, called the poor man's box, existed. It was supplied by "money received for judgments in court, and kept for use of the poor man's box." The following are the fines and penalties paid into it for the year 1619 :—

	£	s.	d.		£	s.	d.
Of John Heard, ...	0	0	20	An Irishman *v*. Dermod Coghlan	0	0	20
Richard Smith, ...	0	0	20	Robert Smith *v*. Field Veege,	0	0	20
Cunningham, an Irishman, .	0	0	20	Richard Glyn *v*. John Braly,	0	0	20
Thomas Porter *v*. Edward Turner	0	0	20	Randall Fenton *v*. Margaret			
Newco *v*. Mat Ellis, . . .	0	0	20	Alleyn, ...	0	0	20
Richard Kingston *v*. Edward				— Battyn *v*. Edward Nicolls,	0	0	20
Porter, ...	0	0	20	John Berry *v*. Blacknell, . .	0	0	20
— Nash, ...	0	0	20	Honora Carthy *v*. Porter, .	0	0	20
Richard Crofte *v*. Henry Johnson	0	0	20				

In 1622 a common council, consisting of twelve members, was appointed. They were chosen by the freemen; and from their ranks the burgesses were to be elected, and from the burgesses, the provost. It was, therefore, necessary from this year to be a common councilman before either of the other two dignities could be obtained. The installation of the provost was one of the great events of the year. What lord mayor's day is to the Londoners, provost's day was to the Bandonians, and something more; for our townsmen enjoyed a luxury to which the inhabitants of the great metropolis are strangers. The London mob cannot cuff their chief magistrate to their liking. Not so the Bandon mob, as they enjoyed unlimited license in this particular. But, curious as it may seem, they exercised their privilege in a way the reverse of the method adopted by modern humanity for displaying its affection or dislike. An unpopular magistrate was permitted to perambulate the streets alone and unheeded. No one would stir a step to give him a dig in the ribs, or strike him on the back or shoulders, or even fling a fistful of coarse flour into his eyes.

The provost was elected at midsummer, and entered upon his duties at Michaelmas. Duly attended by the constables of the north and south side, by the clerk of the market, the bell-ringer, and his friends, he used to walk round the borough boundaries, proclaiming the jurisdiction of the corporation. His worship and his officers all wore new suits of clothes on the occasion; and during the procession, if the new chief magistrate was well liked, he and his staff were accompanied by a crowd of the townspeople, who pelted his worship with handfuls of coarse bran. They took especial delight in showering bran all over his new robes. This was done to some extent as an amusement, but generally to signify that they hoped his year of office would turn out a year of abundance. If he happened to be particularly popular, by blinding him altogether they hoped to let him *see* how they esteemed him. They must have thought that by throwing dust in his eyes they would render him more clear-sighted, and thus afford him a better view of the various objects likely to attract his magisterial vision. Upon reaching his own house, it was customary for him to stand forth, in all the flour of his popularity, and, in all likelihood choking with emotion and bran, he used to thank them over and over again for the many striking manifestations of their approbation; and would tell them, probably with more truthfulness than is usual on those occasions, that he hoped he would never die until he had repaid them for the great favour they had that day conferred upon him.

We have said before that power was given to the burgesses to return two members to Parliament. They soon availed themselves of this privilege; and they sent Sir Richard Morrisson, Knt. (privy councillor, and vice-president of the province of Munster), and William Crow, Esq., of Crow's Nest, Dublin (keeper of the Writs, and chirographer of the Common Pleas), to represent them in the new Parliament, which was to hold its first sitting on the 18th of May, A.D. 1613. For seven and twenty years the faithful Commons had not assembled, and all Dublin ran to see the novel and imposing spectacle.

Amid a flourish of trumpets, Lord Buttevant advanced, bearing the sword of state. The Earl of Thomand followed, with the cup of maintenance; then came the peers of the realm and other notables; the clergy; the archbishops and bishops in their scarlet robes; and last of all, the Lord-Deputy, dressed in the rich robes of purple velvet, which the King gave him, and mounted on a stately charger, trapped with a profusion of gorgeous decorations. The procession set out from the Castle, and proceeded to St. Patrick's cathedral, where the Protestant portion of the processionists listened to a sermon from Hampton, the Primate. Upon the conclusion of the service, they all returned to the Castle; and then ensued a scene which must have impressed the minds of our young legislators with notions widely apart from those with which men, in all ages, have invested the deliberations and decorum of the senate.

The house was a full one. There were two hundred and twenty-six members present, out of a total of two hundred and thirty-two. One hundred and twenty-five of these belonged to the English party, and one hundred and one to the Irish. The English wished to place Sir

John Davis in the speaker's chair, and the Irish preferred it should be occupied by Sir John Everard. Upon a division, it was found that Davis was elected by a majority of twenty-four. During the process of taking the votes, the Irish party, who guessed how the voting would turn out, had resolved to take Time by the forelock, by placing their own candidate in the coveted seat. But the English party had no idea of allowing themselves to be thus tricked. They told Everard that if he did not vacate, "they would pluck him forth." Nevertheless, he clung to the chair still; whereupon Wingfield, St. John, and some others, lifted up Davis bodily, and placed him in the spurious chairman's lap. Perceiving that Davis's colleagues were not to be bullied out of their rights, Everard's friends gave way; and catching Sir John by the collar of his coat, they lifted him out of his uneasy seat. He hobbled out of the house, as well as the sprained leg, which he had received in the fray, would permit; and joined the rest of his party, who had walked out indignantly in a body.

Although the senior member, Sir Richard Morrisson—admitted a member of the King's Inns in 1610—was vice-president of the province of Munster, where he must necessarily have many important duties to discharge, yet he found time to attend to his parliamentary duties also. He was chairman of a committee " to enquire into the fees that were charged by judge's clerks;" and at another time he appears, with eleven others, sitting in committee on a bill entitled, "An Act to assure the lands of Piers Lacye to Sir Thomas Standish."

Mr. Crow, our junior representative,—who built a snug residence for himself near Trinity College, Dublin, which he very appropriately called the "Crow's Nest," and which is memorable as being the house where Sir William Petty accomplished his colossal labour, *The Down Survey*,—did not devote much of his time to his parliamentary duties. Even still, the Crow's Nest leaves a trace of its former being behind it, in Crow Street—a street which derives its name from, and occupies the site of, the old Rookery. Mr. Crow, although he lived near the house, does not appear as often in its journals as his colleague. He sat with eight other members in committee on " a bill against secret outlawries," and upon some others.

O'Sullivan, a county of Cork man, and a grandson of Dermod O'Sullivan, Prince of Berehaven, writes ferociously against this Parliament. On the opening of it, says he, Lord Buttevant carried the sword before the Deputy to the church, to hear the blind ministers of the devil. Again, " the Catholic bishops are. excluded, and the heretic usurpers of their titles and sees vote in Parliament in their stead."

1613.   Inquisitions were first held in Bandon. It was usual in these days, when a ·tenant of the crown died, for the escheator to empannel a jury of the county to which the deceased belonged, or possessed landed property in, and enquire as to what lands he died seized of, and who were his rightful heirs. These enquiries were termed "Inqnisitiones Post Mortem," and frequently escheats. There were upwards of one hundred and twenty of them held here,* principally before William Wiseman, escœtor Domini Regis.

The first jury that sat in Bandon was in the case of James Fitzwilliam Roche, September 10th, 1613; and the last was in Finin O'Driskeill's case, on the 15th of August, 1694. Among the names of those concerning whom the enquiries were held here, are to be found those of Lord Viscount Buttevant, in 1630; Lord David Barrymore, in 1630; John Lord Coursey, 1620; Lord Viscount Cartie, April 31st, 1620; Lord Charles Cartie, September 31st, 1620; Walter Coppinger, Miles, 1639; Lord Viscount Fermoy, September 31st, 1639; John, Lord Baron Kinsale, 1639; Kildare Gerald, Comes; Randal Hurly, 1631; Richard Aldworth, 1630, &c., &c. The reports were generally in Latin. We give the two following as specimens :—

Inq'. Capt. apud de Bandon-Bridge in com. Corke quarto die Octobr' Anni regni dni Caroli, &c., decimo quinto, Coram William Vicecomit Sarsfield de Killmallocke et aliis p. sacrum p. box, &c., qui dic' quod Donnell O'Hearlihy nup de Ballyvorney in com' pred' seitus fuit de feodo de le carrucat' terr' de Ballyvorney pred' val' per anni decem solid'. Et sic inde seitus existens obiit sic inde seitus in anno dni 1637. Et quod Will' McDonnell O'Hearlihy est ejus fil' et heres. Et quod idem Willus fuit plue etatis et maritat' tempore mortis pris sue pd' Postremog Tur pred' dic' quod oia p. miss tempore mortis p. fate Danial tenebrant' de rege nune in capite per service' mil'.

Inq'. Capt'. anno regni dni Caroli, &c., sexto, quarto et decimo die August coram William Wiseman qui die quod Richus Aldworth nup de Newmarket co com' Cork, Miles, Seitus fuit de Feodo de Maner Castra ·Vill et terr de Newmarket p. contin quatuor decem carrucat terr et val p. ann Septem libr. Et de Lismul-coynyn contin quatuor carrucat terr et val p. annum quadragint solid. Et Coolmoata cont tres carrucat terr annui valor triginti solid. Et quod Richus Aldworth mil sic inde seit

---

* See Catalogue of Inquisitions preserved in Court of Chancery; also Inquisitions themselves, Record Tower, Dublin Castle.

existens omia. p. miss dimisit qui busdam Johni Veale tunc av modo
mil Rico Bettesworth et Thomas Searle gen; also to Jephson and Hyde.

The old Protestant church of Ballymodan was built.   It
1614.   consisted of a nave forty feet long by twenty feet wide, and
(at western end) a tower sixty feet in height.   In the tower were two
large windows, one over the other; and in the northern wall of the
church itself, two windows twenty feet high by ten wide, a doorway
twenty feet high by ten wide, and over the doorway a square window
ten feet high by ten wide.   At the east end of the nave was the largest
window, which was thirty feet high and fifteen broad.   Previous to this
church's erection, the Protestants of Ballymodan worshipped in the
church which had belonged to the Roman Catholics, and which was
situated in the old graveyard, at the top of Foxe's Street, in the Irish-
town.

Tradition is fully corroborated on this subject, by an official document
which records the depositions of Mr. Woodner, Samuel Coombes, and
others, " who, being antient men, deposed on their own knowledge, that
the parish church stood in part of the said Irish-town, and that all the
inhabitants of Bandon-Bridge (on the south-side) went to the said parish
church, there being none other parish church save in the said Irish-town;
which was likewise confessed by the defendants.   And also that some of
the burgesses nominated in the Patent, viz. :—Stephen Skipwith,
Thomas Taylor, and William Cecill, worshipped in the same, they
living at the south-side."

The inhabitants grew dissatisfied with the distance of the old church
from their homes.   To quote their own words, " they thought the said
parish church too remote from the town and the other plantations;"
and were naturally anxious to have a church in which none ever
worshipped but those of the purified faith, just like their fellow-
townsmen had on the opposite side of the river.   On applying to Henry
Beecher, he granted them a site for the new church " in the seigniory of
Castle-Mahon, without the town part of the tenement of the said Henry
Beecher, of Castle-Mahon," merely reserving to himself a space in the
new church for a seat.*

---

* A portion of the space reserved by Beecher was subsequently given for a seat
for the provost during his official year, and the rest was assigned by him to his son-
in-law, Charles James, Esq., who was living at Castle-Mahon in 1631, and by whom
it was sold, with the Castle-Mahon estate, to Francis Bernard, Esq., ancestor of the
Earl of Bandon.

It was built by contributions. Some quarried the stone; others drew them; more felled and fashioned the timber; and many gave money. Among stthe latter was Lord Cork, who tells us in his diary, under date September 10th, 1614, "I gave my year's rent of my parsonage of Ballymodan, as a help towards the building of the new church at Bandon-Bridge."

It would seem that the daily increasing number of the settlers soon required that the church accommodation should be extended; and it is highly probable that the transepts and chancel were added by Lord Cork* when he became owner of the incorporated town of Bandon (south-side) by deed of feoffment, from Henry Beecher, dated May 2nd, 1619.

The enlarged building was a plain, unpretending structure; and was entered by a porch, over which was the date of the church's erection in 1614. Inside, it was gloomy and dark. The floors of the nave and transepts were covered by huge high-backed seats, large enough for the owner and his family to stretch at full length and take a comfortable nap, in case the homily was wearisome or too long. At the west window of the nave, and almost touching the ceiling, was the organ, in a gallery set apart for it and the choir. Underneath this was another gallery, which formed a portion of the large gallery which ran along the northern and southern walls of the nave. The transepts also contained a gallery each. Although to modern eyes this sombre, prim old edifice, with its box-stall pews and solemn-looking walls, would seem fit only to be occupied by a serious people, yet such was not the case.

In the olden times this was our fashionable church. It was here the provost sat, with the insignia of his office lying on a scarlet cushion† before him. In an adjoining seat sat the governor of the town; and in various portions of the building were the bright uniforms and the glittering accoutrements of the officers belonging to the various regiments that were quartered here. And many a gay gallant, with the flowing curls of his powdered wig streaming over the collar of his gilt-edged coat, and wearing an ivory or a steel-handled rapier by his side, strutted up the flagged aisle,—holding his cocked hat lightly between his

---

* Lord Cork speaks of having completed Ballymodan Church, and also Kilbrogan.

† After the battle of the Boyne, the cushion was always of orange velvet, bound with the orthodox blue.

jewelled fingers, and looking approvingly on the folds of the ample frill which over-lapped his embroidered waistcoat, or at the Mechlin lace ruffles which encircled his wrists; then when seated, instead of reading reverentially the lessons of the day, he chose rather to exchange furtive glances with the young lady in the big-hooped petticoat, in the gallery. And when the service was over he escorted her home, or walked by the side of some other fair favourite, whose gold-clocked stockings, or whose red-heeled shoes, proclaimed her as one of the belles of the day.

On the 1st of November, 1846, the Hon. and Rev. C. B. Bernard, a descendant of the nobleman to whom Ballymodan Church was so much indebted, preached the last sermon a congregation was ever destined to hear within its walls. The text was, "By the river of Babylon there we sat down. Yea, we wept when we remembered Zion." A crowded and attentive audience listened to the powerful and impressive discourse* which followed.

The foundation-stone of the new church, dedicated to St. Peter, was laid with appropriate ceremonial, by the Earl of Bandon, on the 9th of March, 1847; and the church itself was opened for divine worship on the 30th of August, 1849,† by Bishop Wilson. It is a large and handsome structure, of the decorated style of Gothic architecture, and consists of a spacious nave, with two aisles, two transepts (north and south), a chancel, and a vestry-room. On its north-western extremity is a quadrangular tower, from the top of which a most extensive view of the town and surrounding country is obtained. The lower windows of the church are large, with pointed arches, and divided into three lights by stone mullions. Those of the clerestory consist of two lights, and have flattened elliptical arches. The interior is spacious and imposing. The eight pointed

---

* "What a history," said the preacher, "could these walls unfold! Here, Sabbath after Sabbath, worshipped our common forefathers, 'one Lord, one Faith, one Baptism,' with ourselves. Here listened they to those solemn truths which chasten into holy zeal the spirit which has so long distinguished the town of Bandon —that firmness of principle—that attachment to Protestantism—that honour for the word of God. Here the sorrowing friend or parent has had the full anxiety of a congregation's intercession, following the wanderer in his path of sin. Hither have you brought your children, and consecrated them upon the threshold of their lives—to God. Here, in riper intellect, have you confessed yourselves in confirmation, 'soldiers and servants of the Cross.' Here every detail of your domestic joys and sorrows has been hallowed; while the last resting-place around has been consecrated to you afresh, by tears of separation and hopes of immortality.—(See Sermon preached in the Old Parish of Ballymodan, &c.)

† It was built by Thomas Caroll, from plans furnished by George Welland, architect to the Ecclesiastical Commissioners.

arches, by which the aisles communicate with the nave, stand upon clustered columns of great beauty, and are of a commanding character; whilst the three noble arches which span the entrance to the chancel and transepts are colossal in their proportions, and will not fail to impress the mind of the spectator with their loftiness and grandeur. The roof of the nave and the other portions of the building are of stained oak, and lean for support on trusses, resting on corbels of cut stone. The window of the chancel, the upper portion of which is of elaborate tracery, is divided into five lights by four stone mullions. There is also a large window at the western end of the nave, but it is almost concealed by the organ—a magnificent instrument, presented to the parishioners by the Honorable and Very Reverend Richard B. Bernard. The transepts, which are of similar height to the nave, contain a gallery each, and are lighted by windows of considerable size.

The church contains many monuments. Against the south wall of the nave (west end) is a fine monument, by Flaxman, to the memory of Francis Bernard, Esq., one of the judges of the Court of Common Pleas in the reign of Queen Anne. On a marble tablet, in Gothic characters of raised brass-gilt, is the following inscription :—

"FRANCIS BERNARD, ESQ.,
OBIIT JUN XXIX. MDCCXXXI.
ÆTATIS. SUÆ LXVIII."

The figures at the side, composed of white statuary marble, are of life-size. That on the right represents Justice, in whose countenance the stern requirements of duty are blended with co-mingled feelings of thoughtfulness and commiseration. The goddess is in a sitting posture, and has in the right hand a drawn sword. The elbow of the left arm rests on the knee, and the open hand supports the chin and side-face. On the left is Minerva, helmeted, and reclining on her ægis, on which is the dying head of Medusa, twined with living serpents. In the south aisle (west) is a beautifully wrought altar-tomb of Caen stone, to the memory of James, Earl of Bandon. It is from the chisel of Richardson, of London, and exhibits a full-length figure of the earl, robed, in a recumbent position ; the head rests on a cushion; at the feet is a coronet. On three sides of the tomb are shields of arms ; and on the side fronting the nave is the coat of arms of the Bernards, with supporters, surmounted by an earl's coronet. On the corresponding part (opposite side) a long inscription records the honours and virtues of the deceased peer.

Adjoining this, a handsome monument has been erected by the

parishioners of Ballymodan, to the memory of the Honorable and Very
Reverend Richard Boyle Bernard, Dean of Leighlin. The epitaph
commemorates "his devoted piety, his zeal in the extension of the
gospel of his Saviour, his self-denying liberality in the cause of
scriptural education, and his munificence in aid of the funds raised for
the erection of this church." On one side of the inscribed tablet—on
which is a cinerary urn—is the figure of an angel in alto-relievo, pointing
triumphantly to the words—" Go and do thou likewise." On the other
side—the figure of a boy kneeling, also in high relief. Near this is a
decorated tablet to the memory of Francis B. Sweeny; and in the
south aisle are handsome white marble monumental slabs to the memory
of John Shine, George Thomas, several members of the Honour family,
and to the daughters of the first Earl of Bandon. Close to the gallery
of the south transept is a white marble slab to the memory of Mary
Synge, wife of Rev. George Synge, rector of Kilbrogan. She died
November 23rd, 1684. Mrs. Synge was the daughter of Thomas
Hewitt, Esq., of Clancoole, and her husband was the third son of
George, Lord Bishop of Cork. The following lines were inscribed
beneath a shield on which the family arms were emblazoned, and
which formerly stood beneath the west door of the south transept :—

> " Below—the pride of ancestors—there lies,
> Mouldered in dust, death's lovely sacrifice—
> Her parent's darling, and her husband's pride—
> Whence she was once, a daughter and a bride.
> Lovely without, but fairer much within,
> Her virtues daily triumphed over sin ;
> Thus ripe for nobler joys, she swiftly fled
> To the immortal living, from the dead !

Underneath lies interred the body of Mrs. Mary Synge, &c., &c.

> If grief could speak my loss, or tears retrieve,
> Thy weeping monument I'd ever live."

The floor of the chancel contains no less than sixteen tablets of
variegated marble to various members of the house of Bernard. On
the north wall of the chancel is a monument in the decorated Gothic
style, to Francis, Earl of Bandon. The base is supported by a double-
headed Prussian eagle, crowned, holding a shield with the Bernard's
crest. Above the buttresses is an embattled canopy, bearing the earl's
arms quartered with those of Boyle, with the stag and unicorn supporters
in alto-relievo. The epitaph is in Gothic characters, with illuminated
capitals. Alongside this is a monument in similar Gothic style, to the

Honorable Francis Bernard, lieutenant 9th Light Dragoons, who died whilst with his regiment on active service in Portugal. On the opposite side is a monument also in Gothic characters, to the Honorable Henry Boyle Bernard (fifth son of Earl Francis), cornet 1st Dragoon Guards, who was killed at the battle of Waterloo, on the memorable 18th of June, 1815; and to the east of this is a spacious monument to Catherine Henrietta, Countess of Bandon, daughter of Richard, Earl of Shannon, with an inscription by the Rev. Dr. Lovett, D.D. Upon the east wall, near gallery of north transept, is a monument, with the representation of the burial of Christ, in relief; underneath which is an epitaph to the memory of Thomas Revill Guest. At the south side of the choir, (east end) is an octagonal limestone font, thus inscribed :—

"LAVAET MUNDUS ESTO, R.G. M.Y. J.H. WARᵈˢ. 1719."

On the flat rim :—

"M.Y., 1719, J.H."

Ballymodan was anciently called Bally-budan (that is the place of the little boat). By the latter name it is mentioned in the list prepared by order of Pope Nicolas the Fourth, A.D. 1291; and in which it is rated at seven marks a-year. The parish is a vicarage with cure. It is three and a half miles long by two broad, and contains 7,820 acres. In 1860 the vicar's rent-charge was three hundred per annum. He is also entitled to the rent of ten statute acres of the old glebe land—no residence. Protestant population in 1831 was 2,264; and in 1860, 1,550. In the latter year, also, 162 children attended the schools. The Parish Register does not commence until 1695. The first entry under the head of marriages is dated June 16th, 1695; and records that, on that day, Richard Maddox was married to Sarah Bacchus. Under births, same year, we find Robert, son of Pentecost Tyler; Mary, daughter of Edward Bennett; and under same heading next year (*i.e.*—1696), Alexander, son of Edward Collyer, quaker. Collyer, the Register states, was admitted in the presence of many persons. In 1699, according to Dive Downes, the church was in good repair; there was a sermon every Sunday, very few Papists in the parish, and the sacrament four times a-year. The following is a list of the births, deaths, and marriages to be found in the Registry Book* for several years, beginning with 1695, and ending with 1830 :—

---

* The Registry Book does not contain all the marriages and births in the parish. A great many of the inhabitants were Presbyterians; and many of them were married and had their children baptised by their own minister.

	Births.	Deaths.	Marriages.		Births.	Deaths.	Marriages.		Births.	Deaths.	Marriages.
1695	54	No account	16	1703	64	25	13	1770*	56	62	5
1696	44	28	7	1709	50	38	10	1780	Very badly kept, leaves of Register injured.		
1697	46	16	8	1720	51	30	8	1790	40	26	64
1698	46	37	9	1730	64	101	19	1800	93	96	5
1699	46	38	17	1740	48	158	2	1810	71	53	10
1700	60	28	11	1750	48	107	17	1820	102	32	15
1701	43	44	10	1760	29	53	17	1830	55	43	12

1591.   John Newman was vicar of Ballymodan.   He was also vicar of Brinny.   The rector was Nicholas Thornby.   It was also stated in a M.S., same date, that " Rectoria de Ballimodan spect. ad ab. de Tracton vicar ibm Nicolaus Tompkins."   Another portion of the same document says, " Ecclia de Ballymodan Nich. Thomkyns vic ejusdem Rich. Newman."

1615.   Robert Sutton, vicar.   " Rectoria spectat ad Abbathiam de Tracton."   The vicarage was valued at seven pounds per annum.   Sutton held also the vicarage of Kilbrogan and Desertserges.†

1628.   Thomas Weight, vicar.   In 1630 the cup at present in use was presented.   It is thus inscribed :—

"THE PARISH CHURCH CUP OF BALLYMODAN, IN BANDON-BRIDGE.
BOUGHT IN THE YEAR 1630.
WILLIAM NEWCE, } Churchwardens."
WILLIAM NEWMAN, }

Also a small silver paten, engraved with the town arms.   From all we can learn, this is the oldest church plate in use within the three dioceses.   At all events, it is the most ancient gift presented by Protestants to a Protestant parish church, not only in this county but, probably, in all Ireland.   In 1634 the vicarage had increased in value to forty pounds per annum.   In 1639 the lay proxy for Ballymodan was the widow Turner, who paid three shillings and sixpence yearly.

* In 1770 thirty-six out of the entire number were privately baptized.

† For almost all the particulars connected with the various vicars of Ballymodan, we are again indebted to *Clerical Records of Cork, Cloyne, and Ross.*—Dr. Brady.

Weight had a son (Rice Weight), who was for some time a curate in Bandon; and whose son Thomas, "who served a hard apprenticeship to a clothier in Bandon," became a conspicious member of the Society of Friends, and was the author of the *History of the Quakers in Ireland*— the first work in connection with that body which appeared in this country. Mr. Weight, who came here from Guildford, in Surrey, was ordained deacon and priest by John, Bishop of Oxford, in 1619. He was rector and vicar of Aghlishdrinagh, in Cloyne, prebendary of Kilnaglory, and prebendary of Kilmacdonagh. The year he obtained the vicarage of Ballymodan the Chapter elected him dean of Cork, but the Crown set the appointment aside.

1662. Henry Parr, vicar. He was also rector and vicar of Rathclarin, and vicar of Templequinlan. In 1666 he was appointed rector and vicar of Skull.

1666-7. Peter Hewitt, vicar, upon the resignation of Parr. In 1675 Hewitt became chancellor, and, in 1710, precentor of Cork.

1675. Hugo Jenkins, vicar. Also vicar of Rathclarin, Cannaway, and rector of Ardnegiby. In the margin of the Visitation held in 1679, opposite to his name, is the remark—"Itræ ord. desunt."

1680. John Tom was vicar. He was rector and vicar of Cannaway, vicar of Rathclarin. In 1688 he became vicar of Kinsale, which he retained until his death; holding along with it the prebendary of Iniskenny, and the prebendary of Desertmore. When James the Second landed in Kinsale, amongst those who waited on that worthy specimen of Divine right, and bid him welcome, was the quondam vicar of Ballymodan.* Mr. Tom (who was an M.A. of Peter House, Cambridge,) married Mary [name not known], and had issue four children. She died in 1692. He married secondly, in less than three months afterwards, Deborah Burrowes, widow, by whom he had three sons and one daughter. He died in 1717, and was buried in Kinsale Church.

1681. Hugo Jenkins was restored. He was again deprived in 1685.

1686. Paul Duclos, A.M., vicar of Ballymodan. In 1688 he was admitted to the prebendary of Island, diocese of Ross. Duclos was of an eminent French family, who came to Ireland from Mentz,

---

* Mr. Tom does not seem to have been successful in persuading his Ballymodan parishioners to adopt his political views, as there were none more vigorous and persevering in their hostility to the dogmas of the Divine right of kings, a king can do no wrong, the doctrine of non-resistance, and the other Tom-fooleries of that day, than the people of Bandon.

Department Moselle, upon the revocation of the Edict of Nantes. He
was priested at Cork, September 21st, 1684. He married Frances
Massiott, of Shandon, Cork, in 1682, and had five daughters. He died
in 1717 or 1719.

1692.   Richard Goodman, vicar, upon the resignation of Duclos.
He was son of the Rev. Thomas Goodman, precentor of Ross.
He was born in 1657. He married Hannah [name not known]. From
1682 to 1691 he was one of the vicars-choral of Cork. In 1687 he
was licensed to the curacy of St. Michael's. From 1689 to 1695 he
was rector and vicar of Kilcully. From 1692 to 1696 he was
vicar of Rathclarin; and from 1692 to 1737 vicar of Ballymodan.
He was prebendary of Killanully from 1696 to 1718; and from
1696 to 1737 he was rector of Knockavilly and vicar of Brinny.
From 1705, until his death, he was rector of Kilowen. In addition
to his Cork livings, he was prebendary of Rath, in Killaloe.
There was an assault committed on Mr. Goodman by Alderman Robert
Rogers, of Cork, which was enquired into by the Ecclesiastical Court.
The flagon at present in use in Brinny Church was presented to it by
Mr. Goodman, in 1721. It bears the following inscription :—

"Deo Sacrum. In usum Ecclesiæ parochialis de Brinny. Ex dono
Richi Goodman ibidem Vicarii. Anno Redemptionis, 1721." Also a
Paten, "impensis Richardi Goodman."

He presented two flagons to Ballymodan parish. On one is :—

"The gift of Richard Goodman to the church of Ballymodan, in
Bandon. And He took the cup and gave thanks; and gave it to them,
saying, drink ye all of it.—Math xxxi. 27."

On the other :—

"The gift of Richard Goodman to the church of Ballymodan, in
Bandon. The cup of blessing, which we bless, is it not the communion
of the blood of Christ ?—1. Cor. x. 16."

His father, who died in 1681, had six sons and two daughters. One
of the sons—namely, Thomas—was a vicar-choral of Ross, where he
was licensed to keep school at his residence in the churchyard. When
Richard's wife, Hannah, died, she was buried in a vault at Ross Cathedral,
and it was to his house that lady went on being aroused from the state
of catalepsy in which she lay, by the effort of the sexton to remove a
diamond ring from her finger.* He died in 1737.

----

* For particulars see "The Goodmans," in *Vicissitudes of Families*, by Sir Bernard
Burke, Ulster King-at-Arms.

1737.　William Reader, vicar. In 1741 Reader became vicar of Kinsale; and in 1745 archdeacon of Cork.

1741.　Piercy Meade, vicar, upon Reader's resignation. In 1745 Meade became vicar of Kinsale.

1745.　William Martin, A.M., vicar, upon Meade's resignation. In 1747 Martin and his curate, John Smith,* appeared before the bishop, who decreed that in future "£45 per annum should be paid to Smith, in quarterly instalments, the stipend heretofore being too small for so laborious a cure." Mr. Martin was son of James Martin, of Bandon, merchant, who was provost of the town in 1699, and again in 1713, 1721, and 1724. He entered Trinity College, Dublin, in 1722. In 1726 he obtained a scholarship, and was subsequently A.M. Previous to his appointment to Ballymodan, he was curate of Templeomalus, Templequinlan, and Kilnagross; and in 1737 was curate of Abbeymahon, which impropriate cure he held until his death in 1750. In his will he mentions his brother Edward, provost of Bandon in 1749, and his brother Richard. Administration was granted to the Rev. William Ellis, the husband of his sister Judith, in trust for Ann, daughter of his brother Edward.

1750.　John Dennis, A.M., vicar, upon the death of Martin. In 1776 he became treasurer of Cork. He married Mrs. Elizabeth Bevan, of Kinsale, by whom he had a daughter, Jane, who was married in Ballymodan Church, December 11th, 1768, to James Hussey, Esq., cornet 3rd Light Dragoons. Mr. Dennis died in 1787.

1776.　John Lord, A.M., vicar, per. cess. Dennis. Mr. Lord was probably of the same family as Daniel Lord, prebendary of Kilbrogan. He died in 1795.

1795.　Henry Hewitt, A.M., vicar. In 1767 he was curate of St. Peter's; and in 1770 Thresher's lecturer in Cork. In 1771 he was vicar of Killaconenagh, in Ross. He was buried March 26th, 1803. The Parish Registry contains the following entry in the handwriting of Mr. William Gorman, the curate:—"Reverend Henry Hewitt, the truly worthy and respected vicar of this parish; lamented by all who knew him." In 1768 Mr. Hewitt, on the 12th of December,

---

* John Smith was curate from 1746 to 1749. On the 2nd of June, in the latter year, he was appointed treasurer of Cork. He obtained a scholarship in Trinity College, Dublin, in 1736; was priested in Cork in 1742; and same year he married Elizabeth Lucas, of Desertserges, by whom he had female issue.

married Susan Judith Browne. The ceremony was performed in Kilbrogan Church by the Rev. Michael Tisdale.

1803.   Charles Hewitt, A.B., vicar, brother of his predecessor, was ordained deacon in Dublin in 1761. He was curate of Murragh in 1775. In 1796 he became rector of Ardnegihy, and in 1803 vicar of Ballymodan.

1809.   Robert Montgomery, vicar, upon the death of Hewitt. He resigned in 1813.

1813.   Joseph Jervois, vicar. He was subsequently rector of Ardagh, in Cloyne, where he died in 1856. Upon his leaving Ballymodan, where he was a great favourite, he was presented with a very flattering address. He was provost of Bandon for many years.

1825.   Arthur Knox, vicar. He resigned in 1835, and went to England.

1835.   Henry Fitzallen McClintock, A.B., vicar. In 1846 he became rector and vicar of Kilmichael.

1846.   John Bleakley, A.M., vicar. He obtained his A.B. in 1826; was priested in Cork in 1831; was curate of Kilgarriff, Ross, for some years, and of the Holy Trinity, Cork, in 1843.

The charities of Ballymodan consist of :—

Ten pounds (Irish) per annum, bequeathed by Thomas Harrisson, charged on lands. The amount distributed equally between Ballymodan and Kilbrogan.

Two pounds annually, left by Alderman French, of Cork, to the poor of Ballymodan.

Ten pounds eight shillings per annum, left by Colonel Thomas Beecher, of Sherkin Island. To be expended at the rate of four shillings a week, in bread, for the poor of Ballymodan.

One thousand pounds. Interest thereof to be divided between poor of Ballymodan and Kilbrogan.

Four hundred pounds left by William Moxly. Interest to be divided between poor of Ballymodan and Kilbrogan.

CHAPTER IV.

A JOINT STOCK COMPANY TO MANUFACTURE WOOLLEN CLOTH IN BANDON PROJECTED—THE BEECHERS PART WITH THEIR SIDE OF THE TOWN—NAMES OF MANY OF THE PURITAN SETTLERS—THE ASSIZES HELD HERE—GREAT DINNER GIVEN TO THE JUDGES—THE WALLS—THE MASONS STRIKE FOR A RISE OF WAGES—MURDER—THE FAMOUS HOUSE OF CALL—THE TOWN MILITIA—INHABITANTS COMPLAIN OF HAVING TROOPS QUARTERED ON THEM—ORIGINAL LETTERS OF LORD PRESIDENT VILLIERS—THE EARL OF CORK—SIR WAREHAM ST. LEDGER—THE PROVOST REFUSES TO IMPOSE ANY MORE TAXES ON THE TOWNSPEOPLE FOR THE SUPPORT OF THE GARRISON.

BANDON was by this time a place of considerable size and importance. There were no less than two 1617. thousand English families residing in the town and neighbourhood. These were well acquainted with the manufacture of woollen cloth, and were an industrious and thriving people. A company was formed to establish a cloth factory here in this year, with a capital of three thousand pounds; and their intention was to avail themselves of the skill and intelligence of the townspeople in the manufacture; but owing to the withdrawal of one who undertook to subscribe a third of the sum required, the design fell to the ground "And thus," says Sir Thomas Wilson, "was a project, from which incalculable advantages must have resulted, unaccountably quashed."

Amongst the disbursements of the Bandon Corporation in 1619. this year is the following item :—" To Mr. Harry Beecher, for his half-year's rent, due by ye townes fayers, markets, £7 17s. 6d." This was the last money transaction between Bandon-Bridge and its original founders, the Beechers. Upon the 2nd of May, 1619, Harry Beecher, by deed of feoffment, conveyed " the incorporated town of Bandon-Bridge, on the south-side of the river Bandon," to the Earl of

Cork. Previous to this Lord Cork was the lay impropriator of the parish in which the south-side is situated; and was also part owner of the town itself, having purchased Captain Newce's interest in the northern-side, as appears by deed dated June 20th, 1613. Newce held under Sir Bernard Granville, the original patentee. Sir Bernard, conjointly with his eldest son, Boville, assigned to Sir Lionel Cranfield (afterwards Earl of Middlesex). Lord Middlesex conveyed the same to Sir George Horsey, or Horsley, November 1st, 1623, and Horsley assigned to trustees for Lord Cork, September 20th, 1625;* and thus Lord Cork became sole owner in fee of the town on both sides of the river. It was imperative on the provost to furnish details of the income and expenditure during his official year. The following is the oldest account, as furnished by one of the provosts, and now extant among the corporation papers. , It was furnished by Thomas Taylor, who was "provost in ye yeare of Oure Lorde, 1619" :—

To Mr. Harry Beecher for his half-year's rent due by ye townes fayers, markets, ...	£7	17	6
To Mr. Wright, as much as he paid for the charges laid out by him for the Commissioners of the Peace, for the provost of Bandon-Bridge time being, ...	2	14	9
Paid for my charges to Cork, and man, and the stopping at Cork,	1	2	0
Paid for taking down part of the rails of the bridge, being ready to fall into the river, ...	0	0	6
Paid to Mr. Carey at ye last assizes, ...	0	16	8
Paid Town Clerk for his yearly allowance due at Michaelmas,	2	0	0
Paid to William Fuller for the half bushels and the pecks, . .	0	6	0
Paid to four carpenters for mending the great bridge, . . .	0	15	0
Paid to the Rt. Hon. Lord Boyle, per John Turner, for the use of the fairs and markets on the south-side of the town lately in the possession of Harry Beecher, Esq., due at Michaelmas last past, ...	7	17	6
Also for fairs and markets upon Coolfadda, ...	7	10	0

1620.   This year the colony of New England was planted by the Puritans. Although forced back repeatedly by severe weather, they persevered; and finally sailed from Plymouth on the 6th of September, in the "Mayflower." On the 10th of November they got into Cape Cod harbour, and the next day one hundred and one persons were landed in Connecticut. It is interesting to note that the names of several of those pilgrim fathers are identical with those of several of the Bandon colonists—as Edward Fuller, Thomas Williams, Richard Clarke, Martin, Mullins, White, Warren, Hopkins, Cook, Rogers, Turner, Browne, Gardiner, &c. Puritan settlers had been

* For many of these particulars we are indebted to Francis E. Curry, Esq., the respected agent of the Duke of Devonshire.

pouring in here ever since the settlement was formed, but more especially since peace and order were restored upon the evacuation of Kinsale by the Spaniards; and by this time they had become very numerous. Many of those who settled here had been persuaded to come over by Lord Cork, since he had become connected with the town; and were induced to leave England by the encouragement that nobleman held out to them. They principally came from Taunton and Kingston, in Somersetshire, and brought with them their wives and families. As we have said, they were Puritans; but they belonged to that portion of the body known as the English Presbyterians, and were not so austere and unrelenting in their religious and political views as the Independents. Amongst those who settled here about this time were:—

Allen,	Colman,	Gilpain,	Jerman,	Morris,
Aldworth,	Cork,	Gillet,	Jennings,	Maybery,
Alcock,	Crowe,	Garret,	Joice,	Maunders,
Anstice,	Charley,	Grey,	Jenkins,	Moheway,
Arthar,	Cocker,	Goodchild,	Jeffries,	Newett,
Aveny,	Chambrian,	Gates,	Keene,	Narriarot,
Ball,	Cumber,	Gabriel,	Kendall,	North,
Browne,	Crowder,	Gash,	Knight,	Noole,
Bass,	Dalle,	Good,	King,	Nash,
Baker,	Dolling,	Goodman,	Longe,	Nicolas,
Burchill,	Dawson,	Gosnell,	Leonard,	Olliver,
Banks,	Draper,	Goss,	Landon,	Owgan,
Banfield,	Danger,	Goodwin,	Lashmore,	Osborne,
Butterfield,	Eayles,	Gibson,	Lumbart,	Orchsheare,
Bradfield,	Eastmond,	Hobson,	Leister,	Palmer,
Beech,	Eames,	Hinds,	Ledbetter,	Payne,
Bond,	Elton,	Hendege,	Lyndsey,	Patyson,
Beek,	Elliott,	Hill,	Legge,	Pryer,
Biggs,	Elrington,	Holland,	Lannon,	Patendon,
Barber,	Edwards,	Haines,	Mupesadd,	Provost,
Bignell,	Emerson,	Hunt,	Mutchowe,	Powell,
Burwood,	Everett,	Hide,	Mobbs,	Pifford,
Breerly,	Fleete,	Husband,	Moore,	Peters,
Bisse,	Furrow,	Hobkins,	Maunbey,	Phillipps,
Bannister,	Farnham,	Hurman,	Morgan,	Philpot,
Bayly,	Finch,	Hudson,	Morman,	Piers,
Bradshaw,	Fopp,	Harte,	Maners,	Parrick,
Blewytt,	Fowler,	Hendley,	Michell,	Patch,
Cook,	Ffennel,	Imball,	Mosse,	Price,
Conzell,	Godfrey,	James,	Mills,	Pprott,
Chinnery,	Goodwin,	Jonson,	Mox,	Pinson,
Castle,	Grynnell,	Jue,	May,	Polden,
Chonock,	Grimly,	Joston,	Medley,	Pyne,

Poape,	Roe,	Stoner,	Thornton,	Waye,
Pure,	Reynolds,	Snedall,	Toms,	Wollridge,
Powell,	Rice, ·	Seward,	Thompson,	Wṛite,
Prate,	Rody,	Screenen,	Tape,	Wills,
Quarry,	Redgin, .	Spur,	Truman,	Whitby,
Qoo,	Remnant,	Strong,	Trindor,	Wylde,
Rayoman,	Richardson,	Samson,	Upcot,	Weast,
Rabbet,	Read,	Scatterford,	Usher,	Ward,
Rose,	Sergin,	Stowe,	Varian,	Wright,
Rowbie,	Smith,	Stamers,	Vinson,	Waters,
Rodyan,	Sharry,	Sherrill,	Vinot,	Waldron,
Rowland,	Stoaks,	Shorley,	Vnoles,	Wakefield,
Robinson,	Sparrow,	Slowen,	Wharton,	Winsor,
Ruck,	Salmon,	Symmes,	Withers,	Wells,
Russell,	Small,	Simister,	Winckfield,	Weekes,
Redwood,	Snigg,	Steed,	Weston,	Whelply,
Revel,	Stephens,	Scraggs,	Warley,	Wilmot,
Rufin,	Salle,	Shorten,	Wilkinson,	Wilson,
Riems,	Syle,	Strand,	Wetherhead,	Winthrop,
Rogen,	Seargeant,	Thorne,	Walebauck,	

This was also the first year in which the freedom of the town was conferred.   Some of the entries in the Freeman's original Book are as follows :—

" Azarius Piers, sworn at a court holden on the 20th day of October, 1630, by the provost. for the freedom, at the Feast of the Annunciation of Our Lady, Saint Mary the Virgin, at the sign of the Star.   Henry Jackson, sworn at a court holden the 20th day of October, 1630, by the provost, for the freedom, at the sign of the Star, in manner following, vid.—At the Feast of the Nativity of Our Lord, Christ, hath paid the fee at the Feast of Easter here next following, to the said provost, to the use of the corporation.   Michael Nicholson, late apprentice to Thomas Cook, feltmaker, having served his apprenticeship, was made free of the borough, May 8th, 1631."

It was but natural that Lord Cork, having become owner of
1620.   the incorporated town of Bandon on the south-side, and likely to become sole owner of the north-side before long, should endeavour to bring his new town into notoriety.   Accordingly we find that he induced the authorities to hold the autumn assizes for the county of Cork this year in Bandon.   The Commission was opened at the sign of the Star, and it is probable that their lordships sat and administered justice within sound of sundry demands for noggins of aqua-vitæ and pots of ale.   During their stay here the judges were entertained right royally.   The Star, under whose benign influence they had come to expound and enforce the laws of " our Dred Sovereign Lord, James the King," shone upon a

brilliant feast, and shed a cheerful light, rich with the warm tinting of a hearty welcome, upon all comers. A very interesting view of the good cheer—embracing as it does many of the luxuries of the modern dinner-table—which was provided for their lordships and the country, is to be found in "A note of the particulars paid out by Randal Fenton, provost, Robert Patteyson, John Peters, and the Seargeants, for entertaining the judges and the country."*

	£	s.	d.		£	s.	d.
For eight neate tongues, at 4d.,		2	8	5 hens, 3 cocks, for white broth,		3	4
For churcoles,		3	0	3 turkeys, at 2s. 6d.,		7	6
For egges,		2	0	2 pounds of raisons, at 16d.,		2	8
For dyvers bread and ginger-cakes,		7	8	4 pounds of dried sucker and ginger plate,		10	0
A pound of pepper,		3	0	A sheep to Mr. Newce,		3	0
8 oz. of synnimon, at 4d.,		2	8	A sheep in the market,	1	10	
5½ oz. of cloves, at 9d.,		4	0	Cream and milk,		2	2
A quarter pound of ginger,		0	6	3 cwt. of oyster, to bake, at 8d.,		2	0
3 oz. of nutmegge, at 4d.,		1	0	7 pounds of butter, at 4d.,		2	4
A quarter of mustard,		0	6	4 pigges, at 20d.,		6	8
A bottle of vinegar,		1	0	8 couple of rabbitts, at 7d.,		4	8
4 pounds of loafe shugar,		8	0	A barrel of picle oysters.		3	0
Six mullets,		4	0	4 pounds prewnes, at 4d.,		1	4
8 pounds of currants,		5	4	3 quarts of aqua-vitæ, at 16d.,		4	0
8 pounds sewett, Rich-weaskoll,		2	4	6 playce,		2	6
3 pounds of rice, the Dickenny,		1	6	3 pounds more of loafe shugar,		6	0
3½ pounds of ginger,		7	0	So much pd. Mr. Gookin's cook, 3 days,		10	0
3 dozens of chickens, at 3s. per dozen,		9	0	Paid the cook for four days,		8	0
2 samons, at 2s. 6d.,		5	0	So much to women turnspits,		5	0
2 codd, at 18d.,		3	0	Sums owed myself,		5	0
4 pounds of figge, at 3d.,		1	0				
5 capons, at 16d.,		6	8		£8	11	2

RANDAL FENTON, PROVOST.

There were two other accounts furnished: one by John Blofield and William Browne, and the other by Patteyson and Peters:—

BLOFIELD AND BROWNE'S ACCOUNT.

	£	s.	d.		£	s.	d.
To wood for roasting,		3	6	For a quarter of veal more,		2	6
For a turkey,		2	6	For wine, at several places,	2	10	6
For a calve to roast, at 6d.,		10	0	For butter, to John Blofield,		6	2
For mutton to Richard Wright,		9	0				
For some lambs to him,		7	0		£4	11	2

PATTEYSON AND PETER'S ACCOUNT.

	£	s.	d.		£	s.	d.
Paid by Patteyson to Joseph Lavellan,	1	10	0	A barrel of beer,		19	0
Two cwt. of apples,		1	4	Joseph Clere, his account,		3	8
Paid for butter,		12	2				
Paid for a barrel of wheat,	1	8	0		£4	14	2

		£	s.	d.	
SUMMARY.	My general at	8	11	2	
	The officers,	4	11	2	£17 16 6
	Patteyson and Peters,	4	14	2	

* The figures and amounts we have given in modern characters. The spelling we have given as we found it.

It would appear from the accounts we have just seen, that there was scarcely anything which this country, and—we were going to add—a foreign clime, could produce, that was not duly represented on the festive board. There was one great omission, however, and it must have been conspicious by its very absence—the time-honoured baron of beef. Could it have been that their lordship's metropolitan palates were too fastidious for the old baron, and that nothing would satisfy them but Dickenny rice and pickled oysters? Or was it that meat, which was a savoury viand at the breakfast-tables of the maids of honour of the preceding sovereign, was now only fit food for carrows and idle horse-boys.*

In addition to the great entertainment given by the corporation, Mr. Richard Tickner, the provost, gave another ; and there is no reason to think that every delicacy which graced the corporate board was not present at his. Every thing went on merry as a marriage bell, until it was time to pay the various bills. The townspeople did not object to pay for the entertainment which the corporation produced ; but they did not think it fair to be called upon to pay a shilling of what Tickner expended "avowedly of his own bounty," and for which he had received "the whole and sole commendacions and thanks." Tickner—(who was evidently one of those open-handed, hospitable, good fellows, who are frequently to be met in every age and in every society, and who would be only too happy to feast himself and his friends on all occasions, provided he could saddle the expenses upon others)—boldly said that they should. The dispute was ended by referring the matter to Lord Cork, who wrote the following letter on the subject to Mr. Randal Fenton, Tickner's successor :—

"The townspeople complained that Mr. Tickner levied off them a great sum of money, which he expended in entertaining the judges ; which he bestowed on them as his own peculiar liberality,—and for it was generally received and esteemed,—and not as a gratuity from the corporation. And for that, Mr. Tickner avowed the entertainment to be his own bounty ; and that he had the whole and sole commendacions and thanks for it." He (Lord Cork) concluded his letter by deciding "that the townspeople should not pay for Tickner's entertainment. Lismore, November 15, 1621·"

It is probable that the walls of the town were being rapidly pro-

---

* Spenser tells us "that the idle horse-boy is fit only to be hanged." One would think, after this, that it would be no easy matter to surpass him in wickedness ; " but the carrows," says the same author, " are much more lewde and dishonest."

cceded with at this time. It was only the year before Lord Cork succeeded Beecher as owner of the southern-side, and they were nearly completed in 1625. It would seem, however, that they were commenced immediately after the incorporation, and must have made great progress; for we find that Captain Adderly, who was provòst in 1616, was rated in that year for a house "which he had built without the walls, by the west-gate." Beginning at the south-side of the salmom weirs, they ran south, inclining a little westerly to the roadway in front of Mr. George Fuller's residence—(at this place was west-gate, or Carbery Port); from hence, to south-west portion of Ballymodan churchyard; and thence (still south, with easterly incline), until it reached south-east extremity of Fitzgerald's distillery; thence in a straight line, east, until it arrived about ten yards east of Mr. Pope's corn-store, where it turned sharp to the left, forming the boundary wall of Mr. Swanton's tanyard. Here it crossed the Bridewell river, and ran along its banks, until it reached Mr. William Bennett's house in Castle Street. Here was south-gate (so called because some of the principal roads—Foxe's Street, Warner's Lane, &c.—led from it directly south.) It was named Francis-gate, in addition, in compliment to Francis, Lord Shannon, sixth son of the Earl of Cork; and also Kinsale Port. It continued hence to run with the stream at its base, until it reached the Bandon river. It began again on the northern-side, and skirted Kilbrogan stream, till it reached that part of the North Main Street which fronts the Provincial Bank. There stood water-gate. It was then continued up the Cork road for about three hundred and twenty yards due north, and then went in a direct line—crossing the little stream near Kilbrogan churchyard—to Mr. Hegarty's house, a few yards south of the present meat market. Here was north-gate. It continued again, almost in a straight line, until it arrived about thirty feet to the west of the barracks. It then ran due south, until it reached the bastion in the river, known as the round tower.

The walls were mainly composed of a thick, black slate. That used in building the southern-side was quarried in Ballylanglay. The northern part was composed of a similar material, most of which was brought from Twoomy's glen and the adjoining quarries in the park. There were generally about nine feet thick, and varied in height from thirty feet to fifty. There were six bastions:—one at each corner of the walls, one in the river, and one midway on the south wall. Each of these was mounted with two guns, and flanked the outward surface of the walls completely. There were two postern gates, in addition to the four regular gates mentioned previously. One of these was in that portion of the wall which ran up Cork road, and the other in that part between the bastion to the west of the barracks and the bastion in the river. The openings occasioned by the river itself were protected by iron flood-gates, and by pallisades composed of beams of timber and poles.

The area enclosed by the walls was estimated at twenty-seven English acres. There were three castles* also erected, each of which contained twenty-six rooms. The turrets and the flanks were platformed with lead, and were mounted with cannon. One of these overlooked the gate in Castle Street; another was on the site of the Quaker's meeting house (a few yards east of south-east corner of the butter-market), and the third was on the spot at present occupied by the town-hall.

The two market-houses also were now built. The one at the south-side stretched across the Main Street, from the north-eastern extremity of the piece of ground now occupied by the present building to where the drapery establishment of Mr. Richard Dawson stands. In the centre was a capacious arch, capable of allowing the tallest cartload to pass under; and at the south-side of this arch was a large and deep well, from which the inhabitants in the neighbourhood used to supply themselves with water. After standing about a century, it was taken down in 1721. The market-house on the northern-side adjoined north-gate on the south, and was somewhat smaller than the other. The walls, which were strong and well built, were said (in nearly forty years afterwards, upon excellent authority) to be the best in Ireland. The sum expended on their erection, which must have been very considerable, was raised by a public tax,† aided with very considerable contributions by Lord Cork.

All these defences and improvements, including the completion of the two churches, market-houses, &c., were effected at an outlay of fourteen thousand pounds; a sum which, though large in our day, must in those days have been regarded as enormous. Whilst engaged in these operations, the draw upon Lord Cork's coffers was so continuous and exhausting, that there is reason to fear his lordship was often "hard-

* The device of the Bandon coat of arms is taken from the bridge of the town and these three castles.

† Vide *State Letters of the Earl of Orrery.*

up;" and found it as difficult to raise the wind as many others, who, with equally benevolent intentions, plunged headlong into stone and mortar.

During the progress of the works he frequently visited Bandon. It is related that, during one of these visits, he stayed at the house of an elderly lady named Franklin, whom he had induced to settle in this country, and who lived in Kilpatrick; and being very much pushed for money, he offered to sell her the four ploughlands of Rockfort, Ballina-curra, Callatrim, and Kilpatrick, together with all their royalties, &c., for the sum of fifty pounds.* The old lady agreed; and mounting her palfrey, she had reached as far as Kemeagarah Ford, on her way to town to have the papers prepared, when her good sons heard of her intentions; and running, as if for their lives, they overtook her, caught the palfrey by the bridle, and turned her back; very angrily enquiring of her, "if it was for sticks and stones she was going to give all her money?"

We should have mentioned that during the building of the walls an incident occurred which showed that trade combinations existed, and that those engaged in them looked with as much hatred and distrust upon those who dare violate their rules in those times as in our own. There was a strike among the masons. Their usual rate of wages was twopence-halfpenny a day, but, seeing a long job before them, they could not resist the temptation of striking for "a rise." Accordingly they demanded threepence daily, and "struck" when they were refused. Lord Cork would not yield; so the knights of the trowel, gathering up their tools, marched off in a body to Kinsale, with one solitary exception. This poor fellow refused to accompany them, thinking, probably, that the old wages were better than none at all; and, for aught we know, he might have had a wife and little children, or an aged mother, depending on him for support. Be that as it may, he continued at his work.

The Earl of Cork, being anxious to complete the walling of the town as soon as possible, was obliged to send for the refractory tradesmen, and give the required threepence. Upon their return, they found their former fellow-craftsman still working away; and they resolved on in-flicting exemplary vengeance on him ere that day's sun had set. For this purpose, they had during the day prepared a grave for him in the

---

* These four ploughlands are worth at present about £1,300 per annum.

walls; and, gathering around him when they had stopped work in the evening, one of them hit him from behind on the head with a pickaxe, fracturing his skull and killing him on the instant. They then laid him in his bloody tomb, placing the fatal pickaxe under his head, and his hammer and trowel beside him. Laying a large flag over the enclosure, they quickly ran a course of masonry over it to conceal it; and trusted they had effectually hid for ever this dreadful crime from human eyes.

The unfortunate man was missed, but nobody could tell what had become of him. 'Twas true that mysterious words and ominous shakes of the head had often hinted that there was foul play; and in course of time the facts themselves began to creep out; but there was no one then who cared to busy themselves about what was no particular concern of their's. And one generation handed down to another the story of the murdered mason, who was built up in the walls, until even the very story itself was dimmed and obscured by the long lapse of time.

About five and thirty years ago, two labourers were removing a part of the old town wall, preparatory to the erection of a summer-house. They worked hard, for they found it very difficult to dislodge the stones and mortar out of the bed where they had lain for over two centuries. They persevered; and slowly, stone after stone was loosened from its firm setting, and removed. At last they touched upon something that was likely to reward them for all the toil of their lives. They had met with a large flag, and, upon tapping this with the handle of the pick, it gave out a hollow sound. Visions of Spanish doubloons and crocks piled with gold arose before their eyes. Hard as they worked before, they now redoubled their exertions. The stones and the mortar flew madly about in all directions. The huge flag was seized with a vigour which those who held it never possessed before. It was dragged up on end, and lo!—there were the mouldering bones of the poor mason. There was the fatal pickaxe under his head, and there was his hammer and his trowel lying by his side, just as they were placed on the day of blood. On the right-hand side, corresponding with where his pocket might have been, was a small silver coin of the reign of Edward the Sixth; probably some of the poor fellows earnings. The hammer, trowel, and pickaxe were in a good state of preservation, as was also the coin; but the skeleton, upon being exposed to the air, soon crumbled into dust.

The jurisdiction of the provost and burgesses did not extend beyond the walls; consequently, whenever a poor fellow got heavily into the books of his creditors, and, therefore, thought it necessary to get out of the way, all he had to do was to outstep their worship's judicial limits. In this manner he secured his own liberties by escaping from their's.

There was a notorious house of call in these old times, and it was the resort of all the rakes and all the spenthrifts of the day. It stood just beyond the stream that ran in front of the water-gate, and was consequently outside the liberties of the town. Here was continually a collection of fast and loose characters—drunkards, in every stage of intoxication—swearers, aiming at originality in their impious affirmations—painted strumpets, tricked out in every colour of the rainbow; in fact, the vile human sweepings of both town and country were associated here. All accounts agree in representing it as a regular plague spot. It is even said that the very air above it was saturated with oaths, tobacco-smoke, and maledictions.

But a change—a delightful, moral, and religious change—has come over the spirit of its dream. All the bad and ardent spirits which once haunted the old dram-shop have been long since swallowed up by time. The pedestal upon which Bacchus stood, surrounded by his votaries, is now possessed by Minerva. The altar upon which worshippers placed tankards of nut-brown ale and bottles of aqua-vitæ, is now a platform from which religious discourses are delivered. Even the very site of the old haunt is occupied for purposes differing altogether from those for which it was anciently used. Revival prayer-meetings are now held where words shocking to pious ears were uttered; christian young men assemble where immorality was once supreme; and the Conservative Registration Association holds its sittings where those were accustomed to meet who had but little respect for the rights of property, and who having nothing of their own which they could look admiringly upon under the head of Meum, were only too anxious to lay their hands upon the heritage of Tuam.

1622. On the 16th July, Lord Cork obtained Patents in his own name for the lands which he purchased in this neighbourhood from Sir James Semphill, of Baltees, Scotland. Also for the manors of Ballymodan (*alias* Ballybandon), Castletown, Ballydehob, Clonakilty, and Innoshannon; together with five hundred acres of domain lands.

Bandon had increased so much in population from the extensive immigration before referred to, that we find in this year the town possessed quite a little army of its own. When the King's Commissioners paid their official visit here on the 30th of August, Captain Andrew Kettleby's troop, consisting of sixty-six well-mounted and well-equipped troopers, marched to the parade field for inspection. A body of foot was also on the ground; which, exclusive of its four captains, five lieutenants, and five ensigns, consisted of six sergeants, six drummers, and five hundred and sixty-four rank and file.* The Captains were:—Anthony Stawell, Hubert Nicholas, Richard Crofte, and Anthony Skipwith. This was a valuable frontier garrison in these days. The wild tribes of the O'Crowleys, the Hurlys, the O'Donovans, the McCarthys, and others who roamed in undisturbed possession of the Western Carberries, could never hope to attack Cork with success, or even spoil its lands on the south and west, until they had overcome those sturdy soldiers; and it was next to impossible for them to overcome a well-trained body of men such as these were, who were cemented together by a common interest, stimulated by religious zeal, and glorying in the country they had come from, and the race from which they had sprung.

1625.   The quartering of troops upon towns was a favourite method with the government in those days of providing for the feeding and lodging of its soldiers, without putting itself to much inconvenience or expense. But however satisfactory this plan may have been to the authorities, it was most unsatisfactory to those who had to feed and give up their best bed to the trooper, upon a promise that his keep and housing should be paid for.† As the payments were not satisfactory,—indeed, the only satisfaction they often had was the knowledge of the debt being still due,—the quartering of a garrison upon a town was a most obnoxious measure. The corporation knew this, and they complained of the hardship to Lord Cork. Lord Cork wrote to Sir Edward Villiers,‡ the Lord-President, on the subject, and received the following reply:—

---

* The men were drilled and disciplined by experienced soldiers. In one of the provost's accounts furnished about this time, is the following item:—"Money paid to Sergeant James for his paines in training the townsmen, 10s."

† They were to be paid at the rate of tenpence a day for billeting and dieting a horse soldier and his horse, fourpence halfpenny a day for a foot soldier, and eight-pence halfpenny daily for an infantry officer.

‡ Sir Edward Villiers died September 7th, 1626. On a stone in St. Mary's churchyard, Youghal, was part of an inscription, in Smith's time, with those lines:—

" Munster may curse the time that Villiers came
To make us worse by leaveinge such a name
Of noble parts as none can imitate
But those whose harts are wedded to the State,
But if they presse to imitate his fame,
Munster may blesse the time that Villiers came!"

"Good my Lo,—Be pleased to observe that if I have a little over-burdened one towne, I have alltogether eased another; which I have done by sending none at all to Clonykylte. And those three companies which are at Bandon-Bridge do not exceed one, as I was informed, for the number of them all would not be above a hundred men. And when those whom I have employed about the musters in the country are returned, which I expect daily, I shall be very proud not only to ease them of that towne, but all the rest that have the like relation to your lordship. Desiring to be excused, if, upon every of their dislikes, I do not presently satisfy desires. And this I write to give your lordship satisfaction, but not the townsmen, who, if they had been rational, might have understood by a law I sent there that I meant not long or over-much to burden them.

"And so I rest,
"Yo^{r.} lo^{ps.} servant, to be commanded,
"Youghall, 1625." "E. H. Villiers.

Scarcely was this garrison gone when the town was threatened with another. "I have had much ado," said Lord Cork, "to keep a garrison from coming to the town, to be lodged there, as in all the towns of Munster." In order to show the authorities that there was no necessity for stationing soldiers in Bandon, and thereby escaping the inconvenience and expense of maintaining them, Lord Cork wrote to the corporation, desiring them "to take Anthony Skipwith and Richard Crofte (two of the town militia captains), and go all in person from house to house, throughout the town and liberties, and take a true note of the names of everyone (from fifteen to three-score) in every family; and also what powder, spears, arms, and weapons be in every house. And require all them that have not arms sufficient to furnish their whole family to make a speedy petition for them, in order to keep a garrison from being lodged in the town; and especially in those houses that have not arms for themselves and their people; for, presently after New Year's Day, my Lord-President will be there to see them mustered, which for your own credit I much desire should be considerable. Whereunto, let me entreat you all to use your best endeavours, that it may appear unto his lordship that there is no need to place a garrison there; all in there being sufficient for the keeping of a good watch upon the town. I recommend to you best cares; and yourselves, with my hearty commendationes, to the Almighty. From Cork, this 20th of December, 1625.—Your most assured loving friend, R. Corke."

Now that the inhabitants had a prospect of being permanently rid of a garrison, they turned their attention with renewed vigour to the walling of the town. They were also anxious to supply themselves with a good store of the munitions of war, at reasonable prices; and wrote to Lord Cork on the subject.

"For the munitions," replied his lordship, "which you desire to supply your wants withall, I have brought orders with me from Dublin, from the Master of the Ordinance, to George Pearce, Master of the Stores here, to supply all your defects at the King's rates; and, therefore, send me word what is it you desire. I will give orders you shall have it for ready money, or upon your bills at show of six months to be paid." Concerning the walls, he wrote that, when he would arrive in Bandon, "I shall speak that that shall be satisfactory unto you for your desires touching the walls of the town and those parts that are not finished. I have given fresh orders, as you desire, unto John Louden and John Turner, who are now here with me."

We have stated previously, that it was not unusual for the government to be indebted to the town for the maintenance and lodging of soldiers. The following is one of the accounts :—

First,—There is due to the town, for three months and a half, for billeting and dieting of Sir Francis Willoughby's foot company of soldiers, after the rate of 2s. 6d. a week's allowance for every man, ... £82 3 0
And more, to the town for the diet and expenses of Sir Francis's lieutenant and ensign, ... 0 12 11
More is due.—Three month's and a half to Captain Michael Williams's soldiers, for same time, at same rate, ... 70 19 4
More, for Lieutenant Starky's diet, five months and a half, at 5s. per week, ... 5 10 0

1627.

Lord Cork occasionally shows bad temper in his correspondence with the provost and burgesses of our corporation. In one of his letters, "touching the licences of the victuallers and the stalls in the market," he petulantly addresses our chief magistrate as "Mr. Provost," and at another time as "your lordship." "And wherein for that I have formerly delivered my opinions unto your corporation, I will for this time forbear to write any more, or give Mr. Fenton, the provost, any other satisfaction."

The following were the amounts received this year from the butchers, for stalls in the market :—

	£	s.	d.			£	s.	d.
Bartholomew Harden,		3	0		Christopher Burte,		6	0
Samuel Burchell,		2	0		Nicholas Raymond,		5	6
John Rose,		4	6		Edward Jackson,		4	0
John Bagge,		2	0		Griffin Thomas,		2	0
Thomas Robinson,		4	4		John Ruck,		2	0
Thomas Franklin,		5	6		Richard Maskall,		1	6
Henry Burrowes,		2	6		John Harvey,		2	0
John Loystone,		3	0		William Robinson,		2	0
John Clother,		3	0					

TOWNS IN THE WEST RIDING OF COUNTY CORK.

From the accounts furnished by Henry Turner, the provost, of the payments made by him this year, we extract the following:—

For making clean of the walls against my Lord-President's coming to Bandon-Bridge,	£0	1	0
For whipping a man that stole a sheet,	0	0	6
Mr. Crofte, a year's rent for the Marshalsea,	0	10	0
Money paid to John Fenerston to keep out the beggars,	0	3	0
Paid for whipping a woman,	0	0	4
Paid for whipping of two fellows for pilfering,	0	1	0
Paid more for whipping a gearle (sic),	0	0	4
Paid Sir Thomas Strafford's officers for three troop horse imposed upon this corporation, from the 18th of December, 1627, till June 19th, 1628,	0	17	2

1628. Notwithstanding that the Bandonians had completed their walls, and showed the authorities that they themselves constituted a garrison which was both numerous and well-armed, nevertheless, troops were poured in upon them in such numbers, "that most of the poor inhabitants of the corporation were utterlie ruined thereby." At last they determined they would not stand it any longer; and in a letter to the Lord-President, St. Leger, they plainly told him "that the petitioners, being plantators, are living and residing upon seigniory lands, which ought not to be doubly charged, as now they are." After stating that some householders had already left the town in order to avoid the heavy charges, they informed his lordship that, unless he gave way, they would address themselves "to the King's Majesty for relief, whose royal will and pleasure, we presume, is not that his English new plantations of this kingdom, which with such care have been erected and cherished, should thus be overthrown." St. Leger replied condolingly:—"The worst of those particular sufferings are already past," said the Lord-President; "but, as they have done hitherto, they shall do well to show patience to continue until some compromise be made for the provisioning of the army otherwise, which will not be long; unless the petitioners can by any other means relieve or save themselves, which I shall be glad of."*

In addition to maintaining and billeting the soldiery, the town was also compelled to advance money for their use. The following is a receipt, in acknowledgement for cash paid by the corporation to a cornet of one of the troops of horse quartered here:—

---

* For many of the letters of the first Earl of Cork, several letters of Sir Edward Villiers, Sir Wareham St. Leger, the Lord-Deputy Wentworth (afterwards Earl of Strafford), Lord Inchiquin, Sir Francis Slingsby, and others, now for the first time published, we are indebted to the valuable collection of manuscripts in the possession of the Earl of Bandon.

"Received by me, Richard Seckerston (cornet of Sir Thomas Strafford's troop), of the provost and corporation of Bandon-Bridge, the sum of fifteen pounds seven shillings, it being due for three horsemen of the aforesaid troop, for three weeks and eleven days, beginning the nineteenth of June and ending the last day of September; for the which sum I pass and give my ticket. Witness my hand, the third of November, 1628.

"RICHARD SECKERSTON.

"xv-vii. p. me.

"I have received, likewise, five shillings for the warrant."

Bandon was not the only town in the west of this country upon which soldiers were quartered. There were some sent to Clonakilty, and even to Baltimore. Concerning Clonakilty, the provost of Bandon received the following letter addressed to Captain Oliver Shortall. As this document furnishes us with reliable information as to the manner in which troops were provided for on the line of march in those days, we give it at full length :—

"For as much as I have received directions from the Rt. Honourable the Lord-Deputy and Council to distribute upon the towns of the Province such commanders, officers, and soldiers, as lately arrived in this kingdom under the command of Sir ―――― Crosby, Bart. These are, therefore, to will and require you, Captain Oliver Shortall, to rise with your colours, armes, and baggage, your ensigns, one seargeant, one drummer, and thirty-three soldiers, and to march, after the rate of ten miles a day, the direct way to the town of Clonakilty, there to remain untill you shall receive further directions. And for the avoiding of extortion and oppression, you are hereby willed and required that neither you or any of your officers do depart from your company, upon any cause whatsoever, untill you come to the said garrisson. Hereby also charging and requiring all officers and others the inhabitants of the country to furnish you with *flower* (*sic*), garrons for carrying ; and also to provide for you in the said thoroughfare constant meat, drink, and lodging, such as the country doth afford, for which they are to give their ready money or tickett ; with which provision you are to content your soldiers, without exacting other money or provisions as you will consume. The contrary at your peril. Dated this 17th of September, 1628.

"WAREHAM ST. LEGER.

"To Captain Oliver Shortall, the Officer-in-Chief."

1629.
Although the corporation were sorely oppressed by the maintaining of the garrison, and although the Lord-President assured them the worst was past, yet he afforded them no relief whatsoever. It does not appear that the townspeople carried out their threat of writing to the King; or if they did, Charles does not seem to

nave lightened their burthens, or even to have given them the poor solace of a kind word; for we find that the provost,* despairing of hope from that quarter, boldly took the matter into his own hands, and stubbornly refused to assess any more imposts upon the inhabitants for the support of the troops. This open defiance—this display of contempt for the crowned-head which the Lord-President represented—greatly irritated him. He thought, probably, that it must not be tolerated that those over whom a king reigned by Divine authority should fly in the face of that authority, by refusing obedience to it; and thereby setting an example which may spread to other communities, and eventually imperil, if not destroy, the sovereignty which God hath placed over us. Punishment must be inflicted.

Should he ask, who are those refractory Bandonians? he would be told that they were seedlings, transplanted from the great hot-bed of English Puritanism; and that they contained within themselves the germs of an uncompromising resistance to unconstitutional government. That although they were planted in another soil, yet they firmly took root in that soil. That the sap was speeding through every trunk and every limb; and that, when they spread out their branches, they would, probably, entwine them with those of their genus on the other side of that channel from which they had been brought themselves; and might even yet overshadow the throne itself by the very luxuriance of their foliage.

It must be shown that such a flagrant outrage upon the constituted authorities could not be passed over lightly. Yet it may do more mischief than it could do good to exercise much severity. The latter view was evidently that taken by St. Leger, who contented himself merely with ordering that "one horseman should lye and remain upon the said provost, taking meat, drink, and lodging, horse-meat, fire, and candle-light, and twelve-pence each day he shall there remain, and for so many days as he shall be forced to travel (after the rate of twelve miles a day), until the said money (i.e.—the assessment which the provost refused to lay) be collected and paid."

The townspeople had evidently the best of the encounter in the end, as there is no mention of money being paid in any of the subsequent

* Mr. John Lake, although elected and sworn in as provost in 1628, yet, like all the others, he served the largest portion of his official year the year succeeding. It was in the portion of the year "1629," in which he was provost, that he refused to enforce the tax on the town.

accounts for the maintenance of the soldiery, or even any allusion to their being billetted in the town for several years afterwards.

Upon the departure of the Lord-Deputy for England, Bandon and other corporate towns petitioned Viscount Ely and the Earl of Cork, who had been sworn in as Lords Justices, that they should be assessed as part of the county at large, and not as corporations : in other words, upon the area, and not upon the valuation.

The Lords Justices revised the old enactment, by means of which every Roman Catholic, who was not regularly in attendance at least once in every Sunday in the Protestant parish church, was subject to a penalty of nine-pence for each offence.

We find according to an inquiry held this year at Bandon, before William Wiseman, Esq., that the value of " a greate oake tree" was 11s. 6d. It appears, according to sworn testimony, that Edmund Barrie, of Magowlie, cut down on the lands of Magowlie, since the first of June, 1629, "foure greate oake trees, price, every tree, 11s. 6d. sterling, being p. cell of the inheritance of Andrew Barrett, whereby the saide woods are much spoiled, to the great damage of the saide ward's inheritance."

CHAPTER V.

GRAND ENTERTAINMENT GIVEN BY THE TOWNSPEOPLE TO LORD CORK AND "HIS NOBLE COMPANY"—BALTIMORE SACKED BY THE ALGERINES; ITS HISTORY, CHARTER, PARLIAMENTARY REPRESENTATIVES—THE O'DRISCOLLS—ATTACK ON BALTIMORE CASTLE BY THE REBELS IN 1642—AN ALGERINE ROVER WRECKED IN DUNWORLY BAY—THE WISEMANS—THE SPENSERS—PROSPEROUS STATE OF THE COUNTRY BEFORE THE BREAKING OUT OF THE GREAT REBELLION—BANDON WORTHY OF REGARD FOR "ITS BIGNESS AND HANDSOMENESS"—DOWNDANIAL CASTLE—KILBRITTAIN CASTLE—THE M'CARTHYS-REAGH.

IT was but natural the Bandonians should feel grateful to Lord Cork for the many good services he had performed for them. At their desire he hurried to completion the walling of the town; he enlarged their two churches; he procured for them the munitions of war ·at wholesale rates; and he strove hard with the various Lords-President of the Province to reduce (if not to remove) the garrison, against the burthen of maintaining and paying of which they so strenuously and deservedly protested. Accordingly, when it became known amongst them that Lord Cork intended coming to Bandon, they met together, and invited his lordship and "his noble company" to a grand banquet. His lordship and his noble company cheerfully accepted the invitation; and there is no reason to think that the hosts and their guests did not fully enjoy ·themselves, and part mutually pleased with each other. The cost of the entertainment—which amounted to twelve pounds two shillings and tenpence—was defrayed by public subscription. The following is a list of the names of the subscribers, and the sums contributed by them :—

1631.

	£	s.	d.		£	s.	d.
Mr. Provost Edward Dunkin, .		6	0	Ralph Fuller, ...		2	0
Mr. Newce, ...		16	0	Daniel Seaward, ...		8	0
Mr. Turner, ...		16	0	Thomas Franklin, ...		6	0
Randal Fenton, ...		16	0	Anthony Shepheard, ...		8	0
Mr. Woodroffe, ...		16	0	John Beard, ...		2	0
Mr. Dickenson, ...		9	0	Thomas Atkinson, ...		6	0
Anthony Skipwith, ...		5	0	Robert Patyson, ...		2	0
Mr. Turner, ...		15	0	William Cox, ...		3	0
Robert Tachell, ...		2	0	John Wolfe, ...		2	0
Michael Bull, ...		2	0	Morrough Madden, ...		2	0
William Fuller, ...		2	0	Abraham Savage, ...		2	0
Mr. Brooke, ...		16	0	Joseph Cecill, ...		1	6
Mr. Jenkins, ...		16	0	Thomas Franks, ...		2	0
Thomas Downes, ...		8	0	Andrew Wilson, ...		2	0
William Austen, ...		3	0	John James, ...		2	6
James May, ...		2	0	Thomas Bennett, ...		5	0
Michael Tayler, ...		8	0	John Heles, ...		2	0
Mr. Jefferey, ...		2	0	Edward Turner, ...		2	6
John Orch, ...		2	6	Thomas Adderly, ...		3	0
Jeffery Sale, ...		2	0	Mr. Linscombe, ...		2	6
Ralph Sale, ...		2	0				

The adjoining coasts were harassed by "one Nut, a pirate." This licentiate of Neptune seems to have practised on the sea as if he had a roving commission from his master. Not only did he scour the ocean, but, whenever he could seize upon a favourable opportunity, he was accustomed to make a descent upon the land itself—plundering the inhabitants, and spreading terror and devastation over the entire country. Whenever a force superior to that under his command was sent against him, he set every stitch of canvass, and endeavoured to place as much sea-room between his enemies and himself as possible; and in this he was successful, as his ships were fast sailers, and, in addition, being well manned and equipped, he invariably contrived to escape. So powerful had this sea-brigand become, that the Lord-President informed the authorities that Nut had three ships under his command:—one of twenty of guns, and two of fifteen each; and that on the 31st of May he lay at Crookhaven, where he was joined by his wife, and where he watered and provisioned his fleet.

So unable was the executive at this time to cope with this buccaneer, that although they offered him a free pardon,—so little regard had he for any punishment they could inflict upon him,—some time elapsed before he could be persuaded to pay them the compliment of accepting it.

There are some stories still extant about this famous depredator. One relates that, to protect his plunder, it was customary with him to bury his kegs of gold on various headlands; and then at each place to sacrifice a black slave, whose spirit, it is believed, even still keeps watch over the hoarded treasure.

It was in this year, also, that the Algerine pirates sacked Baltimore. Under the guidance of a Dungarvan fisherman, named Hackett, two of these far-famed rovers covertly stole up to Kedge Island.

The sombre shadows of approaching darkness were creeping over the waning twilight,—the hum and the bustle of day had settled into the quiet and the silence of night,—an air of peaceful repose lay softly on the rugged slopes of the mountains, and on the hills and the valleys and the green fields that stretched around the ill-fated town, ere these dreaded corsairs of Algiers ventured, late on an evening in June, to intrude upon the motionless waters of Baltimore. Noiselessly sliding down the ship's sides to their boats, they pulled with muffled oars to the shore; where they landed, and remained watching, probably with a savage satisfaction, their unconscious prey.

Meanwhile, the inhabitants suspected nothing. After supper, and, perhaps, a social chat by the fire-side, they prepared for bed. In due time the lights which twinkled in their sleeping-room windows began to disappear one by one. Even the last candle, which had lingered long after the others had been extinguished,* and may have been held by a trembling hand over a sick child, or passed before the glazing eyes of a dying husband or a parent, at length vanished in the darkness. And now all was dark and still.

Little did those, who heavily lay in their first sleep, know that almost within arm's length of them was a band of African cut-throats, whose atrocious crimes of rapine and blood had earned for them a wide-spread and a terrible notoriety. In a few minutes they were awake, and realized the dreadful fact that they were slaves. Their limbs were loaded with chains; their houses were ransacked; their wifes and their daughters† were reserved for a horrible fate. Even little children were dragged to the beach amid the shrieks of matrons, and the moans of those, the clanking of whose irons added yet another terror to the horrors of that fearful night.

The town was nearly stripped of its inhabitants; and thus this thriving colony, which could boast of its burgesses, its sovereign, its parliamentary

---

* Tradition states that one candle had continued lighting long after the others had gone out.

† Among those carried off to Algiers was a daughter of O'Driscoll's, and upwards of one hundred of the English colonists who had settled there.

7

representatives, and its opulence,—indeed, the latter had increased so much that the corporation offered to defray the expenses of erecting a pier, and (provided they were furnished with guns) for even the erection of a fort,—received a blow which felled it to the earth, paralysed, and from whence its impotent limbs have since vainly struggled to arise.*

Baltimore (by the Spaniards called Valentimore,† and anciently known

---

* An old ballad is still sung in Baltimore and its neighbourhood. It commemorates the ancient fame of the town, and the unhappy fate of O'Driscoll's daughter :—

"Oh ! Baltimore, thou wer't once the boast
Of the great O'Driscoll and his host :
With thy classic scenes and feudal fame,
It scarcely now deserves thy name.
In thy harbour ships may safely ride—
Safe from the storm, the wind, the tide :
Thy antient castle stands proudly high ;
It speaks aloud of the days gone by.

Within thy walls ruled a chieftain bold,
Whose word was law, as oft was told ;
Where were festive scenes of sport and play,
For valorous chiefs and ladies gay.
Being free from doubt and from worldly care,
They little thought of the danger near,
As the hours did glide merrily on ;
And all enjoyed the dance and song.

O'Driscoll gazed round on sea and land,
And called to his vassals on the strand.
Ready his commands they did obey, .
And launched his galleys into the sea.
He little thought, on that fatal day,
That the Algerines would come that way.
They came on shore, and caused great slaughter,
And carried off O'Driscoll's daughter.

Behold her anguish !   Also her fears !
A poor captive, carried unto Algiers.
Whilst in the harem she stood alone,
And the sun about her brightly shone,
To her flattering tales the Pacha told,
And showed her his pearls and his gold ;
But this virtuous maiden, nobly born,
His love and his treasures she did scorn.

By force she was by him caressed ;
But she plunged a dagger into his breast.
He loudly screamed, and on Allah cried ;
Then fell upon the ground and died !
The sentence was passed that she should die.
She thought of her home, and heaved a sigh.
Resigned to her fate with pious love,
Her stainless spirit found a home above.
Thy pride is gone, and thy glory is o'er,
Ruined and neglected Baltimore !"

† "The bay of Baltimore, in Carbery, is a safe place for ships of any burthen to ride in, and was one of those which the Spaniards much frequented in former times, called by them Valentimore."—See Story.

as Dunashad) derived its name from Beal-tee-more (*i.e.*—the great residence of Beal). It is supposed to have been the site of a sanctuary of the Druids, and to have been a place much frequented by those who venerated the mistletoe and the oak.

In 1413 the O'Driscolls, who lived for a long time previously at Baltimore, and who made themselves obnoxious to the people of Waterford, in particular by the piracy of their vessels on the high seas, as well as when they sought the shelter of Baltimore harbour, were visited by Symon Wickin, Mayor of Waterford, together with Roger Walsh and Thomas Salt (two of the corporate officers); and they contrived to surprise O'Driscoll in his own castle, and to make himself and all his family and followers prisoners.

It seems that Wickin entered the harbour, on a Christmas night, in a Waterford ship; on board of which was a strong force of men in armour. Landing with these, he proceeded to the castle-gate, and called out to one of the warders to tell his lord that the Mayor of Waterford was come into port with a cargo of wine, and called to see him. The message was scarcely received when the gates were ordered to be thrown open, and instantly O'Driscoll and his people were captives.

In 1450, to such a degree of notoriety had the O'Driscolls attained for the worst of crimes, that a special Act of Parliament was enacted against them (28th Henry VI.); in which it was alleged that "divers of the King's subjects have been taken and slain by Finin O'Driscoll, chieftain of his nation, an Irish enemy."

It directed that no person of the ports of Wexford, Waterford, &c., should fish at Baltimore, nor go within the country of the said O'Driscoll with victuals, arms, &c.; and that proclamation be made of this by writs, in the parts aforesaid, under the penalty of the forfeiture of their goods and ships to those who shall take them, and their persons to the King. Also, "that they who receive the said O'Driscoll or any of his men shall pay forty pounds to the King."

In 1461 the O'Driscolls, upon the invitation of the Powers, arrived at Tramore. The chief magistrate and the citizens of Waterford, having become aware of the proximity of their dangerous foes, marshalled themselves in military array, and marched out to meet them. The battle was fought at a place called Ballymacdane; and, after a terrible encounter, the united O'Driscolls and Powers gave way and fled, leaving one hundred and sixty of their number dead upon the field, and several

7—2

prisoners, amongst whom were O'Driscoll and six of his sons. These, with three of their galleys, were brought in triumph to Waterford by the victorious citizens.

In 1537 the Waterfordians, between whom and the O'Driscolls war seems to have been always raging, fitted out a naval expedition, consisting of three armed ships, with four hundred men on board; and, sailing into the harbour, burnt upwards of fifty of O'Driscoll's boats, and set fire to the town and castle, in retaliation for an act of base treachery committed by Finin O'Driscoll and his son, "the black boy."

It appears the O'Driscolls boarded a Portuguese ship laden with a hundred pipes of wine, which were consigned to Waterford merchants; and arranged with the captain (it being very stormy weather) to pilot his ship into Baltimore for three pipes of the precious juice.

Having safely anchored in the harbour, the captain and crew were invited by O'Driscoll to dine at his castle. They, glad to get their legs once more on *terra firma*, joyfully accepted the proffered hospitality, and soon they found themselves in irons. The ship, of course, was plundered; and when the consignees arrived, looking for their wine and revenge, "the black boy" (who was evidently a fine boy in addition,—indeed, one cannot help thinking that he seems to have drawn his inspirations from the "old boy" himself), and twenty-four of his boon companions, contrived to get clear of the ship, after reducing the hundred pipes of wine to twenty-five.

In 1552, *temp.* Edward the Sixth, so much frequented was Baltimore by foreigners, principally for the purpose of fishing, that Parliament advised the King to build a fort, and compel those foreign fishermen to pay tribute.

About the middle of Elizabeth's reign, an English fleet lay becalmed off Baltimore. On being made aware of this, O'Driscoll ordered out all his galleys and boats, and towed the ships safely into harbour. But his kind offices did not end there: he brought all the officers and men ashore with him, to a round of festivities. There was eating and drinking; there was the dance and the song. There was not a harp or bag-pipes for miles around that was not there to swell the volume of sweet strains that never ceased for a whole week. Wine and money were everywhere. In the wantonness of his mirth and hospitality, the host ordered the town well to be cleared out, and for forty-eight hours kept it filled with wine. And, as an inducement to the avaricious as

well as to the thirsty to visit the flowing bowl, he had fistfuls of gold
and silver thrown into it; hence its present name—Tobber-na-Arigid
(the money well).

So pleased were the officers with their bountiful treatment, that, when
they returned to England, they told her Majesty about the way they
were received; and so gratified was Queen Bess with the intelligence, that
she had a letter written to O'Driscoll, thanking him for his hospitality,
and inviting him to come over and see her.

In 1601 Sir Finin O'Driscoll delivered the castle into the hands of
the Spaniards, who supplied it with ammunition, and prepared it for a
resolute defence. Upon the surrender of Kinsale, however, it was given
up, in compliance with the treaty made between Don Juan de Aquila
and the Lord-Deputy.

In 1610 the town and harbour of Baltimore, Innisherkin, "and
divers other parts thereabouts," were such notorious places of resort for
pirates, that even foreign governments complained to James the First
"of that relief and countenance which they pretend the said pirates to
have lately found and received in the said western parts."

The King, who candidly admitted that their complaints were "not
without colours," had peremptory instructions on the subject conveyed
through his English Privy Council to the Lord President and Council of
Munster. The latter, who had previously used their best endeavours to
suppress the existing evils, "yet hath there been little or no reforma-
cion," now took up the matter hotly, and determined to get rid of such
"desperate and dishonest men as resorted thither, of purpose to joyne
and combyne themselves wyth the saide pyrates; and also of suche
shameless and adulterous women as daylie repayred unto them; and
especially of those dyvers taverns, ale-houses, and victualling-houses
that have from tyme to tyme basely and mercenarily entertayned both
those kinds of people."

Amongst the severe measures to which they had recourse, in order to
break up this favourite haunt "of those lewde and wicked pyrates," was
that of unpeopling the island of Innisherken, and the other islands in
the neighbourhood, "and also all such places upon the continent as are
weake, and open to the arrivals of the saide pyrates; only except some
houses and inhabitants as shall be fitly drawn within the guard and
protection of some stronghold or castle."

On the 25th March, 1613, the town was incorporated. The charter provided for the election of a sovereign, twelve burgesses, and a commonality; and empowered the inhabitants to return two members to Parliament, which it continued to do until the Union, when it was disfranchised; and the sum of fifteen thousand pounds, which was awarded to it as compensation for the loss of its privileges, was handed to Lord Carbery, the owner of the town.

The following are the names of the members, and the dates of the returns of those who represented Baltimore in Parliament:—

1613. April 20th.—Sir Thomas Crooke, Knt., Baltimore; Henry Pierce, Esq., Dublin.

1634. June 1st.—Lott Peere, Esq.; Edward Skipwith, Esq. December (same year), James Travers, Esq., *vice* Peere, absent in England on special business.

1639. February 24th.—Bryan Jones, Esq.; Henry Knyveton, Esq.

1661. April 10th.—Sir Nicholas Purdon, Knt., Bailyclough; Richard Townsend, Esq., Castle Townsend.

1692. September 19th.—Colonel Thomas Beecher, senior, of Sherkey; Edward Richardson, gent., Moorestowne.

1695. July 13th.—Colonel Thomas Beecher, senior; Edward Richardson, gent.

1703. August 19th.—Piercy Freke, Esq., Rathbarry; Thomas Beecher, Esq., Sherkey.

1707. Edward Riggs, Esq., Riggsdale, *vice* Freke, deceased.

1709. May 10th.—Francis Langston, Esq., *vice* Beecher, deceased.

1713. October 26th.—Hon. Richard Barry; Michael Beecher, Esq.

1715. November 1st.—Hon. William Southwell; Michael Beecher, Esq.

1721. September 26th.—Sir Percy Freke, Bart., Castle Freke; Richard Tonson, Esq., Dunkettle.

1728. April 27th.—Sir John Freke, Bart., *vice* Piercy Freke, deceased.

1761. November 30th.—William Clements, Esq., Dublin, *vice* Freke, returned for city of Cork.

1768. July 2nd.—Sir John Freke, Bart.; Richard Tonson, Esq., Baltimore.

1775. J. Deane, Esq.

1778. William Evans, Esq.

1781. James Chatterton, Esq.

1783.   Lord Sudley; Richard Longfield, Esq.

1790.   Richard Grace, Esq.

1797.   George Evans, Esq.

The sovereign had the power of holding a Court of Record in personal actions, for sums not exceeding five marks.

In 1628 Captain Oliver Shortall and thirty men were stationed in the town.

In 1629 the inhabitants were greatly perplexed by Walter Coppinger, who obtained an order from the Court of Chancery, by means of which he possessed himself of the manor, castle, and town of Baltimore; in the latter of which the English plantees, who had been brought over by Sir Thomas Crooke, erected sixty houses; and in enclosing and improving lands, &c., they expended altogether no less than two thousand pounds.

The colonists complained loudly against the order of the Chancery Court; and, going before the Lords Justices, they asked if they were to be deprived of what they had laid out upon the tenements and lands which had been leased to them by Sir Thomas Crooke, who was himself a lessee of Sir Finin O'Driscoll (in whose possession, and those of his forefathers, these very lands were for the previous three hundred years).

The Lords Justices ordered Coppinger to appear before them; and then dismissed him, upon his promising to reinstate the plaintiffs upon such terms as the Council Board should think reasonable.

Coppinger, however, did no such thing; for he leased the whole to Mr. Beecher, without providing for his promises to the townspeople. This brought the matter again before the Council, who issued summonses to both Beecher and Coppinger to appear before them. The matter was eventually settled through the intervention of Lord Cork, who advised Beecher either to surrender his lease to Coppinger or estate the tenants during his own term. It is said he preferred the latter alternative, and gave them his own term.

In 1631, on the 20th of June, "the terrible disaster," as Smith calls it, took place, which we have previously mentioned (page 81).

Although Beecher promised to estate the planters during his own term, yet he must either have neglected to do so, or his own term must have been very short, for (in 1636) we find that Coppinger, by indenture of lease bearing date June 30th, granted the castle, village, and town of

Baltimore, together with three carucates of land, to Mr. Thomas Bennett,* of Bandon-Bridge.

It would appear that the townspeople and their new landlord were mutually pleased with each other, as there are no traces to be found of any complaints about the non-fulfilment of promises, or even of any disagreement or misunderstanding between them.

In 1640 the Earl of Strafford was tried for high treason. Amongst the various charges brought against him was that of having arbitrarily imposed illegal taxes on Baltimore, and having quartered soldiers upon the inhabitants until they paid them.

In the great rebellion of 1641, the remoteness of Baltimore from the great slaughter-fields, where the Saxon colonists bravely battled for their lives and properties with those who were thirsting to deprive them of both, did not save it from its share of the common danger. The out-laying colonists were soon driven from their farms, and beggared. The townspeople fared but little better. On one occasion—long before dawn—the rebels approached the town and carried away many head of cattle; and at another time, when the inhabitants were out in the fields harvesting, they stealthily approached and fired close to a hundred shots at them; and not content with even this, they abused them unmercifully in addition.

Those great preservers of the peace,—those sincere devotees of the English crown,—called the English colonists, whose sympathies were undoubtedly with those who manfully resisted the despotism and the religious intolerance of Charles "the king's enemies." "You are rebels, and no Christians!"† shouted the bog-trotting, liberty of conscience loving royalists of Western Carbery, to those who never dared to limit the mercy of an Almighty God to those only who were to be found within the pale of their own church. "They were Puritans" also, and "they were Parliamentary rogues."

If they, however, had carried their hostility no further than firing shots, which do not appear to have wounded any one, and calling names, the Baltimorians would have just reason to felicitate themselves on their good fortune; but such was not the case.

---

* Mr. Bennett was a burgess of the Bandon corporation, having been elected to that office June 12th, 1632, in room of Stephen Skipwith, one of the twelve burgesses named in the charter. On his leaving for Baltimore, the corporation passed a resolution, in which they expressed their regret at his leaving, &c.

† See MS. in Trinity College.

Teige O'Driscoll, of Collimere, and Dermogh O'Driscoll, of Innis-shirkin, at the head of two hundred men, of whom forty were armed with muskets, and had four rounds of ammunition a man, joined with the forces under the command of Tom Coppinger, of Copplebeg; and the entire body, consisting of upwards of three hundred men, inclusive of seventy musketeers, attacked the castle of Baltimore, three hours before day-break, on the 15th of August, 1642.

The castle was full of people. Governor Bennett willingly afforded the shelter of its walls to those hapless creatures whom the rebels had forced from their homesteads, and, when Coppinger and the O'Driscolls marched against it, it contained no less than two hundred and fifteen souls.

The assault was unsuccessful. Indeed, so disheartened were the insurgents at their complete failure, that they drew off before sunrise; and thus the garrison and the helpless inmates escaped without the loss of a life, or even of a drop of blood.

In 1645 Captain Bennett, who commanded a company of foot in the Bandon militia, and who had been appointed governor of Baltimore years before by Charles the First, influenced, no doubt, by the Puritanical principles of his native town, and disgusted with the treachery of the perfidious sovereign who occupied the throne, in conjunction with Captain Muschamp, commandant of the Cork garrison, Sir Hardress Waller, governor of the city, and many others, threw up their allegiance to the King, and proclaimed themselves in favour of the Parliament.

After the rebellion was over Baltimore rapidly recovered, and in less than twenty years after tradesmen's tokens were issued there. One of these bears on the obverse the name of "William Prigg," and on the reverse, "of Baltimore, 1668."

On the 24th of December, 1685, a *quo warranto* was issued against the corporation by Lord Tyrconnell, familiarly known as "lying Dick," and judgment given against them by Chief Baron Rice.

In 1689 James the Second granted a new charter in place of the one of which they were deprived, in which it was recorded that the provost, free-burgesses, and commonality had enjoyed many privileges.

In 1698 the population of the town consisted of only nine seamen, one hundred and eighty-eight fishermen, and eighty-four boatmen, and their families. Amongst the entire number there were only two Roman Catholics.

On the 31st of May, 1703, Baltimore,* which had for some time previously been the property of Edmund Galway, by whom it was forfeited for his adherence to King James, and which is described as a Portreeve town, together with Cony Island and the lands of Rathmore, was purchased at the great sale of confiscated estates in Dublin, by Percy Freke, Esq., of Rathbarry, ancestor of the present owner (Lord Carbery), for the sum of eighteen hundred and nine pounds.

In 1724 this remote place was visited by Benjamin Holme, one of the Society of Friends, on his first visit to Ireland; but, although a man of great zeal and perseverance, he was unable to establish a society there.

The port of Baltimore has still a jurisdiction, which extends over that portion of the coast lying between Galley-head on the east and Mill-cove on the west, and includes the harbour and creeks of Berehaven, Bantry, Crookhaven, Baltimore, and Castle-Townsend, together with all the bays, creeks, rivers, and streams within those bounds.

About sixty years ago an enterprising Scotchman, named Cuthbert, settled here, and expended upwards of two thousand pounds in building and other improvements. But, nevertheless, he could not infuse vigour into its decayed body. It is still a small secluded place, containing less than a dozen houses. However, it is to be hoped that the salubrity of the air, its delightful situation, and its admirable position as a port of call, will again attract notice, and afford it an opportunity of regaining its ancient fame.

The Algerines met with such success at Baltimore, that they were again expected to make a descent upon the coast; and information to that effect was furnished to the authorities by Sir Vincent Gooking. The Lord-President took time by the forelock, and made preparations accordingly. He directed that a beacon should be erected on the promontory overlooking Baltimore, another at Cape Clear, another at Dundeedy, and one upon Crow-head, Dunworly. The latter was to put Bandon and Kinsale on the alert, but more especially to warn the inhabitants of Ibane† and Barryroe, who were told that when they should

---

* John Calvert, baron of Baltimore, proprietor of the State of Maryland, United States of America, took his title from Baltimore in the county of Longford, and not from this place, as is generally supposed.

† Upon the arrival of the English, Ibane (that is "the fair territory,") was wrested from the O'Cowigs by Lord Arundel, of the Strand, as was Barryroe, also the inheritance of the O'Cowigs. In 1406 the then Lord Arundel, who lived at Arundel Castle, Ring, near Clonakilty, derived an income of fifteen hundred pounds per annum from these lands, besides a (by no means inconsiderable) revenue from the rivers, creeks, and harbours which it contained.

see the smoke ascend from the beacon by day, or the flames at night, to march in all haste, fully armed, to Clonakilty; so that, should Ross or Timoleague be threatened, assistance would be near at hand.

One of those Algerine rovers did make its appearance on this part of the coast about this time, but whether it was a portion of the fleet intended for the sacking of Baltimore, or was cruising on its own account, we are unable to say. She was wrecked, however, in Dunworly Bay; and a great number of the glass beads and cylinders (varying from one-fourth of an inch to an inch and a-half in length, and from one-eight to one-fourth of an inch in width), which she had on board, have within the last few years been washed ashore upon the strand of the Yellow Cove, Dunworly.

This portion of the cargo of the old pirate has given rise to a great deal of speculation among the learned. Some affirm that they were identical with those found in and about the Crainogues of the ancient Irish, and were imported for personal ornamentation, centuries before the English invasion. Others think that they were the produce of the robberies of some Egyptain tombs; the blue beads very closely resembling in size and design those of the Scarabeei.

Mr. Vaux, of the British Museum, after showing them to Mr. Hawkins and Mr. Franks, says :—" They have no doubt, whatever, that they all came from the East—probably from Alexandria or Syria." And there were some of opinion that they were mere trinkets, being sent out to some foreign shores in a ship of war which was lost in the bay about the close of reign of Charles the Second.

The conjectures of the latter are somewhat supported by the fact that several of the beads have been found adhering to the guns and timbers of this ill-fated vessel. But their conjectures are again negatived by the discovery that some of the cylinders are impressed with Arabic characters, and therefore could not be intended as playthings for savages.*

Some remains of the robber's ship, as the peasantry call her, and some of her guns, may still be seen in Dunworly Bay. Row to the spot where she has found a home beneath those huge wild waves that roar and tumble in this rock-bound bay, when the sun is in the meridian of its

---

* The whole subject has been lately brought before the public by Dr. Neligan, in a pamphlet entitled " *Ancient Glass Beads and Cylinders found on Dunworly Strand.*"

brilliancy, and when there is not a cloud to fleck a momentary freckle on his beaming face; when the sea is smooth as a mill-pond, and when there is not a breeze or even a breath of air to dull its polished surface. Shading your eyes from the sunlight, lean over the boat's side, and peer intently down into the deep, deep waters, and you will see a dark mass, and the guns of the old rover lying peacefully on the great carpet of white silver sand far below.*

1632. In those days prisoners were punished by being confined in "the cage," and by whipping. The tread-wheel was unknown, and oakum-picking and stone-breaking were not considered a sufficiently moral training to elevate them above malpractices for the future. The cat was the great cynic, whose cutting remarks left impressions on the evil doers which they found it hard to remove. Amongst the items in the provost's "account furnished" for this year, we find :—

	£	s.	d.
For whipping two boys for stealing twist, ...		1	0
Whipping Joe Lowsby and his daughter, ...		1	0

No one will say that it was not right to punish those who were guilty, although the method adopted might be considered a severe one ; but to punish, and that with the whip, those who were only suspected, showed an ignorance of, or a contempt for, that popular axiom in our jurisprudence, which tells us that every one is presumed to be innocent until they are found guilty. A shilling was paid for whipping two women suspected of an offence of which, if guilty, they ought deservedly to be placed outside the pale of virtuous society, as they would now-a-day, but nothing more.

1633. The importance of Bandon at this period as the seat and centre of a Protestant population, and as a *point d'appui* in time of need, is evident from a letter written this year by the Earl of Cork to Mr. Secretary Cook. It is dated April 13th:—

---

* Another ill-starred ship was wrecked not far from the "Rover." She is supposed to have perished in the reign of William the Third; some coins of that monarch's reign having been found among her timbers, and none of subsequent date. She was bound from the coast of Africa, and was leaden with gold-dust and ivory. Tradition asserts that there was an iron chest on board full of gold; and that when the captain found the ship making water, and that crowds of the peasantry were coming off in their boats to plunder, he got the chest on deck, and lashing two or three cannons to it to *sink it*, pushed it over the ship's side. A diver, who went down there some years ago, confirms the account of an iron chest being there, and of some cannon being lashed to it, but whether it contained gold or not he could not tell.

"Upon conference with the commissioners, I have been desirous to satisfy myself whether the works done by the Londoners at Derry or mine at Bandon-Bridge exceed each other. All that are judicious, and have carefully viewed them both, and compared every part of them together, do confidently affirm that the circuit of my new town at Bandon-Bridge is more in compass than Londonderry; that my walls are stronger, thicker, and higher than their's, only that they have a strong rampart within, that Bandon-Bridge wanteth; that there is no comparison between their ports and mine (there being in my town three, each of them containing twenty-six rooms—the castles, with the turrets and flankers, being all platformed with lead, and prepared with ordinance); and the buildings of my town, both for the number of houses and goodness of building, are far beyond their's. In my town there is built a strong bridge over the river, two large session-houses, two market-houses, with two fair churches—which churches are so filled every sabbath-day with neat, orderly, and religious people, as it would comfort any good heart to see the changes, and behold such assemblies, no popish recusant or unconforming novelist being admitted to live in all the town.* The place where Bandon-Bridge is situated is upon a large district of the country, and was within the last twenty-four years† a mere waste-bog and wood, serving for a retreat and harbour for wood-kerns, rebels, thieves, and wolves; and yet now—God be ever praised—is as civil a plantation as most in England, being for five miles round all in effect planted with English Protestants. I write not this out of any vain-glory. Yet as I, who am but a single man, have erected such works, why should not the rich and magnificent city of London rather exceed than fall short of such performances?"

1634.   Lord Wentworth (subsequently Earl of Strafford) was anxious his brother, Sir George Wentworth, should be one of the representatives for Bandon in the new Parliament about to assemble in Dublin, and wrote the following letter to Lord Cork, in order to obtain that nobleman's vote and interest in his favour:—

"To our very good Lord the Earl of Cork, Lord High Treasurer
"of Ireland, &c.

"Allowe our verie hartie commendacions unto your lordship.

"Whereas there are two burgesses to be elected for the towne of Bandon-Bridge to serve at the ensuing Parliament, appoynted to beginne the fowerteenth of July next. And forasmuch as we are desirous that Sir George Wentworth, Knight, our brother, maie be nominated for one of the burgesses of the saide burroughe. We have, therefore, thought

---

* Lord Cork has committed a great error in making this statement. Should the "unconforming novelist" at this time not be permitted to live in all the town, there would scarcely be a house in it inhabited.

† That is in 1609. He represents the site of the town as being "a mere waste-bog, &c." That it was so before Bandon was built, we have no doubt, but a thriving town was on it in 1609. However, it seems his lordship ignored the existence of Bandon-Bridge altogether until he became connected with it.

good to recommende him unto youre lordshipe for that service, that by youre good means and assistance hee maie bee chosen for one of the saide burgesses; whoe, wee' make noe doubte, will well and honestly perform and discharge the trust reposed in him, and that without any charge att all to the place for which hee shall be imployed. And soe leaving to youre lordshipe's good care and consideracion what maie nowe conduce to the furtherance of this service, wee bid youre lordship verie hartily farewell. Ffrom his Majesty's Castle at Dublin, this thirtyeth of May, 1634.

"Youre lordship's loving friende,
"WENTWORTH."

Lord Cork was desirous of obliging the Lord-Deputy by putting in his brother for Bandon, and wrote "to his verie lovinge friende, Mr. William Wiseman," in hot haste, urging him that " he should move the provost and burgesses effectually in his name to intrust him with the nominating of two burgesses for the town, to serve in the next Parliament."

It is not unusual, even in our own halcyon days, for the owner of a town, or for the priest of the parish in which it is, to nominate and virtually return its *quasi* representatives; but then the candidates come to the hustings, and we hear from their own lips all the benefits that are to be showered upon ourselves and our town by returning them.

Lord Cork, however, did not see what necessity there was for those whom he was anxious to nominate to be put to the incon-venience and expense of travelling from Dublin to Bandon and back again, practically to do little more than to say "how do you do" to the burgesses. Neither did he think it at all necessary to mention to them even the names of those whom he intended for the honours of representing them in the new Parliament. He desired that the provost and burgesses should send him " their election, *with a blanke* under their seal, that I may fill it up."

To make their minds easy, however, and to free them from any apprehension of having discreditable persons placed to their account in the coming Senate: "I doe hereby engage my creddit," said his lord-ship, " that I will nominate two able and sufficient gentlemen, such as shall discharge the duties with creddit, and without any charge to the town." He concludes the letter by commending Mr. Wiseman and all his friends at Bandon-Bridge to the Almighty. From Dublin, the last of May, 1634.

It would appear that the Bandonians complied with Lord Cork's wish in this particular, for we find that the representatives chosen were Sir George Wentworth, and "our loving friend" Mr. William Wiseman.

Sir George, as has been previously stated, was the brother of the Lord-Deputy. Mr. William Wiseman, Escœtor dni Regis, held many of his Inquisitiones Post Mortem in the King's "Ould" Castle, in the city of Cork, as well as at Bandon and other places. He was the eldest son of Simon Wiseman, one of the original Bandon colonists, and was appointed a freeman of the Bandon corporation in 1628.

His first wife was Catherine, eldest daughter of the renowned poet Spenser, with whom he lived on the banks of "the pleasant Bandon," as Spenser himself has written it; and in a spacious residence, now, alas! a hopeless ruin, with nothing left but a crumbling wall to represent what was once the Castle of Kilbegge. Here Spenser's daughter yielded up her life; and from within its scarcely defined enclosure, where docks and nettles now flourish in undisturbed luxuriance, her remains were borne to the graveyard of her parish church in Bandon; and there the shadow of the spire of the oldest Protestant edifice in Ireland, uniting with the shade of the chesnut and the elm, spreads a broad dark pall over her grave—a fitting resting place for a child of the immortal bard.* Mr. Wiseman died at Drinagh, in 1639.†

The unexpected fate awaiting one of his descendants has been fulfilled in our own day in the person of a lineal descendent of this Protestant

---

* Spenser's second son, Laurence, died in Bandon in 1654, and was also buried in Kilbrogan. In his will, dated in 1653, he is described as Laurence Spenser, of Camden-Bridge, Youghal. His assets, consisting of feather beds and a few pounds in cash, he left to some friends. The poet's third son, Peregrine, was " firmarius" of the adjoining parish of Brinny. His (i.e.—Peregrine's) son Hugolinus succeeded to the impropriate tithings of Brinny; but, having become a Roman Catholic, he was outlawed by the Parliament, and his property bestowed on his cousin William Spenser, "as next Protestant heir." A William Spenser, also grandson of the poet, was ordered to Connaught, but he appealed to Cromwell; and the latter wrote to the commissioners, stating that William Spenser did profess the Popish religion, but that since he came to the years of discretion he utterly renounced it, at least so he said; but even Cromwell's intercession was of no avail,—it was hell or Connaught with him! Mr. Nathanial Spenser, the poet's great-grandson, through Sylvanus, his eldest son, by his wife Elizabeth, was lay impropriator of Temple-Brady. His (Nathanial's) son Thomas was buried in Kilbrogan in 1729, his son John in 1730, and his son Nathanial in 1732.

† There was a Mr. Wiseman—probably this man or his son—who purchased the lands of Kilmoyleran and Knocks, near Drinagh, from Sir Phillip Percival. At his death, he left those lands to his two nieces:—Susanna, married to Zachary Brady, and Anne, married to William Smith. Smith's son parted with a portion of his lot to Thomas. Ffrench for the sum of thirty pounds sterling, at the rent of one shilling per annum. Brady's eldest son sold his portion of Kilmoyleran and five Gneeves of Knocks to Sir Richard Cox, the Lord Chancellor, for seventy pounds.

representative of the Protestant town of Bandon. A town which has continued so rigidly exclusive to Roman Catholics, that it is within the reach of living memory when members of their church were for the first time permitted to reside in any of the principal streets. Indeed, its notoriety in this respect was world-wide. Who is there that has not heard of the couplet? which says:—

> "A Turk, a Jew, or an Atheist,
> May live in this town, but no Papist!"

The lineal descendant we have referred to is Nicholas Wiseman. Although of staunch Protestant descent, he was born and bred a Roman Catholic; lived the greater portion of his life a priest, and died an archbishop, a cardinal, and a prince of Rome.

Amongst the principal measures brought into this Parliament were:— an Act to prevent and reform profane swearing and cursing; to prevent the ploughing by the tail, and pulling wool from living sheep; and even one to prevent the unprofitable custom of burning corn in the straw.*

The following account, under the head of "A brief note of the receipts and payments for the use of the corporation, the 25th of September, 1636," was furnished by Randal Fenton, provost:—

1636.

	£	s.	d.
Received in money from Ralph Sale, per William Fuller, our treasurer,	0	11	0
Received from the three rates made on the town,	61	4	9
Received from Thomas Franklin for Mr. Fenton, the payment to Lord Cork,	0	5	0
Paid to John Loddin for building the Irish bridge,	5	0	0
Paid to Thomas Wilson for whipping several people,	0	5	0
Paid charges, the first interest in March, to Mr. Crofts, the second interest in August,	12	17	6
Paid charges to Mr. Bennett, a year's interest as his receipt,	8	18	4
Paid for a carpet and several charges belonging to the corporation,	1	7	8
Paid for the charges of the great bridge, to several people,	12	15	5

In a note at the foot is a memorandum stating that William Browne hath agreed to ring the bell at eight of the clock, for twenty shillings yearly, beginning All Saint's-tide, 1637.

The rates generally levied off the town about this time were threepenny rates, and the cost of collecting them was very heavy. Thus we find a threepenny rate, amounting to £46 2s. 6d., reduced by the expenses of collection to £39 9s. 8d.

---

* These old Irish habits certainly demanded parliamentary reform. But what shall we say of the legislative intermeddling which took place in 1447, at Trim, where it was enacted that, if any man wore a moustache, he may be used as an Irish enemy? Everyone who lived in those days knew what that meant.

The bridge leading from south-gate into the Irish-town, and anciently known as the Irish bridge, was built this year by one John Loddin, for the sum of five pounds. In order to procure a foundation, the masons were obliged to imbed blocks of oak, twelve feet long by fourteen inches thick, in the black peat which abounded in the centre, and at both sides of the little river, at this place. Upon these blocks the foundation-stones were laid, and a bridge of two arches erected.

The bridge, which could not have been more than ten feet between the parapet walls, was widened no less than three times, to suit the exigencies of traffic, more especially when wheeled vehicles came into fashion. It was taken down in 1864,* and the present one-arched structure erected on its site.

1639. The Earl of Strafford (previously Lord Wentworth) returned to Dublin, and was re-appointed Lord-Deputy. Immediately he set to work to increase the taxes; and so well did he succeed, that in a short time the revenues of the crown were swollen to £800,000 per annum. But this was not all, as he procured nearly one million sterling in addition as subsidies. But great as the imposts were, they might have been borne if they were expended for the benefit of the country from which they were wrung.

Strafford, however, had no intention of doing this. Having got the money, he proceeded to arm and equip 8,000 foot and 1,000 horse. This large force he raised, not to fight a foreign foe, or to suppress unconstitutional enactments; on the contrary, they were raised to subdue those who opposed unconstitutional enactments; "they were designed," it was said, "to subdue the rebels in Scotland, and to awe the mutineers in England."

He succeeded in making himself obnoxious to two of the most powerful parties in this kingdom. The Presbyterians hated him because he unjustly tendered an oath to them, to avoid the taking of which many of them left Ireland altogether; and the church party, to whom he naturally turned for relief and sympathy, received him very coldly. How could they confide in one who was so loath to part with his intimate friend, Sir Toby Matthews, "a Jesuitical priest," that he brought him to Dublin with him? And it was well known that another friend of

---

* On removing the old bridge, a small copper coin, little more than half an inch in diameter, was found. On the obverse, within a beaded circle, was "Cork Citty," outside of which was another beaded circle containing the date, "1658," and "P. M." (Phillip Matthews), "Mayor." On the reverse, the Cork arms.

8

his, Sir George Ratcliffe, was in close correspondence with Paul Harris, another Jesuit.

Strafford returned to England the next year, and was shortly afterwards arraigned before the peers for high-treason. Amongst the various charges brought against him was one closely connected with our town. The fifteenth article in the impeachment stated :—That he had arbitrarily imposed illegal taxes on the town of Bandon-Bridge, Baltimore,. &c., and cessed soldiers on them till they paid. To this Strafford replied :—That the money levied on the Bandonians was the arrear of their contribution towards the subsidies granted to the King, and that it was levied without force. A Bill of Attainder passed both houses, and on the 12th of March, 1641, he was executed.

Another Parliament assembled in Dublin this year, on the 16th of March. The members for Bandon were Sir Francis Slingsby, Knt., Kilmore, and Anthony Dopping, Esq., Dublin. Sir Francis was recommended to the corporation by the Lords Justices, in the following letter :—

" After our hearty commendacions.

" Whereas there are two burgesses to be elected and sent from Bandon-Bridge to serve at this ensuing Parliament, appointed to begin the 10th of March next. And forasmuch as we are desirous that Sir Francis Slingsby, Knt., may be nominated for one of the said two burgesses, we, therefore, have thought fit to recommend him unto you for that employment, as one whom, we make no doubt, will well and discreetly perform the trust reposed in him, and that without any charge to your corporation. And so leaving him to your good care, and whatever else may most conduce to the furtherance of this service, we bid you very heartily farewell. From his Majesty's Castle at Dublin, this third day of February, 1634.

" Your very loving friends."

The corporation complied with their lordships' suggestion, and gave Slingsby a seat. In a letter to the provost, whom he addresses as " my worthy friend," Sir Francis says :—" I cannot but acknowledge my thankfulness to you for your favourable good intentions in choosing me for a burgess of Parliament for your corporation." He concludes by enquiring " if there be anything that you would have me to do for the benefit of your corporation. If you give me my instructions, I shall willingly do my best endeavour for your advantage and interest, as I have always done."

Our junior member, Mr. Dopping, figures largely in the journals of the house as a practical, painstaking senator ; and he appears to have been as thoroughly Puritanical in every respect as those sturdy non-conforming burgesses who sent him to represent them in the Commons. Indeed, so highly did he stand in the estimation of the honorable commissioners of the Parliament, that when they wanted to ascertain if the Episcopal clergy of Dublin would consent to officiate in their several churches without using the Book of Common Prayer, it was Mr. Dopping they selected for the purpose.

Mr. Dopping must have been known as a useful man before he entered the house, for scarcely had he taken his seat, when he was appointed to sit in committee on one of the first bills introduced during the session. It was entitled " An Act for the examination and settling of fees." Also on a select committee " to consider the best means of strengthening and securing the several plantations in Galway, Mayo, Sligo, &c. ; to consider a petition presented by the inhabitants of King's and Queen's County." And on the 21st of February, 1639-40, the house nominated him, with three others, to draw its order for the expulsion of Joshua Carpenter, member for Carlingford, and Thomas Little, member for Beneher. There was hardly a committee appointed, of any importance, that did not number amongst its members Mr. Anthony Dopping.

His coadjutor, Sir Francis, seems to have been one of the drones of the session ; for we can only find mention of him on two occasions : once when he was appointed with others " to confer with the lords touching their subsidies," and at another time when he sat " to consider the arrest done upon John Johnson."*

1641.　　Forty years had now elapsed since Don Juan D'Aquila surrendered Kinsale to the Lord-Deputy, and, thereby, for a long time damped the hopes of those who expected to profit by civil commotion or a foreign invasion.

During the interval Ireland had been rapidly advancing in wealth and prosperity. A new people had infused energy and new blood into her apathetic and nerveless frame. The country had been dragging its weary wasted limbs, out of the cold barbarous past, into the warm sunlight of civilized life. The change that had been already wrought was marvellous. What was heretofore a swamp or a bog was now

---

* In the account of the savings contained in the patents under the Acts of Settlement and Explanation, we find our senior representative entitled to the full benefits of a judgment and decree to the lands of Moigge, Ballinlaugh, Garrebrickeene, Clydarragh, Kielultane, Ardglasse, and Kilbrey.

drained, and its soft pastures were grazed by well-bred English cattle. The woods and the forest, where the outlaw found a hiding place, and the wolf a refuge, were now the site of an open country, abounding with farm-houses and other signs of improvement.

The trade of the town itself had wonderfully increased. The wool of countless flocks of sheep passed through the hands of the wool-comber, the weaver, the dyer, the cloth-worker, and, finally, of the clothier—who shipped it to England or to foreign markets, and brought back money in its stead. Herds of well-bred cattle also contributed to the wealth of the country. There were butchers and victuallers to dispose of their meat, combmakers and chandlers to manufacture combs and candles out of the bones and fat; and very numerous tanneries, where the tanner and the currier converted their hides into leather, most of which obtained a market elsewhere, and what was left the saddler and the cordwainer turned to profitable account.

Other trades were here also, whose very presence was indicative of the well-being of the inhabitants. There were goldsmiths, to provide gold rings and chains for our Bandon fair; glovers to supply them with gloves, perfumes, and the other requisites of the toilet; apothecaries and chirurgeons, to mix a posset and to bleed the sick; malsters, to supply materials for home-brewed ale; and millers, to grind the corn into flour for bread-cakes. There were inn-holders, in whose hostelries the townsman could regale himself with prawns and broiled oysters, and wash them down with a pottle of sack. There were gardeners to supply his wife with a nosegay; and musicians, to the music of whose lute or spinet he could dance a saraband or a minuet, or accompany with some roundelay which he had learned in his infancy among the orchards of Somersetshire or Devon.

There were members of other trades, too, to supply the requirements of our thriving town. There were bakers, stainers, carpenters, glaziers, blacksmiths, mettlemen, coopers, masons, tailors, feltmakers, pewter-men, barbers, salters, parchment-makers, curriers, cutlers,* &c., &c.

In addition to those who added to the wealth of our Bandon plantation by the labour of their hands, there was a fair sprinkling of yeomen and merchants, and of those whose more elevated social position entitled them to add Miles or Armiger to their surnames. Not only had the trade of the town increased but its size also.

* See Freeman's Book, Bandon corporation.

When Kinsale and Youghal, Wexford, Dundalk, and Belfast, were towns "of small moment," Bandon was worthy of regard for "its bigness and handsomeness."* It ranked with Kilkenny, the seat of the Confederate government, and with Drogheda, which contained, without inconvenience, the large garrison of Sir Arthur Aston. Although it was of considerable extent, the streets and houses were clean and neat, and presented none of that carelessness, and disregard for cleanliness, too often a characteristic of our Irish towns and villages.

Yea, even before our colony had time to recover from the misery caused by the visit of that great devastating monster, whose scorching breath crisped the very earth on which he trod, and who had lapped up countless measures of blood to slake his insatiate thirst, Bandon was "a fine English town."† Its population, "wherein are at least seven thousand souls," was greater than even it is now, and it occupied as large, if not a larger area, than it does at present. All the suburbs we have now were then in being, and we suspect even more. There was one at least, Sugar Lane; for we read that the portion of it adjoining Northgate "was spoiled and pulled down least the rebels should shelter there."

There were many roads striking out from the town in all directions, some of which still remain. One led over Ballylanglay Hill to Innoshannon, and thence on to Kinsale; another up the Cork road to Kilpatrick, and thence over the mountain to "the beautiful city;" another through Gallow's Hill Street, Carey's Cross, and on to Clonakilty; another went up by Barrett's Hill, and turning due north, passed through Kilcrea to Macroom; and another passed through Sugar Lane, and out to Moragh,—here it forked into two branches, one of which led to Newcestown and Castletown, and the other to Enniskeane. Beyond the last place there were no roads. Dunmanway did not exist for nearly sixty years afterwards, whilst the adjoining pretty little town of Ballineen did not contain a house, or had scarcely a name, for close upon a century and a half subsequent to the period of which we write.

When anyone would venture directly overland from the places last mentioned, to Bantry or Baltimore, he should trust by day to whatever straggling bridlepath he could strike upon, and by night to the hollow bark of the squatter's dog, or the glare of the wood-kern's fire, as he and his outlawed companions sat probably preparing their humble meal

* See Dr. Boate's *Ireland*.
·† See a letter in *Mercurius Politicus*.

of horse-flesh. The usual way—in truth, almost the only—method of communication between the seaport towns previously named and Bandon was by the sea. They took ship at Bantry or Baltimore, landed at Kinsale, and marched up.

In those days nearly all the gentry around Bandon were Irish, not only in their sympathies and prejudices, but also by extraction. Some of these were chieftains, in possession of large tracts of country, over which they exercised an absolute control,—hanging up a kern or a gallow-glass to the next tree,—or pouncing upon a neighbour's cattle, would sweep them all off to their bawn with nearly as much indifference as if Anglo-Saxon laws and penalties had never intruded upon the Isle of Saints.

Their dislike of the English, however, did not extend itself to their habits and costumes. The Irish gentry now wore hats, and were habited in broad cloth. They drank wine and beer, and rode on a black or a dun gelding, or a sorrel horse; and, should occasion require it, they could even turn out on a grey nag or a copple bawn. But great as was their advancement, it was as nothing when compared to the prodigious strides accomplished by the corresponding class in the towns; such as the members of corporate and civic bodies. These greatly exceeded them in all the enjoyments of the social circle, and many of them lead a life of almost Oriental magnificence.

They went to sleep upon feather-beds, "with bolsters and pillows to match;"[*] they used spoons made of silver, rested their feet upon stools covered with Turkish cushions, walked upon carpets from the Levant, drank their wine out of silver bowls, wore gold chains, and enjoyed a luxurious ease not always attainable by their representatives, even in our own day.

All the castles in our neighbourhood were at this time tenanted. In our immediate vicinity an ancestor of the present noble proprietor live in the old residence of the Mahowns, and enjoyed all the honours and emoluments pertaining to the lordship of the manor of Castle-Mahon.

Down the river, and in the now old rifted ruin at Kilbegge, Catherine, the eldest daughter of the author of the *Fairie Queene*, experienced all the happiness of domestic life, and looking out from the windows of her mansion, could not fail to behold

" The pleasant Bandon, crowned with many a wood."

---

[*] See inventory of the effects of Alderman Roche, of Cork.

Lower still, a scion of the old house occupied the Castle of Downdanial,* of which scarcely anything now remains, save the large western gable, whose ivy-mantled wall and solitary tower are left, as it were, to mourn over the fallen fortunes of the Barry Oges. Still lower down, Patrick Roche, the senior representative for Kinsale, dwelt in Poulnalonge, from the battlements of which he probably often gazed on the beautiful scenery of that highly-favoured spot.†

In his castle at Kilbrittain,‡ sat the owner of three thousand armed

---

* Downdanial, or Dundaneare, was built in 1476, by one of the Barry Oges, a sept who were seized of the lands subsequently possessed by the O'Mahonys of Castle-Mahon, but which O'Mahonys originally enjoyed the same lands centuries before the arrival of the Barrys in Ireland. The Barry Oges also owned the lands on the southern banks of the Bandon, extending from the Bridewell river down to near Kinsale, and which, after they were deprived, was conferred by the crown on McCarthy Reagh, of Kilbrittain. After the seige of Dunboy Castle, in 1602, Sir George Carew sent some companies of foot to Downdanial, where they remained until ready to leave Munster. About the year 1612 the East-India Company, who paid seven thousand pounds for woods in the neighbourhood, established a depot for smelting iron ore not far from the castle; and Smith says, "the same enterprising company built two ships there of 500 tons each, and also constructed a dock at Downdanial for building more," but this was evidently a mistake. Upon the suppression of the great rebellion, Downdanial Castle, which at that time belonged to Daniel McCarthy Reagh, was granted to Richard, Earl of Cork, and by one of whose descendants—the present Duke of Devonshire—it is still enjoyed. Adjoining the castle is a chalybeate spring, the waters of which were formorly held in great repute by the people in the neighbourhood, by whom they were considered most effectual for removing pains in the stomach, giddiness in the head, colic, and for scrofulous affections. The well, which about two centuries ago was protected by a thick wall, and was roofed with strong flags, is now scarcely recognisable.

† His summer residence was also selected for its scenery, but it was of a different kind. It was built on the steep declivity overhanging File-a-Reel Bay, Dunworly; and so difficult of access was the front of this dwelling, that whenever Mr. Roche wanted to lay in a stock of the good old Spanish wine of these days, he found that the easiest way of conveying it to the cellar was through the roof of the house.

‡ Kilbrittain Castle was built by one of the De Courcys, lords of Kinsale. Although, according to Robert Clayton, bishop of Cork, who in a letter to Lord Egmont (Cork, June 13th, 1744), says he copied an inscription on a stone at the castle; and which, if correctly done, would make it appear that the castle was built nearly a century and a half before the De Courcys came to Ireland. The figures, says the the bishop in reply to his lordship,—who stated some people doubted but that there might be some mistake,—are plainly legible, and cannot be mistaken for any other number than 1035; and what is remarkable, continued he, the figures which make up the date are in the ancient characters. The De Courcys were lords of the manor of Kilbrittain long prior to the McCarthys having become possessed of it. It appears, by a composition of Walter de la Haye, the King's escheator, A.D. 1295 (temp. Edward the First), that the manor of Kilbrittain and Ringroan, with the mills, fisheries, &c., also the lands of Holdernesse Liffyrim, and which, upon the death of John De Courcy (who was killed in 1295, in Inchidonny Island), had fallen to the crown, were restored by the said Walter de la Haye, on a composition of £12 12s. 0d. per annum, to James Keating, in trust, for the use of the said John, Lord De Courcy. It is stated that the way the McCarthys got Kilbrittain was in consequence of one of the De Courcys having borrowed a white ferret from one of them, and, in order to secure the animal's safe return, he allowed McCarthy to hold the castle and lands as a guarantee for the fulfilment of his promise; but the ferret having died, he was

kern.   His territories extended from his castles at Carriganass and Kil-
gobban to where the broad Atlantic ripples on the sanded beach at
Burran and Coolmayne.   Notwithstanding all he enjoyed, he coveted
the possessions of his neighbours, and made frequent incursions upon
them.   He pillaged Ibane; he stripped the Carberries; he ravaged the
Courcies; and even ventured in among the sturdy settlers at Kinalmeaky.
And there is many an old story still rife of the sayings and doings of
Kilbrittain's powerful chieftain, Daniel McCormac McCarthy Reagh.*

---

unable to keep his word, and this McCarthy took advantage of, and kept what he
had.   About the year 1535, Thomas Laverhouse (afterwards bishop of Kildare)
escaped to this castle with a child thirteen years old.   The child was brother of Lord
Thomas Fitzgerald, and a son of the then lately deceased Earl of Kildare.   The
McCarthy Reagh was then dead, but his wife, Eleanor Fitzgerald (Lord Kildare's sister,
and consequently the child's aunt), still lived.   Soon after, this lady married O'Donnell,
of the North; and she made it one of the articles in her marriage settlement with
with him that he should protect her young nephew, and this he solemnly promised
to do.   Shortly after the marriage they returned to Ulster, where they were scarcely
settled when Eleanor became aware that her treacherous lord had arranged to betray
young Fitzgerald.   She saw at once that there was no time to be lost.   She, therefore, sent him away privately to France, giving him one hundred and fifty gold pieces
to bear his expenses.   Finding that he was safe, she then turned on O'Donnell, and
told that worthy that nothing but the preservation of her nephew could have induced
her to marry such a clownish curmudgeon as he was; and, now seeing that he sought
to betray her in that particular, she would stay with him no longer—and left him.
Sir James Semphill obtained patents dated June 27th (13th James the First), A.D.
1616, for holding a fair at Kilbrittain, on the eve of St. Martin's Day, and on the next
day, and a market on every Tuesday.   When the great rebellion was ended, Kilbrittain Castle, which was the seat of one of the most active leaders in that great
revolt, together with part of Coolmayne, Lishinaline, Garranfreene, and other lands,
amounting in all to 4,898 acres were bestowed on Colonel Thomas Long, the same
who, after the retirement of the Lord Lieutenant, Henry Cromwell, from Dublin
Castle, was left in possession of that seat of government, when Cromwell retired to
the Vice-Regal Lodge in Phœnix Park.   It is highly probable that, upon the
restoration of Charles the Second, Colonel Long, like many others who took a
prominent part on the Parliamentary side, were deprived of their grants, and their
lands bestowed on the Duke of York (afterwards James the Second).   It is also
probable that Kilbrittain, like the adjoining Castle of Coolmayne, was bestowed by
James, on his arrival in Ireland, upon Donough McCarthy, Lord Cloncarthy (a
kinsman of the former owner); and that, upon King James's defeat, it was sold with
the other forfeited estates at the great sales in Queen Anne's reign, and bought by the
Hollow Sword Blades Company, who purchased many lands in its neighbourhood, and
bought from them or their assignees by an ancestor of the present proprietor.

* The McCarthys claim descent from Ænghus, who was baptized on the rock of
Cashel by St. Patrick, and who was the first King of Munster who became a
christian.   Ænghus derived from Eogan More, son of Olioll Ollum, who was King
of Munster in the second century; but Keating goes farther back still, and, tracing
them up through Heber the fair (son of Milesius), never stops until he runs them
into the great patriarch—old Noah himself.   One of Ænghus's descendants was
named Carthach, and Carthach's eldest son was named Mac Carthach or McCarthy.
When Fitzstephen, and Strongbow's son Richard, first came over they found Dermot
McCarthy upon the throne of Cork—a kingdom which, at that time, extended to fifty
miles in length and thirty in breadth; and which kingdom one of Dermot's ancestors
had obtained, in 1089, from Turlogh, monarch of all Ireland, who, upon his subjugation of Munster, divided it into two parts.   The northern part, or Thomand, he

About a stone's throw from the Abbey of St. Francis, and close upon the well-wooded banks of the Silver Stream, Sir Robert O'Shaughnessy defended his fortified keep, until compelled to succumb to the well-disciplined forces of Lord Forbes. On the bold bare rock of Ballina-earriga, the towering castle of Randal Oge Hurley raised its lofty head in proud defiance to the Saxon. Its owner joined with, and fought hard for, the rebels, and paid the penalty of ill-success. His estates were forfeited as well as his castle; and Randal Oge remained a hunted outlaw till his death. He now rests in the little moss-grown grave-yard of Fanlobbus, and sleeps his long sleep under the same turf with

bestowed on Conner O'Brian, whilst the southern portion, or Desmond, together with the city of Cork, was conferred on Donogh McCarthy. Upon the arrival of the English, Dermod accepted the sovereignty of Henry the Second, and not only resigned his city into that monarch's hands, but also gave hostages for the payment of a yearly tribute, stipulating in return that he should enjoy the rest of his territories without molestation. We have said he resigned his city, but it scarcely amounts to that; for Cork was then possessed by the Danes, and, of course, he had not the power of giving what he did not possess. He told the English they might take it from the Danes; and when they had succeeded in doing so, he was the very first to try and wrest it from them. The McCarthys at all times ranked high amongst the most considerable families in Ireland; and, in the reigns of several of the English monarchs since Henry's time, they were officially addressed and styled as Princes of Carbery. They remained more or less faithful to English rule for nearly five centuries; but when the great rebellion broke out, the then McCarthy Reagh (Danial McComac, who had been High Sheriff of the county in 1635, and who was even then a member of the Reformed Church), "after obtaining arms from Lord Kinal-meaky in order that he may fight for the English, yet the very next day marched against the town of Bandon." After his fall, the custodium of his lands was vested by the Lords Justices in Lord Kinalmeaky. The additional name of Reagh was assumed to distinguish this family from the senior branch, who dwelt near Macroom and in Kerry, and who were known as the McCarthy Mores. The latter were possessed of very great influence and power, insomuch so, that as far back as 1461 (*temp*. Edward the Sixth), the English were glad to pay them a good round sum annually for protection. We are unable to say in what year the unfortunate Daniel died; but he was alive in 1667, when the French were expected to make a descent upon Kinsale; and when he was represented as near gone into rebellion. He led a wandering life after the taking of Kilbrittain Castle by the Bandonians; sometimes residing at Carbery, and at other times in Bere and Bantry; and, according to Lord Orrery, "amongst the worst lot of people in all Ireland—men that were ready for any villany." He left a son, born in 1625, who went to France in 1647, where he married the daughter of a French count. He died in 1676 (being killed in a duel), leaving two sons, Charles and Dermot. Charles returned to this country, where he married, and died, leaving a son, Owen. Owen died in 1775, and was the father of Charles McCarthy, who was married March 27th, 1749, at Ballymodan Church, Bandon, to Catherine, daughter of Charles Bernard, Esq.,—of the Bernards of Palace Anne; she died in Bandon at the advanced age of 103. Mr. McCarthy, who was a solicitor, was seneschal of the manor of Macroom, recorder of Clonakilty, and also clerk of the crown for the county. He was succeeded by his son, Francis Bernard McCarthy, who married Elizabeth, daughter of William Daunt, Esq., of Kilcascan, and died in 1821, leaving amongst other issue:—Francis B. McCarthy, who married Miss Tresilian, and died leaving an only son, Francis B. McCarthy, late of Bandon; also William Daunt McCarthy, who married Margaret, sister of the Right Hon. Judge Longfield, by whom he had, with other issue:—Elizabeth, who married Arthur Beamish, Esq., late of Mammoor.

many of those who lived in the same eventful period, and shared in the same dangers with himself.

The Irish chieftains were jealous of the growing prosperity of the English colonists. But why should they be so? These colonists were only located upon lands which had been forfeited by those who had raised the standard of open revolt, and who had been put down by a large expenditure of English blood and treasure, and by the assistance of the immediate predecessors of many of these very chieftains themselves.

Instead of being jealous of the settlers, they should, on the contrary, have encouraged those who opened up the country, and who gave them wealth and comforts, in exchange for articles of trade to which they had previously scarcely attached a value. In truth, in this very year the Irish had less reason to complain than they had at any time since Strongbow's arrival; and so well content did they appear to be, that when Lord Muskerry (one of the most powerful chiefs of the Irish Confederacy) heard complaints of the doings of some of his people, "he seemed very zealous for the English, and threatened to hang those who committed them." And his scarcely less powerful kinsman, McCarthy Reagh, of Kilbrittain, having made many professions of loyalty, obtained arms from the governor of Bandon in order to fight for the English.

CHAPTER VI.

THE GREAT REBELLION—WARNINGS OF THE COMING STORM—AN UNSPEAKABLE NUMBER OF IRISH CHURCHMEN FLOCK OVER FROM THE CONTINENT—THE CRUELTIES—THE GLAMORGAN TREATY; THE FIRST ARTICLE CONFIRMS THE ROMAN CATHOLIC CLERGY IN THE POSSESSION OF ALL THE LANDS, TITHES, ETC., WHICH THEY HAD WRESTED FROM THE PROTESTANT CLERGY SINCE THE REBELLION BEGAN—DUPLICITY OF THE KING—CROMWELL ARRIVES.

HE normal state of Ireland, from the arrival of Milesius down to the suppression of the rebellions of Desmond and Tyrone, was that of oppression, rapine, perfidy, and murder. One would have thought that the introduction of Christianity amongst the inhabitants, and the dissemination of its divine precepts among them, would have softened their hearts, and have raised them above their every-day work of rapacity and blood. But it was not so. Speaking of the Irish, " we never read of any other people in the world," says an old writer,* " so implacably, so furiously, so eternally set upon the destruction of one another." He then tells us of no less than six hundred battles fought between themselves, by people of the same country, language, and religion.

Although there was no subject so often dwelt upon by the Irish, in their complaints against the English, as interference with the exercise of their religion, and thereby hindering the practice of its holy precepts among the people; yet, ere England laid claim to a foot of the soil, they systematically violated one of the holiest commands which the Christian religion has given us :—" Thou shalt love thy neighbour as thyself," was not complied with by those who seized upon their neighbour's

---

* P. W.—" Never any nation upon earth anneered the Milesian Irish in the most unnatural, bloody, everlasting, destructive fewds that have been heard of. Fewds continued with the greatest pride, most hellish ambition, &c., followed with the most horrible injustices, rapines, treacheries, murders, &c., for almost two thousand years."

husbands, their neighbour's wives, their children, and annually paid them away in tribute.

Neither was that commandment, which says:—" Thou shalt do no murder," obeyed by a people who slaughtered one hundred and eighteen of their kings; and who burned with such a fury. for dominion or revenge,* that under its influences they are said to have torn out one another's lives.

Century after century rolled by, and yet the country underwent no change. Incursions on each other's territories, lifting cattle,.forays, and internecine wars were just as much in vogue, outside the Pale, in the days of Elizabeth as they were in those of Con of the hundred fights. To the English, all this was the cause of an endless expenditure of blood, and a vast expense. Scarcely had they trampled out the flames of rebellion in the east, when they burst out anew in the west. The rebellion of Gerald, Earl of Desmond, was scarce at an end in the south, when that of Hugh, Earl of Tyrone, began in the north.

After the capitulation of the Spaniards at Kinsale, and the departure of O'Neal and O'Donnell from a country where their path was too often marked " with large columns of fire and dense dark clouds of smoke," Ireland enjoyed a long rest. That tranquility, so necessary for the progress of a State, she enjoyed now for the first time. Peace begat confidence, and confidence begat trade and commerce; and these poured riches in abundance into her lap.

Forests and woods, heretofore the asylum of the criminal and the wild beast, were now the site of busy towns and villages. And there was many a bleak hill-side, whose sod was often stiff with the gore of contending septs, now occupied by a succession of comfortable farm-houses, with their orchards and their cornfields; whilst the green pastures, which but a few years before were covered with rushes and bog-water, and were the daily resort of the widgeon and wild duck, were now grazed upon by flocks and herds of the best English cattle.†

But this was too pleasing a reality to last. Averse to the quietude of peaceful occupations, and glorying in the excitement of war, the native Irish could easily be induced to join with those who could tempt

---

* So intense was the feeling of revenge, that it was not uncommon for an Irish chieftain, when he had slain his adversary, to decapitate him, and have his skull polished and silver-mounted; and from this hideous drinking vessel he used to regale himself on festive occasions.

† Vide—*A Remonstrance of the distressed Protestants in the Province of Munster.*

them with a pretext for hostilities; and there were those who were ever on the look-out for a favourable turn of the tide, and to whom the discovery of a pretext was no difficulty. A complaint against the new plantations, and of the number of new English coming over, was soon upon their lips. But the new English had come to settle upon lands which a fierce and protracted revolt had turned into a desert. That property which had belonged to the partizans of Mountjoy was destroyed by O'Neil; and that property which had belonged to the partizans of O'Neil was destroyed by Mountjoy.

Speaking of the great tract of country forfeited by the northern chieftains:—" All the food the people had," said Moryson, " was taken from them by the rebel soldiers, so that the common sort were driven to unspeakable extremities." Again :—" No spectacle was more frequent in the ditches of towns, and especially in wasted countries, than to see multitudes of these poor people with their mouth all coloured green by eating nettles and docks."

It was into this wilderness "the new English" had come; and because the six counties, escheated to the King by the rebellion of Tyrone and Tyrconnell,—a rebellion which took the best army in Europe, and the expenditure of two millions sterling, to suppress,—were disposed of to those who undertook to improve the lands, and to plant them with an industrious and loyal people; and because, forsooth, there was a rumour that the colonizing principle would be extended, those who had never even simulated loyalty unless constrained by circumstances, and who scoffed at industry and trade, must needs get incensed at the preference shown "the new English;" and hence the new plantations were in the fore-front of Irish grievances.

The other great cause of complaint was the persecution of their religion. Although there were acts in the statute book intolerent of the free exercise of Popery, yet for years before they were a dead letter.* Roman Catholic mayors presided over cities; Roman Catholic sheriffs presided over counties. Some of the Roman Catholic justices of the peace, who sat upon the bench, and some of the Roman Catholic lawyers, who practised at the bar, had never taken the oath of supremacy or allegiance to the King, whose laws they promulgated.

Indeed, so anxious was the government to conciliate those turbulent

---

* See Lord Lowther's speech at the opening of the High Courts of Justice, Borlace, Sir John Templer's *History of the Irish Rebellion*, and various other works.

subjects, that concessions made to them were refused to the religionists
of the State; and they were allowed to enjoy a licentious freedom in the
doctrines and rituals of Rome, at the very time when Protestant non-
conformists writhed under the whip at the tail of a cart, when red
hot irons seared their cheeks, when the executioner's knife slit their
noses up, and scooped out their ears, because they refused to comply with
the formularies of the Church of England.

They enjoyed their full share of the State's honours also. They had
their earls and viscounts, their barons and baronets; they had their
burgesses to introduce measures into the Commons, and they had their
nobility to ratify them in the Lords.

The clergy, one would think, ought to have been content with all
this liberty to their laity, and with publicly celebrating their religious
rites without being interfered with. But they were not satisfied yet.
The most severe anathemas of the Church of Rome—a church proscribed
by law—were uttered against those who dared to attend the worship
of the church of England—a church established by law. But the
Romish clergy had no idea of stopping short even at this. They must
go farther still, and actively interfere in civil affairs. They opposed
the judgments of the courts of law, and they absolutely compelled
their people to disobey the decisions of the judges, when they were
not in accordance with their wishes.

They had a regular Romish hierarchy, complete in every detail,
established all over the kingdom; and its jurisdiction was as potent as
if Pope Urban the Eight resided in Dublin Castle. In every province
in Ireland they had an archbishop; in every diocese, a bishop; in
every parish, a priest. There were abbeys, nunneries, religious houses
everywhere, and they were filled with nuns and monks, Jesuits and
friars. Even the metropolis, the official residence of the government
itself, was so overrun with those several orders—more especially the
friars, who abounded in every variety, shod and unshod, black, white,
and grey—that Father Harris, in his published work, humorously
remarked:—" That it was as hard to find what number of friars were
in Dublin as to count how many frogs there were in the second plague
of Egypt."

Even in a few years after the death of Elizabeth, such was the
number of places of Roman Catholic worship and resort in and around
Dublin, that Barnebe Ryche could not refrain from saying, in 1610:—

"Let the wind blow which way it list—east, west, north, or south—Dublin is so seated, that a Papist may go from the high cross with a blown sheet, right before the wind, either to an idolatrous mass within the town, or to a superstitious well without the town."

Yet the cup of their contentment did not overflow. Now that they enjoyed the free exercise of their worship to its fullest extent, they wanted to enjoy the livings formerly attached to that worship also.* This could be best effected by a revolt;† and when was there a time more opportune for a revolt than the present? England and Scotland had been at war, and Scotland was victorious; and now England herself was divided, and trembled at the approach of a much greater war—a war between the people of England and her Parliament on the one side, and the royalists of England and her King on the other.

Materials for a revolt were not wanting. We cannot forbear asking, when were they? 'Tis true that the old Irish septs, who had maintained a protracted struggle with the Saxon for nearly four centuries and a half, were crushed and dispirited, but they were not extinct. Their organization was still effective and formidable. They had to lead them, chieftains, to whom descended traditions of the heroism and achievements of a long line of forefathers; and they had their bards to sing passionate recitals of the many wrongs they endured.

'Twas easy to fan these combustibles into a blaze; and no one was better adapted for that task than Roger Moore,‡ who had been sent over for that very purpose from Spain. "After some very little time spent in salutations," says Lord Maguire, "Moore began to discourse of the many afflictions and sufferings of the natives." And after referring to Lord Strafford's government,—which, by the way, pressed with as much severity on the English inhabitants as on the Irish, and probably more

---

* In the very first article in the peace made between the English and the rebels,—the Glamorgan Treaty,—the Catholic clergy were to hold, "henceforward and for ever," all the tithes, &c., which they had wrested from the Protestants since the 23rd of October, 1641; and to get back those which the Protestants had retaken from them during the same period. When the Pope's legate came over, he refused to sanction any peace that did not stipulate to restore the livings of the Protestant clergy to his priesthood.

† Mr. Sacheveril mentions the names of several priests who told him that the priests, Jesuits, and friars of England, Ireland, and Spain, and other countries beyond the seas, were the plotters, projectors, and contrivers of this rebellion; and that they have been these six years in agitation and preparation of the same. MacMahon, bishop of Clogher, admitted to the Earl of Strafford that, so far back as 1634, he, with others of his order, were engaged in soliciting aid for it.

‡ So popular was Moore with the peasantry, that they put their trust, they used to say, in God, our Lady, and Roger Moore.

so, and, therefore, not a grievance peculiar to themselves,—he mentioned the plantations ; and then told them that if the gentry of the kingdom were disposed to free themselves from the like inconvenience, and get good conditions for themselves for regaining a good part (if not all) of their ancestral estates, they could never desire a more convenient time than that time.

Although Maguire may have agreed with him as to the opportuneness of the time, yet he hesitated to join in an enterprise so often productive of forfeiture and the scaffold.   Moore saw this, and, changing his ground, he began again.   He put before him that he was overburthened with debt ; that his estate was small, whilst that of his forefathers was large.   That the estate of his forefathers would be restored to him for the most part, if not altogether ; and, as if to silence any whisperings of conscience about drawing the sword on those who had never harmed him, he was told that the welfare of the Catholic religion depended on it.   " I hear from every understanding man," says Moore, " that the Parliament intends the utter subversion of our religion."

With the prospect of the sponge being applied to his debts, and his estate increased in this world, and the happiness that must most assuredly be his, for fighting for the welfare of the Catholic religion, in the next, what could Maguire do ?   To enrol himself in that noble phalanx, who would rob his creditors at the same time that they would enrich his church and himself ; and he did so.

Warnings were not wanting of the coming storm.   More than eighteen months before, Sir Harry Vane acquainted the Lords Justices that information had reached him from abroad, which had been substantiated by the King's ministers in Spain and elsewhere, to the effect :—" That of late there had passed from Spain, and probably from other parts, an unspeakable number of Irish churchmen, for England and Ireland, and many good old soldiers ; and that, among the Irish friars in Spain, a whisper runs as if they expected a rebellion in Ireland."   Sir Henry Bedingfield foretold it the previous April, and even on the 11th of October itself.

Sir William Cole gave the justices and council notice " that there was a great resort made to Sir Phelim O'Neil's house, also to Lord Maguire's. That the latter made several journeys within the Pale and other places, and had spent much of his time in writing letters and sending despatches abroad.

But it was not until they were informed by Owen O'Connolly, on the evening of the 22nd of October, that it was the intention of numbers of Irish noblemen and gentlemen to take Dublin Castle on the following morning, October 23rd (the feast of St. Ignatius Loyala, the founder of the Jesuits), and possess themselves of all his Majesty's ammunition, that they opened their eyes.

The magnitude of the danger they were in alarmed both the council and the justices, and they instantly set to work. They had the gates of the city closed. They removed themselves into the Castle for better security. They had Lord Maguire, Colonel MacMahon, and other leaders, arrested; and they issued a proclamation, calling on all the good and loyal subjects in the kingdom to arm and betake themselves to their own defence.

The insurrection was begun in the north by Sir Phelim O'Neill; and his very first act showed how little dependence could be placed on his honour by those who fell into his hands, and must have created misgivings in the minds of many as to the sincerity of the professions of those amongst whom he was so conspicious a chief. Inviting himself and some of his followers to the house of Lord Caulfield, who was always glad to see him—they sat down to supper; but scarce was the entertainment half over, when he ordered his lordship and his family to be seized and bound. His castle was gutted before his eyes, and his servants were murdered.

The other chiefs arose also at the same time, in their own localities. The O'Riellys (one of whom was a member of Parliament, and another high-sheriff of Cavan) took possession of that county. The MacMahons seized all the forts in Monaghan. Newry, with its magazine of seventy barrels of powder, was betrayed to Magennis.

When Lord Ranelagh returned to his presidency in Connaught, he found Mayo, Leitrim, Roscommon, and Sligo in open rebellion; and before he was there long, several of his towns were burned, and he himself was shut up in Athlone Castle the entire winter. The O'Farrels overran Longford; Kells and Navan succumbed to O'Rielly; Naas, Kildare, and Trim were also seized; and before the month of November was at an end, Drogheda, a walled-in town, not many miles distant from the seat of government itself, was beseiged by fourteen thousand men.

Munster was the last to rise; but it was not until the last day of the

9

old year that it did anything. On that day the rebels seized on Cashel, and the next day on Fethard. Encouraged by this beginning, Clonmel, Dungarvan, Kilmallock, Waterford, Limerick, and every town in Tipperary, rushed to arms.

At first the Irish made a distinction between the Scotch settlers and the English. "The Scotch," said they, "are new comers; and, besides, they have suffered persecution for their religion like ourselves." But this was a piece of strategy. The true cause of this simulated friendship was least the Scotch should unite with the English, and crush the rising in Ulster.

The new comers were kindly treated for about ten days,—until, in fact, the English were nearly all destroyed,—and then their turn came. From that time out it did not matter at which side of the Tweed a British Protestant was born. The cruelties they committed were diabolical, and were aimed "at extirpating out of this island, not only the Protestant religion, but also your Majesty's most loyal subjects;"* and so effectual was the progress made in carrying out this design, that, before the end of March, no less than one hundred and fifty-four thousand of the Protestant inhabitants had lost their lives.†

It is true that all those had not their brains knocked out; neither were they all hanged or shot; but thrusting men and women, with the helpless offspring who clung to them, without either food or fuel, and *stripped stark naked*,‡ out into the bitter winter season of "1641," and forcing them to remain there until they fell dead with cold and hunger, was a less humane, but a more wholesale method of destroying them than either of the former. Thousands perished thus!

A more expeditious mode of getting rid of them was also in high

---

* See a letter from the Lords-Justices and council to King Charles the First.

† Ibid, also life of Bishop Bedell, Dr. Maxwell's Examination, &c. We are aware that the numbers mentioned in the Lords-Justices' letter are considered grossly exaggerated by some writers; and even Sir William Petty thinks they did not exceed thirty-seven thousand. But let any one look through the thirty-two folio volumes of depositions sworn before the commissioners, appointed under the great seal to take the evidence of sufferers from the rebellion, and he will there read the testimony of witnesses from every part of Ireland concerning the droves of people continually being led to the slaughter. Considering all those killed by actual force; by being driven out in the cold, where they perished; those that died broken-hearted and by hunger; it would appear that the computation made by the justices is rather within than outside the mark.

‡ Some of these miserable people having procured straw, endeavoured to hide a portion of their nakedness; but the rebels used to amuse themselves by setting the straw on fire, regardless of the intercessions or the shrieks of the sufferers.—See depositions of John Major, of Kilkenny.

favour. At Portadown, upwards of a thousand were brought out in parties of forty each, and pushed over one of the broken arches—into the river; where those that continued struggling with their fate " were knocked on the head, and so after drowned, or else shot to death in the water."

Thousands were hanged; thousands were smothered in ditches and turf-pits; thousands were knocked on the head, or piked to death. Multitudes were burned alive; many were buried alive; and so fiendish had the Irish become from familiarity with their horrible occupation, that it afforded them pleasure to hear their victims speak from the grave, ere the clay had choked them.*

Some had their eyes plucked out; some their hands cut off. Even little children, whose innocence and helplessness should have touched a pitying chord in a parent's heart, fared no better. Two children were hanged—one at the neck and the other at the girdle of their mother, who, poor woman, was herself also hanged; and with them (in hellish disport) their enemies hung up a dog and a cat.†

Some were fed upon by swine; others by dogs;‡ and more of them had their brains dashed out. And it is on record that another little sufferer was absolutely boiled to death in a caldron.‖ But some were not even satisfied with this wholesale extermination. They must obliterate every trace of England's connection with Ireland. The English names of places must be replaced by Irish names; and penalties must be inflicted upon those that speak the English tongue.

The people, upon whom these atrocities were perpetrated, had been living on the most friendly terms with their Irish neighbours. When any of these were sick or in distress, they administered those comforts and gave that assistance which the sick and the distressed stand in need of. They did not excite their susceptibilities, by drawing invidious comparisons between their race and religion and those amongst whom they had settled. They had done nothing that could arouse a revengeful feeling, or even said anything that could provoke a retort; yet, ere many hours, that confidence, through which they had beheld them for years, disappeared from before their eyes, scared away by the thick, red mist that arose from the blood of their fathers, their wives, their children.

* See Dr. Maxwell's Examination.
† Depositions of the Rev. William Hewitson, county Kildare.
‡ Vide Sir John Temple's *History of the Irish Rebellion.*
‖ Ibid, page 156; also Sir John Borlace's *History of the Irish Rebellion.*

Some of those active in the organization of the great outbreak were averse to the shedding of innocent blood. "Let us banish the English out of Ireland," said they, "as the Spaniards banished the Moors out of Spain!" To this it was replied:—"That if they were expelled the kingdom, they would return back, full of revengeful thoughts, to recover their losses."

Nevertheless, influential men among the moderate party, such as Lord Muskerry and many others, did succeed for a short time in restraining their followers within the bounds of the Spanish policy. But there were others who hounded them on—to overleap them. They were told that the bodies of those who would be killed in the war would be scarce cold ere their souls would be in heaven.[*] That the penalties of excommunication would fall upon them, should they harbour or relieve any Scot, English, or Welshman; and Father Mahony,[†] in his *Disputatio Apologetica,* assured his readers, "that the Irish are engaged by a divine, humane, and natural precept, unanimously to join and extirpate heretics,[‡] and to shun communion with them."

It would be impossible, within the limits of one short chapter, to give even a very brief account of the numerous battles and encounters that took place almost daily, between the Protestants and Roman Catholics, throughout the kingdom. We will merely remark that they were

---

[*] See Sir John Temple.

[†] Cnogher O'Mahony was born in Muskerry, county Cork. He was a Jesuit, and an active member of their Order. He published the *Disputatio Apologetica de Jure Regni Hiberniæ adversus Hæreticos Anglos,* in 1648, under the assumed name *Cornelius de Sancto Patricio.* The intention of the work was to make it appear that the sovereigns of England were not entitled to Ireland; and that, supposing Charles the First to have had a right originally, it lapsed, owing to the fact of his being a heretic. So fierce was Father Mahony's hatred to the English crown, that he recommended his countrymen to kill all of those who sided with it, should they even be his own co-religionists; and when they had rid themselves of their enemies, to set up a king of their own. Although the *Disputatio* was ordered to be burned, by order of the Supreme Council, at Kilkenny, yet it remained unnoticed by the clergy until 1666, several years after the rebellion had ended,—when, in fact, the dissemination of its doctrines could do no more harm.

[‡] In his tour through Ireland, in 1644, Boullaye Le Gouz, "who was of the French nation, and a good Catholic," records an instance of the bitter spirit possessed by the Irish priesthood at this time, not only against those of their fellow-christians who differed from them in matters of faith, but even against a nation who cheerfully afforded them a home, and who knelt at the same altar with themselves, because she dared to tolerate any of her own people when they ventured to think for themselves. "At Lord Ikerims," says Le Gouz, "I met at supper, a friar, who had a mortal dislike to the French. He could not refrain from giving vent to his antipathy in my presence: stating that, as we had no Inquisition in France, we were but a set of reprobates, and partial to heretics,—whom, instead of tolerating as we do, we ought rather to exterminate, as the progress of the Catholic faith could not co-exist with this pestilent sect, whose very name ought to be abhorred by the people."

numerous, and fought with varying success,—the fickle goddess leaning at one time to the Saxon, and at another time to the Celt,—and then pass on to the peace made " by the Earl of Glamorgan, by virtue of the King's authority under his signet and signature, on behalf of his Majesty, and Lord Mountgarret, Lord-President of the Supreme Council of the Confederates, Lord Muskerry, and others, on behalf of the King's Roman Catholic subjects and the Catholic clergy of Ireland."

The first article in the agreement was solely in reference to the Roman Catholic clergy, who, in their anxiety to secure the livings of the Protestant clergy, threw into the back-ground those grievances upon which Roger Moore was never tired of expatiating. It was agreed "that the Roman Catholic clergy of this kingdom, henceforth and for ever, shall hold and enjoy all such lands, tenements, tithes, and hereditaments, whatsoever by them enjoyed or possessed within this kingdom since the 23rd of October, 1641."

From this it is evident that they were to be confirmed for ever, not only in the lands, tithes, &c., which they had wrested from the English, and which they then held, but also all that they at any time possessed since the breaking out of the rebellion; so that the lands, tithes, churches, parsonages, &c., retaken from them, were obliged to be handed over to them again.

The second article stipulated that two-thirds of the emoluments of those tithes, &c., possessed, or to be possessed, by the clergy, was for the ensuing three years to be employed in equiping an army for his Majesty's use.

The third was that the Lord Lieutenant, or any one else in authority under his Majesty, shall not disturb the professors of the Roman Catholic religion in the possession of their churches, lands, tithes, &c., until the King's pleasure be signified for confirming and publishing the same.

And the fourth was, that an Act of Parliament should be passed according to the tenure of these agreements; and that, in the meantime, the clergy shall enjoy the full benefit of the agreements made with them.

There was also an agreement made at the same time between Glamorgan and the same parties, on behalf of the Confederate Roman Catholics, in which it was certified that the professors of the Roman Catholic religion " shall hold and enjoy all and every the churches by them enjoyed, or by them possessed, since the 23rd of October, 1641. That Roman Catholics shall enjoy the free and public use of their religion. Shall be exempted from the authority of the Protestant clergy. That these our clergy shall not be molested in the exercise of spiritual and ecclesiastical jurisdiction over the people. And the Confederates bind themselves in return to bring ten thousand men (one half armed with muskets, and the other half with pikes) to any part in Ireland, to be shipped for his Majesty's use in England, Scotland, or Wales."

This treaty of peace, known as the Glamorgan Treaty, was kept with great secrecy from the King's Protestant subjects. Charles was unwilling that it should get abroad that he had concluded negotiations with their hereditary foes—for ten thousand men; and that these were to be brought to England, and let loose upon those who had resisted his religious intolerance, his illegal taxes, his tyranny, his despotism.

Notwithstanding the precautions that were taken to keep the treaties hidden from public view, yet their contents soon got abroad; copies of them having been found in the pocket of the Titular Archbishop of Tuam, after he was killed—in an attack made by him at the head of some troops on the town of Sligo.

The papers were sent to the Parliament, and they ordered them to be printed and published to the whole world. The contents amazed everybody, and overwhelmed with confusion those who loudly proclaimed that a King could do no wrong.

The King's most devoted adherents, his Lord Lieutenant, and his zealous cavaliers, could not be persuaded that he was in earnest. How could he that could do no wrong allow the lands, that were reclaimed by the untiring industry of his Protestant subjects, to be wrested from them, and the livings of their clergy to be appropriated by those whom they looked upon as idolaters? Could he who could do no wrong shake the red hand of the murderer, who smote to death tens of thousands of his best subjects? Could he tell him that he may keep his spoils, and never even reproach him with his slaughters? Could he still grasp that gorestained hand, whilst he bargained with its owner for more blood, and yet do no wrong?

The Parliament were enraged, and sent a strong remonstrance on the subject to Charles, who, in his reply, stated that he had heard of it with extraordinary amazement. "That it was true he was anxious to procure a peace in Ireland; but not such a one as would compromise his honour and conscience, or the safety of his Protestant subjects. That Glamorgan was bound up by our positive commands from doing anything but what you (the Parliament) should particularly and precisely direct him to, both in the matter and manner of his negotiations."*

The King's commission to Glamorgan, however, gives all this a flat denial. His Protestant subjects, about whose safety he was concerned, are not named, or even referred to; his honour and conscience are nowhere to be seen; and "Glamorgan being bound up by our positive commands from doing anything but what the Parliament should particularize and direct him to do"—was an invention of his own. On the contrary, Glamorgan was told "to proceed with all possible secrecy; and for whatsoever you shall engage yourself, upon such valuable considerations *as you in your judgment shall deem fit*, we promise, on the word of a King and a Christian, to ratify and perform the same that shall be granted by you, and under your hand and seal, the said Confederate Catholics having, by their supplies (the promise of ten thousand men to butcher the English non-conformists), testified their zeal to our service; and this shall be in each particular to you a sufficient warrant."†

In order to save appearances, and avoid, if possible, the charge of Popish predilections, "our trusty and right well-beloved cousin," Edward, Earl of Glamorgan, was impeached of suspicion of treason, and committed to prison; but when Charles,—who, forsooth, "was exceedingly angry at the first news of this affair,"—cooled down, and calmly considered "that the earl's error proceeded from excess of loyalty, and that all this was done to hasten the considerable succour of ten thousand men unto him," his insulted Majesty was at length appeased; and he sent the erring earl a most kind and gracious letter, containing great assurances both of favour and friendship.‡

Notwithstanding the confidence placed in him by the King, and the great friendship he entertained for him, yet his trusty cousin must have trespassed seriously on his forbearance, for scarce was Glamorgan out of gaol, when away he went again to Kilkenny, and resumed the negotiations interrupted by the untimely discovery in the pocket of the Titular of Tuam.

There was another peace perfected between the Marquis of Ormond

---

* Vide—His Majesty's letter about the Earl of Glamorgan's Peace.
† See Warrant from the King to the Earl of Glamorgan.
‡ Cox.

and the Confederates, on the 30th of July; 1646 but as this did not provide sufficiently for the liberty and splendours of religion, in accordance with the exalted notions of the Nuncio, the poor bantling was knocked on the head, ere it entered on the third week of its sickly existence.

Many subsequent attempts were made by Ormond to patch up a peace, in order that he might procure assistance for the King, but they ended in nothing; and shortly after he surrendered Dublin to the Parliament, and left the country in disgust.

Meanwhile, disunion began to prevail in the Irish army. The old Irish, or Nuncio's party, under Owen Roe, said that they were better soldiers and better Catholics than the old English or Confederate party under Preston. From words they proceeded to acts. On the 11th of June, 1648, Owen Roe proclaimed war against the Supreme Council of the Confederates at Kilkenny, and on the 20th of the same month the Confederates proclaimed war against Owen Roe.

Lord Ormond went again to Ireland, and finally arranged a peace with both lay and clerical belligerents; "but it exacted such conditions," says Cox, "as rather hastened than prevented his Majesty's ruin." Before the good news had, however, reached London, he, in whose favour it was concluded, had expiated his crimes on the scaffold.

There were now no less than five armies in this distracted kingdom, all acting independently of each other, and all with different objects in view. There was the Royal army, under the late King's faithful Lieutenant, the Marquis of Ormond. Castlehaven and Preston commanded the Confederates. Jones commanded for the Parliament. The Nuncio's forces were led by Owen Roe O'Neil; and the united troops of the English and Scotch Presbyterians were under Montgomery and Sir George Munroe.

Sieges and surrenders, advances and retreats, skirmishes and battles, were daily occurrences. The impoverished country was still more impoverished, and the misery of its people was increased by the confusion and disunion that prevailed everywhere. Such was the state of affairs when Cromwell arrived in Dublin!

His first act was to issue a proclamation against swearing and drinking; and his next was to enjoin his soldiers not to do any injury to any person, unless found in arms or employed by the enemy. He invited the country people to bring their provisions into his camp, and that they should be paid for them in hard cash; and proclaimed that all those who would act peaceably and quietly should have liberty to live at home with their families, and be protected in person and estate. By these, as well as other judicious measures, he soon begat strength and confidence.

After the capture of Drogheda, Cromwell marched south. City after city, and fortress after fortress, fell before him; and the Protestant inhabitants of Bandon, Youghal, Cork, and other towns in Munster threw open their gates to him, and bid him welcome.

Upon his return to England, Charlemont, Limerick, Waterford, Galway, and some few insignificant places, were all that remained to the great army of the Confederated Catholics. Before very long, these were in the hands of Coote and Ireton; and on the 26th of September, 1653, it was officially announced "that the rebels were subdued, and the rebellion appeased and ended."

Thus ended the greatest effort that was ever made by the people of this country to rid themselves of English rule. An effort, which was conceived in order to take advantage of a nation's distress,*—born in treachery, baptized with blood, fed on carnage,—and after a vigorous existence it was overcome, and placed in a felon's grave!

* "England's adversity is Ireland's opportunity!" is a cry with which our own ears are not unfamiliar.

CHAPTER VII.

FIRST APPEARANCE OF THE REBELLION IN THE COUNTY OF CORK—THE FIRST GOVERNOR OF BANDON-BRIDGE—NAMES OF THE IRISH GENTRY IN THIS LOCALITY WHO WERE INDICTED AT THE GREAT SESSIONS HELD AT YOUGHAL—OLD CLEAR AND HIS FORTY SPARTANS—THE BANDONIANS PURSUE A BAND OF MARAUDERS INTO KERRY—MASSACRE OF THE CONGREGATION AT COOLE CHURCH—COMMISSIONERS SENT TO BANDON TO TAKE THE EVIDENCE OF THE SETTLERS CONCERNING THEIR LOSSES IN THE REBELLION—THE CESSATION—THE GLAMORGAN TREATY—THE ORMOND TREATY—THE BANDONIANS PROTEST AGAINST SUCH PACKED TERMS OF PEACE—A MINT ESTABLISHED IN BANDON.

THE rebellion made its first appearance in this county at Glandore; where, we are told, several of the English were gagged to death; and where, in fiendish sport, the rebels forced a Presbyterian clergyman to eat a piece of his own flesh. The flames soon spread far and near; and the outlaying settlers flocked into Bandon, the only walled-in town to the west of Cork. Here they remained huddled together, when death strode in amongst them; and from despondency at the loss of all the industry of their lives, or the hopelessness of their prospects,—or, it may be, from the overcrowding of themselves,—they fell unresistingly into his embrace; and before the rebellion was one year old, one thousand of them lay buried within the churchyard walls.

When loyal men were so scarce, and when the exertions demanded of them were so great, it could not be expected that the Bandonians, who were pre-eminent for their loyalty to England, would remain indifferent spectators of the dreadful acts of rapine and blood which were being perpetrated around them. Accordingly, they formed themselves into a regiment of foot,* and a troop of horse; and no body

---

* For particulars of the exploits of the valiant Bandonians, see, in this work, history of the South Cork regiment of militia, chapters 22 and 23.

of men in Ireland, similar in number, did the State more excellent service.

There were many cruelties and murders committed by the insurgents in our neighbourhood, and these, for the most part, upon people who carried no arms, and who shunned the very sight of blood. Margery White, whilst detained a prisoner at Daniel Mac Carthy's door, was run through the body with a spit;* another unhappy woman was half hanged, then she was cut down, and her body was trampled upon by horses until her protruding intestines presented a revolting sight.

The chief magistrate of Clonakilty, a gentleman who lived on the best of terms with his Irish neighbours, and who felt such confidence in them, that not only did he refuse to avail himself of the protecting walls of Bandon, but he absolutely preferred residing amongst those whose ample promises of security he must have deemed unnecessary. This fearless reliance on their humanity—a piece of generous good faith which would have found a responsive chord in the breast of a cannibal—was of no moment with them. Laying hands on him, they made him drink till he sickened; they then compelled him to swallow what his stomach had ejected, and then they hanged him.

Mrs. Stringer and Richard Mewdon, whilst returning to Bandon, were seized by Mac Carthy Reagh's troop of horse; and, having been tied back to back, endured such torture from the tightness of the cords " that they earnestly cried and prayed to Mac Carthy that he would either unbind them or take away their lives quite."† He did unbind them; and they were then placed in a large dungeon under the castle wall, from whence they were brought on the following morning and rebound for two days more, at the end of which time Mewdon was brought to the gallows (which seems to have been a fixture at Kilbrittain, " having been firmly built within sight of the castle, for hanging the English"), and executed. When the rope was removed from poor Mewdon's neck, it was placed round Mrs. Stringer's. Her earthly career was being brought to a close, and in a few minutes her corpse would be swinging in the air, had not one of her own sex (the mother of Mac Carthy, who had been looking on out of one of the castle windows) made an effort to save her, and sent a priest to her, who asked her what religion she was of. Although the gibbet loomed over her, and although the fatal

---

* See MS. in Trinity College.

† See Mrs. Stringer's Depositions in Trinity College.

halter was adjusted for its horrible purpose, the poor woman boldly avowed that she was a Protestant, and, moreover, that she would die one.*

Lord Cork did not forget to see after the defences of Bandon. 1642. In a letter to Lord Goring, dated January 6th, he says :—"My son, Kinalmeaky,† had been at his own town of Bandon-Bridge before this time, but his lady having been stayed here (Youghal) these three weeks by contrary winds; but so soon as her foot is on ship board, his foot shall be in the stirrup to go to Bandon-Bridge, of which town I hope he shall give a good account, for he hath a fair rising-out in the town and the suburbs thereof; and I have put up portcullises for the strengthening of the gates, and planted six pieces of ordinance for the better defence thereof; for, I thank God, I have so planted that town as there is neither an Irishman nor Papist within the walls; and so can no town or corporation say."

On the 12th of January Kinalmeaky arrived, and was appointed the first governor of Bandon-Bridge. At the time of his arrival matters were in a pitiable plight. The rebels had ventured within two miles of the town, and swept away all the cattle with them to Muskerry. They also plundered Castletown, Enniskeane, and Newcestown, from the effects of which the latter place never recovered; and they overran the whole country, ravaging and laying waste whatever they could lay their hands upon. So utterly abandoned had these miscreants become, that even Lord Muskerry‡ (their own commander), executed several of

---

* Many Protestants, who had been induced to declare themselves Roman Catholics in the hope of saving their lives, were immediately put to death least they should again become heretics.

† Louis Boyle (Lord Kinalmeaky), second son of the first Earl of Cork, was born on the 23rd of May, 1619; and on the 28th of May, 1627 (when he was only eight years old), he was created Baron of Bandon-Bridge and Viscount Boyle of Kinalmeaky. He married on the 26th of December, 1638, the lady Elizabeth Fielding, third daughter of William, Earl of Denbeigh, but had no issue. Lord Cork, in a letter to Mr. Marcombes, (his son's tutor), gives an account of his marriage. He says :—" On St. Stephen's Day, my son, Kinalmeaky, was married in the King's chapel to the lady Elizabeth Fielding, daughter of the Countess of Denbeigh. The King (Charles the First), gave her away in marriage unto him, and the Queen presented her with a jewel, valued at fifteen hundred pounds, which the King, with his own hands, put about her neck, and did the young couple all honours and grace, both with revelling, feasting, and bringing to their bed in Court." Upon the accession of Charles the Second, long after Kinalmeaky's death, his widow was created Countess of Guildford.

‡ Donogh Mac Carthy More (Lord Muskerry), "a facetious fellow, and a good companion," owned the castles of Macroom and Blarney. He married a sister of the Duke of Ormond, and was general of the Irish forces in Munster. He took a very prominent part in the great rebellion, for which all his estates were forfeited by Cromwell; but subsequently, through the influences of the Duke of Ormond, the

them for thieving ; and did what amounted to the same thing with more of them,—" he sent them to Bandon, where they soon met with their deserts."

The rebellion spread with such rapidity through the Irish gentry in this county, that at the quarter sessions held on the second of August in this year at Youghal, before Lord Cork, who presided as Custos Rotulorum, assisted by his three sons, Dungarvan, Kinalmeaky, and Broghill, no less than eight noblemen and eleven hundred· gentlemen in the counties of Cork and Waterford were indicted for treason. Among those indicted and outlawed in the King's Bench from our neighbourhood were* :—

Arundell, Garrett, Agludullane.
Arundell, Garrett, Darrig.
Barry, Redmond, Lisgriffin.
Barry, Nicholas, Drinagh.
Barry, John, Drinagh.
Baldwin, Walter, Garanancomy.
Baldwin, Henry, Macroom.
Barry, William McShane, Burren.
Barry, William, Lislee.
Barry, John, Downarhug.
Barry, John, Downededy.
Barry, William, Downededy.
Barry, Richard, Downededy.
McCarthy, Cormack, al. McReagh, Kilbrittain.
McCarthy, Florence, Castle-Donovan.
McCarthy, Donogh, Kilbrittain.
McCarthy, Teige, al. O'Downy, Dunmanway.
McCarthy, Teige, al. O'Norse, Togher.
Carthy, Dermot McTeige, Dunmanway.
Carthy, Florence McDonnell, Banduff.
Carthy, Donell McFynyn, Banduff.

McCarthy, Florence, Derry.
Carthy, Florence McDermody, Maddame.
O'Crowly, Teige McDavid, Dromiclough.
McCarthy, Cormack, Manche.
McCarthy, Oge, Manche.
McCarthy, Donell, Manche.
Carthy, Owen McDonogh, Cahirkirky.
Carthy, Donell McOwen, Cahirkirky.
Crowly, Donell McTeige Oge, Skeaff.
O'Crowly, John McTeige, Skeaff.
O'Crowly, Redmond McTeige, Skeaff.
O'Crowly, David, Shynagh.
O'Crowly, Fynyn McDavid, Kinneagh.
Carthy, Donogh McFynyn, Maulbracke.
Carthy, Cormack Fynyn, Boultinagh.
O'Crowly, Teige, Skeaff.
Carthy, Cnogher McDermody, Knockycullen.
— Shily, his wife.
O'Crowly, Donogh McTeige, Skeaff.
Carthy, Teige McFynyn, Curry-Crowly.
Carthy, Cnogher McDermody, Garranure,

---

greater portion of them were restored by Charles the Second, by whom also, in 1658; this most active and zealous rebellious chieftain was raised to the earldom of Clancarthy; and a special act was incorporated with the Act of Settlement, entitled " an Act for restoring Donogh, Earl of Clancarthy, and Charles, Viscount Muskerry, to their blood and honours; and for investing and settling them in their several estates." Lord Clancarthy died in London, August 5th, 1665. By his wife he had three sons:—Charles, Callaghan, and Justin. Charles (Lord Muskerry), died some weeks before his father, having fallen in the great naval engagement which was fought with the Dutch in Southold Bay, June 2nd, 1665, being killed by a cannon shot,—the very same which killed Richard, third son of the Earl of Cork, and Berkeley, Earl of Falmouth, the three of whom were officers on board the same ship with the Duke of York (afterwards James the Second), with whom young Lord Muskerry was a great favourite. He was buried in Westminster Abbey. Upon Clancarthy's decease, he was succeeded by his grandson, Charles James, the only surviving son of Lord Muskerry; and he dying a minor, was succeeded by his uncle, Callaghan. He married Elizabeth, daughter of the Earl of Kildare, by whom he had four daughters and a son (Donogh the fourth earl).

* See MS. British Museum.

Carthy, Kragher Dermody, Maddame.
O'Carthy, Dermod McDonogh, Maule-
    bracke.
O'Coghlane, Phillip, Enniskeane.
O'Crowly, Humphry Oge, (Yeoman),
    Enniskeane.
McCarthy, Donogh (Lord Viscount
    Muskerry), Blarney.
McCarthy, Charles, Castlemore.
Carthy, Teige McCormack, Aglish.
Carthy, Cormack McDonogh, Court-
    brack.
McCahir, Cowne, Kilcrea.
Creagh, Patrick, Kilcrea.
Cloddagh, Cormack, Misshaneglasse.
Cloddagh, Owen, Misshaneglasse.
O'Donovan, Donell, Castle-Donovan.
O'Donovan, Donell Oge, Castle-Donovan.
O'Doogan, William, (Yeoman), Mosshan-
    glasse.
Hitchcock, John, Kilmurry.
Hodnett, Edmund, Courtmacsherry.
O'Hea, Thomas, Pallice.
O'Hea, William Oge, Pallice.
O'Hart, Teige, Knock.
Hodnett, James Fitz-Edmund, Court-
    macsherry.
Hurly, Randal, Ballinacarriga.

Hurly, Randal Oge, Ballinacarriga.
Hurly, William, Ballinwarde.
Hurly, William, Lisgubby.
Hurly, Ellen (widow), Grillagh.
Hurly, Daniel Oge, Kilbrittain.
O'Houghlin, Dermod McFynyn, Rath-
    drought.
Hurly, James, Ballinwarde.
Totane, Daniel McTeige, Kilmaloody.
Totane, Dermod McTeige, Kilmaloody.
Totane, Mahowne McTeige, Kilmaloody.
O'Keiffe, Keffe, Killeollman.
Long, John (High Sheriff), Mount
    Long.
Long, John, junior.
O'Leary, Kilcaskan.
O'Leary, Cornelius McDonogh, Grange.
O'Leary, Donell, Grange.
Murphy, Donogh, Brinny.
O'Mahown, Cnogher, Leamcon.
Nugent, Redmond, Castletown.
McOwen, Teige, Carhue.
McOwen, Dermod, Knockanroe.
Power, Robert, Castletown.
Roch, Patrick, Poulnalonge.
Roch, James, Kippagh.
Roch, Edward, Castletown.
McSwiney, Owen, Misshaneglasse.

From the names and localities just mentioned it will be seen that Bandon was hemmed-in on all sides. It was like a glade surrounded by a dense forest. Should our townsmen endeavour to pierce the rebel lines, they should confront the Rochs and the McCarthys on the east, and the Hurlys, the O'Donovans, and the McCarthys on the west. It was even worse in the north and south. The McSwineys, the Cloddaghs, and the McCarthys lay between Bandon and the country to the north; and the Arundells, the Barrys, the Hodnetts, and the McCarthys between it and the country lying to the south.

The rebels did not remain content with merely drawing a cordon around Bandon. Occassionally some of them ventured up to the very walls of the town, and drove away the cattle. The McCarthys, from Kilcrea, having heard that the Bandon and Kinsale troops of horse would leave Bandon on a foraging expedition at a certain hour, resolved to take advantage of their absence, and come in here on a foraging expedition of their own. Accordingly, they came in and drove away all the cattle they found grazing outside the walls; and were proceeding leisurely homewards (probably congratulating themselves on their good fortune), when the Bandon troop, which, by some mischance, were delayed beyond the hour appointed for setting out to meet the Kinsale troop, became aware of what was going on, and followed in pursuit. They came up with the marauders at Brinny-Bridge. The cattle were soon the property of their former owners. They then fell on the spoilers themselves. They made no resistance, but fled at once into Kilmore bog for safety, where fifty of them were overtaken and killed.

Upon another occasion, the rebels from Carrigadrohid, having ascertained that the Bandon men were away somewhere, advanced in regular order to attack the town, which was but very poorly defended, having been entrusted to the charge of old Ralph Clear, and a guard of forty men. Old Ralph heard of their approach, and instead of allowing the enemy to waste their strength on the defences, he depended on a piece of strategy, which may be commended simply on the grounds of its success. At the head of his forty Spartans, he walked boldly up Barry's Walk, and along the old road to Macroom, to meet the foe. In a short time he met with two of the enemies advanced scouts, who had been sent forward to reconnoitre and see if the Bandonians were on the alert. With these old Clear, who pretended not to know who they were, entered into friendly conversation. Perceiving that their office was not apparently suspected, they became somewhat emboldened, and asked him was he going to fight the Irish forces with such a handful of men. " Oh ! " said he, " we are only the advanced guard of our party. The main body are gone round so as to get into the enemies rear, and prevent their escape ;" adding, with a confident shake of the head, " that not a man of them but would be dead and comfortably damned before starlight."

Seeing the effect this piece of bravado had upon his hearers, he ordered his men to halt and see to their pieces, as they would not have long to wait for the signal now. This was enough for the scouts. They quietly slipt away ; and, having got out of musket range, they ran with tremendous haste till they reached their main body, where, pale with fright, they told all that they had heard. This had such an effect on the adventurers from Carrigadrohid, that they fled in consternation, and in so much disorder, that, when the Bandon people arrived at the bottom of a steep hill near Gurteen House, they found one poor fellow lying dead upon the road, who, in his eagerness to escape, had fallen headlong, and absolutely broken his neck. There were some doggerel lines composed on this affair, a few of which we have been enabled to collect :—

" This gallant old sword and forty more
   Made all the rebels run before;
And old Dromaun*—oh! he laughed like fun,
   To see the cowardly rascals run.
He saw the place where the rebel fell,
   And cried:—' Here's one of them that's gone to hell;
If we caught the rest, you'd plainly see,
   We'd send them to keep him company.' "

The Bandon people did not always remain on the defensive, either. They also ventured out; and not only cut the hostile cordon, but, upon one occasion, absolutely followed the foe all the way into Kerry. It appears that the chief of Ardtully Castle, at the head of a strong force, penetrated into the Carberries, and, encouraged by his great success there, marched into Kinalmeaky; and having collected a great spoil, both in prisoners and in cattle, was making off to his wild retreat in the fastnesses of Kerry. But the Bandonians were determined he should not escape so easily. Setting out, alone and unaided,† they pursued the Kerry men in hot haste through Inchigeela, through Lacka-laun, and up through the sullen hills, which seemed to frown upon the intruding steps of the audacious Sassenach. They came up with them on a heath-grown flat, within three miles of the chieftain's home; and immediately the fight began. For some time the contest was maintained on either side with great spirit. After all the fatigue and the danger the marauders had undergone, better almost that they should perish where they stood than be deprived of their spoils—and that within sight of their very doors! To the Bandon men victory was every-thing. If vanquished, they would be followed by an exultant foe; and how could they expect to escape through forty miles of a country abounding with bogs and woods, and inhabited by those whom the news of their overthrow would convert into an active enemy, who would confront them at every step? They knew this, and they knew that defeat was death.

Both the contending parties fought desperately. The towering mountains, where the silence was seldom broken save by the croak of the raven or the crow of the grouse, now resounded with the fierce shouts of a bitter strife. At length the Lord of Ardtully fell, and he

---

  * Dromaun was a nickname for old Clear.

  † The Bandon regiment of militia were away at this time. The Kerry expedition, and other enterprises undertaken about this period, were performed by the towns-people themselves.

lay pouring out his life's blood on the heather.   His devoted followers lay scattered in scores all round him; and their dying moans, mingling with his own, proclaimed that the Bandonians were the victors.*   The victory was complete.   The Bandon men secured all their prisoners and all the cattle, and they returned to their homes, through a peaceable country, unmolested.

The rebellion was raging in every part of the country.   The strong castle of Limerick was compelled to yield to the rebels.   The castles of Askeaton and of Castlematrix were obliged to do the same.   The garrison of Claughleigh surrendered to Richard Condon, upon promise of quarter and protection as far as Castlelyons; notwithstanding which, some of them were made prisoners, and the rest were murdered.

The garrison at Coole, which consisted of thirty-six of Lord Barrymore's troopers, hearing of what Condon had done at Claughleigh, fled to the parish church of Coole for safety.   Entering hurriedly, they barricaded the doors.   It is Sunday morning, and the terrified Protestant inhabitants of the neighbourhood are assembled within its walls.   On their knees, they are pouring out their souls before Him who gave them; and they are beseeching the great giver of all good to soften the hearts of those who are thirsting for their innocent blood.   In less than half-an-hour after the sacred edifice is surrounded.   They hear their death-knell in that demoniac yell, which pierces their very brain.   In tremor, the helpless flock rise from their knees, and bid each other a hurried farewell.   The troops would not surrender without a promise of quarter.   They asked but for their lives, and the lives of the poor sufferers who stood around them.   This is granted.   They require a guarantee.   "The word of a soldier and a Christian!"

Enough!   And now hope beams in every eye, and joy overspreads every face.   The doors are thrown open; and groups of men, whose faces portray a fiendish expression, rush in, armed with pike and sword; and their blood begins to flow.   It will suffice to say, that the little purling stream, whose silvery tones often tinkled in the ears of those whose eyes are now fast glazing in death, was soon swelled and reddened with their

---

* The late Sir John Warren, on a portion of whose Kerry estate this sharp encounter took place, intended to open a few of the graves, and ascertain if the tradition, which stated that the dead were buried with their arms, was correct.   He was deterred, however, from carrying out this intention, owing to the difficulty of procuring a sufficient number of men, duly provided with crowbars, &c., to remove the enormous stones which the piety of the friends of those who had fallen had placed over their last resting-place.

10

blood.   Two only escaped.   Lacey jumped through a window, and made off.   The other—namely, Mr. John Hutchings,* the gentleman upon whose lands the church stood—lay stretched on the ground with the rest, apparently dead, having received a great many wounds.   After sunset, however, the cold air gradually restored him.   Conscious of all he had seen, he remained for some time motionless; but he listened, and listened eagerly, and there was no pacing sentinel.   Occasionally a breeze disturbed the stiffened tresses, still moist with agony and blood, which lay on the matron's clammy, cold brow, or spread the golden locklets over a baby's face.   But there was no voice.   Not even a timid whisper stole over that silent group, and asked, in a low tremulous tone, and in God's name, if any friend was there.   Taking courage, he at last ventured to look out from the gore-stained portals, and there was no human being or a light to be seen anywhere.   Moving away from the ghastly companionship of those who are now far beyond the reach of human troubles, he was overtaken by a travelling tinker, with whom he struck a bargain, giving him his own clothes in exchange for those of the tinker and his paraphernalia.   Putting those on, and slinging the budget across his shoulders, he contrived to reach the nearest loyal garrison in safety.

So confident were the government of being able speedily to crush out the rebellion, that four months had not actually elapsed ere they empowered commissioners to proceed through Munster to ascertain the losses of the Protestant settlers.   The commissions were issued under the great seal, by the Lords Justices; and the commissioners were directed to take evidence, upon oath, of all those sufferers who should present themselves for examination.   Dean Grey and archdeacon Bisse were the two that came to Bandon.   They sat here in the February of 1642, and again in the following October; and from the depositions sworn before them, we have been enabled to collect much interesting matter connected with the greatest effort ever made by the Celt to eject the Saxon.

Dean Grey died peaceably in Bandon; but poor Bisse was waylaid and murdered on the road between Cork and Youghal, by one Garret, of Dromaddath.   For a long time his papers were believed to have been lost.   All of them were missing in Temple's time; "and it is owing to their seizure by the rebels," says Cox, "that there is no full

* The last of the Hutchings family, who lived in the neighbourhood of Coole Church, was Thomas Hutchings, Esq., of Mohera.   His daughter, Bridget, married Mr. William Dalton, of Castlelyons, and died in 1825.

account of the losses and murders in Munster." Although their existence was unknown to the public until not many years since, nevertheless, they were carefully preserved all through.

Mr. Gething tells us some particulars of their history in his evidence before Jenkins Lloyd, at Kilkenny, in 1652. After mentioning about Bisse's death, he states, "that Lord Inchiquin sent to his lodgings in Youghal, and got the trunk and papers wherein the examinations taken were contained; and his lordship finding occasion shortly after to repair unto the King, then at Oxford, and understanding that there was, at the same time, agents with his Majesty, both from the British Protestants and the Irish rebels, he carried the trunk with him, intending to make use of it—to make known to his majesty the proceedings of the Irish; but his lordship finding occasion to return without using it, because of the prevalency of Irish agents at court, it was (as deponent believed) entrusted with Lott Peereigh—Perry—(formerly secretary to Sir William St. Leger), since deceased, whose wife and son resided at or near Audley, and in the county of Cambridge, where it was taken great care of. And that he had heard orders were given for sending the trunk to Sir Phillip Perceval, at London." Mr. Gething concludes his evidence by remarking, "that Mr. Thomas Bettesworth, agent to the Protestant forces in Munster, can say something about it."

1643.   In the opening campaign of this year, Sir Charles Vavasor, who succeeded to the governorship of Bandon upon the death of Lord Kinalmeaky, resigned his appointmennt, and was replaced by Colonel Rowland St. Leger.

To show the confidence that existed here in the ultimate success of the English in the rebellion, we may mention that a lease was executed on the 23rd of May in this year, by Richard, Earl of Cork, to Matthias Anstis, of the premises described as situate, lying, and being in the lands of Coolfadda, in the borough of Bandon aforesaid, &c.

Upon the 15th of September a cessation of arms was agreed upon for twelve months, between the Marquis of Ormond on the King's side, and Lord Muskerry, Sir Lucas Dillon, Sir Robert Talbot, and others, on the part of the Irish. It was agreed that each party should keep possession of what they then held. The arrangement agreed upon for the county of Cork was:—"That a line was to be drawn from Youghal to Mogeely, thence to Fermoy, on to Mitchelstown and Liscarroll, and thence to Mallow. From Mallow to Cork, Carrigrohane, Rochfordstown, Bandon,

Timoleague, and thence along the coast to Youghal." All outside this boundary, on the land side, the rebels were to remain in undisturbed possession of.

September 15th, the date of the first cessation, Richard Boyle, the great Earl of Cork, died at the college of Youghal, in the seventy-seventh year of his age. Sir Richard Cox, speaking of him, says:— "The noble Earl of Cork (Lord High Treasurer), was one of the most extraordinary men either that this or any other age produced, with respect to the great and just acquisitions of estates that he made, and the public works that he began and finished for the advancement of the English interest and the Protestant religion in Ireland,—as churches, alms-houses, free-schools, bridges, castles, and towns (*vide* Lismore, Tallagh, Clonakilty, Enniskeane, Castletown, and Bandon),—insomuch, that when Cromwell saw the prodigious improvements in a country where he little expected to see them, he declared " that if there had been an Earl of Cork in every province in Ireland it would have been impossible for the Irish to have raised a rebellion."

On the 24th of November in the previous year he made his will, and in it directed " that a free-school, and an alms-house for six men, be erected, of lime and stone, sawn timber and slate, in the place where he caused the foundations to be dug at Bandon-Bridge ; and where, before the troubles, he had great part of the squared timber, hewn stone, and other materials brought for finishing that good work ; and this to be done so soon as it should please God to send peace in this kingdom." In addition to this, he also left instructions for the erection of a strong substantial bridge, as follows :—" And for that I much desire the good increase and prosperity of Bandon-Bridge and the inhabitants thereof, whom I have ever much tendered and respected, I do, therefore, declare it to be my will that there be a very strong and substantial bridge of lime and stone, with my arms cut in the stone to be set upon the wall thereof, erected over the river Bandon, within the town, where the timber bridge now stands."

For the carrying out of this intent, he entrusted the provost for the time being, and other friends, to take the charge upon them, " that it might be gracefully, strongly, and substantially done, without any fault or deceitful work, as other bridges of late have been." He likewise bequeathed ten pounds per annum to the poor of Bandon, Coolfadda, and Clonakilty.

1644. The Confederates, as the Irish called themselves, broke most of the articles of the treaty; and the English were daily alarmed by intelligence of fresh conspiracies. In particular, there was a conspiracy planned by a friar named Matthews, and some others, to betray the city of Cork into Irish hands. Upon the discovery of this, and other designs of a similar nature, Lord Inchiquin was asked by the colonists to repudiate the cessation. They did not understand why they should be called upon to preserve religiously their side of the agreement, when those with whom they made the agreement, and who were equally bound to preserve it in its integrity with themselves, broke through it whenever they thought proper to do so.

A "manifestation," containing a strong remonstrance against the armistice, was sent to the Parliament from this country, signed by Lord Inchiquin, commander of the Protestant forces in Munster, Lord Broghill, governor of Youghal, Sir William Fenton, Knt., Lieutenant-Colonel William Brockett, governor of Kinsale, Lieutenant-Colonel Thomas Searle, governor of Bandon, and Serjeant-Major Muschamp, governor of the Fort of Cork.

Inchiquin did respond to the wishes of the memorialists, and put an end to the truce in Munster; and the Parliament being made aware of what he had done, not only sanctioned his proceedings, but showed a more substantial mark of their approval still, by conferring on him the Lord Presidency of Munster.

1645. The Confederates felt such confidence in their stability at this time, that they sent ambassadors to foreign nations. In France they were represented at various times by Mr. Rochfort, Father Hartigan, Colonel Fitzwilliam, and Mr. Godfrey Baron. They received in return, MM. La Monarié, Du Maulin, and Talloon. They deputed to Spain, Father James Talbot; and received from that country the Count of Berehaven (O'Sullivan Bere), and Don Diego de la Torres. To the Pope they despatched Mr. Richard Beling, and the bishop of Ferns; and obtained from his Holiness, Peter Francis Scarampi, and the bishop of Firmo.

Father Hartigan, the French representative, carried on a very extensive correspondence with the Irish Supreme Council, specimens of which we subjoin from some of his reverence's intercepted letters :—

That my Lord Abbot Montague said to him, in his ear, "that he should write to your lordships not to trust most of the English, *even the very Catholics of whom have more national than religious thoughts.*" That the Queen, talking of Ormond, said :—" It was hard to trust, believe, or rely upon any Irishman that is a Protestant, for every such Irishman that goes to church does it against his conscience, and knows in his heart he betrays God." " That Ormond is a viper, and an idolater of majesty." " That Clanricarde got something from Essex, his brother-in-law, otherwise he would be for the Catholics." " That they should write down the words uttered at table, and even in conversation, by Ormond, Clanricarde, and Inchiquin." " That Clanricarde robs more from the Catholics than even the villainous Scots." " That Castlehaven is rather nationally than religiously inclined." " That the King is easy, and not to be trusted." "That the Queen will be cast upon the Irish ; and, therefore, advises them to play the cunning workman."

As regards the Queen, it is but fair to state, that in one of her letters to Lord Digby, she says that many things written by this divine " are lies."

After Charles's flight from Oxford, he secretly sent over the Earl of Glamorgan to conclude a peace with his rebellious Irish subjects—with those who, in fact, had all but extinguished the Protestant settlements in the country with the settler's blood. As this treaty of peace (best known as the Glamorgan treaty) is a document now rarely met with, we have much pleasure in laying copious extracts from it before our readers :—

" Articles of agreement made and concluded upon and between the Right Hon. Edward, Earl of Glamorgan, and in pursuance and by virtue of his Majesty's authority, under his signet and royal signature, bearing date at Oxford, tho 12th day of March, in the twentieth year of his reign, for and on behalf of his most excellent Majesty on the one part, and the Right Hon. Richard Lord Viscount Mountgarret, Lord President of the Supreme Council of the Confederate Catholics of Ireland, Lord Viscount Muskerry, &c., for and on behalf of his Majesty's Roman Catholic subjects and the Catholic clergy of Ireland of the other part.

" The Earl of Glamorgan doth grant, conclude, and agree with Lord Mountgarret, &c., that the Roman Catholic clergy shall and may, from henceforth and for ever, hold and enjoy all such lands, tenements, tithes, and hereditaments whatsoever by them respectively enjoyed within this kingdom, or by them possessed at any time since the three-and-twentieth day of October, 1641 ; and also, all such lands, tithes, &c., belonging to the clergy within this kingdom, other than such as are actually enjoyed by his Majesty's Protestant clergy."

By the second article :—

" It was agreed on and concluded by Lord Mountgarret, &c., that two parts in three of the lands, &c., mentioned in the preceding article, be disposed of and converted for the use of his Majesty's forces, employed in his service, for three years next ensuing the feast of Easter; and the other third part to the use of the clergy; and so the like disposition to be renewed from three years to three years by the said clergy during the war."

" It was also accorded and agreed on behalf of his Majesty, his heirs, &c., that his Excellency the Marquis of Ormond, Lord Lieutenant of Ireland, or any other authorized, or to be authorized by his Majesty, shall not disturb the professors of the Roman Catholic religion in their present possession of their churches, lands, jurisdiction, or any other matters articled by the said earl; and furthermore, that an act shall be passed the next Parliament according to the tenor of the agreement and concessions herein expressed."

By this treaty, it will be perceived, that the rebels were confirmed for ever, not only in the possession of all the lands and tithes which they had wrested from the Protestant settlers, and which they then held, but also all that they at any time possessed since the breaking out of the rebellion; and, in addition, the church lands and tithes in the possession of laymen in this kingdom. So that all they took possession of they were to keep; all that his Majesty's loyal subjects repossessed themselves of from them were to be surrendered to them; and " the lands and tithes, other than such as are actually enjoyed by the Protestant clergy" (that is the church lands and tithes belonging to the laity, and which the Roman Catholic clergy did not at any time possess since the 23rd of October), they were also to have.

In order to properly estimate the concessions made by the King, our readers should bear in mind that, save the few castles held by the Bandonians, and some few others scattered up and down through the country, and the city of Cork, Youghal, Kinsale, and Bandon, all the rest of Munster was in the hands of the rebels; besides nearly the entire of the other three provinces.

So well pleased were the Confederates with their side of the bargain, that in a few days after the whole assembly unanimously voted " that they would send the King ten thousand men; and would refer to his Majesty's pleasure such things about religion as Ormond either hath not power or inclination to grant."

The Confederates belonged to the national party, or those who, having obtained what they required, were content to remain under the English crown. The religious party, on the contrary, were anxious to remove

Ireland altogether from under British rule—not for the purpose of forming it into a separate kingdom, but to make it a dependency of the Court of Rome.

At the head of the latter party was the Pope's Nuncio, John Baptiste Rinuccini, archbishop and prince of Firmo, "who, arriving in the nick of this business," says Cox, "quite altered their measures and confounded their affairs;" as it was, this prelate, at the head of the clerical party, stirred up those animosities between the Irish and the old English—animosities which may have slept, but which were never forgotten.

The Nuncio landed at Kenmare on the 22nd of October, bringing with him two thousand swords, five hundred petronels, twenty thousand pounds of powder, and five or six trunks of Spanish gold. In his train were twenty-two Italians, and several ecclesiastics. The vessel, which brought over this precious freight (a frigate, carrying twenty-one guns), was chased by Captain Plunket, in a ship belonging to the Parliament; and, had not a fire broken out in the cook's galley, the Puritanical old salt would have sent his Grace of Firmo and his clerical friends— certainly not to Kilkenny.

At Kilkenny he was received by the Supreme Council with transports of delight, and was conducted with great state to the castle; and here, in the great hall, he made a grand speech; and among other things he did religiously swear "to do nothing prejudicial to the King." Nevertheless, he refused to countenance any agreement between his Majesty and the rebels, that did not stipulate to restore the tithes to the priesthood; and he wrote a peremptory letter to his friend, the Titular bishop of Kildare, to the effect that if the Supreme Council should agree with Ormond he would quit the kingdom, and take all the bishops with him.

The English were not aware of all these secret negotiations between Glamorgan and the Supreme Council until after the defeat of the Irish at Sligo, upon which occasion the Roman Catholic bishop of Tuam was killed, and in his pocket was found a copy of the articles of peace, which, says Cox, "displayed such a quantity of intrigue as amazed the whole Protestant party."

On the 18th of March another peace was made between the
1646. Marquis of Ormond, the Lord Lieutenant, on behalf of the King, and Lord Muskerry, on behalf of the rebels; the substance of which, in reference to our subject, was :—That all attainders, indictments, out-

lawries, issued since August 7th, 1641, to the prejudice of the Roman Catholics, their heirs, &c., should be null and void. The fifteenth article ran thus :—

" It is further concluded, accorded, and agreed by and between the said parties, and his Majesty is graciously pleased, that an Act of Oblivion be passed in the next Parliament, to extend unto all his Majesty's subjects of this kingdom and their adherents, *of all treasons and offences,—capital, criminal, and personal,—and other offences, of what nature, kind, or quality soever, as if such treason or offences had never been committed, perpetrated, or done.* That such act shall extend to all rents, goods, chattels, prizes, &c., taken since the 23rd of October, 1641."

It was also agreed that certain places of command in his Majesty's army, and of honour and profit in the civil government of the kingdom, be conferred on his Roman Catholic subjects. In consideration of these wholesale favours, the Confederates bound themselves to raise ten thousand men to assist the King in England.

This treaty, made by Ormond at the instance of Charles, seems to be the foulest act committed in that monarch's most unrighteous career. It was a base compromise, and for the vilest of purposes. To prolong a war with his own Parliament,—the chosen representatives of his own people, whose interests they shielded, and in defence of whose constitutional rights they stood together,—Charles negotiated with those who were longing for the opportunity to wrest Ireland from the English crown, and whose fierce hostility to their English fellow-subjects was reflected in the broad stream of English blood which flowed from one end of Ireland to the other. And yet, to hire a horde of cut-throats, and let them loose upon the Puritans of England, he covenanted with these murderers to forgive them their murders, and to allow them to retain the property of their victims.

In order to gratify his hatred against the Parliamentarians, he seemed to disregard every other consideration. Honour and duty were as nothing in the scale; his thirst for vengeance out-weighed them all. For this he overlooked the sufferings of the settlers; for this he was content to let their blood sink in the earth and their wrongs *in oblivion.* For this act alone he deserved to be discrowned. It proclaimed him a traitor, and it almost sanctified the stroke that took off his head.

It appears that rebels and tithe-owners were the only approvers of this treacherous treaty. The Supreme Council of Kilkenny were almost unanimous in its favour. The clergy of the Established Church, too, applauded it to the very echo, "and made a grateful remonstrance of thanks to his Excellency for his care of religion and the kingdom." Their approbation, however, is easily accounted for, by the difference between the Glamorgan treaty and the Ormond as regards tithes; for by the former the Roman Catholic party were to keep all the tithes, &c., which they at any time possessed since the breaking out of the rebellion, but by the latter they were reserved for the Protestant clergy—*hence Ormond's care of religion and the kingdom.*

The news of the peace was received with acclamation by the insurgents everywhere, except in Waterford, Limerick, and Clonmel. In Waterford the heralds were so unwelcome, that no person would show them the mayor's house; and when they did succeed in finding his worship, that worthy flatly refused to make any move in the matter just then; and the mob told the heralds that if they did not be off, they would send them away packing, "with withes about their necks."

On their arrival in Limerick, the mayor of that city received them very courteously; and, having called a council, they resolved on proclaiming the peace at once. But Father Wolf, and the sheep of his pasture, resolved they should do no such thing. Accordingly, they proceeded up to the high cross; and Father Wolf threatened the bell, book, and candle-light to any one who should dare adhere to the treaty. Nevertheless, the mayor and corporation began to proclaim the peace with the usual formalities; but the mob of liberals drove them away with hideous outcries; followed them into the mayor's house; hunted them from room to room, and having wounded severely the chief magistrate and several of his adherents, the liberals concluded the business liberally, by liberally helping themselves to what they thought worth carrying away from the houses of the mayor and his friends. During all the tumult, Father Wolf was with his innocent flock. "Kill, kill, boys," he used to say to the sheep, "and I'll absolve you!"

The people of Bandon, too, were dissatisfied with the peace; and—in connection with Cork, Youghal, and Kinsale—they sent the Lords-Justices a remonstrance, stating:—"That his Majesty has been misguided and seduced by sinister and corrupt means, and with a lavish expenditure of that treasure and those estates which your petitioners have been dispoiled of; by which subtle and serpentine courses the Irish quashed and depressed all opposers and accusers, and removed all impediments to their devilish end of exterminating the English." Towards the conclusion of this spirited remonstrance the petitioners take higher ground, and they boldly tell my lords :—" That before they concluded a peace, they should have consulted the Parliament of England, or debated the matter with them in council."   They go on to state :—" That, finding how they are in all likelihood of being over-borne by the power and potency of their adversaries, they do beseech your lordships to call to mind that his Majesty hath, by his Royal assent unto an Act of Parliament, obliged himself not to grant any pardon or terms of peace to the aforesaid rebels without the consent of the Parliament of England ; and that, accordingly, your lordships should not suffer any part of his Majesty's honour to be betrayed to clemency, in assenting to such packed terms of peace as they have already contrived to draw your lordships into, without the consent of the said Parliament of England, and without admitting your petitioners to the free and full debate of the case."

We are not surprised to find that many men of influence and character should leave a cause represented by a prince who outraged every honourable feeling, and forfeited every title of respect.   Indeed, we are surprised how any of the English, in this country at least, could sympathize with one who grasped in amity the red hand of the murderer of more than half their kindred, and linked himself with those who stripped them of the fruits of all the industry of their lives.

Amongst those in this country who broke off all connection with the Royal cause, were :—Sir Hardress Waller, commander of Cork city ; Captain Muschamp,* commander of the Cork garrison ; Thomas Bennett,

---

* When the authorities had determined on getting the Roman Catholic inhabitants out of Cork, they resolved on effecting their purpose in as peaceable a manner as possible.   It would never do to remove the greater portion of the citizens by force— in fact, it could not be done.   They, therefore, had recourse to stratagem—and stratagem will often win where sheer brute force will fail.   The authorities knew this, and they adopted a ruse, which, for novelty and success, has been seldom surpassed.   Captain Muschamp strolled into the city one day about dinner-time, and, pretending to be more than half-drunk, he swaggered into the mayor's house, and invited himself to dinner.   Coppinger was glad to see him.   Muschamp was not the less welcome because he had come without a formal invitation, and down he sat to his worship's hospitable entertainment.   The sack went round, and the claret and the usquebaugh ; and cups were drained in bidding the unexpected guest a hearty welcome.   After a time, they began to talk on the all-absorbing events of the day.   Every man spoke out.   What did any one care ?   That frigidity and reserve, which prudence tells us to exercise in a mixed company, thawed before the warm glow of the juice of the generous grape.   Muschamp spoke out, too.   " Well, Master Mayor," said he, " if that it should please God that the Parliament in England should have the best of it in this war, and that the Parliament ships were in the harbour of Cork, if you and the rest of you would not take the covenant to be true to the King and Parliament, I protest I would, with the great ordinance in the fort, beat down all the houses in Cork about your ears."   " Treason !" shouted Coppinger, as he and

governor of Baltimore Castle; Robert Salmon, of Castlehaven Castle; and Captain Robert Gookin.

The Bandon people having heard that the Lord President was about placing a large garrison in their town, sent him a remonstrance, in which, amongst other matters, they complained of the disorderly conduct of some of his troops. Inchiquin, in his reply, date October 14th, says :—"I shall endeavour to do you this favour, to place in your garrison all the old men that are best acquainted therewith, and will be most orderly and safely governed; and to that end shall send the rest of Sir Arthur Loftus's regiment unto you, with a new company raised by Lieutenant-Colonel Woodley, but of old men, whom I shall desire you to receive into the garrison, and to billet and accommodate in the same proportion with this company."

The townspeople did not confine their complaints to the garrison alone; they complained of their having to contribute towards the support of the governor, Colonel Thomas Hill. It is true that twenty pence weekly was apparently a small amount, but it will not appear so to those who will bear in mind that this, with other imposts, was levied

---

his guests rose in fury to their feet. "Treason!" shouted they all, as they collared unfortunate Muschamp, and hurried him before the governor. The governor heartily thanked them for their loyalty and the promptitude with which they seized the traitor. "It is time," said that functionary, "to look about us, when we have the chief officers that are put in trust with matters of such concernment, as he was (being governor of the King's fort), should speak such treasonable words; and, therefore, Master Mayor, you shall have my best assistance; and such punishment shall be inflicted upon him as martial law will permit." A court-martial assembled at once. Treason in an officer, filling such an important post as "governor of the great fort outside South-gate," must be made an example of. Witnesses were produced who swore to his treasonable words. He was found guilty by a board of indignant officers, and he was sentenced to be hanged next day at a certain hour. As the appointed time drew near, crowds began to assemble. There were a great many anxious to feast their eyes on the death-struggles of an avowed Parliamentarian. "Arn't you coming out to see Muschamp hanged?" was, probably, the greeting with which those, who wished success to the united royal and rebel cause, met one another on that welcome morning. When the period arrived for the execution (which was to take place some distance outside the city walls), the sheriff appeared; and then the unhappy prisoner was brought forth, guarded by a strong body of musketeers. When they had almost reached the fatal spot, Muschamp looked around him, and, perceiving that his late host and his fellow-guests were all present, and also the principal men of the city,—or at least those of them upon whose active hostility to the Parliament he could count upon,—"Halt!" cried a stentorian voice, and instantly the prisoner was free. Stepping to the front of his musketeers, Captain Muschamp ordered the principal citizens to be made prisoners, and carried to his fort for safe keeping. Meanwhile, the city gates were shut, the draw-bridges were drawn up, and thus those who had gone out were unable to return to their homes. A proclamation was then published, announcing that if the Irish made any resistance they would be shot down; and, moreover, that if any English were killed in that broil, the chief men of the city would be hanged over the walls, which, we are told, did so terrify the Irish that they were all glad to be quiet.

off a people who, to use their own words, " were utterly undone from the many pressures and extortions practised upon them ;" whose lands were wasted ; whose trade was annihilated, and whose resources, after six years of a devastating civil war, must have been reduced to a cypher, if not exhausted altogether.

" It hath been represented unto me by Colonel Thomas Hill, governor of your corporation," says Lord Inchiquin, in a letter to the provost, " that you have lately protested against the payment of that weekly exhibition, which you have formerly satisfied towards his support in that command. Whereby I am occasioned to put you in mind that, upon the complaint of the many pressures and extortions practised upon you by former governors, I did, for your ease and for your instance, repose the trust of governing that corporation in this gentleman, whereby you not only seemed to be abundantly satisfied, but did also, of your own free consent, submit to the payment of twenty pence weekly towards his subsistence." He concludes his letter by telling them " that they may get worse ; and that, in case they did resolve to stand in their own light, I must then let you know that I stand engaged to interpose so far as that, during his continuance amongst you, the rent of any house he shall think convenient to live in must be free unto him, and the charge thereupon borne by the corporation."

The government were sorely pressed for funds from the commencement of the rebellion ; and, although there were many matters of vital importance to engage their attention, there were none of such moment as that of procuring means for the maintenance of the army. As they could levy no money off the country, they resolved to establish a mint of their own, and coin it. To do this, the Lords Justices and council met and issued the following order :—

" That we find it of absolute necessity, for the relief of the officers of the army, that in the case of extremity wherein we now stand, all manner of persons, of what condition or quality soever, dwelling in the city or suburbs of Dublin, as well within the liberties as without, within ten days next after publication of the said order, do deliver, or cause to be delivered, half or more of his, her, or their plate to William Bladen, of Dublin, Alderman, and John Pue, one of the sheriffs of the same city, taking their hand for receipt thereof, to the end use may be made thereof for the present relief of the said officers."

To this an assurance was added that payment should be made at the rate of five shillings for such silver plate " as is of true touch ;" and interest at the rate of eight per cent. per annum, until the debt was discharged.

Permission to establish a mint was subsequently extended to other towns, and from those mints issued "siege pieces," or money of necessity.   There was one established this year in Bandon, under the direction of Lord Broghill.   The Bandon coins, all of which were of copper, were about the size of a farthing, and about half as thick ; containing, on the obverse, the Bandon bridge, within a linear circle, outside of which was a beaded circle, but without the three castles which are generally represented in the Bandon arms ; and between the circles just mentioned, " THE CORPORASION."   On the reverse, enclosed by a linear circle similar in size and form to the other,—three castles ; and between the circle and the beaded one outside, " THE BANDON ARMS," with the date, 1646.   There was another of an irregular octagonal form, having on one side the letters " B. B.," within a circle of small lozenges ; on the other side, three castles within a similar circle ; weight, thirty-one. grains.   The letters " B. B." signifying Bandon-Bridge ; and the same letters, indented, occur as a counter-mark on some of the tokens issued in Bandon in 1670.

On the 16th of December a report of the state of Ireland was made to the Parliament, from which it appeared that there were four thousand foot and three hundred horse in the garrisons of Cork, Bandon, and Youghal.

1647.   The Irish Parliament, which had been prematurely brought to a close by the outburst of the great rebellion, resumed its sittings on the 26th of March, and on the 30th proceeded to business. The first act of the house was to appoint a committee to draught a letter to be sent to the committee of the Derby House, in London, on behalf of Captain Thomas Plunkett; and the first act of the committee was to appoint one of the members for Bandon—our old friend, Anthony Dopping—to prepare it.   Mr. Dopping, nothing loath, applied himself to the task with his usual industry, and with such dispatch that it was brought up the same day, before the rising of the house.   From the report, which was rather a lengthy one, we gather that Captain Plunkett gave one thousand pounds for the protection of the city of Dublin and the relief of several garrisons, and that the committee were so pleased with his patriotism, that they recommended that the thanks of both houses be given to him.   Some few days after, Mr. Dopping presented a petition to the house, stating:—"That upon the 6th instant, Sir Erasmus Burrowes and Sir William Gilbert were spoken to at a committee of both houses, to view the guard in the Castle; that they, repairing to the guard, found only six men upon guard and one sentinel at each gate; that they asked of a corporal of Captain Peisley, who had command of that guard, who showed him the said eight men, and told them that there were two upon the Castle; that immediately Captain Peisley coming in, they, in a civil manner, demanded of him where his officer was, who told them he went out to recreate himself, and would come bye and bye; that Sir Erasmus told him the guard was very slender, and some of his soldiers Papists, and were ill-affected, and were gone to the enemy; that Peisley, in a very high manner said, they lie that say so; and that there is a great stir with a company of flickards and babblers, without cause."

After reading the report, the Rev. Mr. Birch, chaplain to the Lord Lieutenant, was called in to know his answer concerning the matter, and some words in the petition. Mr. Birch, however, stood on his privilege as chaplain to his Excellency, and refused to give the house any information; whereupon a committee was appointed to wait on the Lord Lieutenant, and carry with them Mr. Dopping's petition.

Mr. Dopping was a member of several other committees also: as, "To consider the advisability of not billeting soldiers on members of Parliament;" "To congratulate the commissioners that had been sent over by the Parliament, and to acknowledge in the name of both houses their hearty thankfulness for their zeal and care in sending supplies for the relief and preservation of this kingdom;" and "To peruse the Articles exhibited against William Chappell, bishop of Cork and Ross, late provost of the College of Dublin, and his answer thereunto," &c.

Notwithstanding all the care and diligence displayed by our junior representative in the discharge of his duties, yet we find that Master Anthony was caught napping at last; for on a roll-call of the house, on the 21st May, he and thirty-three others were fined one shilling each for being absent.

Although, as we have said, our junior representative was most assiduous in the performance of his duties towards his country and his constituents, yet, like many of our parliamentary representatives in our own day, he did not think the interests of that very important digit— "number one"—beneath the consideration of an Irish M.P. Accord-

ingly, we find him looking about him; and with such success, that he
was enabled to induce the house to pass a bill, entitled "An Act for
securing three messuages or houses,* with three gardens and one orchard,
with the appurtenances, situate in St. Bride's Street, in the City of
Dublin, unto Anthony Dopping, gentleman, for threescore years."

Of our senior member, Sir Francis Slingsby, we have been unable to
discover any trace.

On the 18th of June the house adjourned. Letters of protection
were conferred by Lord Inchiquin upon those of the Irish party who
contributed to the support of his army; and copies were sent to the governors, mayors, provosts, &c., of the different districts, cities, and towns
under his authority. One of these, granted to Walter White of Kinnallea, we subjoin :—

"BY THE LORD PRESIDENT OF MUNSTER.

"WHEREAS, I have protected Walter White, gent., upon his lands in
the barony of Kinnallea, he contributing to the Protestant party. These
are, therefore, to will and strictly require all commanders, officers, and
soldiers, be they horse or foot, and all others whom it may concern, to
forbear arresting, suing, or impleading the said Walter White in any
court or courts, for any manner of debts, claim, or demand whatsoever,
due by bill, book, or other ways. Whereof they may not fail at their
ensuing peril. Dated the eleventh day of March, 1647.

"INCHIQUIN."

Notwithstanding the local mints, and the assistance procured by letters
of protection, the Lord President was still at his wit's end for money
and means. In a letter to Mr. Robert Bathurst, the provost of Bandon,
dated Cork, January 24th, he states :—"I have already borrowed of the
officers of Colonel Blunt's and Sir Arthur Loftus's regiments money to
pay their men for the week ending this day, which is all they are able
to send me; and now, their being no other way left to maintain them
this ensuing week, I am enforced to desire the assistance of the inhabitants of that town, as I have done the like of this [Cork] and
Kinsale, who have very willingly and largely contributed unto the
relief of those garrisons in their extremity; and shall, therefore, desire
that you will cause so much money to be raised in that town as the most
equal and indifferent now. That you can as well pay those two
regiments for this next week :—Colonel Blunt's men two shillings a

---

* We presume these were some of the houses taken from Roman Catholics found
residing in the city.

piece, and ten pounds amongst Sir Arthur Loftus's regiment; and accordingly pay it unto them, and before the end of that week I shall take those men from you. My only endeavour, in the meantime, being to get enough of oaten meal made in a readiness for carriage into the field, and then to draw them abroad; being unwilling to continue any burthen upon you any longer than unavoidable necessity doth counsel me; and herein expecting you will not fail," &c., &c.

The town granted the money, and receipts were passed to the provost for the amounts. We give the two following:—

" Received of the provost of Bandon, forty shillings, for the use of the lieutenants, ensigns, and staff officers, this 24th of August, 1647.

" CHARLES ELSYNGE."

" Received of the provost of Bandon, fifty shillings, for the use of lieutenants, ensigns, and staff officers, this third day of ———, 1647.

" JAMES RIDDOR."

The new provost, Mr. Abraham Savage, felt the burthen of supporting the garrison as acutely as his predecessor, Mr. Bathurst; and, in a letter to Governor Searle,* requests that he would have the sick and wounded men removed from the town into an hospital; and that he would have one of the regiments, at least, removed from the town.

In reply, the governor said:—" I think the sick and shot men were better to be continued in their quarters than to be removed into an hospital. As for getting a regiment removed, I shall endeavour it, but I fear I shall lose my labour; but I assure yourself I will do the utmost I can to comply with your expectation." He then informed our chief magistrate " that the day of public thanksgiving is put off by the general consent until Thursday next, and I desire you to acquaint the magistrates with the same, and all the corporation." He concludes " by praying that the corporation will have the thirty pounds ready for Monday be-times." The letter is dated December 3rd, 1647, and signed,

" Yours to do your service,

" THOMAS SEARLE."

Notwithstanding that the townspeople were desirous of being rid of " the sick and shot " soldiers, and were also convinced that they had a

---

* In an account of the particular savings contained in the patents under the Acts of Settlement and Explanation, we find the sum of £4,826 6s. 10d. assigned in trust to Sir Randal Clayton, for Mrs. Jane Searle, being the amount of arrears due to Colonel Thomas Searle, deceased.

regiment too much billetted upon them, they were ordered to prepare quarters and credit for two more.

"By virtue of an order from the Lord President of Munster, I do hereby desire the provost and inhabitants of Bandon-Bridge to procure credit for the officers of the regiment under the command of Colonel Blunt, and the officers of the regiment under the command of Colonel Knight, for which the Lord President doth engage himself to make payment out of the first money that shall arrive. The number of officers to be quartered are hereunder written, this 21st day of December, 1647, for which I do hereby undertake that satisfaction shall be made according to my Lord's letters, only for their diet.

"THOMAS SEARLE."

COLONEL BLUNT'S OFFICERS.*	COLONEL KNIGHT'S OFFICERS.†
Captain Kirle.	Captain Richards.
Lieutenant Alexander.	Lieutenant Brady.
Lieutenant Blunt.	Lieutenant Lone.
Lieutenant Morse (absent).	Lieutenant Erwin.
Lieutenant Austin.	Lieutenant Plumer.
Lieutenant Browne.	Lieutenant Cavanagh.
Lieutenant Harrisey.	Lieutenant Tucker.
Lieutenant Chambers.	Ensign Elliard.
Ensign Woods (absent).	Ensign Mason.
Ensign Somersett.	Ensign Peach.
Ensign Symons.	Ensign Cossior.
Ensign Mallory.	Ensign Garner.
Ensign Morrill.	Ensign Loftus.
Ensign Hawkins.	Ensign Hamilton.
Ensign Giles (absent).	Ensign Holland.
Ensign Halfaicker.	Benjamin Cox, Marshall.
Ensign Pottye.	John Comyn, Waggon-master.
Henry Causen, Marshall.	———, junr., Marshall.
James Wood, Waggon-master.	
John Bignall, Chirurgeon.	
Charles Elsynge, junr., Marshall.	

1649.   On the 23rd of February the Nuncio set sail from Galway, and returned to Rome. The General Assembly at Kilkenny were so displeased with his conduct, that they directed their speaker to write him a letter, ordering him to quit the kingdom; and enclosing him, at the same time, a schedule of the grievances which he caused. They threatened, in addition, to impeach him before the Pope; and they concluded, by warning every one not to communicate or correspond with

---

* Colonel Charles Blunt appears on the roll of 1649 officers, but not in the Act of Settlement, or in the savings under that Act; or even in the Court of Claims. He was attached to the Parliament, and his name was furnished to the government of Charles the Second in "A list of those officers who joined in betraying the towns of Munster, and are now in command."

† Colonel William Knight obtained a grant of lands under the Act of Settlement and Explanation. His name also appears on the list of certificates to adventurers and soldiers, preserved in the office of the Chief Remembrancer of the Exchequer.

him. Upon his arrival in the holy city he had an interview with his his master. "Temerarie te gessisti," said his Holiness. This rebuke is said to have grated so severely upon the sensitive feelings of the poor Legate, that it killed him.

Now, that the prince of Firmo had turned his back upon our shores, the Irish fought vigorously on the Royalist side; and there are not wanting writers who would fain persuade us that they were warmly attached to the first Charles. But we very much question the warmth of that attachment, as well as its sincerity; particuliarly when we note that it was in this very prince's reign they got up this—the greatest rebellion of all; and in whose reign, also, it was that their Supreme Council at Kilkenny gave written instructions to Sir Nicholas Plunket to offer his kingdom of Ireland—first to the Pope, and, if refused by him, then to every other Roman Catholic potentate in Europe, including even the Duke of Lorraine. And yet we find some writers term them "Royalists;" and, indeed, as such they had the boldness to petition Charles the Second for the restoration of their estates!

Royalists, forsooth! What pretty Royalists were Owen Roe O'Neil, Rinuccini, Father Wolf, Sir Phelim O'Neil, and the other worthies who took a prominent part in the great events of the day!

"The English colonists," say the writers referred to, "were rebels." Was it the English colonists sent emissaries all over Papal Europe, and organized the most gigantic conspiracy that ever threatened English rule in this country? Was it at their instigation that hosts of priests and friars flocked into this country from abroad? Was it by their desire that the Irish rebelled against the supremacy of England, on the 23rd of October, and in a short time caused the death of over one hundred thousand of their kith and kin?

That the colonists did fight against Charles—is true; but not until he had justly forfeited every prerogative of a king; until he had sided energetically with those who had wrested from them all the fruit of the toil of their lives, and then sanctioned the robbery; and who had, with a fury almost Satanic, swept numbers of their inoffensive women and children into an early grave!

When he stood up in their gory ranks, arrayed against those whom Queen Elizabeth and his own father had induced to settle upon the devastated lands of Desmond and Tyrone, they strove resolutely against him; and fought as fearlessly against the traitorous King, as they did

11—2

against those who boasted of such leaders as Father Wolf and Sir Phelim O'Neil.

No! On the contrary, the Irish hated both the English and their King; and in this they were consistent, for every generation that preceded them—from the time the English came here down to their own time—did the same. That they formed an alliance with Charles—no one will deny; but it was not for the purpose of benefitting him, but of dragging from him terms which they well knew his English subjects would never concede to them.

They were also influenced by another motive—that of crushing the Puritans. On this subject the royalists and the rebels were united; they were both sincere in their professions of enmity to them; and it would be difficult to say—now—which of the two burned with the most intense hate towards them. They both foresaw that, if the Puritans won, the "divine right" nonsense of the one had as little chance of attaining to favour and success, as the cruel misdeeds of the other had of escaping a severe—but well-merited—punishment.

CHAPTER VIII.

OLIVER CROMWELL LANDS IN DUBLIN—HE STORMS DROGHEDA—HIS CAREER IN THE
SOUTH—SEVERAL OF THE MUNSTER TOWNS PRONOUNCE FOR HIM—BANDON IS THE
FIRST TO MAKE THE ATTEMPT—CROMWELL VISITS BANDON—THE ROMAN CATHOLIC
BISHOP OF ROSS HANGED AT CARRIGADROHID CASTLE—SIR RICHARD COX AND HIS
DESCENDANTS—TRIAL OF MAC CARTHY-CRIMEN, OF BALLINAROHUR CASTLE, BEFORE
HIGH COURT OF JUSTICE IN BANDON, FOR THE MURDER OF MR. BURROWES AND
HIS FAMILY.

A NEW chapter in the history of this great civil war now opens before us. After eight years of a prolonged and desperate struggle,—after a wholesale destruction of life and property,—neither of the combatants were victorious. The Supreme Council of the Confederated Irish still sat at Kilkenny, and their armies garrisoned most of the towns of Munster. The Royalists were also in arms, and held Cork, Bandon, Youghal, and other important places in the same Province. To these two—various causes added three more. Owen Roe O'Neil commanded the army of the Nuncio and the clerical party in the North. The Scotch and English Presbyterians had an army of their own, which would neither ally itself with the Royalists or with the Irish; or even with those whose religious and political opinions were almost in unison with their own—the Parliamentarians. And, lastly, the troops which Colonel Jones and Sir Charles Coote commanded in Dublin and Derry for the Parliament.

'Twas on a memorable day in August—a day that will survive in our annals for ever—that Oliver Cromwell landed in Dublin. He brought with him eight thousand foot, four thousand horse, twenty thousand pounds in hard cash, a large park of artillery, and all the other requisites for carrying on war on an extensive scale. Notwithstanding that Oliver's attention must have been fully occupied in making the necessary preparations for arming, provisioning, and equiping such a formidable force, yet he did not overlook—what was of paramount importance in his eyes—the religious instruction of his soldiers. Every file was served out of store with a Bible; and such a horror had he of profane swearing, that one of his first proclamations —as Lord Lieutenant of Ireland—was directed against it.

Cromwell did not come here to look about him. On the 2nd of September he was before Drogheda.

Ormond had left nothing undone to strengthen this place. He placed four hundred men of his own regiment in it; also the regiments commanded by Sir Edward Verney, Colonel Birns, Colonel Warren, Colonel Wall, Lord Westmeath, Sir James Dillon, and Lieutenant-Colonel Cavanagh; amounting together to three thousand four hundred foot and two hundred horse, all of whom where under the orders of Sir Arthur Aston (late governor of Oxford), a man of great military experience and reputation. So confident was Sir Arthur of being able to maintain his position, that he wrote to Ormond—to assure him—that he "would find the enemy play; and that the garrison being select men, and the town so strong, it could not be taken by assault." Oliver, however, soon effaced this impression from his mind; for, having besieged the place *on one side only*, and then even without the formality of a regular approach, he began the construction of his batteries on the 9th of September, and the very next day—at five in the evening—stormed the town. Although his men were twice beaten off, and their leader (Col. Cassells) slain, yet—nothing daunted—he attacked it the third time, commanding in person,* and carried it.

Most of the garrison were put to the sword, amongst whom was Colonel Boyle (one of the Cork family); and the rest, amounting, it is said, to not more than thirty, were transported to Barbadoes.

The terrible slaughter at Drogheda so terrified the neighbouring garrisons, that Dundalk submitted immediately—as did several forts and castles.

---

* Oliver was a brave man. It is related, that once—during his Scotch campaign —he was riding near Glasgow at the head of a body of horse, when a Scotch soldier, who was planted on a high wall, fired at him, and missed him. Oliver, without slackening his pace or drawing a rein, turned contemptuously round in his saddle:—" Fellow," said he, " if a trooper of mine missed such a shot as that, I'd give him a hundred lashes!" He then rode on, leaving Sawney amazed at the cool way he took this attempt on his life. This, as Mr. Pinkerton remarks, was a rare example of true courage.

In justice to Cromwell, it is but right to state that, previous to opening fire on the town, he sent the besieged the following laconic message :—" Surrender, and quarter.   No surrender, no quarter."

When Owen Roe heard that a place so strong and so well secured as Drogheda was taken, and that in such a summary manner :—" Well, exclaimed he, with a great oath, "after that, if Cromwell stormed hell, he'd take it too !"

Having returned to Dublin, Oliver marched southwards ; and, having taken Arklow, Ferns, Enniscorthy, and other places, he arrived at Wexford on the 1st of October, and summoned the town to surrender. But the governor (Colonel Synot) gave a reply, which made it evident that his only object was to gain time.   In this Cromwell, who also bided his time, indulged him ; so that Lord Castlehaven found it easy to introduce a regiment of foot into the town, and—in three days after —Lord Ormond was able to send in another force, consisting of a thousand men, under Sir Edmund Butler.   Nevertheless, this last reinforcement was not within the walls two hours, when Captain James Strafford surrendered the castle.   Cromwell instantly had the guns turned on the town, which so terrified the garrison and the inhabitants, that they fled from the walls in dismay, and endeavoured to effect their escape by the river.   The besiegers took advantage of the fright they were in ; and, raising the scaling-ladders, they ran up the walls and took the town by storm.   Upwards of two thousand of those found in arms were put to the sword.

From Wexford, Cromwell hastened to Ross, into which Lord Ormond had thrown one thousand five hundred men.   But scarce had the guns began to play—when the garrison began to capitulate.

" I demand liberty of conscience," said Taffe, the governor, " for those who intend to remain in the town !"

" I meddle with no man's conscience," replied Oliver, " but if by liberty of conscience you mean liberty to exercise the mass, I judge it best to use plain dealing, and let you know—that where the Parliament of England have power—that will not be allowed."

Taffe, being unable to prevail upon the stern Independent, was obliged to accept the proffered terms, and march out ; taking with him all his men, save about six hundred who took service with Cromwell.

In the meantime, the chief towns in our county had revolted to the Parliament.   The city of Cork was the first to begin.   It appears the movement originated there with some officers, who waited upon Colonels Townsend, Warden, and Gifford—the three colonels who were under arrest for showing disaffection to the royal cause. The officers told them "that they were undone unless they would stand by them, for they would else be slaves to the Irish." "Bring us a sword each, and a brace of pistols," said they, "and we will live to congratulate ourselves upon our success, or perish in the attempt!" The arms were brought to them; and—descending the prison steps sword in hand—they were met by the guard, who, with loud cries of "We are with you too!" fell in behind them, and marched to the main guard. There was no difficulty in getting them and the Protestant citizens to pronounce for them also; and then—with one simultaneous shout—they demanded that the Irish should be driven out of the city. This was speedily effected; and on the next morning Major-General Sterling, and the few that remained of his way of thinking, were also placed outside the gates.

Although, as we have said, Cork was the first town in Munster to declare for Cromwell, Bandon was the first to make the effort. Ere the officers had asked the colonels to stand by them, some prominent townsmen, and some officers of the Bandon militia, had resolved to seize on the Royalist guards, and deliver up the garrison. The attempt was made by a party of civilians, on the forenoon of the 16th of November, under the command of Captain Braly and Lieutenant Berry. At first they were successful, having seized upon the guards at West-gate; but the other posts not being attacked at the concerted time, the Royalists were on the watch, and Braly and his valiant comrades were assailed by overwhelming numbers, and made prisoners.*

In about three weeks after this another design was on foot, "to seize the governor, officers, and guards, and secure the town for the Parliament and the Lord Lieutenant—Cromwell;" and having taken possession of two houses near the sally-port at the north side of the town, the conspirators plainly told Courtnay (the governor) that it was vain for him to oppose, as they were resolved to deliver up the town. Courtnay seemed to have thought so too; and he asked them not to deliver him up also, until he had some time to make conditions for himself and his party. This was agreed to, and at the end of the specified time he surrendered.†

---

* See history of the Bandon militia in this work, chapter 22.
† See M.SS. Carte-papers, Bodleian Lib., Oxford.

The throwing open of the gates of these Munster towns was of the greatest benefit to Cromwell. It convinced him that the inhabitants were with him; and they furnished him with comfortable winter quarters for his hard-worked troops.

This hostile demonstration for the Parliament, and the gaining possession of those garrisons by their generals, without losing a drop of blood, greatly incensed the Royalists. "It was a treacherous revolt of the Presbyterian English, which garrisoned most of the towns of Munster." And Lord Ormond—in a letter to Charles—thought it was too bad "that Bandon, Kinsale, Youghal, and other places, should be all betrayed to him [Cromwell] without one stroke struck!"

The Presbyterian English* did garrison most of the towns in Munster; but in our town, whatever may be said of the garrison, there is no doubt but that the inhabitants themselves were thoroughly Puritan. Hence it was, that from the moment they became aware of the negotiations going on between the King and the rebels, they mistrusted him. They could not be expected to look favourable upon—much less to fight side by side with—those whose hands still reeked with the blood of their dearest kindred. And what claim had the Royalists upon their allegiance and affections?—Royalists who were willing to secure the Irish enemy in the possession of all the property they had wrested from them, and to forgive them for all their offences, of what nature or quality soever, as if they had never been committed.

Their very stomachs sickened at the mention of the unholy alliance between their King and the rebellious Irish. The alliance itself was an unnatural one, and it was both hypocritical and hollow on both sides. What cared the Irish for a King; who, when they thought themselves strong enough to do so, hastened to offer his kingdom of Ireland—first to the Pope, and subsequently to nearly every other Roman Catholic crowned-head in Europe? What cared the King for those whom he knew looked upon him as an intruder; and who had just made a prodigious effort to shake off the sovereignity of England for ever. Charles joined them in order to procure assistance to crush those who resisted his autocratic enactments in England; and they

---

* Although the Presbyterian English separated themselves from the Royalists, yet the latter did not taunt them "with their religion." They were not, however, so lenient to the Scotch Presbyterians, whom they accused of having "a scurvy religion;" and assigned that as the reason why they agreed so well with those who had none at all.

joined Charles in order that—when he had accomplished his vicious purpose—they could the more easily rid themselves of him, and scoop out of the earth the very fibres of the roots of those colonies which the prudence of preceding princes had planted in Ireland.

Cromwell selected Youghal as his head-quarters during the winter of 1649. He frequently left it, however, on tours of inspection to the various garrisons that were quartered throughout this county, and those adjoining. On the 17th of December he first came to Cork, accompanied by Lord Broghill; and after Ireton's arrival—in two days after—he proceeded to Kinsale; and from thence to our own town.*

Tradition asserts that he was greatly pleased with the strength of this plantation, and the devotion of its inhabitants to the cause of England; and, speaking about that great nobleman who was so closely identified with Bandon, he is reported to have said: "That if there had been an Earl of Cork in every province in Ireland, it would have been impossible for the Irish to have raised a rebellion!"

Oliver came several times to Bandon, and always put-up at a little two-storied house—that then occupied the site upon which at present stands the residence of Mr. T. Bennett—in the South Main Street; and in a little bedroom of which (at the western end)—one who in a short time was destined to become one of the most powerful potentates of Europe—often retired to rest, or to muse, perhaps, over his anticipations of the future. Such importance did a subsequent owner of the little tenement of two stories attach to everything connected with Cromwell's visit to the town, that when the house was taken down— about the beginning of this century—to make room for its present successor, he had the boards of the little bedroom carefully removed, and relaid in the new edifice; and—with no small interest—we have looked on those old time-worn mementoes of a by-gone age,—mementoes, too, closely-associated with the presence of Oliver Cromwell.

On the 29th January Cromwell broke up his winter quarters, and marched for Ormond's head-quarters at Kilkenny.

1650.

His march was one continued triumph. He occupied Clogher; Roghill Castle succumbed without a struggle; Fethard, contrary to all the rules of war, was summoned by candlelight, and surrendered before daylight; the garrison at Cashel fled when they heard of his approach. At

---

* For particulars, see history of the Bandon militia, chapter 22.

Callan, Oliver was joined by Reynolds; after placing a garrison there, he then fell back upon Fethard and Cashel.

Meanwhile Colonel Hewson, who commanded the Parliamentary garrison in Dublin, had made his way—at the head of two thousand foot and one thousand horse—into Kildare; and, having taken Leighlin-Bridge (on the river Barrow), at last effected a junction with Cromwell before Gouran. Gouran Castle was strong; and was thought so much of by the enemy, that it was occupied by a portion of Ormond's own regiment, under Colonel Hammond, a distinguished Royalist. Hammond sent a stern negative in reply to Oliver's order to surrender. The batteries were immediately placed in position, which so terrified Hammond's men that they mutinied, and gave up their officers, a priest, and the castle itself, on being allowed their lives. The next morning Hammond and all his officers—save one only—were brought out on the parade-ground, and shot; and the unlucky priest, who had been chaplain to the Roman Catholics in the regiment, was hanged.

On the 22nd March Cromwell arrived before Kilkenny, and the same day demanded that the city and castle should be given up to him; but the governor (Sir Walter Butler) refused. After a vigorous resistance —extending over some days—he began to negotiate; and on the 28th of the same month he capitulated.

Cromwell's army now spread itself in all directions, collecting provisions, levying contributions, and reducing the small garrisons scattered throughout the country.

Colonel Hewson's party attacked Castledermot; but the Irish shut themselves up in a strong tower, having burnt the greater part of the castle the day previously, and they refused to come out. Whereupon Hewson piled a lot of faggots and other combustibles against the door, and set fire to them. In due time the inmates cried for mercy— and they surrendered. Amongst them were three friars and one Captain Sherlock, who is described as "a bloody tory."*

After the capture of Kilkenny, Cromwell proceeded to invest Clonmel,

---

* Sherlock was not the only "bloody tory" to be met with in those days. In fact, they over-ran the whole country; and the authorities were often at their wit's end how to get rid of them. The ordinary price set upon a tory's head was forty shillings; but if he happened to be a great tory—like Sherlock—the reward offered was often as high as thirty pounds. In a proclamation, dated October, 1655, the following sums were offered for the apprehension of the under-named tories—alive or dead:—For blind Donough, £30; Dermot Ryan, £20; James Leigh, £5; or for any other tory that shall be brought by any countryman to any governer of a county or precinct—dead or alive,—forty shillings.

but here the resistance he met with was not only obstinate but successful. Such were the number of his men that perished in the very first assault, that he determined on starving out the garrison—rather than on hazarding another attempt. Meanwhile, he sent pressing instructions to Lord Broghill to come to his assistance at once; but scarce had Broghill arrived, when intelligence reached him that the Titular bishop of Ross was on his way—at the head of five thousand foot—to compel him to raise the siege. He instantly dispatched Lord Broghill—with two thousand horse and sixteen hundred foot—to intercept him. On the line of march, with a portion of his force—consisting of six hundred horse and four hundred foot—he overtook Lord Muskerry, marching to join the bishop at the head of one thousand horse and two thousand foot, and fell on him at once. Both sides fought furiously. Many of the Irish strove hard to reach Lord Broghill, shouting at the top of their voice:—"Kill the fellow in the gold-laced coat!" And they would, in all probability, have done so, had not a supernumerary lieutenant come to his aid, and saved him. After a desperate struggle, the Irish at length gave way, leaving behind them six hundred dead and a great many prisoners.

On the morning of the 10th of April Lord Broghill came before Carrigadrohid Castle, and found it occupied by some of the bishop's troops. Here he left his foot to over-awe the garrison, and hurried on with his horse to Macroom. The Irish, aware of his approach, burnt the castle, and then joined their main body, which lay encamped in the park. Broghill immediately dashed at them with great spirit; and with such success, that they broke and fled—leaving a great many dead,* and several prisoners. Amongst the latter were the high-sheriff of Kerry and the bishop himself.

In those days there was not much time consumed in a tedious process of law; nor were there many opportunities afforded an ingenious counsel to pick holes in an indictment. A file or two of dismounted troopers presented their petronels at the high-sheriff's breast, and soon that functionary was beyond the reach of any benefit he may be entitled to by a decision of the twelve judges in his favour.

The bishop, Lord Broghill took with him to Carrigadrohid; and he there offered him his life if he would induce the garrison in the castle

---

* Colonel John Barry—Fitz-William—(who succeeded his grandfather, John Barry of Liscarrol, and was married to Alice, daughter of the first Earl of Cork, and relict of the Earl of Barrymore) was killed fighting on the English side.

to surrender. He accepted the proffered terms; but, when brought within talking distance of them, he told them to hold out to the last. Broghill did not appreciate the joke; he ordered a gallows to be erected forthwith; a rope was put round the bishop's neck, and he was hanged on the spot.

But the loss of his life did not even save the castle; as it was soon afterwards taken, and by a very simple contrivance. The sentries posted on the watch-tower saw teams of oxen dragging heavy ordinance, and slowly approaching the castle walls. "What," probably thought the terrified warders, "shall become of us, when these walls are battered about our ears! If not seized and shot on the instant, we may be hanged like a dog!" And a fearful instance—fresh in their memories, if not yet before their very eyes—told them that the opposing general was not incapable of using the halter. They surrendered. The heavy ordinance were balks of timber, fashioned to resemble cannon.

Emboldened by Lord Broghill's success, Cromwell again assaulted Clonmel, but was driven back. Again he rushed at the breach; and both sides maintained the fight with great fury until the darkness prevented them seeing one another. The inhabitants were now weary of the struggle, and believing that Oliver would be victorious in the end, they gave up; and the next day Cromwell marched into the town.

The taking of Clonmel was his last achievement in Ireland. Despatches had reached him from the Parliament, urging him to return home. He gave the command to Major-General Ireton, the Lord President of Munster,—the same who shortly after also succeeded him as Lord Lieutenant of Ireland; and embarked for England, at Youghal, on the 29th May. On the 4th of June following he entered the Parliament, when Mr. Speaker (by order) " gave him the hearty thanks of this house, for his great and faithful services unto the Parliament and the Commonwealth."

Now that the war was drawn to a close, people breathed more freely; and they began to turn their attention to other matters, from which they were diverted by that momentous struggle which had absorbed all their time and attention for the previous nine years. The inhabitants who had lived outside the walls of our town thought they had a right to be exempt from the rating assessed upon those who lived inside. They complained that it was an oppression to assess them, and that they ought not to be asked to contribute any longer. The inhabitants who lived within the walls thought differently; so they joined issue, and went to law.

The cause was tried before a jury, on the 26th of September. The plaintiffs were :—The provost, free-burgesses, and commonalty of Bandon-Bridge; and the defendants :—Francis Boyle, Esq.,* Thomas Ellwell (Ensign), Roger Grimley, Thomas Hogan, and all the other tenants of the said Francis Boyle, and inhabitants of the Irish-town. As the jury could not agree, another was empannelled; and the case was re-heard. Mr. Clement Woodroffe (the provost), Mr. George Fenton, and Mr. Abraham Savage appeared for the corporation. Mr. William Thivey (agent to Mr. Boyle), Ensign Grimley, and Thomas Ellwell, for the inhabitants of the Irish-town.

It was alleged by the plaintiffs that, according to the patent of King James, "all the castles, messuages, lofts, mills, houses and edifices, structures and carthlaghs, places, lands, tenements, and hereditaments whatsoever, with the appurtenances, on both sides of the river, sliding or running under the bridge of the said town, adding thereto, or being within the said town or village, or points of the same, shall henceforth and continue one free and entire borough of itself." They then produced Mr. Woodner, Charles Coombes, and others, " who being antient men," deposed, on their own knowledge, that at the time the Letters-Patent were granted there were some structures in that place (*i.e.*—the Irish-town); and, moreover, that Samuel Fenton had a house there, which was subsequently occupied by one James Ellwell. Woodner and Coombes also averred that the parish church stood in part of the said Irish-town, and that all the inhabitants of Bandon—on the south-side of the river—went to the said church, there being no other parish church save in the said Irish-town, and that some of the burgesses nominated in the Letters-Patent (viz. :—Stephen Skipwith, Thomas Taylor, and William Cecill—they living at the south-side of the town) worshipped in the same. Plaintiffs, in addition, tried to prove that Ballymodan was also called Bally-bandon, thereby endeavouring to show that the whole parish was

---

* Francis Boyle, fourth son of the first Earl of Cork, was created Viscount Shannon in 1660, and died at a very advanced age in 1699. It was this gentleman who so valiantly distinguished himself at the battle of Liscarroll in 1642, upon which occasion he nearly lost his life in rescuing the body and charger of his brother, Lord Kinalmeaky. The title expired with his grandson, but was renewed in 1756, and conferred upon Henry Boyle, Esq., of Castlemartyr, the grandson of Lord Broghill, first Earl of Orrery.

incorporated. Finally, they proved, from entries in the rate-books of 1614 and 1628, that Ellwell and Witherhead—although living in Irish-town—paid the same rates as those residing inside the gates.

The defendants admitted that Ellwell and Witherhead did reside in the Irish-town, but the rates they paid, they alleged, was for property within the walls. That Irish-town was part of Ballymodan, but not of Bandon-Bridge. That it belonged to William Murray at the time of the incorporation; and that from him it was subsequently purchased by the Earl of Cork. And Coombes admitted that when Captain Adderly was provost he was rated for a house he built outside the walls, by West-gate; and that he was acquitted of the payment thereof, as it stood not upon the corporation.

The plaintiffs, in reply, urged that the house referred to by Coombes was built since the erection of the walls, and that that altered the case.

As regards Ballymodan being *alias* Bally-bandon, Lieutenant John Langton deposed that he read over many records and always found it written Ballymodan; and did not find it "*alias* Bally-bandon," until he hath kept court there.*

Even if they were rated, the defendants insisted that it was only during the war, and not in peaceable times. And to show that they were recognized as being outside the bounds of the corporation, they brought forward Mr. Edmunds, who stated that Mr. Richard Crofts, provost in 1617, showed him the bounds of the corporation, and told him it went no farther than the little river.†

Mr. Daniel Roch confirmed the testimony of Edmunds, and said it was only intended to incorporate that portion of the town built on what was forfeited to the crown by the attainder of one Mahowne, whose lands were bounded by the said river running by the East-gate.

The plaintiffs showed that this could not be the case, as a small portion of the lands within the walls, and already incorporated (viz.: the lands south of the little river) never belonged to Mahowne.

But, replied the defendants, Lord Cork being the owner of those lands south of the river, and within the walls, consented thereunto for the good of the corporation, by setting the walls on that side of the hill southwards.

---

* Lieutenant John Langton was seneschal of the manor of Ballymodan, and was also an officer of the Bandon militia. He married a sister of Francis Bernard, Esq., of Castle-Mahon. *Vide* Langton, Bandon militia.

† Now known as the Bridewell river.

Upon proof of this being demanded, the defendants were unable to produce any.

Both sides having at length thoroughly exhausted every proof and argument they possessed, the court decreed :—That the church being in the Irish-town rendered it a town, otherwise it would be a hamlet. It was, therefore, determined that all the lands, tenements, and hereditaments on both sides of the river Bandon,—in both the parishes antiently called by the name of Ballymodan and Kilbrogan, and now known and called by the name of Bandon-Bridge,—shall be deemed for evermore a part of the corporation; and even in all equity, said the judge, those who availed themselves of the protection of the walls, and who could not have kept anything from the enemy during the war, ought in all conscience contribute towards the safe-guarding of Bandon-Bridge. The judgment was pronounced by John Cooke, Chief Justice of Munster.

The year that witnessed this great internal commotion amongst our old townsmen, witnessed the birth of a child within our walls, destined to become a great man, and a far more eminent lawyer than the Chief Justice himself. On the 26th of March, the Honorable Sir Richard Cox, Lord High Chancellor of Ireland, was born.. In his autobiography, he tells us that his grandfather, Michael Cox (the first of the family who settled in Ireland), was the younger brother of an honest family, which had for some hundreds of years held a good copyhold near Bishop Cannings, in Wiltshire. Michael's third son, Richard, married Kathrine* ("a pretty black woman, as I have been assured"), daughter of Walter Birde, Esq.,† three times sovereign—and for a long time recorder—of Clonakilty ; and by her had the subject of this memoir.

Before he was three years old, however, he lost both his parents. His father, whilst walking with one Captain Norton, was suddenly set upon by him, and stabbed ; and his mother took grief so much to heart at his loss, that she fell into consumption, and died the following winter. John Birde (his mother's brother) then took charge of the little helpless orphan, and, when he was of sufficient age, sent him to school to Mr. Thomas Barry, of Clonakilty. At fourteen years old he began to

---

* Kathrine was previously married to Captain Thomas Batten, who was killed at the siege of Dungarvan, in 1642, having been shot through the forehead.

† Walter Birde was educated at Oxford. He was not only a good scholar but also understood music, and was said to be an excellent performer on the bass-viol.

learn logic, and when barely fifteen he left school; and not having the means to take out his degree at Trinity College, he spent the next three years in idleness,—during the whole of which he scarcely ever opened a book, unless *Heylin's Cosmography*, or the very few works on history or theology to be had in the town.

He attributes all his success in life to a principle of honesty, and a regard for religion, sincerity, and virtue; in connection with which he relates the following :—" I owed a cob [a Spanish dollar, value 4s. 6d.], which by driblets I had lost at the truck-table, and being dunned for it, I stole one from my uncle; but being checked by my principle, I restored it immediately, and resolved to take some lawful course to pay that debt, and furnish myself with more money. That very night I proposed to my uncle, who was seneschal of several of the Earl of Cork's manors, that I might have his permission to practise as an attorney; which being granted, I got enough to pay my debt the first court day."

His success encouraged him to proceed, and before he attained the age of eighteen he was an attorney of great repute in all the local courts. Shortly after this he resolved on becoming a barrister. Accordingly he proceeded to London, and entered himself as a student at Gray's-Inn in 1671; and in two years after was called to the bar.

On his return to Bandon he united himself to a wife and a law-suit. However disposed people may be to run after the former, there are few to whom the latter is an attraction. Nevertheless, to a young active lawyer, a law-suit may present itself in a different light. He may not only gain his cause, but gain notoriety and fame. This was the view he took of it; and had his anticipations been realized, all would have been well. But, unfortunately, they were not. The suit went against him; and such an effect had this upon him, that he absolutely threw up practice, returned to Clonakilty, and went farming.

But the growing of corn and the rearing of cattle had little or no attraction for a man of his active and ambitious temperament. Accordingly, he shook off the rustic indolence which pastoral ease produces, and began again. He was also stimulated to this by the numerous family which his illusory dowered wife, Mary Bourne, brought him.

He now took up his residence in Cork, where his industry and abilities soon drew him into notice; and such was his success, that the very first year of his residence there he realized upwards of five hundred pounds. His practice continued to increase, and in a short time he was enabled not only to keep his coach and live in a style befitting his position, but to purchase estates.

Upon the resignation of the recordership of Kinsale by William Worth,* he was appointed to that office through the interest of Sir Robert Southwell. In addition to the great industry and skill exhibited by Mr. Cox in mastering his case, he was possessed of a seductive and persuasive eloquence—an eloquence so attractive and telling, as to earn for him the appellation of the silver-tongue of Munster. But the time was fast approaching when he should forego his honours and emoluments, and leave the country altogether.

On the return of the Earl of Clarendon from the Lord-Lieutenancy of Ireland, in 1687, he was succeeded by Lord Tyrconnell. Cox saw in this appointment an attempt to reverse that policy which fostered the Protestant interest in this country; and he well knew that, in the hands of an unscrupulous partizan like "lying Dick," no means would be spared to render the effort a success. He, therefore, resolved to leave as soon as he could; which he did, and went to live in Bristol. Here time hung heavily on his hands; but he was determined not again to relapse into listlessness and inactivity. He undertook to write a history of a country which his infant years had seen emerging from a great civil war, and which his mature years saw hurrying into another. He began his history of Ireland in Bristol. The first part was published in London, in 1689, and entitled *Hibernia Anglicana;* and the second appeared in 1690, but was not brought down further than 1653. Some think that its continuation from that year was in manuscript, but this is generally believed to be a mistake.

When the Prince of Orange landed at Torbay, there were thousands who rejoiced at the news; but—with the fate of Monmouth before their eyes—they hesitated to bid him welcome. Cox was not one of these. With a fearless disregard of the consequences, he hurried up to London; and took a most decided and active part in promoting the revolution. He wrote a pamphlet, proving the urgent necessity of placing the crown upon William's head, and of sending speedy relief to the Protestants in Ireland. And after the proclamation announcing that William and Mary had ascended the throne, he published *A brief and modest Representation of the State and Condition of Ireland.*

---

* William Worth was the first recorder of Cork. He was subsequently second baron of the Irish Exchequer.

His numerous good services were not suffered to go unrequited. He was made Under Secretary of State; and soon after accompanied King William to Ireland.* He was present at that memorable encounter at the Boyne, and by his sagacity was enabled—even on the tented field—to render valuable assistance to his royal master.

It appears that the night before the battle an Irish officer deserted from the enemy; and, being brought before William, stated the number and position of the Irish with such confidence, that the King got uneasy, and told Sir Richard Southwell, his Irish Secretary of State, that James's army were certainly more numerous than he imagined. Southwell immediately went to Cox, and told him what his Majesty said. "Never mind," says Cox, as he hit upon a plan of testing the Jacobite officer's estimate of numbers, "let him be carried through the camp; and then let him inform the King how many men he has with him." This was done; and after being conducted through the several divisions of the Protestant army, he was led to William; and he stated to him that he had—at least—more than double the number of troops he really had. King William saw at once that his new ally was a poor authority in such matters, and gave himself no further concern on the subject.

When the King reached Finglass, a little village within two miles of Dublin,—which he did on the 5th July,—he established his headquarters there. And the next day—upon his return from the city—he issued a proclamation, in which pardon and protection were promised to all labourers, private soldiers, farmers,—as well as to all townsmen and mechanics,—who remained at home; or would surrender their arms and return to their dwellings on or before the 1st of August. The tenants of loyal landlords were told to pay their rents as heretofore; but those who held under the disloyal were directed not to pay anybody, until the Commissioners of the Revenue should duly acquaint them as to who were to be the new owners. The proclamation also declared that those who took an active part in aiding or fomenting the rebellion shall abide the consequences. This celebrated document, which plainly intimated to those in arms against the new Sovereign what they had to expect, was drawn up by Cox; and so exactly was it

---

* Richard Cox, of Clonakilty, appears on King James's Black List of "Persons who have notoriously joined in the rebellion and invasion of this kingdom, are hereby adjudged traitors, convicted and attainted of high-treason, and shall suffer such," &c.

in accordance with the King's own views, that his Majesty was heard to say :—"That Mr. Cox had exactly hit his own thoughts."

When Waterford surrendered, Cox was appointed to the recordership of the city.   But this was only a move to a step still higher; for on the embarkation of his royal patron at Duncannon—in a few months after—he was raised to the Bench ; having been sworn in—on the 15th of September, 1690—as one of the Justices of the Common Pleas.*

The month after he took his seat as a judge he accompanied Robert Rochford, Esq., (one of the Commissioners of the Great Seal) on a Commission of Assize and gaol delivery, to Ardee and Drogheda.   In the March of 1691, the Lord Chief-Justice Reynell and Mr. Justice Cox went as Judges of Assize to Cork and Waterford ; and such was the number of "protections" granted by them at this time, that—in those two counties alone—they amounted to no less than twenty-four thousand.

He had hardly been a judge six months, when he was appointed to an office differing remotely from the usual requirements of judicial life, and demanding a rare foresight, combined with a promptitude and vigilance, which no man—but one possessed of a sagacious understanding and a resolute will—would be fit to undertake.   Although the country swarmed with rapparees, disbanded soldiers of James's army, and the numerous disaffected people who overspread the west of this county, nevertheless, Cox was not deterred by the magnitude of the task before him from entering actively on his duties.   He was selected to fill the post of Governor of the County and City of Cork, on the 1st of May, 1691 ; and on the fourth of the same month he arrived at the scene of his labours.

He proceeded at once to raise and equip eight regiments of dragoons, and to increase the three militia regiments of the county to nine companies each.   Success attended his efforts.   Not only did he protect a frontier extending from Tallow to Sherkin Island—about eighty miles—from the incursions of the Irish without, but he also inflicted a wholesome chastisement on those within.   Upon the latter, he tells us, his troops did much execution and great service ; and took from them so much plunder—ten thousand pounds worth, if not more—as set many of the soldiers on their legs after the war."

---

* The salary of a judge of the Common Pleas—this time—was about £400 per annum.

Although the governor was entitled to a tenth of all the spoil, he refused to take any of it; "contenting himself with acting like a true Englishman, whose heart was in the cause." So pleased was the Government with this act of Cox's disinterestedness, as well as with the talent and energies he displayed in the discharge of his onerous duties, that they presented him with one hundred and fifty pounds, and permanently reduced his quit-rents to half.

Not only were the authorities grateful, but also those whose lives and possessions he protected from destruction. He received the warmest expressions of gratitude, says one of his biographers, from the numerous persons whose property he saved from devastation and pillage.

On the 12th of April, 1690, he was made Deputy-Governor of the Royal Fishery Company; and the next day a member of their Majesty's Privy Council. Upon his return to Dublin from the Summer Assizes in the South—where he went circuit with Judge Reynell—he was knighted by Lord Sidney, the Lord Lieutenant.

In 1693 he was elected a member of the Philosophical Society, upon which occasion he read an essay on the geography of the counties of Antrim and Derry. The same year he visited England, where he met with a very favourable reception from the Lord Treasurer (Godolphin), and the other members of the Government; and received at their hands a substantial proof of their approbation of his services,—they having nominated him on the commission of Irish forfeitures, at a salary of four hundred per annum.

"The strict equity," says Wills, "with which he resisted an oppressive partiality on one side, and the urgency of menace and corruptions on the other, soon drew upon him the clamorous accusations of those by whom the just forfeitures of the recent struggle were looked on as a prey, and the no less dangerous resentment of the leaders of popular feeling."

It was no hard matter to raise a powerful set against him; and when everything was decided by the movements of intrigue, his displacement was a matter of course. One occasion is honourably distinguished, in which an effort was made to seize on the estates of several gentlemen of the county of Galway, in defiance of the articles of the capitulation. Cox insisted on the manifest injustice of such a violation of a solemn treaty, and—by an arbitrary order in council—he saved the Galway gentlemen from losing their estates.

Soon after this a manœuvre was made to destroy Sir Richard's credit with the King, by voting that the forfeitures in Ireland were mismanaged. The effort was a failure, and served to raise the reputation it was designed to destroy.

Cox defended himself against a formidable string of accusations—by statements so full, so well vouched, and so forcibly put forward—that the vote was lost.

In 1694 he went circuit with Chief-Justice Pyne; upon which occasion he came to Cork, where such was the number of rapparees and other lawless people put on their trial for capital offences, and found guilty, that no less than eight-and-twenty of them were condemned to be hanged or burned.*

Upon his retirement from his troublesome and unenviable commissionership in 1698, he turned again to literary pursuits; and—amongst other things—published an essay for the conversion of the Irish. He also wrote his views on a bill then before the Lords, to prohibit the exportation of Irish woollens.

Upon the death of Lord Chief-Justice Hely, of the Common Pleas, in 1701, Cox was promoted to the vacant post; and soon after to a seat in the Privy Council.

The same year his daughter Mary was married to Mr. Allen Riggs;† and the year preceding, his eldest daughter, Amy, married Sir William Maunsell,‡ a Welsh baronet.

When King William died, Sir Richard Cox was sent for by Lord

---

* Mr. Freke, of Rathbarry Castle—now Castle-Freke—was high-sheriff at the time. In her journal, Mrs. Freke (his wife), speaking of this Assizes, says:—"He [Mr. Freke] kept his first Assizes in the city of Cork, where I was with him; and had two-and-twenty proper, handsome men, in new liveries, to attend him, besides those that ran by his horses' side. The two judges were:—Lord Chief-Justice Pyne, and Sir Richard Cox." Again:—"Amongst those sentenced to death was a young Englishman (an only son), whose life I begged—it not being for murder, and his father an estated man in Dorsetshire."

† After Riggs' decease, she married, in 1716, the Rev. Nicholas Skolfield, vicar of Fanlobbus and Drinagh.

‡ Sir William Maunsell agreed to settle an estate in Wales, of the yearly value of £450, on his wife. When this was done, her father was to pay Maunsell her fortune of £1,000, and to allow Lady Maunsell one hundred a-year during her life. Sir Richard was very fond of his daughter Amy, and made her several presents. He gave her a bed and bedstead, for which he paid £37; a chaise, which cost him £10, &c., &c. He was also very kind to Sir William, and paid many of his debts. Amongst the rest, he paid Lawless, the poultry-man, £1 2s. 5d.; Gaskin, for coles [sic], £12 0d. 7d.; Mr. Day, for Coffy [sic], £4 17s. 6d.; Mr. Baker, for sope [sic], £4 16s. 1d.; Alderman Ffrench, for a furnace, 18s. 9d.; Johnson, the attorney, £1 3s. 0d.; for two hundred of turf, at Clonakilty, £1, &c., &c.

Methuen, to consult with him on Irish affairs, but more particularly to consider what measures should be laid before the Irish Parliament; and it was by his advice that, at this time, the first bill was introduced for the recovery of small debts in Ireland; and it was through his exertions the English Parliament legalized the exportation of Irish linens direct to the colonies.

When Mr. Methuen (the Irish Lord Chancellor) was sent as ambassador to Portugal, Sir Richard Cox was appointed to his high office; and thus, by pursuing, as he says, the principles of honesty, religion, sincerity, and virtue, he attained to the highest legal honours in the power of the State to bestow,—having been, on the 6th of August, 1703, sworn in as Lord High-Chancellor of Ireland.

Four days after this he issued writs for the meeting of Parliament on the 21st of September; and, in that great senatorial assembly, the once humble Bandon orphan boy took precedence of the highest nobles of the land, and occupied the enviable position of Speaker of the House of Lords.

The same year the Lord Mayor, Recorder, Sheriff, and Aldermen of Dublin waited on him with the freedom of the city, and presented it to him in a gold box of considerable value.

In 1705 Sir Richard and Lord Cutts were appointed Lords Justices; the Duke of Ormond being the Lord Lieutenant.

In 1706 he was created a baronet by Queen Anne; and the same year he subscribed twenty-five pounds towards repairing one of the churches in Bandon—"being the town where I was born."*

In the April of 1707 the Earl of Pembroke succeeded to the Lord Lieutenancy; and the following June Cox resigned the seals† into his lordship's hands, who assured him that he would not accept them unless with the design of returning him adequate compensation.

One of the objections of the Whigs to Cox's remaining in office was—that he was opposed to the repeal of the Test Act.‡

---

* See his autobiography.

† New seals were sent from England to Sir Richard; the old ones then became his as a matter of right. These weighed upwards of one hundred ounces; and those of the Common Pleas, which also lapsed to him (weight, twenty-five ounces), he got made into a handsome silver bowl, with the Ormond arms on one side, and his own on the other. This, together with the gold box he received from the Dublin corporation, he desired should be preserved as heir-looms in the family.

‡ Cox was a consistant opponent of all those outside the Pale of the Church of England. On this subject, he says:—"The ministry of England having, as I sup-

After vacating his office, he remained some time in Dublin, ready to face any investigation which his enemies might make into his conduct.

They did not keep him long waiting. Numerous accusations were brought against him; all of which he replied to so fully and powerfully, that his accusers retired from the contest—irritated and confused.

He again returned to the country and resumed his pen. He wrote *An Address to those of the Romish Communion in England*; also, *An Enquiry into Religion, and the use of reason in reference to it.*

In 1710, on the displacement of the Whig ministry, he came back to public life, and was made Lord Chief-Justice of the Queen's Bench; which post he filled until the death of Queen Anne, when he and the other Tory judges were obliged to retire.

In 1715 he was called before the Irish Parliament to answer several charges brought against him; but—after a full and patient hearing—he was honourably acquitted of all.*

Again he returned to Dunmanway, where he spent his time in improving his estates, in study, and in acts of charity; and he died there on the 3rd of May, 1733, in the eighty-fourth year of his age.†

"He was endowed with many personal advantages," writes Wills, "and many great qualifications for the professional career in which he rose to eminence."

Sir Richard left a large property to his descendants. Whilst a practising barrister his income was large, and was subsequently much

---

pose, a design to repeal the test here as to Protestant dissenters, and render them capable of holding offices, which it was truly judged I would never promote." Again :—" I was a firm churchman, and stopped a bill for liberty of conscience, by saying I was content every man should have liberty of going to heaven; but I desired nobody might have liberty coming into government but those who would conform to it."

* Cox concludes his autobiography with a sentiment—the truth of which must have more than once forcibly impressed itself on his mind :—" Experience," says this eminent statesman and lawyer, " has convinced me that one ought not to put too great trust in men."

† Sir Richard maintained that name for hospitality for which Dunmanway was famous in former days. Amongst other proofs of which, is the following lament, which we extract from Crofton Croker's interesting researches in the South of Ireland :—" My love and darling, though I was never in your kitchen, yet I have heard an exact account of it. The brown roast-meat continually coming from the fire; the black boilers continually boiling; the cock of the beer barrel for ever running; and if even a score of men came in, no person would enquire their business, but they would give them a place at your table, and let them eat what they pleased, nor would they bring a bill in the morning to them. My love and friend, I dreamed, through my morning slumbers, that your castle fell into decay, and that no person remained in it. The birds sang sweetly no longer, nor were there leaves upon the bushes; all was silence and decay! The dream told me that our beloved one was lost to us; that the noble horseman was gone—the renowned Squire Cox!

larger. His expenditure was in a style befitting his position—but nothing more. All the rest of his income he invested in the purchase of estates.

We have already seen that, even previous to his appointment to the recordership of Kinsale, he had become a land-owner, and from that period—until his death in 1733—there is scarcely a year that he did not add considerably to his possessions.

Sir Richard had four daughters, and two sons—Richard and Michael. The latter was archbishop of Cashel in 1754. He married Anne, daughter of James, son of William, Earl of Inchiquin, and had issue. Richard—the great Sir Richard's eldest son—predeceased him, having died in 1725. He married a daughter of Dean Pomeroy, and left an only son.*

Richard—the second baronet—succeeded, upon the death of his grandfather, in 1733. This gentleman was noted for a blemish, which not only detracted considerably from his personal appearance, but rendered him unwilling to take an active part in the various public events of his day.

It appears that, in the reign of William the Third, there lived in the wild mountainous district of Glounacreme a celebrated Tory, named Donough-na-Malan-bawn (Denis of the white eye-brows). This daring outlaw was the terror of the adjacent country for miles around. No one was safe from his depredations. One time he would burst in the door of a farm-house, and—with horrid threats—demand the farmer's money; and, at another time, he would drive away his cattle, and secrete them in lonely defiles—known only to himself.

Emboldened by repeated success, his audacity prompted him to pay a predatory visit to that great incarnation of law—the veritable Lord Chancellor himself. His usual good luck attended him. He had picked out some of Sir Richard's best cows, and was in the act of driving them

---

* Arthur Pomeroy, Dean of Cork (of the Pomeroys of Engeston, in Devonshire), was educated at Westminster School, and subsequently was a Fellow of Trinity College, Cambridge. He came to Ireland in 1672, as chaplain to the Earl of Essex, Lord Lieutenant of Ireland. He married Elizabeth, daughter of Sir John Osborne, county Waterford, and had issue—besides a daughter married to Richard Cox—a son John, who was rector of St. Paul's, Cork, and archdeacon of that diocese. This John, in 1716, married Elizabeth, daughter of Edmund Donellan, of Roscommon, and by her had, with others, two sons—Arthur and John. Arthur was raised to the Peerage, as Viscount Harburton; and John became a Lieutenant-General, and a Privy Councillor of Ireland.—See *Clerical Records of Cork, Cloyne, and Ross.*— Dr. Brady.

off, when the alarm was given; and Sir Richard's steward—a smart, active fellow, named Shannon—calling to his aid two or three good-men, upon whom he could rely, followed in pursuit.

Finding that Sir Richard's men were on his trail, Donough abandoned the cattle, and endeavoured to escape with his life. But Shannon was resolved not to rest quiet with the mere recovery of his master's property. He now saw a chance of ridding the neighbourhood of this audacious scoundrel, and he determined on doing so if he could.

Failing in his attempt to reach his old quarters, Denis made straight for Inchigeelagh, with Shannon and his party at his heels; and arriving on the edge of one of the lakes, he dashed in, and tried to baffle his pursuers by lying amongst the rushes.

But there were those now on his track who were not to be baffled by ordinary obstacles. Paddling through the water and mud in search of him, he was at length found; and they returned with their prisoner in triumph to the manor-house.

Many were anxious to see the notorious bandit, and crowds hurried to the impromptu tribunal before which he was arraigned. Amongst those who made their way there—anxious to set eyes on this notorious marauder—was the wife of Sir Richard's eldest son. This lady was far advanced in pregnancy at the time; and so much was she affected by the sight of the ill-looking ruffian, that she fainted on the spot.

In some time after she gave birth to a son—the second baronet; and it was found the child's eye-brows bore a strong resemblance to those of Donough-na-Malan-bawn.

Sir Richard was collector of the Port of Cork, and member of Parliament for the borough of Clonakilty. In 1702 he was born; and in 1725 he married Catherine, youngest sister of George Evans (first Lord Carbery). He died in 1766.

He was succeeded by the Rev. Sir Michael Cox, his second son. In 1772 he died, and was succeeded by Sir Richard Eyre Cox, his only surviving son. He married Maria, daughter of John O'Brien, Esq., and niece of the Marquis of Thomond; by whom he had an only daughter—Maria. Sir Richard was drowned—by the upsetting of a boat—in a little lake adjoining the town of Dunmanway, on the 6th of September, 1784.

It seems that the young baronet, like many a young man of large fortune, had more time on his hands than he well knew what to do with.

He was tired of hunting, of shooting, of cards; in fact, of all the ordinary resources of a country gentleman's life. At last a piece of intelligence reached him, which promised a new pastime. He was told that one of those indefatigable missionaries—sent out into the world by John Wesley—was about visiting Dunmanway for the first time.

To lay hands on the unfortunate man, drag him to the adjoining lake, and there half-drown him, would afford rare sport, and help to ingratiate him with the mob at the same time. Accordingly he commenced his preparations; and the day before the preacher was expected he got his boat into the lake, and took an oar himself. Whilst pulling away vigorously, the oar suddenly snapped, and he fell back with great force. Owing to the awkwardness of those that were with him, in their efforts to pull him up, combined with his own unskillfulness, the boat heeled over. His companions struggled for the banks as fast as they could, but made no attempt to save him.*

Cox was lying at the bottom of the boat when it upset; and it is thought that, in turning over, he must, in falling out, have received a blow from it which stunned him, or was forced by its weight into the mud,—the water not being more than three or four feet deep where the accident occurred. When the body was recovered, life was extinct.

The Wesleyans, of course, saw in the untimely fate of the young baronet a signal mark of the displeasure of Providence. If Cox had not taken out his boat, and made arrangements to half-drown one of their preachers, he would not be drowned himself.

'Twas because he had laid his horsewhip across the shoulders of a priest, said the Roman Catholics.

No! said the Established Church people, 'twas because the oar which he used was made on a Sunday, and from a limb cut off one of the venerable elms in the churchyard.

The poet who wrote his epitaph, however, entirely disagrees with the views of the three important bodies of religionists just mentioned. "*De Mortuis nil nisi bonum,*" was his motto, as appears by the following inscription :—

* In Stewart and Revington's life of the Rev. Adam Averell, it is stated that there were many persons present who could swim, but, being awed by a dark cloud which at that time overspread the lake, no effort was made to save him.

" Beneath this stone, in death's cold arms is laid,
   In youth's fair bloom untimely snatched away;
Whose upright soul, approaching heaven surveyed,
   And would not risk it to a longer stay.

" Pure were the feelings of his generous mind;
   His liberal soul of bounty knew no end;
In him the helpless long were taught to find
   A husband, son, a father, and a friend."

Upon the death of this Sir Richard, the title devolved upon Sir Richard (grand nephew of the second baronet), he being the grandson of Colonel Michael Cox, by Anna Maria, only daughter of Daniel Shea, of the West Indies.   He was lost on his way home from Bengal, the ship having foundered, and all hands perishing.   He was succeeded by his brother,

Sir John, the sixth baronet.   Sir John was born in 1771, and died December 23rd, 1832.

Sir George Matthias Cox, Major-General in the Bombay army, succeeded upon Sir John's decease.   He died on the 28th of June, 1838, and the title passed to

Sir Richard, of Castletown, county Kilkenny.   He was son of Michael Cox, of Castletown, by Mary, daughter of Henry, first Lord Dunalley.   He died in 1846, and was succeeded by his uncle,

Sir Francis Cox.   Born 1769; married in 1803, Anna Maria, second daughter of Sir John Ferns.   He had no male issue.   Upon his death, in 1856, his nephew,

Sir Hawtrey, the tenth and present baronet, succeeded.

1652.   Fleetwood,—who became Cromwell's son-in-law, having married the widow of Ireton, who had died of the plague at the siege of Limerick,—was appointed Commander-in-Chief of the army in Ireland.   He was also entrusted with the civil government; but conjointly with four commissioners of the Parliament, namely :— Edmund Ludlow, Miles Corbet, John Jones, and John Weaver.

Amongst the very earliest proceedings of those associated with Fleetwood was that of erecting a high-court of justice, for the purpose of trying those who had performed the first great act in the drama with blood-stained hands.

Commissioners for this purpose were soon sent to several places. Mr. Justice Cook went down to Kilkenny, and opened his court within a building—the walls of which often rang with the declamations of the Irish confederacy.

Lord Chief-Justice Lowther sat in Dublin, and condemned to death Sir Philip O'Neil,—a monster, who, as he himself admitted, was an accomplice in the murder of no less than five thousand of his Protestant fellow-subjects.

Commissions were also opened in Waterford, Cork, &c. ; and one was held in our own town. The commissioners who sat here were :—John Clerke, John Wheeler, and Peter Wallis. No small portion of the evidence taken before them had reference to the case of Mr. John Burrowes, of Balliniscarthy.

Mr. Burrowes held some lands under Dermod-McDaniel Carthy,* *alias* Mac-ni-Crimen, of Ballinorohur Castle ; and upon those he was residing when the rebellion broke out.

It appears he was an extensive sheep farmer, and also possessed cows and horses. But these did not remain long in his possession. Mr. Edmund Hodnett, a gentleman of wealth and station, and who lived on his estate at Courtmasherry, seized on no less than eleven hundred sheep belonging to him and his neighbour, Henry Sampson.

After this, Burrowes foresaw what he had to expect. Having taken his property, he thought the next thing they'd take would be his life. Urged by the instinct of self-preservation—an instinct which rises above all others in the human breast—he applied to his landlord, who lived not a mile distant, to shelter him and his family from the fury of the storm, before whose overwhelming might many a hope fell prostrate for ever ; whose track was marked by roofless homesteads ; and whose very roar—surly and terrifying as it was—was almost stifled by the moaning of men, and the wail of women.

Mac-ni-Crimen did shelter them for a time ; but growing tired of his charge, or wishing to be rid of their pitiful faces, he brought them to the Irish encampment at Killavarrig Hill ; where poor Burrowes, together with his wife and two sons, were taken to the rear of the rebel lines and hanged, by order of Mac-ni-Crimen, their protector.

The whole country was indignant at this gross outrage on the laws of

---

* He was one of the Mac Carthys—Mac-ni-Crimen—a sept of the McCarthy Reaghs, of Kilbrittain. Dermod was married to a daughter of Randal Oge Hurly, by his wife, Catherine Collins. Hurly lived at Ballinacorriga Castle, a few miles to the south of Dunmanway. Tradition states that Faenah Crimen, an ancestor of Dermod-McDaniel, issued leather money from his mint, at Balliniscarthy. Mounteen Castle was built by one of the McCarthy-Crimens, in 1446. Upwards of twenty-eight feet of this castle was taken down to build a house (long since in ruins) for the Rev. Mr. Stawell. A gold ring was found near Mounteen some years ago. It is thus inscribed :—" I live if I [marry you, understood] if noe I dye."

hospitality, and "a general rumour prevailed that Burrowes was basely hanged by Mac-ni-Crimen." The feeling against him was so general and so strong, that he was afraid even to stay within his own castle walls. He fled to the neighbourhood of Dunmanway; and lived for some time at Kildee, within sight of his brother-in-law's castle, hoping by this means to escape the vengeance of those who professed the same religion, and belonged to the same race, as the murdered Burrowes.

Being asked why he left Ballinorohur, he replied that he was timorous to live in his castle, for fear of the garrison at Bandon-Bridge.

The property Mr. Burrowes left behind him soon found its way into strange hands. Dermod Mac Ffinen Reagh got his nag; but the lion's share Mac-ni-Crimen reserved for himself. He admitted that he had three of his trunks, and that they contained gowns of serge, linen, and other apparel; also that he had brass pots of his, pewter dishes, a flock-bed, a feather-bed, a ring, and some household stuff, which Mac-ni-Crimen thought it unnecessary to particularize.

In reply to a question about their money, he averred that he had not seen any of it, except one twenty shillings, which he borrowed from Mrs. Burrowes. That, although the Burroweses were taken to Killa-varrig, it was not he took them there. That it was some of the soldiers belonging to his son (Captain Mac-ni-Crimen's) company who carried them before McCarthy Reagh. In addition, he intimated very plainly that they deserved their fate. The reason why Burrowes was put to death, said he, was because he gave one Tom Stephens, a shoemaker, five pounds to go to Bandon and inform the Bandonians of the weakness of the castle; and that—two days before the death of Burrowes—one Richard Willoughby accused him of it. Moreover, that Burrowes did admit to him (Mac-ni-Crimen) that he sent Stephens to Bandon, but that he gave him no money, or sent him to give any intelligence to the townspeople; and that the wife of Burrowes confessed as much, and no more.

A Newcestown man, named Harrisson, a private in Captain Wood-house's company (Bandon Militia) stated that "he lived in Bandon—being a soldier in Captain Woodhouse's company; and, whilst there, he met Stephens, who told him that Mac-ni-Crimen told Burrowes that he was overpowered by a stronger party, and he must be hanged. Where-upon Burrowes said:—'This is not the promise you made me, or else I might have gone away with the rest of my friends.' Mac-ni-Crimen said he could not help it."

A statement of McCarthy Reagh's—at that time an outlaw, and on the run for his life—was handed to the commissioners. If this statement was true, Mac-ni-Crimen was as innocent of the death of poor Burrowes and his family as those who were not born at the time.

It was McCarthy Reagh's soldiers took the prisoners out of Ballinorohur Castle, and brought them before him. That they (the Burrowes) confessed their treachery to him. That he referred their confession to his commanders, who caused them to suffer. That Mac-ni-Crimen was not even at home when Burrowes was taken away; neither was he present, or even privy to their censure or suffering, to his knowledge.

According to this testimony, it was McCarthy Reagh's commanders caused the Burrowes to be put to death; but according to the evidence of Mac-ni-Crimen's wife, it was McCarthy Reagh, who not only signed the order for their execution, but wrote it.

McCarthy subsequently explained this. He admitted he did write an order for their execution, but it was after they were dead; the order being given upon the importunity of Mac-ni-Crimen's wife, who began to grow apprehensive least a day of reckoning should come.

McCarthy, as he acknowledged, was present at Killavarrig on the day of the murder, and so was Mac-ni-Crimen.

An eye-witness, who was there, relates "that he well remembers when the latter came up and asked McCarthy what he should do with the Burrowses; whereupon McCarthy, who had just heard of his own castle at Kilbrittain being taken, fiercely replied :—" Go you and them to the devil, and afterwards where you will !"

The upshot of the matter was that the commissioners believed Mac-ni-Crimen to be the murderer, and they hanged him accordingly.

Although high-courts of justice—Cromwell's slaughter-houses the Irish called them—were, as we have said before, held in several places in Ireland, for trying those accused of having taken part in the fearful slaughter at the commencement of the great outbreak; yet such was the number of those who had been cut off during the previous ten years, or had perished by pestilence, or had fled from the country, that not more than two hundred were left to perish by the hands of the executioner.

CHAPTER IX.

THE COUNTRY A DESERT—WOLVES ARE NUMEROUS—THE FORFEITURES—WHAT IT COST TO SUPPRESS THE REBELLION—NOT A SINGLE TENEMENT SEIZED IN BANDON—MANY OF CROMWELL'S TROOPERS SELL THEIR GRANTS FOR A TRIFLE—HELL OR CONNAUGHT—HOW CROMWELL QUIETED THE COUNTRY—WHAT HIS COMMISSIONERS THOUGHT OF THE PRIESTS—CROMWELL'S SON, HENRY, ORDERS LANDS, VALUED AT £200 PER ANNUM, TO BE CONFERRED ON THE BANDON CORPORATION—CHARLES THE SECOND DEPRIVES THEM OF SOME OF THEIR GRANTS.

AND now the mighty wave, which had rolled with a devastating sweep from one end of Ireland to the other, had subsided into a tiny ripple. The troubled waters—which had long tossed a reddened spray on their angry surface—were again pellucid; and one may see peace and prosperity—tranquilly awaiting the signal to come up—lying on the silver sands below. But the country was a vast ruin. A traveller might journey thirty miles along the public roads and not see a human face. When Cromwell's troopers were on the line of march, they used to wonder when they saw smoke arise from a chimney, or saw a light at night. Wolves roamed about unmolested; their hereditary enemy—man—was absent; and the wolf-dog,* whose deep bay often rang along the wooded hill-side, or who had often kept faithful watch and ward at the Irish chieftain's castle-gate, had accompanied him, or his sons, to a distant land.

The few persons that were occasionaly to be met with in the rural parts were wandering orphans, whose fathers had embarked for Poland or

---

* Such was the number of wolf-dogs taken away by the Irish officers on their quitting this country for Spain and other places, that the tide-waiters at the different ports received peremptory instructions to seize on all dogs who were about to leave with their masters, and send them to the public huntsman of the district, in order, if possible, the diminish the daily increasing number of wolves.

Spain,* and whose mothers had died of hunger; or were miserable old people, who would quarrel over a putrid carcase raked from a stagnant pool; and some of whom were seen to eat human flesh, cut from the corpse of a fellow-creature, that lay broiling on the fire before them.

Such was the destruction of life, of property, and of everything that tends to make a nation great and prosperous, that it was thought a great portion of the kingdom must necessarily remain a waste for many years to come; whilst others were of opinion it would take ages to restore some of it to the high state of cultivation it had attained to before the war.

The fences were broken down; houses were levelled to the ground; drains, that had carried off the superfluous moisture, were choked; the ditches were filled with briars and rushes, and the meadows with weeds; the dock and the thistle flourished in fields where—in happier days—the wheat shook its golden plume. The wild duck rose lazily from what had once been an ornamental lake; and the flower-garden, where the blooming rose commingled its delicate perfume with the rich fragrance of the honey-suckle, and the savoury aroma of the thyme, was now the home of crawling creatures who trailed their slimy bodies through the rank grass, and of noxious animals, who burrowed holes in the ground, and fed on carrion. Silence was everywhere, and it remained unbroken— save when the raven croaked as it soared into the sky; but the lively twitter of the birds, the buzzing hum of the bee, and the low of cattle, were absent. The latter were nearly all destroyed.

In a letter from the commissioners for Ireland to the English council, they state that " the stock of cattle in this country are almost all spent, so that four parts in five of the best and most fertile lands in Ireland lie waste and uninhabited."

To remedy this evil, cows and sheep were imported from Wales; and

---

* Colonel Christopher Mayo obtained permission to raise, by beat of drum, three thousand Irish soldiers for the service of the King of Spain. Don Ricardo White shipped no less than seven thousand, in detachments, from Waterford, Kinsale, Bantry, and Limerick, for the same prince. Colonel Edward Dwyer commanded three thousand five hundred foot in the pay of the Prince de Conde, and Lord Muskerry took five thousand of them to Poland. Between 1651 and 1654, thirty-four thousand Irish soldiers embarked for foreign ports; and it is computed that about forty thousand left altogether. The regiments, headed by their pipers, marched to the different shipping ports; the hills, as they marched along, perhaps, echoing the mournful strains of :—

" Ha til, ha til, ha til, ha til, mi tulidh."
" We return, we return no more."

See *Cromwellian Settlement of Ireland.*—Prendergast.

so anxious were the authorities to foster their increase, that it even required a license to kill a lamb.*

Those who were the cause of all this ruin and waste, paid the penalty of their misdeeds. Numbers of them had fallen in the field, with arms in their hands. Numbers of them perished in a famine of their own creating; and others were crowding the sea-ports, on their way to distant shores.

As nearly all the Irish gentry, and the greater portion of the old English residents, both within and without the Pale, had united against British rule, the forfeitures were immense. It was found, upon a careful survey, that there were in Ireland, of forfeited lands, 4,758,657 plantation acres;† of these, there were given :—

	Acres.
To adventurers‡	396,054
To the officers and soldiers	1,442,839
To the officers that served his Majesty against rebels in Ireland prior to 1649	278,041
The Duke of York, as regicides' lands	111,015
To Protestants, on provisions by Acts of Settlement and Explanation	383,975
To the bishops, for their augmentations	118,041
Reserved to his Majesty as undisposed of, being set out to adventurers	14,006
Left of coarse lands undisposed of—title of which is doubtful	73,578
Restored to innocent Papists	965,270
Restored to them by special provisions in Acts of Settlement and Explanation	408,083
Set out to them upon their transplantations to Connaught and Clare	667,755
	4,758,657

* " Upon the petition of Mrs. Alice Bulkeley (widow), and consideration had of her old age and weakness of body, it is thought fit, and ordered, that she be, and she is, hereby permitted and licensed to kill and dress so much lamb as shall be necessary for her own use and eating,—not exceeding three lambs for this whole year,—notwithstanding any declaration of the said commissioners of Parliament to the contrary.— Dublin, March 17th, 1652."—*Cromwellian Settlement of Ireland.*

† A plantation acre consists of one hundred and sixty perches, each perch containing twenty-one feet.

‡ The adventurers were those who had advanced several sums of money on the credit of the Act of 17th (Charles the First), for the encouragement of adventurers, whereby it was, amongst other things, enacted :—That such rights, titles, interests, &c., as the rebels in Ireland, or any of them, had, on the 23rd of October, 1641, when the rebellion broke out, or afterwards should have, in any lands or other hereditaments, shall be forfeited to his Majesty; and should be deemed adjudged, vested, and taken to be in the actual and real possession of the said King, his heirs and successors, without any office or Inquisition thereof to be found. And for reducing the rebels, and distributing their lands amongst such persons as should advance money and become " adventurers " in the reduction, two and a-half million of acres were to be assigned and allotted in the following proportion, viz. :—Each adventurer of £200 was to have a thousand acres in Ulster; of £300, a thousand acres in Connaught; of £450, a thousand acres in Munster; and of £600, a thousand acres

From this it will be seen that nearly half of the forfeited estates were restored to their former owners; and the rest,—namely, 2,717,549 acres,—valued averagely, good and bad as they were, at a shilling an acre (their full value in those days), gives a yearly income of £135,877 9s. 0d. Computing the cost of subduing the rebellion at £22,191,258—Borlace's estimate*—it will be perceived that the lands retained by the government cost them over one hundred and sixty years' purchase.

Now, when we remember that the ordinary rate of purchase for lands was but ten years, there is no one can accuse the authorities of either cupidity or unnecessary severity.

The forfeitures in the county of Cork amounted to 98,000 acres; exceeding those of every other county in Ireland—save Cavan, where they amounted to 163,000 acres.

In our own immediate neighbourhood they were most inconsiderable. In the parish of Ballymodan, in which lies the southern portion of the town, the only lands escheated were:—Classafree and Ballinlough, belonging to Daniel McCarthy-More; Lissefooke, owned by Daniel Coppinger; Knockamortela, by Daniel McOwen Carthy; and six gneeves of West Tulle-Eland, the property of Charles McCarthy-Reagh; and in Kilbrogan—the parish containing the northern portion of Bandon—there was not a seizure made of a single foot of ground.

The loyalty and—we may add—the devotion of the "ancient and loyal borough" to the English interest was more conspicuous than that of any other town in the whole kingdom—save, perhaps, a few in Ulster.

Tenements and messuages were wrested from the rebels in Dublin—the very seat of the government itself; in Galway, in Limerick, and in Waterford; and, in the very county in which we live, there was not a town of note—but one—that did not contain many rebellious subjects.

---

in Leinster (English measure). Each acre was to pay a yearly quit rent to the crown, as follows:—In Ulster, a penny an acre; Connaught, three-halfpence; Munster, twopence-farthing; Leinster, threepence. And every adventurer who, within three months after allotment, that shall possess, in Leinster, a thousand acres; in Munster, fifteen hundred; in Connaught, two thousand; and in Ulster, three thousand, was to have power to erect a manor, with a Court Baron and Court Leet, and all other privileges belonging to a manor, deodands, fugitive's goods, &c.

* This amount is made up of specie sent over from England, deficiencies in customs and excise, money expended in raising armies, purchase of provisions, clothing, arms, loss of rents, &c., &c., independent altogether of the losses caused by the destruction of houses, orchards, corn, cattle, improvements, household stuffs, &c., &c.; and the loss of life, which was enormous.—See Borlace.

Several premises and houses were taken from disaffected people in the city of Cork; in Bajse Street, and near the Clock-gate, in Youghal; every house in Cloyne; and in the very town adjoining us—our next-door neighbour, in fact—there were houses in Cork Street and outside the Cork-gate, in the Market Place and outside Nicholas'-gate, in High Fisher Street and in Low Fisher Street,—in truth, Kinsale was almost entirely bereft of its old proprietors, by reason of its active partizanship with the disloyal.

We have said that every town of note in this county contained many rebellious subjects, but one—that one was Bandon. There was not a rebel lived within the walls* on either side of the river that flowed through the centre of the old borough; or that was the owner of a street in it, or of a lane, or of a house, or even of a pig-stye. And although the population was large—larger even a dozen years before the rebellion broke out than it is at the present day—there is not on record the name of a single individual, descended from any of the plantees, charged with showing sympathy to, much more co-operating with, those who would exterminate their kith and kin.

The town was free from forfeitures, but not the county. In the adjacent parish of Innoshannon:—Knockawroe, Drounkeene, and Curranure, belonging to Daniel McCarthy-More; Ballymountaine the property of Charles McCarthy-Reagh; Coolmorine, Farrencarrigg, Raghnaroughy, Knockmullane, Cloherane, and Controverty, of Patrick Roche, of Poulnalonge (Shippool Castle), Killinecallen ahd Annaghmore, of John Long, of Mount-Long, high-sheriff of the county in 1641; Cornitrishane and Rincurran, of Phillip Barry Oge; Dunkerine, of Robert Oge; Curraghboy bog, of Phillip Barry. In the parish of Rathclaren:—The lands of Ballycatten, Clonderine, Burren, Ardacrow, Rathclaren, Clonduffe, Shanakiel, Garrenffreene, part of the estate of McCarthy-Reagh, Ffinen McDermod, and Daniel McCormac Carthy; Gortnahorna and Garrangroorig, belonging to James Coppinger; Maulmane, to Daniel McOwen Carthy; Knocknamartela, to Owen McFfinen Carthy; Gloreene and Lisheeneleigh, to Florence McCarthy. In Desert:—Maulbrack, belonging to Donogh Oge Murphy; and the lands belonging to Joan Regan,

---

* There was a Dr. Desmond, John Splaine (who is described as a Frenchman), and Teige Carthy; these were deposed against as being rebels, or having uttered rebellious sentiments; but they had fled almost before the rebellion began, and could not be caught. They lived in the suburbs, as no Irish or Roman Catholics were permitted to reside inside the walls.

McFfinen Carthy, James Roche, McCarthy-Reagh, Dermod O'Mahowne, Collohan McKnoghan Carthy, Murrough McSheehy, &c.

1653. When peace was firmly established, the army was no longer necessary, and the disbanding of the regiments began. The surveys of all the escheated lands being finished, the district which had fallen to the lot of a regiment was marked out. Commissioners, who were appointed for the purpose of carrying out the allotting there, attended on a certain day;* and there, in the presence of the officers and men, the drawing was proceeded with. As each lot was drawn, it was opened and read aloud, in the hearing of all present. It was then filed, and its contents duly recorded. They then drew another lot, and so on, until all were completed;† after which they crossed over into the lands of the regiment whose lands began at the boundaries of the former, and so on.

The plan of setting down each regiment by itself, and not mixing them up together, had many advantages. The officers and men knew one another—an *esprit de corps* bound them together. A comrade would be more likely to assist a comrade than a man he never saw before; and should their services be again sought for, the whole regiment could take up arms, and march at a moment's notice.

The officers and several of the men seemed to have taken to their new mode of life well enough; but the majority of the latter did not value their grants. It may have been that they were reluctant to undertake the labour which their farms required, or were unable or unwilling to supply the capital necessary to purchase cattle or build a house; or they may have preferred returning to England. Be that as it may, they did not care about them.

One heedless fellow is said to have staked an estate worth, at the present day, over a thousand per annum, upon the turn up of a card; and his comrade is reported to have parted with the adjoining estate to the winner for five jacobuses and a white horse. Of another, it is

---

* See *Cromwellian Settlement of Ireland.*

† If the allottees could not agree among themselves about their various allotments, they used to box for them (*i.e.*—resort to the lottery-box). It is from this circumstance the term boxing is derived—a term now applied only to those who settle their disputes not with the box, but with the fist. In the *Cromwellian Settlement of Ireland* is an extract from an order, which states:—" Or if the discovered forfeitures may be set out at unequal rates, whether there shall be a free and open boxing for them indifferently, as whereby one that has received his clear satisfaction in Munster may box for the dubious lands of Ulster."

told, that he disposed of his grant for a broad sword and a silver tobacco stopper ;* and a body of horse soldiers are alleged to have actually handed over the entire of their allotments, to the captain of their troop, for a barrel of ale.

Although, in the eyes of several of the new owners, those estates were scarcely worth anything, it was with great reluctance the old proprietors parted with them. Crossing the Shannon, and setting down in the wilds of Connaught,† was nearly as bad as death itself.

It was in the banquetting hall of yon dismantled castle that the forefathers of the late owner used to entertain the great head of their house, and his princely retinue, with almost regal pomp. It was from that window, which looks towards the west, that its late possessor had oft, in his boyish days, watched the setting sun flush the neighbouring plains with a blended colouring of crimson and gold. It was through that great gate his fathers rode out to the foray and the chase ; and it was through those portals they were borne, one by one, accompanied by a long line of sorrowing clansmen, to their graves.

They knew that they must abide the chances of war—especially a war began by themselves ; and now that they were vanquished, at an enormous outlay of blood and treasure, they could not reasonably expect to escape the consequences of their own avowed and deliberate acts. Nevertheless, they clung to the old sod with a tenacity irreconcilable with the recklessness with which they periled it. Although instructions were given that they should be settled upon lands as nearly as possible resembling those they had lately held, yet they could not endure the thought of transplanting, and they inundated the commissioners with applications to be left stay behind.

Margaret Barnwall had long been troubled with a shaking palsy; Mary Archer had an aged father who would be suddenly brought to his grave, wanting his accustomed accommodation ; Lady Margaret Atkinson

---

* Vide Crofton Croker's *South of Ireland.* Cromwell's troopers tempted purchasers in every direction. In the neighbouring barony of Muskerry, one Thomas Crooke assigned to John Bayly, his heirs, &c., the lands of Castlemore, 234a. 3r. 8p., and Cloghduffe, 240a., subject to an annual crown rent of £7 4s. 3d., for the sum of fifty pounds.

† It is stated that in one immense district, containing thirteen hundred ploughlands, there were only forty that were inhabited. Even the castles that were in the country were either blown up by gunpowder or demolished. It appears, by the petition of Edmond Dogherty, mason, that he was paid by the Loughrea commissioners at the rate of fifty shillings each for demolishing thirteen castles.—*Cromwellian Settlement of Ireland.*

was of great age; Elinor Butler was a widow, and had a helpless family; the Dowager Lady Lowth was of great age and impotency; John, Lord Baron Power, of Curraghmore, for the twenty years past was distracted and destitute of all judgment; Lord Viscount Ikerrin had great weakness and infirmity of body. Others sought to be left off upon the grounds that they had performed important services for the government, and were reluctant to go to Connaught least their lives should be endangered on that account. Robert Plunkett had given information against several prisoners now in the Marshalsea, and, therefore, he was afraid to risk his safety in Connaught. This was a very common excuse. Major Cavanagh and his brother, according to their own account, were most inoffensive to the English; Mrs. White used to entertain English officers at her house; Mary Butler gave information of an ambushment of the Irish to cut off the English, &c., &c.*

Many, as we have said, begged to be allowed to remain at the English side of the Shannon, but others stubbornly refused to stir a foot. This was not to be borne. The commissioners were determined to let the Irish see they were in earnest. Accordingly, a court-martial sat in St. Patrick's Cathedral, Dublin; and amongst others brought before them was Mr. Edward Hethrington, of Kilnemanagh. Hethrington was accused of a breach of the Declaration Order of the 30th of November, and for disobedience to several commands to transplant. He was found guilty and hanged; and least there should be any mistake about what he was hanged for, a placard on his breast, and another on his back, plainly informed the public it was " for not transplanting."†

It fared ill enough with those who did transplant, and thereby preferred the alternative of Connaught to hell. Upon their arrival in Connaught, some sold their assignments for a trifle, and endeavoured to to make their escape. Their altered circumstances had such an effect upon others that they lost their reason. Others, in despair, killed themselves; and more, leaving allotments and all behind them, fled in horror to Spain.‡

---

* Vide *Cromwellian Settlement of Ireland*.

† Ibid.

‡ See *The wail of the Irish Catholics, or the groans of the whole clergy and people of Ireland, in which is set forth an epitome of the cruelties practised upon the Catholics of Ireland by the Godless English, under the arch-tyrant, Cromwell, the usurper and destroyer of the three realms of England, Ireland, and Scotland*, by Friar Maurice Morison.

As a great many of the male population in the kingdom, who had survived the great rebellion, had either joined the armies of foreign States or were forced into exile, the number of women remaining behind were vastly in excess of the men. In order to save the former from immorality, and, at the same time, afford them an opportunity of earning their bread, it was ordered :—" That Irishwomen, as being too numerous now,—and, therefore, exposed to prostitution,—be sold to merchants, and transported to Virginia, New England, Jamaica, or other countries, where they may support themselves by their labour." Many of them were accordingly sent over; and so acceptable were they to the sugar-planters, that Cromwell wrote to the Major-General of the forces in Ireland to try and secure no less than a thousand young Irishwomen for Jamaica alone.

It was no difficult matter, at this time, to procure plenty of females to whom employment would be advantageous in many respects, as there were crowds of young widows and deserted wives wandering about in the neighbourhood of cities and towns, without any visible means of living. Boys and girls were also in request, but the women were preferred, provided " they were marriageable, and not past breeding."[*]

By getting rid of the surplus population, the commissioners expected to get rid of those who would be likely to prove a source of annoyance to the plantees in Ireland; and, by the same stroke of policy, hoped to place them where they could effectually assist the planters in America.

With this intent, they sent over agents to England, and contracted with various parties for a supply of labour for the Transatlantic colonies. They agreed with Messrs. Sellick and Leader, of Bristol, to furnish them with two hundred and fifty women of the Irish nation, between the ages twelve and forty-five, and three hundred men, between twelve years old and fifty, to be taken to New England.[†] They agreed with Messrs. North and Johnson to deliver them all the wanderers—men and women— and such other Irish, within the precincts of the governors of Carlow, Kilkenny, Clonmel, Wexford, Ross, and Waterford, as could not prove

---

[*] *Cromwellian Settlement of Ireland.*

[†] These were to be shipped at Kinsale, and to be procured in the country within twenty miles of Cork, Youghal, Kinsale, Waterford, and Wexford. Lord Broghill thought the county of Cork could supply them all. Accordingly, orders were issued for the county to be searched for the requisite number of wanderers and persons who had no ostensible means of livelihood. When seized, they were to be taken to Kinsale.

they had a settled course of industry,—all children in the hospitals and workhouses, and all prisoners,—to be transported by them to the West Indies.

Henry Cromwell, in reply to a letter from Mr. Secretary Thurloe, stated that from one thousand five hundred to two thousand boys, from twelve to fourteen years of age, could be supplied; adding, "we could well spare them; and who knows but it might be a means to make them Englishmen—I mean Christians." In fact, such was the number of people sent to the West Indies by the commissioners, that—so late as the beginning of the present century—traces of them were to be found there; and in one place in particular—the Island of Mountserrat—the Irish tongue was a common means of communication.*

Although Ireland was cleared of a great deal of her old inhabitants, she was not deprived of them all. Neither was it the intention of the Parliament that she should, as appears by the Act for the Settling of Ireland, in which they declared that "it was not their intention to extirpate the whole nation."

Many of those who refused to cross to the Irish side of the Shannon took to Torying. Although they were well aware of the penalty attached to being caught, nevertheless, those outlaws were both daring and desperate. They used to "run out" from the mountains, plunder and murder the new settlers, within hail of the English garrisons, and then retreat to their almost inaccessible hiding-places.

Cromwell resorted to severe measures to suppress these marauders. When Symonds and his two sons—who had been faithful soldiers of his—had settled close to the garrison of Timolin, the Tories attacked them in the open day, and barbarously murdered one of the sons, he issued peremptory orders to send all the Irish inhabitants of the town of Timolin, and all those dwelling in the neighbourhood—without even one exception—straight to Connaught.

One would think this wholesale punishment would be sufficient to quiet a country—for a generation or two at the least; but it was not so. Soon after another murder was committed at Lockagh, in the same county; and Cromwell became more rigorous still. All the Irish on the townland were seized, and tried by court-martial. Four of them were hanged for the murder, or—what appeared to him just as bad—not exerting themselves to prevent it; and the rest, amounting to thirty-

---

* *Cambrensis Eversus.*—Ed. Dr. O'Kelly.

seven, including two priests, were transported in one batch to the sugar plantations of Barbadoes.

Murder, however, was not the main object of the Tories. They may kill a hundred Englishmen, and still be without a meal of victuals. It was the Englishmen's sheep, their oxen, and their cattle, that they wanted, and they pounced upon these with the rapacity of ravening wolves.

To follow the marauders to their bogs and wilds would be an act of foolhardiness, which would, probably, cost the pursuers their lives; therefore, some other means must be found to stay those desperadoes. When the Tories* drove away a lot of the settler's cattle, the value of them was demanded from those of their kindred who lived under English protection; and, if not paid, it was levied off their goods and chattels. Should the authorities, however, not be able to identify the spoilers, or should the relatives of the spoilers be too poor to pay, then the amount was assessed upon all the Irish in the barony where the murder, or robbery, or outrage, was committed. Nor was it always confined even to them. The Irish, through whose baronies the Tories passed and repassed on their predatory excursions, were also forced to contribute, unless it was proved that they strenuously opposed the marauders; or should, by following them with hue and cry, or by giving notice to the next garrison, prove that they were in earnest.

The Irish priesthood were always looked upon with suspicion by Cromwell. "It had now been manifest, from many years' experience," said the commissioners of the Parliament, "that Popish priests held it to be their duty to estrange the minds and affections of the people from the authority and government of the English Commonwealth."

During the rebellion, whenever the ardour of the Irish began to flag, their clerical leaders were sure to stir it up anew. They were amongst the first to take up arms, and amongst the last to lay them down. The authorities were well aware of this; and of the great influence they possessed over their flocks, and how they used it. Consequently, whenever any of the rebellious forces sought to make terms with the Parliamentarians, the latter—whoever else they may stipulate to show mercy

---

* The plundering propensities of these daring desperadoes are still held here in felonious remembrance. Should the cat run off with a kidney or a mutton chop intended for breakfast, one may expect to see the cook give chase; and should she not be able to catch her, the chances are that she will avenge herself upon the feline miscreant by calling her a " Tory."

to—invariably excepted the priests. As high as twenty pounds was offered for the discovery of some of their hiding-places, and it was often death to give them a night's lodging. When they were caught, they were generally delivered over to some person who would pay the reward offered for their apprehension, and undertake—at the same time—to send them to some country at peace with the Commonwealth.*

But it was found many of them made their way back again. To prevent this, the commissioners began transporting them to Barbadoes, in order "to prevent them returning to their own and the people's destruction." Notwithstanding that Ireland must have been a most uncomfortable place for Romish ecclesiastics to live in at this time, yet they were most unwilling to leave it. Several—who were prisoners at Carrickfergus—offered to become Protestants, if they were permitted to remain behind. Rather than quit the kingdom, Father Neterville preferred the ghastly companionship of the dead—for a whole year—in his father's tomb. Father Forde lay hid among the rushes and tall grass of an immense bog, where he celebrated mass, and imparted a rudimentary instruction, to the few people who contrived to escape the quick eye of the Cromwellians, and visit him in his unwholesome den. In spite of all the precautions used, said Father Quin,† no wild beast was ever hunted with more fury, nor tracked with more pertinacity— through mountains, woods, and bogs—than the priest.

When the commissioners were rewarding those who had fought manfully in the great struggle from which the country had just emerged, they did not forget Bandon. In a letter from the Lord-Deputy (Henry Cromwell) and Council—dated February 15th, 1657—to the Surveyor-General of Lands, they direct him to prepare forthwith a particular of lands of the yearly value of two hundred pounds sterling; and that a patent may be granted for the same, provided they (*i.e.* the corporation) give a general release of all of what is due to them from his Highness. In compliance with these instructions, the following lands were bestowed on the town:—

No.
1. The lands of Rine and Lackyduffe, containing 365 acres, formerly the property of Daniel Carty,* I.P. [Irish Papist].

---

* *Cromwellian Settlement of Ireland.*

† Vide *Canbrensis Eversus.* annotated by Dr. O'Kelly. Father Quin was an eye-witness of the events which he describes. See *State and Condition of the Catholics of Ireland, from the year* 1652 *to* 1656, by Father Quin, of the Society of Jesus.

2. Tughidullane and Ballintemple, containing 201 acres, formerly the property of Garrett Arundell,* I.P.
3. Dorrery, containing 106 acres, formerly the property of Dermod Cullinane,* I.P.
4. West Croony and East Bally-mac-William, formerly the property Dermod Carthy,* I.P.
5. Bally-mac-Redmond, containing 88 acres, formerly the property of Teige Mac Shane Crowly,* I.P.
6. Richardstown, *alias* Richfordstown, formerly the property of John Oge Shea, I.P.
7. Concanmore and Ballyuargan, containing 201 acres, formerly the property of Andrew Arundell and Edmond O'Shea, I.P.
8. Ballinglannig and Attery, formerly the property of Charles McDaniel Carty,* I.P.
9. Cardonybeg, formerly the property of Owen McDermot Carty.*
10. Curryleigh, containing 194 acres, formerly the property of James Fitz-Edmond Barrett.*
11. Chirryheghy, containing 200 acres, formerly the property of James Coppinger and of Richard Hale Coppinger.*
12. [Illegible], formerly the property of Nicholas and James Gold-lyinoge.*
13. Killnocehsheny, containing 141 acres; West Ballneady, 162 acres, barony Barrett's, formerly the property of Daniel McCarthy.*
14. Pallice,† containing 68 acres, Barony Barryroe, formerly the property of Daniel, I.P., and William O'Shea, I.P.
15. Lislee, containing 322 acres, formerly the property of William Barry,* I.P.
16. Agha, containing 422 acres, formerly the property of William Barry,* I.P.
17. Kilbarry,‡ one ploughland and a half, barony Muskerry, formerly the property of Lord Muskerry.*

---

* Those marked thus were indicted for treason at the great sessions held at Youghal, on the 2nd of August, 1642, before Lord Cork and his sons; and were subsequently outlawed in the King's Bench.

† The lands of Pallice, Lislee, and Agha, were leased for a term of twenty-one years from the 21st November, 1658, to Edward Yeemens.

‡ Claugh-mac-Cow was let on behalf of the corporation, by Samuel Browne, Esq., provost (he was also a captain and an attorney), to Teige Oge, Bantry, Moyle Murry McNeale, and the rest of the tenants on the lands, for half-a-crown an acre.—Date, 1657. This ploughland, together with Currybihagh, Kilbarry, Cooleduffe, and Pollericke, were not of the lands given to the town to secure it £200 per annum; they were in addition to those given for that purpose. Currybihagh contained 240 acres. Previous owner—Lord Muskerry—was subject to a rent of £10 yearly to the Government. The patent is dated April 21st, 1657. It sets forth that it was "An agreement between the commissioners, for the setting of lands, houses, &c., belonging to his Highness and the Commonwealth, and Samuel Browne, Esq., provost of Bandon, on the other, about the lands of Currybihagh; one ploughland set unto him for the use of the corporation, consisting of 240 acres,—formerly belonging to Lord Muskerry,—lying in the barony of Muskerry, for the sum of ten pounds per annum."

18. Cooleduffe, barony West Muskerry, formerly the property of Lord Muskerry.*
19. Pollericke, one ploughland, barony Muskerry, formerly the property of Lord Muskerry.*

The portion of Lord Muskerry's estate, which was conferred on the Bandonians, was subject to an annual rent of £22 10s., which became due on the 1st of May, and was received by the high-sheriff of the county—"By virtue of authority of assistance directed to him out of the Court of Exchequer."

When Lord Muskerry was restored to his blood and honours by Charles the Second, he was also restored to the greater portion of his estates; and, amongst the rest, to the five ploughlands last mentioned. The Bandon burgesses complained sadly of this; and they declared that by reason of their poverty—caused by taking away that which they had well-earned—they were unable to wage law with Lord Barrymore,* a nobleman of whom they justly complained that he had endeavoured to deprive them of lands bestowed on them by patent.

Lord Orrery, who always stood by them, now exerted himself again on their behalf; and with such success, that he obtained an order from his Majesty to the Chief Governor of Ireland, to set out some lands to the Bandon corporation in lieu of those that were restored to the the Earl of Clancarthy. The corporation wrote a warm letter of thanks to Lord Orrery on this occasion, in which they refer to "his lordship's many noble favours;" and well they might. Notwithstanding that they were entitled to compensation for the lands taken from them, yet they were too much tainted with Cromwellianism to be in favour with the Stuarts. Although—as we have just seen—Charles did write to the Lord Lieutenant to reprise them, the latter never did so.

Several of Cromwell's troopers settled in and about the neighbourhood of Bandon, where many of their descendants are to be found at the present day, and possessed, too, of many of the characteristics of their famous forefathers. Colony after colony of Englishmen have come over to this country from time to time, but we have had no body of settlers possessed of such hostility to the native Irish as the Parliamentary soldiery.

---

* Lord Barrymore endeavoured to deprive them of the lands of Rine and Lacky-duffe, but Lord Orrery decided in favour of the corporation. Nevertheless, Barry-more took possession again; and when Captain Freke entered by force as tenant of the corporation, and repossessed himself of the lands, Lord Barrymore had him indicted and tried for it at the Bandon Quarter Sessions.

This may have arisen from their having witnessed the wholesale destruction of property effected by them, and the slaughter of the thousands of people—the vast portion of whom they could never accuse of doing them any harm—which they accomplished by the various means previously described.   From whatever cause it has arisen—it has existed, and exists still.

CHAPTER X.

BALLINACORRIGA CASTLE—RANDAL OGE HURLY AND HIS DESCENDANTS—TEIGE MAC CARTHY-DOWNY, OF THE TOOHER—PATRICK ROCHE (FITZ-RICHARD), SHIPPOOL CASTLE.

ALL the Irish gentry—in this and the adjoining neighbour-hoods—who sided with the rebels in the last great war, were dispossessed. Foremost amongst these was Randal Oge Hurly, of Ballinacorriga Castle. His father also (Randal Oge Hurly) married Catherine, daughter of O'Cullinane of Timoleague, who was physician to Mac Carthy-Reagh of Kilbrittain Castle, and was one of the family of the O'Cullinanes—a family which had for many generations supplied physicians to the royal house of the Mac Carthys.*

This Randal Oge,† who built the castle of Beallenecarrigy in 1585, died in 1631, as appears from an Inquisition held in Bandon on the 16th of September in that year, and was succeeded by his son, Randal Oge. The castle is a strong, square tower, nearly one hundred feet in height, and stands on the crest of a bold, bare rock, which rises upwards of forty feet above the waters of an adjoining lake. A few yards in its front is a small circular tower. This formerly guarded an angle of the wall which enclosed the castle, of which not a trace is now to be found, as the wall itself, and the three other towers at the other angles, were removed to aid the building of the adjacent flour-mill. The lower part

---

* So notorious was their skill in curing the many ills which the flesh is heir to, that whenever a poor fellow was past all hope, one would often hear it said that even an O'Cullinane couldn't save him.

† He had a daughter married to Dermod McDaniel Carty, *alias* Mac-ni-Crimen, of Ballinoroher Castle. The same who was hanged at Bandon for the murder of Mr. Burrowes and his family.—See chapter 8.

of the interior of the castle does not differ materially from those of similar structures to be seen elsewhere; but the upper floor contains two large windows, and these are adorned with various illustrations, in relief. On the arch of one is a representation of the Crucifixion, and the Virgin and child; and on the other, the letters R.M. CC. (the initials of Randal Murrilah* and Catherine Cullinane), the date of the castle's erection, a ladder, a heart transfixed with crossed swords, a scourge, a cock, and a pot.

The ladder, the heart, and the scourge, we could easily refer to incidents in sacred story, but the cock and the pot fairly puzzled us. We could not make out head or tail of the cock and the pot. At one time we imagined the pot was typical of the caldron of boiling oil into which St. John was thrown at Patmos. Then we thought it had some reference to the great feast of Belshazzar; and then again we supposed it to be allegoric of the pot of manna in the ark of the tabernacle in the wilderness; but as for the cock, we felt convinced at once that he symbolized the triumph of Christianity,—that he represented, in fact, Christianity crowing over prostrate Paganism.

All our conjectures, however, were wrong, as appears by the following tradition—the tradition upon which those two emblems are founded, and which has the merit of being devoutly believed by a great many. After mentioning the well-known circumstances connected with the seizure of Christ, and his being brought into the palace of the high priest, the legend asserts that Peter, who staid in an outside apartment, was warming himself by the fire; and after stating the fact, as given in Holy Writ, of the three denials given by him of any knowledge of our Lord, it avers,—that scarce had he uttered the last denial, when a cock, who was being cooked in the pot for the high priest's supper, on the fire near which Peter stood, suddenly jumped out of the boiling water upon the floor, and crowed in his face!

---

* Murrilah—the Irish of Hurly—is supposed to be a corruption of Murircillah (the great small flood). The name is said to have been derived from the following circumstance:—The two sons of an Irish chieftain were out hunting one day along the banks of the Bandon river; when the stag, which they were pursuing, came to the river, he dashed in, and swam to the opposite side. The two young men—who were step-brothers—speedily arrived at where the stag crossed over, and the eldest of the two reined up his horse, being afraid to trust himself in the swollen waters. The younger asked him why he did not cross over. He told him he was afraid to do so. "Oh, its only a Murircillah!" said the young horseman, as he fearlessly plunged in, and got safe across. In some part of this country the Hurlys are still called Murrilahs, or Urrilahs, and in other places Hurly is pronounced Murly.

It does not, however, say whether the truth-loving chanticleer emerged from his warm corner scalded to the bone with indignation and hot-water; or whether he was dressed, as at present, with his liver tucked under one wing, and his masticating apparatus under the other. It simply unpots him, places him right in front of Peter, and there it leaves him.

The castle, as has been previously mentioned, was built in 1585, and —if what we have been told is correct—at a comparatively small cost to the founder; but by a contrivance which, however ingenious it may have been, had neither honesty, nor even the semblance of fair-play, to recommend it.

Having quarried the stone, and collected all the other materials necessary for going to work, he sent in every direction for stonecutters and masons. These were very unwilling to go to him. Where the building was to be erected was in a remote place in the wilds of Carbery; where no human face was scarcely ever seen, save that of the wood-kern, or some unhappy outlaw who was flying from place to place, with a price set upon his head; and where the silence of the night was oft-times broken by the ominous screech of the owl, and the howlings of hungry wolves.

Nothing could coax the workmen to move except high wages. These Hurly readily promised; and in course of time a considerable number of artificers arrived, and went to work. Randal took great care of them. He had cabins erected for their accommodation; he laid in a goodly store of oxen and hog's meat; and made them as comfortable as circumstances, in that out of the way place, would allow.

The men worked hard, and with a good-will. Randal Hurly treated them well, and they were determined to treat him well in return. Occasionally a married man drew some of his wages to send home to his family, but the great bulk of what was due to the men was left untouched. They looked forward with pleasure to the large sum that would be theirs on the completion of the edifice; and how he might turn his to the best account, may have often engrossed a poor fellow's thoughts when he ought to have been asleep.

At length, when the castle was finished, and everything completed within and without, Randal Oge gave a great feast. Not only were all the workmen invited, but also all the tenants and gallow-glasses belonging to himself and his kindred. There was no one refused—all accepted

14

his hospitality; but it was observed that the tenants and gallow-glasses of Randal and his friends came fully armed, thereby to add additional lustre to the splendour of the great banquet that was to celebrate the completion of the grandest of all the castles of the Murrilahs.

After they had all enjoyed a bountiful meal, and had drunk the health of the founder of Ballinacorriga in bowls of usquebaugh, Randal told his guests to come outside the walls. They readily came, expecting to find fresh incentives to fun and frolic out of doors. He then ordered the gates to be closed, and the gallow-glasses to be drawn up under arms. Calling his workmen to him, he desired them to produce their tally-sticks, in order that he may see if he owed them anything. As each man produced his stick, Randal produced a set-off in the shape of board and lodging; and many of them, he alleged, were in his debt.

What could they do? They dare not utter an angry word; and the two or three who ventured to look cross, got an unmistakable hint, in the form of a dozen pike-heads placed in such disagreeable proximity to to their ribs, that they regretted even that display of disapprobation of the method Randal Oge adopted of paying off his creditors.

Having gone through all the claims, or at least as many of them as were presented to him, he ordered the workmen to leave his country at once, telling them that if he caught any of them there after nightfall— then he pointed significantly to the grim warriors who stood behind him. The poor masons understood him thoroughly, and they put many a weary mile between them and Ballinacorriga Castle before the sun arose next morning.

Catherine O'Cullinane, the wife of the founder of the castle, is traditionally stated to have been a great lady. The prevailing weakness of the sex is said to have been strongly exemplified in her. She was vain and over-bearing. Indeed, so fond was she of display, that she rarely ventured outside the threshold of her lordly residence without being accompanied by a bevy of young maidens,—some of whom acted as her train-bearers, and others were in attendance to pay that obeisance which the dignity and unbending hauteur of their almost royal mistress demanded.

Her haughtiness is still often the theme of many a winter fireside in Eastern Carbery, and there is no "ould story" fills the chimney-corner with a more attentive group of listeners, than that which has for its subject the Ban-Tierna of Ballinacorriga.

The peasantry glory in her.   Looking back, through the gloom with which intervening centuries have shadowed the past, some of them still see the old harper sitting on the stone bench in front, near the castle-gate; and see his fingers glide over the strings, as he sings of the foray and the chase, and of red battle-fields—where oft a chieftain of their race fell in the fierce fight.   Others behold that comic-looking piper playing a humorous tune for the crowd of dancers, whose boundless merriment never seems to tire; and more look on the Tierna riding out of the great gate of the bawn, with his huntsmen and his horses, his carrows and his dogs—and quickly recognize among the latter a leash or two of tall, wiry-haired animals to hunt the wolves, now nightly becoming more dangerous.

The "stranger" was almost unknown then throughout the length and breadth of Hurly's country.   These were the good old times, when Catherine O'Cullinane was in the heyday of her glory.   Her memory is still treasured up in the affections of the people in the neighbour-hood, and they pay her the unaffected homage of their hearts.

Nevertheless, the Ban-Tierna was not absolute perfection, even in their eyes; her haughtiness must draw down a severe punishment upon her—and it did.

Late one night, a poor beggar woman—followed by her children—knocked at the castle-gate, and asked for alms.   Catherine herself looked through the wicket, and demanded to know what she wanted. She was a widow, and sought for food and a night's lodgings for herself and her helpless offspring.

"Begone!" quoth the great madame, "this is no time to be wander-ing about the country, seeking for charity."

"Oh, my lady, don't turn me away!   The clouds bode an ill night, and I have seven little children."

"You have seven little children! and, pray, whose fault is that?" was the cruel response of the Ban-Tierna, as she banged out the wicket in her face, and secured the fastenings with her own hands.

"Listen, Ban-Tierna!" shrieked the distracted woman.   "Listen!" Then putting her lips to a crevice in the door, she slowly uttered, in an impressive tone:—"The next time that you are brought to bed, may you have as many children at the birth as I have altogether!"

Some months after, Randal Oge was returning from hunting; and, on approaching the castle, he observed a woman carrying a large basket

14—2

towards the adjoining lake, who, on seeing him, appeared much confused. Riding up, he inquired what she had in that basket.

"Nothing but Cullinanes,* your honour," quoth she—dropping a deep courtesy.

"Cullinanes!" roared he; "and who dare send any of my Cullinanes to be drowned, without first asking me? Show them, immediately."

The terrified woman obeyed; and, on looking into the basket, Hurly saw six male infants—all newly born. The messenger threw herself on her knees, and told all,—beginning with the beggar-woman's curse, and ending with the statement—that scarce had he left on that morning, when his wife was confined of seven sons. One of these she kept, and the others were on their way to the lake when he stopped her.

Taking the woman with him, he went to the cabin of one of his most trusted retainers, and directed that the six infants should be provided with nurses as quickly as possible.

He bound those in the secret not to open their lips on the subject to any one, as they valued their lives, and then rode home. Ere he had time to dismount, he was told the good news. "He could hardly have reached the other side of Moneneurig bog that morning, when the Ban-Tierna was seized with the pains of labour, and in due time she gave birth to a son."

Randal appeared overjoyed with his good fortune; and rushing up the stone staircase, and along the dark corridor—which is even still in tolerable preservation—he entered the apartment where Catherine lay; and, taking her by the hand, congratulated her upon her safe delivery, and thanked her warmly for adding another scion to the Murrilahs.

Years rolled past, but not even a whisper reached the Ban-Tierna's ears, from which she could glean that her scheme was either frustrated, or even known. For aught she knew, the remains of her helpless infants were lying placidly beneath the surface of that sheet of water, upon which her eyes must have rested every time she looked out of the southern windows of the castle.

Those that knew her well, thought that of late they could occasionally detect a shade of melancholy spread itself over her fine, commanding face; and they thought, too, that her haughtiness had more of defiance, and less of the air of conscious superiority about it, than formerly.

On the seventh anniversary of the birth of the young son above

---

* (i.e.) Pups.

referred to, Randal Oge Hurly gave a grand banquet to all the neighbouring chieftains and their wives, and to many of his friends and retainers. Great preparations were made. Oaken tables extended through the centre of the great hall, creaking under the weight of the beef and the huge baskets of bread which were piled upon them. Round the walls were ranged shelves, upon which were placed vessels of usquebaugh and the best meiodh of the Carberries ; and at the head of the hall was another large table, at right angles with the others. Upon this were haunches of venison and tankards of claret for his principal guests.

When the Ban-Tierna occupied her customary seat, all those invited were assembled ; and all that was now required to begin the feast was the presence of the child, in whose honour the great entertainment was given. After waiting for some time, and wondering what could have detained him, he at length made his appearance, accompanied by six other boys of similar size and appearance, and dressed in every particular like himself.

Who are they ? anxiously inquired every one of his neighbours. No one could tell. Where did they come from ? No one knew. Meanwhile they moved with slow and measured pace up to where the great lady of the castle sat. Scarcely did their young innocent faces meet her eye when her brain reeled. "Oh, God !" thought she, " are those six children, whom I have consigned to destruction, come up from the depths of that lake to reproach me, in the noon-tide of my splendour, with their murder ?" She fainted.

The consternation and excitement became intense. Many of those who never knew what fear was amid the clash and din of arms, now shook with sheer terror ; and the shrill screams of the women, mingling with the hoarse voices of the men, produced an uproar—the like of which was never heard within the walls of Ballinacorriga before or since.

After some time, the Ban-Tierna was restored to consciousness; and Randal Oge, placing his hand affectionately upon her shoulder, bid her be of good cheer, and he would explain all. Silence was proclaimed by a hundred voices, and in an instant everybody was noiseless and still—so eager were they to hear the solution of this all-absorbing mystery.

Hurly then detailed every circumstance connected with his meeting the woman with the basket, the placing the children at nurse, his contrivance for having them presented to their mother on their seventh birthday, and concluded by endeavouring to impress upon the minds of all present, the moral,—that at any time, and under any circumstances, they should never refuse a beggar-woman a night's lodging, or turn her away empty-handed from the door.

Upon the death of this Randal Oge, in 1631, he was succeeded by his son, Randal Oge, who was one of the first of the Irish chieftains to take up arms in 1641 ; and in the first great official record of those who rebelled against English rule, his name appears.

On the roll containing the " names of persons indicted of treason in ye county of Corke, att the sessions holden att Youghall, ye second of August, 1642," is to be found that of Randal Hurly, of Beallenecarrigy, together with that of his son, Randal ; William Hurly, of Ballinwarde, also James Hurly, of same place ; William Hurly, of Lisgubby ; Donogh McDonel Hurly, of Bummeonderry ; Daniel Oge Hurly, of Kilbrittain ; James Hurly, of Grillagh.   Even the very women of the Hurlys fled to arms in that memorable uprise ; for, on the list referred to, we find them represented by Ellen Hurly, of Grillagh—Ighteragh.   All these were not only indicted for high-treason, but they were subsequently outlawed—women and all—in the King's Bench.

Randal Hurly took an active part in the rebellion.   Not only was he present at the various encampments of the rebels—aiding and abetting— but he had them encamped at Ballinacorriga, and was privy to the murder of an English soldier there.

It appears that when McCarthy-Reagh's troop of horse lay at Ballina-corriga, news reached them that a quantity of corn was about being conveyed from Enniskeane to Bandon.   To intercept this, the quarter-master and thirty horse were detached ; and, upon their return, they met five of the English party at Desert Church.   These fought manfully, and never gave up until two of their number lay dead ; the other three then surrendered upon quarter.

The rebels kept their word with the Rev. John Snary (who was the rector of the parish of Kilbrogan, and also of Desert), and with Ralph Clear, a Bandon man, who was with him, but they carried Owen McDermod Carty to their camp at the castle, and there they hanged him ; alleging, as an excuse for their gross breach of faith, " that they had a law amongst them,—that if any Irishman did serve on the English side, and was taken, he should be hanged."*

---

* Examination of Donough McCormick Carthy, taken before John Wheeler, &c., at Bandon-Bridge.

Hurly possessed a good-sized estate, all of which was forfeited. In addition to his castle and lands in the parish of Kilmeen, he owned Ardcahane, granted to Captain Jeacock, in the parish of Fanlobbus, and the three ploughlands of Yeaden-Carrow, granted to John Sicklemore and William Blackbourne; Ardeah, Kilcashane, and Buddermine, granted to Benjamin Crofts, in the parish of Ballymoney. He was a married man, and had a family, consisting of six sons. Of these, two became priests; two more died unmarried—having been killed during the rebellion; and of the two surviving,—one was Randal Oge, his eldest son, and the other was father of two sons (one of whom was Jeremiah Hurly), and of a daughter, who married her cousin, one of the McCarthy-Crimens.

Jeremiah was called Dermod Tresalia (Jerry the light-footed). He is said to have owned Mounteen Castle, and also Ballinorohur; and it is possible he may have possessed himself of them in James the Second's time; but he could not have held them long. He fought on the Irish side in the Williamite wars, and returned home after the siege of Limerick, bringing two English troop horses with him. He married, but died issueless; and was buried in the graveyard of Clogough, in the parish of Kilmalooda—an ancient and picturesque burial-place, on a rising ground, overlooking where the blind river unites its fortunes with the Arrigadeen; and the rough stone, with the rude inscription, which marks the place of his interment, may still be seen on the eastern side of the entrance from the river.

His brother was father of seven sons and three daughters. Two of the sons (namely:—James and Jerry) were within the walls of Limerick during the siege in William's reign. Of these, James was called Shamus Atrooher (James the marksman). It was this James who killed the six troopers between Bandon and Clonakilty.

It seems the soldiers heard of his whereabouts, and came to the very house he was in; and actually made inquiries of him concerning his noted self. He readily undertook to guide them to where the celebrated freebooter lay concealed, and contrived to draw them off the main road into the intricacies of a huge turf-bog. He then managed to give them the slip; and, while the unfortunate men were vainly endeavouring to flounder their way out of the soft slush, he shot every one of them. Their bodies were subsequently recovered, and they now lie buried in Desert churchyard. He is also said to have shot another soldier, who was attempting to take liberties with a young woman, at a place called Fourchill. He was at the time at Granard, and saw what was going on. Loading his piece, he took deliberate aim, fired, and the soldier fell dead.

Shamus Atrooher was married, and had several sons. Of these, James and Randal were priests. The former died soon after his ordination, but Randal lived many years, and died at Clonteada, near Kinsale. Others of his sons (Daniel, Jerry, John, and Patrick), all grew up, and married; but most of their descendants have left Ireland, and settled in England and America, where they may be found amongst the labouring classes, fighting the battle of life for their daily bread. He had also a son, Michael, who married, and left, amongst other children, a son Michael, who had, with others (the descendants of whom are now residing in the neighbouring parish of Desertserges), a son Daniel, who married, and had also a son Daniel, who was the father of Daniel Hurly, a respectable and industrious mechanic, now resident in Clonakilty.

Randal Oge—the eldest son of Randal Oge who forfeited his estates, and grandson of Randal Oge who founded the castle—was indicted for high-treason at the sessions held at Youghal, as previously stated. He married his cousin, Ellen Collins (or Cullinane), daughter of one of the great family of physicians who lived near Timoléague. This lady's father was known as "Cool-Yeakel en ore" (the golden tooth), in allusion to a gold tooth he wore in the front of his mouth.

Randal Oge fought on James's side at the siege of Limerick; and on the departure of the Irish forces for France, under Sarsfield, he accompanied them there, leaving his wife behind. She was disconsolate at his departure, and grieved sorely after her beloved Randal. Nothing could persuade her but that she would see him once more. That he was coming back to her, was told to her in dream after dream. The zephyr, which lurked among the trees, whispered it to her as she passed along. The storm roared it in her ears. Old crones, who were never known to be out in their prognostications, averred he would be home soon; and sick people, who were half on their way to the grave, saw him approaching—but yet he never came.

We are unable to say whether he fell, fighting in one of those brilliant actions which has immortalized the career of the Irish brigade, or sunk, broken-hearted, into a premature grave.

In an agony of grief, poor Eileen used to bemoan him; wringing her hands, and rocking herself to and fro :—"Oh! I wish I had a young smart messenger," she used to say, "that would run out, and come and tell me that Randal Oge is coming with his golden sword in his hand."

Great as were the exertions of Randal Oge Hurly in the great rebellion, yet they would count almost for nothing when compared to those of Teige McCarthy-Downy. There is not a single one, among the hundreds of Irish chieftains who flew to arms in the west riding of this county upon the memorable uprising referred to, whose name is more frequently to be met with than his. Wherever there was a rebel encampment, a marauding excursion, a skirmish, a fight, or a pitched battle, or where any of these were even expected to come off, there was Tiege McCarthy-Downy, of the Togher. He was at his great kinsman's— McCarthy-Reagh's—gathering, at Killivarrig wood, when Mr. Burrowes and his family were hanged ; he was at Enniskeane, at Ballinacorriga, at Kilbrittain—near which place he caught an unfortunate Bandonian, whom he stripped naked, and so ill-used that he died in a few days. He carried away all the horses and cattle belonging to another, to the value of £130, and he was heavily in the books of many others ; and there is no doubt but that his Bandon creditors told the simple truth when they stated to the commissioners, in 1642, that "they expected no money of the said Teige O'Downy."

His hatred of the English crown extended itself—not only to the English people, but to their religion. "Luther and Calvin invented your new found religion," said he to an orthodox Christian, whom he wanted to turn Papist ; and, moreover, that unless he (the deponent) would turn to the holy mass, he would be damned. As for Englishmen, he vowed "that he would not trust one of them upon any occasion whatsoever, any more than he would a Turk, who did deny Christ."

The hostility of some Irish chieftains to the English crown, however unjustifiable it might have been, could be accounted for. They sought to repossess themselves of estates which they had lost, either through extravagance or crime ; and it was "now or never" with them. But his was wholly unaccountable, and exhibited, on his part, the basest ingratitude. The very Dunmanway estate which he possessed was a grant from the English crown, only fifty-two years before, to Teige McDermod Carthy—whom he inherited from—for the valuable services which Teige had rendered England during the great Desmond rebellion.

Sir William Burghley, in a letter—which Teige himself was the bearer of—to the Lord-Deputy Fitz-William, after stating that it hath pleased the Queen to extend her grace and favour to him, said he was to have a grant made to him, and to his heirs (male), of the town, castle, and lands of Dounemoenway, in the county of Cork, as in her Majesty's special letters written to you in their behalf more at large appeareth.

The McCarthys of Glounacreme were a sept of the royal house of McCarthy, and had the affix of Downy to distinguish them from other branches of this illustrious family,—as the McCarthys of Banduffe, the McCarthys-Crimen, the McCarthys of Ballea, the McCarthys-Reaghs, the McCarthy-Spoinochs, &c.

Teige had a large estate, and upon it were two castles,—Dunmanway and the Togher.*   The latter of these was his favourite residence; and it was as Teige O'Downy, of the Togher, old chroniclers love to speak of him.   He was hospitable in the extreme.   Even in those days—when almost every man of note kept an open house, and when inscriptions on the neighbouring cross-roads invited the wayfarer to the next castle to come and eat—one would think, that where hospitality was so generally practised, it would come to be looked upon as a matter of course,—and so, in fact, it was; but the hospitalities of Teige O'Downy were on such a gigantic scale that they out-topped all others.†

Some of his people arrived at Togher one day with a large booty of beeves and sheep, which they had driven out of O'Sullivan Beare's country, without even having the manners to say to him, "By your leave," or "The top of the morning to you, Mr. O;" and having safely housed them in the bawn, they set out on their way home.   They had got but a very short distance, however, when they stretched themselves on the banks of the Bandon river—which flows near Togher—and began to drink out of the running stream.   Teige, who had only just returned from hunting, saw them from one of the upper windows of the castle, and roared out to

---

* Togher—a wedding gift—did not originally belong to the McCarthys.   It was acquired by one of them in marriage with an heiress of a family of considerable wealth—supposed to be one of the Fitzgeralds—who lived in that part of Carbery.

† To this day, in the neighbourhood of Togher, the peasantry, in "keening" at a wake or a funeral, frequently refer to Teige's hospitality, and the wealth and varied attractions of his castle and lands.   One of these laments, which has been kindly procured for us by a friend to whom we are much indebted for reminiscences of Dunmanway and its neighbourhood, speaks of the grassy meadows of Togher; where the sheep were, with their snowy fleeces; over which thousands of bees hummed during the live-long summer day; where the flowers bloomed in rich and gay variety; of the river, where sported the salmon and the trout; and of the owner of all—Teige McCarthy-Downy—whose large heart would bleed if a man had not enough to eat and to drink.

them to desist. He then ordered his steward to bring out several casks of his best Spanish wine, and empty them into the still waters of a portion of the river that lies within the ledges of two projecting rocks—since known as Teige's punch-bowl. Here the thirsty kern drank, drank, and drank till they could neither see, sit, or stand. Indeed, so great was the quantity of the precious liquid poured in by his orders, that it is asserted that even the very fishes in the river—including the eels and the water-rats—were all blind drunk ; and that, for the most part of the entire week, they did nothing but beat and scold one another like Christians. Even an old sow, we are told, who was out next morning taking her constitutional meander along the banks of the river, got so overpowered with the very odour of what was unavoidably spilt in unheading the casks, that she had to be led home and rolled into her bed by a half-a-dozen of her interesting progeny.

His extravagance was unbounded. Anything he desired to have, he would have, if it was in his power to accomplish it. He was so pleased with the first coach he ever saw, that he wanted to buy it of the owner. The latter, who was probably pleased with the comfort and dignity of his new conveyance, was reluctant to part with it ; but Teige would have it, and at last it became his for four ploughlands.

Although very attentive and kind to others, yet he was very grateful for any kindness or attention shown to himself. Returning to Togher one day, he sat down to rest himself upon a stone at the Comorefortera Pass. A tenant of his, who lived close by, seeing upon what his master was seated, immediately took off his big frieze mantle, and insisted on placing it under him. This act of consideration on the part of the poor peasant so pleased O'Downy, that he absolutely made him a present of the whole ploughland of Inch.

But although he was generous and hospitable to a fault, yet the possession of these and other good qualities did not exclude some of the worst. He was tyrannical, cruel, and unrelenting.

One Sunday morning a young countryman was hurrying to Kilbarry chapel. Fearing he would be late, he crossed one of the Togher meadows, as a short-cut. O'Downy saw him ; and sending some of his men in pursuit, he was seized, and brought before him. The young man—who was a widow's only son—readily admitted the trespass ; and having stated his reasons for intruding, solemnly promised he would never do so again.

But his promises and excuses were of no avail. Teige had made up his mind, and who was there that dared to interfere with him? There was no jury to interpose its calm decision between the accused and his accuser and judge; and there was no appeal to another tribunal from the dictum of an Irish chieftain, who repudiated British laws, and withstood the influences of British civilization. Before ten minutes had elapsed the body of the unfortunate youth was swinging from the gibbet*—which was a fixture at Togher, and some portion of which can even yet be seen on its northern wall.

His tyrannical disposition extended itself to members of his own immediate family, as well as to his unfortunate kern, whose feelings and whose lives were in those days of little consequence to any one but themselves. It is said that he banished and disinherited his eldest son for what he considered an unpardonable oversight—if not an act of cowardice.

Two Spanish officers, who were "on the run" from the King's troops, arrived one day at Togher. Teige, who could never be reproached with loyalty to the English crown, gladly received them, and when he ascertained that they had done something which compelled them to hurriedly withdraw from the sway of the English authorities, we may fairly assume that the cordiality of his welcome, and his respect for themselves personally, underwent no diminution.

It happened, just about the time of their arrival, that O'Downy's eldest son had a falling-out with one of the O'Sullivan Beares. The Spaniards, who were made acquainted with all the circumstances of the case, were asked what ought young O'Downy to do, and they replied that he ought at once send O'Sullivan a challenge to fight a duel—volunteering, at the same time, to become his seconds. He accepted their kind offer; and obeying their directions, he sent the summons, which O'Sullivan— who was as pugnacious as any other well-disposed and respectable Milesian—unhesitatingly accepted.

The combatants, accompanied by their respective seconds, met in a grass-field on the banks of the Bandon river—a mile or two from Teige's residence; and after a desperate contest, O'Sullivan fell. The two

---

* A small portion of the iron-work that was used to support the gibbet still occupies its old-position. The gibbet itself remained until about the close of last century, when it was removed, and thrown into Poolgurrum—a deep hole in the Bandon river. We are told that on a bright summer's day this souvenir of Teige's day and generation may still be discerned, lying peaceably on the gravel beneath the water.

Spanish officers who stood by O'Downy were also slain; but O'Sullivan's two seconds were unharmed.

Now if young O'Downy had attacked and killed both of these, or even got killed himself in making the attempt, O'Downy would have thought well of him; but the young fellow had neglected to do so—he may have forgotten it, or thought that he had quite enough of it already. Be that as it may, he permitted them to walk off unmolested, and thus omitted an opportunity of avenging the death of his father's Spanish guests.

Teige never forgave him. Not content with ordering him never to show his face to him again, he compelled him to quit the neighbourhood altogether; and regretted he was unable to deprive him of his consanguinity and his name.

Togher is a large imposing-looking edifice, about eighty feet in height and sixty in breadth. It is built on the southern bank of the river Bandon, and on a piece of ground gently shelving to its waters. It was evidently inhabited long after Teige ceased to be its owner;* and the diamond-shaped chimney-tops, and some of the windows—intended, no doubt, as improvements—do not harmonize with the solid, massive style of the rest of the building. We visited it not long since. Pushing open a rough timber door, we stood in the banquetting-hall of the O'Downys. The roof was gone, and the masonry, that towered high above us on all sides, looked gloomy and dark. Nevertheless, we could not but gaze with a deep interest on those old walls—walls that have again and again rang with the rude revelry of Celtic chiefs, and often echoed the sad and sweet tones of the pipe and the harp.

As we entered, a sow and her bonnives rushed at us from their stye, in this very apartment, where O'Downy or some ancestor of his may have haughtily received the herald of the Lord-Deputy, and told him that he refused to hold any intercourse with "the stranger." We groped our way into the shomera bud-dough—a dark prison, embedded in dense masonry, and not more than eight feet high and as many broad. Alas! how strangely human joys and human woes often jostle one another in the great eddying stream of life. With only a wall between

---

* There are some still living who remember when the grounds about the castle exhibited an appearance of having been previously stocked with choice trees, and well kept. The gravel walks, branching off in many directions, could easily be traced. There were several old fruit trees in what was once the orchard; and there were exotics tastefully planted on the belt of green sward that lay between the castle and the river.

him and the boisterous merriment of the carouse, what must be the
feelings of the wretch doomed to perish on the morrow from that fatal
beam overhead; or, worse still, to be dragged out, amid the scoffs and
sneers of his conquerors, and piked to death? Or can we be surprised
that the blood should bound through his veins when, through an air-
slit in his thick prison walls, he hears the O'Downy pour into the greedy
ear of his Ban-Tierna, tales of his recent deeds of valour; and that he
should listen with a fluttering heart to their exultations over the fall of
his kith and kindred? True that he is weak, but he is not powerless.
The clanking of his irons hushes their song of triumph, and reminds
them of a fate that may one day be their own.

Within living memory Togher had a roof and a tenant. The roof
was of slate, and the rafters, as well as the joists which supported the
various floors, were of native oak. These were very strong, and they
contained many iron hooks, said to have been used in Teige's hospitable
days as meat holders.

The tenant was an old schoolmaster—a man of considerable repute in
his day; and one who, in fact, lived ahead of his age, as he abolished
altogether the use of the stick and the lash within the sphere of his
jurisdiction. He endeavoured to instruct the youth intrusted to his
care by placing their errors before them; and then, giving them time
and place for reflection, he trusted to the children's own good sense
to correct them. Accordingly, when one of his pupils mistook the
letter B. for a bull's foot, or could not—for the life of him—tell how many
beans made five, or forgot how to make a pot-hook, our Philomath used
to send young ignoramus up to the top of the castle-tower; where, far
elevated above the disturbing influences of the school-room, he may
calmly meditate on the bad use he was making of his time; or, if so
disposed, could take a bird's-eye view of his own prospects, as well as
those of the neighbouring farmers.

All went on very well. The boys, we are sure, were a great deal
more intelligent, and not one whit worse conducted, than those who
were beaten stupid by the rod and the whip; and the master's reputation for kindness, as well as for learning, was known far and wide.

One day, however, put an end to all. A little fellow was up on the
tower atoning for some misdeed, when he cried out that his head was
going round; and, before assistance could reach him, he came tumbling
down through the joists, the flooring of which had been long previously

ripped off for fire-wood ; and as he fell from story to story, his body was caught by the iron hooks, and frightfully mangled.

The country-people were indignant.   Flocking in from all the adjoining townlands, they cut away all the joists, they ejected the un-fortunate schoolmaster, and they built up all the entrances to the castle.

It could not be expected that an active, untiring enemy like Teige O'Downy could escape the vigilance of Cromwell—neither did he.   In common with a great many others who had robbed and despoiled the English colonists, and waged open war with England herself, all his estates were seized and conferred upon military officers, and upon those on whose loyalty the authorities could rely.

Killronan, Ballinhalewig, and Bohinagh, were granted to the See of Dublin, Arthur Ormsby, and Lord Kingston ; the three ploughlands of Dunmanway and two gneeves of Togher—1,460 acres—were bestowed on Colonel William Arnopp; another lot, consisting of 780 acres, on Lord Kingston ; and Awe, another lot, containing 744 acres, on Robert Maude.   Alderman William Barker got O'Cullane, and a portion of the Drumalinagh estate—upwards of 1,600 acres. Patrick Allen got another portion, containing 590 acres ; and Lord Kingston* got 260 acres of same lands.   The latter also got Inshy—466 acres—and a portion of Awe—780 acres.   Togher Castle,† together with the ploughland of Togher, Monerage, Drumdedga, Coramuck, Corancooly, Callyroheene, Gortenure, and Naskin—in all 3,468 acres—were bestowed on Captain Edward Hoare and Lieutenant Abraham Hoare.   Colonel Arnopp got Coolemarty-West, in addition to his previous grant ; and the Earl of Cork got all the rest.

O'Downy lost 12,814 acres altogether.   Of these, 11,464 were in the parish of Fanlobbus ; in Inchigeelagh, 813 ; in Killmacomoge, 117 ; in [illegible], 320 ; and in Drinagh, 100.

The descendants of O'Downy are now believed to be extinct ; the last survivor of them, it is said, having died in the person of Charles McCarthy—an old man who lived many years ago.   McCarthy was

---

* Lord Kingston could not complain. His grants in the county of Cork alone amounted to 261 townlands, containing 20,852 acres.

† About twenty years ago a valuable gold ring was dug up by a labourer in the neighbourhood of the castle, on which was inscribed :—

> " Me hart an i
>   ontel i dy,
>   C. Mc Carty."

proud of his descent from old Teige ; and, among other proofs of his being his heir as well as his lineal descendant, he used to exhibit the Togher title-deeds,—records which were carefully preserved, and handed down from father to son, in the hope that, one day or other, circumstances may arise which may replace the McCarthy-Downys in the Castle of the Togher.

> "And thou, proud Togher, waste and worn
> By fate, by time, thou'rt lost and lorn.
> On a fair bank on Bandon's stream
> Thou standest still—but like a dream.
> Thy life is fled ; sped away,
> Like shades of night, 'fore rising day.
> On the old ground thou dwellest yet,
> Lingering where thy glories set.

> "The harvest moon thy crumbling walls
> Doth lave with mellow light. Thy halls
> Are lonely ; and the owl and bat
> Flit where noble chieftains sat.
> Thy wassail bowl, thy harp, thy horn,
> All, all, are gone, not to return ;
> Thy buckler's broke ; thy glave is rust,
> And thy lordly owners—dust ! dust !"

Patrick Roche—Fitz-Richard—of Poulnalonge, was also among those who were indicted for high-treason at Youghal, and subsequently outlawed. He was the son of Patrick Roche, also Fitz-Richard, of Poulnalonge, upon whom a post mortem Inquisition was held on the 2nd of May, 1633, and descended from Phillippus Roche,* de Kinsale, Armiger, who obtained a licence from Henry the Eight, in 1544, to bring provisions from England, " to the intent that the said Phillip Roche, &c., should buylde a castell neer unto the ryver of Glasselyn, in the coun of Cork."

Roche (Patrick Fitz-Richard) was the junior representative for Kinsale in the Parliament which held its sittings in Dublin Castle in 1639.   He

---

* Phillip Roche, described as of Serrell and Rahane, was the sixth son of David (who was the son of Maurice, by Amy, daughter of Maurice, Earl of Desmond,) and Beatrice, his wife [Beatrice was the daughter of Ralph, Earl of Strafford, and Duke of Buckingham]. David (Phillip's father) was twice married—firstly to More, who is thought to have been the daughter of O'Brian Strogh, and secondly to Joan, daughter of Walter Butler, *alias* McWilliam. We are not aware of any issue that he had by his first wife, but by the second he had ten sons (Maurice, Edmund, Ulick, Theobald, William, Phillip, Garret, Edward, James, John,) and two daughters, one of whom married the Lord of Carigoguinal, and the youngest, Ellen, married —firstly, McCarthy-More, and secondly, Lord Barry.

joined in the rebellion at its very outset, and at its conclusion he found himself without either castle or estate.

In Innoshannon—the parish in which he lived—he lost Coolmorine and Cloherane, granted to William Hodder; Farrancarrigg and Raghnaroughy, granted to Humphry Baggaley in trust for the '49 officers; and Poulnalonge Castle, conferred on John Herrick.*

Shippool Castle was commenced in 1544, and completed within three years, as appears by the certificate† attached to the following recognizance entered into by Phillip Roche, to our Lord, King Henry the Eight, dated December the 4th, 1544 :—

"The condicon of this recognizance is such :—Where^{as,} our said Sovereign Lord the King's most excellent Ma^{tie,} at the contemplacon of the Rt. Honorable Sir Anthony St. Leger, Knight, one of the gents. of the Privy Chamber, and his Grace's Lord Deputy of Ireland, and his most Honorable Council of the same, granted to—as above bounden—Phillip Roche a lycens to carry out of the realme of England two hundred and fiftie quarters of malt and five hundred quarters of beans, to the intent that the said Phillip Roche, his heirs, executors, administrators, and assigns, should buylde a castell neer unto the ryver of Glasselyn, in the coun of Cork; if the said Phillip, his heirs, &c., within three years next after the date of the above within recognizance, doo buylde, or cause to bee buylded, the Castell of Shepespool guardable; and, upon the p-fection of the same, bring, or cause to be brought, before the King's Highness, Chancellor of this his Majesties realme of Ireland, in his Grace's High Courte of Chancerie, a certificate or testimoniale of the Maior of the cittie of Corke and the towne of Kensale, sealed with the common seal of the saide cittie and towne, that the saide Phillip, his heirs or assigns, have buylded up, made up, and clerly furnished the said castell," &c., &c.

The Herricks, who succeeded the Roches, lived in the castle until 1787. The late Captain William H. Herrick was born there, and his father's sister, Jane—mother of the celebrated Rev. William Hickey, rector of Mulrankin, Ferns, best known as Martin Doyle—was married within its walls, to the late Rev. Dr. Hickey, of Murragh.

Shippool Castle,‡ which consists of a square tower, with modern

---

* The grant to Herrick was enrolled June 20th, 1666. In the same patent he had conferred on him the lands of Lishyday, Castlelavard, Northlefoney, Ballidina, part of Skynegore, and part of Slevegolan.

† Roche bound himself in the sum of two hundred pounds that he would have the castle completed within the specified time. Having done so, the bond was cancelled.

‡ On the northern bank of the river, and close to the castle, is a soft chalybeate spring, which was in high repute so far back as the reign of James the First, for its anti-scorbutic qualities. It was also widely known for curing rheumatic complaints. Upon being tested-with gall, the water became of a deep purple colour; and upon the water being evaporated, a deposit of ferruginous matter was obtained.

gables and chimneys, is delightfully situated on the steep decline of a nobly-wooded hill; and so close does it approach to the Glasslyn of bluff King Hal, that occasionally—at full spring-tide—its southern wall is touched by the gentle swell which creeps noiselessly along the swollen waters of the Green river. Springing from the eastern and western walls—on the inside—is a stone arch, formerly bomb-proof. On the top of this was the kitchen, and underneath it was the drawing-room—the concave surface of the arch forming its ceiling. This was at one time a very handsome apartment. Under this was the dining-room, in which—as well as in the drawing-room overhead—was a handsome bay window, opening out upon the river. Looking from one of these in the olden time, one could gaze upon the primeval forest stretching far away to the distant west, and to the south and east; whilst, far below one's feet, the pleasant Bandon glided by—perhaps, bearing on her fair bosom a rude contrivance or two, composed of a frame-work of stout osiers, held together by thongs cut from raw hides, and covered with horse-skins, in which wild and half-naked creatures—who were owned by a Roche or a Mac Carthy—lounged, as they fished for eels and salmon.

During the long absence at sea of the late Captain Herrick, R.N., the fine old chimney-piece, which for upwards of two centuries and a half formed one of the principal ornaments of the drawing-room, was stolen, and also the beautiful cut limestone arches of the bay windows. The latter were even a greater loss than the former, as the bomb-proof arch partially rested on one of them; and when the limestone arch was removed, the great arch commenced to crumble away.

The keep was on the basement story of the small round tower at the north-west corner of the castle, and was entered by a square aperture in the centre of the floor above. It was constructed in the form of a beehive, so that when once an unfortunate wretch was imprisoned within its walls, it was impossible for him to climb up its concave sides, and escape. It was accidentally discovered when the family were removing to their new residence in 1787; and, on peering down into its gloomy depths, some human skeletons were seen lying at the bottom. Some of these were, in all probability, the remains of unhappy beings who had been confined in this noisome cell at an early period, and others were the remains of those who were thrust—whilst yet alive—into the ghastly companionship of the bones of those who were there before them.

What pen can describe the feelings of one of those thrice-wretched sufferers, as he stretches out his weary limbs upon the floor, clammy with the decayed covering which has dropped from those hideous frames —grim skeletons!—through whose huge eyeless orbs voiceless and invisible spirits are staring at him continually, and whose long flesh-less arms are threatening every moment to clasp him in their repulsive embrace.   Perhaps, too, as the sleep of death creeps softly over him, fancy carries the poor colonist* back to his snug farm-house; to his wife, wondering what could have delayed him so long; to his little children, who are eagerly asking about him ; to his cattle ; to his well-filled haggard ; and a smile may have rippled over his wan features, as he beholds the prosperity which his industry has achieved.   He awakes again.   He implores for mercy, but there is no pitying ear to listen to him ; there is no cherished hand, now, to wipe his reeking brow.   He is surrounded by an unearthly group ; and amid those fetid relics of humanity his last sigh steals away.

In addition to the lands forfeited by Roche in the parish of Inno-shannon, he was also dispossessed of the townlands of East and West Dunworly, in the parish of Lislee.

In that portion of the coast lying between the Old Head of Kinsale and the Galley Head is a deep indentation, known as File-a-Reel Bay. Bounding this on the west is a bold headland on Dunworly ; and half-way down its rugged slopes, and over-hanging the angry waters which rush in here from the Atlantic, was the marine residence of the former owner of Poulnalonge.   Some traces of this old dwelling, and some of the old garden walls of this favourite summer residence of the Roches, are still to be seen ; and many a butt of sack, and many a tun† of the best Spanish wine, was emptied beneath the old roof-tree at File-a-Reel.

Its loss was acutely felt ; and one member of the family, at least, is said never to have lost sight of the sunny home of her youth—where she spent many a happy hour, ere the machinations of her own kindred swept away the support of her declining years, and flung her on the world a beggar.

It is related that—several years after Dunworly changed owners—Roche's sister, Mary (an elderly lady), arrived from Kinsale, and dwelt

---

* They are believed to have been the remains of some of the Protestant colonists, incarcerated there during the great rebellion by Roche.

† The price of a tun of wine in those days was fifty hides.

in the old castle of the O'Cowigs—a ruin which occupies the causeway connecting Horse Island with the mainland, and which is still in tolerable preservation. From this secluded home she was accustomed to walk—usually in an excited state—several times a day, to the bold promontory of Crow Head. In mild weather, shading her eyes from the light, she used to gaze intently, for hours together, far out to sea. But when the storm raged; when the thunder bellowed o'er the world of waters; when the waves, lashed into a fury by the western winds, bounded madly up the black, sullen cliffs, as if to drag them from their rocky bed and hurl them into the yawning gulf beneath—and finding the black weather-beaten old front, which the tempests of thousands of years have assailed in vain, as unshaken as ever, roll precipitately back again into the troubled deep, roaring with rage at beholding their own impotency; it was then she was in high glee. Upon the crest of the highest crag she was to be seen, with her long hair streaming wildly in the wind, and her white garments—anon wrapped tightly round her body, and anon fluttering like a loose sail in the gale; and then her voice might be heard—out-topping even the deafening din of the billows —as she upbraided the King of Spain for not sending his men long before to her assistance. She was supported by the neighbouring peasantry, who were accustomed to place in her daily path such supplies of eggs, potatoes, and fish, as their humble circumstances would afford. Her clothing was supplied by those relatives who occasionally called to see her; and by some of whom, after her decease, her body was taken round the coast in a boat to Kinsale. The county-people used to look on her with great awe; and many of them were uncertain whether they ought to class with the dead or with the living—Ban-Teirna banna-vailte, or the White Lady of the Cliffs.

The two ploughlands of Dunworly (*alias* Downevourleage) were bestowed on Sir George Hamilton, of Donalong, county Tyrone, and of Nenagh, in Tipperary. Sir George—ancestor of the Marquis of Abercorn—was created a baronet in 1660. He married Mary, third daughter of Walter, Viscount Thurles, and sister of James, first Duke of Ormond. He was vice-president of the province of Munster, under Lord Inchiquin, the lord-president; and was father of George, commonly called Count Hamilton, who married Fanny Jennings—equally celebrated with her sister Sarah, the renowned Duchess of Marlborough, as one of the most fascinating belles of the court of Charles the Second. Upon

Count Hamilton's decease, his widow married the notorious Dick Talbot, Duke of Tyrconnell, lord-lieutenant of Ireland under James the Second.

In the Dunworly patent, in addition to what is usually bestowed, the crown conferred on Sir George, his heirs, executors, &c., "All the reversion and reversions to which it was entitled; with waters, water-courses, fisheries, and all its rights, privileges, advantages, emoluments, and hereditaments, &c., whatsoever, to the said premises, or to any part or parcel thereof, belonging or in anywise appertaining." Indeed, so comprehensively worded was the patent, and so lavish was it of the crown rights, that one cannot help thinking Sir George, who was an influential government official, must have framed it himself.*

Although these lands, as we have said, were granted to Hamilton, yet they were bestowed on him subject to a charge of £120, due to Captain John Sweete, of Timoleague, for which sum they had been mortgaged by Roche. Captain Sweete, having purchased Sir George's interest, became sole proprietor; and took up his residence at Dunworly, at a place called the Corrig, where some remains of "The White House" are still shown.

Sweete is said to have been very active in hunting the Tories; and it is said that, whenever he could lay hands on any of these unfortunate freebooters, he brought them with him to the White House; and having placed them under the permanently-erected crossbeam, he had a skewer —upon which was a transfixed potato—firmly inserted in their mouths, and in this position they were hanged.

Captain John Sweete disposed of the estate to William Sweete, who —dying intestate—was succeeded by his son William. William, by his will (May 26, 1697), left Dunworly to his son William, who— dying a minor and issueless—was succeeded by his sister, Jane Sweete, who married Robert Tresilian, of Ballinadee.

---

* When lately placed in the hands of the commissioners for investigating the title of the present owner to unclaimed wreck of the sea, the commissioners unhesitatingly confirmed the rights of the applicant to same.

CHAPTER XI.

THE LORD-LIEUTENANT (CROMWELL'S SON-IN-LAW) ARRIVES IN BANDON—THE
QUAKERS FIRST VISIT THE TOWN—CROMWELL DIES—HIS REMAINS DISHONOURED—
HIS TWO SONS—IRELAND MORE PROTESTANT IN THE REIGN OF QUEEN VICTORIA
THAN IN THE DAYS OF CROMWELL—DR. BRADY (OF BRADY AND TATE'S VERSION OF
THE PSALMS) BORN IN BANDON.

ABOUT this time the corporation began to enter actively
1654. upon the performance of their civic duties. Many
matters, that were pushed out of view by the
urgency of military necessity, were now looked after and
attended to. There was a bye-law passed to regulate the markets. In
summer, they were not to be opened before eight in the morning, and
they were to be closed at five in the evening. In winter, they were to
be opened three hours before mid-day, and closed three hours after.
Another bye-law directed that the streets should be kept clean ; and—as
if to show that, however palatable their new duties may be to them,
they should not prevent them attending to what was of great service to
them heretofore, and may be again—they appointed a committee,
composed of the following, " to see after the courtyards of their
garrison" :—

Messrs. Brooke,	Withers, William,	Dunkin,
Bennett	Beamish,	Deane,
Woodroff,	Smith,	Fuller,
Hewett,	Bathurst,	Poulden,
Withers, Nicholas,	Landon,	Jackson.

A great deal of evidence was taken at Bandon this year, relative to
"the reudition for the Parliament," in the month of November, 1649.
Lieutenant Edward Berry, Abraham Savage, John Smith, and Nathaniel

Clear, were examined,* and they deposed to many particulars about the organization that was got up, for the purpose of seizing on Governor Courtnay and the troops under his command; and, having expelled the incongruous combination of Royalist and rebel, the conspirators intended to secure the town for the Parliament and the Lord-Lieutenant (Cromwell).

1655.   The Lord-Lieutenant (Charles Fleetwood)—who married Bridget, widow of Major-General Ireton, and daughter of Cromwell—attended by his council, arrived in Bandon on the 1st of June. After " a gallant dinner, which Major Hodder, the Governor of Kinsale, did provide in the fort for his Excellency and the council, with all them that attended (saving the clerk of the council and some others, who dined at Mr. Southwell's), the Lord-Deputy and council did ride to Bandon—a fine English town. Staid there that night. Saturday, the 2nd of June, Dr. Worth† made an excellent sermon. After dinner they came to Cork again. Little business was done at Bandon."‡

The first Quaker that ever visited Bandon made his appearance here this year. His name was Francis Howgill. He was received by Edward Cook—a gentleman of great local influence, and who was the cornet of Oliver Cromwell's own troop of horse, which, at that time, lay in Bandon. He was also land agent to the Earl of Cork. Mr. Cook accompanied Howgill " on the first day of the week to the public worship-house of the town, where the said Francis declared truth among the people ;"|| and he invited him to hold a meeting at his house in the evening. This he gladly assented to ; and a great many people being assembled, Howgill stood up, and boldly proclaimed the true gospel; and with such beneficial results, that many admitted, there and then, that he was right; and they proved the sincerity of their assertions by at once joining the Society of Friends.

Amongst those were :—Edward Cook, and his wife Lucretia Cook, Daniel and Sarah Massey, Robert and Mary Mallins, William Smith, Catherine Smith, Matthew Prin, William Driver, Joan Frank, Thomas

---

* Much of the evidence will be found in the history of the South Cork light infantry, chapter 22.

† Dr. Edward Worth (subsequently bishop of Killaloe). His wife, Susanna, became a Quakeress; "and, though she suffered much from her husband, lived and died in unity with the Friends."

‡ Vide—A letter in *Mercurius Politicus*, dated Cork (in Ireland), June 4th, 1655.

|| See Weight's *History of the Quakers.*

Biss, &c., &c. Several of the men just mentioned were soldiers in Cromwell's troop of horse.

Mr. Cook proved a true convert. "He embraced the truth with his whole heart," says Weight, "and retained it."

On the following Saturday, Cook, in company with Edward Burrough, Francis Howgill, and Captain James Sicklemore, proceeded to Limerick, where they were treated scandalously. Indeed, it would appear as if the authorities were unwilling to hearken to any interpretation of the Scriptures save their own, as they had Cook and his companions "thrust forth through the gates, by order."

In some years after, the founder of the body, George Fox, visited Bandon, where he had an extraordinary vision.

"Being in Bandon, there appeared to me, in a vision, a very ugly-visaged man, of a black and dark look. My spirit struck at him in the power of God; and it seemed to me that I rode over him with my horse, and my horse set his foot on the side of his face. When I came down in the morning, I told a friend the command of the Lord was to me to ride to Cork."

Although the religious opinions and proceedings of the Quakers were assailed without mercy, and although they were compelled to put up with a great deal of ill-usage, nevertheless, they would not always tamely submit to be insulted. They sometimes retorted very sharply, and with such acrimony and vigour, as proved them to be no contemptible opponents.

In a book written by one of them at this time, the writer, who was evidently endowed with the tongue of a fish-fag, called the Church of England, Satan's synagogue. She was Mrs. Babylon's looking-glass; and she was mounted upon the beasts, and agoing with speed in the wide way of destruction.

After this charitable piece of information, the author—who seems convinced there could be no doubt as to *his* ultimate happiness—acquaints us that his book is written by a servant of Christ, whose name is written in the Book of Life.

The religious ardour of the body extended itself to the female members of the sect as well as to the males. Barbara Blaugden absolutely went up to the Lord-Lieutenant, and bid him beware that he was not found fighting against God. Her anxiety to do good induced her to follow many of her misguided fellow-Christians into the steeple-houses; where, we are told, " she opened her mouth;" and even to pay a visit to the judges of the land.

She naturally surmised that their lordships had souls as well as other people; and she did not see why their future should not concern a spiritually-minded person, as well as the future of those whom their lordships condemned to be hanged for sheep-stealing, or for doing a grievous bodily harm, or for murder. She, therefore, appeared before the court, and vainly strove to move them to righteousness. But the justices were not only unmoveable, but ungrateful. They not only refused her motion, but they ordered a detainer to be lodged against her on the spot, and she was incarcerated forthwith.

The Bandon congregation of Friends was never numerous or influential. It struggled on for about one hundred and fifty years, and then died out in the person of Tommy Weldon—a fat, Quaker-like little fellow, who died about the year 1807. His was the last interment in the Quakers' burying-ground; after which it was ploughed up, and turned into a potato-garden—the produce of which was so unctuous and creamy, that many of the people who boiled the potatoes declared that they saw some of Tommy Weldon's fat floating on the top of the pot.

The following are amongst the names of those Friends who worshipped in Bandon during the continuance of the Society here :—

Edward Cooke,	Robert Mander,	Abraham Uncles,
Daniel Massey,	Edward Russell,	Gideon Cocker,
Robert Mallins,	Joshua Russell,	Henry Hussy,
William Smith,	Eliazer Hutchinson,	Obadiah Hutchins,
Matthew Prin,	Isaac Weymour,	Thomas Weldon.
William Driver,	George Mansfield,	
Thomas Biss,	Mansfield Westcomb,	

1658.   On the 3rd of September—a peculiarly lucky day in his own estimation—died Oliver Cromwell. There was no sovereign that ever wore the crown of England caused her to be so much respected among neighbouring nations, and among distant ones, as Cromwell.[*] He compelled them to pay his ambassadors the same honours they did when a king was on the throne. " It is to the nation and not to the persons of kings," said he, " that the respect is due." It is stated that, as Protector of England, he insisted on signing his name before that of the haughty Louis the Fourteenth, of France; and Cardinal Mazarin

---

[*] " He was the greatest prince," says Macaulay, " that has ever ruled England."

(Louis' great minister) openly declared that he was more afraid of Cromwell than of the devil.

The stubborn Dutch were all submission to him.* The Swedes took great pains to obtain his friendship. The Pope was so much in dread of him, that he ordered processions to be made through the streets of Rome, in order to avert the roar of his avenging cannon.

He commanded the Duke of Savoy to stop the massacre of his Protestant subjects; and the very moment his Grace received the order, he hastened to obey it. All Italy, and those States of Africa which had dared to commit depredations upon British ships, he punished so effectually, that they are said to have trembled at the very mention of his name.

The remains of the Protector were buried with great state, in a vault in Henry the Seventh's chapel, in Westminister Abbey; where they lay until Saturday, January the 26th, 1666, when they were dug up—to please a prince under whom England became almost as insignificant a member of the political system of Europe as the petty Republic of San Marino ;† who was debased by indolence and by vice ;‡ who lived all his life professedly a Protestant, and died professedly a Papist ; who received large bribes from a foreign king, for betraying the honour and the interests of the country he was called upon to govern. Such was the man that now occupied the place of Cromwell.‖

Early on the night of Monday, January 28th, Cromwell's coffin, and

---

* When news of Cromwell's decease reached Amsterdam, the city was illuminated; and children ran through the streets, shouting for joy, and crying out that the devil was dead.

† Macaulay.

‡ When De Ruyter sailed up the Thames with a broom at the mast-head, and when the smoke of the English ships of war, which lay burning at Chatham, could be seen from the very windows at Whitehall, Charles is said to have dined with the ladies of his scraglio, and spent a portion of the evening in chasing a moth round the supper-room.

‖ Cromwell's memory is still greatly reverenced in Bandon. A short time since, the comparative merits of Oliver Cromwell and of William the Third were the subject of conversation in a workshop here. "William was a good and a great man, undoubtedly," said a smoke-begrimed smith, who was one of the principal speakers. "Bah! but, what was he to Oliver? He wasn't fit to hold a candle to him. Cromwell," said he, laying down his sledge, and looking thoughtfully at those he was addressing, "was specially raised up by the Almighty to destroy the idolaters; and that was the boy that He could rely on to do it. Do you think," cried he triumphantly, as he again seized his huge hammer, "that if Cromwell was still alive, you would have ever heard of a Phœnix boy or a Fenian? Or do you think that if Stephens (the Irish head-centre) was under the charge of one of Oliver's Puritans, he could leisurely walk out of Richmond gaol?—Bah!"

also that of Henry Ireton (his son-in-law), were taken on two carts to the Red Lion, in Holborn, where they remained for the rest of the night. Bradshaw's was disinterred next morning—being the anniversary of the death of Charles the First. All three were then drawn on sledges to Tyburn. Upon their arrival, the coffin lids were broken open, and the bodies dragged out, and hanged upon a triple gibbet until sunset.* They were then taken down, and beheaded. The mutilated bodies were flung contemptuously into a hole that was at the foot of the gallows; but the heads were set upon poles, and placed on the top of Westminster Hall.

It does not appear at what time these poor relics of humanity disappeared from their unenviable position, but two of them, at least, were there more than twenty years after; for when Sir Thomas Armstrong was executed in 1684, his head was placed on a spike between those of Cromwell and Bradshaw.

Oliver was succeeded in the Protectorate by his eldest surviving son, Richard. Republicans, as well as Cavaliers, grossly abused the new Protector in their songs. He was the meek Knight; he was tumble-down Dick; he was Queen Dick.

Henry, the Lord Lieutenant of Ireland, was Cromwell's other surviving son. His wife was Elizabeth, daughter of Sir Francis Russell, of Chippenham, in Cambridgeshire; by whom he had five sons and two daughters. The highest testimony is borne to his talents and virtues by many eminent men.

Mr. Luson says, that his government in Ireland was so mild and equitable, that he acquired a great degree of esteem even from many persons of high rank in King Charles's interest. Dr. Leland says that Henry was penetrating, just, and generous. Neal, that he was a wise and discreet governor, and brought the nation into a flourishing condition. Cardinal Mazarin declared that he admired Henry Cromwell very much. He was a great man, even in those great days, says Dr. Gibbons. Even the great Protector spoke highly of his merits. He was a governor, said his illustrious father, from whom I myself might learn.

Neither the Lord-Lieutenant or the new Lord Protector enjoyed their

---

* A gentleman who was present has left a detailed account of the appearance of the bodies. He says Cromwell's was wrapt in green cerecloth, and looked quite fresh.—See Noble's *House of Cromwell.*

high positions long; and they vacated them without any show of resistance, or even giving their opponents any trouble.

In "The Rump Carbonaded," a ballad which was very popular at that time, the meekness of Oliver's two sons is contemptuously spoken of:—

> "But young Dick and Harry—not his heirs, but his brats—
> As if they had less wit and grace than gib-cats,
> Slunk from their commands like a pair of drowned rats;
>   Which nobody can deny.

> "The sound of a rump, ne'er heard before
> In their addle pates, did so whistle and roar,
> That straight they took themselves to the back door;
>   Which nobody can deny.

In another song :—

> "And King Oliver's sons—
> Like prince-playing w——e sons
> That on too high parts had ventured—
> They tripped with a hiss
> Of the State properties,
> And exeunt two fools as they entered."

1659.   Dr. William Petty,* physician-general to the Parliamentary army in 1652, was sworn in a burgess of the Bandon corporation. He was also elected to represent the town in Parliament. It is to him we are indebted for the laying down survey—familiarly known as the Down Survey—a task which he undertook in December, 1664; and with the aid of his friend, Thomas Taylor, Esq., he accomplished the measurement of two millions and eight thousand acres of forfeited lands by the month of March, 1666.

It is through him, also, that we are made acquainted with the population of Ireland in 1641, and subsequently; and, from the facts furnished by his labours, it is apparent that,—notwithstanding all that has been written and said about the destruction of the Irish population in the fearful struggle that began in 1641; of all those that were put to the sword by Cromwell; of all those that perished by famine; that lost their lives in the new penal colony of Connaught; that went of their own accord, or were forced into exile,—so prodigious was the

---

* Dr. Petty's eldest son was created Earl of Shelburne—a title now borne by the eldest son of the Marquis of Lansdowne. The first Lord Shelburne's eldest daughter married Francis, eldest son of Judge Bernard, and died without surviving issue. She predeceased her husband, whose grand-nephew, Francis, was the first Earl of Bandon.

number of English who lost their lives at that time, or were compelled to fly the country, that the Protestant population in Ireland was less, in proportion to the Roman Catholic population, after the conquest by Cromwell than it was before the rebellion broke out.

Now, when we bear in mind that thousands of adventurers, soldiers, and others—all of whom were Protestants—had come over and settled upon the forfeited lands in this country after the conquest, some idea may be obtained of the wholesale extermination aimed at, and which was well-nigh accomplished.

In 1641 there were two Protestants in Ireland to every eleven Roman Catholics; whereas, after Cromwell became victorious, there was only the same number of Protestants to every sixteen Roman Catholics.*

In common with many others, we have been accustomed to look at the era of the Protectorate, as the era when the Protestant inhabitants of this country were more numerous in proportion to the Roman Catholic inhabitants than they were in any other portion of our history; but this we find is an error. Who would have thought that the Protestant population in our own day is greater, in proportion to that of the Roman Catholic, than it was when Ireland was lying prostrate at the feet of the victor,—in other words, that Ireland is more Protestant in the reign of Queen Victoria than it was in the days of Cromwell? According to the last census (1862), there were not ten Roman Catholics in Ireland to every two Protestants.

As far as we have been able to discover, the oldest tradesman's token issued in Bandon bears the date of this year. On the obverse is a house, with gable fronts, three stories in height. Each gable contains a doorway on the ground floor; and between the doorways is the shop-front, consisting of three round-headed windows, and containing two or three rows of shelves, running their entire length. On the apex of the triangle formed by each gable-roof, and straight above the entrance door, is the figure of a bird—supposed to represent a wren, the crest of the occupying tenant. The obverse also bears the following inscription :—" IOHN WREN, OF;" on the reverse, " BANDON-BRIDEWELL," and the date, " 1659."

Nicholas Brady was born on the 28th of October, this year (1659), in Bandon. He was the son of Major Nicholas Brady, of Richmond,

---

* Dr. O'Kelly, of Maynooth, says the population of Ireland in 1641 was, according to Petty, 1,466,000 Catholics; being to Protestants as eleven to two. After the conquest by Cromwell the proportion of Catholics to Protestants, according to the same, eight to one.

Surrey, and also of Bandon, by Martha, daughter of Luke Gernon, Esq., second Justice of the Presidency Court of Munster. His (the Major's) father was Nicholas, second son of Hugh Brady (the first Protestant bishop of Meath), by his second wife, Alice, daughter of Sir Robert Weston, Lord Chancellor of Ireland.

. The bishop died in 1584, and the next year his widow married Sir Jeffrey Fenton, by whom she had a son, Sir William Fenton, and a daughter, Alice, who became the second wife of Richard Boyle, the first Earl of Cork.

Nicholas Brady, the subject of this memoir, was educated by Dr. Tindall, of Cork, until he was twelve years old ; he was then sent to Westminster School—at that time under the presidency of Dr. Busby. Young Brady applied himself diligently to his studies ; and with such success, as to become a favourite with the celebrated head-master. He was elected king's scholar at Westminster, and subsequently to a studentship at Christ Church, Oxford. Having remained there for three or four years, he removed to Dublin—where his father at that time resided—and obtained from the Dublin University the degrees of B.A., M.A., and D.D., successively. He was ordained priest at Cork, in September, 1687, by Bishop Whetenhall, who appointed him his chaplain. In 1688 he was made prebendary of Kilnaglory, rector of Kilmeen, vicar of Drinagh, and also vicar of Castleventry, in the diocese of Ross; all of which he resigned in 1692.

During his residence in Cork he became conspicuous for his advocacy of the divine-right of kings, non-resistance, and other doctrines then greatly in vogue with the Absolutists. And it was, we may safely assume, owing, in a great measure, to this that he occupied so favourable a position in Jacobite estimation.

It was certainly fortunate for the Bandon people that such was the case ; for when Major-General McCarthy had taken their town, and was about to execute ten of the ringleaders of the black-Monday revolt— after which Bandon and its inhabitants were doomed to the flames— Brady interposed ; and, by his influence, was enabled not only to bar the cruel intentions of McCarthy, but, in addition, to procure very easy terms for his fellow-townsmen.

In 1690, being deputed by the Bandonians to seek the assistance of the English Parliament in removing some grievances of which they complained, he went to London ; where he met with such success as a divine, that he was induced to leave Ireland and settle there altogether.

In a short time he became one of the most popular preachers in the city; and a vacancy having occurred, he was appointed the church of St. Catherine Cree, and also to the lectureship of St. Michael's, in Wood Street. The rectory of Richmond—where he completed the versifying of the Psalms—was conferred on him the same year; and, in addition, the wealthy living of Clapham. For some time, too, he had spiritual charge of Stratford-upon-Avon.* His first appointment to a chaplaincy was to that of the bishop of Cork. He then become chaplain to the Duke of Ormond. After that he was chaplain to William and Mary; and, finally, to Queen Anne.

In 1692 we find him first distinguishing himself as a poet, when he was declared the winner of the prize ode then annually competed for on St. Cecilia's-day; the matter and finish of which was so much admired at the time, that it was set to music by Harry Purcell, and performed amid great applause. He also preached a sermon in St. Bride's Church, on sacred poetry, which he afterwards published under the head of *Church Music Vindicated*. He published, in addition:—

The Rape, or the Innocent Imposters; a tragedy. London, 1692.

A sermon preached at Whitehall, before the King and Queen, upon the 23rd of October, 1692.

A sermon preached at the funeral of the poet-laureate (Thomas Shadwell, Dryden's successor); on Revelations, pt. v. 13, c. xiv.

A sermon on the death of King William.

Sermons.—Three vols.:—London, 1704, vol. one; 1706, vol. two; 1713, vol. three.

A thanksgiving sermon for the victory of Blenheim.

The Æneid of Virgil, in verse; four vols, 1726.

Sermons.—Three additional volumes published after his death by his eldest son; 1730.

But it is principally in connection with Brady and Tate's version of the Psalms that his name has been transmitted to posterity. The first portion of this rhythmical arrangement of the sacred songs of David appeared in 1695, and was entitled *An Essay of a new version of the Psalms of David, consisting of the first twenty, by N. Brady and N. Tate.*† After three years this was followed by the *New Version,*

---

* It was an easy matter to get preferment at this time, as several hundreds of the clergy of the Established Church threw up their livings rather than swear allegiance to William, or acknowledge him as their sovereign.

† Nahum Tate was born in Dublin in 1652. Scarcely anything is known about him until he went to reside in London, where he led a very idle and dissolute life.

completely fitted to the tunes used in Churches; but the supplement containing the Church hymns, was not completed until 1709.

Throughout his whole life, Dr. Brady was held in the highest esteem, "as a man and as a minister." He is described as a person of most obliging, sweet, affable temper; a polite gentleman, an excellent preacher; and, as a poet, the two centuries that have almost since elapsed have failed to produce anything deemed worthy of replacing the harmonious and devotional style of Brady and Tate's version of the Psalms.[*] He was married on the 29th of June, 1690, to Letitia, daughter of Richard Synge, who died archdeacon of Cork in 1688, and grand-daughter of Edmond Synge, who was translated from Limerick to the See of Cork in 1663. By her he had issue—four sons and four daughters. He died in London on the 22nd of May, 1726, and was buried on the 26th of same month, in Richmond.[†]

1660. Charles was scarcely seated on the throne, when the Irish presented him with a petition, setting forth their loyalty during the late war, and urging—as a matter of right more than as a matter of favour—that they be restored to their estates. The English heard of their intended design; and so far from placing obstacles in their way, they asked that the whole subject be fully investigated. The council readily agreed to this, and appointed a day for the purpose. Lord Orrery, Lord Mountrath, and some others, represented the English, and Sir Nicholas Plunkett, and several of his fellow-sufferers, appeared for the Irish. The King himself presided. Amongst those of the council present were the Duke of Ormond and the Lord Chancellor.

Sir Nicholas commenced by endeavouring to show what his party had endured for their loyalty to his Majesty. How they were dispossessed of their lands, and the hard privations they met with in the transplantation scheme.

He adopted no profession, and contrived to support himself by writing verses, and dedicating them to some of the principal men of the day; one of whom (Lord Dorset) procured for him the office of poet-laureate, vacant by the death of Shadwell in 1690. In addition to a number of miscellaneous poems, Tate was the author of no less than nine plays; one of which—an adaptation of *King Lear*—had a successful run for several years. He died within the unhallowed precincts of the Mint, where he fled to avoid his numerous creditors.

[*] It would be difficult to say, at this time, what part each of them performed in the work so inseparably connected with their names. But looking at the characters of the two men, we may lawfully presume that it was Brady supplied the strain reverential, and Tate the rhyme.

[†] His funeral sermon was preached by Dr. Thomas Stackhouse, author of the *History of the Bible*.

Upon this, Lord Orrery rose, and produced a paper—which Plunkett did not deny to have been written by himself. This proved to be an order made by the Irish Supreme Council, in which they unanimously resolved to prosecute Ormond (the King's Lord-Lieutenant) with fire and sword. He also produced another document issued by the same council to Sir Nicholas and another, to go to the Pope, and in their name to offer him the kingdom of Ireland. If his Holiness refused, then they were to tender it to the King of Spain. In case he should not take it, then to the King of France. If rejected by him, to the Duke of Lorraine; and, if declined by him, then to any other prince they liked, provided he was a Roman Catholic. Holding up the two papers in his hand, Orrery triumphantly remarked that those men were not likely to prove good subjects who offered to give away the kingdom from his Majesty. The King perfectly understood their loyalty, and he declared that he was fully convinced that the Irish got only what they deserved.

1661. A new Parliament assembled at Chichester House, Dublin, on the 8th of May, from which we miss the familiar presence of our old friend, Mr. Anthony Dopping. The representatives for Bandon were:—Robert Georges,* of Kilbrew, county Meath, and John Reade, Esq., Coolerelonge.

The Lord Primate (the Speaker of the House of Lords) made a great speech at the opening of this Parliament, in praise of the great, good, and and virtuous Charles the Second. "And is not this place then," said his lordship, "a Mount of Transfiguration? Hath not our dread Sovereign Lord the King, of whom the world is not worthy, been banished into foreign countries, so that he might take up that expression:—'The foxes have holes, and the birds of the air have nests, but the son and undoubted heir of three kingdoms—nay, the native and lineal king of them—had not a place to rest his head in.' But, praise be to that God! that—at the same time He made a stone to be his pillow—sweetened his repose with heavenly visions."

Infamous as this was, it was surpassed by the arrant blasphemy of Bishop Down. Speaking of Charles the First:—"The person murdered," says that prelate, "was not the Lord of Glory, but a glorious lord,—Christ's own vicar, His lieutenant, and vicegerent here on earth.

---

* In James the Second's reign, Dr. Georges was deprived of a large estate which he held under the Act of Settlement; and which had previously belonged to a Mr. Barnwell, by whom it was forfeited for the active part he took in the great rebellion.

Albeit, he was inferior to Christ as man is to God, but yet was his privilege of inviolability far more clear than was Christ's; for Christ was not a temporal prince—His kingdom was not of this world—and, therefore, when He vouchsafed to come into this world, and to become the son of man, He did subject Himself to the law. But our gracious Sovereign was well known to be a temporal prince—a free monarch—to whom they did all owe and had sworn, allegiance. The Parliament is the great council, and hath acted all and more against the Lord and Sovereign than the other did against Christ. The proceedings against our Sovereign were more illegal, and, in many things, more cruel."

The only matter of importance that occupied the attention of the members, during the eight sessions through which this Parliament lasted, was the great Act of Settlement—an Act upon which the titles of most of the estates in this country were based until the introduction of the Court of Encumbered Estates. Our senior member, Dr. Georges, was the person entrusted with the presentation of the Act of Settlement to the King.

1662.   In order to extricate themselves from their difficulties, the Bandon corporation—who were at this time much in want of money, and deeply in debt—intended levying a heavy rate on the town, when the undermentioned citizens came forward and generously contributed the sums affixed to their names :—

	£	s.	d.		£	s.	d.
Clement Woodroffe, . .	47	0	0	Abraham Savage, junr., . .	10	0	0
John Landon, ...	47	0	0	William Wright, . . .	10	0	0
John Poole, ...	20	0	0	Robert Blanchett, ...	10	0	0
Thomas French, ...	20	0	0	John Brayly, ...	10	0	0
John Polden, ...	20	0	0	Nicholas Wright, ...	10	0	0
Jonathan Bennett, . . .	10	0	0	John King, ...	10	0	0
Mathias Percival, . . .	10	0	0	Abraham Savage, ...	7	7	0
Edward Turner, ...	10	0	0				

In the accounts furnished the corporation by Captain Browne, who became provost on the 29th of September—this year—we find the following items :—

	£	s.	d.
Paid Counsellor Cox (Sir Richard), for drawing deeds, . . .	2	9	6
Paid the Bellman, for whipping five persons, ...	0	5	0
248 feet two-inch plank, for gaol, ...	2	8	0
John Nash, for ironwork, ...	2	3	6
For mending Water-gate lock, ...	0	2	3
For turf and candles for the guard, ...	3	9	0
John Nash, for East-gate lock, ...	0	2	0

THE RIGHT HONORABLE FRANCIS BERNARD ... NETTLES BERNARD
Judge of the Court of Common Pleas

CHAPTER XII.

JUDGE BERNARD AND HIS DESCENDANTS—THE FRENCH EXPECTED—LORD BARRYMORE CLAIMS SOME OF THE CORPORATION LANDS—PROVOSTS' ACCOUNTS—LOSS OF AN ENGLISH SHIP OF WAR ON THE NEIGHBOURING COAST.

FRANCIS Bernard, familiarly known as Judge Bernard, was born at Castle-Mahon, Bandon, A.D. 1663. He was the eldest son of Francis Bernard, high-sheriff of the county of Cork in 1676, and great-grandson of Francis Bernard, the first of his family who settled in Ireland (*temp.* Queen Elizabeth).

For several centuries before this offshoot from the parent tree was planted here, the Bernards were domiciled in England. When William of Normandy landed in Sussex, in the memorable year of Grace, 1066, among the mail-clad warriors who accompanied him was Sir Theophilus, who is described as "a valyant knyghte of German descent." Sir Theophilus—who was the son of Sir Egerett—had a son, Sir Dorbred, who was the first to assume the surname of Bernard, and whose son, Robert Fitz-Bernard (in 1172), accompanied Henry the Second to Ireland; and so high did this officer stand in that monarch's estimation, that—when Henry left for England—he entrusted Fitz-Bernard with government of Waterford and Wexford.

"Fitz-Bernard was appointed lord,
By Henry, over Waterford."

Sir Henry Bernard (the christian name of Henry became a general favourite with the Bernards, in compliment to their royal patron) was grandson of Sir Francis Bernard, who married Hannah, daughter of Sir John Pilkington, and was a lineal descendant of Sir Dorbred's. He lived at his ancestral seat—Acornbank, in Westmoreland—where his

16—2

forefathers had been seated for many generations.   He married **Anne**, daughter of Sir John Dawson, also of Westmoreland, by whom he had four sons,—Robert, William, Francis, and Charles.   Francis, his third son—who settled here in Elizabeth's reign—married and had two daughters (one married Sir George Reynolds, and the other Percy Freke, Esq.) and a son Francis, lord of the manor of Castle-Mahon, where he resided previous to the breaking out of the great rebellion in 1641. This Francis married Alice, daughter of — Freke, Esq., of Rathbarry Castle, by whom he had seven daughters (Elizabeth married Captain James Burrell; Kathrine married Francis Beamish, Esq., of Kilmalooda; another married Lieutenant John Langton; Ellinor married Captain William Holcombe—whose eldest daughter, Jane, married William Sweete; another was married in 1660, by the Rev. Thomas Weight, in Ballymodan Church, to her cousin, Captain John Freke, of Garrett's Town; Mary married Captain John Poole, of Mayfield; and Anne married Reuben Foulkes, Esq., of Youghal) and one son **Francis**. Upon the death of his father—will dated December 21, 1660—

Francis succeeded. He married—marriage settlement dated **December** 5th, 1661—Mary, daughter of Captain Arthur Freke, and grand-daughter of Sir Percy Smith, by Mary Boyle, sister of Richard, first Earl of Cork, and had issue :—Maria married Eusebius Chute, of Ballygannon, county Kerry; and, secondly, Francis, son of Sir David Brewster, of Brewsterfield, same county.   Anne married Robert Foulkes, Esq., Youghal.   She died in 1754, leaving the bulk of her property to her nephew, Stephen Bernard, who then became owner of Prospect Hall, county Waterford. Elizabeth married the Rev. Samuel Wilson, of Little Island, county Kerry.   Mary married Edward Adderly, Esq., of Innoshannon, son of Edward Adderly, by Mary, daughter of the Lord Chief-Justice Sir Matthew Hale.   And two sons,—Francis, the judge;[*] and Arthur, progenitor of the Bernards of Palace Anne, who, on the 22nd of December, 1695, married Anne Power (or La-Poer), "att the castle of Lismore, in the great dining-room, about eight of the clock on Sunday night."

The father of Francis, the judge, lived in the most eventful period of our history.   From the time that McCarthy-Reagh marched on Bandon at the head of three thousand men, in the February of 1642, until the

---

[*] A portrait, in oils, of the Judge (from which our engraving is taken) is at Castle-Bernard; and also one of Arthur, copied from the original for which he sat to the celebrated Hogarth.

town threw wide its gates to one of Cromwell's generals, in November, 1649, he held a commission in one of the companies of foot raised by the Bandonians for the service of the State.

It does not appear, however, that he served after Colonel Courtnay—the Royalist governor—and the troops under his command were compelled to march out. Neither does he seem in any way to be connected with the unsuccessful attempt made a few weeks before, " to seize upon the governor, officers, and guards, and to secure the town for the Parliament and the Lord-Lieutenant (Cromwell)."

Mr. Bernard's name appears on the roll of officers known as the 1649 officers; that is, on the roll of those to whom arrears of pay were due prior to the 5th of June, 1649.

His military services were rewarded with a grant, under the Act of Settlement, of Knockane-Ideene, for which he passed patent, December 10th, 1669. These lands, which are on the southern banks of the Bandon river, adjoin the town of Ballineen, and have been ever since enjoyed by his descendants.

As a private gentleman he was highly esteemed; and, as an impartial, active, and judicious magistrate, perhaps, the best proof that can be given of the good opinion entertained of him in those respects, even by those from whom he differed widely in religion and politics, was the request conveyed to him in the April of 1688, by the provost of James the Second's Bandon corporation, from the council chamber of James's Grand Jury of the county of Cork, "that he should make cognizance of the high-constables, overseers, and undertakers of works for the barony of Kinalmeaky, for which they have not given any account; accordingly the said Grand Jury do entrust," &c.

In 1690 he died—having been killed whilst heroically defending his castle against an assault made upon it by a strong party belonging to Colonel Charles McCarthy's regiment of foot.† Upon his decease, he was succeeded by his eldest son,

Francis, the subject of this sketch. Judge Bernard was born in peaceable times. The great storm which had raged for nearly a dozen years, was succeeded by a profound calm. The turbulent waters which had flooded this unhappy country, bearing terror and destruction on their angry surface, had settled into the stillness of a mill-pond. The fired and the blood-stained walls of the colonist's home was replaced by a new and

---

* For particulars see chapter 14.

handsome residence.   The low of cattle and the bleat of sheep told that flocks and herds again trod the soft pastures.   The traveller listened with delight to the ploughman's peaceful whistle, and the milkmaid's song, as he passed along the high-road, or made his way through shady lanes and green fields, to his journey's end.

The Judge, as we have said, was born at Castle-Mahon—an ancient fortalice which belonged to the O'Mahonys; by one of whom, it is said, to have been built in the reign of King John, and which occupies the site of the rath in which St. Fin Barr was born, and resided with his parents nearly thirteen hundred years ago.   Here the future senator and lawyer read the classics until he was nearly ready to enter college.   He then went to live for some time with Dr. Wilson, of Little Island, Kerry, (the husband of his sister, Elizabeth), under whom he completed his studies.

He entered Trinity College, Dublin, on the 20th of April, 1679, as appears by the Entrance Book, in which he is described as " Franciscus Bernard, Pensonarius, filius Francisci Bernard, natus annos sedecim, natus in Comit Corcagiæ, educatus sub ferula Magistri Wilson."   His college tutor was the Rev. Samuel Foley.*

After obtaining his degree of A.B., and completing his terms as a law student, he was called to the Bar.   Being a hard reader, and a pains-taking and clever man, he soon rose to eminence.   Before he was twenty-nine years old he was recorder of Clonakilty—having been sworn into that office, September the 7th, 1692, in room of Richard Cox (afterwards Lord Chancellor of Ireland), who resigned.   Before he was thirty-one years old he succeeded John Dowdall in a similar office in Kinsale; and had even attained to the recordership of the important city of Bristol whilst still a very young man.

Like many other eminent lawyers—both before and since his day— he was desirous of obtaining a seat in Parliament.   He may have thought that those daily conversant with the working of the laws may perform a useful part in framing new laws, or in moulding the old to the requirements of the age.   Be that as it may, his wish was soon gratified.

---

* The Rev. Samuel Foley—son of Samuel Foley, Esq., of Clonmel, county Tipperary—became a Fellow of Trinity College, Dublin, in 1677, chancellor of St. Patrick's in 1689, precentor of Killaloe in 1691, dean of Achonry the same year, and bishop of Down and Conner in 1694.   He died May 22nd, 1695.   His brother, Samuel Foley, was appointed prebendary, rector, and vicar of Kilbrogan, Bandon, in 1704.

He was not more than one week recorder of Clonakilty, when the sovereign, burgesses, and commonality of that corporation assembled, " pursuant to a receipt directed to them, to choose two burgesses of the most discreet and the most sufficient men of the said town, to be and appear at the next Parliament, to be held at Dublin on the 5th of October, 1692 ;"· and the said suffrain, burgesses, &c., freely and unanimously chose Colonel Percy Freke and Francis Bernard, Esq.

On the 28th of October, 1693, Mr. Bernard was sworn a free burgess of the Bandon corporation,* in lieu of Sir William Moore, deceased ; and in 1695, he—in conjunction with Mr. Riggs, of Riggsdale—was elected to represent his native town of Bandon in the new Parliament about to assemble in Dublin.

That the Bandonians should select him as one of their representatives was just what one would expect. He was a fellow-townsman, and one they were proud of. He was a distinguished lawyer ; and had been a member of the late House of Commons. His religious feelings, his political principles, were the same as their own. Their interests were identical.

Both were oppressed† and vanquished under James the Second ; and both were free and exultant under William the Third. Under a Popish king they were dispoiled of their goods, and compelled to fly from the country to save their lives. Under a Protestant king their properties were protected and their lives were safe.

His supporters placed implicit confidence in him ; and their confidence was not misplaced. Before the House had well sat, he presented a petition from his constituents, setting forth :—" That they disarmed the garrison of Bandon, and seized upon the town for his Majesty's service ; and that afterwards, being overpowered by Major-General McCarthy and twelve thousand Irish, they were forced to ransom ten of the principal townsmen from execution, by compounding for fifteen hundred

---

* Mr. Bernard obtained civic honours in various other places. He was appointed a burgess of Castleconnell in 1690 ; of Clonakilty in 1692 ; Bandon, 1693 ; Belfast, 1700 ; and Dunleer in 1707, He was presented with the freedom of the city of Kilkenny in 1705 ; and of the city of Cork in 1725.

† Mr. Bernard was attainted by King James. His name appears on " The list of those who are hereby adjudged traitors, convicted and attainted of high treason ; and shall suffer such pains of death, penalty, and forfeitures respectively, as in cases of high-treason are accustomed, unless such persons shall deliver themselves up the 10th of August, 1689." His estates were forfeited, as were also those of his father and brother. These, however, were all restored upon the accession of William and Mary.

pounds, which they borrowed from English merchants at Cork, who had lately sued out execution against the petitioners for three thousand pounds, principal and interest, to their inevitable ruin, unless relieved by the House, &c.   They, therefore, prayed that the Lord-Deputy should be asked to intercede for them with his Majesty for a grant of some portion of the Earl of Clancarthy's estate,* as a recompense for their services and sufferings in the late troubles."

He also presented a petition from Richard White, stating:—"That he was one of the persons who became bound for eight hundred pounds of the money borrowed for the said town of Bandon, and that his whole substance hath been taken in execution for same; and praying that his deplorable condition be taken into consideration."

But he did not rest satisfied with the mere formality of presenting the petition.   He urged the House to take the matter up; and, in all probability, told the assembled Commons that they should allow no hurt to befall those valiant subjects of their Majesty, who appeared so early and so vigorous in so good a cause.

His appeal was successful.   The House appointed a committee, composed of twelve of its members, to hear evidence and report.   The committee† did so; and the report, which was brought up by Sir John Broderick, set forth:—"That the committee were fully satisfied that the suffering inhabitants of the town of Bandon appeared very early in defence of his Majesty and the Protestant interest in this kingdom, and disarmed a garrison of Irish, consisting of two companies of Irish and one troop of horse.   That they were besieged by a body of twelve thousand Irish, under McCarthy and the Earl of Clancarthy.   That they were forced to pay fifteen hundred pounds for the preservation of themselves and the said town from fire.   And finally recommended that

---

* They probably hinted at that portion of Lord Muskerry's estate which Cromwell gave them, and which Charles the Second restored to Muskerry's grandson (Lord Clancarthy).   Prior to this, they were willing to accept compensation out of General McCarthy's estates (Lord Mount-Cashel).   In a letter from Captain James Waller (Governor of Kinsale and Deputy Vice-Admiral of Munster) to Sir Robert Southwell, he says that Major Love (his brother-in-law) was employed to obtain of the government compensation out of General McCarthy's estate, for the money the corporation of Bandon were compelled by him to pay upon the surrender of that place.

† The committee consisted of:—

Mr. Waller,	Colonel Beecher,	Mr. George Rogers,
Sir John Meade,	Mr. Riggs,	Mr. Richardson,
Mr. Solicitor-General,	Sir Francis Blundell,	Sir St. John Broderick,
Mr. Bernard,	Mr. Robert Rogers,	Colonel Purcell.

the debt should be satisfied out of Lord Clancarthy's estate, or some other of the forfeitures in Muskerry."

Upon the report being read, the House passed a series of resolutions, and gave directions to Mr. Bernard to introduced a bill founded upon them.

The bill was not long in preparation. Neither was it long in passing through the House. It had hardly passed through one stage, when it passed into another—and so on, until it passed through all. Though it may get thus far, it may then be shelved for years. But this was not a measure, in our representative's opinion, to be thus treated; neither was he the man to permit it. Scarcely was the last formality complied with, when he was with their Excellencies the Lords Justices, pressing that the bill should be at once sent to England to obtain the royal signature. His urgency prevailed; and in a short time the bill returned an Act of Parliament.

The only portion of the committee's report which the House did not adopt was that recommending that the money should be raised off some of the Muskerry forfeitures. The House preferred it should be raised off the province of Munster, which was accordingly done; and thus his Bandon constituents, as well as their descendants and successors, have ever since been relieved from a debt of two thousand five hundred pounds, mainly, if not entirely, owing to the energy, the perseverance, and the unfaltering devotion of their zealous and worthy representative, Mr. Francis Bernard.

Two years after he first sat for Bandon, he married. His wife was Alice, grand-niece of that uncompromising Republican, General Ludlow,* and only daughter of Stephen Ludlow, Esq., one of the trustees

---

* The Ludlows took their surname from the Castle of Ludlow, in Shropshire. Stephen Ludlow—ancestor of the Earls Ludlow—was son of Henry Ludlow; and he (Henry) was the son of Sir Henry Ludlow, of Maiden-Bradley, county Wilts, by Letitia, daughter of Thomas West, sixth Lord Delaware. At the restoration, General Ludlow fled to Switzerland, where several attempts were made to assassinate him and other English refugees, at the instigation of the Stuarts. It was well for him he escaped from England, as he would have been, undoubtedly, one of the very first to share the fate of his valiant companion in arms, Major-General Harrisson, "who was so barbarously executed, that he was cut down whilst yet alive, and saw his bowels thrown into the fire. Chief-Justice Coke—another friend of his, who had been solicitor for the High-Court of Justice at the trial of Charles the First—was dragged to the scaffold upon a hurdle, upon which was the head of Harrisson, with its ghastly face uncovered, and turned towards him. Coke met death like a man. He declared that, "as to the part he had taken in the action, he was most ready to seal it with his blood." Mr. Peters, Mr. Scot, Colonel Scroop, Colonel Jones, and several others—relying upon the Act of Indemnity, and the proclamation calling on

appointed by the 11th of William the Third, to carry out the trusts in connection with all rectories impropriate, tithes, vicarages, glebes, and advowsons, forfeited by those who were found guilty of acts of rebellion.

In 1703 he was again returned for Bandon, along with Richard Georges, of Meath (subsequently Quarter-Master General of Ireland); and in 1713 he sat for Bandon for the last time. On this occasion his co-representative was Mr. Bladen, of Albany Hatch, in Essex.

In politics, Mr. Bernard professed himself a Tory; and his friends being seldom in office—and even then but for a short time—a fitting opportunity was not afforded them of placing him in that position to which his abilities eminently entitled him. But, although opposed to the Whig adminstration, his opposition was not very vigorous, and was never factious. Notwithstanding that he would remove them from the management of affairs, yet he approved of many things that they did. And it was but natural that he should. A Tory king seized on his estates, and also on those of his father and brother; and a Whig king restored them. It was under a Tory government a debt was imposed on his fellow-townsmen—" to their inevitable ruin, unless relieved;" and it was under a Whig government that they were relieved, and their inevitable ruin averted.

We have said he approved of many things the Whigs did. Indeed, he would seem to have been more of a Whig than of a Tory. Writing to a friend in 1714, he says:—" I have as great a value for the Revolution as the most perfect Whig in the world. Again:—"I am determined to stand by the present government as long as I have life, or an acre to lose in the service."

Although warmly in favour of a bill that was brought into the Commons for establishing a new bank in Ireland—a valuable measure which the government supporters threw out, " they having got up such a public clamour throughout the whole kingdom that there was no standing against the torrent, and we were knocked down by a majority, without either argument or debate ;"* and although he severely censured

them to surrender themselves within fourteen days, under the penalty of exception from the benefit of the said act for life and estate—came out boldly from their hiding-places, and unreservedly placed themselves in the royal hands. But they soon had reason to regret what they did; for, with the characteristic mercilessness and treachery of this branch of right divine, they were quickly seized upon, and nearly the entire number hanged and quartered.

* Vide—Judge Bernard's letters to Right Hon. Edward Southwell.

the government for granting a patent to Mr. Wood, for supplying a
deficiency in the copper coinage of this kindgom—yet such was the
high opinion entertained of his judgment and honour by the very head
of the government to whom he showed no mercy on this point, that
the Viceroy sent for him, and spent three hours discussing the matter
with him.   In a letter to the Right Hon. Edward Southwell, Mr.
Bernard tells us a great deal of what passed at that interview, and that
"it ended in the Lord-Lieutenant being convinced that it was not
possible for him to give any currency to Wood's halfpence; and that, if
he could not obtain a power from the other side to assure the people
that they should be freed from them, it would be impossible for him to
do the King's business."   In a week after, the Viceroy sent for him
again; "and then told me, that since I had been so free with him as to
break my mind to him, he had discoursed with the Lord Chancellor and
Connolly, and that they had concurred with me in everything; and
that he was convinced and satisfied that the method I proposed—and
no other—could give him credit, and render the King always easy; and
then treated me with so much confidence, as to show me his letter to
the Duke of Newcastle upon the subject, which pressed the easing of
us from Wood's coin."   So thoroughly did he share in the indignation
which Drapier's letters aroused in the public mind at this time, "that
he didn't care to show himself at Court until Wood,* as well as his
coin, be laid aside."

In 1705 Mr. Bernard was made Justice and Commissioner of the
County Palatine of Tipperary, by the Duke of Ormond; and on the
retirement of William Witshead, Esq., he was appointed to the office of
Solicitor-General, on the 3rd of July, 1711.   In 1724 Lord Carteret,
the Lord-Lieutenant—although of opposite politics—sent his secretary
to him, with the offer of the post of Prime Sergeant, just vacant by
the death of Robert Fitzgerald; and this—to use Mr. Bernard's own
words—"being done in so kind a manner, that I accepted of it; though

* Mr. Wood obtained a patent in 1723, to supply a deficiency of £108,000 in the
copper coinage of Ireland.   Dean Swift, under the signature of M. B. Drapier,
attacked the government for granting Wood this privilege; and such sensation did
his letters excite, that the patent was cancelled, and Wood was compelled to leave
the country.   The public mind was greatly incensed against Wood and the government at this period.   Archbishop Boulter, in one of his letters to the Duke of
Newcastle, Secretary of State, says:—"We are at present in a very bad state, and
the people so poisoned with apprehensions of Wood's halfpence, that I do not see
there can be any hopes of justice against any person for seditious writings, if he
does but mix somewhat about Wood in them.

it will not add any profit, but is attended with the trouble of going circuit—which I have declined for some years past." Upon the death of Charles McCruthers, he was appointed to his place; and took his seat upon the Bench, as one of the Judges of his Majesty's Court of Common Pleas, June 26th, 1726; and there he continued to sit, giving great satisfaction to the Bar and the public, until two days before his death —which occurred on the 29th June, 1731.

As a lawyer, he was not remarkable for the possession of any conspicuous forensic powers; but he stood high for a profound knowledge of the law, for keen penetration, and for sound judgment. Archbishop Boulter, who was a contemporary of his, says :—" He was allowed to be a profound lawyer, and man of integrity; and as such—when the rage of party cooled—his merit was taken notice of, by promoting him to a judge's place."

As a practising barrister he was much sought after. In the journals of the Irish House of Commons, we find permission asked from that assembly—at various times—that he should be allowed to appear as counsel before the Lords. He was leader in the celebrated case of Lord Limerick v. Annesley, when he appeared for the plaintiff; also in the great Appeal case of Sir Humphry Jervis v. Offley. He appeared for the petitioner in the Chancery suit of Bayly against Charles McCarthy, and in a great many others.

As we have before remarked, Mr. Bernard was a man of keen penetration and sound judgment; but in no portion of his career were those qualities more perceptible than during the sale of forfeited estates— which began about the year 1702. The sale continued for years, as the estates to be sold were enormous; and as the biddings were often inconsiderable, the commissioners were unwilling to force too many of them together into the market.

That the biddings should be small—and reach, perhaps, to not a quarter of what they would in settled times—ought not to surprise us. We should remember that the effects of the rebellion, which was put down in 1692, were still felt in 1702. It was true that a great portion of the capital, which fled from Ireland to escape being laid hands upon by Tyrconnell or his royal master, had returned; but its owners were still frightened, and they hoarded it. Suppose it was invested in the purchase of those estates; and suppose Anne—who, two years before, lost the only child she ever expected would succeed her—should die, as she now was, childless; or should abdicate in favour of her brother, the Pretender*—for whom she entertained a strong affection; or should leave him the throne at her decease? And should he become James the Third, was it improbable that he would reverse the attainders, and restore to their estates those who suffered years of poverty and disgrace for their siding with his father? Putting aside the principle of gratitude, had he not a precedent in his own family, to show him how he ought to act? Were there not many of those who adventured their money for lands here in his grandfather's reign, or who had obtained grants for valuable services, deprived of these lands in his uncle's reign? And was it likely that the son of James the Second—who was taught to abhor a heretic from his cradle—would protect Protestant purchasers in the possession of estates from which Roman Catholics had been ejected?

Hence it was that the prices obtained were apparently insignificant; but—considering the circumstances at the time—were in reality their full value. We are acquainted with the rental of a property bought at this time for a sum less than it annually produces now. Yet the great inducements given to buyers, by the low prices procured for the lands, were not sufficient to coax some of those who brought them to keep them. The Blarney estate was purchased by Sir Richard Pyne—who, from his official position as Lord Chief-Justice, would reasonably be thought to be nearer the sources of correct information than the ordinary buyer—but he quickly disposed of his purchase to Mr. Jeffries, at a sum less than he paid for it himself. The Hollow Sword Blades Company, who bought immense estates in this country, got rid of them as well as they could.†

Mr. Bernard was able to see before him. He knew that no inconsiderable portion of the English aristocracy and landed gentry, nearly

---

* "Oh, my brother! my poor brother! what will become of you?" was among the last exclamations of Queen Anne.—(Vide *Queens of England*, Miss Strickland.) Again—same work :—"The suspicions of the tendency of Queen Anne to the cause of her brother led the Whigs to a resolution of dethroning her, which, there can be little doubt, they would have perpetrated long before, had it not been for the moderation of her measures. Glanville (the member for Hythe) was heard to declare, 'that the Queen and her ministers' designs for the Pretender were well known; and the opposite party had resolved that the Queen should not remain on the throne one fortnight; for which purpose they had sixteen thousand men in readiness—not, he added, to begin first, but to resist the intrusion of the Pretender.'"

† Those who purchased under the Hollow Sword Blades Company were secured by two English Acts of Parliament,—the Irish Trustee Act, and a special Act obtained by the Company to make good the titles of those who purchased from them.—See Boulter's Letters.

all the inhabitants of cities and towns, and tens of thousands of the intelligent freeholders and yeoman, were deadly opposed to the crown of England being ever again placed upon the head of a Stuart. If, however, the Pretender was called back, and governed in accordance with the wishes of his people, he knew he need not fear for his purchases; and should he not do so, he knew well that the same power which deprived his father of his crown, and his grandfather of his head, was still in being. He saw all this, and he bought boldly. He invested close on thirty thousand pounds* at the sales; and when these were over, he purchased a large portion of the Earl of Anglesea's grants in Bantry and the Carberries; the town of Macroom, its manor and castle, the manor of Kilcrea, the manor of Blarney, and the conservatorship of the river Lee, and the fishings therein, from the Hollow Sword Blades Company. In 1708 he bought from Hester, widow of Thomas Gookin—her six daughters joining in the sale—the lands of Killountain (*alias* West Gully), Currymachane, Brittas, and Gaggin; and from many of those who longed to be rid of what they had. And the largest estate in the largest county in Ireland testifies that he was right.

He died, as has been previously stated, on the 29th June, 1731; and in a few days after his remains were removed from Dublin, and arrived at Castle-Bernard. Here they staid until next day, when they set out for their final resting-place; and were laid in the family vault, in the chancel of Ballymodan Church; and a magnificent white marble monument, by Flaxman, was erected to mark the spot where they lay.

The Judge was the father of a large family, and was a kind and considerate parent. On one occasion, preliminaries were arranged for a marriage between his eldest son and the daughter of the Earl of Barrymore; yet, when he found that the young gentleman didn't care much about the young lady, he broke it off. "I do not find," said he, in a letter to one of his friends, "that he has any inclination to proceed in the matter; and God forbid that I should press him to act against his inclinations in an affair of so much consequence to him." On another occasion he objected to his sons travelling, because he was told the distemper abroad rendered it unsafe.

He was as kind a brother as he was a father. When his sister Eliza-

* We need scarcely remind our readers that thirty thousand pounds in our day is by no means commensurate with a similar sum nearly two centuries since.

beth, who married Dr. Wilson, fled from this country upon the arrival of Tyrconnell as Lord-Lieutenant, and escaped to England with her husband and children, where poor Wilson soon after died, leaving his widow and a little boy and girl totally unprovided for, Mr. Bernard at once sent for her; and although money was very scarce—it having almost quitted the kingdom in despair—nevertheless, he provided liberally for her relief; he allowed her a handsome income, to maintain herself and her children; he paid all the expenses of educating the latter, and, in addition, undertook to provide suitably for them when they were grown up.

He left behind him six sons and one daughter, namely:—

Francis, his heir, born in 1698, of whom presently.

Stephen—of Prospect Hall, county Waterford—a barrister, born in 1701. He was elected to represent Bandon in 1727. In 1734 he was appointed to the recordership of Kinsale, in succession to Mr Jephson Busteed; which office he filled for many years. He died at Tarbes, France, in 1757. He was unmarried.

North Ludlow, major 5th Dragoons,[*] born in 1705. Married Rose, daughter of John Echlin, Esq., of Echlinville, county Down; and, secondly, Mary, eldest daughter of Richard, Viscount Fitz-William, and widow of Henry, ninth Earl of Pembroke and sixth of Montgomery. It was this lady brought the Fitz-William estates into the Pembroke family. She died in Dublin, and was buried in St. Mary's Church in that city. North Ludlow also died in Dublin, April 15th, 1768, having had issue by his first wife:—Charles, who died young; James, who succeeded his uncle Francis, the squire; and two daughters—Mary, married at Ballymodan Church, August 26th, 1756, to Isaac Hewett, Esq., of Clancoole; and Eliza, married January 14th, 1766 also at Ballymodan Church, to Richard Sealy, Esq., of Richmond.

Arthur, William, John; and one daughter, Elizabeth, who married James, third Viscount Charlemont, and was mother of James, fourth Viscount and first Earl of Charlemont, commander-in-chief of the "volunteers" in 1779. She married, secondly, her cousin, Thomas Adderly, Esq., of Innoshannon. She died in 1743.

Francis—best known as Squire Bernard—was the Judge's eldest son

---

* Richard, Viscount Molesworth was the colonel. Lord Molesworth was also General and Commander-in-Chief of the Forces in Ireland, and Major-General of the Ordinance for the year 1751.

and heir. He succeeded upon the death of his father in 1731. He was elected to represent Clonakilty in 1725, in room of Richard Cox, Esq., of Dunmanway, deceased; and in 1766 sat for Bandon. In 1722 he married Anne, daughter of Henry, Earl of Shelburne,* by Arabella, daughter of Charles, Lord Clifford, son and heir-apparent of Charles, Earl of Cork and Burlington. This lady did not survive long, as she died in her thirty-first year, having had a son, who predeceased her.

Had this youth survived, he would have been the largest landed proprietor in the British isles; as, in addition to the very extensive estates of his father, he would, upon the death of his uncle, Lord Dunkerron, and his infant son, have inherited the vast patrimony of his grandfather, Lord Shelburne—containing upwards of one hundred and thirty-five square miles—as next heir; and which, after his death, Lord Shelburne bequeathed to John Fitz-Maurice, the second son of his sister Anne, by Thomas, twenty-first Lord Kerry (ancestor of the Marquis of Lansdowne).

Although the Squire lived in an age when every man of wealth and station had an embroidered coat or vest on, wore frills and rich ruffles of Mechlin lace, and was decked out with valuable jewels, yet he was conspicuous, in his time, for the costliness of his habiliments, for the lustre of the rubies and garnets which glowed on the hilt of his rapier, and for the size and brilliancy of the diamonds which glistened on his fingers, and on his shirt-front and shoe-buckles.†

---

* Henry, Earl of Shelburne, was the second son of the celebrated Sir William Petty, by Elizabeth, daughter of Sir Hardress Waller. In the north aisle of the chancel of Wycombe Church, is a monument to his memory, with the following inscription:—"To the memory of Henry Petty, Earl of Shelburne, son of Sir William Petty. His Lordship married Arabella Boyle, daughter of Charles, Lord Clifford, son and heir-apparent of Charles, Earl of Cork and Burlington, by whom he had issue:—Julia, who died unmarried, aged twenty-three years. Charles, who died at the age of twelve years. Anne, who married Francis Bernard, Esq., of Castle-Bernard, in the kingdom of Ireland, and died aged thirty years, leaving no issue. James, Lord Viscount Dunkerron, died in the fortieth year of his age; Elizabeth, his wife, in her thirty-third; and with their only son, who died an infant, lie buried underneath this monument."

† Long before his time, expensiveness of attire was fashionable, and had reached an extreme, which, even in the gayest part of the last century, would be looked upon as outrageous. In the reign of James the First, the Duke of Buckingham used to walk about, dressed in a suit and cloak of uncut velvet, encrusted all over with diamonds to the value of eighty thousand pounds. The ladies were even worse. At the wedding of the Princess Elizabeth (daughter of James the First) with the Count Palatine of Germany, Lady Wotton wore a gown, the embroidery of which cost fifty pounds a yard; and Lady Arabella Stuart had a dress on which cost fifteen hundred pounds, and jewelry, the price of which would be represented now-a-days by a sum equivalent to between one and two millions sterling.

He made great improvements at Castle-Bernard.   It was he who planted the rows of colossal beech, which stretch from the western entrance of the demesne to the east end of the castle.   He built an eastern front to the old fortalice, where his forefathers had lived the previous century; and which his grandfather had improved by throwing down the bawn walls which surrounded it, and enlarging and modernizing the windows; and which building his father (the judge) enlarged by the addition of a handsome brick* front, facing the river; and which, when completed, the entire was by him named Castle-Bernard.

When Dr. Smith was collecting materials for his history of the county of Cork (first published in 1749), he visited Castle-Bernard. "The house," said he, "has two regular fronts; the walls are of brick, with Corinthian pilasters, coignes, and beltings of Portland stone.   There are fine gardens on three sides of it, adorned with fountains, statues, and other decorations.   That on the north is a most delightful spot, called the water-garden, with cascades, jets d'eau, &c.   The apartments are well disposed.   Adjoining is a very noble park, which is about four miles in circumference.   The Bandon river runs through it, being divided by several islands, sweetly wooded, as are most of the upper grounds."   Then quoting from Pope's *Windsor Forest*, he says :—

> " Here hills and vales, the woodland and the plain :
> Here earth and water seem to strive again ;
> Here waving groves a chequered scene display,
> And part admit, and part exclude the day.
> Here in full light the russet plains extend ;
> There wrapped in clouds, the bluish hills ascend."

But even the far-famed attractions of the royal grounds at the King's castle at Windsor—although depicted in immortal song by the greatest poet of the eighteenth century—failed, according to the opinion of the eminent topographer above referred to, to rival the beauties of the sylvan scenery here.   " But this park," says Smith, " may be truly said to be pleasant beyond any poetical description."

In addition to the beech planted, leading to the west-gate of the demesne, the Squire planted two rows of beech trees, extending from the new front which he built almost to the very church gate at Bally-

---

* The bricks were made from the clay of the field that lies on the southern bank of the Bandon river, between that charming bower known as Lady Harriet's cottage, and Baxter's-bridge.

17

modan. The townspeople took fire at this. They did not object to his planting all the lands intervening between the fair-green and Castle-Bernard—amongst other reasons, perhaps, because they had no control over them, as they formed a portion of Mr. Bernard's estate—but they strenuously resisted the planting and enclosing of that portion of their common where the trees stood.

After a protracted struggle, in which both sides showed strong feelings, the Squire was obliged to give way; and so chagrined was he at the discomfiture of this pet project, that he uprooted not only the trees complained of, but also all those which formed the continuation of his new eastern entrance; and, packing up, he transferred himself and his establishment to England, and never set his foot in this country again.

Upon his arrival in London, he took up his residence in Spring Gardens, and shortly after he purchased Bassingbourne Hall, in Essex, from the family of De Bassingbourne, by whom it was erected. He almost re-built this old mansion; and when completed, it resembled Palace Anne—a beautiful residence raised by his uncle, Arthur, some years previously, on the southern banks of the river Bandon, and a few miles to the west of the town. Bassingbourne was tastefully planted, and had a large ornamental lake in front of the house.

But even the allurements of his country seat, and of Spring Gardens, were not sufficient to prevent him travelling a great deal abroad. He visited most of the principal cities in Europe, where he spent large sums in collecting many valuable pictures and articles of virtu. He died at his town residence in Spring Gardens, March 19th, 1783, aged eighty-five years; and was buried with much heraldic pomp and display.

By his own particular desire, his body was drawn to Lokeley Church, near Bassingbourne, by six of his favourite grey mares; and upon the conclusion of the beautiful and impressive service for the burial of the dead, his costly-draped coffin, with its mountings and armorial bearings, all of solid silver, was laid in a vault in the chancel. He was succeeded by his nephew,

James, eldest surviving son of his brother, North Ludlow. James was born in 1730; and in 1752 he married Esther, sister of William Smith, Esq., of Headborough, and relict of Major Gookin. She died in 1780.

Mr. Bernard was first elected provost of Bandon in 1764, in which year he also served the office of treasurer to the corporation. He was again provost in 1768 ; and again in 1776.

During his long connection with the Bandon corporation—which continued to his death—he was most assiduous in the performance of his duties ; and during the time he served as provost, so anxious was he to be always on the spot, that he used to leave Castle-Bernard altogether, and reside within the walls.

When the great flood, which happened here on the 15th of January, 1765, swept away old Bandon bridge, and flooded the lower parts of the town—causing great loss and distress amongst the poor inhabitants who lived there—he came forward and volunteered to supply the corporation with whatever funds they should deem necessary to afford the sufferers relief.

One who saw a great deal of the world, and who was well acquainted with every surface which humanity presents to the eye, thought highly of Mr. Bernard. " Though he is far the richest person in these parts," said John Wesley, " he keeps no race-horses or hounds, but loves his wife and home, and spends his time and fortune in improving his estate and employing the poor. Gentlemen of this spirit are a blessing to this neighbourhood. May God increase their number !" Speaking of Castle-Bernard :—" It has a beautiful front," said he, " resembling that of Lord Mansfield's house, at Carnwood ; and he (Mr. Bernard) has opened part of his lovely park to the house, which, I think, has now as beautiful a situation as Rockingham House, at Yorkshire."

Mr. Bernard first sat for the county in 1783. On this occasion there was a great contest, and at the close of the poll Mr. Bernard stood at its head. There being :—

For James Bernard, ... 1665
   Lord Kingsborough, ... 1198
   Richard Townsend, ... 978
   Sir J. C. Colthurst, ... 209

He again sat for the county in 1790, and again Lord Kingsborough was his colleague ; but he (Lord Kingsborough) was unseated, upon a petition presented against his return by Mr. Morris.

As has been stated previously, he married the widow of Major Gookin.* This lady had by Gookin two sons—Robert and Waller.

---

* The Gookins (originally Gokin, Gockin, Cockin,) were from Canterbury, Kent ; and down to A.D. 1700 their posterity continued within a circuit of five miles of

Waller died a child in 1751 ; and Robert, a mere youth, was accidentally killed* at Castle-Bernard, in the summer of 1760.

It appears that young Gookin, with a love of sport common to all little boys, ascended to the top story of King John's tower; and whilst standing near a window, through which bats and swallows used to fly in and out of the apartments which they had made their own, he made a stroke at a swallow with the battle-door which he held in his hand; he missed his aim, and in endeavouring to repeat it he stepped back, when he unfortunately fell through the trap-door through which he had come up, and received such severe injuries that he died on the second day after.

Mr. Bernard had by his wife two sons and five daughters, namely:—

Francis, his heir, of whom presently:

Charles—born in December, 1762—died before his father.

Rose, born March 8th, 1758, married—November 13th, 1773—William, Lord Riversdale, by whom she had seven sons and one daughter ; and, secondly, Captain Millerd, of the 55th Foot, by whom she had no issue.　She died May 26th, 1810.

Esther, born March 17th, 1759, married—December 2nd, 1775—Sampson Stawell, Esq., of Kilbrittain, and died leaving issue.

---

that city.　Vincent and Daniel Gookin were contemporary with Richard Boyle, first Earl of Cork, who was a native of Canterbury, in 1566.　Daniel Gookin founded a colony in Virginia at his own expense.　Vincent came to Ireland : he became Sir Vincent Gookin.

Sir Vincent married a daughter of Sir Thomas Crooke, Bart., by whom he had two sons—Vincent and Robert ; and after her decease he married again, and had several children.　Upon the death of his father,

Vincent succeeded.　He died without issue, and was succeeded by his brother,

Robert Gookin.　He married Mary Smith, by whom he had four children—Vincent, Robert, Mary, and Anne.　Mary married Morgan Bernard, and had Steward Bernard (who married his first cousin, Dorothy Gookin, by whom he had John Bernard, of Bernard's Hall) ; and Anne married Abraham Lamb, and had Vincent Lamb (ancestor of the Lambs of Kilcoleman).

Vincent Gookin succeeded his father, and dying issueless, his brother,

Robert, succeeded.　He married Hester Hodder, and had one son Robert.　After her death he again married, and had two children—Vincent and Dorothy—and dying, left

Robert his successor.　He married Dorothy Waller, and by her left a son, Robert, and dying,

Robert (i.e.—Major Gookin) succeeded.　He married Hester Smith, daughter of Percy Smith, Esq., of Headborough ; and dying, in 1752, left two sons—Robert and Waller.　The Gookins lived for a long time in Ibane, and later are described as of Courtmasherry ; and many of them (including Major Gookin and his two sons) are buried in the churchyard of Lislee.

* It would seem from the date of the deed executed by his co-heirs—John Bernard, Esq., of Bernard's Hall, and Vincent Lamb, Esq.—that this unfortunate event occurred previous to the month of July, 1760.

Mary, born in 1760, married Sir Augustus Warren, Bart., and died November 14th, 1825, leaving issue.

Charlotte married—September 3rd, 1785—Hayes St. Leger, Viscount Doneraile. She died September 2nd, 1835, leaving issue.

Elizabeth married, in 1785, Richard Acklom, of Wiseton Hall, Notts, by whom she had a daughter, Esther Acklom (who, in 1814, married John, Viscount Althorp, who, upon the death of his father in 1831, became Earl Spenser).

Mr. Bernard died* in Dublin on the 7th of July, 1790, and was succeeded by

Francis, born November 26th, 1755. He represented Bandon in 1783, in conjunction with Lodge Morris, Esq. He was created Baron Bandon on the 30th of November, 1793, having declined a peerage twice previously. The patent states that the honour was conferred for the distinguished services, loyalty, and fidelity of himself and his ancestors.

He first took his seat in the Lords on the 25th of March, 1794. He was introduced by Lords Lismore and Donoughmore; and on his Patent of Peerage being read and delivered to him with the usual formalities, he was sworn, and took his seat as a baron. In two years later he was made Viscount Bandon, on which occasion he was introduced to the House of Peers by Lords Harburton and O'Neil; and on the 6th of August, 1800, he was advanced to the dignities of Viscount Bernard and Earl of Bandon.

In 1798 he pulled down the two fronts added to Castle Bernard by the Judge and the Squire, and built a spacious mansion a little to the east of the old castle, with which it is connected by a long corridor.

A tourist, who visited this place before the additions and improvements were completed, says:—" The new portion of the castle contains some large rooms. The corridor is ninety feet long; the library, an oval room, forty feet; the dining-room, thirty-six feet by twenty four; the hall, thirty feet square; drawing-room, thirty-six feet by twenty-four. All these rooms are eighteen feet high. The length of the entire building

---

* His body was brought from Dublin, and interred in Ballymodan Church. The account of the expenses is still extant which was furnished for supplying fresh horses at the various stages on the way down, and of the payments made to " keeners," fresh relays of whom met the funeral at specified places, and took the "keen" from the previous lot, who returned to their homes; and in this way the lamentation was kept up unceasingly, day and night, from the moment the coffin was brought out of the house where Mr. Bernard died, until it was entombed in Bandon; a period which in those days, and under the circumstances, must have at least occupied a week, if not more.

is two hundred feet. The rooms are ornamented with many family portraits, and historical portraits and pictures, and many good specimens of the ancient masters."

The same writer also gives a description of the grounds. "The demesne," he writes, "is ornamented by an extensive sheet of water, and rare trees and shrubs. The deer-park on the north-side, through which the Bandon river runs, has some splendid ancient oaks, and extends two miles in a western direction, where the river forms an island, which is tastefully planted; and from a rustic cottage a fine view of the distant mountains is obtained. The gardens cover eight acres of land, and have large green and other houses for pines and other plants. The most ancient portion of the castle was built in the reign of King John. Various additions have, from time to time, been made," &c., &c.

In a lengthy poem, containing no less than one hundred and seventy-seven lines, which appeared in the *Hibernian Chronicle* in 1793, the author, who was evidently enraptured with "the successive beauties" of Castle-Bernard, says :—

> " Where Castle-Bernard sees with glad surprise,
> At every wish, successive beauties rise.
>
>   *   *   *   *   *   *   *
>
>   *   *   *   *   *   *   *
>
> Romantic scenes, that rise at every view—
> Scenes ever dear, and scenes for ever new.
> Ye guardian hills, that round the prospect rise,
> And lose your spiry summits in the skies.
> Here cumbrous oaks a fringy train appear—
> The slow-reared charge of many a fostering year—
> With shelving arms, that cast a glimmering shade
> Along the vale irregularly spread ;
> Their ample trunks, with creeping ivy twined,
> Laugh at the tempest, and outbrave the wind.
> The towering ash its pliant branches spreads,
> And limes, soft, blooming, rear their nodding heads.
> The stately fir; the waving beech that grows,
> O'er sloping borders, in ascending rows.
>
>   *   *   *   *   *   *   *
>
>   *   *   *   *   *   *   *
>
> See !—where the vale draws down, the hanging wood
> In twilight arches o'er the winding flood,
> Bent to the wave—what new creations rise !
> Banks, flowers, and woods that point at other skies.
> Here fair Bandonia rolls, a sleepy tide," &c., &c.

On the 12th of February, 1784, Mr. Bernard married Catherine

Henrietta—who died July 8th, 1815—only daughter of Richard, Earl of Shannon, by whom he had :—

James, the second Earl.

Richard Boyle—in holy orders, D.D., and dean of Leighlin—born September 4th, 1787, died in 1850. Previous to his entering the church, he represented Bandon in Parliament in 1812, and continued to sit until 1815, when he accepted the stewardship of the Chiltern Hundreds.

Francis—Lieutenant 9th Light Dragoons—born February 27th, 1789, died at Coimbra, in Portugal, in 1813.

William Smith, born September 13th, 1792, was colonel 17th Lancers. Served many years with the 1st Dragoon Guards, in which regiment he obtained his troop. He was the first representative for Bandon after the passing of the Reform Bill in 1832. He again sat for Bandon in, 1857, and continued to sit until his death in 1863. He was high-sheriff of the county in 1820; was provost of Bandon in 1824, again in 1826, 1828, 1830, 1832, 1836, and, finally, in 1841, after which the corporation was abolished. He married (in 1831) Elizabeth, daughter of Lieutenant-Colonel Gillman, of Clancoole, Bandon.

Henry Boyle, cornet 1st Dragoon Guards, killed at Waterloo, born 1797.

Charles Ludlow, born 1805, died January 21st, 1861.

Catherine Henrietta, died in 1850.

Charlotte Esther, married (in 1816) Hayes, Viscount Doneraile, by whom she had a son—the present peer.

Louisa Anne, died in 1851.

The Earl died in November, 1830; and was succeeded by his eldest son,

James, the second Earl, D.C.L., F.R.S., lord-lieutenant and custos rotulorum of the county of Cork, and a representative peer. Born June 4th, 1785. He first sat for Bandon in 1820, and again in 1830. He married—March 13th, 1809—Mary Susan Albinia, daughter of the Honorable and most Reverend Charles Broderick, D.D., archbishop of Cashel, and had issue. He died October 31st, 1856, and was succeeded by

Francis, the present peer.

Charles Broderick, born January 4th, 1811, lord bishop of Tuam, Killalla, and Achonry. Married—July, 1843—the Honble. Jane Grace, sister of George, seventh Baron Carbery, and has issue :—Percy Broderick, born September 17th, 1844 ; James Boyle, born December 22nd, 1847.

Henry Boyle, born February 6th, 1812, colonel 87th South Cork Light Infantry. Married—January 18th, 1848—Matilda Sophia, youngest daughter of Lieutenant-General Charles Turner.

Catherine Henrietta.

Francis (the present peer) succeeded upon the death of his father in 1856. Born January 3rd, 1810. He first obtained a seat in Parliament, January the 6th, 1831, having only attained his majority three days previously ; on which occasion he succeeded his father in the representation of Bandon, he having become Earl of Bandon by the death of Francis, the first Earl.

He was again returned on the 7th of May—same year—for the new Parliament summoned to assemble on the 14th of June, but retired in a few weeks. On the 2nd August, 1847, he again sat for Bandon, and continued to represent the town until the decease of the late peer in 1856. On the 16th of August, 1832, he married Catherine Mary, sister of Thomas Charlton Whitmore, Esq., Apley Park, Salop (he married Louisa Anne, daughter of Charles, Marquis of Queensbury, by Caroline, daughter of Henry, Duke of Buccleuch), and has issue :—

James Francis, Viscount Bernard, born September 12th, 1850.

Mary Catherine Henrietta, married—July 1863—Richard Aldworth, late colonel 7th Royal Fusileers.

Louisa Albinia.

Charlotte Esther Emily.

Emma Harriet.

Adelaide Mary Lucy.

Kathleen Frances.

1666.   It appears that Samuel Browne, provost, and Mr. Francis Bernard, were directed to examine the accounts of Mr. Clarck, master of the House of Correction.

Among other matters which were brought under their notice, was a statement to the effect that Mr. Clarck had given no security for the property of the county which was entrusted to him. In reference to this affair, Lord Barrymore wrote the following letter :—

" To my very loving friend, Samuel Browne, provost of Bandon,
          and Mr. Francis Bernard, Bandon,

" Gentlemen,

     " I understand by Mr. Clarck, master of the House of Correc-

tion, that on account of some information which ye hath received, that no security was given for the stock of the county, ye were ordered to call him to account; I do hereby certify that Redmond Barry, Esq., and Ensign Richard Peard, of Castle-Lyons, were security for the said Richard Clarck; and it (the said security) was taken by me, by order of the Justices at the Sessions. I do further desire ye not to proceed any further in the accounts; in regard, I am now going to Charleville, where the Lord-President shall receive satisfaction how the county stock is employed by him. "Yours,
"Kilnokerry, April 5th, 1666." "BARRYMORE.

As some of the old proprietors had been already restored to their estates, and as the government intended to restore many more, the Bandon corporation began to grow uneasy least they should be deprived of the lands bestowed on them by Cromwell, or that the rents payable by them should be increased. In answer to a letter of their's on this subject, to their senior representative, Dr. Georges, they received the following reply:—

"Honoured Sir,
"I have that due sense of my obligation to yourself and your corporation, that I can omit no opportunity that may give me occasion to express my gratitude to you both. And though I had many friends and relatives that I am inclinable to gratify, yet upon the last disposition of his Royal Highness's lands in the county of Cork, for this following year, I have only preserved your interests—I mean the land which was last year let to your corporation—being not yet in a capacity to procure them to be confirmed, and settled upon you as part of what is secured to you by the last law. I have, however, upon your agreement with Sir Kirle and Colonel Townsend, engaged them that the interest of your corporation should be continued, without any increase of rent for the following year; which you may, if you see occasion, inform them from me. And if you observe any inclination in them to fail in that engagement, let me receive notice thereof; and I hope, before the period of this year, I may be able to secure your corporation better in this particular, which, I pray, assure them. From him who is
"Their and your most affectionate friend and humble servant,
"April 21, 1666." "ROBERT GEORGES.

A great portion of this year was spent in making preparations to receive the French, who were almost daily expected to make a descent on our neighbouring coasts. Lord Orrery (the Lord President of Munster) was particularly active. He devoted a great deal of his time to Kinsale;[*]

[*] Some idea of the kind of town Kinsale was at this time may be inferred from the fact that, in the following year, out of forty houses in Higher Fisher Street, and also in Lower Fisher Street (the two principal streets in Kinsale), thirty-one were built with stone, and roofed with slate. The other nine were also built with stone, but they were roofed with straw.

at which port, he was informed by the Duke of Ormond, the enemy intended to land. Orrery lost no time in setting that place in order. He laid a boom across the channel, constructed bastions and curtains, erected earthworks upon the ramparts, placed six thousand pounds weight of biscuits in the fort; employed " a good chirurgeon and two mates, with a chest of medicine, to clap in there ;" sent to Limerick for two hundred hand-grenades, and set to work all the basket-makers in Bandon, making gabions and dust-baskets.

As soon as he had rendered Kinsale defensible, he hastened up to Bandon—"the frontier town of the west"—where he called out three companies of foot and a troop of horse. During his stay here he had an interview with some of the principal gentry in the west of the county, who readily came forward and offered to assist him with four hundred foot and three hundred horse, which he gladly accepted. To this force was subsequently added Armitage's company of foot, also Wade's and Stawell's.

Of the officers, and of others who solicited appointments, Orrery speaks creditably enough, with one exception :—" Gookin is rich, a man of good brains, and fit to command horse. Townsend has money and brains also. Gifford, although very stout, is very poor, yet he is as able to command foot as Townsend. Moore is a good horse officer, and an honest man ; but as for Lieutenant-Colonel Arnop, he is somewhat crazed."

Several of the Dutch prisoners taken during the war were lodged for safety in Bandon, where the government agreed to pay them a penny a day each for their support; but this miserable sum was not only insufficient for the purpose, but it was, in addition, paid so irregularly, that the unfortunate Hollanders would, in all probability, have died of hunger had not the townspeople liberally assisted them.

There was a great deal of wrangling, and even actions at 1667.   law, between our corporation and Richard, Earl of Barry-more,* about the lands of Ryno, Lackyduffe, Ballynargan, and Concan-more. The former claimed them by Letters Patent from the King, and the latter as lord of the manor of Timoleague, to which manor the lands anciently belonged; also by an exemplification of an inquisition taken at Kinsale some time before, which Mr. Flemyn (his lordship's agent) insisted on calling a patent.

---

* Captain John Sweete, of Timoleague, offered the corporation fifty pounds per annum for these lands—a fair rent in those days.

In order to settle the differences between them, and put an end to the vexatious and expensive proceedings both sides were engaged in, Lord Orrery wrote to Lord Barrymore as follows :—

"My Lord,
"Finding by the complaint of the inhabitants of Bandon, that, notwithstanding the several civil actions which I have wrote to you about the differences between your lordship and them for the lands which they lay claim unto, there is not anything done for the determining of it, I have appointed the last of this month for the hearing of the defence concerning these lands; and do desire your lordship to be here with your proof and evidence at such time.   I have ordered Captain Browne, on behalf of the inhabitants of Bandon, to be here also, and to produce his patent, and what else he can show for those lands, that I may do therein according to right.
"I remain your lordship's friend and servant,
"Charleville, 19th July, 1667."   "ORRERY.

The parties accordingly did appear on the appointed day at Charleville; and, in addition to the exemplification of the inquisition previously referred to, Lord Barrymore produced a witness—Edmund Arundell—who offered to swear that he himself, as well as his father, used to pay a heriot per annum for these lands to Lord Barrymore.   Browne, on behalf of the Bandonians, replied by producing his Majesty's Letters Patent for the lands, and several other lands; and proved that the said lands were the property of several "forfeiting Irish Papists." The case was a plain one.   Orrery decided in favour of the corporation in full, and ordered Richard, Earl of Barrymore—within ten days after sight of the deed—to restore the lands, &c.

The corporation let the lands to Captain Freke, and put him in possession of them, by an order bearing date May 10, 1670 :—

"To WIT, We, the provost and burgesses of the borough of Bandon, whose names are hereunto subscribed, authorize William [illegible], of Bandon, to give full and plenary possession of the lands of Ryne, Lackyduffe, and Ballynegan, and all tenants, houses, gardens, orchards, &c., in the barony of Ibane and county of Cork, unto Captain John Ffreke, of Knocknameal, in said county, as tenant to the provost and corporation.
(Signed)   "JOHN POOLE, Provost.
"THOMAS BEAMISH."

Captain Freke was not one month in possession when Lord Barrymore began again.   Notwithstanding Orrery's decision against him, he still claimed the lands as his; and actually levied a distress on them for sixty pounds, which, he alleged, accrued due to him as chief rent since 1641.

"I have been this day at Ringe,"

(writes Freke, in a letter addressed to "Brother Poole,")

"and I find my lord has gotten possession of the house by threatening the people, and pretending he had authority to have it by right of the old inquisition you have seen. As may appear by this letter of Robert Hopper's to me last night, he hath put a padlock on the door, but nobody was in the house when I was there; but, as I came through Timoleague, I was told he had appointed a man, and he goes there this night. He did not meddle at all with the stock on the lands, but he had driven all my sheep at Concanmore, for sixty pounds he pretends is due to him out of that ploughland for forage and chief rent ever since 1641. So if you or Captain Browne go or send to Charleville, I may get a special order that you may feed or graze the lands of Ringe, Lackaduffe, Concanmore, and Ballinglanvig—with all your interests of in chief rents—quietly; and also to command all his tenants to forbear gathering forth these when he is come; for, truly, I dare not venture any stock until such an order is gotten. I sent all my sheep this day to Rosse, and will bring more there until after the shearing, by which time I hope things may be quiet. As for the house, I think you may get an order for it again. This I thought good to acquaint you of, which is all from he that is

"Yours to command,

"JOHN FREKE.

"Bandon, June 8th, 1670."

Whether the provost and corporation again wrote to Lord Orrery on the subject, or whether it was upon their advice Captain Freke acted when he reoccupied the house and lands, does not appear. At all events, he did enter upon the lands, and by force possessed himself of them. For this he was indicted and brought to trial before William Meade, Robert Bathurst, and the other Justices who were assembled at the General Quarter Sessions of the year, held at Bandon. We are unable to say what the decision of the Bench was, but, at all events, it prevented any more litigation for some years.

1670.   The following is the account furnished by Captain John Poole, of the disbursements made by him during his provost-ship :—

	£	s.	d.
"My expences at ye Assizes, when wee had a tryall (Earl of Barrymore's business),	1	10	0
For posting of letter at same tyme,	0	3	8
My expences at ye Summer Assizes,	1	0	0
Paid a footman for coming from Cork with a lettr.	0	2	6
Expences on my journey to Charleville,	1	10	0
For making eight halberts,	2	16	0
For gravelling ye bridge,	0	0	6
For ye Rock of Inishanon,	3	0	0
Mr. Francis Borne, for a yard and interest on £9 10s.,	0	19	0

For whipping a boy and woaman,* 0 2 0
A man for goeing to Cap^{tn}. Hungerford's, ... 0 0 10 .

1676. By this time lands do not seem to have increased much in value. By a lease dated August 19, 1676, we find that the Earl of Cork demised the entire townland of Granoore to Dermod McFinen Carthy, husbandman, " without fine or interest, and all the appurtenances; and, in as large a manner as possible, excepting royalties, free-ingress, and regress; for the term of twenty-one years, for the sum of ten pounds lawful money of England—to be paid at the southern market-house in Bandon, on the 25th March and 29th of September. And also, every Michaelmas, two-and-sixpence in lieu of two fat capons; and also, on the death or alienation of said Dermod, forty shilling in lieu of a heriot; and also to do suit at the manor, Enniskeane, and to grind his corn at the said Earl's mills, of Manch; and also to keep one able man and horse, armed with swords and pistols, to attend said earl's musters, and for defence of town and country. Lease to be void if lands let to any but of British extraction.

1681. Mr. John Watkins, who was provost this year, was also provost the year following; and had been provost ten years before, having succeeded William Chartres in 1672. His account of receipts and disbursements for 1681 is as follows :—

RECEIPTS.

	£	s.	d.
Received from Cap^{tn}. John Freke, in money, at two several times, ...	8	5	9
Received of Mr. John Sweete, at two several times, ...	12	17	4
By customs for ye year, ...	34	0	0
By a rate, ...	19	15	6
	£74	18	7

DISBURSEMENTS.

	£	s.	d.
To money paid for the customs, ...	17	0	0
Captain Poole, for waiting on commission of army, ...	0	9	0
Money paid for billetting the soldiers, proclamation and expenses, ...	0	6	0
Paid for whipping several rogues, ...	0	9	0
Paid the bellman, ...	6	0	0

* The same chivalrous forbearance that signalizes the present age, in dealing with that portion of our humanity known as the fair sex, and which would fain impress upon us that a woman can do no wrong, did not prevail in those rude days. Joan Booth, for instance, who only a few years previously was brought before the provost and burgesses for making use of her tongue too freely—a lingual accomplishment, by the way, not even yet quite out of fashion—was ordered to be ducked in a horse-pond; but, upon her submission upon her bended knees, and her promising never to call Mr. Hethrington " a base rogue " again, her penance was remitted for the present.

Paid John Nash for halburds for ye town's use, ...	3 11	0
Paid Frank Moyers for one year's interest, ...	5 0	0
For a lock for the stocks, ...	0 1	0
Concerning the powder alleged to be found, ...	1 11	0
William Lisson, for mending the cage, ...	0 2	7
Mr. [illegible] and Carey, for ye Irish-town bridge, ...	1 10	0
Jonathan Sloane, for mending ye bridge, ...	0 0	6
Money for commissioners of army, ...	2 15	0
Paid for ye rates-collecting, ...	0 10	0
My own salary, ...	10 0	0
The marshal, for Thomas Olliffe, ...	1 6	9
Money paid two assizes and four sessions, ...	12 0	0
Paid Cornelius Conner, churchwarden, ...	1 15	7
Money paid insolvencies, ...	1 0	6

£67 7 11

There were great floods in the winter of this year; "the hill of Killary," it is said, "hath been washed down, and hath *chocked* [*sic*] up the river, and by its means made the land in the great road* leading from thence to Bandon impassable for man or horse, in winter;" and Bandon bridge was so "put out of repair" by the last great floods, that it took thirty pounds to restore it.

1682. As Lord Orrery—who had decided against Lord Barrymore's title to the lands rented from the corporation by Captain Freke—was now dead, Lord Barrymore probably thought he had now a good chance of asserting his presumed rights. Accordingly, he again brought his claims forward; and prevailed upon the authorities to issue a commission to take evidence. It was signed by Lord Berkley (the Lord-Lieutenant of Ireland), and directed to William Warner, Francis Bernard, and Thomas Hungerford. We have not been able to discover any account of their proceedings, but it would seem that they were unable to add anything to what had been previously known.

In Dunworly Bay—a portion of our neighbouring coast—a shipwreck occurred ; although a shipwreck is not, unfortunately, or ever has been, of rare occurrence on our shores, yet the loss of a ship of war not more than a dozen miles from our town is an event in our history. We are well acquainted with the scene of this occurrence; and for a long time before any record of it appeared in print, or even was known to exist, tradition had made us conversant with many of the particulars.

---

* Much as our forefathers suffered from floods, the people in the west of England were worse off, and even in times much later. Thomas Prowse, M.P., told the House of Commons in 1752, that in the neighbourhood of Taunton the roads were so bad that he verily believed it would cost as little to make them navigable as it would to render them fit for carriages to travel upon.

A great many years ago we inquired of an old peasant what was the name of that ledge of rocks jutting out into the sea at low water.

"Cannon Point," said he; "and the reason it was called so was because one of the King's ships struck on it, and went to pieces, leaving many of her cannon strewn about where she lay."

He also told us that several of the cannon may still be seen on a bright summer's day lying at the bottom of the little bay, within the ledge of rocks we have referred to. He was unable to recollect the ship's name, but he knew it was that of a bird; but what bird, he could not call to mind, although he had often heard it when a child.

In a summer or two afterwards, in company with a few boys of our own age, we happened to be strolling about the rocks in the vicinity of Cannon Point, at low tide.

"Suppose we go out, and try and see the guns at the point," cried one who was weary of unsuccessful crab-hunting.

"Oh! that's just it," replied we all; and away we flew over the intervening space, as fast as our legs could carry us.

Laying ourselves flat on the rocky rim of the little bay, we looked eagerly into its deep waters, but we could see nothing; a breeze had rippled their surface, and the sunlight skipping from one tiny wave to another, rendered it impossible to fix a steady gaze into the mysterious depths beneath.

"Let us strip off and dive down," said one of the youthful inquirers; thinking, naturally enough, that the best way to ascertain the truth of the old stories we had heard was to go down and judge for ourselves.

"Agreed!" burst simultaneously from the lips of all; and, jumping up, we began to undress at once.

We had not proceeded very far with our task, when one little adventurer suddenly remembered that his mamma gave him strict injunctions not to attempt to enter the water until he was rid of his cold; and then he favoured us with a hard cough or two, as if to show us he was still far from being well. Another, for the life of him, could not open his necktie, therefore, he couldn't get his shirt off; and, of course, no one could expect him to go diving with it on. And another felt convinced that if he got his boots off, he could not get them on again.

"Well," we replied, "do as you like, we will make the attempt at all events."

Plunging in, we swam to the opposite side of the little bay, not many yards in width; and, taking in "a big breath," we went in headforemost, and in a few seconds reached the bottom. We plainly saw guns of various dimensions, and came up to the surface with the good news.

After a little rest we again went down, and caught hold of a large gun by the muzzle with our hand—and it was probably the first human hand that had touched it since the reign of Charles the Second—and, groping about with the other, we laid hold of what we believed was a round shot. Leaving go our hold of the gun, we hoped to raise our well-earned prize with both our hands, but having nothing to hold by, we were quickly borne up to the surface. Again we made the attempt, and succeeded in laying hands on another gun, but felt too exhausted to continue below.

From that time to the present—although we have promised ourselves over and over again that we would pay another submarine visit to those mementoes of the old ship—we have not yet done so.

The ship was the "Lark" frigate, and belonged to the British navy. She was lost on the spur of rocks mentioned previously, at eight o'clock on the evening of Thursday, the 25th of November, 1682.

The following account of the disaster, by no less a personage than the captain himself, was lately found by a friend of ours, among the Carte M.SS in Bodleian library. It is headed

THE LARK FRIGATE;

A NARRATIVE FROM YE 23RD OFF NOVEMBER, 1682, TO YE 25TH OF YE SAME.

Between three and foure O Clock on Wednesday Morning wee fell in between ye Blasketts and ye Skellecks wch ly off to ye westward-most part of Ireland, ye wind being at S. S W. Wee got oure tacks on board and stood away to ye E. ward, and about foure in ye afternoon we had ye river of Kilmare open. Ye wind being at S an easy gale which occasioned us to lagg much into ye bay, the same time we went about to ye westward, Ye wind wearing and halling two or three points, occasioned our tacking very often. Off ye Cape Dersey lyeth three isle, about two leagues into ye sea bearing S. W & N. E wch wee could not reatch; but att nine att night wee went between ye two westwardmost Ile steering away E. b S & E S E then ye wind coming to ye W. S. W we went away S & S b. E, till day, for to keep clear off the land, and as soon as ye day appeared we halled away E. & E. b. N. along shore, very fine weather, wth ye wind at S. S. W and made every headland; and about foure in ye afternoon my mate Will Hendley who was about a twelve month scince Master of His Majestys ship Garland, and served in ye ship three years under ye command of Captⁿ Hodder who recommended him to me by letter for being a very able piolate for ye coast of Ireland, that having been there stationed for three years the saide William Hendley telling off me and all my officers, how able he was to harbour ye shipp in King-saile, and several other partes of Ireland; I never having been upon the coast, consented thereunto for the piloting off ye shipp into ye saide harbor of King-saile, wch he undertook wth all willingless, affirming that having made ye old head, as he thought he would carry ye shipp in ye darkest night y^t could be. About six O Clock wee came up wth ye headland, wch ys called ye Seaven heads,* wch he was very confident was ye old head of King-saile, and halled close on board ye northermost shore, and told me our best way would bee to goe up before ye towne, ye wind being out att sea, it would not be safe to ride any lower. I told him ye safest and best place I was for, but when we came to have but six fathoms water I told him I liked not ye shoulling of ye water soe fast, and he told me it was ye Mede, wch is a bank att ye going in off King-saile harbor. But soon after ye water grew shouller wch came to five and four fathoms water, wch meade me call to him manny times and tell him wee had best come to an anchor. He still was positive, and told me he should come to deeper water but I being afeard of ye danger w_{ch} afterwards happened, I halled up our fore-saile and lowered our top-sailes, ye water still shoulling very fast; but before I could stop ye shippes way notwthstanding I braced all aback and let goe our anchor, ye shipp running aground to all oure great misfortune, about eight O Clock att night and ye setting off ye moon and ye top of high-water. I fired manny gunnes for assistance, but not any body came to us, in a long time that could doe us any service. And immediately after wee struck we lowered oure yards and top-mast and got oure small anchor into our boate and run it out with two hausers upon one end into sixteen foot water and brought y^t to ye capstan and endeavoured all wee could to save ye shipp, but ye tide ebbing very fast from us and a storm of wind coming at S S E wee could do noa good, and then wee concluded ye best way toe save ye shipp would be toe cut oure maine and four mast by ye board, wch I accordingly did and by Gods assistance may bee ye savinge off ye shipp. Ye storm continued untill eleven on Friday morning att wch time ye shipp having been full of water, for manny hours before yt, wee were forced all toe stand on ye quarter deck to preserve oure lives. About five in ye morning ye boate went ashore wth nine men wch they affirm broke from ye shipps side, and about eleven they came off wth ye boate att wch time I commanded not a man to goe in, but wth orders. Ye men accordingly obeying, soe that att three times I cleared the shipp except six of us, myself and the Doctor being ye last on board except three men left to guard and keep ye country people from ye shipp. Sir Richard Ruth, Captain Hopson and Captⁿ Deering came from King-saile toe my assistance and manny men off ye two shipps and about one O clock in ye afternoon I went on shore to advise wth them for ye better saving off

---

* This was a mistake, it was the Galley head.

18

ye shipp and stores.   This is ye Testimoney of subscribers hereunto
mentioned.

JOHN MOYLE Chyrg   ⎫   The bay where wee received oure mis-
THOMAS PARSONS Gunner ⎪   fortune* is called by the name of Timo-
HENRY MOULD Boatsw^n   ⎬   league bay, about eigh myles N. W from
ROBERT FRANCIS Carp^ter ⎭   the old head of King-saile.

1683.

A very severe frost visited Bandon, which lasted for many
weeks during the winter.   So intense was it, that an instance
is mentioned of a potato being found in the middle of a ball of woollen
thread, stiff with frost, long after the frost itself had disappeared.

The hearth tax chargeable in this locality was this year two shillings
per hearth, as appears by an allowance made the farmers of the tax of
two shillings per hearth for each hearth in the guard-houses of the
Bandon garrisons.   They contained eight hearths, and the amount remitted was sixteen shillings.

Amongst the presentments of the Grand Jury for 1683, we find that
a Quaker named James Woode, and another named Cook, are described
as vagrants, going about to seduce his Majesty's subjects under the
pretence of religious meetings; and that they congregate several fanatics
in Youghal and Mallow, to the scandal of the Protestant religion, and
in contempt of the government.

---

* There is no such place in any ancient or modern map of Ireland as Timoleague
bay.   However, it is but natural that he should call the place where he received
"his misfortune" by that name, as Dunworly bay was not mapped at that time;
and, besides, it is only two miles distant from the town of Timoleague itself, therefore the writer may well be pardoned for calling a bay so close to the town by the
name of the town.

CHAPTER XIII.

THE MILITIA DISARMED—THE PROTESTANT INHABITANTS TERRIFIED—THE OLD
RANDON CHARTER SET ASIDE—THE NEW CORPORATION—KING JAMES'S IRISH
MILITIA—THE BLACK MONDAY INSURRECTION.

E have now come to another great epoch in our history.
1685. When England rebelled against the Stuarts in
the reign of Charles the First, the Irish took advantage of that event, and rebelled against England.
Now that England rebelled against the Stuarts in the reign of James
the Second, the Irish readily took advantage of a similar opportunity,
and rebelled again. But the great mistake made by them in the former
struggle was not repeated by them in this. In the previous one they
did not warmly espouse the royal cause, but in this one they did.

In the vast uprising in 1641, they first fought against the Royalists;
then they joined them; then they broke faith with them; and then they
betrayed them.* In this one, however, they were united with them
before James set his foot on Irish soil, and after he left it.

They now enrolled themselves under the royal banner; and it was
but what one would expect. James had become a Roman Catholic, and
had taken to his new profession with the zeal of one who was stimulated

---

* Owen Roe, the generalissimo-in-chief of the Irish, left the Royalists, and
entered into a treaty with their powerful opponents (the Parliament) for mutual
assistance; and by virtue of his league with them, General Farrell (the Parliamentary general) had the arms and ammunition restored to him which Inchiquin
(the Royalist general) captured from him.—(See Cox.) Again:—The army of the
Supreme Council deserted the King's service—most of the Irish being seduced by
their clergy—so that at length their pretended loyalty became the scorn of their
enemies.

by prejudices which he had long laboured to conceal, and now, having thrown the reins on their neck, he let them run riot.

If they could not obtain a favour from a sheep of their own flock—from one who humbled himself at the same shrine with themselves—how could they obtain a favour from one who believed the faith avowed by the members of their church to be an idolatrous and damnable superstition?

If James reverenced his religion, he would, at least, respect his co-religionists; and would, of course, restore them to those estates from which they had been ejected by their heretical oppressors. Scarcely had he mounted the throne when the Irish began. Reports from various quarters poured into the authorities that private meetings were held, where violent language and fierce threats were uttered against the Protestant inhabitants. Indeed, so thoroughly convinced were the government of the great movement in progress, that Lord Granard (one of the two lord justices) became so alarmed, that he desired to be deprived of his post; and he was not content to retain it, until James wrote with his own hand, assuring him that nothing should be done in Ireland prejudicial to the Protestant interest.

The great obstacle to the successful over-running of the country was the militia. Talbot, who had been appointed lieutenant-general of the army towards the close of the last reign, had been successful in de-protestantizing it, and now he turned his attention to the militia—a force which was more powerful than the regular army; whose ranks were filled with the sons and grandsons of Cromwell's old Ironsides; a body of men whom nothing could induce to change their religion or countenance the policy of the new regime. Therefore, they must be got rid of.

Accordingly, under the pretence that many of the Irish Protestants were privy to the Duke of Monmouth's designs, instructions were forwarded to Ireland to disarm the militia; and they were ordered to deposit their arms in his Majesty's stores. This being accomplished, the rest was easy.

A petition was presented to Lord Clarendon (the new lord-lieutenant) demanding that all the outlawries occasioned by the great rebellion should be reversed. Archbishop Boyle (the lord chancellor) had the seals of office almost snatched out of his hand. Three Protestant judges were removed without a reason being assigned for their removal, and three Roman Catholics—Nugent, Daly, and Rice—put in their places, without even being asked to take the oath of supremacy.

A cloud of informers arose everywhere. One Major Lawless caused Sir Edward Moore, Edward Riggs (subsequently one of our Parliamentary representatives), and thirty-three others* to be indicted for high-treason. Moore's treason consisted in his being a good Protestant; whilst Riggs, who was also a Protestant, was accused of saying that if he could not live quietly in Ireland, he would go to England.

The Protestant population were terrified. Numbers of the northern Presbyterians disposed of their effects, and fled to New England. A great many of the southern gentry—in fact all those from every quarter who could fly—escaped out of the country as fast as they could. Those that remained behind were insulted and robbed.

"We'll make you as poor devils as when you first came to Ireland!" was in the mouth of every fellow who, from laziness or extravagance, was in the very condition to which he was anxious to reduce his Protestant neighbours.

When rents were demanded, the tenants would coolly tell their landlords they had nothing to give them, as they had spent their last farthing in arming themselves and their sons for the service of King James. At other times they would invite them to drink damnation and confusion to all heretics, especially the Prince and Princess of Orange. But they did not even confine themselves to these civilities. They indulged in unmeasured abuse. Their favourite appellation for a Protestant was—"You dog!" but if they wished to concentrate every vengeful feeling they possessed into one phrase, they would hiss from between their teeth—"You Whig!" It is no wonder, then, that those who could contrive to leave Ireland should do so.

Ever since Talbot was sent over here as lieutenant-general, the peaceably-disposed inhabitants were becoming uneasy; but now that he had been appointed lord-deputy of Ireland, they would stay no longer.

Amongst those who managed to escape from this locality were :—

			Annual income.
Bernard, Francis, sen.,	. . . .		
Bernard, Francis, jun.,	. . . .		
Beecher, Thomas,	. . .	wife and seven children,	. . . £897
Cox, Richard,	. . . .	wife . six children,	 160
Crofts, George,	. . . .	wife . children ten,	 260

* They were all tried and acquitted, and the verdict of Not Guilty had such an effect upon poor Lawless that it broke his heart.

			Annual Income.
Daunt, Joseph, .			£100
Freke, Percy, .	wife .	one child, .	520
Gilman, Robert,	wife .	children six,	120
Gash, Joseph, .			140
Gookin, Mary, .	spinster		100
Gookin, Robert,	wife .	one child, .	300
Gookin, Vincent,	wife .		500
Hewitt, Thomas, .			140
Heyrick, Gersham,			250
Honner, Joseph,	wife .		147
Jervis, Samuel, .			120
Lucas, Nathaniel, .			126
Moore, Sir Emanuel, .	wife .	two children	650
Riggs, Edward,	wife .	children five,	800
Synge, Rev. George, .	wife .	two children,	100
Stawell, Jonas, .	wife .	two children,	600
Travers, Robert,			140
Wade, Richard,			100
Warner, Thomas,			150

Not only those who left the country, but those who came into it, were looked upon with no friendly eye even years before Tyrconnell's arrival.

A lady,* who lived in this neighbourhood, tells us in her journal, that in the July of 1681, her husband and herself, on their landing from Bristol, were brought before the mayor of Cork, and accused of being " plotters in England, stole over."

As soon as Clarendon resigned the sword of state, Tyrconnell went actively to work. Sir Charles Porter was dismissed for saying he would not allow himself to be made a tool of for uprooting the Protestant interest in Ireland; and Sir Alexander Fitton†—a man who had been convicted of forgery, but had atoned for all his misdeeds by becoming a Roman Catholic—was appointed in his place.

Soon after—desirous of filling all the corporations with his co-religionists—he had a *quo warranto* issued against every corporate town in Ireland; and he employed Rice, the chief baron,‡ and Nagle, the

---

* Under date of July 26th, 1681, Mrs. Freke writes:—" I came to Bristol and took shipping at Pill, *incognito;* and by God's great goodness and mercy to me through such turbulent times, we [Mr. Freke and herself] both came safe to Cork the Saturday following. Being both of us guarded before the mayor there—for plotters in England, stole over—to be searched by the present mayor; who being one Mr. Covett [Richard Covett], well known to my family, was over and above civil to us, and treated us like a gentleman, and bound himself for our loyalty; and commanded all our things on ship-board to be presently delivered to us, and the city of Cork to give us the respect due to our quality, to the amazement of all beholders."

† This worthy stated in open court that he believed there was not one heretic in forty thousand who was not a villian.

‡ Sir Stephen Rice, before his elevation to the bench, was in good repute as a lawyer; but it was for his inveterate hostility to the Protestant interest and the Act

attorney-general,* to carry out his designs. Those worthies set to work with a zeal equal to his own, and after two successive terms, there was scarcely an old charter remaining.

New ones were immediately issued to replace those which had been condemned, and new officers were elected, but these are said to have been, for the most part, such inconsiderable and beggarly fellows, that they were unable to pay the fees demanded of them.

The sheriffs were as bad. Some of these are described as being men "without freeholds, and without sense." And one of them— Turlogh O'Donnelly, who served two years as high-sheriff of Tyrone— is stated to have been so deficient in common honesty, that when his son stole some bullocks from his neighbour, Mr. Hamilton, he brought them to his father's (the sheriff's) house; but that high functionary, instead of instantly restoring them to the owner, had some of them killed for his own use; and the rest, in due course, would have shared the same fate, had not Hamilton discovered who the thief was, and where the cattle were. The live ones were given up to him, and a bond was passed for sixteen pounds for those which the sheriff eat; but when Mr. Hamilton sued that worthy for the amount, he—in order to avoid being arrested—enlisted as a private soldier.

By the charter conferred upon Bandon, one Teige McCarthy was appointed provost; and twenty-four burgesses were, at the same time, elected to sit with him.

When news was brought that Daniel McCarthy-Reagh would arrive in Bandon from Cork on a certain day with the new charter, also that he intended raising money off the town, and, if possible, enlisting soldiers there for James, several adventurous spirits from the town, accompanied by some people from Kilpatrick, resolved on awaiting his approach on the banks of the Brinny river, near the bridge—where they pretended to be fishing—having previously determined on making him a prisoner, and burning the new charter with all becoming honours. By some mischance McCarthy heard of their design, and contrived to get safely within the walls with his precious charge.

Good news travels fast enough, but bad news generally out-runs it.

---

of Settlement that he was principally known. Concerning the latter, a favourite expression of his was, that he would drive a coach and six horses through it.

† Richard Nagle (subsequently knighted and made secretary of state by James) was originally designed for the priesthood, and spent some years among the Jesuits, with the intention of becoming one of their Order.

Not only did the rumour of McCarthy's arrival speedily reach them, but an additional piece of most unwelcome intelligence also. They were told that not only had the charter come, but that the bearer of it was accompanied by an idolatrous priest, who had with him a veritable link from the chain of St. Peter.

The charter they thought was, in all conscience, bad enough, the presence of a Popish clergyman was still worse, but that Bandon should afford a sanctuary to an infamous Romish imposture was unbearable.

After making use of language which revealed the intensity of their bitterness, many of them calmed down, and looking at their critical position, they listened to reason; but a blue-black Presbyterian among them would not listen to anything. "That charter—that priest—oh! if he had his will, he'd——! but that link from the iron chain—that symbol of unfettered thought." After wearying himself by the vehemence of his denunciations against relics, and against all those who dared to bring them within the immaculate walls of Bandon, "By the solemn League and Covenant," said he, "if I can lay my hands on it, I will make a bob of it to catch eels with!"

Although the individuals selected by Tyrconnell to fill the corporate and civil offices were in general chosen from a class who had little means, and less reputation, yet so far as Bandon was concerned, those appointed under James's charter were not inferior in social position or substantial wealth to any corporate body that preceded them. The provost, Mr. Teige McCarthy,* was a member of one of the oldest and most respectable houses in the kingdom. Of the burgesses, one was a colonel of a regiment of militia, which he had himself raised for the service of King James, and, subsequently, sat in that turbulent Parliament called into being by that monarch on the 7th of May, 1689. Another commanded his company of foot in the same cause; and nearly all the rest were taken from precisely the same rank in life as those whose duties they were now called upon to perform.

McCarthy having arrived at the scene of his future labours, immediately proceeded to business; and having removed Mr. John Nash— the provost of the Protestant party—he, on the 20th of March, was duly sworn into the provostship. The following were nominated the same day as free-burgesses :—

---

* Teige McCarthy, of Aglise, was deprived of his estate, valued at three hundred and fifty pounds per annum, for his adherence to King James. It was sold at the great auction of forfeited estates in 1703, and bought by James Hingston, of Cork.

Teige McCarthy, provost.
Colonel Charles McCarthy,
Captain Arthur Keefe,
Teige McCarthy, jun.
Thomas Knight, merchant,

Joseph Chamberlaine,
Ralph Chartres, apothecary,
Murtogh Downy,
Edward Collyer, merchant,
Daniel Conner, jun.

To these, on the next day, were added four more—Cornelius Connor, James and Edward Rashleigh, clothiers, and John Goold, merchant.[*]

Hugh Donovan was sworn sergeant-at-mace. His securities were Richard Edwards, innkeeper, and John Murphy.

Following the example of their predecessors, the new corporation also appointed constables to preserve the peace. On the north-side of the town they had Solomon Pope and Abraham Beere, together with Robert Gyles and Thomas Blewit as assistants; and on the south-side, Jeremy Biggs and Attiwell Woods, with William Walker and John Barther as their assistants.

The new provost, although an ardent admirer of James, yet did not permit the interest he took in that prince's welfare to blind him to his own; for we find that upon the very day after he took the oaths, he demanded and obtained from the corporation treasurer fifty pounds, being, as he said, the amount expended in procuring the new charter, and ten pounds to compensate himself for the interest he took in obtaining that boon for the inhabitants.

In two days after (March 23), the following, having taken the oath of allegiance to James the Second, were admitted to the freedom of the town :—

Abbott, William,
Barther, John,
Balten, Matthew,
Biss, Thomas,
Browne, Samuel,
Barrett, W., shoemkr,
Connell, J., carpenter,
Corker, John, cooper,
Cullinane, J., mason,
Cooke, Robert,
Denison, Thomas,
Drapier, I., clothier,
Davis, John, sen.,
Davis, John, jun.,
Edwards, R., innkpr.,

Edwards, Josias, carpenter,
Garret, Robert,
Galvin, Danl., tailor,
Husband, John,
Humphries, David,
Harris, John,
Joyce, Thomas,
Humphries, William, button-maker,
Langton, Aaron,
Litton, William,
Martin, Walter,
Murphy, Denis,
Hungerford, J., tiler,

Mahony, John,
Malone, Hugh,
Polden, Thomas,
Roe, Robert,
Reagan, Darby,
Richardson, William,
Sullivan, David,
Splaine, Robert,
Sabery, Thomas,
Sullivan, Timothy,
Scannel, W., mason,
Woods, Attiwell,
Wright, William,
Wholehane, Darby, carpenter.

[*] Joseph Chamberlaine, Ralph Chartres, and Edward Rashleigh refused to serve, and fled for safety to England. Henry Curtin, William Harding, and Daniel Doolin, were elected in their stead.

From these names, it will be seen that out of the entire population only forty-two could be prevailed upon to recognize James as their king; and even of these some were evidently new arrivals—as Murphy, Mahony, Wholehane, &c.

Now when we consider that, at the very time we write of, all the civil and military power of the kingdom was in the possession of those from whom the Bandonians could expect no favour, and who could at any moment have seized their goods, and incarcerated themselves, without their motives being challenged or their authority disputed, we are amazed to find how any people, helpless as they were, would have dared to resist the supreme authority of those in whose hands were their very lives. Probably they had convinced themselves that the success of James and his allies was but a temporary one, and that it must fly before the advance of a Protestant army and a Protestant king; or, it may be, they despised that prince and the cause he was identified with so utterly, as to prefer the alternative of ruin, beggary, or even a violent death, to any acknowledgement of him—however slender, superficial, or insincere. The authorities were well aware of this feeling, and of its intensity, and on the 1st of June they issued the following proclamation :—

"WHEREAS, several summonses have of late been given to the inhabitants of this corporation to appear and take the oath accustomed for freemen, and forasmuch as they refuse and contemn the said summonses. Now we, the said provost and majority of the burgesses, having taken into consideration the wrong and injury that happen unto the corporation thereby, do, and by our mutual assents and consents have ordered that every person, of what trade soever, shall pay six shillings and eightpence sterling per day for using every such trade or occupation, either private or public, after the fifteenth day of June next after the date hereof; and the same to be levied on their goods and chattels, and to be disposed of according to law; or their bodies to be imprisoned, through the choice lying in the provost."

Another proclamation, more peremptory still, was issued in three weeks afterwards, directed against those " who do stand out, and refuse to take the oath." But this was also unheeded; and all that the summonses and proclamations could wring out of the reluctant townspeople was the addition of six names to those already mentioned, namely— Robert Langley, Thomas Browne, John Long, Jeremy Biggs, Thomas Williams, and Richard Clarke.

Although the treatment they received at the hands of their fellow-citizens was sufficient to discourage them, nevertheless they persevered, and performed their duties with zeal and ability. They passed a bye-law, by which sixpence was charged on every cow, bull, or ox coming into the town markets; on every sheep, veal, and pig, twopence; and on every lamb, a halfpenny. The tolls of the fairs and markets they let to one Daniel Hurly, for £34 per annum, as appears by the following :—

"WHEREAS, there was a lease formerly made by the Right Honble. the Earl of Cork to Thomas Polden, provost of Bandon, and to his successors, provosts of the said town, of the tolls and customs of the fairs and markets of the said town, for a term of years yet unexpired of the said lease. Now we, Teige McCarthy, provost of the said town of Bandon, and the burgesses of the same, whose names are hereunto subscribed, do demise and set the said tolls and customs, with the issues, rights, and profits to the same belonging, unto Daniel Hurly, of the said town, for the term and time yet to come and unexpired of the said Earl's lease, at the rent of thirty-four pounds sterling per annum; payable at Michaelmas and Ladyday, by equal portions, and according to reservations in the said Earl's instructions. In witness whereof, we have hereby put our hands and seals this fourteenth day of April, 1688.

	Teige McCarthy, provost,	McCarthy-Reagh,
Copia vera examinat	Dermot McCarthy, free-burgess,	John Walsh,
p. me.	Arthur Keefe,	Daniel Connor,
	Denis Leary,	John Goold,
Jor. Coghlan,	Thomas Knight,	Francis Riordan,
dep. town clerk.	Joseph Chamberlaine,	Mortagh Downy."
	Charles McCarthy,	

The provost received a letter from the high-sheriff of the county, informing him that he, together with the undermentioned justices of the peace, were appointed by the Grand Jury at the Spring Assizes, 1688, "to take cognizance of the high-constables, overseers, and undertakers of works in the several baronies, and for which they have not given any account."

David Nagle, for ye town and manor of Mayallo.
Martin Supple, Esq., Youghall.
Sir Richard Aldworth, Knt., Duhallo.
Richard Nagle, Esq., Fermoy.
James Mansor, Esq., Candons and Clongibbons.
John Power, Esq., Orrery and Kilmore.
John Barry, Esq., Ibane and Barryroe.
The Sovereign of Kinsale.
Sir Boyle Maynard, Knt., Kinatalloon.
Sir Richard Hull, Knt., Imokilly.
Garrett, Goold, Esq., Barrymore.
Charles McCarthy, of Cloghroe, Muskerry.
John Barrett, Esq., Barrett's.
Nicholas Browne, Esq., Bantry.
Edward Kenny, Esq., Kinalea.
Teige McCarthy, provost, Bandon-Bridge.

Francis Bernard, Esq., Kinal-meaky.

Sir Edward Moore, Carbery East.

Jonas Stawell, Esq., Courceys.

John Ffolliott, Esq., Kerrieurrihy.

Daniel O'Donovan, Carbery West.

1687.

When Lord Clarendon left Ireland in February, 1687, he was accompanied—from Dublin alone—by no less than fifteen hundred Protestant families, who preferred leaving home under many disadvantages, rather than face the danger which threatened to engulf them if they remained. Tyrconnell had long been delayed on the English side by contrary winds—believed by many of the Protestant party to be the act of a benign Providence, which, by hindering him coming over, allowed them to profit by the delay, and make their escape. At last he reached this country in safety. His arrival here as lord-deputy was burlesqued by some wag* in the following verses:—

> " Ho, broder Teague! dost hear de decree,
>   Lilli burlero, bullin a la,
> Dat we shall have a new deputie?
>   Lilli burlero, bullin a la.
>   *Chorus.*—Lero, lero, lilli burlero, lero, lero, bullin a la;
>   Lero, lero, lilli burlero, lero, lero, bullin a la.

> " And he will cut de Englishman's troate.
>   Lilli burlero, bullin a la,
> Dough, by my shoul, de English do prate,
>   Lilli burlero, bullin a la.
>   *Chorus.*—Lero, lero, &c.

> " Dat de law's on dere side, and Crish knows what,
>   Lilli burlero, bullin a la,
> But de King is wid us; and yerra! why not?
>   Lilli burlero, bullin a la.
>   *Chorus.*—Lero, lero, &c.

> " And if de dispense do come from de Pope,
>   Lilli burlero, bullin a la,
> We'll hang Magna Charta and dem in a rope,
>   Lulli burlero, bullin a la.
>   *Chorus.*—Lero, lero, &c.

> " For de good Talbot is made a great lord,
>   Lilli burlero, bullin a la,
> And bringing brave lads wid him from abroad,
>   Lilli burlero, bullin a la.
>   *Chorus.*—Lero, lero, &c.

---

* Said to be Lord Wharton, an old Puritan who fought on the Parliament side.

" Who all in France have taken a big sware,
    Lulli burlero, bullin a la,
Dat dey're damned if dey'll have a Protestant heir
    Lilli burlero, bullin a la.

Chorus.—Lero, lero, &c.

" Arrah, Teague ! but why does he stay behind ?
    Lilli burlero, bullin a la,
Is it Luther keeps him back wid his Protestant wind ?
    Lilli burlero, bullin a la.

Chorus.—Lero, lero, &c.

" But see ! de Tyrconnell* is now on shore,
    Lilli burlero, bullin a la,
And we shall all have commissions galore,
    Lilli burlero, bullin a la.

Chorus.—Lero, lero, &c.

" And he dat will not go straight to de mass,
    Lilli burlero, bullin a la,
Won't we turn him out—de heretic ass,
    Lilli burlero, bullin a la.

Chorus.—Lero, lero, &c.

" Dere was an old prophecy found in a bog,
    Lilli burlero, bullin a la,
Dat Ireland would be ruled by an ass and a dog,
    Lilli burlero, bullin a la.

Chorus.—Lero, lero, &c.

" And now dat prophecy is come to pass,
    Lilli burlero, bullin a la,
For Dick Talbot's de dog, and Shamus de ass,
    Lilli burlero, bullin a la.

Chorus.—Lero, lero, &c.

Soon after his landing he visited Cork, where he was sumptuously entertained by Christopher Crofts, the mayor.

A great many complaints were sent over to England against him, insomuch so, that James thought it right to summon him over to meet him at Chester. His departure revived the drooping spirits of the English ; but this gleam of sunshine did not last long, as he soon came back, and took to his old courses without being in the least diverted from his purposes by his visit to England.

---

* Tyrconnell was one time suspected of being a spy of Cromwell's. In a letter of his to the Marquis of Ormond (dated Antwerp, 1655), he says he merits a better opinion than he finds is held of him by some of the King's ministers, to be Cromwell's only intelligence here.—Carte Letters of Ormond.

The Irish having all the civil as well as military power in their own hands, and having secured Ireland, as they thought, they resolved to send help over to James. Accordingly, three thousand of Tyrconnell's choicest troops went over.

To complete their body, he withdrew the garrison at Londonderry; and neglected to put one in its place, not dreaming that the men of the town would dare refuse admission to any garrison he should at any time choose to send there.

Having recruited, so as to fill up the vacancies caused by the forces sent to England, he ordered the Earl of Antrim, with his newly-raised regiment of twelve hundred men, to take possession of the city.

Whilst this body was on the march, Colonel Phillips sent one James Boyle to Derry, recommending the inhabitants to shut the gates and refuse them admission.

This they had already resolved on, and on the 7th of December the 'prentice-boys tried their 'prentice hands on the drawbridge, and the memorable siege of Derry began. The townspeople were also urged to this dangerous proceeding by a report which was extensively circulated, and believed by every one who heard it, that the Irish intended a general massacre of the inhabitants on the 9th of December; but we suspect that the landing of William at Torquay, on the 5th, did more to influence them than the advice of Phillips, or the fear of any danger to apprehend from the soldiers of Antrim.

The great encouragement given to the disaffected by the new deputy, induced them to start up everywhere. Bands of men—many of whom had long been on the run for robbery or murder—were now formed into corps of militia, and were often commanded by those who, but a short time before, were cow-boys, clowns, or Tories. Fellows who had been accustomed to put straw in their brogues to keep out the cold and the wet, now wore three-cornered cocked hats, and shuffled about oddly in their military jack-boots.

Should any of the class from which these militiamen were drawn exhibit any lack of zeal or sympathy for the cause, they were not overlooked by their clergy.

One who was conversant with the south of Ireland at this time says, that no person, from fourteen years old up to eighty, was allowed to attend mass unless he was furnished with a knife sixteen inches long, and a large half-pike; and should he neglect, or not comply with their

injunctions, a terrible punishment was exacted :—he was excommunicated; cast off for ever; flung outside the Pale of Christianity in this
world, and damned, without doubt, everlastingly in the next; or else he
should pay a fine of seven-and-sixpence.

Influenced by their own passions, as well as by those of others, these
lawless militia roamed about the country, devastating and destroying
everything. In every direction the smoke from a burning farm-house,
or a blazing haggard, told where they had been.* The carcases of sheep
and oxen, slaughtered by them in pure wantoness, were left to rot on
the highway, and taint the atmosphere for miles around.

If a Protestant was seen to look joyous, or even to smile, he was a
Whig, and ought to be piked ; and if he was seen going to, or returning from, his place of worship, he was a heretic, and ought to be burned.

Blood was freely shed too. One who lived then might behold one of
the dominant party parading on the public road, holding a pike above
his head, on which was transfixed a human tongue, and crying out,
" Who'll buy a Protestant's tongue ?" These, and such-like proceedings,
spoke volumes of what the country and its industrious inhabitants had
to expect under the new rulers.

It is no wonder then that the Protestant farmers—many of whom
could remember the great rebellion—should fly from their fields and
homesteads, and flock to the nearest walled-in town for protection.

1689.   Bandon was this time garrisoned by a troop of horse and
two companies of foot, all under the command of Captain
Daniel O'Neil, who held the town for King James.

On Saturday, the 16th of February, 1689, Captain O'Neil issued a
proclamation, which was read at the market-house in the South Main
Street, and at the one adjoining North-gate at Kilbrogan, calling on the
inhabitants to deliver up all their arms and ammunition within three
days.

At the expiration of the allotted time, finding that his orders were
but very partially obeyed, he communicated with Lord Clancarthy,†

---

* Ireland abounded at this time with large farms, all of which were plentifully
stocked with sheep and cattle. Mrs. Freke states that, when she and her husband
let Rathbarry (now Castle-Freke) in 1684, the lands maintained two thousand five
hundred sheep, seven hundred lambs, and in addition to coach horses and saddle
horses, supported thirty working horses, plough oxen, and three hundred beasts of
the pail (i.e.—milch cows), besides young stock.

† Donogh McCarthy (fourth Earl of Clancarthy) was the only son of Callaghan,
by Elizabeth, daughter of the Earl of Kildare, and was grandson of Donogh, Lord

who readily promised to assist him, stating that he would be with him from Cork about noon on the following Monday—February 25th— bringing with him six companies of foot.

The Bandon people having timely notice of this, and being, moreover, encouraged by the proclamation announcing that the Prince of Orange had ascended the throne, resolved not only on preventing the entrance of the six companies, but on turning out those they had within.* They were also stimulated to this resolve by a report—

Muskerry, the first Earl of Clancarthy (the Lord Muskerry who distinguished himself on the Irish side in the great rebellion). He was married when not quite sixteen, to the lady Elizabeth Spenser—a child of not more than eleven years old— daughter of the Earl of Sunderland, then secretary of state to Charles the Second. Shortly after his marriage he removed to Ireland, and lived principally at Macroom Castle, where he continued to profess the Protestant religion, in the doctrines of which he had been carefully brought up at Oxford under the tutelage of the archbishop of Canterbury, until James the Second landed in Kinsale. When Cork was obliged to submit to the victorious Marlborough, Clancarthy was taken prisoner, and, on being sent to England, was imprisoned in the tower. After being detained there for three years, he escaped to St. Germains, where he was graciously received, and entrusted with the command of a corps of Irish refugees. His estates, which amounted to ten thousand a-year, were forfeited, subject, however, to two annuities—one to his wife, and one to his brothers. Of these, the greater portion were bestowed by William upon the Duke of Portland's eldest son, Lord Woodstock. Great efforts were subsequently made by Lord Sunderland, and other influential people in England, to have this forfeiture reversed, Clancarthy being represented to the King as a faultless person ; and they, probably, would have succeeded, had not the Grand Jury of the county of Cork, instigated by Sir Richard Cox (then a Justice of the Common Pleas), forwarded to the court a strong memorial against any clemency being shown to him, on the grounds, amongst other matters, of his practices against the Protestants, his inveterate hatred to the English interest, and the little probability of ever seeing an English plantation in those parts if he was restored. " If he be restored," says Cox, in a letter to Sir Robert Southwell, " this country is undone, and the people swear they'll go to the Indies." The remonstrance of the Grand Jury, backed up by the zealous support of Lord Sydney and the Earl of Burlington, prevailed. Clancarthy was ordered out of the kingdom, but had a pension of £300 a-year allowed him on condition that he would never take up arms against the Protestant succession. He went to reside at Hamburg, where he purchased a little island, in which he died in 1734, leaving two sons—Robert and Justin. Upon his death, his eldest son, Robert, became fifth Earl of Clancarthy. He petitioned George the Second to restore him to his estates—at that time worth one hundred and fifty thousand pounds per annum—and the King was so favourable to his suit as to send letters of recommendation to that effect to the lord-lieutenant. But the new owners speedily took the alarm, and memorialized the English Parliament against the project. The end of the matter was a compromise. Clancarthy got a sum of money in hand, and was promoted to the command of his Majesty's ship of war, the " Adventure." Being suspected of a leaning towards the Stuarts, he vacated his command and joined the French. Louis XV. entertained him handsomely. He gave him apartments in his own palace, rank in the army, and gave him a pension of a thousand a-year. Nevertheless, his love for England was so great, that he removed to Boulogne-sur-Mer, as he used to say, in order that he might live and die in sight of his native country. He died in 1770, in the eighty-fourth year of his age, leaving two sons—both officers in the French service—nothing but his name. They died, as is believed, issueless.

* We think the Bandon people showed more prudence in their resolve than their brethren of Derry. The latter rose on William's landing ; but the Bandonians first

which had probably more weight than even the disarming itself—that O'Neil had declared that the Sunday after Clancarthy's arrival should witness the celebration of mass in the parish church of Kilbrogan.

At the period of which we write, a portion of the space now occupied by the present main entrance to Kilbrogan Church was the site of an old two-storied house, whose big bay windows, high pointed gables, and conical roof, formed an appropriate residence for its well-known inhabitant.

The tenant-in-chief of this gloomy-looking domicile was an elderly lady, called Katty Holt. Tradition represent her as a thin, skinny, wicked old woman, whose tongue never stopped unless she was asleep —and even then it was at best but a guess that such was the case, as some asserted that in her soundest slumbers she kept it going—whilst others state that it was only when she opened her big, old bible, and slowly ran her eyes over some of its pages, that it was in reality at rest.

One so fond of talking must, of course, be fond of gossiping; and, in order to gratify this innocent propensity, she used to allow her neighbours to pass through her house, in their direct path to the church.* This being found very convenient, many availed themselves of her kindness, and afforded Katty thereby unlimited opportunities for a chat. In course of time the passage became such a regular thoroughfare on Sundays, that numbers were able to go in and out without attracting more than ordinary notice.

The leaders of the movement took advantage of this; and on the return of the congregation from noon-day service on the following Sunday, they privately went up stairs. Being all assembled, their first act was to appoint old Hardinge† chairman; after which they unanimously agreed on disarming the garrison at cock-crow the next morning.

Arrangements were then made for perfecting the design. Those who were present undertook to induce all those on whom they could rely to join them. They were to report progress at stated intervals up to ten o'clock that night, by which hour it was hoped every detail would be

---

waited to see how he would be received, and finding he was proclaimed king, they seized on the first opportunity to declare in his favour.

* Our local readers must be aware this was a great favour to the people in the neighbourhood, as otherwise they should pass through the North Church Lane, the only regular entrance at that time to Kilbrogan Church.

† Supposed to have been the Rev. John Hardinge, M.A. and D.D.—the same who (*circa* 1653) engaged in controversy with Dr. Worth, of Cork, on infant baptism.

satisfactorily arranged.   Finally they separated, after entrusting to the church bell of Kilbrogan the ominous duty of announcing on the coming morn that the very eventful moment had at length arrived. They all slipped away as quietly as they had entered.   One or two went out by the front door, but the greater portion got into the little gardens abutting on the churchyard, and thence into the houses of those neighbours on whose fidelity they could rely.

These in their turn also became emissaries; and in a few hours all the male inhabitants were enrolled*—the Rev. George Synge, of Kilbrogan, "Ould Andy Symes,"† of Ballymoney, and the few of those who preached and practised the doctrine of non-resistance, alone standing aloof.   The Presbyterians—and even the peace-loving Quakers‡— joined in the movement to a man.

It may seem odd that the only one of the fair sex entrusted with the secret was Katty; but this was accounted for by the simple reason that it could not be helped.   However the conspirators made a great parade of their confidence in her, pretending to consult her upon what they had resolved upon, and deliberating with her as to what they should do.   All went on smoothly enough, until some one asked what they should do with the prisoners.

---

* Another account is that the conspiracy was organized in Kilbrogan Church, after noon-service on Sunday; and that, in order to prevent any inkling of their intentions from getting abroad, the conspirators turned out all the women—relying upon that popular fallacy that a woman cannot keep a secret.   One young woman, however, who happened to be a servant at Edwards' Inn, where Captain O'Neil had his quarters, contrived to hide herself under one of the seats, and heard all; and her heart being probably smitten by the jack-boots and feather of the gallant O'Neil, she watched anxiously throughout the night;.and when she heard the first stroke of the bell, she ran up to his room and urged him to fly for his life. He had only time to throw on a few articles of clothing, when a loud knocking was heard at the front door.   He hastened as fast as he could to the door leading into the back premises; and once in the yard, it was but the work of a minute to scale the wall and be off.   Notwithstanding, he had a very narrow escape, as he was pursued for several miles, and nearly overtaken.

† Rev. Andrew Symes, who spent a great deal of his time in Bandon, was appointed rector of Ballymoney upon the death of the Rev. Isaac Mansfield in 1688. He was born in 1662; married at St. Fin Bar's, Cork, to Bridget Doherty, in 1692; and died in 1718.   Although very corpulent, he was active and strong.   Whilst running a foot-race on one occasion with another stout defender of the church militant, he so far distanced him, that when he arrived near home—in a fit of generosity to his opponent—he snatched up a couple of bystanders, and tucking one under each arm, he continued the race thus weighted; and arriving victoriously t the winning post, he claimed and received the stakes.

‡ One of these was subsequently arrainged before some of the Society of Friends at Cork, and asked why it was that he, a Quaker, could join in such an enterprize. "I know I am a Quaker," quoth the follower of George Fox, "but I also know I'm a Bandonian."

"Prisoners!" screamed she, stamping her foot wickedly upon the ground, and looking forked-lightning, "Oh, bring them to me—the popish varlets!—and see if I don't scratch their eyes out!"

After spending many anxious hours, the Bandon men dispersed to their homes; where some quietly retired to bed, whilst others anxiously continued awaiting the first cold, pale streak of the coming day—a day which would probably see them revelling in all the joys of recently acquired freedom, or, perhaps, throw its long, silent shadows on their newly-made graves.

The day broke; the cock crew; but the church bell didn't ring. This was owing to a desperate encounter taking place between Jack Sullivan, the sexton, and his wife, Nancy. Jack didn't like the job. If they gained the victory it would be all well enough, but if they didn't—here he pulled up the waistband of his sheep-skin breeches, and after scratching his head as if to irritate his meditative powers into full play, he was more than half disposed to go home again. Nancy arrived just at this crisis in the fate of James's garrison.

Having missed Jack from her side, she thought that he must be engaged in something more than usually important when he would slip away without telling her a word about it; and like all sensible married women, she thought that a husband ought to have no secrets from his wife. In a few words he told her all. She warmly approved of the design, and urged him to do his duty like a man. But Jack wouldn't.

"Then I'll do it myself," she cried, rushing forward to seize the bell-rope; but he prevented her.

And now a regular hard fight took place between them; but where is the wife that's not victorious in the end? and Jack's case was no exception to this rule. Nancy proved to be the queen of trumps, and descending upon the knave of spades, she dealt him such a bad hand as to render it a losing game for him to continue opposed to her any longer. Then following up her lead, she bounded over his prostrate body, and rang the bell, crying out at the same time—"O Lord, spare not the Philistines!"

The bell tolled out a loud encouraging sound. The Bandon men rushed out, and the garrison which was quartered on the inhabitants was disarmed. All the horses, accoutrements, arms, and ammunition were taken, but, we regret to say, with loss of life.

It was not the intention of the Bandon people to have shed any blood on this occasion, but owing to the darkness of the morning and the confusion caused by the sudden rush, eight of the soldiers, who had seized their arms and continued to make resistance, were unfortunately killed. Of these, three—namely, Sergeant John Barry and two privates of the troop of horse—being Protestants, were buried in Kilbrogan; the other five were buried in the graveyard attached to the Roman Catholic chapel in the same parish. The disarmed men were conducted outside North-gate, from whence they all proceeded to Cork.

It was owing to these events having taken place on a dark Monday morning that the inhabitants of Bandon have been called "Black Mondays;" and the neighbouring peasantry still stoutly affirm that ever since a black cloud hangs over Bandon.· The town is called "Southern Derry," because the people of Bandon rose in the South just as the townspeople of Derry did some weeks previously in the North.

The "Black Mondays" did not long enjoy the fruit of their victory; as, shortly after, Major-General Justin McCarthy* (an officer who had served many years with distinction in the French army), together with the Earl of Clancarthy and twelve thousand men—amongst whom were the four regiments of Clancarthy, O'Brien, Dillon, and Owen McCarthy— marched against them from Cork.

The Bandonians could make no resistance. They had no arms, save the few muskets and swords taken from the men under O'Neil's command, and the six old rusty pieces of ordinance sent them nearly fifty years before by the Earl of Cork—and which, if induced to go off at all, were more likely to prove dangerous to themselves than to their enemies. They had no hopes of assistance from any of the towns in the neigh-

---

* Major-General Justin McCarthy (Saorbhreathach), afterwards Lord Mount Cashel, was the youngest son of the celebrated Donogh (Lord Muskerry), first Earl of Clancarthy. He was severely wounded and taken prisoner at the battle of New-town-Butler by the Enniskilleners. Having made his escape, he went to France. where he commanded the six Irish battalions—called, after him, the Mount Cashel brigade—which were sent to replace the seven battalions of French that arrived in Ireland under Count Lauzun. The Mount Cashel brigade was composed of three regiments—the Mount Cashel, the O'Brien, and Dillons—each of which consisted of two battalions, containing sixteen companies of one hundred men each. Upon their landing at Brest, they were sent into Savoy, where they distinguished them-selves under Marshal de Catinat. They also obtained particular notice at the battle fought at Marseilles in 1693. Mount Cashel did not long survive his arrival in France, having died within twelve months from his landing at Barège, from the effects of a wound received in the chest whilst valiantly fighting with his brigade in Savoy. Upon his death, his regiment was conferred on De Lee; and it was sub-sequently known as Bulkeley's regiment.

bourhood, as their inhabitants had been long since disarmed. Under these circumstances they were almost at the mercy of the besiegers.

McCarthy surrounded the town, and peremptorily demanded that the leaders of the late revolt should be given up to him. The besieged replied that they had no objection to treat about delivering the town into his hands upon honourable terms; but as for giving up their leaders, their answer was—" No surrender !"*

This spirited reply, however, availed them nothing; for McCarthy having taken the town, was about to lead forth ten of the principal men to execution, after which he intended destroying not only the town, but also the inhabitants, with fire; all of which he would most assuredly have done, were it not for the interposition of their fellow-citizen, Dr. Brady—who being a recognized follower of King James, and an ardent admirer of the theories then in vogue with the Jacobites, had great influence with that party, by which means he was enabled to induce McCarthy to come to terms; and these were of so mild a nature, that he must have had the dictation of them himself, as the Bandonians were only asked to pay fifteen hundred pounds—cash down—and to reimburse the officers, troopers, and soldiers for their losses and the damages they sustained. There was not a word about hostages or the demolition of the walls, as mentioned by Smith.†

The greater portion of the money was borrowed from some of their Protestant friends in Cork—amongst whom was Mr. William Chartres, an alderman of that city—and some from their fellow-townsman, Mr. Cornelius Conner.

To secure the repayment of this sum, and whatever interest might accrue from time to time, the following, with others, passed their bonds, and became personally liable for the entire amount :—James Dixon, John Nash, Saul Bruce, Thomas Forster, and Robert White.

The articles of peace were signed on the 2nd of March, 1689-90, by

---

* " *No Cede*" has since been added to the town arms. It is supposed to be engraved on a stone over the centre arch of the bridge, looking east.

† Although there is no reference in the treaty of peace to the demolition of the walls, as stated by Dr. Smith in his history of the county of Cork, yet a portion of them were thrown down—perhaps after the treaty was signed. That they were thrown down is evidenced by a presentment passed at the Cork Assizes, December 9th, 1690, which states that " it is ordered that the inhabitants within four miles of Bandon contribute their labour towards the erecting and securing of the walls of the said town, thrown down by Papists." In 1700 another presentment passed the General Quarter Sessions held in Bandon, " for making up the walls of Bandon by the labour of the Popish inhabitants of Kilbrogan."

Major-General McCarthy, on behalf of King James, and Dixon, Nash, Bruce, and Forster, on behalf of the townspeople.

When Tyrconnell heard the arrangement that had been come to, he wrote to McCarthy on the 10th of March, stating "that he was sorry a treaty had been entered into with the people of Bandon until the authors of the disturbance were brought to justice;" and—in allusion, probably, to the unwillingness of the Protestant soldiery to do anything injurious to the Bandonians—he adds :—" The army we shall new-model when the King arrives ; and till that be done it is impossible to make them useful."

When Chief-Justice Nugent,* who presided at the Cork Spring Assizes this year, became aware of the articles entered into with the Bandonians, he cancelled them at the instigation of no less a personage than King James himself ;† who, upon his arrival from Kinsale during the sitting of the court, was made aware of all the circumstances connected with the revolt, on hearing which he became so exasperated with those who dared to raise the first standard of defiance in the South—and that, too, at a distance of only nine miles from the very sea-port town where he was daily expected with a French fleet, and an army second in discipline and equipment to none in Europe—that he order indictments for high-treason to be prepared against them on the spot.

The Grand Jury, constituted as it was of men to whom the very name of Bandon was odious, could not be expected to show them either justice or mercy. Accordingly true bills were found ; and the Bandon men would soon be arraigned for the highest offence known to the law, and soon after on the scaffold have to undergo death with all the dire concomitants of a conviction for treason, were it not for the urgent intercessions of the same Dr. Brady, who, not more than a fortnight

---

* Chief-Justice Nugent—created by James, Baron Nugent, of Riverstown, county Westmeath, in 1669—was the second son of the Earl of Westmeath (the same who was deprived of his titles and estates by Cromwell, for the active part he took in the great rebellion). His appointment to the chief-justiceship was for him a lucky one, as he was enable to decide whether the attainders and forfeitures which left himself and his friends outlaws and beggars should be reversed or not. Previous to Tyrconnell's arrival he was a man of no repute, and was only known amongst his brethren at the bar by his roguish tongue and his little knowledge of the law. He married Mariam, daughter of Henry, Viscount Kingsland. He was outlawed by William the Third. He died in 1715.

† "About seven in the evening," says Dean Davis in his journal. "I got into the park [London], and received an account that King James, in Ireland, proceeded very severely against the Protestants ; and, notwithstanding that he had promised a pardon to the men of Bandon, many of them were indicted at the assizes, and had capias's issued against them."

before, had used his good offices with General McCarthy on their behalf, and who was now called upon again to go over the same ground with James.

But the man he had to contend with this time was the reverse of the former. McCarthy was a man of good sense, and a soldier; James was a religious bigot and a poltroon. Over and over again the humane divine reminded his king that the act of his general was the act of himself; but he could scarcely be prevailed upon to listen to them, and all Brady gained by his mediation was the delay of a few days.

The royal mind was as unshaken as ever; and when the merciless monarch did set out for Dublin, he left peremptory instructions behind him to have the Bandon rebels severely dealt with.* Nugent, only too glad to carry out his Majesty's views in these particulars, ordered them on their trial at once.

There they stood, unflinching and undismayed—although there was no gleam of hope to soften the gloom of that destiny which now appeared inevitable. Before them sat the Irish Jeffries, and beside him was the gibbet. But the darkest hour is that which precedes the dawn.

McCarthy, who had signed the terms of capitulation on behalf of James, and who felt himself bound in honour to maintain his promises with the Bandon people, could not look on himself in any other light than that of an accessory to their murder if he did not energetically interfere. Accordingly he urged the Chief Justice to abide by the peace he had made; but finding importunities of no avail with that worthy, he walked in contumaciously upon the bench, and dared him.†

Thus menaced and overawed, Nugent, " who had resolved on serving them as he served Mr. Browne," gave way. The trial was postponed for a time, when it was again heard—but before a tribunal where opposing counsel were represented by contending armies, where the leaders on both sides were kings, and where the point at issue was the welfare of nations. This court sat upon the never to be forgotten banks of the Boyne.

The names of these old Bandon heroes, over whose devoted heads

---

* It is stated that James was heard to say that he would trust no Protestant; that all the Protestants of Ireland were Cromwellians, and deserved to have their throats cut; that they stunk in his nostrils, &c.

† This was not the first time General McCarthy bullied the bench. On another occasion he threatened the judge (Sir John Meade), because he refused to direct the jury to bring in a verdict of guilty against certain prisoners then arraigned before him.

the sword of Damocles hung so long, were subsequently inserted in the Act of Attainder, and are as follows :—

Arthur Bernard, Castle-Mahon, Bandon.	Henry Jones, Bandon.
Ralph Chartres, Bandon.	Thomas Ware, Nucestown.
Ralph Clear, ,,	Phillip White, Brinny.
John Sullivan, ,,	William Ware, Nucestown.
Thomas Dennis, ,,	Sampson Twogood, Bandon.
Robert Gookin, Kilcoleman.	Samuel Sweete, ,,

We mentioned that Chief-Justice Nugent had resolved on serving the Bandon men as he served Mr. Browne; and had he done so, the Bandonians would have had good reason to complain of his cruelty and atrocity, as well as that of his royal master.

Mr. Browne's case was a melancholy one. It appears that, some short time before James's arrival, Nugent had pronounced it treason for any Protestant to keep arms, or even to wear a sword, after the King's proclamation. Many did so notwithstanding, as they had no other means of protecting themselves and their property from the continued attacks of the rapparees and other lawless bodies, which at that time roamed about the country unmolested. Mr. Browne, a county of Cork man, was one who retained his weapons, and being seen in company with some men who were armed, he was pursued. He was soon overtaken and brought before Judge Daly at Limerick. Upon examining into the case, Daly, who saw nothing unconstitutional in a man's being prepared to defend himself when attacked, dismissed him, considering him innocent of any charge that could support an indictment. Nevertheless he was arrested again, and tried for the same offence before the Chief-Justice at the Cork Assizes.

At first Nugent was disposed to take the same view of the matter as Daly, although it was he himself who pronounced the retaining of arms to amount to treason; but he probably thought that, where it was proved the arms were held only for purposes of defence, the keeping of them would not amount to a capital offence. Be that as it may, after a consultation with King James, who was then in Cork, he proceeded vigorously against the unfortunate accused; and an accommodating jury brought in a verdict of guilty against him.

Everybody thought that James's only object was to have an opportunity of showing his clemency. That he wished, in fact, to inaugurate his arrival in Ireland with an act of grace—a harbinger of the mild and conciliatory policy he intended to pursue here. But it was far otherwise. Notwithstanding that the miserable man's wife and his six little children threw themselves at his feet, and implored him to exercise his royal prerogative of mercy in their favour, he rejected them.

Maddened at the thought of losing her husband, the unhappy woman went amongst her friends; and making interest with every one she could, again she flung herself at James's feet, and besought his pardon; but this effort of her's was more than unavailing, for, adding insult to injustice, he spurned her.

The unfortunate man was first half hanged, then his bowels were torn out, and his body cut into quarters.

This one act of atrocity and bad policy disgusted and confounded many of those who oscillated between their own good sense and the doctrine that a king can do no wrong.

It was useless to look for a change in him; and wherever the news reached, the hearers became convinced that James was as bigoted, as brutal, and as bloodthirsty as ever.

James the Second sailed from Brest on board the St. Michael, and landed at Kinsale on the evening of Wednesday, March 12th.*

It is said that Tyrconnell was opposed to James's coming to Ireland, and even sent over Lord Mountjoy and Chief-Baron Rice to put him against it. But he did not anticipate any success, as he felt convinced the French court would oppose his wishes with all their power. "For that court," said Tyrconnell, "minds nothing but its own interest; and they would not care if Ireland was sunk in the pit of hell, so they could but give the Prince of Orange but three month's diversion. But if the King be persuaded to ruin his fastest friends to do himself no service, only to gratify France, he is neither as merciful, nor so wise, as I believed him to be. If he recover England, Ireland will fall to him as a matter of course; but he can never expect to conquer England by Ireland.† If he attempted it, he ruins himself to do himself no kindness, but rather to exasperate England the more, and make his restoration impossible."

---

* A presentment was passed at the Cork Spring Assizes for raising the sum of £420 off the county, to supply the French fleet that brought James over with fifty fat oxen and four hundred fat wethers, "as a small acknowledgment of the universal thanks due to officers and seamen for transporting his Majesty hither."

† An old poet tells us the reverse. He says:—
> "He that would England win,
> Must with Ireland first begin."

CHAPTER XIV.

JAMES was rapturously received on his landing by the entire
of the Roman Catholic people, and by some of the Protestants that remained in the locality—amongst whom was
the Rev. John Tom, vicar of Kinsale. He was accompanied
by ships of war, carrying two thousand two hundred and five men.

On the 14th, five thousand more debarked. They were commanded
by Count Lauzun and the Marquis de Lacy. In their place James sent
back a similar number of Irish; and on the same day he set out for Cork,
where, on the next Sunday, he heard mass in a chapel belonging to a
monastery on the north side.

During his stay in Cork he was the guest of Major-General McCarthy.
the commander of his forces in the South. The general's residence*
was in the South Main Street (at that time one of the most fashionable
localities in the Munster metropolis); and here the last king of the
royal line of Stuart—a dynasty which occupied the throne of England
for upwards of a century, and which had long previously worn the im-
perial purple in a neighbouring kingdom—lived for more than a week.

The day after his arrival in Dublin—then a city of about 30,000
inhabitants—he issued a proclamation, summoning a Parliament to
meet him at the King's Inn on the 7th of May.

The representatives chosen by the Bandon corporation to sit in this

---

* The house remained standing until about the year 1828, when it was taken
down to make room for the Arcade—a thoroughfare not now much frequented, and
which runs from the South Main Street to Great George's Street.

Parliament, "according to his most gracious Majesty's writ in that behalf," were Charles McCarthy, Esq.,* of Ballea, and Daniel McCarthy-Reagh, Esq.

The election was held on the 23rd of April, in the Tholsel or court-house, situate on the south side of the town, and the return was endorsed by the signatures of those who were present, namely :—

Daniel McCarthy, Deputy-Provost.	Daniel Conner.
Manus McCarthy-Reagh.	Andrew Callaghan.
Charles McCarthy.	John Walshe.
Dermod McCarthy.	Thomas Knight.
Henry Riordan.	Denis Leary.
Cornelius Conner.	William Hore.
Edward Collyer.	Cornelius Perry.

* Charles McCarthy—a kinsman of Lord Clancarthy—was a colonel of militia in James's army. For his attachment to that prince, his estates, valued at six hundred and thirty-five pounds per annum, were forfeited. He was also one of the burgesses mentioned in the charter conferred on Bandon by James. The corporation elected him provost for the year 1691 ; and he would, in all probability, have discharged the duties of that office were it not for the success of William the previous year. He died on the 20th of May, 1704, and was buried in Kilcrea Abbey. The McCarthys of Ballea were a sept of the great house of McCarthy-More. Amongst the Irish gentry who left this country for France after the capitulation of Limerick, was one of this family. He was a very small man, but very active ; and so expert was he with the sword and pistol, that he had no superior. A French officer, meeting him one day, made some uncomplimentary remarks on his stature. This nettled the peppery little Irishman to such a degree, that after retorting as vindictively as his scarcely intelligible French would permit, he sent the censorius Gaul a challenge to fight. The latter—who was both tall and powerful—had heard of McCarthy being a crack-shot, and also that he was able to handle his toledo. Nevertheless, he cheerfully accepted the summons to single combat, and named the sword as the weapon of his choice. He may have been influenced to this resolve by his being aware that he was twice the size of his diminutive opponent, and, there-fore, that he afforded the latter twice the chance of sending a bullet through his body than he had of performing a similar favour for him ; and that, on this very account, his size, which would tell against him with the pistols, would tell for him with the sword—as his height, and consequent length of arm, would give him a considerable advantage over his little antagonist. Both men were on the ground at the appointed time, and set vigorously to work. Every thrust the Frenchman made at McCarthy the latter dexterously parried, and afterwards gave back one in return before the big Gaul could recover his guard ; but though he drove the point of his weapon straight at his heart more than once, and at other times cut through his clothing in efforts to spit him under the ribs, 'twas of no use—he did not even draw a drop of blood ; and his tall opponent stood as erect as ever. At last the sharp eye of the wife of one of the Irish soldiers who was present, and who was beginning to grow apprehensive for the fate of her gallant countryman, detected—or, as some say, only surmised—that the doughty Gallican had armour on beneath his uniform. Quick as thought she addressed McCarthy in the mellifluous vernacular of his native hills—"Arrah, sir," said she, " can't you stick him where we stick the sheep in ould Ireland !" Looking towards where the voice came from, he smiled his thanks, and began again. After a feint or two, he made a desperate lunge at his adversary's neck. The point of his sword severed the carotid artery, and tore open the flesh with such force as to produce a wound which gaped into the very bone. A thick stream of blood gushed out, warm and strong, and soon the poor Frenchman was beyond the reach of all human aid.

During the sitting of this Parliament several bills were passed, two of which involved very important interests. One of these was for repealing the Act of Settlement, and the other for transferring the greater portion of the tithes from the Protestant to the Roman Catholic clergy.

Of the peers, only fourteen obeyed the summons, amongst whom were the four Protestant bishops of Meath, Ossery, Limerick, and Cork. By the revision of old attainders, however, and new creations, seventeen more were added.

James's great want was a want of money; and in order to supply this, he had resource to coining. As he had none of the precious metals to convert into the circulating medium, he had to supply their place with any kinds of metal he could lay hands on. A cracked pot, or a broken frying-pan, worthless pieces of cannon, knockers of doors, brass candlesticks, and old kettles, were carted to the mint; and in a short time lumps of metal, coined to represent close on a million and a-half sterling, but not worth a sixtieth of that sum, were in circulation.*

A royal ordinance pronounced them legal tender. Hardly any one dared to refuse them; and those who did summon up courage, and declined to part with their goods, valued in twenty guineas, for a bag of pot-metal half-crowns—in reality not worth seven shillings—were seized and brought before the provost-marshal, who swore at them, confined them in dark cells, and by threatening them with the gallows, compelled them to submit.

On a bright sunny morning in April (1690), occurred the darkest disaster that as yet befell the citizens of the ancient and loyal borough of Bandon. Ever since the capitulation of the town—just thirteen months before—the townspeople lead a very peaceable life. Knowing that they were helplessly at the mercy of their hereditary foes, they did nothing that could afford a pretext for violence, or an excuse for extortion; whilst so thoroughly were they stripped of all their

---

* The amount issued nominally was £1,396,799. After the battle of the Boyne, Lord Coningsby found £22,489 in the mint, which he valued at £641 19s. 5d. It is stated that fourpennyworth of brass metal was made pass current for five pounds sterling; and, as if this was not enough, the half-crowns were subsequently transformed into five-shilling pieces, and the shillings reduced to half their former size. Any one refusing to take them at the value set upon them by James, ran every chance of being hanged. After the accession of William, this coinage was reduced to its proper value, by a proclamation announcing that thenceforth a five-shilling piece should pass for one penny, a half-crown for three-farthings, and a shilling and a sixpence for a farthing each.

weapons by General McCarthy, that not a single musket, or even a charge of gunpowder, was to be had in the whole town.

On Sunday morning it was usual to throw open the gates, in order to admit the numerous Protestant colonists to attend divine worship. The gate at the northern side—called North-gate—invited the stubborn Presbyterians, who had settled along the upper banks of "the fair Bandon," to enter its friendly portals on their way to the plain, unpretending meeting-house, which at that time occupied the site of the present court-house.

The other gates were equally accommodating to the outsiders. West-gate led to Ballymodan Church, whilst East-gate, at the other end of the town, conducted the settlers on the Innoshannon side to the studiously unassuming place of worship belonging to the Society of Friends.

It was a calm, clear day. The last peal of the church-going bell of Kilbrogan had settled into a prolonged booming sound—and even that was slowly softening into silence. The grave-looking sextoness of the Presbyterian chapel, with her clean tidy apron on, and her neat but unassuming cap, had put her head outside the chapel doors for the last time to see if, perchance, some undecided straggler, or some over-worked neighbour's wife, had thought it not yet too late to join in the sacred services of the Sabbath morn. She could see no one. The streets that lay before her were empty. There was not a voice, or even a footfall, to ruffle the solemn stillness of the scene. Above her was the blue sky—the first, perhaps, that she had seen since the summer of the preceding year—and around her danced the golden sunbeams, all joyous and fresh, from their long winter prison. She softly closed the door, and thought, as she did so, that surely this was indeed God's holyday.

The Rev. Mr. Hardinge occupied his own pulpit on that Sunday morning; and with the foresight almost of a seer, had selected as his text, "Let not your hearts be troubled : ye believe in God; believe also in me."

He had not been preaching for more than ten minutes, when the sextoness, who fancied more than once that she had heard a subdued noise resembling the shuffling of feet, quickly left her seat, to see if there was anything amiss. Scarcely had she opened the door, when back she started with a shriek, followed by a horde of savage-looking men, whose wild gesticulations and ferocious yells contrasted strangely with the staid and reverential deportment of those amongst whom they had thus suddenly come. Pouring in, with their pikes waving above their heads, their long knives unsheathed, and ready for any atrocity, resistance was out of question.

What could the people thus surprised do? If any of them dared to look even angry, in an instant a dozen skeans were at his throat; whilst others, not so accessible, felt that their lives hung upon the caprice of those whose levelled muskets were pointed at their heads.

Having secured all the outlets, and rendered escape impossible, McCarthy,* who commanded them, ordered his men to keep silence; then taking his seat as one of the congregation, he crossed his legs, and apparently paid strict attention to Mr. Hardinge's discourse.

Meanwhile, the old minister—faithful to the trusts committed to him, and nothing daunted by the presence of one who held a colonel's commission under King James, and who had under his orders, and in that very place, those who would not hesitate to enter his pulpit and imbue their hands in his blood—proclaimed the divine precepts as heretofore, and pounded and expounded the various heads under which he had classed his subject, with just the same earnestness for the spiritual welfare of his hearers as he had done for the forty years preceding.

After remaining about a quarter of an hour, McCarthy stood up and directed his followers to turn out, save those who were necessary for keeping the congregation in safe custody.†

Colonel McCarthy's design of surprising the town was well planned, and successfully executed. Being an inhabitant of Bandon for no small portion of the two previous years, he was aware of the gates being left open on Sunday mornings, and of the strong prejudices entertained by the inhabitants of doing anything, even in their own defence, on the Lord's-day. He took advantage of this, and waiting till the church bells stopped ringing—by which time his soldiers, who had marched in with him before day-break, and concealed themselves in the bogs of Callatrim, were rested and refreshed—he stole up with them to North-gate; and parties having been previously told off for certain posts, all they had to do was to march in and take possession.

---

* Colonel Charles McCarthy, the senior representative for Bandon in King James's Parliament.

† There was a little girl named Mary Morris present on this eventful morning; and such was the impression made upon her youthful mind by all she witnessed, that she was enabled to state the most minute particulars in seventy years afterwards.

A strong force occupied both churches. That in Kilbrogan was accompanied by three Irish pipers.* One of these fellows impiously sat on the communion-table, where he struck up " the King shall enjoy his own again," in triumphant style, beating a tattoo by way of accompaniment upon the leaf of the table with his long hairy legs, and with just as much composure as if he were seated upon the edge of his native bog-hole, and was playing a tune for the boys at the wake of some mutual friend.

Another fellow squatted on the circular bench in front of the communion-rail, with his dilapidated hat jantily set on the side of his head. Here he sat, whilst—with eyes brimful of fun and humour—he played " Lilli-Burlero," and the " Humours of Bandon." The latter he seemed much to relish, dwelling upon some of the notes in a style peculiarly grotesque.

But the third seems to have been the most amusing of the lot. He took up his station in front of the pulpit, and signified by his pipes what he thought of the discourse. If he had heard anything that pleased him, he'd make the pipes utter three or four jocular squeaks, musically intimating his satisfaction ; if otherwise, he'd lower his tubes, and give out a deep melancholy drone of disapprobation.

Meanwhile the congregation looked on ; and though at any other time or place the ultra-comic nature of the scene might have produced shouts of merriment, yet, considering the orchestra selected by the pipers, and the circumstances under which the musical matinee was performed, we must not be surprised at the solemn silence maintained.

Upon McCarthy's arrival the pipers were ordered out of the church, and permission given to the women and children to return to their homes ; but the men were all made prisoners.

The people at Ballymodan Church were similarly treated, the men alone being detained.

After spending some hours in pillaging the town, they conveyed all their plunder and their prisoners into the castle that up to about fifty years ago occupied the piece of ground on the right of the court-house, and upon which at present stands the town-hall.

The property seized on them was not much; as the townspeople had carefully concealed the most of their valuables on the approach of

---

* One of the pipers was subsequently arrested and brought before Shane Dearg ; but before the non-commissioned officer, in whose custody he was, had time to even narrate half the details connected with his arrest, the unfortunate man was on his way to the gallows.

General McCarthy; and the times being very disturbed ever since, they prudently left them remain where they were.

The prisoners, however, were both numerous and respectable; every man for whose ransom they expected anything being secured. The rest, not being considered of any value, were permitted to go at large.

In the meantime various other parties were scouring the country, pillaging and bringing in prisoners. One strong party made a fierce onslaught on Castle-Mahon; but Mr. Bernard, who had often smelt powder during the great rebellion, was not to be easily disposed of. He was an old soldier, who had passed through many a bloody struggle with the Bandon militia—a regiment in which he had served many years. It was not probable that he, who had been rewarded with a grant of land by Cromwell for his services against men who were led by experienced officers—whom long campaigning had converted into trained soldiers, and who had resisted the arms of England for a dozen years— would now lower the red flag which flaunted defiance from the battlements of King John's tower, and surrender to a parcel of vagabonds whose acquaintance with the art of war scarcely extended beyond loading and firing a musket, and brandishing a pike.

Mr. Bernard, who had timely notice of the enemies approach, had his retainers and several of the neighbouring farmers—many of whom had borne arms with him more than forty years before—armed and ready; and when the trumpeter appeared on the esplanade in front of the castle, and demanded that the castle itself and all its stores should be given up to his gracious Majesty King James, and that the garrison should come forth and deliver themselves up as prisoners, he bid them begone for a set of knaves.

Seeing that they could obtain nothing by peaceable means, they marched up boldly to the main entrance, hoping to overawe the warders, and again demanded a surrender; but a universal " No!" assailed their ears from every quarter.

Not a whit disconcerted by the firm negative, they attempted to batter in the great gate; but a well-directed discharge of musketry from within stretched some lifeless forms on the pavement. Hurriedly withdrawing themselves for a time outside the range of the hostile bullets, they again advanced. Every window was pushed violently and shaken, in order to effect an entrance. Every door was attempted to be forced for the same purpose, but there was no stirring them.

Meanwhile, the sentries—a chain of whom were posted on the open ground in the front, with orders to pick off every one who should appear in any of the windows and attempt to fire on those who were striving to get in below—were nearly all shot. In fact, all any one of besieged had to do was to rest the muzzle of his piece on the window-sill, take good aim, touch the trigger, and down would drop one of the enemy—either howling with pain from a wound which would probably prove fatal, or a corpse.

The garrison, no longer deterred from putting their heads out of the windows, now opened a murderous fire on the foe beneath. They could not withstand this. Should they remain much longer, they must all be killed. They knew this, and with one simultaneous rush they took to their heels.

But although they were disheartened, they did not despair. Possessing themselves of the out-houses in the rear, they kept up a continuous discharge of fire-arms at every opening through which a ball could enter. At length, seeing that victory was as far off as ever, they ceased firing, and ran to the banks of the river at the town side. Finding the water too deep there, they made the best of their way* to the ford which lies a little to the east of the rustic bridge which at present spans the river in the deer-park. Before they left, however, they inflicted a severe loss in killed and wounded upon the stubborn defenders of the little garrison, amongst whom was Mr. Bernard, the owner of the castle, who valiantly lost his life in its defence.

The dead Irish were collected and removed shortly after to a stable, where they were covered with straw ; and the next day they were buried in an old but long disused graveyard, some traces of which may still be seen in the adjoining lands of Killountain.

Another party surprised the house of Mr. Francis Banfield, of Shinagh. Finding the door unfastened, they easily obtained admission, and rushed in. They found him standing near the kitchen fire talking to his wife, and ordered him " to come along !" The poor man hesitated, not well knowing what to do; upon which one of the marauders presented his musket at his head, and would most assuredly have stained his

---

* A few years ago, in cleaning out a pond which lay in the track of the fugitives, the remains of a few old swords, from twelve to fourteen inches long, and the blade of a pike, were discovered imbedded in the mud at the bottom. It is not unlikely that these fragments, pronounced by competent authority to belong to weapons of that period, were the remains of some thrown away by them in their flight.

hearth-stone with his brains, had not his wife bounded forward, and throwing her arms around him, received the discharge in the upper portion of the left arm; which not only shattered the bone, but tore open the entire shoulder, and no small portion of the chest. They then dragged him outside the door; but leaning forward to take one last look at her who had probably lost her life in order to prolong his, he perceived her lying near a chair—her pale face, and the white-washed wall against where she lay, being smeared with her blood. He implored the leader to be allowed to whisper but one affectionate farewell—to breathe but one word into her ear before they were separated probably for ever—but his reply was a stroke of a halberd, which laid open his face from the check bone to the chin, and covered him with blood.

His cattle were all driven away, his effects were destroyed, and he who rose up on that morning in affluence and in happiness, closed his weary eyelids that night a disconsolate husband and a beggar.

After all the prisoners were brought together, McCarthy addressed them, as well as those friends who had come to see them off. He told them " that all he and the others on the same side with him wanted was their own. That he would not dispossess one of them; for—so help him God !—he knew no one he would prefer as a tenant to any of them ; and that what he merely required was that they should pay him their rents for the future instead of Lord Cork."

Early on the following morning, those prisoners whose friends were unable or unwilling to pay the required ransom were marched off, strongly escorted, to Kerry, where they were confined in a Protestant church.

During the time of their incarceration—which was about four weeks —they were tolerably well treated and fairly provisioned, but in a primitive manner. If their captors wanted to supply them with beef, they would drive in a cow, telling them there was the meat, and let them divide it between them. Potatoes and wood were literally showered down on them through a hole in the roof; and water was supplied them by being passed through a small aperture in one of the closed-up windows.

The women and children who were left behind did not fare near so well as those who were taken away. They were imprisoned, and in dread of being murdered. It was no uncommon thing for their guards, in some of their fiendish freaks of humour, to drag out four females, and placing a pack of cards in their hands, order them to play for their lives, telling them that they intended to kill them all, but that they would begin with the unsuccessful.

This state of things continued about a month, when McCarthy—who had been in daily apprehension of King William's arrival, and considering that, in such a case, the prisoners would be likely to embarrass his movements, and otherwise prove a serious incumbrance should James be worsted—resolved on restoring them their liberty. This he did, contenting himself with exacting the promise of a ransom so small, that it did not exceed in amount a fiftieth part of what he had previously demanded.

At the same time he sent peremptory orders to his garrison in Bandon to withdraw from the town, and join him without delay. The men fearing from such haste that something dreadful was about to happen, or that they would be surprised on their way home, evacuated the place in a perfect panic, taking nothing with them but their arms and accoutrements; having buried in and around the castle in which they had been quartered all the plunder they had collected in the town and country during their sojourn.

Although we could not expect to find those half-civilized militiamen possessed of any species of forbearance—impressed, too, as they had been with the conviction that their country and their forefathers had suffered centuries of oppression at the hands of the English—yet, in one respect, they behaved towards their female captives in a manner which would favourably contrast with any garrison in our own day similarly circumstanced.

When the Bandon men returned from their captivity, many of them, being joined by others, formed a volunteer corps. They elected their own officers; and, after a little hasty training, they hastened northwards to meet Schomberg, intending to join the King when he landed.

William did not keep them long waiting. On the 14th June he arrived at Carrickfergus, and immediately proceeded to Belfast, which he entered amid loud shouts of "God save our Protestant King!"

The night came, says Macaulay, but the Protestant counties were awake and up. A royal salute had been fired from the castle at Belfast. It had been echoed and re-echoed by guns which had been placed at wide intervals for the purpose of conveying signals. Wherever the peal was heard, it was known that King William had come. Before midnight

20—2

all the heights of Down and Antrim were blazing with bonfires. The lights were seen, and gave notice to the outposts of the enemy that the decisive hour was at hand.

After enduring many hardships, of which fatigue and hunger were not the least, our little band of heroes reached the rendezvous at Lough-brickland in safety. Here they were joined by some of those neighbours and fellow-townsmen who had eluded Tyrconnell's vengeance by escaping to England; and they had now accompanied the King to Ireland. Amongst these were:—Colonel Beecher,* Colonel Moore, Colonel Tonson, Bryan Wade, &c.; and amongst those who travelled up all the way from the South to join the ranks of the Protestant King, were:—Robert Stukely, William Atkins, Thomas Sloane, Gosnell, Swanton, &c.

The Bandonians were attached to the auxiliaries from Londonderry; with whom they followed Soames's Blues into the water, and by whose side they remained fighting throughout the day. At this distance of time we are unable to mention any special acts of valour performed by them, as tradition only briefly relates that they fought like men; but we may fairly assume that they were not behind their heroic brethren of the maiden city in all the qualifications essential to make a brave soldier.†

After the battle was over—seeing that their military services were no longer requisite, and acting upon the principle that all was fair in war—our volunteers roamed over the battlefield in quest of riderless horses, and whatever else they might consider legitimate trophies of war. In this they only followed the example of their superiors. Lord Coningsby, for instance, is said to have taken three hundred head of cattle and several horses, which James's army left behind, without rendering any account of them to the King. After securing a number of horses, sufficient almost to mount the entire band, they marched for Bandon, led by one of their valiant non-commissioned officers (Corporal Sloane), whose only qualification for the important post which he then held—at

---

* Colonel Thomas Beecher, lineally descended from Phane Beecher, the founder of our town, married Miss Turner, a Bandon lady. He served during the battle as an extra aide-de-camp to King William, who was so pleased with his services, that he presented him with his own watch upon the field. Colonel Beecher sat for Baltimore in 1692, and for which place he continued to sit until 1709, when he died.

† They do not appear to have been very roughly handled by the enemy, as the only casualty that we have heard of was that which befell "Bill Atkins," who had the little finger of his right-hand carried off by an Irish bullet.

least, as far as can now be ascertained—was that his charger was equal in value to the mounts of nearly the others, having belonged during the day to an Irish officer of rank, many of whose accoutrements were still affixed when captured by the gallant volunteer. The horse was subsequently called "Billy Boyne "—" Billy " in compliment to the King, and " Boyne " in reference to the locality where he changed masters.

No news had been received in Bandon for several days after the battle. The townspeople were on the tiptoe of expectation ; but they had been punished with such severity on a recent occasion, that they were afraid to make any manifestation of their sympathies. At last, upon the Monday succeeding the great events of the preceding week, various conflicting rumours reached them. One report prevailed that William was killed by a cannon-shot early in the fight, and that all his army were slain or taken prisoners. Another was that the Irish had been routed with great slaughter, and that several of their generals were in the hands of the victors.

With minds full of gloomy apprehensions, they knew not what to do. What if James should be the conqueror? Then farewell to the labour of many a weary year ; farewell to the fields made fruitful by their industry ; farewell their altars, their liberties, their all. But should William be victorious, then all would again be joyous and happy.

Whilst in this uncertain state, and with hope and fear alternately predominating in their breasts, a young man arrived, exhausted and almost breathless; and announced, with a terrified look, that a large body of cavalry were coming down Kilpatrick-hill, and conversing with one another in a foreign tongue.

In an instant consternation was in every face. Their utter helplessness, now thrice apparent, convinced them that they could be none other than the French, who were coming to take possession of their town ; whilst the remembrance of all they had suffered not yet three months since had such an effect upon the women who were present, that several sunk on their knees, and they prayed to a merciful God to remove them out of this world, rather than that they should again witness scenes similar to those with which they were unhappily too familiar.

But this despondency was not of long continuance. The gloom which overspread their saddened faces broke ; then passing away, hope's effulgent beams shone forth, when into their midst hobbled an old soldier named Delaroy*——one who had long served his country in foreign lands, and who had often looked death in the face in many a hard fight.

Having pushed his way into the crowd, and learned from the young man all the particulars he could collect as to the uniform and accoutrements of the approaching troops, he finally asked if they wore any ornaments on their head-dress.

" Oh, yes !" said he, " they have silver bugles in front of their caps."

" Then huzza !" shouted the old veteran, throwing his crutch into the air, and bounding with very joy, " them be the Dutch horse, and many and many is the time I seed them fellows afore in the Low Countries."

Meanwhile the cavalry approached ; and having arrived where the cross-road meets the north-eastern extremity of Kilbrogan glebe, they halted, and sent forward a trumpeter with a letter to the authorities, by which it appeared that the force consisted of two troops of Ginkell's horse, who had been sent by William to garrison the town.

One troop passed along Kilbrogan Street, and into the town through North-gate; the other passed down the old Cork road, and thence in by the Water-gate.

We need scarcely say that they were both thankfully and triumphantly received.

Whilst the troop that passed through Cork road was on its way down that steep suburb, a gaily-dressed young man was seen riding up Foxe's Street on a white horse. The quick eye of the Bandon volunteer who accompanied the troopers as a guide soon espied him. On inquiring who he was, a bystander informed him it was Lord Clancarthy. Instantly dismounting, he placed the muzzle of his piece on an adjoining fence, and fired. The ball is said to have hit its mark, but owing to the great distance its strength was spent, and it did no harm.

The garrison with which Clancarthy occupied the town after McCarthy's departure were almost in as great a state of trepidation as the Bandon matrons on the approach of the foreign horse. Their arrival would decide their fate. If they belonged to King James, the day was their's. If they belonged to King William, the day was lost;

---

* Delaroy was not only lamed in both legs from wounds, but also lost one of his eyes from the same cause. Nevertheless, he is represented as being a first-class marksman, and upon one occasion is stated to have killed two men with one shot.

and they must either quietly settle down to peaceful pursuits, or quit the country.

But however disposed they may be to bend to circumstances, their clergy were for fighting it out to the last.

"If the Williamites do come itself," says Father Crowly to his congregation on the preceding Sunday, "every man of you that dies fighting will go straight to glory."

When William's men did come, or were nearing the walls, the garrison ran. Some of them followed Lord Clancarthy, and at first went towards the sea-side, but eventually turned their footsteps to Cork and Kinsale, where they arrived unmolested; but the greater portion of them left by West-gate.

Amongst those who accompanied the latter was Father Crowly, who, in his efforts to place as much ground as possible between himself and the new comers, got helplessly imbogged in a piece of soft ground at that time known as Spratt's marsh. Here poor Father Mick floundered, and floundered in vain. He could not get his feet out of his boots, and he could'nt get his boots out of the bog.

"Tiege," cried he to one of Clancarthy's men who was hastening by, "stay and pull off my boots, and God will bless you!"

"Yerra, I thought yer reverence would stay behind and earn your share of the glory you tould us about on Sunday last!" says Tiege, without waiting to give a tug at his confessor's leathers, or even stretching out a helping hand to extricate him from the fix he was in.

Throughout all Bandonia there was great rejoicing for the great victory at the Boyne. High and low, Episcopalian and Non-conformist, old and young, felt relieved from a thousand apprehensions. That government which had begun with the spoilation of their liberties, then attacked their properties, and before long would take their lives, was an end.

Exultation was everywhere. The name of the great deliverer was in every mouth. The farmer drank his health in a pot of beer; the squire* wished him long life in a bumper of claret; the clergyman

---

* Up to the close of the last century there was scarcely a gentleman of position in this neighbourhood, or throughout the west of this county, who ever thought of rising from his dinner-table without drinking to "the glorious memory." He first gave thanks to God for the good things which He had made his, and then he drained his glass to the memory of him by whose exertions he was enabled to enjoy them. Even at the present day it is not of rare occurrence here at a festive gathering—especially should this event occur on the first or on the twelfth of July—for the

prayed for him from the pulpit; the townspeople paid him the highest compliment they could—they likened him to Cromwell. Every one had something good to say of, or something great to wish to, glorious William. But sincere as they were in their ardent loyalty, and loud as they were in their laudations of their new king, the parish-clerk of Kilbrogan excelled them all.

When the first lesson was concluded on the Sunday after the news of William's victory had been received in Bandon, "Let us sing," says old Eldad Holland, "to the praise and glory of William, a psalm of my own composing :—

"William is come home, come home;
William home is come;
And now let us in his praise
Sing a *Te Deum.*"

He continued :—"We praise thee, O William! We acknowledge thee to be our king!" adding, with an impressive shake of the head, " and faith, a good right we have, for it is he who saved us from brass money, wooden shoes, and Popery !" He then resumed the old version, and reverentially continued to the end.

Old Eldad was one of those quaint, old-fashioned people, whose notions of propriety differed widely from those entertained in our own day. He did not see why the clergyman should have all the talk to himself, and yet he did not like to interrupt him. When he withdrew, however, to the vestry, Eldad used generally inform the congregation of anything that he thought would interest them; but instead of addressing them in the orthodox style as "dearly beloved brethren," he used simply say, "Boys."

"Boys," said he on one occasion, "I suppose you heard that the first of July will fall this year on a Sunday, so the battle of the Boyne is put off to next day. I'm sorry to tell you also that the Ballymodan side won the toss this time, and so we're to fight for King James. Humph! May the devil scald him !"

---

host, after inviting his guests to "fill up," and seeing that they did so, to rise to his feet, and pushing back his chair, so as to give him full room, say:—"Gentlemen, as we are all loyal men here, I give you the glorious, pious, and immortal memory of the great and good King William."

CHAPTER XV.

THE ANNIVERSARY OF THE BATTLE OF THE BOYNE IN DAYS OF YORE—ANECDOTES—
THE BANDONIANS REBEL AGAIN—THEY DECLARE JAMES'S CHARTER NULL AND
VOID—THE IRISH ATTACK CASTLETOWN—GOVERNOR COX'S PROCLAMATION—
SARSFIELD'S DIVISION EMBARKS AT CORK FOR FRANCE—THE FORFEITURES.

THE celebration of the battle of the Boyne was an important event in the annals of Bandon in the days of "auld lang syne." What the 25th of December was in mid-winter, the first of July was in mid-summer. The former was the great winter festival; the latter was the great summer festival. The date of the battle itself was a great time-mark with the inhabitants. For more than a century after people used to relate how that their fathers, or their grandfathers, or their great-grandfathers, were born, or were married, or died, so many years before or after the battle of the Boyne. A man obtained the lease of his farm, or of his house, or his people "came over," so many years before or after it.

The first of July was a grand holiday. Months before the day broke on that memorable morning—before the sun showed a portion of his broad, bright red face above the shoulder of yon eastern hill, and peeped furtively into the grey valley below as if to see if there was any one awake or up before himself—thousands were eagerly looking forward to "the first."

It came at last. Old quarrels were speedily forgotten; old friendships were quickly revived. Those between whom a coolness had existed now shook each other cordially by the hand. A man one had never seen before would put a foaming tankard in his hand, and invite him to drink to the glorious William. The buxom country lass, who blushed when, for the first time, her eyes met those of the stalwart young fellow who insisted on walking a part of the way home with her a year ago, was now all blushes and smiles, as he pressed her hand, or whispered in her ear.

It was a glorious day.* Heaven's huge azure vault was suffused with rich light. The golden beams of the great luminary quivered and sparkled in the warm, still air. Its light was everywhere. The stones and and pebbles which lay in the beds of brooks and rivers looked large and soft in the midst of the soft mellowish glare that surrounded them. Splashes of bright light lay scattered on the moist ground, and on the damp green moss, that were to be found in dark recesses in the woods and groves; and luminous spots and patches of it—sprinkled, as if by invisible hands—dappled the lacquered surface of the ivy leaf, the holly, and the laurel.

Early on that morning Bandon was astir. The cannon on the walls were fired at intervals of a few minutes, and each successive "bang" swelled and roared along the valley, and echoed and re-echoed among the surrounding hills, announcing that the day had begun. The bell of Christ Church sung it in silvery tones. The bell at Ballymodan boomed it. Simultaneously with this announcement, standards were hoisted. A large orange flag flaunted from the belfry of old Kilbrogan; a similar one waved from the roof of Ballymodan. A blue flag floated from a tall spar placed over the centre arch of the bridge. Orange and blue, purple and violet, red and yellow—in fact, flags and ribbons of every colour, save green and white—streamed from lofty oaks planted in commanding situations. One tree stood just outside the Water-gate, another stood at Kilbrogan-cross; there was one on the quay—now known as Cavendish-quay; there was one on the western extremity of the South Main Street, another at its eastern extremity; there was one on Shannon Street bridge, and another in the Irish-town.

People were soon in the streets. Many of those who had arrived after a long journey the night before were busy watering and feeding their horses, so that they may have the day uninterruptedly to themselves.

The townsmen were busy too. Every door, every window, every sky-light, was being decorated by them with branches of oak; whilst their mothers, or their wives, or their sweethearts, stood by, twining tasteful garlands of marigold and sweet-william.

---

* Tradition says, "the first" was never known to be wet or cloudy.

The roads leading into the town swarmed with country-people. There was not a village, or a hamlet—almost every house poured its tributary into the live stream that swept by. Margery and Mabel, Sukey and Bess, in kirtles of blue or red stuff, and wearing a bunch of roses and sweet-william in their bosoms, trouped on, accompanied by young men who wore sprays of oak and orange lilies in ther hats. Men and women—some of whom were advanced in years—were there on foot and on horseback; and many a comfortable-looking matron rode by, sitting on the big padded pillion affixed to her husband's saddle. Scarce a door they passed that had not an oak branch and a cluster of orange lilies placed above it in honour of the day; and people too old to travel, or who were obliged to stay at home to mind the house, were out on the wayside, huzzaing to every group that went by, or making the air resound with the enlivening strains of "The Boyne Water."

About eleven o'clock the streets were lined with crowds of pedestrians. Precisely at that hour the gates at the market-house at Ballymodan side were flung open, and a corps of drums and fifes passed out, playing loyal tunes. They were followed by a long line of men wearing sashes and shoulder-knots of the favourite colours, marching four deep.

After traversing the South Main Street, Castle Street, and the Irishtown, they arrived at Ballymodan Church, by Bridewell Street and Church Street. Here several entered and heard divine service; but by far the greater number of them being Presbyterians, they marched to their own meeting-house.

At the same time another large body, also headed by drums and fifes, marched from the market-house at North-gate, out to the end of Sugar Lane, across the fields to Barrett's Hill, and thence down through the North Main Street, to the bottom of Water-gate; and returning the same way again, they halted at Kilbrogan Church gate, detaching the Presbyterians, who formed no inconsiderable portion of their rank and file.

At one o'clock, all the religious services being over, they all met at the bridge. Here they were divided into two hostile camps. Those who lost the toss, being for King James, possessed themselves of the bank of the river on the Ballymodan side, extending from the bridge to the piece of ground now occupied by the gas-works. Whilst William's party—the party who won the toss—held the Water-gate side, beginning also at the bridge, and extending down to where the Messrs. Cornwall's brewery now stands.

After reviewing, shouting, speeching, and huzzaing, "Billy Boyne" would be led forth arrayed in all his battle-field accoutrements. He would have his Boyne saddle-cloth on, his Boyne holsters and silver-mounted pistols, and all the other trappings that rendered him so attractive the evening corporal Tom patted him on the back and vowed he should accompany him to the sunny South.

Being led along the ranks, "Billy" used evidently feel vain of his position. He used to curvet, he used to prance, and look as proudly at his old Boyne regimentals as if he was born every inch a soldier. Finally he was brought in front of the stand of colours, where he was mounted by "Schomberg"—one of the Boyne volunteers usually doing duty for the old marshal on these occasions—and "Schomberg" having addressed his followers in suitable terms, used to conclude by pointing to "their persecutors" on the opposite bank, and then charge resolutely into the river, followed by all his forces. When about half way across, bang would go a shot from one of the persecutors, and slap-bang would go "Schomberg" into the water. At this the Williamites would become desperate. They would plunge through the stream, foaming with rage, and should they lay hands on "their persecutors" at this moment, they would probably discover that playing the Jacobite even in joke, with the Bandonians for opponents, was an amusement not always safe to indulge in. The admirers of brass money and wooden shoes knew this well, and by the time "Schomberg's" comrades reached the shore, they had become invisible.

When the great attraction of the programme was over, the people dispersed for dinner. Provident house-wives from the country sought out retired spots; and opening their provision baskets, helped those whom they had invited to join them to piles of bread and beef, and then allayed their thirst with foaming jugs of cider and home-brewed ale. Others who had friends in the town, staid with them; or they crowded the inns and alehouses, and washed down a hearty meal with rum and beer.

As time wore on the thoroughfares began to fill again. Music and singing were heard in every direction. Now it was the joyous tones of the hautboy and fiddle invited the dancers to a saraband or a minuet; then a sweet voice sang a roundelay to the thrumming notes of the spinnet, and then a burst of sounds, from dozens of hoarse throats, roared :—

> " July the first, in a morning clear, one thousand six hundred and ninety,
>   King William did," &c.

The fireworks were exhibited about nine in the evening, and proved a great source of amusement to every one; after which the cannon on the town walls announced that the day was ended.

Nearly every one in this locality—during the close of the seventeenth century, the whole of the eighteenth, and the first quarter of the one we live in—heartily joined in celebrating the Boyne anniversary. Indeed, such was the anxiety of a gentleman—who is still affectionately remembered by some of our old citizens—that his unaltered devotion to the principles associated with the memory of King William should be exhibited, and that, whilst lying in his last resting-place, his very remains should as it were display those loyal emblems he so often paraded whilst alive, that on his dying bed he gave peremptory orders to his next of kin to pay the sum of ten pounds yearly to an individual whom he named, provided he decorated his grave every 1st of July with orange lilies.

We should have stated that "Schomberg's" horse was not forgotten. When the great toast that was given at every dinner-table, and was drank over and over again, was first proposed, a full bumper of the best October was poured into the horse's bucket, which he used to drink off with all the gusto of a real true-blue. Poor "Billy" died about the year 1708, and was publicly buried in the churchyard of Ballymodan; and 'tis said that many a wet eye became wetter, and many a sad heart sadder still, as the stones and clay covered for ever the inanimate form of the once gay and joyous old Boyne campaigner, "Billy Boyne."*

The custom of celebrating the Boyne anniversary by a sham fight continued until the year 1809; and the last "Schomberg" we have any account of was the late Mr. William Banfield, of Shinagh. The planting of oak-trees, with paintings of William crossing the Boyne, continued until the passing of the Party Processions Act; whilst the practice of decorating the churches with flags and streamers remained until 1858. And the only traces we have now of these by-gone celebrations are the few harmless shots that are fired on the eve of the old anniversary.

---

* For many years afterwards "Billy Boyne" was a favourite name for a pet horse; and even now its corruption—"Billy Boy"—is not altogether forgotten.

The battle of the Boyne, one of the most important in its results that has ever been fought in this country, was celebrated in a song which bears evident traces of having been written by an eye-witness—indeed, it is thought to have been written by one of the famous Enniskilleners who was present—and it still retains much of its former popularity.

AIR: THE BOYNE WATER.

"July the first, in a morning clear, one thousand six hundred and ninety,
King William did his men prepare—of thousands he had thirty—
To fight King James and all his host, encamped near the Boyne water;
He little feared, though two to one, their multitudes to scatter.

"King William called his officers, saying 'Gentlemen mind your station,
And let your valour here be shown before the Irish nation.
My brazen walls let no man break; our subtle foes we'll scatter;
See that you show good English play, this day at the Boyne water.'

"His officers they bowed full low, in token of subjection.
Said they 'My liege, you need not fear, we'll follow your direction.'
He wheeled his horse; the hautboys played; drums they did beat and rattle;
And 'Lilli burlero' was the tune we played going down to battle.

"Both foot and horse we marched on, intending them to batter,
But brave Duke Schomberg he was shot, as he crossed over the water;
And when King William he perceived that brave Duke Schomberg falled,
He reined his horse with a heavy, heavy heart, and the Enniskillen men he
        called.

"'What will you do for me, brave boys; see yonder's men retreating!
Our enemies encouraged are, and our English drums are beating;
I'll go before, and lead you on.   Boys, use your hands full nimble;
With the help of God we'll beat them down, and make their hearts to tremble.'

"The Enniskillen men, they did not know it was their King spoke to them,
But when informed of their mistake, they bowed full low unto him.
'We'll go before; stay you behind, and do not cross the water;
Old Britain's lamp shall clearly shine, and our enemies we'll scatter.'

"We formed our body at the ford, and down the brae did swatter;   .
And each man grasped his fellow close as we passed through the water.
But—oh, my stars!—had you been there, when we their trench came under:
Sulphur and smoke darkened the air, and the elements did thunder.

"King William he did first advance where bullets sharp did rattle.
The Enniskillen men bore noble hands, and soon renewed the battle.
Then lionlike we made them roar; like chaff we did them scatter.
King William pressed his way through blood that day at the Boyne water.

"My Lord Galmoyle within a crack of our fore-front advanced.
Both great and gay, in rich array, like prince's sons they pranced.
In a full body they came down, with broadsword and caliver,
With whip and sword, most Jehu-like, as the devil had been their driver,

"Within ten yards of our fore-front, before a shot we fired.
But a sudden snuff they got that day; they little it desired;
For men and horse fell to the ground, and some hung on their saddles,
And many turned up their forked end—as we call 'coup-de-ladles.'

"Prince Eugene's regiment was the next, on our right-hand advanced,
Into a field of standing wheat, where Irish horses pranced;
But the brandy ran so in their heads, their senses soon did scatter,
They little thought to leave their bones that day on the Boyne water.

"We turned about our foe to flank, intending them to batter;
But suddenly they did us spy, and fast began to scatter.
The Irish they ran first away, the French they soon did follow,
And he that got fastest away, was, aye! the happiest fellow.

"'Oh see! Oh see! cried Dermot Roe. Oh, help, dear Lady Mary!
By my fet, we're all dead men this day, if we do longer tarry!'
They threw away both fife and drum, and firelock from their shoulder.
King William's men pushed them hard, to smell the English powder.

"I never saw, nor never knew, men that for blood so gaped;
But yet I'm sure that from three to ten of them that day escaped.
We formed the French* on our left wing, the enemy to batter;
And glorious was our victory that day on the Boyne water.

"Both man and horse lay on the ground, and many there were bleeding.
I saw no sickles there that day, and yet there was lots of shearing.
But still the faster we pursued, the more we did them scatter.
Our hearts were to each other bound that day at the Boyne water.

"Had Enniskillen men got leave that day, when they their foes defeated,
For to pursue the enemy that from the field retreated,
Ten thousand broguineers and more would not have been much cumber,
Nor James's men have rose again, by the third part of their number.

"Now praise God, all true Protestants, and heaven's great Creator,
For the deliverance that He sent, our enemies to scatter.
The church's foes shall pine away, like churlish-hearted Nabal;
For our deliverer came that day like the great Zorobabel.

"Now praise God for all, true Protestants, and I will say no farther,
But had the Papists gained the day, there would have been open murder.
Although King James, and many more, were not that way inclined;
Yet it was not in their power to stop what the rabble they designed.

"Both France and Spain they did combine, the Pope and Father Peter;
They thought to steep a rod in brine, Great Britain to whip completer;
But Providence to us was kind—sent William to cross the water;
Who broke the rod and their black design, and their bones lie at the Boyne
water."†

---

* The Huguenots.

† The Rev. Dr. Hume, to whom we are indebted for this copy of "July the First,"
thinks verse nineteen was subsequently added by some smart member of an Orange
lodge.

The song best known in the South, and which we now give, first appeared in 1814, and from that time up to the present it has to a considerable extent supplanted the former, which was the original song, and which was known in the North ever since the great event which it purports to commemorate. It is said that the circulation of the latter is in a great measure due to the large woodcut in the centre of the broad sheet, along the margin of which it was printed :—

"July the first, in Oldbridge town, there was a grievous battle,
Where many a man lay on the ground, by cannons that did rattle.
King James he pitched his tents between the lines for to retire,
But King William threw his bombshells in, and set them all on fire.

"Thereat enraged, they vowed revenge upon King William's forces,
And oft did vehemently cry, that they would stop their courses.
A bullet from the Irish came, which grazed King William's arm—
They thought his Majesty was slain, but it did him little harm.

"Duke Schomberg then, in friendly care, his King would often caution,
To shun the spot where bullets hot retained their rapid motion;
But William said he don't deserve the name of Faith's Defender,
Who would not venture life and limb to make a foe surrender.

"When we the Boyne began to cross, the Irish they descended;
But few of our brave men were lost, so nobly we defended.
The horse they were the first crossed o'er, the foot soon followed after;
But brave Duke Schomberg was no more, by crossing o'er the water.

"When gallant Schomberg he was slain, King William he accosted
His warlike men for to march on, and he wou'd be the foremost.
'Brave men,' said he, 'be not dismayed, at the loss of one commander,
For God will be our King to-day, and I'll be general under.'

"Then bravely we the Boyne did cross, to give the enemy battle;
Our cannon, to our foe's great cost, like thundering claps did rattle.
In majestic style our King rode o'er, his men soon followed after,
And 'twas soon we put our foes to rout, the day we crossed the water.

"The Protestants of Drogheda have reason to be thankful,
That they were not to bondage brought, they being but a handful.
First to the Tholsel they were brought, and then to Millmount after;
But brave King William set them free by venturing over the water.

"The cunning French near to Duleek had taken up their quarters,
And fenced themselves on every side, just waiting for new orders;
But in the dead time of the night they set their tents on fire,
And long before the morning's light to Dublin did retire.

"Then said King William to his men, after the French departed,
'I'm glad,' said he, 'that none of ye seem to be faint-hearted;
So sheath your swords and rest awhile, in time we'll follow after.'
These words he uttered with a smile the day we crossed the water.

> " Come let us all, with heart and voice, applaud our lives' defender,
>   Who at the Boyne his valour showed, and made his foe surrender.
>   To God above the praise we'll give, both now and ever after,
>   And bless the glorious memory of King William that crossed the water."•

" The Boyne Water," " July the First," and a few others breathing the same spirit and full of the same aspirations, were almost the only tunes known here for a very long period—in fact down to the times we live in.

A few years ago, when a portion of her Majesty's —— regiment was quartered in Fermoy, a company, consisting of a drummer and fifer and the usual number of rank and file, were sent to a little country town in Tipperary. The captain who commanded was a French Canadian, and a Roman Catholic; and he not only regularly attended his place of worship whilst stationed there, but he was also on terms of friendly and social intercourse with the clergymen of his persuasion, not only where he was quartered, but in the neighbourhood.

A little chapel, recently built in a hamlet a few miles distant, was about being formally opened for divine service; and the priest, knowing Captain G——, asked him for the loan of his musical staff for the occasion, in the hope, that when it became known that a military band was to take a part in the grand ceremonial of the consecration, numbers would come who would otherwise stop away.

The band—such as it was—was given, and welcome. Accordingly, on the appointed day, the drummer and fifer (two young Bandonians, who had not been very long in the service) were present, and also several of their comrades. There was no programme given to them; and the only order they received was that at a given signal they should begin to play.

When all was ready, and when the proceedings reached that point where the music was to be introduced, the priest gave the signal, and the drum and fife commenced.

• Some of the evils that fell on old Ireland by the successes of William are still preserved in a little poem, written by one Guliclimus O'Callaghan (a Kanturk schoolmaster), beginning with :—

> " Bad luck to ould bandy-legged Schomberg ;
>   King William, and Mary, also !
>   Oh ! 'tis they that did water ould Ireland
>   With bloodshed, an' murther, an' woe !"

Scarcely, however, had poor Guliclimus finished his interesting recital of Erin's woes, when he was pounced upon by some of Scragvenmore's troopers, and mercilessly put to death.

21

The reader will naturally expect to hear that the sacred music of Mozart, or of Handel, or of some other great composer, was performed, or at least attempted—although the instruments were the profane ones we have mentioned; or even one of those sweet, plaintive melodies with which the surrounding hills and valleys were not unfamiliar. No! they did no such thing. They struck up the boisterous and defiant strains of "The Protestant Boys!" As if this was not enough to stretch the forbearance of the large assembly present to the very last thread, they were then favoured with "Rise, sons of William, rise!" and they concluded—what they intended as the first part of the day's musical entertainment—with "Croppies, lie down!"

The priest was almost breathless with timidity and rage—and no wonder. He trembled least his indignant people should rush on the heretical instrumentalists, and annihilate them. He was greatly incensed to think that the very first hymn that should ascend before that altar, and find a responsive echo along that roof—a roof that was raised by the pence and piety of the Irish Roman Catholics—should be "The Protestant Boys!" How did he know but that "Rise, sons of William, rise!" was an invitation to the Protestant wolves to come in and devour his Catholic sheep? "Croppies, lie down!" was, if possible, worse. It may do very well for the black North, or for an Orange lodge; but in a Catholic sanctuary, raised in the most Catholic county in most Catholic Ireland, for two miscreants in the Sassenach army to stand up, and in their very midst, and in the midst of everything they looked upon as sacred, to tell them to "lie down!" far exceeded anything he had ever heard of for audacity, impudence, and irreverence. If Captain G—— was a Protestant, he would not half mind; but for a Catholic captain to———!

A grave complaint was made to head-quarters, and the two Bandonians were placed under arrest, and brought before a court-martial. In their defence, they stated that the music being left to themselves they played those tunes they could play best. Perhaps they thought, too, that as they were good enough for the people of Bandon, of course they ought to be good enough for them.

The affair eventually blew over, and the drummer and fifer received strict injunctions never—under any circumstances—to play any of those obnoxious tunes again.

The orthodox colours, as well as the orthodox music, were greatly in vogue in Bandon, and the old folk hardly knew any others.   Even many of those whose business it was to be familiar with every pigment in general use showed a lamentable ignorance in this respect.

A sign-board swung over the door of an ale-house, on which was a painting representing an orange cow giving blue milk; another sign-board had a yellow salmon on it, with violet-coloured fins and tail; and over a little inn in one of our suburbs was another, with a tableau emblazoned upon it of a gentleman on horse-back, drinking a pint of ale at the door of "mine host." The gentleman, who was dressed in blue, sat on an orange horse, and drank " the glorious, pious, and im-mortal memory,"* in red ale, out of a purple pint. Indeed, some of our old people even still are so familiar with the name and the Boyne exploits of William the Third, that it would take very little argument—especially when their memories are quickened by something more exhilarating than tea and coffee—to persuade them that they were personally acquainted with him of the glorious memory, and were eye-witnesses, if not participators, in the great struggle that was decided on the memorable first of July.

We are acquainted with an old townsman who avers that he not only saw William, but was talking to him; and, moreover, that he himself performed an important service for the Protestant cause on that eventful day.

After Schomberg was killed, says he, the Irish began to gain ground. King William perceived this, and saw there was not a moment to be lost. "Where's Ned Lisson?" cried the King, standing up in his stirrups and looking anxiously about him. "Here, your Majesty," answered Ned, emerging from a cloud of smoke; and passing on to where his royal master was, he stood and presented arms with as much composure as if he was at after-breakfast parade. "Ned," said his' Majesty, "tell the Enniskilleners to cut away the Irish centre at once." Away Ned ran, glad to be bearer of such gratifying directions—often being obliged to hop and skip, least he should trample on the body or limbs of many a poor fellow whose fast glazing eye told he would soon be a stranger to the strifes and troubles of this world; and running up to the gallant horsemen from Enniskillen, gave them the King's com-mand to cut away the Irish centre; "and I could'nt help saying,"

---

* Dr. Peter Browne—appointed Bishop of Cork in 1709—wrote a pamphlet against the custom of drinking "the glorious memory." He said it was impious.

says the old Boyner, "and their two wings also," adding, by way of palliation for meddling with his instructions, "sure they might as well finish them all when they went about it." Well, away they went straight at them, and before you could whistle the first line of "July the First!" they lay stretched upon the grass by the dozen. "Yerra, ar'nt them Enniskilleners the devil entirely!" said the temporary aide-de-camp, rushing up to where the great deliverer stood surveying their bloody work. "Yes, Ned," said King William, with an applauding look, "one would think them fellows were Bandonians!"

Coins struck in William's reign are prized here as mementoes of him and of the eventful times in which he lived. His watch—which he presented to a brave soldier on the battle-field at the Boyne—has descended to its present owner, who resides in this county, as a family heirloom. And a suit of clothes worn by the great Protestant King when a boy is carefully preserved in a glass-case, and forms a prominent feature among the attractions of a valuable collection of curiosities and works of art in the possession of a lady who lately resided in this neighbourhood.

The success of King William entailed ill-success on King James. What brought life to the hopes of one prince carried death to those of the other. But though the important victory gained by William resulted in the surrender of Drogheda and the evacuation of Dublin, yet—excepting what he had marched through from his landing, and the district held for him by the Enniskilleners—all the rest of Ireland was as hostile to him as ever.

The royal banner of the Stuarts still floated from the battlements of Cork. A similar one streamed over the fort and barracks at Kinsale; over Limerick, over Galway, and over dozens of other garrisons in the south and west.

Under these circumstances, one would have supposed the Bandonians —who had suffered so much and so often, and that within a short period —would have remained quiet; more especially as, within a few miles of where they stood, Sir Edward Scott commanded a body of foot—twelve hundred strong—in James's interest. Colonel O'Driscoll's regiment, too,—composed of men raised in the west of the county, and with whose fathers and forefathers the Bandon people had been striving for the ascendency for generations—was equally near. And Cork—the city from which marched the troops which surrounded their walls in thousands not yet eighteen months before—was as devoted and vehement in the same cause as heretofore.

Notwithstanding that everything was against them, and that they had no friends to give them even the poor encouragement of their sympathy in all that portion of the kingdom extending from the southern limits of Dublin to Cape Clear, and from Wexford to Kilkee, yet on the 16th of July—months before the mortars of Marlborough threw bombshells from Cat-fort into Cork, or the battery at the Red Abbey tore a breach in its walls—they assembled themselves together; and stimulated by that undeviating attachment to the Protestant cause, which defeat could not overturn or bloodshed extinguish, they courageously came forward, and again rebelled against the sovereignity of King James. And, as if already conquerors, they triumphantly decreed:—

"That the new charter brought and produced by Teige McCarthy, under the government and under the broad seal of this kingdom, had become null and void; and that the old charter be revived and stand in force. And by virtue thereof we have assembled ourselves together in the former house, and elected and appointed Mr. John Nash to be provost of the borough for the year to come; he first taking the usual oaths, and the oath of loyalty to our gracious sovereigns, William and Mary, King and Queen of England," &c.

This defiant edict was dated July 16th, 1690, and was signed by Edward Turner, Christopher Grinway, Isaac Browne, and Daniel Beamish.

It will be seen, from the date just mentioned, that the corporation of James lasted within a few days of two years and four months.

Throughout the whole of their career—save in the one instance of directing that the sum of 6s. 8d. should be levied off every one objecting to become free of the corporation, and thereby refusing to swear allegiance to James the Second—they acted with a leniency that could not reasonably be expected from them. Indeed, they would seem to have carried conciliation almost to the verge of partizanship with their enemies, in their efforts to humour the prejudices of the stubborn people over whom they were placed; and so far did they strain points in this particular, that in the most sensitive of all our prejudices—our religious feelings—it was those of their opponents they sought to gratify, and not their own.

Throughout the entire of our rule here, there is no reference to any Roman Catholic clergyman having been admitted to reside within the walls until the 24th of June—a few days prior to the eventful 1st of July—when that permission was for the first time bestowed on Father Michael Crowly; but not until he produced an order from King James —so that even this small concession to a minister of their own faith was not granted by them either as a right or a favour, but solely because the aforesaid Father Crowly presented a mandate from his gracious Majesty in that behalf.   This was their last recorded act.

The following is a complete list of the free-burgesses in 1689, authenticated by the signature of the provost for that year :—

Danl. McCarthy-Reagh,	Andrew Callaghan,	Charles McCarthy,
Charles McCarthy,	John Walshe,	Francis Garvan,
Edward Collyer,	Daniel Crowe,	Denis Leary,
Thomas Knight,	Denis Riordan,	Cornelius Leary,
Cornelius Connor,	Arthur Keefe,	Kadogh Leary,
Murtogh Downy,	William Hore,	James Purcell,
Edmond Barret,	Thomas Curtin,	Dermod Keohane,

ROBERT CASEY, provost.

Upon the 2nd of October Marlborough arrived in Kinsale, and the very next day attacked the old fort; which he valiantly assaulted, and took by storm—killing the governor (Colonel O'Driscoll) and two hundred of his men; and others, amounting to two hundred and fifty, he took prisoners.

Charles-fort was then summoned, but Sir Edward Scott (the governor) pertly replied that it would be time enough a month hence to talk of surrendering.   Marlborough immediately set to work at the trenches, and constructed batteries.   After a fortnight's cannonading, the Danes, who were posted on the east side, breached the walls; and the English, who were on the northern side, had previously possessed themselves of the counterscarp; then a mine was sprung, and the enemies works seriously damaged.   When everything was ready for the assault, Scott surrendered; the garrison, which consisted of twelve hundred men, being permitted to march to Limerick with all their arms and baggage, but leaving their stores behind—amongst which were one thousand barrels of wheat, one thousand barrels of beef, forty tuns of claret, and large quantities of sack, brandy, and strong beer.

Having made his brother (Brigadier Churchill) governor of the fort, he placed his regiment in winter quarters in Bandon, Kinsale, and Cork, and then returned with the fleet to Portsmouth.

Previous to setting sail, he held a levee in Cork, where numbers of

William's loyal subjects went to pay their regards; amongst whom was Mr. Gosnell, of Kilpatrick, who waited on him at the head of a cavalcade composed of his wife and twenty-one children. But Gosnell paid dearly for his loyalty; as the rapparees took advantage of his absence, and having entered his house, they burnt it to the ground; and so effectually was this performed, that, when the owner returned, all he was able to discover among and *debris* was the left-hand of a woman and two pewter plates.

At this time the large district to the west of Bandon was almost entirely in the hands of the rebels. These were for the most part composed of trained men who had served under King James, and were led by officers who lacked none of the qualities of brave soldiers. They marched through the country, headed by their pipers; and they caused great terror and alarm amongst the outlaying colonists. So numerous were they, and such confidence had they in themselves, that they ventured to attack villages, and even towns.

Five hundred men, belonging to O'Driscoll's regiment—a division of which was so roughly handled by Marlborough at Kinsale—under the command of young Colonel O'Driscoll, attempted to burn Castle-Townsend; but they were repulsed by Townsend and his brave little garrison of thirty-five men with such success, that the O'Driscolls beat a hasty retreat, leaving twelve of their dead behind. Nevertheless, they again renewed the attack, but with results still more disastrous. This time they fled, leaving O'Driscoll (their young colonel), Captain Teige Donovan, Captain Croneen, Captain MacRonaine, and thirty rank and file dead upon the streets, and many wounded. MacRonaine behaved well. It was mainly owing to him that the Irish were brought up to face the little garrison; but the stuff of which his men were made of may be inferred from the fact that several of them advanced to the attack with bundles of straw tied round their bodies to protect them from the hostile bullets.

Towards the close of the year, MacFineen, having broken out of Cork goal, collected about four hundred men, and marched to Enniskeane. Finding this place guarded, he proceeded to Castletown, in which was a little garrison of thirty dragoons, under the command of a lieutenant. These fought stubbornly and successfully for a long time; but their ammunition being all gone, and five of their number killed, they surrendered on quarter. Although the lieutenant had his life promised to him, nevertheless he was set upon by these wretches, and murdered in cold blood.

1691.   Owing to the greatly disturbed state of the country, Mr. Justice Cox—who had been appointed governor of the county and city of Cork the month preceding—issued a proclamation, forbidding all Papists of this county to be out of their dwellings from nine at night till five in the morning; or to be found two miles from their places of abode, except in a highway to a market-town, and on market-days; or to conceal arms and ammunition, on pain of being treated as rebels. That hue and cry should be made after murderers and robbers. That all persons should on their allegiance enlist themselves into the militia. That none should traffic, correspond with, or send provisions to the enemy; or shelter or entertain Tories, rapparees, &c. That no protected person should desert his habitation, or go to the enemy, or otherwise absent himself above three days, on pain of imprisonment of his wife and family, and the demolishing of his house. And, lastly, it pronounced impartial justice without distinction of nation.

Limerick capitulated. On the 3rd of October the treaty was signed. It contained no less than forty-two provisions, the most important of which was permission to James's adherents to leave the kingdom. They were also allowed to take with them all their chattels, &c. Similar permissions were granted to other garrisons, and to every one who wished to leave Ireland.

As soon as the peace was signed, four thousand five hundred foot marched into Cork under the command of Sarsfield; and after remaining there about a month,* they sailed for France, and landed at Brest on the 3rd of December.

D'Usson and Tesse also arrived at Brest about the same time, with four thousand seven hundred and thirty-six—exclusive of officers—from the Shannon direct, in transports belonging to the squadron under M. de Château Rénaud. Shortly afterwards Major-General Wachop

---

* Whilst staying at Cork awaiting transports great numbers of them deserted, in consequence of accounts which had reached them of the ill-usage which had been received by those who had preceded them. Such was the effect of the bad news, that three whole regiments refused point blank to go on board. The embarkation itself was a most distressing spectacle. Numbers of the wives and children of the soldiers, who had accompanied them to Cork for the purpose of sailing with them, were not even allowed to go near the ship's side to bid them good-bye; and when several of the poor creatures caught hold of the boats, imploring to be carried to their husbands, they were roughly thrust aside. Some who followed the boats into deep water held on for awhile, but, their hold gradually relaxing, they let go and were drowned; and others, who continued their grip, had their fingers chopped off.

left with about three thousand more, in English ships; and these were followed by two companies of King James's body-guard.

According to the report of the commissioners, all the Irish troops—including officers—that followed James to France amounted to nineteen thousand and fifty-nine; but great as this force may seem, it was only the nucleus of a greater. The Irish gentry who had eluded the vigilance of Cromwell, or had been restored or permitted to enjoy their estates by Ormond, were now hopelessly ruined by the forfeitures under William—some idea of the extent of which may be surmised from the fact that in our county alone they amounted to two hundred and forty-four thousand acres*—and they left Ireland in crowds, taking their dependents and many of their former tenantry with them. Indeed, so great was the number of these voluntary exiles that landed in France during the next half century, that it is computed—upon calculation made at the French war-office—that from the landing of James's army, up to and including the battle of Fontenoy in 1745, upwards of four hundred and fifty thousand Irishmen laid down their lives in the service of France.

* The entire confiscations in Ireland amounted to near 1,700,000 acres. Two hundred and ninety-seven houses in Dublin, thirty-six in Cork, and one hundred and twenty-six in other towns. There were also sixty-one mills, twenty-eight patents for fairs and markets, seventy-two rectorships, with their tithes and rents, six ferries, and a great number of fisheries. Also vast numbers of sheep and cattle, which were only valued at £135,552; but they were worth much more, as in this calculation a horse was set down at only twenty shillings, a sheep at half-a-crown, and other animals proportionally low.

CHAPTER XVI.

CAPTAIN NASH (ALIAS SHANE DEARG)—THE SUGAN—PRIEST-HUNTING—THE BLACK
CAT—A NEW PARLIAMENT—BACHELORS TAXED—NUCE'S BYE-LAW REVIVED—THE
GREAT AUCTION OF FORFEITED ESTATES.

MR. John Nash, a captain* in the Bandon militia, was
1691. provost of the town this year. Although the
battle fought at the Boyne virtually decided the
contest between James and William for the possession of
this kingdom, yet the friends of the former continued to disturb the
country for years afterwards. It is true that every succeeding year
saw them get weaker and weaker. Those who were soldiers in 1690
and 1691 became Tories in 1692 and 1693, and common thieves from
that out.

At this period the state of the country could not be worse. Skirmishing between armed parties, attacks on military out-posts—even sieges
—were not uncommon; whilst so infested was this neighbourhood with

---

* Captain Nash was also provost the preceding year (1690), from the 16th of
July, when the corporation of James was deposed; and was the provost elect for
1688, but was obliged to give place to Teige McCarthy, who produced the new
charter and initiated a new policy. He was subsequently provost in 1703, when
Nuce's bye-law was revived and a preamble prefixed, beginning with :—" Whereas,
several Papists and other loose persons have presumed to bring their families into
the corporation of Bandon-Bridge." In 1711 he again filled the office; again in
1723; and lastly in 1724. He took a great interest in the welfare of his native
town, and was one of the four who signed the articles of peace on behalf of the
Bandonians with General McCarthy; upon which occasion he and others made themselves personally responsible for the large sum of money borrowed on account of the
town, and for which some had their effects seized, and others were imprisoned. To
a fund for the payment of these liabilities he contributed the emoluments of his
provostship more than once. He took a very active part, too, in getting a market-
house erected at the south-side; and throughout the entire of the thirty-six years
he was connected with the corporation, there was no member of it more anxious to
promote its success or increase the prosperity of those entrusted to its care.

deserters from Sarsfield's division—whilst it lay in Cork awaiting transports—and disbanded desperadoes let loose upon society by the surrender
of Limerick, that those living in the country parts could not count on
being alive in twenty-four hours ; and their property was not in reality
worth the trouble of protecting it.

Should an outlaying settler require anything from the neighbouring
market-town, he would do without it, or wait until an armed caravan
passed his door; and then either accompany it, or get some one to execute
his orders for him.   Whilst so afraid was he of his cattle being carried off,
that he used to guard them all the day with a loaded musket ; and at
night-fall, by driving them to his own dwelling-house, and barricading
the doors and windows, he and the members of his family hoped, by keeping a constant watch all through the night, to protect them from some
rapparee or Tory who may covertly make his way through the thatch,
or gain admission in some other unceremonious fashion.

To grapple with this desperate state of things, Captain Nash was
armed with strong powers by Governor Cox.   He was aware of what
he was to do, and he was aware of how to do it.   A desperate case he
well knew required a desperate remedy.   A rough customer could
appreciate rough usage; but rose-water usage would be thrown away
upon him.   Treat him kindly, and he would persuade himself you were
afraid of him.   Show him mercy, and it was because you felt he was
your superior.

Captain Nash was one of those men whom the exigencies of those
times created.   A flaw in an indictment, a misnomer, hair-drawn dis-
tinctions, and other minutiæ which a microscopically-eyed lawyer may
be able to discover, he pooh-poohed altogether.

If Teige Carthy was charged with a robbery, which he felt persuaded
he committed, he did not think him innocent of it because his christian
name was spelt with two G's in it instead of one; or if Dermot Crowly
was guilty of murder, he could not understand why he should be
pronounced "not guilty," because he was described as of a certain
place, whereas he lived somewhere else.   He believed when a fellow
committed a robbery, or a murder, he ought to be hanged, and he hanged
him accordingly.

He set to work vigorously ; and such havoc did he make amongst the
outlaws and rapparees, and such terror did his numerous executions
inspire, that the neighbouring peasantry still shudder at the very mention

of his name. The children lie motionless in their cots. And " If you don't be good, I'll send for Shane Dearg!" is a threat well known to nurses in a district in our neighbourhood to terrorize the most unruly piece of juvenile humanity into quietness.

Amongst the Irish he was known by a great many names. He was Ould Jack, Jack the Devil, Hanging Jack, and Ould Nash ; but he was most familiarly known as Shane Dearg (pronounced Shawn Dhorrig), or Red Jack—red, as some say, in reference to all the blood he spilt; whilst others contend it was owing to the colour of his hair.

In his day there were but few gaols, and certainly no reformatories. So that when a prisoner was brought before a country justice of the peace, that functionary had scarcely an alternative between letting him go or hanging him ; and the latter presented many advantages to which the former could lay no claim. If he was let go he could commence a fresh career of crime, and it may be difficult, if not impossible, to lay hands on him again ; but if he was hanged, he would not do any more harm, and the militia need not turn out to give him chase. Therefore, if he was guilty, putting a rope round his neck and swinging him from the next tree was considered the shortest and the most economical mode of disposing of him.

At first it was customary for Mr. Nash to try the accused, to investigate all the evidence *pro* and *con.*, and ascertain if the prisoner was really, or even probably, guilty of what he was charged with. But as time wore on, and as their numbers increased, he gradually became convinced that every one caught wandering about the country was either a Tory, a rapparee,* or a thief.

---

* A little after ten o'clock one morning, a rapparee—a big, burly fellow—walked into the house of a man named Merry, who lived at Clancoole, about a mile from the town; and, drawing a stool to the fire, sat down, and demanded his breakfast. There was no one in the house but Merry's wife ; and she knowing it would be useless for her to try and dislodge such a formidable intruder by force of arms, resolved to effect it by stratagem. Accordingly she put on a pleasant face, set a bowl of new-milk on the table alongside of him, and handing him a good-sized piece of oaten cake, she bid him eat away, and welcome. When she perceived his meal was drawing to a close, she went into the yard and brought in some bundles of hay, and began to make a sugan. " Yerra, couldn't you help me with this?" said she to her unbidden guest. He readily rose up to do so ; and taking the outstretched stick from her, he began to twist. As the rope lengthened—she, meanwhile, feeding it from the hay on the floor—he pushed back and back, and passing over the threshold, he continued twisting away. As soon as she found that he was some distance outside the door, she suddenly sprang forward, and slapping it out, she hastily bolted it ; and then securing it effectually, she ran up stairs, and opening the window, roared murder and fire. In a short time her husband and sons, who were in the neighbourhood, came running to her assistance ; and the rapparee taking to his heels, made off as

From this time out he became content with a very superficial examination, and sometimes with none at all. And at length became so callous, as to issue his orders in such a careless manner, or to speak so unintelligible, as to be often misunderstood.

A rapparee, who had been captured by a sergeant's guard of the Bandon militia, was brought before him one day. In reply to some queries put to him, the prisoner stated that he was a poor weaver on his way to Bandon in quest of employment.

Upon hearing this, one of the guard stepped forward, and said he could prove the accused was no weaver.

"Oh, never mind, never mind!" said Old Jack, "we'll soon know all about that!" Taking a piece of string from his desk, and walking up to him:—"Come, my good man!" said he, "tie a weaver's-knot for me with this, and I'll let you go."

The unfortunate man was dumb-founded. He was no weaver, and knew no more about weaver's-knots than he did of what was discussed at the last cabinet council held at Kensington; so he held down his head, and was silent. Old Nash returned to his desk and resumed his pen.

Some time after, the sergeant, who had made several ineffectual attempts to catch his worship's attention, at last called out in a rather impatient tone:—"Well, sir, what am I to do with the prisoner?"

"Oh, hang him!" said he. "Take him out of that, and don't bother me with him!"

The sergeant possibly misunderstood him. However, true to the letter of his instructions, he did take him out of that, and strung him up forthwith.

The place of execution at that time was North-gate, from a beam across the arch-way of which the condemned underwent their doom.

On the very next morning his worship was out taking his customary walk, and happening to pass through North-gate, observed the body of the rapparee suspended from the fatal beam.

"Gatekeeper!" shouted he, "who is that fellow? and what brought him there?"

---

fast as he could. This exploit of Mrs. Merry's is preserved in an Irish song, and may be occasionally heard in the chimney-corner of some cabin in the vicinity of where it occurred. The first two lines are:—

"The old woman put me out
    When twisting the hay rope."

The gatekeeper explained to him that he was the man who was hanged the evening before by his orders. He paused for awhile, in all likelihood reflecting upon the dreadful mistake that had been committed.

"Well, well," said he, "if he didn't deserve it this time, he probably did at another!" He then quietly resumed his walk.

On another occasion, a man was brought before him just as he was about sitting down to dinner.

"Is this a rapp?" quoth Old Jack to the non-commissioned officer in charge.

"Yes, sir!" was the reply.

"Well," said he, "you can hang him now, and by the time you think dinner is over come back, and I'll enter the particulars!"

In these two instances, however, the prisoners were accused of being rapparees; but in the following the unfortunate man was not even guilty of being accused. He was put to death not for what he did, but for what he could do.

Being out one day with a detachment of the militia, he overtook a fine, handsome young man walking along the road.

"Take that fellow up," cried Jack, "and hang him!" pensively remarking, "if that chap was vexed, he could do mischief!"

The man was seized, marched into Bandon, and hanged the same evening at North-gate.*

He had even the temerity to hang a priest—Father Sheehan—a piece of indiscretion, we need scarcely say, which no statesman of our day would have the hardihood to attempt. And so anxious was he lest by any means he should be balked of his clerical prey, that he did not even wait until he would arrive at his favourite North-gate, but hung him up at the very first cross-road he came to.

Such terror prevailed amongst the class to whose radical reformation the ministerial labours of Old Nash were devoted, that when any of them were captured, their first inquiry was before whom they were to be brought; and on learning it was Shane Dearg, "Oh! may the Lord have mercy on us now!" was the usual exclamation of these unhappy men—well knowing that when brought before him their existence in this world might be computed by the time they occupied in marching from his worship's presence to the gallows.

---

* Previous to his execution he admitted he had been a soldier, and as such served within the walls of Limerick.

Incredible as these stories may appear, yet they are devoutly believed in this locality. And we have heard them from such a variety of sources—all corroborating each other by abundant testimony in every particular—that we have no doubt as to their general truth. The peasantry in our neighbourhood to this day believe that he was capable of any atrocity.

Not long ago we encountered an old fellow who was sunning himself on the side of the road; and having heard that he knew a great deal about the old people, we were very glad to make his acquaintance. After a few preliminary queries as to our friend's health, the prospect of the approaching harvest, the probability of pigs being up, &c., we proceeded to business.

"Tim," we inquired, "did you ever hear of Shane Dearg?"

"Oh!" cried Tim, rousing himself a bit, and looking eagerly at us, "is that the fellow that used to hang all the people long ago?"

"We replied that it was."

"Wisha, by gonnies!" said he, "I did so."

We then asked him why it was he used to hang all the people.

"By gor!" said he, "for being Papists."

We could not help reflecting on the enormity of hanging a poor fellow because he could only believe up to the orthodox mark, and no further. However, we continued.

"But, suppose a man said he was no Papist." Here we thought we had old Tim.

"Och, by gorra," said he, "that wouldn't do him either; for then he'd have him hanged for telling a lie!"

The apparent necessity for such severe measures having passed away, and every disaffected person being either hanged off or otherwise disposed of, Old Jack turned his attention to the no less secular, but yet more irreverent, pursuit of priest-hunting.

By an act of the Irish Parliament it was ordered that the Roman Catholic clergy should appear before the authorities at stated times, and have their names and residences duly registered; whilst those who refused to comply with these injunctions were proclaimed, and rewards offered for their apprehension.*

In these pastoral pursuits, Red Jack was one of the most successful

---

* One hundred pounds were offered for the apprehension of a bishop or a priest, and prosecuting same for saying mass.

sportsmen of the day.   There was no follower the clergy had who more
closely adhered to them.   He was always at their heels.   And there was
scarcely a day that he did not pounce upon some sacerdotal delinquent—
either catching him before he broke cover from the sheltering roof of
some poor peasant, who risked his life in giving him a night's lodging,
or else running him right down through sheer exhaustion.   At all
events he was scarcely ever without a priest or two to his credit.

He was at last, however, cured of this propensity of clinging to the
skirts of the clergy in a manner so singular and efficacious, that not
only did he give up hunting priests, but he absolutely used to secrete
them in his own house.

He asked a large party to dinner one day, amongst whom were some
of the neighbouring gentry, several Protestant clergymen, and a poor
priest—then in his safe custody, and to whom a good dinner in those
bad times was a rarity.

After the covers were removed, the host commenced carving the leg of
mutton which lay before him, and soon threw a piece to a large Tom
cat that had taken his accustomed seat by his master's side.   His
reverence happening to look that way caught pussy's eye.

"Holy Moses!" said he, "look at the cat!" and immediately rose
from the table, telling his host, at the same time, that he must excuse
his remaining any longer.

The guests were greatly amazed, and anxiously inquired of each
other what was the matter.

"Oh! that hell cat!" cried the priest, looking daggers at black
Tommy.

"Why, man," said Mr. Nash, "that cat is domesticated in the family
these many years, and he is very fond of me!"

"I don't wonder at his being fond of you," quoth his reverence,
"for a good right he has;" deliberately adding, "I assert that cat to
be none other than the devil!"

At this Old Nash became very indignant, and after swearing a great
deal, concluded by telling the priest he'd make him prove what he
stated.

"That I will readily do," said the latter, "and in a very short time,
too, if you will allow me to send for my stole and books."

This was assented to; and the messenger having speedily returned
with the necessary articles, his reverence put on his vestments and

began to read. As he did so, it was observed that the cat began to swell. The priest read on, and the cat swelled on, until at last black Tom grew as large as a two-year old heifer; and then, at a sign from his reverence, suddenly appeared in his own proper person.

There could be no mistake about him. Old Clooty was there, with his orthodox appendages *in extremis*. There were his horns, his tail, and his cloven foot.

The priest then—in order to afford the company a better opportunity of inspecting the latter—ordered him up on the table, and made him show his hoof all round.

The devil most uncourteously took advantage of his elevation, and gave all the company a long lecture upon the evils arising from heresy and schism; but addressing himself particularly to the clergymen present, he told them, that as regarded the high-church party he wouldn't say a word against them, as he could see but little difference between them and the real clergy, but as for those low-church fellows, and those vagabond Puritans, if any of them were ever sent to his dominions, he'd———!

Here he became so excited that the good priest interfered, and changed the subject.

He then went through a variety of interesting manœuvres, and concluded by speaking in seven different tongues, and displaying a proficiency in the acquisition of ancient and modern languages truly wonderful.

" Wisha, puss!" said Old Nash, who could scarcely persuade himself that his old favourite was in reality the dreaded personage he now appeared to be, " is it possible you're the devil ?"

" Wisha, by jabers!" said puss, scratching his head, and familiarly addressing his old master, " there's no use in denying it any longer, Shane Dearg," said he, " I am !"

Old Jack made a rush at him, and if he could have only laid hands on him North-gate would have been his inevitable doom. Being unable to catch him, he could only vent his vengeance in abuse—which he did unsparingly, and with a right good-will. But the devil was more than his match. He scolded him horribly in return; and after hurling at him all the obnoxious terms he could muster, he wound up by telling him that he was as cruel as Nero, not a bit better than Cromwell, and almost as unfeeling as an attorney.

Nash, of course, was greatly annoyed, and obliged to seek the assistance of the priest to have him removed; and although the latter and his fraternity owed no debt of gratitude to him, yet—kind and forgiving man as he was—he readily assented, and black Tom was ordered not only to quit the house, but also the parish, and never to put his foot within its precincts again. He obeyed—in fact, tradition furnishes many instances where the devil bows to the decision of the Roman Catholic clergy without a murmur—and rushing up the chimney in a volume of smoke, like Luther, he disappeared.

So pleased were all the company with the forbearance and Christian disposition showed by the poor priest, that a subscription was immediately entered into for putting a roof upon his chapel at Moviddy; whilst so overjoyed was old Nash, that there and then, before them all, he vowed that he would never raise his finger, or say an angry word, to a priest again.

We by no means wish to be considered as guaranteeing the authenticity of the last story; but we might just as well think of denying the infallibility of the Pope as to seem for one moment to doubt its truth. The peasantry in our neighbourhood believe every word of it devoutly, and they would look with no small share of mistrust upon any one who would hesitate to give it full credence.

After giving up priest-hunting, he took to the less arduous duty of burning houses. It was enjoined on all people to be in their dwellings from nine at night until five in the morning; or, if not found within, or a satisfactory reason given for the absence, they were themselves liable to be punished and their houses burned.

It was often very difficult to catch the offenders, but their houses were always to be found; and although in our day it would seem a burning shame to set fire to a poor man's house for any offence, yet old Nash made light enough of it.

Whilst on one of these fiery excursions, he saw a poor peasant digging potatoes in a field adjoining the road. He called the man to him; and seeing he had on a new sheep-skin breeches, he ordered him to take it off and exchange it for an old broken one with one of his men.

"Now, Dermod," said he, "you can keep that well-aired garment; for you looked so over-heated in the other, I was greatly afraid lest you should catch cold!"

There are numberless other stories concerning him still floating about in our neighbourhood, but we have given enough to show the exceptional man, which exceptional times, for exceptionable purposes, may be expected to produce.

He died in 1725, in the seventy-fifth year of his age ; and so much was he detested by the Irish, that their malignity followed him even beyond the grave.

It was extensively reported—and is believed by many even now—that after death he went to a certain place ; and the devil, seeing him approach, cried out to some of his imps :—" Run, run, heap more coals on the fire, here is old Nash !"

He was not interred in the family burying-place at Brinny, lest, as some say, his remains should be exhumed and dishonoured by the country-people.

He was buried in Bandon ; and underneath an almost illegible tombstone, and a few feet outside the southern transept of Kilbrogan Church, reposes all that is mortal of the renowned and celebrated Shane Dearg.

1692. On the 23rd March a proclamation was issued, announcing that the war was over. This was exactly twenty-two months from William's landing at Carrickfergus.

In Elizabeth's time the insurrection lasted fifteen years, and the great rebellion of 1641 took no less than twelve years to suppress ; and yet this was more extensive than either of the others, the Irish having possession of cities—such as Cork and Dublin—and forts and garrisons, which they never once occupied in the great revolt last referred to.

On the 5th of October a new Parliament assembled at Chichester House, Dublin. The members for Bandon were Sir William Moore, Rosscarbery, and Edward Riggs, Esq., Riggsdale. Of our senior member we can discover nothing in the journals of the House, save that he obtained permission to go into the country on private affairs ; and of our junior representative we scarcely know more, except that he sat on a committee of grievances.

1693. On the 28th of February, Tom Dennis, an attorney practising in our corporation court, was not only prohibited from appearing before the court again, but " was also committed to goal for evil words spoken."

From all we can gather from the MSS. in this matter, it seems that Tom had a most outrageous temper. For aught we know, he might

have been stung into a fury by the opposite attorney; perhaps taunted
with talking nonsense by the bench, or so inflated with illusory notions
of his own greatness as to forget his duty to his betters. Be that as it
may, he attacked Mr. James Dixon—one of the burgesses—in open
court, and called him "an old rogue, an old knave, and an old rascal;
and that, were it not for his grey-hairs, he (the said Tom Dennis) said
he would break his (the said old Dixon's) pate." Of course such evil
words, even from such a privileged individual as an attorney, could not
be endured for a moment—particularly as they were addressed to one of
the most honourable dignitaries of the judicial seat. Accordingly the
provost, free-burgesses, and commonalty assembled in solemn conclave,
and by mutual assent and consent they put Tom out of court and into
the Marshalsea.

A new Parliament assembled in Dublin on the 27th August.
1695. Our Bandon representatives were Edward Riggs, Esq., Riggsdale, and Francis Bernard, Esq., Castle-Mahon. There were a great
number of bills and petitions introduced during the several sessions
through which this Parliament extended, amongst which were :—

> A Bill for taking away the *Writ de heretico comburendo*.
> A Bill to fix the value of brass money at the time same was bor-
> rowed during the late troubles.
> The Petition of Margaret Maxwell—a poor distressed widow—on
> behalf of herself and four small children, praying the House
> to take her sad and deplorable condition into consideration;
> her husband being tried and executed for treason in the late
> King James's government, for no other reason but for endea-
> vouring with others to defend themselves against the rapparees.
> The Petition of Folliott Sherighly, praying the House to consider
> the services done by him in securing the muster-roll and
> books of entry of the Irish army after the rout at the Boyne,
> whereby the commanding officers who served in the Irish
> army were known and outlawed.
> A Bill to prevent Protestants turning Papists, or intermarrying
> with them.
> A Bill to prevent Papists becoming solicitors.
> A Petition from the inhabitants of Bandon, setting forth their
> grievances under King James, &c.

Bachelors were taxed this year. We really hope some member of
our legislature will introduce a measure on the all-important subject of
bachelor taxation. Of what earthly use is he—the snarling, selfish,
cold-hearted piece of unfeeling humanity? He does not help to
increase the subjects of our gracious Queen, as all good people are in

duty bound to do, and thereby produce additional consumers of the various excisable articles in daily use ; and in this way contribute his share toward the relief of the state, and towards paying the very policeman who interposes his baton between him and the honest indignation of the fair sex.

Although we approve of the principle of free-trade, and will candidly admit that every man ought to be allowed to dispose of himself as he may deem fit, yet there are exceptional cases, and where legislative interference amounts to a positive necessity. Why should the executive —which we entrust with unlimited powers for increasing the weal of our fellow-countrymen—suffer one of them to be dismally moping his way through the streets, with his coat buttoned probably over his buttonless shirt, and his cold, blue nose and his lustreless eyes turned up to the wet clouds, as if he—wretched outcast !—expected to find sympathy there, when he may have a comfortable wife for the asking ? and, in due time, if he has only ordinary luck, he may have a dozen or so of interesting little children—all striving, perhaps, at the same time, to make a horse of his paternal knee, and running up various accounts for edibles, clothes, boots, shoes, pinafores, &c.—that would do any parent's eyes good to behold.

We would undoubtedly place a confiscating tax upon all such odd and singular fellows, and would consider ourselves amply borne out by the jurisprudence of our own day. Have we not an act on the statute-book interfering with the liberty of the subject, and that to such an extent as to impose fine and imprisonment upon him for attempting to terminate his miseries and his existence at the same time ? And yet no one cries out against it. If then the legislature is justified in interfering to keep a man miserable, how much the more is it justified in laying hold of a wretch by the collar, shaking all the crumbs of bread and bits of string out of his pocket, and saying :—"Sir, you must—you shall—we'll force you to be happy !"

1697.   The Quakers were at this time pretty numerous in Bandon. We have seen an interesting relic of their presence in our town in this year, to wit—a marriage certificate ; and as we are aware that anything connected with this respectable body during their stay here will interest our local readers, we readily lay it before them.

SOCIETY OF FRIENDS.

"John Ferishe was born the sixteenth day of ninth month, 1676, in ye town of Malverton, Somerset, England. Joan Taylor (his wife), was born ye tenth day of eleventh month, 1674, in ye town of Banbury, Devonshire. They were married in ye Friends' meeting-house, at Bandon, the twenty-fourth day of sixth month, 1697."

1698.

In this year there were only one hundred Roman Catholic clergymen in the county and city of Cork; and of these, before the year ended, seventy-five emigrated—their expenses being defrayed by the government.

At the General Sessions of the Peace held here, it was found by the Grand Jury that Teige Dash had a harper playing in his house on the sabbath-day, contrary to the act; also that Will Barrett is a common swearer and blasphemer.

1702.

Captain Nash became provost for the third time. Nuce's bye-law, prohibiting Roman Catholics from following any occupation in the town, or even living there, was revived and amplified this year. This interesting relic of the policy pursued when political and religious animosities filled the contending parties with a rancour so fierce that it was implacable, and created a thirst for vengeance in either side which nothing but the utter prostration of its opponent could appease, we now give :—

BOROUGH OF
BANDON-BRIDGE.

" At a general assembly of the provost, free-burgesses, and commonalty, met together in the Tholsel or court-house, situate on the north-side of the said borough, the fourth day of February instant, Anº Domi, 170⅔. After debate had between them, concerning the removing of all Irish Papists out of the said borough and liberties thereof, it was, by the general and mutual assent and consent of the said provost, free-burgesses, and commonalty, consented and agreed upon in manner and form following (that is to say)—That we, the provost, free-burgesses, and commonalty of this borough, being very sensible that it has been, time out of mind, a custom within the borough that no Irish Papist should inhabit within the liberties thereof; yet, notwithstanding, there has of late several such Irish Papists crept in, and do still inhabit within the liberty of this borough. For remedy whereof, we, the said provost, free-burgesses, and commonalty do resume our ancient privilege, and make it a bye-law : That if any Irish Papists, now inhabiting within the liberties of this borough, being warned to depart and remove out of the said liberties aforesaid, upon pain of forfeiting whatsoever the present provost shall think fit, provided it be under three pounds six shillings and eight-pence (£3 6s. 8d.) sterling, he, or they, or any, or all of them, having first due notice given them, and a time to remove, not exceeding ten days after such notice. And if any one of them shall, after such due notice given as afore-said, to the same aforesaid, presume to remain and inhabit within this borough, that then their goods shall be answerable to pay any such sum as shall by the provost be laid on him or them, for his or their contempt; which said sum or sums so levied shall be for the use of the said corporation, to be laid out as the said provost shall see occasion. And ·if, for the future, any who is or shall become a freeman of this borough shall let or set a house, or houses, to any such said Irish Papists, within the liberties aforesaid, any such freeman shall forfeit three pounds six shillings and eight-pence sterling; to be levied by order of the provost for the time being, when any freeman shall presume to set or let a house to any such Irish Papists, and being so levied shall be for the use of the corporation. And if any one who is a freeman of the said borough that shall or will oppose the turning out of any such said Irish Papists out of the liberties thereof, according to the ancient custom aforesaid, and will refuse to join in turning out the said Irish Papists, or any of them, shall be thought and looked upon as enemies to the borough, and for ever be adjudged incapable of being either provost, burgess, or freeman of the commonalty within the borough of Bandon-Bridge, as aforesaid."

By way of giving this additional significance, the following was added:—

"The contents of the within bye-law is the full and general assent and consent of the whole court assembled this fourth day of February, Anº Domi, 170$\frac{3}{4}$, to which they have subscribed their names as followeth.

And, further, that this bye-law be, by counsel-at-law, put into due form of law.

COMMON COUNSEL.	BURGESSES.
Samuel Browne.	James Dixon.
Isaac Browne.	Christopher Grinway.
Andrew Langton.	Thomas Polden.
Abraham Savage.	Saul Bruce.
Attiwell Wood.	James Martin.
Thomas Linscom.	William Bull.
Daniel Conner.	John Nash, provost."
James Rice.	
Richard Willoe.	
Edward Millington.	

All the members of the corporation present signed the above document, with two exceptions—William Bull and Abraham Batten; and, so indignant were the provost, free-burgesses, and commonalty with them, "for wilfully refusing" to affix their names to the bye-law, that a court immediately sat to expel them.

There was another bye-law also passed, beginning with:—

"Whereas several Papists and other loose persons have presumed to bring their families into the corporation of Bandon-Bridge, and the liberties thereof, without the knowledge and consent of the provost, free-burgesses, and commonalty of the said borough," &c., &c.

A new Parliament assembled in Dublin. The representatives for Bandon were Francis Bernard, Castle-Mahon, and Colonel Richard Georges,* Kilbrew, county Meath. Both our representatives served on a great many committees, and were two of the most active members of the House. The importance of encouraging trade seems to have engaged the attention of the House. Amongst the various measures introduced with this intent were :—

1703.

A Bill to encourage the making of earthenware in this kingdom.

To encourage the importation of iron and staves.

To prevent the destruction of the fry of herring, salmon, and other fish.

To oblige all persons in this kingdom to bury in woollen garments.

To improve the hempen and flaxen manufactures in this kingdom, &c.

There were a number of petitions presented, with various objects in view. There was one from the sovereign, burgesses, and commonalty of Kinsale, praying " that the lighthouse at the Old Head near Kinsale may have light continued on it as formerly." From the poor people of the baronies of Muskerry, complaining that the high and petty constables of said baronies made them pay twice over the taxes laid upon them. And one from a number of young gentlemen, complaining of the several frauds and abuses committed on them by one Timothy Salter, who keeps the Royal Oak Lottery.

A great portion of the estates confiscated in consequence of the late rebellion were disposed of this year, in pursuance of an act passed in the English Parliament (11th and 12th William the Third), entitled:—
" An Act for granting an aid to his Majesty, by sale of the forfeited and other estates and interest in Ireland, and by a land tax in England, for the several purposes therein mentioned."

It was enacted that all the honours, manors, lands, possessions, and hereditaments within the realm of Ireland—whereof any person or persons who stood convicted or attainted of treason since the 13th day February, 1688 ; or who should be convicted of treason before the last day of Trinity term, 1701 ; or who had been slain in actual rebellion since the 13th of February, 1688 ; or who at that time were seized, or possessed, or entitled to, on said day, or at any time since, of estates and interests, &c. ; or of any person or persons who possessed in trust for

* Colonel Georges—subsequently a lieutenant-general—was for a long time quarter-master of the army in Ireland. In this Parliament he was elected for Ratoath and Coleraine as well as for Bandon, but preferred to sit for the latter.

them, or for any of them, on the 13th of February, or at any time since; or whereof the late King James the Second, or any in trust for him, or to his use, was seized or possessed, or interested in at the time of his accession to the crown of England—should be invested in Francis Annesley, James Hamilton, &c., &c., to the end that the same might be sold and disposed of, to and for such uses as are expressed and declared by the said act.

At the great auction, which commenced in March and ended in June, an immense number of estates were disposed of. The average of a life interest was six year's purchase; and of a fee, thirteen years.

Amongst the principal purchasers in this county were:—Alderman John Newenham, of Cork, who purchased some townlands forfeited by Ignatius Gould; Sir John Meade became the owner of Michael Casey's estate; Sir Richard Cox, of Dunmanway, was the purchaser of a part of the estate of King James; Piercy Freke, of Rathbarry, was the successful bidder for another portion of King James's estate, and also for that of Edmund Galway; Daniel Conner, of Bandon-Bridge, bought a portion of Justin McCarthy's property, and also of Ignatius Gould's; Francis Bernard, of Castle-Mahon, bought several thousand acres which had belonged to Lord Clancarthy; and "the governor and company for making hollow sword-blades in England," who were by far the largest purchasers in this county, on the 23rd of June, 1703, became owners of no less than 55,000 acres—a portion of the vast estate of the unfortunate nobleman whose name we have just mentioned.

The wholesale destruction of woods about this time was much complained of. It is said that on Lord Clancarthy's estate alone no less than £27,000 worth of timber was wantonly destroyed. Full-grown trees could be bought for sixpence a-piece; and when purchasers could not be found for them at that trifling sum, they were allowed to rot, as no one would take the trouble to remove them.

Up to this time the country, which was well-timbered, presented a park-like appearance. Barren mountains and valueless lands were covered with tall, stately trees—a portion of the primeval forest that was allowed to remain—but now they were all cut down, and the hills and valleys were stripped of the graceful foliage which had been their pride and their protection centuries before Strongbow and his audacious adventurers cast covetous eyes on this green isle; and this district has ever since exhibited that naked look for which it is noted to the present day.

Two reasons are assigned for this réckless waste. One is that the purchasers of the escheated estates were afraid they would be dispossessed in case the Pretender ascended the throne, and that they were eager to repay themselves as much of their purchase-money out of the lands as fast as they could. The other was that they were felled lest they should afford protection to the Tories and rapparees.

Gibraltar was taken this year. A Bandon man—Captain Jumper—was one of the first who rushed into it, sword in hand.

In the next chapter we give all the particulars we have been enable to collect of our famous townsman—a man to whom England is in some measure indebted for the possession of the renowned key of the Straits.

CHAPTER XVII.

SIR WILLIAM JUMPER—BYE-LAW OF THE CORPORATION TO PREVENT ANY ONE TEACHING A POPISH APPRENTICE—THE LAST PRESENTMENT PASSED IN THIS COUNTY FOR KILLING WOLVES—THOMAS WIGHT—A TURK, A JEW, OR AN ATHEIST.

AMONG the crowd of heroes which the British navy has produced, there are few (if any) more conspicuous for that daring and cool intrepidity which has rendered "Jack" the best fighter, as well as the best sailor, in the world, than the subject of this memoir. One of his biographers tells us that he was a most active, diligent, and brave man ; but Charnock is more laudatory still. "Few men," writes he, " who have not lived to attain the rank of commander-in-chief, or at least that of flag-officer, have ever acquired so much renown as this gentleman."

Sir William Jumper was a Bandonian. His parents* lived in an old-fashioned, bay-windowed house, which—up to about three-quarters of a century since—occupied the piece of ground upon which at present stands the boot and shoe establishment at the south end of Bridge Street ; and in this house Sir William was born. His family, which may be classified under the term "respectable," and was well-connected,† had sufficient interest with Admiral Lord Dartmouth to obtain for him the appointment of second lieutenant on board his lordship's own ship, the " Resolution," of seventy guns. He soon left the " Resolution " for another ship—in fact during the next six years he held commissions in several, and in all of them he acquitted himself with credit and distinction.

---

* His aunt was married to Sir Francis Page (a judge of the King's Bench). Sir Francis, who lived to be eighty years of age, died in December, 1741.

† On the 24th of February, 1651, arms were granted to William Jumper. *Arms :*—Ar, two bars, Sa—between three mullets—gu. *Crest :*—On a wing—Arg, two bars, Sa.

Early in 1694 he obtained command of the "Weymouth;" and in the following June fell in with a large privateer belonging to the French—with whom we were at that time at war—and captured her ; and before the month ended he captured another.

The "Weymouth" was but a fourth-rate, and we can easily imagine what a fourth-rate was upwards of one hundred and sixty years ago. Nevertheless, on the 31st of the following August, he attacked another ship, manned with a large and efficient crew, mounted with twenty-eight guns, and commanded by one of the bravest officers in the French navy.

The "Weymouth" did not hesitate about what she'd do.   She boldly sailed up to the enemy, grappled with him, and Jumper and his men leaped on board.   There was a long fight, and a desperate one. Discharging their fire-arms, they closed with one another, hand to hand. It was now cutlass against cutlass, and pike against pike ; but the obstinacy, the daring, and the expertness of the British sailor told in the end.   The Frenchman hauled down his colours, but not until thirty of his men lying dead, and nearly an equal number writhing in their last agonies on the deck, convinced him that to carry on the contest any longer must only result in a useless expenditure of more blood.

The next year our hero made prizes of two more privateers ; and very shortly after of another, which he fell in with outward-bound from St. Malo, and which was much his superior in size, in metal, and in her complement of men.   But these advantages disappeared before the daring spirit of Jumper.   Placing his ship alongside the Frenchman, he knocked his masts overboard, killed dozens of his crew, and after a stubborn resistance the stubborn Gaul hauled down his colours and struck.

Victory followed quick upon victory, and success upon success—his daring and his deeds were the theme of every mess-table in the service to which he belonged ; but "a domestic affliction awaited him, capable of overshadowing all."

It appears that he had to put into Plymouth to victual and refit for another cruise ; and so anxious was he to have this done under his own eye, that he never quitted his ship during the whole time she lay in port.

His wife, Catherine (who was daughter and heiress of —— Browne,

Esq., Ireland), lived on board with him up to the day named for sailing; then bidding him farewell, she stepped into the pinnace with his friend, Captain Smith, of the "Portland," and made for the shore; but by some mischance the boat upset, and both she and Smith were drowned.

Jumper felt the blow most acutely, and for some time he was inconsolable. But he knew that grieving could not recall the past. He soon longed for his favourite element again, and for his favourite pursuits, and he determined to devote himself to his country more than ever.

Returning to active service, fortune again smiled on him, and he chased and captured prizes, and boarded ships of war, with the same uninterrupted success as heretofore.

On the 10th of January, 1701, he was appointed captain of the "Lennox," a ship of seventy guns, and a crew of four hundred and forty men; and was ordered to join the squadron under Sir George Rooke, which he accordingly did, and weighed anchor with the Confederate fleet from Spithead, on the 19th of June, 1702.

The object of the expedition which Rooke commanded was to seize on Cadiz, and by this means to prevent the French from possessing themselves of the Spanish West India Isles; or even if they did possess themselves of them, to render their permanent occupation impossible.

The expedition was a failure, and the design was abandoned. Cadiz could not be approached whilst the Spaniards held Matagorda-fort. And although the fort was attacked, and a battery of cannon played on it, the Spaniards would not stir an inch.

Rooke was greatly blamed for his want of success in this affair, and also for his remissness in not burning the enemy's ships and destroying his towns. Burnet charged him openly with this, and stated that before Rooke set sail from England he had in a manner determined not to do the enemy much hurt. Sir George's friends denied this, and endeavoured to justify his conduct by alleging that he thought it downright madness to expose the lives of the Queen's subjects when they might be spared to better advantage; and, moreover, that the Spaniards must think the English had a strange way of showing their affection for them when they'd begin by cutting their throats. Nevertheless, the outcry raised against him was so fierce, that he was obliged to appear before the House of Lords, and reply to the charges brought against him.

Although the Cadiz expedition did not add to the fame of Rooke, whose flag floated from the mizen of the " Royal Sovereign," it was otherwise with the captain of the " Lennox "—his track was as brilliant as ever. In this attack, writes Charnock, he took a more prominent part than any other naval commander—successfully executing the arduous services entrusted to him with the most spirited address.

When the admiral had embarked his troops, and was preparing to return home, news was brought to him that the Spanish galleons—for the capture of which a squadron had been fitted out under Sir Cloudesley Shovell—had reached Vigo, escorted by a French squadron under the Count de Château Rénaud. Rooke at once assembled a council of war, composed of the flag-officers of the combined English and Dutch fleet, and they resolved to crowd all sail for Vigo at once, and attack the enemy.

When they arrived off the mouth of the harbour, they found that the entrance to it—which was not more than three-quarters of a mile wide—was well defended. On the northern side was a battery of twenty guns, and on the southern side was a platform mounted with twice that number. In addition, there was a stone fort with ten guns, and garrisoned with five hundred French troops. But this was not all ; stretching from shore to shore was a boom made of ships' yards and top-masts, lashed together with three-inch rope ; and over this again was wound a stout coil of hawsers and cables. And as if even this was not enough, there were five ships—carrying between sixty and seventy guns each—moored inside the boom, and with their broadsides fronting the entrance ; so that, should an enemy's ship near the boom, she had to face five broadsides at the same time, as well as receive the fire of the fort and the batteries on either side.

Fifteen English ships, ten Dutch men-of-war, together with all the frigates, fire-ships, and bomb-vessels, were told off for this desperate enterprise. In order to capture the battery and fort at the southern side, and thus divert the fire of fifty guns from the attacking squadron, Ormond landed with two thousand five hundred men—a detachment of which, consisting of five hundred, under Lord Shannon, stormed the platform of forty guns, and carried it.

The governor of the fort was furious. Throwing wide his gates, Sozel determined to drive the English before him. But though his gates lay open to allow his men to charge out, it seems not to have occurred to him that they afforded the enemy an opportunity to charge in. This they did without hesitating; and pouring in, sword in hand, they forced the garrison—which consisted of French and Spanish troops—to lay down their arms.

As soon as the British flag was seen floating from the platform, the ships advanced. Vice-Admiral Hopson, in the "Torbay," spreading out all his canvas, dashed boldly against the boom, and broke it. Scarcely had he time to congratulate himself upon his success, when he was grappled by a French fire-ship, and was within an ace of being destroyed; as it was his sails were on fire, his fore-yard burnt to charcoal, and his larboard-side severely scorched. But this was not all; an incessant discharge of round shot and small arms rained on the unfortunate "Torbay." Her top-mast was splintered to pieces, several of her ports were knocked in, and one hundred and fifteen of her gallant crew were shot and drowned.

When intelligence reached the fleet outside that the boom was in two, in they come. Bakenham, in the "Association"—a ninety-gun ship—lies broadside on to the battery of twenty guns on the northern side, and keeps pounding at it until 'tis silent. Wyvill, in the "Barfleur"—also a ninety-gun ship—drops anchor opposite the stone fort, until captured by Shannon's grenadiers.

And now the struggle is between the French fleet, backed by whatever assistance the Spanish galleons could give them, and the united English and Dutch. The latter had a double duty to perform—to destroy the French fleet, and to save the Spanish galleons—and well they did it.

Measured by the magnitude of the victory, the loss of the Confederates was inconsiderable. The enemy lost fifteen French men-of-war, two frigates, a fire-ship, and seventeen of the coveted galleons. Of these, four French ships of war and six galleons were taken by the English, and five galleons and six French ships of war by the Dutch; and the rest, consisting of five men-of-war and six galleons, were either sunk or burned.

Although the gold ships were discharging cargo the previous twenty-five days, yet there remained a magnificent sum to reward the victors, as they got possession of goods valued at no less than five millions of our money, and two millions in hard cash.

The "Lennox" was one of that gallant squadron which sailed into Vigo harbour on that memorable 12th of October, 1702, when signalled

by the British flag on the enemies forty-gun battery to " come on !"
and her captain was one of those who " took a prominent and active
part in the enterprise."

On the 9th of May, Jumper again left England with the fleet under
Sir Cloudesley Shovell, and in fourteen days arrived at Portsmouth,
bringing with him a French East-India ship, valued at one hundred
thousand pounds.

His repeated services were now deemed worthy of being prominently
noticed by the State. Accordingly, in little more than a month after
his return (that is, on the 1st of July, 1703), he was knighted* by
Queen Anne.

On the 14th of June, 1704, the ships of war under the command of
Sir George Rooke, after chasing a large French squadron into Toulon,
repassed the Straits of Gibraltar; and in two days after were joined by
the squadron under Sir Cloudesley Shovell.

Rooke had now a large fleet under his command. To spend the entire
summer doing nothing would raise a loud outcry against him at home,
and, in all probability, bring him again before the Lords. Therefore
something must be attempted.

A council of war sat, and several schemes were discussed. It was
proposed to attack Cadiz again; but Cadiz could not be taken without
a large army, and they had only a small one. But they must attack
some place; and at last they resolved that Gibraltar should be the
place.

Three reasons influenced them to this. By making a sudden dash at
it as it then was, there was some chance of taking it, whereas if it was
properly provisioned and garrisoned they could never hope to do so.
If they could seize it, it would be of the greatest importance to them
during the war; and the capture of such a renowned fortress would
cover the conqueror with glory, and furnish materials for the brightest
page in the history of the annals of Anne.

On the 21st of July the fleet sailed into Gibraltar Bay, and, before
sunset, eighteen hundred English and Dutch marines landed under the

* One account says it was for his conduct at Gibraltar he was knighted. Another,
that it was for his bravery at Malaga; but we are convinced it was for his speedy
return with the rich French prize, as well as for his gallantry at Vigo and elsewhere;
and in this we are fully sustained by information kindly furnished to us by the naval
authorities at Somerset House, which places beyond all doubt the date of the knight-
hood. If it was conferred in 1703, how could it be for services which he did not
perform until the year after at Gibraltar and Malaga ?

Prince of Hesse upon the isthmus connecting Gibraltar with the mainland.

When the debarkation was completed, Hesse called on the governor to surrender; but he replied that he would defend the place to the last. There was nothing done that day; but on the next morning, as day broke, Rooke opened with a terrific cannonade; and so well was it kept up, that in less than five hours there were fifteen thousand round shot and shell poured in one continuous stream into the town.

This terrible fire began to tell in due time; but especially upon the defences at the south mole, and from which several of the enemy were seen to run.

If I could but seize and hold those defences, thought the admiral, the town must be mine.

He immediately sent orders to Whittaker to man his boats and make the attempt; but Captain Hicks and Captain Jumper, who lay nearest the mole, forestalled him.

Seeing the Spaniards fly, they wasted no time in sending for instructions or waiting for orders; they lowered their pinnaces into the water, rowed rapidly to the shore, and bounded into the coveted fortress, sword in hand.* But scarcely had they gained the inside when the ground heaved beneath their feet, and in a second two lieutenants and a hundred of their men were blown into the air; and although they could not tell but that in a moment or two they would share a similar fate, nevertheless, they doggedly held possession of the great platform until Whittaker's boats arrived; then massing together, they stormed the redoubt that lay between the mole and the town, and carried it.

Again the governor was called upon to surrender. He did so; and the greatest fortress in the world was ours.†

These were no idle times for sailors. Scarcely had they fought one engagement when they began to prepare for another. In less than three weeks after the taking of Gibraltar, Rooke sighted a French fleet under the Count de Toulouse, and on the morning of the 13th of August he came up with them.

---

* It is said that when Jumper got in he ordered a marine to take off his jacket, and hoist it on the top of a pole, to serve as a flag. On seeing this substantial proof of possession, the Spaniards became greatly disconcerted, and Whittaker's men redoubled their exertions to come to the aid of their heroic brethren-in-arms.

† Battery No. 6 in Gibraltar is still called Jumper's battery, in compliment to our gallant townsman.

The English and the Dutch fleets consisted of fifty-three ships, having on board nineteen thousand three hundred and eighty-five seamen and marines, and carrying two thousand nine hundred and thirty-five guns. Of the ships there were two fourth-rates, a fifth-rate, a sixth-rate, and two fire-ships, that did not fire a shot, having been ordered away to windward before the action began.

The French had fifty-two ships and twenty-four galleys, carrying three thousand five hundred and thirty-three guns, and manned by twenty-four thousand one hundred and fifty-five men. They had also nine frigates, a similar number of fire-ships, twelve French galleys, and eleven Spanish galleys.

A little after ten o'clock in the forenoon Sir George bore down on the enemy; and after a little dexterous manoeuvring on both sides, he ran the fighting signal up the mainmast, and the battle began.

Sir Cloudesley Shovell, running before the wind, separated himself from the centre, and attacked the French van under the Marquis de Vilette. Behind Vilette's van was a second line under the Duke de Tursis.

Foremost in Sir Cloudesley's front was the "Lennox." Three times she fought three French ships in succession, and three times she was victorious. A damaging cannonade was maintained by both combatants. "The fire," says a French writer, "was most extraordinary on both sides;" also, that "the Marquis de Vilette had so roughly used the van of the enemy, that five of their ships were obliged to quit the line. Of those the most roughly used was the 'Lennox;' whose gallant commander—Captain Jumper—was severely hurt, and nearly a fourth of whose entire crew were either killed or wounded."

Sir Cloudesley Shovell, in his letter in the *Complete History of Europe for* 1704, substantially confirms the portion of the French account we have just given. "The ships that suffered most in my division," says he, "were the 'Lennox,' 'Warspight,' 'Tilbury,' and 'Swiftshire;' the rest escaped pretty well." Again:—"Notwithstanding, the engagement was very sharp, and, I think, the like between two fleets never has been in any time. There is hardly a ship that must not shift one mast, and some must shift all."

The fight did not end until night. Both sides claimed the victory, but neither had any of the fruits of victory to show.

Our fleet endeavoured the next two days to renew the fight, says an English writer, but the French avoided it.

On the morning of the 26th, the wind having again shifted to the east, says a French writer, gave the English a fair opportunity to renew the fight, but they did not think fit to approach.

In fact, the two fleets were like two big school-boys that thrashed each other well—they had sufficient pluck in them to fight again if they were forced to do so, but they would rather not.

Both sides suffered severely. Of the English, two thousand seven hundred and nineteen were either killed or wounded; and of the French, three thousand and forty-eight.

This was the great battle of Malaga.

As soon as Jumper had recovered from his wounds, he was on board the "Lennox" again; and soon after he performed a good service for his country, although not exactly in the fashion he was accustomed to.

Whilst lying in the port of Lisbon, waiting to convoy a fleet of merchantmen to England, intelligence reached him that the garrison at Gibraltar were about to mutiny, owing to their pay being considerably in arrear. Sir William acted with his usual energy and promptness. He at once sent off some of his ships with what specie he could collect. The soldiers naturally enough thought that this was but a portion of the rest now daily expected. At all events, they made a hasty submission, returned cheerfully to their duty, and thus, as is said, probably preserved that important fortress to the English crown.

The last account we have of him at sea was when he accompanied Sir Cloudesley Shovell's squadron homeward-bound, and arrived off the Land's End on the 22nd of October, 1707. On that fatal day, Sir Cloudesley's own ship, as well as two others under his command, foundered off the Scilly Isles, with upwards of two thousand men on board; but his good fortune accompanied the commander of the "Lennox," as usual—he escaped into Falmouth unhurt.

On the 22nd of the following January he quitted his brave old ship, at Chatham. He was now nineteen years afloat, nearly all of which he spent in active service—and that at a time when active service meant something more than full pay.

It was but reasonable, after the many sanguinary struggles which he had taken a part in, that he should at length seek rest; or, it may be, that his wounds impaired his strength, and incapacitated him from the vigorous action of his younger days. Be that as it may, he retired into private life; where he enjoyed the handsome pension generously bestowed on him by Queen Anne, and where he remained until 1714 —when he was appointed resident commissioner of the navy at Portsmouth. He did not hold this office long, as he died in the March of the following year (1715).

Some time after the death of his first wife he married again,* but it does not appear that he left behind him any offspring to inherit a name rendered illustrious for bravery, for daring, and for promptness of action; and although, in the attributes just mentioned, Britain produced, and again and again produced, his equal, she has never produced his superior.

1706.   A bye-law was passed by our corporation, to prevent any one teaching a Popish apprentice, or any one of the Popish religion, any trade, mystery, or occupation; "and if any person or persons shall offend by employing such persons, he shall be deemed an ill-member if he do not discharge him before the 1st of May next. And if any person, &c., transgress for the future, he shall be turned out and discharged, and not thought worthy to inhabit within the said corporation; and that the sum of three pounds six shillings and eight-pence be levied by distress and sale of goods, as a fine, upon each person so offending.—Daniel Conner, provost."

1710.   This year the last presentment passed the Grand Jury for killing wolves in this county. It is said that the wolf for whose destruction the money was voted was killed near Kilcrea Abbey. Wolves were not unfrequently seen long after this in the woods on both sides of the Bandon river; between Bandon and Kinsale, and the remote parts of the country, particularly between Bantry and Bere-haven, there were many of them.

1713.   At the General Quarter Sessions held at Bandon, on the 12th of January, an address was voted to the Queen's most excellent Majesty, as follows:—" We, your Majesty's subjects of the county, most humbly beg leave to approach your royal person," &c. It then went on to congratulate her on the safe and honourable peace which her Majesty had obtained for the relief and comfort of the people. Also, " that we are thankful to God for the late blessings of the late happy revolution, and are firmly resolved to stand by the succession in the illustrious House of Hanover. So we do not think the remem-

---

* This lady survived him. She subsequently married Nathaniel Ware, of the county of Cork, and died issueless.

brance of the one, or the prospect of the other, any motive to abate our duty and allegiance; and we hope that neither Popery or seclusion can prevail with any other of your Majesty's subjects to abet or assist any pretender to your Majesty's crown and kingdom, and to disturb or elude your legal successors." This address was signed by the high-sheriff (Richard Cox, Esq., Dunmanway), many justices of the peace, clergymen, grand jurors, &c.

1714. A deaf mute, named Robert Long, was born here this year. By dint of industry, and a little assistance, he became acquainted with some branches of mathematics. He understood astronomy; he could calculate eclipses, manufacture globes, maps, &c. A wheel barometer of his make was shown, and some tables made by him for computing the motions of the planets.

1715. Upon the death of Queen Anne a new Parliament was summoned to Dublin. The members for Bandon were:—Francis Bernard, Castle-Mahon, solicitor-general, and Martin Bladen,* Albany-Hatch, Essex (Mr. Secretary Bladen).

Immediately upon the sitting of the House a complaint was made that Richard Croker, high-sheriff of the county, did not make a return in due time of the members elected to serve for the borough of Bandon-Bridge.

Mr. Croker replied that he was unable to attend in Bandon owing to illness; but that he sent his sub-sheriff in due time to Mr. James Jackson, the provost of the said town, for the indenture and return; and that the said provost had been negligent in not returning the same.

Upon this Mr. Jackson was immediately ordered to attend at the bar of the House on a certain day, " touching the complaint of the high-sheriff;" and being duly sworn, made a defence which was considered so unsatisfactory, that it was proposed " that James Jackson be taken into the custody of the sergeant-at-arms;" this, however, was negatived on a division.

1723. The original market-house on the southern side was taken down, and a new one built on the same site; towards the erection of which Lord Burlington gave the sum of twenty-two pounds per annum for five years—being his portion of the tolls of the town.

The new building was fifty feet in length (clear of the walls), and

---

* Arthur Bernard, of Palace Anne, brother of Francis, the senior member, was elected as his brother's co-representative, but refused to serve.

stretched forth his hand in the work of the gospel. And
ful preaching Wight's convictions were reinvigorated—H
friends and his fear of the bewitching Quakers vanishe
forth he was resolved to become a Quaker himself:

He endured a great deal of persecution from his old co
he became a jest and a by-word with them: but he bo
Christian. He also displayed great skill in shunning unr
troversy, and in not wasting his words on those whose wo
induced them to keep their eyes firmly shut against the li
contrary, instead of looking after these unprofitable peopl
after his own spiritual improvement, and he sacrificed himse
to sobriety, solitude, silence, and the Bible.

After some time he came out boldly, and standing up co
he proclaimed the plain truth, in the plain language, and i
clothes of the Society of Friends; and emboldened by his w
success, he flung timidity to the winds, and was not ashame
that he was a Quaker.

In the year 1670 he married, and in process of time had a
family. His increased responsibilities induced him to att
closely to his business—which was not confined to the cloth
alone, he being also engaged as a commission agent—and in
hood Wight would have been in a short time a wealthy man; h
been providentially stopped in his sinful career by an illuminati
from heaven, which threw a great deal of light into his dar
causing him to reflect much, and satisfying him "that he cou
heir to two kingdoms at once." He saw his great danger, an
thorough Christian, he flung all his worldly gains to the wi
devoted himself entirely to the truth.

Being an able scribe, he was appointed clerk to the meetings
and for the province of Munster. He was also the compil
historical account of *The first rise and progress of the truth in the*
which he perfected in the form of annals, up to the year 1700.

He was, says his biographer, a man of exemplary life a
versation, a pattern of plainness, and a diligent attender of
both at home and abroad.

He was seized with an indisposition, which proved mortal on t
month of 1724, under which he showed great composure of m
resignation to the Lord's will.

twenty in width.   The main entrance consisted of five archways, each
of which was six feet in height, and whose sides were formed by the six
pillars upon which the ornamental portions of the front rested.   The
yard to the rear was enclosed by a wall, that on the southern side being
twenty-five feet high.   The entire was completed by Marmaduke
Young, junior, for one hundred and twenty pounds and the materials
of the old building.

1724. Thomas Wight (author of the first *History of the Quakers
in Ireland*) died this year, at the advanced age of eighty-four.
He was born in Bandon in 1640.   His biographer tells us that he was
the son of Rice Wight, minister of the town of Bandon; who was the
son of Thomas Wight,* also minister of the same town, and who came
here from Guildford, in Surrey.

It appears that young Wight's father (Rice Wight) was a very
zealous clergyman of the Church of England, in the principles of which
he brought up his children with great care; but his son Thomas, "who
served a hard apprenticeship to a clothier in Bandon," hearing of a
Quaker's meeting which was to be held in the neighbourhood of the
town, attended it out of pure curiosity; but finding that the people sat
silent a long time, he got uneasy, and began to think that he might be
bewitched if he staid any longer, for he had often heard that the
Quakers were witches.

At length Francis Howgill stood up and uttered these significant
words :—"Before the eye can see, it must be opened; before the ear
can hear, it must be unstopped; and before the heart can understand, it
must be illuminated."

Upon these truisms Howgill delivered an excellent discourse, which
made such a deep impression on young Tom's mind, that he became
deeply convinced of the truth of what he had heard.   But the prejudices
of education and the reproaches of his relatives very nearly effaced
those good impressions; and in all probability young Tom would have
relapsed into Church of Englandism, had not Edward Burrough

---

* Thomas Wight, A.M., was ordained deacon and priest by John, Bishop of
Oxford, October 23rd, 1619.   In 1620 he became prebendary of Kilmacdonogh,
Cloyne; and in 1628 vicar of Ballymodan, Bandon.   In 1634 he was appointed
prebendary of Kilnaglory.   From 1628 to 1649, rector of Aghlishdrinagh.   In 1628
he was elected dean of Cork by the chapter, but the crown declined to ratify the
appointment.   Dr. Brady, from whose valuable records we have derived the above
information, thinks Wight was induced to settle in this country by the Boyle
family.

stretched forth his hand in the work of the gospel. And by his powerful preaching Wight's convictions were reinvigorated—his dread of his
friends and his fear of the bewitching Quakers vanished—and henceforth he was resolved to become a Quaker himself.

He endured a great deal of persecution from his old companions, and
he became a jest and a by-word with them; but he bore it all like a
Christian. He also displayed great skill in shunning unnecessary controversy, and in not wasting his words on those whose worldly interests
induced them to keep their eyes firmly shut against the light. On the
contrary, instead of looking after these unprofitable people, he looked
after his own spiritual improvement, and he sacrificed himself altogether
to sobriety, solitude, silence, and the Bible.

After some time he came out boldly, and standing up courageously,
he proclaimed the plain truth, in the plain language, and in the plain
clothes of the Society of Friends; and emboldened by his well-merited
success, he flung timidity to the winds, and was not ashamed to admit
that he was a Quaker.

In the year 1670 he married, and in process of time had an immense
family. His increased responsibilities induced him to attend very
closely to his business—which was not confined to the clothing trade
alone, he being also engaged as a commission agent—and in all likelihood Wight would have been in a short time a wealthy man, had he not
been providentially stopped in his sinful career by an illumination direct
from heaven, which threw a great deal of light into his dark mind,
causing him to reflect much, and satisfying him "that he could not be
heir to two kingdoms at once." He saw his great danger, and, like a
thorough Christian, he flung all his worldly gains to the winds, and
devoted himself entirely to the truth.

Being an able scribe, he was appointed clerk to the meeting in Cork,
and for the province of Munster. He was also the compiler of an
historical account of *The first rise and progress of the truth in this nation*,
which he perfected in the form of annals, up to the year 1700.

He was, says his biographer, a man of exemplary life and conversation, a pattern of plainness, and a diligent attender of meetings
both at home and abroad.

He was seized with an indisposition, which proved mortal on the ninth
month of 1724, under which he showed great composure of mind and
resignation to the Lord's will.

1727.   A new Parliament assembled in Dublin. The members for Bandon were:—Brigadier the Hon. George Freke, and Stephen Bernard, Castle-Bernard. Brigadier Freke died in 1731, and was succeeded by Bellingham Boyle, of Glenfield, Rathfarnham, Dublin. The return of both these representatives was indentured by William Lapp, the provost, and several of the burgesses. Thomas Evans and Edward Hoare, Esqs., were also returned for the town, their return being duly authenticated by John Bourne, provost elect, and many of the freemen.

Upon these returns being sent up, the House ordered that the clerk of the crown do attend immediately and take off the file the indenture by which the said Mr. Evans and Mr. Hoare were returned. It was further ordered that the said Mr. Evans and Mr. Hoare have liberty to petition the House within fourteen days, if they think fit, in relation to the election of the said borough.

1728.   The Quaker's meeting-house in Bandon was built. It is still in existence, having long survived the last of the Quakers. Previous to its erection the first meetings were held at the house of Mr. Edward Cook, cornet of Oliver Cromwell's own troop of horse, which lay in Bandon when Howgill and his friends arrived. After that they were held at the residence of Mr. Daniel Massey; and after his time, the then Earl of Cork allowed them to meet in one of the three castles erected by the great earl, which occupied the piece of ground now partially covered by a green-house attached to the residence of the late Mr. T. Bennett. After the castle was taken down the meeting-house was erected on a portion of its site.

1729.   Dean Swift spent some time in Bandon. Whilst here, he had ample opportunities of learning many of the characteristics of those amongst whom he lived; and it is to the information thus acquired we are indebted to the motto so devoutly believed to be even still in existence on the walls of Bandon, and which a celebrated political orator stated in the British House of Commons, not many years ago, "that he had read it there with his own eyes." Even yet, it is no unusual thing to see a travelling-capped tourist pull up at the "Tandem Emergo" of the big bridge, and in the "sub auspiciis Johannis Travers," insist on recognising,

"A Turk, a Jew, or an Atheist,
    May live in this town, but no Papist."

There is scarcely a corner of the earth that these lines have not reached, and been quoted as a specimen of the rank bigotry and intolerance supposed to prevail here in former days. Nay, we should not be surprised if some future tenant-right orator of Tongataboo were to conclude a forcible speech in favour of the Tongataboo compulsory valuation clause, by, in some way or another, lugging in this famous couplet. It is not generally known that the original stanza contained fourteen lines; and as this is very rare—we believe we are favoured with the only copy extant—we place it before our readers :—

> "A Turk, a Jew, or an Atheist,
> May live in this town, but no Papist.
> He that wrote these lines did write them well,
> As the same is written on the gates of hell.
> For Friar Hayes, who made his exit of late,
> Of * * * some say. But no matter for that—
> He died; and, if what we've heard is aright,
> He came to hell's gates in a mournful plight.
> 'Who's there?' says the sentry on guard. Quoth the other,
> 'A wretched poor priest, sir! a Catholic brother!'
> 'Halt! instantly halt! Avaunt! and stand clear.
> Go, be damned somewhere else; you shan't be damned here!
> We admit no such fellow, for a wretch so uncivil,
> Who on earth would eat God, would in hell eat the Devil!'"

Although these lines are now believed to have been written by the witty Dean, local tradition says otherwise. It asserts that the first two lines were in reality written on one of the gates of the town, and that some Jacobite wag wrote underneath them,

> "He that wrote these lines did write them well,
> As the same is written on the gates of hell."

And that it was to turn aside the point of the Jacobite's lines the rest were added—either by the writer of the two first, or by some one of the same way of thinking. It may be observed that the lines beginning with "For Friar Hayes" are not of the same metre as the four preceding, and this, to some extent, supports the traditional account.

1734. James Martin succeeded the Hon. Henry Boyle as provost. Wine and turf were cheap in these days, as appears by the following extracts from the accounts, under head of disbursements, furnished by him to the corporation.

	s.	d.
For a bottle of wine, ...	1	2
Ten loads of turf, ...	1	2
Six loads ditto, at 1½d., ...	0	9
To Mr. Sealy, for four bottles of wine, .	4	8

CHAPTER XVIII.

CLONAKILTY—TIMOLEAGUE—COURTMASHERRY—ENNISKEANE—BALLINEEN—
KINNEIGH.

ABOUT twelve miles from Bandon lies the town of Clonakilty.   It is situated in the parish of Kilgarriff, and in
the eastern division of the barony of East Carbery.   Up
to nearly twenty-five years ago Clonakilty was spelt
Cloughnakilty, and previous to that it was Cloughneekeelty (that is,
according to some, the stone* of Kilty—a family of that name having
occupied the site on which the town stands before any houses were
erected there).   Others derive it from Cluan Callow (the harbour of
the valley).   Another derivation—and probably the correct one—is
Cluan Keeltha (the harbour of the woods).†

In all likelihood the town was founded by some of those who came
over to the new colony on the banks of the Bandon towards the close
of Elizabeth's reign, as the names of many of its first inhabitants are
common to both settlements—one brother settling in one place, and
another in the other.

That they were English, and that they professed the same religious
and political opinions as their fellow-colonists at Bandon-Bridge, may
be looked upon as equally certain.

Amongst the first that settled here were :—

---

* It is stated that the stone from which the term Clough is derived may still be
seen at the side of the street opposite the court-house, and adjoining the entrance to
the butter-market.

† We take this opportunity of acknowledging our obligations to our friend,
Zachariah Hawkes, Esq., for much interesting information to be found scattered
throughout these pages.

Anstice,	Chappell,	Hare,	Strangway,
Bird,	Cotter,	Hyman,	Sears,
Baker,	Corker,	Jobson,	Snowe,
Borrell,	Dyer,	Linscombe,	Slyman,
Bailey,	Fisher,	Martin,	Sheapheard,
Baylis,	Fowler,	Mills,	Small,
Browne,	Glover,	Morgan,*	Stukeley,
Barrone,	German,	Merry,	Vigers,
Broughton,	Harris,	May,	Wallis,
Bareham,	Hart,	Patterson,	Worralls,
Bodge,	Holloway,	Pratt,	Ware.
Cleveland,	Hutchins,	Spiller,	

The town was of some importance as early as 1605; in which year—according to Smith—it was incorporated. That a representative body of some sort did really exist at that time appears from a petition dated July the 5th, 1605, and addressed to the authorities at Cork, "from the portreeve and corporation of Cloughnakilty."

In 1613, however, a charter was granted to the town by James the First, by which the inhabitants were incorporated as the "sovereign, free-burgesses, and commonalty of the borough of Cloughnakilty."

The charter, which was a lengthy document, appointed Sir Richard Boyle—and, after him, his heirs and successors—as "lord of the town;" and authorized him to elect, nominate, and choose one of three names to be presented to him by the burgesses, who were to assemble for that purpose on St. James's day, July 25th; and the person nominated by him† was to be sworn as sovereign on the following St. Luke's day, October 18th.

The lord of the town also appointed the recorder, who, as well as the

---

* The Rev. James Morgan—probably a descendant of Morgan, one of the first settlers—was born in Clonakilty in 1741. He wrote the life of the Rev. Thomas Walshe (a distinguished preacher among the Wesleyans), and other works. He died in Dublin at the early age of twenty-seven. He is described in a MS. lately in our possession as "a scholar, clear head, neat and clean man."

† On one occasion "the lord of the town" neglected to select a name from those presented to him in the usual way, whereupon the corporation laid their case before an eminent lawyer—Mr. Francis Bernard, solicitor-general. I have perused (said counsel) a copy of the charter of Cloughnakilty, which was laid before me by Captain Snowe; and as the charter is worded, I am of opinion as followeth, viz.:—That if the corporation has done its duty by nominating three persons on St. James's day, and presenting their names to the lord of the soyle in due time, and his lordship has neglected to signifie to the corporation the person he designs should be sworn suffrain before the day of swearing, then, and in such case, there being a neglect in the lord of the soyle, the right of election is, as I can conceive, devolved on the corporation, and they may elect and swear in a magistrate on St. Luke's day. This opinion was endorsed by a very competent authority. "I am of the same opinion," says Sir Richard Cox, ex-Lord-Chancellor.

sovereign, was a justice of the peace for the borough and liberties—the latter embracing a district of three miles long by three in breadth, with the old chapel in the middle of the town for its centre. In addition, the sovereign and recorder were also empowered to hold a court of record for the recovery of debts and the determining of pleas, not exceeding twenty pounds late Irish currency.

A manor court was held on the third Wednesday in every month by a seneschal, where debts could be recovered to the amount of forty shillings.

The corporation consisted of a sovereign and burgesses. The burgesses were never to exceed twenty-four in number, or to be less than thirteen. As vacancies would occur amongst them they were to be filled up from the freemen, and the freemen themselves were to be nominated by the burgesses. The corporation was to be assisted in the performance of its duties by a sergeant-at-mace, three constables, a toll-collector, and a weigh-master.

The right of sending two members to Parliament was also conferred on the town by this charter; and this privilege it continued to exercise until the passing of the Act of Union in 1800, when it was disfranchised.

The first two members returned for Clonakilty were :—Sir Edward Harris, Knt., Cahirmoney, and Sir Henry Gosnell, Knt. Their return is dated May 3rd, 1613.*

---

* The following is a complete list of those who represented the town from 1613, when it sent its first two members to Parliament, down to, and including its last :—

1613 (May 3rd).—Sir Edward Harris, Knt. ; Sir Henry Gosnell, Knt.
1634.—Sir Robert Travers, Knt. ; Phillip Manwaring, Esq.
1639 (February 24th).—Sir Robert Travers, Knt. ; Peregrine Banastre, Esq.
1661 (April 8th).—Joshua Boyle, Esq., Castle-Lyons ; Arthur Freke, Esq.
1692 (September 1st).—Sir Percy Freke, Bart., Castle-Freke ; Francis Bernard. Esq., Castle-Mahon.
1695 (August 12th).—Sir Percy Freke, Bart. ; Bryan Townsend, Esq., Castle-Townsend.
1703 (September 1st).—Sir Ralph Freke, Bart., Castle-Freke ; Lieutenant-Colonel George Freke.
1713 (October 28th).—Sir Ralph Freke ; Brigadier-General George Freke.
1715 (October 17th).—Sir Ralph Freke, Bart. ; Brigadier-General George Freke.
1717 (September 1st).—Richard Cox, Esq,, Dunmanway (vice Sir Ralph Freke, deceased).
1725 (September 26th).—Francis Bernard, junr., Esq., Castle-Mahon (vice Cox, deceased).
1727 (October 16th).—Francis Bernard, junr., Esq. ; Sir Richard Cox, Bart., Dunmanway.
1761 (May 1st).—Richard Lord Boyle, Castle-Martyr ; Sir Richard Cox, Bart.
1761 (November 27th).—Henry Shears, Esq., Golden Bush (vice Lord Boyle, returned for the county of Cork).
1766 (February 15th).—Matthew Parker, Esq., Youghal (vice Cox, deceased.)

When the great rebellion broke out in 1641, Clonakilty suffered severely. It had no walls to protect it, and it was therefore almost at the mercy of any persons who choose to walk in and help themselves to the property of its inhabitants.

On one occasion, Joan Barry* marched into the town at the head of three hundred women, and ransacked every house that was in it. There was no opposing these Amazons. With one weapon in their fist, and another between their teeth, they could bewilder as well as pommel their antagonists. Quickly they overspread devoted Clonakilty. Like a swarm of locusts they pitched upon everything. The curiosity and the pillaging proclivities of Joan's "red shanks," left nothing escape them. These unwomanly women stuffed everything into their bottomless wallets. Candles and taffety were in all likelihood wedged in with silks and pickled pork, whilst salt fish and ribbons were in juxta-position with pots of pomatum and new-laid eggs.

After bringing her regiment of rebels together, they set out for home; but whether they fell in or fell out on the line of march—whether they helped one another with their knapsacks, or scrawled one another's eyes out—we are unable to say. At all events they walked off, leaving many a full heart behind them, and an empty shelf.

On another occasion she commanded upwards of a hundred men and women, and again attacked the town.

But Joan was not the only one who visited Clonakilty with bad intentions. Teige O'Hea, of Kilgarriff, made off with the cattle of one townsman, and, in conjunction with Garrett Arundell, of Ring, he robbed another.

Cornelius O'Crowly† disarmed another settler, and he stripped him

---

1768 (July 7th).—Richard Longfield, Esq., Castle-Mary; Riggs Falkiner, Esq., Cork.
1776.—Thomas Adderly, Esq.; A. Wood, Esq.
1784.—Charles O'Neil.
1792.—Sir J. C. Colthurst.
1793.—Viscount Boyle.
1794.—J. Hobson, junr.
1797.—Thomas Prendergast.
At the Union, Lord Shannon—a descendant of the first lord of the town—was awarded £15,000 as compensation for the disfranchisement of his town.

* Joan Barry was a widow lady. She lived at Mucrus, and was the mother of David McPhillip Barry, a captain in the rebel army.

† Teige O'Hea, Garrett Arundell, and Cornelius Crowly were indicted for treason at the great sessions held at Youghal, August 2nd, 1642, and outlawed subsequently in the King's Bench.

and his wife and three children, in the beginning of the month of February, and left them, "with divers others, to the number of five-and-forty,"* to shiver in the cold.†

Donogh O'Shea, of Ring, robbed another townsman, and then took away his clothes.

Dermod Duffe took a man's coat and hat away, and "then took some necessaries from his pocket." And "one Tom Barry," who pretended to be a friend of another Clonakilty man, kept two trunks full of clothes, two brass kettles, a sword, a brass skillet, and divers other small things which he was entrusted to take care of by a poor fellow whose wife the rebels murdered the year before.

Several of the townspeople made their escape to Bandon; and one of them (Walter Bird), contrived to take the charter and other corporation documents with him; but many of them remained—amongst others, Mr. Linscombe, the sovereign. He, poor fellow, was a very quiet, inoffensive man, and the Irish—with whom he appeared to be a favourite—assured him that there was no fear whatever of him; and we have no doubt but that several of the leaders of the great movement in this quarter‡ intended to dispossess the colonists of their lands, and redress some of their alleged grievances—but no more. But when once their followers had tasted blood, their thirst became insatiable. Laying hold of Mr. Linscombe, they forced him to drink until his nauseated stomach rejected the fluid, and then they hanged him at his own door.

During the siege of Rathbarry Castle, an effort was made to relieve it by a detachment of the Bandon militia, and the Scotch regiment commanded by Lord Forbes. Upon their arrival in Clonakilty, one company of the Bandonians and two of the Scots remained behind in the town. Being suddenly attacked by the Irish, the Scotch companies were cut to pieces, but the Bandonians forced their way to the old Danish fort on the road to Ross, where they defended themselves until the return of the troops who marched to Rathbarry; then uniting with

---

* See MSS. Trinity College, Dublin.

† Amongst those stripped were:—John Justice, of Clonakilty, and his son Edward; Mills and his son, and his son's wife and three children; Chapman Sheapheard, his wife and children; Ellen Duffill, Mabel Hollowell, Mary Wan; — Cotter. They were stripped in John Baker's house in Clonakilty, on the 10th of February, 1642.

‡ Lord Muskerry, for instance, who took a very prominent part in the rebellion, hanged several of his own followers for thieving.

them, they all fell on the rebels, upwards of six hundred of whom were destroyed.*

The town never recovered from the effects of the ill-usage it received in the great rebellion.

Before 1641 the town flourished greatly, says Smith; but being then burned down, it has since but slowly recovered.

In 1679 tradesmen's tokens were issued at Clonakilty. One of these, at present in the collection of an eminent numismatist, has, on the obverse, the coat of arms of the issuer, and on the reverse, "Cloghnikilty, PE. IB. farthing."

A *quo warranto* was issued against the corporation by Tyrconnell, and the old charter set aside. A new one was then conferred on the town, dated July 12th, 1688, in which one Daniel McCarthy was appointed sovereign, and twenty-four burgesses were nominated with him. This did not remain long in force, and the town resumed its original charter again.

On the 11th of April, 1691, five hundred of the Irish soldiers in James's service attacked the town, but they were valiantly repulsed by the garrison, which consisted of fifty dragoons and twenty-four men belonging to Captain Fenwick's company of foot.

The two oldest documents to be found at present among the records of the Clonakilty corporation have reference to the election of John Townsend as sovereign of the town :—

BOROUGH OF CLONAKILTY. At a court of record held in the borough the 25th of July, 1675, Thomas Gookin, the present sovereign, John Townsend, and William Warner, Esquires, being free-burgesses of the said borough, were chosen and elected to be presented to the Rt. Hon[ble] Richard, Earl of Cork, to the end that one of them may be nominated and appointed by his lordship to be the sovereign the next ensuing year, according to his Majesty's most gracious grant in that behalf.

John Sweet, junr.	Thomas Gookin, sovereign,
David Jerman.	Richard Cox, recorder.
Abel Guilliams.	John Townsend.
Walter Harris.	John Birde.
William Warner.	Richard Travers.
Cornelius Townsend.	Samuel Jervois.
John Freke.	Edward Jenkins.

The following oath was administered to the sovereign on St. Luke's day, October 18th :—

---

* For additional particulars of this affair see chapter 22.

You, A. B., shall well and truly serve the King's most excellent Majesty, his heirs and successors, in the place or office of the sovereign of the borough of Clonakilty for this year to come, or for so long time as you shall continue sovereign of the same within the said year. You shall truly and indifferently administer justice, right, as well to the poor as to the rich, without any respect, dread, gain, reward, favour, or affection. You shall delay no man's case to be depending before you, other than the laws of the land shall admit; and finally, as in these, so in whatsoever else that may or shall concern your said place or office, you shall well and truly do, or cause the same to be done to the uttermost of your understanding and knowledge—so help your God.

The return of the sovereign was duly certified as follows:—

BOROUGH OF CLONAKILTY. At a court held for the borough, the 18th day of October, John Townsend, Esq., one of the free-burgesses of the borough, pursuant to the nomination and appointment of the Rt. Honble Richard, Earl of Cork and Burlington, Lord High-Treasurer of Ireland and lord of the said borough, was sworn sovereign of the said borough for the next ensuing year, and had the ensigns of authority delivered to him before the late sovereign and the under-named burgesses:—

John Sweet.	Richard Cox, recorder.
Cornelius Townsend.	Emanuel Moore.
Thomas Gookin.	Jonas Stawell.

1678.

Jonas Stawell, sovereign. The tolls of the fairs,* markets, and customs were let for five years, at the rate of nine pounds yearly, to James Barry and John Spiller; "and if they find their bargain hard, they may surrender at the year's end. The freemen are not to pay custom for anything they buy, except on market and fair days." It does not appear that Barry and Spiller found their bargain hard, as—upon the expiration of the five years—they entered into a new contract with the corporation, and agreed to pay the increased rent of twenty pounds annually.

1687.

The records contain no account of the transactions of the corporation from this year until February 4th, 1692; when Mr. Charles Gookin was elected burgess. It is highly probable that the interval was occupied by the proceedings of James the Second's corporation; and that, upon the restoration of law and order under William, nearly everything connected with their civic connection with the town was destroyed. The only thing about them that has survived, is that John Hull, who was sworn in as sovereign for the year beginning

---

* Three fairs are held under the old charter—April 5th, October 10th, and November 12th; and two more were established by patent dated July 11th, 1788—namely, on June the 1st and July the 3rd.

in October, 1687, was set aside by Tyrconnell's new sovereign—Dan McCarthy.

1692.

On the 7th of September, Francis Bernard, Esq., was sworn and admitted recorder, before Thomas Gookin, Esq., sovereign, and Piercy Freke, Bryan Townsend, and Edward Jenkins, burgesses; pursuant to the Earl of Cork's order, dated July 7th, 1692. Mr. Bernard was appointed in place of Richard Cox, who was made a judge of the Court of Common Pleas. A week after Mr. Bernard was appointed recorder, he and his cousin-german—Colonel Piercy Freke—were elected to represent the town in the new Parliament that was t.... assemble at Chichester House, Dublin, on the ensuing 5th of October.

BOROUGH OF CLONAKILTY.

Pursuant to a precept directed to the sovereign, bu... gesses, and commonalty of this borough, returnable ... 18. Monday, the nineteenth day of this instant, grounded upon the ...ed Majesty's writ of summons, to choose two burgesses, of the most discr... and the most sufficient men of the said town, to be and appear at t... next Parliament, to be held at Dublin on the fifth day of October nex... we, the said sovereign, burgesses, and commonalty, have freely an... unanimously elected and chosen Colonel Piercy Freke and Francis Bernard, Esq., recorder of the said borough, to serve in the said Parliament, this fourteenth of September, 1692.

John Jermyn (treasurer).
Alexander Arundell.

Thomas Gookin, sov{n.}
Francis Bernard, rec{dr.}
Richard Travers.
William Warner.
Edward Jenkins.

Samuel Jervois.
Abel Guilliams,
Bryan Townsend.
Piercy Freke.
Samuel Jervois, jun.

1699.

A stringent rule was passed against forestallers buying before ten in the morning.

"Whereas several foreigners, on market days, in the morning, engrosses the several provisions and commodities brought thereto, to the great detriment of the inhabitants of the said borough. We therefore find and present, that any person not living within the said borough, that henceforth shall buy or earnest anything brought to the said market before the hour of ten o'clock in the forenoon, shall pay to the poor of the parish the sum of one shilling out of each crown laid out or earnested for the same, and such proportion to be paid to the church-wardens, to the use of the said poor, for the time being; and that no townsman buy for any foreigner, under any pretence whatever, under the penalty aforesaid."

The same year that they imposed this penalty of twenty per cent. upon all sums expended by foreigners in Clonakilty market, the corporation were determined to show that they looked after the morals of their people as well as after cheap food. "We find and present," said

24

those chaste burgesses, "that Honora Keliher is reputed to be a common w——e, by having two bastards by two several persons, and humbly desire as such she may be prosecuted." But they did not confine their solicitude merely to cheap provisions and morals—they looked after the health of their people also. They gave directions "that the dunghills which are now in the streets, to the great nuisance of all the neighbourhood, be removed within three weeks; and that, for the future, no dunghill lie in the street from the making of the same, upon pain and penalty of one shilling.

A resolution of the burgesses this year shows us how they managed to keep up the roads in their vicinity in those days. We find and present," said they, "that the road leading from Clonakilty to Timoleague—between the lands of Cahirgale, Gullames, and of Trerrery—ought to be repaired; and that three men out of each ploughland, living within the corporation, repair the same." Should they, or any of them, refuse to come, "they must pay a shilling each, to be levied by the corporation constable. Mr. Herbert Baldwin and Capt. Richard Hungerford to oversee the work, that it is properly done. The said men to appear at the work with spades and shovels." When the road, however, lay within the jurisdiction of the corporation, it was repaired out of a rate levied off the townlands within the liberties. Thus, when the road from Clonakilty to the strand, through the lands of Laconagubbodane, was out of order, twopence per ploughland throughout the corporation was passed to restore it; the money to be levied by the petty constable.

1706. Robert Travers, sovereign. Before Travers was elected, he promised "to finish that part of the market house that now is lathed within-side, glaze the said house, and hang up the bells, upon his own cost and charge within his year."

1715. Michael Beecher, who had been nominated sovereign by the lord of the town, could not attend to be sworn on St. Luke's day, "he having the gout."

Originally Clonakilty was built in the form of a cross; but, as trade increased, streets sprang out in every direction, and crossing the Farlah, formed another town on its southern banks.

After the manufacture of woollens had ceased, Clonakilty became celebrated for its linen yarn; and on market-days large sums were expended in the purchase of this—for over two centuries its staple product; but the yarn trade, too, has died out, and the town now relies for support on its dealings with the farmers in its neighbourhood.

The parish church, which was situated on an eminence overhanging the present Main Street, was built by the first Earl of Cork,* who also. planted the town with English Protestants. In 1679, although there was no other church for the Protestant inhabitants of Inchidonny, Templebrian, Desert, Killkerran, Rathbarry, and Ardfield, to worship in, yet so much was it suffered to fall out of repair, that the Grand Jury of the county were obliged to come to its relief, and pass a presentment, levying the sum of eight shillings off every ploughland in the parishes just mentioned, to render it suitable for divine service.

The present church, which is a plain, unpretending structure, was built on the site of the original church, which was taken down in 1818. It is capable of accommodating five hundred persons, and was erected at a cost of £1,460.

Clonakilty contains also a Presbyterian church—a very handsome edifice, erected within the last few years; a Wesleyan chapel, which has been recently enlarged and beautified; and a Roman Catholic chapel.

The bay, to which the town has given its name, is spacious but ill-protected. In Smith's time, its eastern boundary was formed by one of the Dunworly headlands;† on the west it was bounded by Dunny Cove. The water was eight fathoms in depth on the Dunworly side, five on the western side, and no less than twelve fathoms deep across the mouth of the bay.

TIMOLEAGUE.

Timoleague lies about eleven miles south of Bandon. It was formerly spelt Tagumlag, Tymulagy, Tymoleague, &c., and it derives its name from the Tee Molaga (the house of Molaga),‡ an Irish saint, who lived in A.D. 665, and to whom the abbey, built in the beginning of the fourteenth century, was dedicated. The town of Timoleague, and much

---

* " * * Clonakilty, wherein he hath built a fair, new church, and made a plantation—all of English Protestants. See *Particulars of the first Earl of Cork's Commonwealth Works.*

† At present this headland forms the eastern boundary of what is now known as Dunworly Bay.

‡ St. Molaga was a native of Fermoy, and his principal monastery there was called Tulach-Min Molaga. His festival day was on the 20th of January. It is not known when he died, but he was alive in A.D. 665, having survived the great plague which raged in that year.

of the adjacent country, anciently belonged to the Hodnetts—an English family who settled here from Shropshire; and prior to their advent it belonged to the O'Cowigs.

In the reign of Henry the Third a great battle was fought at Timoleague, between the Hodnetts, under Lord Phillip Hodnett, and the Barrys, under Lord Barrymore; when the former were routed, and their leader, Lord Phillip, killed.

The Barrymores then became its owners, and they and their descendants retained possession of it until some years since, when it was purchased by the late Colonel Travers.

When the site of the town of Bandon was "a meer waste bog and wood, serving for a retreat to wood-kerns and wolves," Timoleague was a town, and contained more than a dozen hostelries, where Irish gentlemen and Spanish merchants could rest, and regale themselves with a refreshing cup of sack, ere the former set out on their way to Cork or Kinsale, or the latter went into the market-place, and bartered their wines and olives for the hides and butter for which the town was famous.

In 1589 (*temp*. Queen Elizabeth) Timoleague was known as a seaport town, and in that year was mentioned in conjunction with Kinsale; both being described as "market and haven towns, the furthest not a myle from the maine sea."

The importance of Timoleague towards the close of the sixteenth century may also be inferred from another fact, namely:—that excepting Bandon, Timoleague was the only town in the west riding of the county deemed suitable for holding courts of inquiry concerning owners *in capite* deceased; what they died possessed of, and who were their lawful heirs, &c. And although the "Inquisitiones Post-Mortem" were much more frequently held in the former than in the latter, yet an inquisition was held in Timoleague nearly twenty years before one was heard of in Bandon. The first jury that was empanneled in Bandon was in the case of James Fitzwilliam Roche, September 10th, 1613; the one we have referred to as being held in Timoleague was in the case of David Barry, and bears date April 12th, 1594.

In the great rebellion Sir Robert O'Shaughnessy held the castle* and town of Timoleague for the rebels, but was compelled to lower his flag to Lord Forbes. Forbes neglected to garrison it; and it was again

---

* Said to be built by the Morils, A.D. 1206.

occupied by the Irish, who were again forced to surrender it to Colonel Myn, on the 1st of July, 1643.

Most, if not all, the Irish gentry in the neighbourhood of Timoleague were at this time actively engaged in the vast civil strife that was convulsing the kingdom from one end of it to the other. John Oge Mac Redmond Barry,* of Dunworly, William Barry, of Lislee, James Barry, of Dunworly, William Barry, of Glanwirane, were in open arms against the English; and William Barry, of Agha, had collected stores, and had two houses in Butlerstown full of corn, to furnish the rebels with supplies.

In 1649 Captain Sweete and his company of foot were quartered in the castle; and being anxious to join the Parliament, he wrote to England to say so, and desired that some shipping should be sent into the bay. Inchiquin, who seems to have had some inkling of his designs, ordered him and the force under his command to shift their quarters.

Should Sweete do this, his scheme would have been frustrated; he therefore called on the Rev. John Godfrey,† of Timoleague, and requested him to get up a petition in the name of the gentry and respectable inhabitants of the locality, and present it to Lieutenant-General Barry, urging that Sweete and his command be allowed to remain with them.

The petition was duly presented, and its prayer assented to; and thus the parliamentarian was afforded the desired opportunity, and of which he availed himself, " to secure the castle of Timoleague for the English interest."

Cromwell confirmed him in his command, and he remained governor of the castle until November, 1652.‡

Whilst Sweete's company lay in the castle, some of McCarthy-Reagh's

---

* John Barry, of Dunworly, William Barry, Lislee, James Barry, Dunworly, &c. There were no less than five Barrys from Dunworly indicted for high-treason at the great Youghal sessions, and subsequently outlawed.

† The Rev. John Godfrey, in 1639, was curate to the Rev. Robert Snowswell, who was vicar of Fanlobbus and rector of Ballymoney. At the time Captain Sweete obtained his assistance he was curate to the Rev. John Eveleigh, who was vicar of Timoleague from 1634 to 1663. Godfrey had a son, John, also in holy orders, who was born in Bandon in 1639. This Rev. John was rector of Kilmeen, prebendary of Currograngemore, vicar of Drinagh, &c.—Vide *Clerical Records of Cork, Cloyne, and Ross.*

‡ Captain John Sweete was awarded the sum of £809 16s. 0d. for his services. This sum was assigned to Randal Clayton in trust for him.

troop of horse came into the locality, demanding that meat should be sent to Kinsale fort; but they were set upon by a small detachment from Sweete's force, consisting of Sergeant John Barnes, George Woods, Robert Hooper, George Reinor, Daniel Seaberry, and some others; who succeeded in capturing six or seven of McCarthy's troopers, together with their arms, and eight or nine horses.

On another occasion, between fifty and sixty foot, sent into Ibane by Colonel Crosby, the governor of Kinsale garrison, drove off two hundred cows and beeves.

Captain Sweete heard of it, and nothing daunted by their superior numbers, he dispatched Sergeant Barnes, and a little force consisting of Privates Seaberry, Warner, Stephens, Viner, Dennie, Patch, Hooper, and Teige O'Monoghane, to go in pursuit, and rescue the cattle.

The abbey was built in A.D. 1320, by Daniel McCarthy, prince of Carbery. It is stated that the ground upon which it was erected was previously occupied by a building belonging to the Morils, and taken from them by the McCarthys. In 1373, William Barry, lord of Ibane, was buried there. In 1400 it was given to the Franciscans of the Strict Observance. In 1484, in accordance with a bequest of William Galwey, of the city of Cork, the friars of "Tymulagy" received a portion of six pecks of salt and six stone of iron.

Edmund de Courcey* added the handsome Gothic tower, which is seventy feet high, and which is still in excellent preservation; and to him the abbey was also indebted for the dormitory, infirmary, and library. He died in 1518, having bequeathed for the use of the friars many valuable books and much plate.

De Courcey was held in high esteem by Henry the Seventh, whose rights he strenuously defended against the efforts of Lambert Simuel and Perkin Warbeck. Indeed, so greatly was he respected by Henry's government, that when Sir Richard Edgcomb arrived in Dublin after Warbeck's rebellion, to administer oaths of fidelity and allegiance to the principal personages in Ireland, he sent for De Courcey to consult

---

* Edmund de Courcey had been a monk in Timoleague Abbey. He was subsequently raised to the See of Clogher, and was the first prelate of English descent that ever wore the mitre in that diocese. He was appointed to Clogher by Pope Sixtus IV., in June, 1484, and to that of Ross, in September, 1494. He died in March, 1518, at a very advanced age, and was buried in his beloved abbey. He was brother of Nicholas de Courcey, baron of Kinsale (he died in 1474), and was uncle of James, Lord Kinsale—a nobleman from whom he received much assistance in the great additions and improvements which he made to the abbey in which he first took his vows.

with him, and deemed the administration of oaths in his case as altogether unnecessary.

Provincial chapters were held in the abbey in 1552, and again in 1563; and by an inquisition held shortly after, it was found that it possessed only four acres and a-half of land, but derived a large income from tithes. The land was given to Lord Inchiquin, and the greater portion of the tithes to Trinity College, Dublin.

Father Mooney, provincial of the Irish Franciscans, visited the abbey in 1603. Speaking of it, he says:—

"The church was, indeed, a splendid edifice, having a spacious choir, aisle, lateral wing, and magnificent tall tower. The cloister was very beautiful, square, richly arcaded, and covered with a platform, on which there was a suite of apartments—comprising chapter-room, refectory, and the guardians' ample chamber. Along with these the convent had also its dormitory, kitchen, cellars, and other appurtenances, which made it one of the noblest houses of our Order in Ireland. When I visited the place, the entire edifice was still standing, though sadly in need of being repaired; for, indeed, it had suffered much from the ruthless Vandalism of the English soldiers, and also from the sacrilegious rapacity of William Lyons, Protestant bishop of Cork, and a certain Doctor Hanmer, an Anglican minister. During the late war, a body of English soldiers, consisting of one hundred infantry and fifty horsemen, halted before Timoleague, and, entering the church, began to smash the beautiful stained-glass windows, and destroy the various pictures about the altar. It so happened that the carpenter, whom our friars employed to look after the repairs of the sacred edifice, was present on this occasion; and seeing the impiety of those creedless mercenaries, he addressed himself to our holy founder thus:—'St Francis, in whose honour this house was built, I know that thou art all-powerful with God, and canst obtain from him whatsoever thou askest. Now, I solemnly swear that I will never do another day's work in this monastery, if thou dost not take speedy vengeance on those sacrilegious wretches who have destroyed the holy place.' And, indeed, it would appear that the poor man's prayers were soon heard; for, on the following day, when the soldiers had struck their tents, after doing such serious damage to the church and monastery, they were encountered by Daniel O'Sullivan, prince of Bear, who, with a small force then under his command, fell upon them, and cut them to pieces. Dr. Hanmer, whom I previously mentioned, destroyed the dormitory in 1596; for he came in a small vessel to Timoleague, in order to procure timber for a house which he was building near Cork; and having learned that the friars' cells were wainscoted with oak elaborately carved, he pulled asunder the rich wood-work, and placed it aboard his vessel. But his sacrilege was duly avenged; for his ship had hardly put to sea, when a gale sprung up, and sent it with its freight to the bottom. Lyons, the Protestant bishop of Cork, was an unrelenting enemy to our convent of Timoleague, and never spared that beautiful house when he required

building materials.   In 1590, having commenced building a mill, he
and his *posse* made a descent on a mill belonging to our friars, which stood
on the Arrighideen, and carried off the hammer-stones and machinery ;
which he re-erected in his own neighbourhood.   Soon afterwards,
however, an inundation swept away all his work; and many who
witnessed the fact attributed it to the indignation of Heaven."

Notwithstanding the severity exercised towards the friars, they
seemed to have taken up their abode within the old walls whenever a
favourable opportunity presented itself.

When the great rebellion was raging, there were friars residing in the
abbey ; and when that great revolt was finally crushed by Cromwell,
amongst those that suffered for their partizanship with the rebels were
" the ffryers of St. Ffrancis's Order," at Timoleague.   They had but
one acre of ground—" now a garden"—and this the relentless Oliver
deprived them of.   Again :—When James the Second showed unmistakable signs of attachment to the Church of Rome, the friars were to
be found there once more.   Even in April, 1696—years after the
departure of the last of the Irish soldiers for France—it was announced,
upon official authority, that four friars were then living in the abbey.

From that period up to the present it has only been used as a burying-place ; and such has been the rage for interments there, that, on
several occasions, the bones of many of those deposited within its
hallowed precincts have been removed to make room for fresh inmates.

All these bones and skulls were collected, and arranged in the form of
a wall; and, up to about twenty-five years ago, they were the first to catch
the visitor's attention on his entrance to the graveyard.   At present, the
lower portion of this crumbling structure can still be seen, but it is so
overgrown with moss as to escape the eye of the ordinary observer.

The building itself is in a very fair condition, and is at this day in a
better state of preservation than it was nearly a century since.*   For
this it is solely indebted to the late Colonel Travers, who, at considerable expense, repaired and strengthened the walls, and by these and
other means kept it from falling.   So that to this gentleman it is owing
that a feature prominent in the landscape for over five hundred years is
yet in being, and the student and the tourist can still visit and admire
the venerable abbey of Timoleague.

The buildings are nearly entire, says Lewis, except the roof, surrounding three sides of a court sixty yards square.   On the east is

---

* See engraving in Grote's *Antiquities of Ireland.*

a church, with a nave and choir (the former thirty and the latter fifteen yards long). From the division a transept opens to the south, more than twelve yards long ; and on the south of the nave is the open arcade extending round one side of the transept, and supported by seven irregular arches, resting on cylindrical and square pillars, without capitals. The windows are round in their style and elevation. The east window is composed of three lofty lights, divided by stone mullions. The south window of the transept is also of three lancet-shaped lights, and the great west window of two. On the east side of the south transept is an oratory, with light and elegant windows ; and those of the nave are pointed, square-headed, obtuse, and ogee. The division or screen between the nave and choir is by a lofty arch, on which rests a small, light, square tower, sixty-eight feet high ; and beneath this tower is a narrow and curious passage, similar to those leading to the rood-loft in the English cathedrals. The dormitories, refectory, and other domestic offices, are remaining.

There are several tombs belonging to old Irish families of distinction to be found within the walls. That of the McCarthy-Reaghs, of Kilbrittain Castle, is in the centre of the choir. Near this is a monument to one of O'Cullinanes, with the following inscription :—" *Hic jacet bonus vir dominus Thade O' Culleane al Totan cum suis filiis eorum et successoribus. Requiescant in Pace. Amen.* A.D. 1635." There is also a tomb of the De Courceys, barons of Kinsale. Eugene O'Hagan, bishop of Ross, Apostolic vicar of Clement the Eighth, and who was killed in the fight on the banks of the river Bandon, in December, 1602, is interred in the north-western angle of the cloister. Allen Patrick O'Fihelly, of the Order of Friars Minor, " a man famed for his great learning," is buried here. John Imurily, who succeeded De Courcey in the See of Ross, and died in 1519, also found a resting-place within these walls, and many others of lesser note.*

Famous as this old abbey is, it may have been more famous still, by contributing to the literary lore of our country's history ; and in all probability would have done so, were it not for a piece of heartless Vandalism, inexcusable even in school-boys and pigs.

It appears that, about twenty years ago, a new master arrived to take

---

* The Barrys, O'Learys, Regans, O'Heas, O'Donovans, &c., bury their dead here still. In the will of Daniel O'Donovan, made in August, 1629, he directed that " hise bodie be buryed in ye abbeye of Tymulagy."

charge of the National School at Timoleague. In order to ingratiate himself with his pupils, and generate a good feeling in the school to the schoolmaster, he granted a half-holiday. The play-ground at that time was the abbey and graveyard. It was a bright, sunny day in July; and the boys, who had just got rid of an ill-grained pedagogue, and received a kind, considerate man in exchange, were more than usually merry and frolicsome. Some raced with their bare feet over the marble slab, underneath which lay many a grim chieftain of the McCarthys; others peered courageously into the gloomy vault, which contained the dust of several of the descendants of the champion of England in the reign of King John; and more scaled the walls, and chased one another along their dangerous summits. Whilst running on the top of one of the latter, one little fellow trod with his heel upon a flag, and it gave out a hollow sound; he trod again, and the sound was more hollow still. Calling two or three of his companions to him, they resolved to raise it, expecting that underneath they would find gold goblets and other valuables, which the monks may have secreted there in the old times. At length they succeeded in tumbling the guardian stone into the nave below, but, instead of gold goblets, all that they beheld was an old parchment book. Descending with this, they collected all their school-fellows around them, and through sheer vexation—intermingled with that strong love of mischief common to young scholastic humanity all the world over—they kicked the musty volume from one end of the village to the other, and then back again. At last, when almost tired of maltreating it, they flung it into a puddle, where they pelted it with stones to prevent it floating. Then something more exciting catching their attention, away they ran. One would think its misfortunes had now drawn to a close, but it was not so. Scarcely had the boys gone away when a sow and her bonnives paid it a visit. We are unable to say whether materfamilias, or any one of her bewitching offspring, was ambitious of being looked upon as " a learned pig," but certain it is that they one and all seem to have been bent on making their own of what the school-boys had unintentionally spared. One interesting little porker was observed to hold several of the leaves determinedly between his teeth, whilst another bonnive—literally of the same litter —tore more than half of them away from him; and then both literati, retiring with what they had to a neighbouring sink, literally devoured them. A gentleman residing in the vicinity heard on the same evening

of what had occurred, and although he was ready to give almost everything he possessed for the old MS., all he was enabled to procure was a
portion of the cover; and thus perished a manuscript which may have
been as welcome to the student of Irish history as the *Psalter of Cashel*
or the *Annals of the Four Masters.*

When the abbey was in its glory, and when those ivy-mantled ruins,
now tenanted by the bat and the owl, were occupied by numerous
Franciscan friars, it must have been delightful—at full tide, on a waning
summer's evening—to listen to the vesper-hymn pouring from out the
painted windows of the cloister, and rolling with melodious swell down
through the echoing woods which at that time embosomed the estuary of
the Arigadeen; and listen on, and hear the last lingering note grow
soft and faint—and yet softer and fainter still—as it slowly crept along
to the great ocean that lay asleep outside the dark cliffs of Lislee.

On the strand, between the abbey and Barry's Hall, a light chalybeate
spring was noticed upwards of a hundred years ago. The water is free
from sulphur, and easily lathers with soap. It is said to be good for
indigestion, loss of appetite, and for strengthening the stomach. On
the eastern side of the town is another chalybeate spring, but its waters
are not thought to be so salubrious as the former. It is dedicated to
the Virgin Mary; and on the 8th of September was formerly much
frequented by the peasantry, who had great faith in the efficacy of its
waters.

In 1726, Benjamin Holme, a very zealous member of the Society of
Friends, visited this place, and preached to a very attentive congregation.

There was formerly a pig market held here on every Thursday, but this
has fallen into disuse for a great many years, and the market-day itself
was almost forgotten. It has of late again been brought into notice by
Robert Travers, Esq., the present proprietor of the town, who has established a market there for the sale of lump butter, and with considerable
success.

Through the interest of David, Earl of Barrymore, a patent for fairs
was obtained to be held at Tymulagy, on the 28th March, July 5th,
August 21st, and on December the 7th.

In a field on the side of the road between Timoleague and Dunworly
are the ruins of an hospital for lepers, of which little now remains save
the northern wall. In digging the foundations of this building—which
was erected by one of the McCarthys—tradition asserts that the work-

men were frequently not only interrupted, but absolutely driven away, by the groans of some fiends who were buried there; and who were unwilling to be disturbed, even for so charitable a purpose as the erection of a house of refuge for those who were looked upon with almost as much horror as themselves.

COURTMASHERRY.

Courtmasherry is upwards of two miles to the south-east of Timoleague. It is a very pretty marine village, and is most agreeably situated on the southern-side of Courtmasherry Bay. It consists of one long street, whose windings in and out, with the graceful curvature of the water upon whose shores it is built, renders its aspect varying and attractive. The portion of it principally occupied by visitors contains many good-sized, comfortable, and cleanly dwellings; and they are built at the foot of a well-wooded hill, which almost surrounds the village on three sides—screening it from the scathing east wind, as well as from winds from the south and west.

Although, as we have said, it consists but of one street, yet that street contains houses but on one side; the other side being open to the sea. And thus the invalid in his easy chair, or the recluse, is enabled in one look to gaze upon the sparkling waters of the harbour, the white sands of Flax-fort and Burran, the embattled towers of Coolmaine, and the distant lighthouse on the "Old Head."

Should the visitor desire it, there is nothing to prevent him sauntering through silent groves and dark-embowered arcades, on his way to "the Point." Here, reclining on a bed of green moss, he may bask in the sun,—as he perhaps, listens drowsily to the shrill whistle of the wild sea-mew, as she soars rapidly in the air, and then swooping down, rides on the swelling wave; or he hears the soft sea-breeze nestling among the leaves of the ash and the oak behind him; or he gazes on the world of waters that stretch from where its waves heave lazily at his feet, out far, far out, until its blue tints blend with the blue of the cloudless sky above. Occasionally, too, he sees a white sail—like the wing of a great white bird—shining a long way off in the horizon, and he wonders from what sunny clime it has come, and whither it is speeding. Oft, too, he beholds a fishing-smack, with its black hull and its brown outspread canvas, slowly passing and repassing before him; and now and then a long line of smoke points to some modern giant ploughing his way through the resisting main, on his way to that great empire which those of our race have founded in the distant West.

In the reign of James the First, Courtmasherry was spelt Courtneshry, and, up to a few years since, Court-mac-Sherry (that is the court of Mac Sherry, according to Smith, who states that it was built by a Shropshire man named Hodnett; and that he, wishing to drop his English patronymic and become wholly Irish, assumed the name of Mac Sherry).

Others state that it was an Englishman named Foley, whose Irish name was Mac Scaruig, who gave this place his name. Another derivation is "Cluan an uishga geel" (the harbour of the white waters); and another is "Cuirt na nuishire" (the court of the oysters)—in reference to the great oyster bed that was here formerly.

In former days all the neighbouring lands belonged to the Hodnetts, who, as we have stated previously, owned Timoleague; and who had also large possessions near Queenstown, where one of them built Belvelly Castle, and resided there.

The Hodnetts remained in possession of Courtmasherry until the suppression of the great rebellion, when Edmond Hodnett, who years before was outlawed—as was also his son, James Fitz-Edmond, and his brother, Richard, of Barrireagh—and who then represented the Hodnett family, was dispossessed by Cromwell; and most of his lands bestowed on Captain Robert Gookin, who received a grant of Abbey-Mahon and nineteen ploughlands in the vicinity, and subsequently (March 20th, 1656-7) seven ploughlands more.

At the restoration, however, Gookin, who was a most zealous Cromwellian, fearing he would be dispossessed, passed his grants to Lord Orrery—then in high favour with the King—who obtained letters patent for them in his own name, dated March 2nd, 1660; and from him Gookin took a lease, which expired in 1760.

There were but few men in this district displayed more activity in that great effort of the Irish in 1641 to throw off the English yoke than Edmond Hodnett. Scarcely had he declined the invitation to move into the English quarters, when he appeared at the head of four hundred men, and, in conjunction with William Barry, of Agha, prepared to attack a government ship that was coming into the harbour. He drove away sheep and cattle belonging to Mr. Gookin, to the value of £2,000. He seized five horses, twenty cows, and eleven hundred sheep belonging to Mr. Henry Sampson, and, in addition, all his corn and household stuff. He possessed himself of the house, the goods, and estate of poor Burrowes, who shortly after was hanged at Killivarrig wood by Mac-ni-Crimen, of Ballinorohur; and the weapons which he brought away with him he gave to the rebels. And when an unhappy wretch, flying for his life from his friend, William Barry, arrived at Courtmasherry, and got into a boat, Hodnett took away the oars, and then told him if he did not be off, he'd cut his throat.

When the day of retribution came he lost everything. He was deprived of Ringe, Ballycarriga, Milmanie, Lisletemple, Callinagh, Ballyreagh, Killmaramosse, Ballygallman, Ballycurdy, &c. And there are not a few hardy fishermen and humble peasants dwelling along the adjoining coasts, whose selves and whose fathers for several generations have never spoken a word of English, and yet, with a pardonable pride, they still retain the Christian names and the surname of the old Shropshire family from whom they are sprung—a family who were living at Courtmasherry when Christopher Columbus was on his way to the unknown shores of the New World, and who exercised almost kingly authority in Ibane and Barryroe for centuries before a plantee set his foot in O'Mahony's country, or Bandon-Bridge had even a name.

Captain Robert Gookin obtained a lease of Courtmasherry from Lord Orrery, and he and his descendants lived in a house, the site of which is now occupied by the residence of the ladies Boyle.

When Gookin's house was being levelled some years ago, two quaint-looking old bottles, with R. Gookin, 1718, inscribed on them in raised characters, were discovered under the foundation-stone, unbroken, and carefully sealed. Upon being opened they were found to contain a dark, tasteless fluid, supposed originally to have been claret.

Between Courtmasherry and Timoleague are the ruins of Abbey-Mahon. It was founded by the Bernardine monks, and stands close to the waters of the bay. It was endowed with the eighteen ploughlands* which constitute the parish of Abbey-Mahon. But these were only granted to it whilst it was being built; and when it would be finished, the monks were to look for their support from other sources.

It was never completed. The dissolution of monasteries was decreed

---

* In 1634 the tithes of the eighteen ploughlands were valued at £80 per annum. In that year the curate was Benjamin Hearice—Harris, and for performing all the duties he was rewarded with the sum of forty shillings yearly.

and enforced before it was roofed, and the lands which Lord Barrymore
bestowed to aid in its erection, being then the property of the abbey,
were escheated.

ENNISKEANE.

Enniskeane is ten miles to the west of Bandon, and is situated on
the northern-side of the Bandon river. It derives its name from Ennis-
Keane (the inch of Keane.) This Keane was Keane Mac Moyle More—
one of the O'Mahonys—a sept who were long connected with this
locality, before McCarthy-More obtained a grant of Iniskean, Blarney,
Muskerry, &c., from the crown.

In the great rebellion, McCarthy-Reagh, of Kilbrittain Castle, and
his sons, quartered themselves in the neighbourhood for some days; and
whilst there, deliberated with Teige O'Downy, Teige O'Norse, and other
notorious rebels, on the furtherance of their designs. And it was during
their stay here that Mr. Meech, and "one Holbrooke"—both of the
parish of Moragh—together with thirteen other English (including men,
women, and children), were brought into McCarthy's camp.

After being carried away, up and down, their captors grew tired of
them; and, as the deponent* "had been credibly told, and believeth
the truth thereof, they were knocked on the head by the rebels with
stones, and murdered;" after which they were buried in a field belonging to Mr. Snowswell, the rector of Ballymoney.

In 1678 tradesmen's tokens were in circulation here. One of them
bearing this date, has on the obverse, "Henry Wh . . . n [Whelan],
merchant," and on the reverse, "in Eniskean, His PENNY."

Upon the 11th of April, 1691, Enniskeane would have been the
scene of a dire tragedy, had not a few of the Bandon militia, under
Major Wade, and some troops of horse belonging to Colonel Coy's
regiment, opportunely arrived and prevented it.

When Brigadier O'Carroll drew off with his four regiments from his
unsuccessful attack upon Clonakilty, he fell upon Enniskeane—which
was at that time garrisoned by forty-four men of Sir David Collier's
regiment, under the command of Ensigns Lindsey and Daniel. This
little force manfully held the streets for some time against the overwhelming numbers opposed to them; but finding that the Irish
inhabitants were letting in O'Carroll's men through their back-doors,

---

* See Mrs. Stringer's depositions, Trinity College, Dublin.

they all retreated to one house, which they barricaded, and resolutely defended.

Although the resistance they made was a gallant one, and ought to have elicited the admiration even of an enemy, yet there was "no quarter" for them. Faggots were placed round the house, and the flames were to accomplish what the prowess of fifteen hundred men could not achieve; and, in all likelihood, would have done so, had not Major Wade and ten of the Bandon militia arrived at this critical time.

Although this mere handful of men could apparently be but of little assistance, yet the help they rendered the besieged was great. Notwithstanding that the rebels had a hostile cordon surrounding the little garrison, and notwithstanding that there was a distance of six hundred yards between the ill-fated house and the outside barrier, yet the undaunted Bandonians unhesitatingly entered the rebel lines, and forced their way to Collier's men.

We presume the Irish would have never allowed one of these militiamen to pass through alive, were it not that they supposed further assistance was close at hand—and so it was; for some time after, Major Ogilby galloped up at the head one hundred and fifty horse, and dashed at them. The enemy fled in disorder; Ogilby followed hot-foot, and slew seventy-two of them in the pursuit.

There was formerly a weekly market held here every Thursday, but this has long since fallen into disuse.

The manor of Enniskeane was one of the largest in the county. It contained no less than eighty ploughlands, situated on both sides of the Bandon river.

The following is a "a list of the fees chargeable "*:—

		£	s.	d.
BILL OF COSTS FOR THE PLAINTIFF.	Attachment and service, ...	1	2	
	Drawing and entering declaration, ...	1	6	
	Attorney's fees, ...	3	4	
	Re-attachment, ...	0	10	
Motion and rule for the defendant to answer, ...		1	4	
Copy of the same, ...		0	6	
Drawing and entering replication, ...		1	0	
Motion and rule for the defendant to rejoin, ...		1	4	
Copy of the same, ...		0	6	
Making up the issue, ...		2	6	
Motion for the venire, ...		1	0	
Venire and special service, ...		3	0	

* The same fees were chargable in the manors of Clonakilty and Ballydehob, of which Mr. Snowe was also seneschal. Mr. William Snowe was agent to Lord Cork, and swore to the correctness of the above, May 15th, A.D. 1718.

	£	s.	d.
Evidences of rejoin and swearing certificates, ...	1	2	
To the jury and bailiffs on verdict, ...		4	6
Attorney, pleading fee on trial, ...		3	4
Motion for judgment on verdict, ...		1	0
Entering verdict, ...		1	0
Execution and service, ...		2	0
Bill of costs, ...		0	4
Motion and rule for service for or against the bails, ...		2	0
Service fees and service, ...		2	0
Copy of bail's plea, ...		0	6
Drawing and entering answer thereto, ...		1	6
Motion of judgment for want of plea, ...		2	6
Execution and service, ...		2	0

		£	s.	d.
BILL OF COSTS FOR THE DEFENDANT.	Application and copy of declaration, . . .		0	10
	Drawing and entering answer, ...		1	0
	Attorney's fee, ...		3	4
Motion and rule for replication, ...			1	4
Copy of same, ...			0	6
Drawing and entering rejoinder, ...			1	0
Attorney's trial fee, ...			3	4
Evidence's expenses, and swearing such, ...			1	2
Motion for judgment and verdict, ...			1	0
Entering the same, ...			1	0
Execution and service, ...			2	0

BALLINEEN.

About an English mile to the west of Enniskeane is the pretty little town of Ballineen. It consists of one long street running east and west, and of another street starting from its centre, and running due south to the Bandon river. At one time it belonged to the Earls of Cork—one of whom parted with it to the Heathcote family.* From the Heathcotes it was purchased by an ancestor of the present Earl of Bandon, from whom, and his successors, it was held for a long time by lease, during which period it made little progress; but upon the expiry of the term—about twenty years ago—it came into the immediate possession of the late Lord Bandon, and since then it has been almost rebuilt.

It now contains a handsome market-house, a new court-house, one or two hotels, a Wesleyan chapel, a boys' and a girls' school, a new glebe house, and a beautiful new church.

The latter is a Gothic structure, with belfry, spire, and two porches; over one of which is the arms of the late Earl of Bandon impaled with those of Brodrick, and over the other, the arms of the Rev. Robert Meade, the late rector.

---

* At present represented by Sir William Heathcote and Lord Aveland.

their pastoral clay was not almost wholly restricted to those effeminate addenda to the modern dinner-table, tea and coffee; the next day the shepherd of Kilmeen would feast his late host and the shepherd of Desertserges; and the latter, the day following, would share his hospitality with the two former; then the pastor of Ballymoney would begin again, and so on. The good care they took of one another helped to carry them all beyond the allotted three-score and ten. From one fact alone we may infer to what a great age some of the rectors in former days used to attain to, namely:—that the three parishes above mentioned were possessed by rectors; and by adding together the time that three of them—one from each parish—were in holy orders, the sum total will be found to want only thirteen years of being no less than two centuries.

There are three entrances to the graveyard from Ballineen. That on the right is the circuitous route used by the Episcopalians, on their way to the grave with the remains of those of their persuasion; that on the left is the still more circuitous route belonging to the Roman Catholics; but the direct route—the short cut, in fact—is the exclusive property of the Methodists and Presbyterians.

Ballineen, at which is a station of the West Cork Railway, is not more than an hour and a-half's journey by rail to Cork; and is a clean and healthy town. Standing on a gentle eminence, a low chain of hills effectually screen it from the northerly winds; whilst its position—overhanging the Bandon river—enables it to intercept the fresh breeze as it rises off the water, and to temper it with the warm air which gushes to it from the south. All the lands lying north of Ballineen—for several miles—are the property of Lord Bandon.

Some years ago this large district enjoyed a very unenviable notoriety. Illicit distillation was carried on there to a great extent; and, we regret to say, murder was not of unfrequent occurrence also. But since it has passed into the hands of the late Earl—and those of his successor, the present proprietor—a great change has been effected for the better. Those amongst whom were many who spent their time in unlawful pursuits, and many at whose door grave charges were laid, were removed, and their places filled by an industrious, orderly, and contented tenantry; and we doubt if this extensive tract of country has since furnished a single case deemed sufficiently important to be sent before the criminal judge of assize.

About thirty years ago a noted fairy-woman, who was then in the full-bloom of her fame, lived in Ballineen. Her reputation had spread far and wide, and it was nothing unusual to see pilgrims all the way from " the beautiful city " visiting at the shrine of Moll Carroll.

All her nights she spent with the fairies, with whom she was a great favourite, and to whom she used to relate every bit of gossip she could lay her tongue to. And she was equally fond of them; and so she ought. When many of her poor neighbours were obliged to be off to Mohn-drohid bog before day, with kitches on their backs, to purloin a handful of bog stuff to help to manure their gardens, or to form an antiseptic couch for the pig, Moll could lie in her bed, fine and soustha, and take her two or three fine cups of elegant strong tea, and her couple of fine fresh eggs, for her breakfast. Besides, her house was one of the best furnished in the whole street. Her bed had curtains to it; there was a looking-glass on the table, where Moll could take a quiet survey of her rubicund visage, without being disturbed; and there was a chest of drawers, with brass handles to it, in which she kept her Sunday clothes and her bran-new blue cloth cloak. Then, as to the kitchen, which was used as a parlour and drawing-room as well, the splendid dresser was all ablaze with emblazoned basins, and plates, and cups and saucers, and tea-pots, and egg-cups. There was a settle there, which was painted a bright red; and there were chairs to match; and there was a geranium crock on a saucer in the little window; and as for the walls, they were papered all over with ballads and pictures. Amongst the latter was a grand engraving of the Great Liberator striking the shackles from off the manacled limbs of weeping Erin: and another containing a representation of Adam and Eve standing on each side of the tree of Knowledge, with their scanty fig-leaf aprons on, and throwing a wistful eye at the big scarlet apple that hung so temptingly from one of the branches.

Although Mary used to spend all her nights with the fairies, yet she was sometimes seen in her bed before cock-crow, and by those, too, who naturally thought she ought to be elsewhere at that witching time. On one occasion a traveller, who had come a long way to consult her, told her secretary—one Dan Hart—that he peeped in through a hole in the door, and saw her in bed.

" You didn't," said Dan.

" I did," said the pilgrim.

"Yerra! whisht, ye fool, you!" said Dan—who, when he found that the man wasn't to be persuaded against the evidence of his two eyes, promptly changed his tactics—"that was only her body you saw there; she was away herself. Tell me," says he, "didn't you ever see a snail's shell lying on the ground empty, and the snail himself walking about the place minding his business?"

Mary's fees were regulated by those great commercial principles which tariff the prices of everything—demand and supply. When trade was very brisk, she was known to demand half-a-sovereign for a single consultation; and when it was the other way, she would take a dozen of eggs, or a weight of potatoes, or a bottle of cream.

The queries put to her were on a variety of subjects—on love, on marriage, on death—but her principal business was in carrying messages to and from those lately deceased to their relatives on this side of the Styx, and *vice versa*. It was a great point with her to pick all she could out of her clients before she uttered her communications; and then form a sort of flexible reply, that could be twisted to suit any question. Thus, in answer to a young woman who would ask her, "Who will I be married to?" she'd often say, "To a man with a green coat." Now this would answer for a policeman; or it would do in case she died unmarried, for then the green coat she'd be wedded to would be the grass on her grave. Or, should she say to some one with hair over his mouth, her prediction would be considered verified if the applicant marched off with one of the South Cork Militia, or evaporated with a medical student, or was goose enough to cut away with a young tailor, or made a pet of a tom-cat or a Skye terrier.

Mary did not confine the advancement of temporal interests by spiritual means entirely to herself; she allowed herself to be made the medium for promoting the temporal interests of others as well, when she was properly paid for it. A strong farmer died, and left his buxom young widow in comfortable circumstances. She soon had many suitors; but there was one whom she looked upon with a sweetness which spoke volumes in favour of his chances of occupying the place vacant by the demise of poor Mick. Another lover, seeing the direction of the current, hurried off to Moll; and the very next morning she went to the widow, and told her she saw Mick the night before, and that he was as mad as a hatter at the thought of Johnny ——— getting his ground, and his cattle, and his wife; and that if he had to come back to the world again, and take possession of all he had before, he'd do so rather than that ommedawn of a devil—who didn't know how to take a butt of pratees to the market—should have any of his substance. "If she wants to get married," says Mick's ghost, "let her take and marry James ———, a decent honest boy, that she needn't be ashamed of. But, by this and by that"—and he crossed his fingers, said Moll, as he spoke—"I'll never consent to any one else!" The widow, who never cared a trauneen about her deceased lord, and who didn't want to see his face any more, never dared to disobey him when he was alive; and now that he was dead, she felt it doubly incumbent on her to be obsequious. Accordingly she sent a message to the man of her husband's choice, by Moll herself; and in a few days—preliminaries being arranged—they were married.

Her secretary—Dan Hart—was of the greatest assistance to her. A poor woman came looking for her one day, from the Cove of Cork. Dan immediately put himself in her way; to whom she told that her husband was at sea, and that she had heard no tidings of him for a long time, and she wanted to know if he was drowned. The assistant, having heard her story, made her sit down by the fire, and warm herself. And then, under some pretence or the other, he slipped out the back-door, and made straight for the public, where Molly sat communicating with the spirits which were confined within the four walls of the glass bottle that stood before her, and told her all the woman told him. She shortly after returned home; and walking straight up to the strange woman, looked carefully into the palm of her hand.

"Your husband gains his living by ploughing the salt seas, ma'am," says Mary.

"Och! then, you're right, ma'am," says the poor mariner's wife.

"And you want to know," says Moll, peering closely into the centre of her hand; "you want to know," says she, slowly, "if he's alive."

"Och! wisha! then," says the poor woman, "that's the very thing that brought me up all the way here; and shure you must be a wonderful woman entirely, entirely, to be able to tell that."

"Well," says Moll, putting out her hand, into which the sailor's wife placed five shillings, "there'll be a great change come over you before you see him again; and as for his grave, you'll never be able to kneel on his tombstone, and say a rosary for the dead."

The woman set out for home, distressed, of course, at the confirmation of her worst suspicions, but sounding the praises of the extra-ordinary fairy-woman of Ballineen as she passed along.

Moll had a roaring trade of it for a long time; but during the famine years, and since, the fairies do not seem to have taken scarce any interest in sublunary affairs—here, at least; and, as a consequence, the trade declined so low, that for some time previous to poor Moll's death it had almost ceased. And when poor Moll did cross over in the ferry-boat, and drop her courtesy in fairyland, her divining-mantle does not appear to have fallen upon the shoulders of any successor.

The celebrated Kinneigh steeple stands in a wild country, a few miles from Ballineen. It is rather a singular structure, being hexagonal in form from its base to a height of fifteen feet, and circular from that up. An old legend states that it was built in one night by two angels; but that it was never finished, owing to an old woman—who certainly had no right to be out star-gazing long after midnight. Be that as it may, she most unexpectedly made her appearance at the back-door of a neighbouring cabin—when, like all honest people, she should have been fast asleep in her bed—and frightened them. Away they flew; but whether it was that the spell under which they laboured was broken by the old lady's unwarrantable intrusion, or that they flew off in a fit of indignation at having their workmanship overlooked by human eye, has not transpired.

Two or three miles to the north-east of the steeple is Castletown (or Poldenstown, as it was formerly called), the property of the Earl of Bandon; and near the steeple—the steeple is in fact its belfry—is the new parish church of Kinneigh, an edifice in no small degree indebted to the liberality of the nobleman just mentioned. The church which originally stood here occupied the site upon which the late parish church stood. It was founded by Saint Macomoge, and was the cathedral of a diocese that existed before the English invasion. For some time previous to that event, the appointment of a bishop to the See of Kinneigh was discontinued, and it was united with Ross.

Bishop Downes visited Kinneigh in 1700. Speaking of the church, he says:—" 'Tis supposed the church was formerly a cathedral. A stone in the south-west corner of the church is considered very sacred, which the Irish swear upon. This church is accounted amongst the Irish very sacred. There is a tradition amongst the Irish, that formerly, in the the churchyard, there was a well that had great medicinal virtues; and that the concourse of people being very chargeable to the inhabitants, they stopped it up."

The remains of old buildings and Danish forts abound in this locality. Not long since, one of the latter—which is said to communicate subterraneously with the steeple—was opened by Colonel Bernard ; but he was unable to enter in consequence of the quantity of foul air that continued to pour through the aperture. It was subsequently opened by another gentleman ; but the foul air was still present in large quantities, and had such an injurious effect upon two of the workman, that they took ill and died.

A new glebe house was lately erected at Kinneigh, and occupied by the Rev. Godfrey Smith, prior to whose time there was no resident since the days of old Bellingham Swan. This old clergyman flourished in an age when there were many specimens of a class which it is to be hoped are now altogether extinct, namely,—those who prized the sheep of their pastures more for the value of the wool that grew on their backs, that for any pleasure they received in feeding them. Old Swan lived to be ninety-five ; and to the day of his death he used to keep a large brass blunderbuss over his mantelpiece, which he used to exhibit to his friends as " God's vengeance against Popery." In his younger days he was a curate of Dean Swift's. He died on the 2nd of October, 1798 ; and, it is said, that for several weeks after his death he was represented as being alive, in order that his representatives might be entitled to claim the tithes which would become due on the 1st of the following November.

CHAPTER XIX.

DUNMANWAY—SKIBBEREEN—BANTRY—CARRIGBUIE—ROSSCARBERY—MACROOM.

UNMANWAY is seventeen miles west of Bandon. It derives its name, according to Dr. O'Donovan, from Dun-na-m-bean (the fort of the gables or pinnacles). Others derive it from Dun-own-bwee (the fort of the Yellow river)—in reference to a stream of muddy water that flows through it. And another derivation, by one who was considered an excellent Irish scholar, was from the compound Irish word signifying the fort of the yellow women (the yellow women being the term applied by the Irish to the Spanish soldiers who garrisoned the fort,* in contempt of the colour of their skin, and the cloaks which they wore).

The castle of Dunmanway was built by Catherine, daughter of the Earl of Desmond, lady of Hy— Carbery, "a charitable and truly hospitable woman," who died in 1506.

When the vast estates of Gerald (the Red Earl of Desmond) became vested in the crown, owing to the war waged by that nobleman and his confederates for years against England, the Queen wrote to the Lord-Deputy (July 18th, 1590), directing that the castle and lands of Downemoenwye, in the county of Cork, be granted to Teige McDermod McCarthy, in consequence of the favourable report made of him by Sir Walter Raleigh.

In pursuance of her Majesty's wishes, Sir William Burghley—her secretary and treasurer—wrote the following letter on the subject to Sir

---

* A short time since some Spanish coins (*temp.* Ferdinand and Isabella) were dug up where Dunmanway Castle stood—which castle occupied the site of the fort garrisoned by the Spanish soldiers.

William Fitz-William, the lord-deputy, into whose hands it was placed by Teige himself, who was the bearer of it from Elizabeth :—

"After my very hearty commendations to your lordship :

"Whereas, it hath pleased the Queen's Majesty to extend her grace and favour to this gentleman—the bearer hereof—Teige McDermod Carthy, so far forth as to grant unto him, and to his heirs (male), the town, castle, and lands of Downemoenwye, in the county of Cork, as in her Majesty's special letters written to you in this behalf more at large appeareth. I am to let your lordship understand that her Highness, the more to show her princely consideration towards him in respect of his good service and loyalty, for which he hath been much commended, and in the hope of the continuance of the same, is very pleased that, in the grant which is to be passed unto him, he shall be charged but with the services of ten footmen, and with a rent of forty shillings sterling by the year, besides the tenure of knight's service; of which her Majesty's pleasure your lordship is to take knowledge, for in her letters directed to you there is mention made of new arrenting the lands by a new survey, without any certain rent first named, which her Majesty's pleasure is now, as shall be as is aforesaid. I very heartily bid your lordship farewell. From Greenwich, the 25th of June, 1590."

When the great rebellion broke out, Teige McCarthy-Downy, who inherited the town, castle, and lands from the grantee, sided energetically with the Irish against England; and, upon its suppression by Cromwell, all his possessions were forfeited, and his Dunmanway estates—which consisted of the three ploughlands of Dunmanway, two gneeves of Togher, the west side of Awe, and the western portion of Coolsnarty, in all 2,932 statute acres—were bestowed on Colonel William Arnopp, subject to a quit rent of £22 12s. 6d. per annum.

Pierce Arnopp—the colonel's son—after charging the estate with ten pounds annually for his wife during her life, and with a perpetual annuity of twenty pounds to Dean Pomeroy, sold it to Sir Richard Cox for a thousand and fifty pounds.

The town of Dunmanway owes its existence to the want that was felt for a resting-place for the troops on the line of march from Bandon to Bantry, and also to the necessity that existed of occupying with a loyal colony that wide region which stretches out on both sides, from the base of the great range of mountains that run through the Western Carberies.* The government, accordingly, afforded every facility to Sir

---

* Tradition relates, that previous to the building of Dunmanway, the large tract of country lying between Ballineen and Dunmanway was covered with a vast forest, in which many a wayfarer lost his way in his efforts to reach Baltimore or Bantry, in his journey to or from Cork or Bandon; and in some places the trees are said to have been so close together, that one might travel seven or eight miles, by passing from one tree to another, without once touching the ground.

Richard Cox to plant this place with English.   He was granted a patent for holding fairs and markets.   And so sanguine was he of success, that he erected a handsome stone bridge, consisting of six arches, over the Bandon river, at his own expense; and effected other improvements— among which were roads, one of which (the one that lead to Bandon) was pushed forward with such zeal and perseverance, that it was completed in six days, although two miles of it ran through a bog.

In A.D. 1700 he had no less than thirty English families residing in his new town, all of whom he kept employed at remunerative work.

The parish church at this time was in Fanlobbus graveyard.   One who saw it the year before (1699) says :—" The church is covered, but many slates are off.   No pulpit or seats.   About half the church is ruinous."

The necessity for a place of worship in Dunmanway—where divine service was performed in one of the settler's houses—was felt so strongly, that Sir Richard Cox was determined, if he would not be allowed to have the church of the parish in his new settlement, to build a chapel-of-ease there ; and, in furtherance of this design, he put down his name for a hundred pounds.   And Mr. Patrickson, who also felt warmly interested in the matter, put his name down for another.

When Queen Anne—whose lord chancellor Sir Richard was—came to the throne, he procured an Act of Parliament, by means of which the parish church was for the future to be in Dunmanway.

Accordingly, one was speedily erected there, and dedicated to St. Mary, in compliment to Mary (Lady Cox).   It was a plain structure, and continued to be used as a parish church until 1821, when it was taken down, and the present edifice, which cost £1,100, erected on its site.

The old church, which, it is said, was well filled on the sabbath-day with a *well-looking*, industrious, thriving people, contained several monuments to the memory of various members of the Cox family, including one to the great Lord Chancellor himself.

The chalice and paten used in it, and still in use in its present successor, were presented to it by the distinguished man who may be looked upon as its founder.   The chalice is thus inscribed :—

"THE GIFT OF Yᵉ RIGHT HONᵇˡ·
SIR RICHARD COX, KNT. AND BART.,
LORD CHIEF-JUSTICE OF IRELAND,
TO ST. MARY'S CHURCH IN DUNMANWAY,
EASTER, 1714."

Sir Richard made great efforts to introduce the growth and culti-vation of flax into Dunmanway. He knew that if the inhabitants were to rely solely on agriculture for their support, the assistance they would derive from it would be not only insufficient, but precarious. He there-fore went energetically to work to introduce an industry which would furnish extensive employment, at good wages, independent of it altogether. He bestowed prizes on those who bought and sold the largest quantity of linen manufactured in the town and its neighbour-hood. He rewarded the girls who excelled at the wheel in the spinning-school. He gave sums of money to the best workmen, and to the most diligent apprentices; and a good house was granted, rent-free, to the employer who the previous year manufactured the best linen, and the greatest quantity of it; and, in addition, the table of honour was hung over his door, with the following inscription in letters of gold:—

"DATUR DIGNIORI.
This house is rent-free, for the superior industry of the possessor."

He also had an inspection every May-day, on the green, of all the spinning-wheels worked in the town, "which made," says Dr. Smith, "no inelegant entertainment, to see so many young creatures rescued from want, idleness, and misery, decked out in decent apparel, earned by their own industry; and, to countenance this review, the young ladies of the best distinction in the neighbourhood exhibited their skill in spinning in this public assembly."

In 1748—the year, probably, in which the doctor visited Dunman-way—he informs us that, according to a moderate calculation, there were four hundred hogsheads of flax-seed sown in the west of the county. And speaking of the number of machines in the town, and of the goods turned out by them, he says:—"Here are a considerable number of looms at work for linen (as well chequered as white), diapers, fustians, handkerchiefs, girt-web, &c."

Although the first Sir Richard did much for the introduction and prosperity of the linen trade, yet it did not attain the same strength and dimensions in his time that it did in that of his grandson and successor.

In less than twenty years after his death the houses in the town had more than doubled; the population had run up from five hundred and fifty-seven to eight hundred and seven; and the flax and woollen wheels had increased from one hundred and thirty-eight to two hundred and fifty-four.

The following is a list of the prizes awarded by Sir Richard Cox—the second baronet—for the year ending December 31st, 1750 :—

	£	s.	d.
" Will Curry got the master's premium of	5	0	0
James Archibald, the journeyman's of	2	0	0
Louis Grizza, the apprentice's of	1	0	0
Robert Wallis, for buying most cloth last July,	5	0	0
Will Curry, for selling most,	3	0	0
George Gribble, for buying next most,	3	0	0
Leonard Hewetson, for selling next most,	1	0	0"

In 1724, Benjamin Holme—a member of the Society of Friends—travelled through the west of this county, and, amongst other places, visited Dunmanway.

"At Dunmanway, in the market-house," says Wight, "he had a large and satisfactory meeting, notwithstanding Skofield,* the priest of the place, made some disturbance."

In 1751 Dunmanway contained a population of seven hundred and ninety-nine; of these, four hundred and ten were Protestants, and three hundred and eighty-nine Roman Catholics—a decrease of eight on the gross population since 1749.

Sir Richard—the second baronet—accounts for the deficiency, and the absence of a progressive increase, by stating that the ramblers and sojourners are all gone, and the people remaining are fixed and settled. There was one item in the decrease, however, which consoled him for the diminished sum total :—" The decrease is amongst the Papists who in 1749 were four hundred and two, and in 1751 are three hundred and eighty-nine."

Although the Roman Catholics decreased, the Protestants increased. Sir Richard was quite exultant at this. " But, blessed be God !" said he, " the Protestants increase. In 1749 there were but four hundred and five, and in 1751 they are four hundred and ten—an increase of five ; one indication of the thriving of the linen manufacture, which in this country was very properly called the Protestant manufacture."

In 1769 Sir John Cox obtained a patent, dated July 20th, in that year, for holding an additional fair in Dunmanway on the 17th of September, and for holding a market on Saturday.

There was also a charter school here, which was established by the first baronet, for the maintenance and education of forty children. He

---

* Skofield or Scofield, " the priest of the place," was vicar of Fanlobbus and Drinagh from 1718 to 1746. In 1716 he married Mary, widow of Mr. Allen Riggs, and daughter of Sir Richard Cox, the first baronet.

granted two acres of land for the erection of the school, rent-free; and he endowed it with eighteen more, at a small rent. In addition to which he furnished stone and slates for the building; he paid the cost of its erection; and he directed that the sum of twenty pounds be paid every year out of his estate for its support.

The old mansion-house—which was built by the Lord Chancellor, and in which he and his descendants resided for many generations—stood a few yards to the rear of the site occupied by the present court-house. It is represented as being pleasantly adorned with handsome avenues and good plantations of fir, elm, lime, chestnut, and some beech.

The castle, which, as we have said, was built by the daughter of Thomas, Earl of Desmond (son of James), stood at the western end of the town, and was approached by a broad path—now called the Castle-road. There is not even one stone left upon another of this famous old fortalice, which was raised by the hospitable and pious Catherine Fitz-gerald; as its walls, and its very foundations, were uprooted some years ago, to furnish building-stone for the erection of a flour-mill in the vicinity.

While the workmen were engaged in this work of demolition, and blotting out every trace of this—the first stone castle that was ever erected in this part of Carbery—they came upon a subterraneous chamber. Carefully removing the superincumbent earth and rubbish, they descended into the granary. It was from this reservoir the Geraldines, and their successors, the McCarthys, drew supplies for the kern and the gallow-glasses; at the head of whom they often struck terror into the heart of some neighbouring chieftain, or engaged in the hopeless enterprize of endeavouring to drive out the stranger who had settled amongst them, and who called their country his own.

The granary contained several compartments, and these were nearly all filled with native wheat. The compartments themselves were in perfect order, but the wheat, which time and circumstances had shrunk and discoloured, was found to be as hard as shot, and quite as black.

At a short distance from the town, at a place called Drumrastel, Smith found a light chalybeate spring. "This water," says he, "has never been drunk, and therefore its virtues are not well known, except that it may agree with many delicate habits, where a large proportion of the mineral would be too rough."

To the north of this well is the townland of Deneens. Here, on the very summit of the Yew-tree Mountain, once stood a famous tree.   It was a tall and graceful-looking specimen of the old Irish yew; and its bulk was such, that, at a distance of two yards from the ground, it had a circumference of no less than eighteen feet.   This time-honoured relic of the historic past—this forest giant, which stood sentry amid those lone mountains century after century, with its tall head strained toward heaven, as if to catch the first glimmer of the return of that age when the harper oft sat at its feet and sung love ditties the live-long day, or celebrated in harmonious verse the bravery and success of the proud chieftain who lived in the great castle on the banks of the Bandon, and whose hospitable door was ever open—this venerable tree, among whose branches the sunlight may have played when a McCarthy sat on the throne of Cork, was ruthlessly cut down, and hacked into lengths of about seven feet, nearly all of which were then divided into blocks of a convenient size, and hawked about Dunmanway to be sold for fire-wood.   One of these, however, was rescued from the degradation of heating the shins of some Dunmanway barbarian, by a gentleman, who had a bedstead made of it.   Another Christian saved another length for some similar purpose; but all the rest experienced the fate intended for the whole—it was chopped up and stuck under the pot to boil potatoes.

Living almost beyond those boundaries where British laws were supreme, the requirements of the people of Dunmanway compelled them to extemporize a code of laws of their own.   If a man beat another at Ballybwee fair, or at Ballygurteen, or anywhere else in the neighbourhood, his friends, in due time, demolished the assaulter's house; or they waylaid him on his way from the market-town, and either beat him within an inch of his life, or killed him outright.   At all events they gave him, at the very least, two blows for the one he gave the other.

Although this may be considered a rude way of punishing the aggressor, yet it had a very salutary effect; and, as a consequence, an assault was never heard of,—unless occasionally at mating time, before Lent, when some jilted rustic would beat the brains out of his successful rival; or unless in a fair, honest, open faction-fight, when the combatants could indulge in the luxury of murdering one another without any one stepping in between them to spoil sport.

The same principle was acted upon in civil cases.   If a man owed another two or three pounds, and would not pay it, the creditor served him with a fairy process—*Anglice*, he stole his cow. And if the cow did not pay forty shillings to the pound, he spirited away a two-year old heifer or a couple of sheep, until his self-imposed decree was satisfied. So well was this understood, that when a man missed his cow, or his sheep, or his heifer, he took the hint, and went straight to the plaintiff's house and paid the money; and he would be greatly surprised if, on the following morning, he did not see all his cattle grazing in his own fields when he got out of his bed.

This fairy process system was greatly in vogue here for a long time, and it was found to be a much more economical, as well as a much more expeditious method, for the recovery of small debts than the cumbrous one now in use. Instead of waiting until the quarter sessions would come round; then having to travel, perhaps, twenty miles to go to the court—attending there from day to day until the case would be called, and at the same time being obliged to keep a strict watch lest the defendant, by an hospitable half-gallon or two, would induce your principal witness to forget all he knew about the affair—to say nothing about your having to pay an attorney to state your case for you; and then having to sit still while the opposite attorney bullied and abused you— so that (as a Dunmanway man once remarked to us) if you met a dog in the street, he'd pass you by without looking at you, for fear the neighbours would think he had such a disreputable acquaintance; and after all, perhaps, be dismissed on the merits besides; all this could be avoided by a simple process under the Fairy Summary Jurisdiction Act.

The utility of this proceeding was so apparent, that some of the local justices not only thought well of it, but they recommended it. When any one would go to the Rev. William Sillito—who was a magistrate as well as a divine—and tell him that such a one owed him money, and that he was anxious to get it, he would recommend them to lose no time, but go and serve him with a fairy process before day-break next morning; and if the complaint was that his cow, or his horse, or anything that was his, was stolen during the night, his first query would be, to whom do you owe money? and on ascertaining who he was, he would recommend him to pay him at once, and then, if he did not get back his chattels in a day or two, to come to him again.

A few miles to the north of Dunmanway is the new parish church of St. Edmund's. It is dedicated to St. Edmund, and consists of a nave fifty-four feet long by twenty-eight broad, a chancel, a vestry-room, a bapistry, and a spire ninety feet in height. It is built on a little rocky eminence, and in the centre of a valley which lies within the arms of those huge mountains from whence flow the Ilen and the Lee, the Bandon and the Bride. Passing round the building to the northern wall, we look northward, and before us is a lofty chain of hills, tinted to their utmost height with the bloom of the gorse and the heather; whilst on our left, stupendous Owen, with its huge rough head turbaned by the very clouds themselves, scowls in silent anger, and adds yet another dark hue to the sullen waters of Colkinoor. This beautiful little edifice, with its pale yellow spire pointing heavenward, and its emblazoned windows, illuminated with suggestive scenes from sacred story, seems like a party-coloured battle flag, which religion and civilization hath planted in triumph upon a territory which they had wrenched from the rude grasp of uncultivated nature, and that, too, in. her lurking-place amid those solitary Alps.

SKIBBEREEN.

Skibbereen—formerly Skubbareen—lies upon the southern bank of the river Ilen. The portion of it called Bridgetown is in the parish of Abbeystrewry, but the main portion of the town is in the parish of Creagh. Its site, and the country around for miles, anciently formed the domain of Gortnaclough—a fief belonging to the great sept of McCarthy-Reagh, of Kilbrittain Castle. After its forfeiture by the McCarthys in the great rebellion, it was granted under the Act of Settlement to William Prigg and Samuel Hall, who, in addition to "the town of Skibbereen and its appurtenances," got portion of the lands of Ballygumagh, Gortniclough, part of Smorane, and part of Coronea.

The patentees, like many others who got grants in those days, were anxious to obliterate the old names; accordingly they dropped Skibbereen and substituted New Stapletown, and by this name it is referred to in the patent, which mentions "Skibbareen to be for ever called New Stapletown."

As New Stapletown it is also mentioned in the patent obtained by Prigg and Hall in 1681 (temp. Charles the Second), for holding two fairs (one on the feast of St. Peter, the other on the feast of St. Andrew) and two markets (one on Wednesday, and one on Saturday). There was also a patent for holding fairs granted to Richard Townsend, dated March 1st,

26

1778. The earliest date that we have found of any interest in connection with Skibbereen is that of 1544, when Florence Magther was presented to the rectory and vicarage of Creagh by Henry the Eight; "the late incumbent being an Irishman."

In 1699 Bishop Down visited this place. "The chapel at Skibbareen," said he, "was formerly the market-house, and was consecrated about the year 1686, by Dr. Wetenhall, bishop of Cork. It stands in the parish of Abbeystrewry. I preached at Skibbareen on Sunday, August 13th. I lodged at my lady Catherine Barclay's house. The Earl of Orrery," continues the bishop, "has the entire impropriation. Hence it was that the vicar was obliged to levy heavy and very obnoxious fees for his support. When the man of a family or a widow dies worth five pounds, the sum of thirteen shillings and fourpence is demanded as a mortuary; and if he dies worth less than five pounds, then his second best suit of clothes, or six shillings in lieu thereof."* The church in which divine service was performed was burned down in James the Second's time, but was put in good repair in 1695, at a cost of twenty pounds.

The Quakers built a meeting-house in Skibbereen in 1696, and used to attend there on Sundays and Thursdays. The congregation, however, was not numerous, and in its palmiest days did not consist of more than eight families.

There was formerly an extensive trade carried on here in the manufacture and sale of woollen and linen cloth, which has altogether ceased. It is still, however, known as a seat of the provision trade—large quantities of butter, corn, pigs, and cattle being annually disposed of in its weekly markets and fairs. It is very advantageously situated for a trade of this kind, being in the centre of a wide and improving district, and only two miles distant from where the river is navigable at Old Court for vessels of two hundred tons burthen. Facilities are afforded by this water-way of exporting its produce, and, by means of lighters, landing in its very streets the various imports which the town and country require.

BANTRY.

Bantry derives its name from Ban-tra (white strand), from the whir shingly fore-shore in front of it. Others derive it from Beant Mac

---

* See *Clerical Records of Cork, Cloyne, and Ross.*—Dr. Brady.

Fariola (a descendant of the O'Donovans and O'Mahonys—two septs who formerly possessed all this country).

Bantry was the name at one time applied to two settlements—Ballygobban (or Oldtown) and Newtown, where Ireton had a fort with bastions erected, and to which the present name of the town was given.*

These divisions were so distinct and apart that each had its own fairs. The Earl of Anglesea, who obtained under the Act of Settlement a grant of 96,284 acres of the forfeited estates in the baronies of Beere and Bantry, procured a patent, dated March 15th, 1679, for holding fairs at Ballygobban; namely:—on May 29th and 30th, August the 10th and 11th, and on October the 4th and 5th ; and markets on Wednesdays and Saturdays. And John Davis acquired a patent, March 10th (13th William the Third), for holding a fair on the 2nd of November and the day following, at Bantry.

The importance of Bantry, in a military point of view, was recognized even by one in whose hand the pen was a far more powerful weapon than the sword ; and that, too, long before our Gallican neighbours selected it as a point from whence they could annoy England.

So far remote as Elizabeth's time, the poet Spenser, in his view of the state of Ireland, " written in dialogue verse between Eudoxus and Irenœus," in reference to the thousand " souldiours" who he would quarter in "Mounster," makes Iren say :—" I would have a hundred of them placed at the Bantry, where is a most fit place not only to defend all that side of the west part from forraine invasion, but also to answer all occasions of troubles to which that country, being so remote, is very subject."

Bantry was unfortunately very subject to troubles. Its remoteness from the seat of authority, and the difficulty of getting to it, encouraged the Irish chieftains resident in its neighbourhood to revolt on " all occasions."

During the Desmond insurrection, the garrison at Bantry was attacked by Lord Barry and one of the McSwineys.

After the surrender of the Spaniards at Kinsale, Sir George Carew— the Lord-President of Munster—made his way out to Dunboy Castle, and took that valiantly-defended fortress, after a very hard and prolonged fight, by storm ; and also another castle of the O'Sullivans, which stood in Whiddy Island, and which was subsequently destroyed by Ireton.

---

* Newtown subsequently lost the name of Bantry, and it is to Ballygobban the name of Bantry is at present applied.

In 1641 the English settlers here were stripped of everything they possessed. Nat Mayher lost his interest in the lands which he held under O'Sullivan Beare; his household goods, his pewter, his brass, &c. All the horses and cows belonging to Tom Veyford were driven away by the rebels—two of whom had such a regard for the eternal welfare of Anthony Blunt, that they wanted him to turn Papist. But when Anthony—who was determined to remain an orthodox Christian—told them he wouldn't, those who complained that they were not allowed liberty of conscience said they'd make him! Christopher Spearing was deprived of property to the amount of eighty pounds and upwards. And Agnes Tucker—a widow lady, who lived in Whiddy Island—complained that O'Sullivan's people went into the houses of several of the Protestant inhabitants, and took away their bibles.

If it was for the purpose of making themselves acquainted with their contents one would be almost disposed to forgive them, but those zealous religionists acted as if they believed the word of God was opposed to the knowledge of God—whose word they, in common with all other denominations of Christians, admitted it to be; and yet, says Mrs. Tucker, they threw them on the strand, and then most contemptuously threw stones at them.

When the rebellion was over, a great many of the Irish soldiers were permitted by the Commonwealth to enlist into the armies of several nations in amity with it. A large force, consisting of no less than seven thousand men, were shipped for service under the King of Spain by Don Ricardo White; and of this body many divisions embarked at Bantry for Spanish ports in the May of 1652.

Arthur, Earl of Anglesea, who, as has been previously stated, obtained a grant of most of this country, had several of his lands erected into the manor of Bantry, and more of them into the manor of Altham; as appears by a private signet, dated Whitehall, February 6th, 1679, and duly enrolled. By this instrument the lands in the barony of Bere and Bantry (with others) were erected into the manor of Bantry, and other lands in the said barony were erected into the manor of Altham, with two thousand acres in each for a domain. Power to create tenures; to hold Courts Leet and Baron, and a court of record; to build prisons; to appoint seneschals, bailiffs, gaolers, and other officers; to enjoy all waifs, &c.; to impark three thousand acres or more in each manor, with free warren; to build tan-houses, and dress leather; to hold (weekly

Wednesday and Saturday market, and three fairs, &c., at Ballygobban, in the manor of Bantry; to appoint say[assay]-master and clerk of the market.

The desirability of having a fort at Bantry forced itself upon the attention of Lord Orrery (the lord-president of Munster). That great soldier and statesman recommended that the fort which he himself caused to be erected there should be garrisoned with a hundred men, in addition to the sixty it then contained; thus confirming the opinion given by Spenser, nearly a century before, as to Bantry being "a most fit place to defend all that country from foreign invasion."

In a letter to the Duke of Ormond, dated Charleville, May 25th, 1666, Lord Orrery, speaking of the fort at Bantry, says:—"It is a small one, but regular, and consists of four small bastions, the faces of which are but forty-eight feet long, and the planks eighteen; the curtain ninety feet long. All the stoccadoes, which were on the inside on the brick of the graff, and placed there in the nature of a false bray, are rotted away, the guns unmounted, the drawbridge broken, and but one company of sixty men in it, commanded by Captain Manly. This fort is the furthermost western garrison of this county; and we have no garrison between it and Cork—which is about forty English miles. It stands over against Whiddy Island, in the bottom of the Bay of Bantry. This place must immediately have one hundred men sent to it more than the company now in it, the drawbridge and pallisadoes forthwith mended, the guns mounted, more ammunition sent to it, and one month's victuals at least for one hundred and sixty men put into it; for this being the frontier garrison of the west, ought to be well provided."

The duke agreed with the views of the Munster lord-president; and in "an estimate of the charge for putting into repair his Majesty's chief fortifications and places of strength throughout the kingdom of Ireland, made October, 1677," says, concerning Bantry:—The fort is built of lime and stone, consisting of bastions. In it are houses built for two hundred men, but are all out of repair, and some wholly unroofed; walls defective, gates and drawbridge decayed, the dry graff round the fort to be cleared; all which to repair will cost £400. In this fort must be mounted, on standing carriages, eight guns, which will cost £56; making new platform, £15; and for repairing the magazine, £80.

The following is a list of the guns and other munitions of war in the fort at the time:—

	ft.	in.		ft.	
Demi-culverin (large),	7	8	Falcon scald,	6	
Ditto,	8	10	Falcon scald,	8	
Saker,	8	0	Round-shot for culverin, eight.		
Saker (unserviceable),	8	0	For demi-culverin, fifty-seven.		
Mynion scald,	7	0	For saker and mynion, thirty-two.		
Mynion scald,	6	4	Standing carriages (unserviceable).		

Lord Orrery thought that Bantry and Berehaven should be carefully guarded. Not only did their waters afford a secure retreat for the descent of a hostile fleet, but the country was inhabited by a large population impatient of British rule. "I know no place in Ireland," said Orrery, in a letter to the Lord-Lieutenant, in 1665, "so fit to begin a rebellion in as this place,—both for the multitude of ill-people in it, the fastnesses of the country, and the good, unguarded harbours in it, from whence, out of France, they may be there in forty-eight hours." In another letter, he says that West Carbery contains "great crowds of ill-affected Irish." Again, that in those parts of Carbery, and Bantry, and Beere, "he was assured, that there was a great number of the worst sort of people in Ireland—that they were ready for any villiany." The bad opinion which his lordship entertained of West Carbery, Beere, and Bantry, in two years after—when he had more experience, and better opportunities of knowing the people—extended itself still further. "I am certain," said the acute and observant lord-president, "that there is not such a pack of rogues in all Ireland as those in the west of this county."

In 1689, the Count de Château Rénaud cast anchor in Bantry Bay; and landed a supply of money and military stores for the use of King James. Admiral Herbert, who had received orders not to allow any assistance to reach the south of Ireland from Brittainy, heard that the French were in the bay; and, although their fleet consisted of twenty-eight ships of war and five fire-ships, he boldly sailed in to attack them. Not only did Château Rénaud's squadron greatly out-number him in men and guns, but he had the additional disadvantage of having the wind against him. After exchanging some broadsides with the enemy —which seems not to have hurt either party—Herbert, seeing no probability of being able to beat the Frenchman, circumstanced as he then was, judiciously stood out to sea; and the Frenchman, instead of following him, absolutely drew in closer to shore. Both fleets claimed the victory. The House of Commons passed a vote of thanks to its admiral for what—to make the most of it—was but a drawn battle, if it could be even called a battle ;* and King James was so overjoyed, that he had bonfires lighted, and a *Te Deum* chanted, in honour of the great victory gained over the English fleet by the French.

In 1697, some troops in the service of William the Third arrived from Flanders, and landed here.

On the 14th of December, 1796, another French fleet sailed from the shores of France to Bantry Bay, having on board twenty-five thousand men, under the command of General Hoche. Owing to a thick fog, which lasted some days, they were enabled to escape the British fleet which was on the look-out for them ; and by Christmas-day, the greater portion of them, consisting of thirty-six sail, with several thousand men on board—together with forty-one thousand one hundred and sixty stands of arms, twenty pieces of field artillery, nine large siege guns, mortars, howitzers, sixty-one thousand two hundred kegs of powder, seven millions of ball cartridges, seven hundred thousand flints, &c.— were safely in the harbour. Finding that the whole country were up in arms against them, and that a determined spirit of resistance filled every loyal breast, they held a council of war ; when, after much discussion, it was decided to land the soldiers, under the guidance of some Irishmen who had accompanied them. But, upon further reflection, they thought that by this time troops must be on the march from every quarter upon Bantry ; that the peasantry—at least, that portion of them who had anything to lose—were decidedly hostile to them ; and that in the perplexity they were in they had not even their general to consult, they finally determined to put to sea again—which they accordingly did, on the 2nd of January, 1797, having just remained nine days.†

---

* It took place in that portion of the bay between Great Island and Mintervary.

† As soon as the French fleet were recognized in the offing, Mr. James Sweeney —who subsequently attained the rank of major, and died a few years ago—was sent off in hot haste with the intelligence to Cork. Mr. Sweeney, who was a Bandonian, knew all the short-cuts in the country well ; and he got to his destination in an almost incredibly short space of time, completely using up the three horses which were kept in waiting for him along his route. In the hurry of starting, he forgot to lock up a favourite little dog, and did not know that he was following him until he was many miles on his journey. The little animal accompanied him all the way to Cork ; and when Mr. Sweeney had delivered his dispatches to the authorities, and gave them all the information he was possessed of concerning the great event that brought him from Bantry, he hastened to see after his little escort. He found him lying on his saddlecloth in the stable where his horse was put up, prostrate, and gasping for breath ; upon seeing him, "poor Pompey" made an attempt to get up and greet his old master as usual, but the effort was too much for him ; he fell back, and after a few feeble struggles he was dead. Mr. Sweeney carefully wrapped poor Pompey in the

Near Bantry formerly stood a Franciscan abbey, which was founded by Dermot O'Sullivan in 1460. Where it stood is still known as the Friar's Hill, and the burial grounds that anciently surrounded it are still in use; but of the old building itself there is not even a stone left. Although none of the remains of the old priory were in existence in Smith's time, yet such was not the case some years before. When Dive Downs visited Bantry in 1699, he spoke of its ruins, and said they were within a short distance of the town. The ruins, when he wrote, must have included standing walls, and even a roof of some kind, for we find by a presentment passed by the Grand Jury of the county, only three years before, that there were then two friars living there.

At the close of the seventeenth century, the country beyond Bantry was still wild and barbarous. It did not contain a single Protestant place of worship, nor was divine service according to the rights of the the Reformed Church ever heard, in all that extensive region stretching from Bantry to the confines of the county of Cork, and from thence to Glanerought in Kerry—a distance of at least twelve miles from the eastern boundary of that county. Eagles brought forth their young in its fastnesses, and wolves prowled about in its plains and valleys. Even the people who lived there were but little better than savages, and a journey through O'Sullivan Beare's country in the reign of William the Third would be almost as great a feat as a journey into the interior of of Africa would be now. When the bishop of Cork set out from Bantry for Berehaven, he returned by the same route; preferring on both occasions to trust himself to the waves in an open boat, rather than face the dangers of a passage over-land; and when he brought his life out of that country, and came safe to Cork, he thanked God.*

When the fishing was good, Bantry prospered; and when the fish ceased to frequent the bay and the coasts adjoining, the town gradually kept sinking from bad to worse. Pilchards, herrings, haak, and sprats were at one time taken here in great abundance; but for the last fifty years the take of fish of any kind did not pay the expenses. It was during the middle of the last century that fishing was remunerative in

cloth on which he lay; and on his way back to Bantry he had his family burial-place in the churchyard of Ballymodan opened, and with his own hands he laid the remains of his faithful little companion amongst the dust and ashes of his own kindred.

* See *Clerical Records of Cork, Cloyne, and Ross.*

Bantry. In 1749 Mr. Richard Meade, an enterprizing fish-merchant in the town, proved to the satisfaction of the Dublin Society that he caught and cured on his own account, in that year, no less than three hundred and eighty thousand fish of various kinds; and Mr. James Young, another trader, saved, the previous year, two hundred and thirty-one barrels of sprats, and four hundred and eighty-two thousand herrings. A valuable sand, thickly strewn with coral, and a tourist traffic in the summer months, are the chief support of Bantry now.

The neighbouring bay conferred the title of Viscount Berehaven upon the Berkleys, and subsequently upon the Chetwynds; and Bantry itself gave the title of earl to the Ropers, a family now extinct. At present the earldom of Bantry is borne by the Whites, of Bantry House, one of whom, in 1734, married Martha, daughter of Rowland Davis, dean of Cork and Ross; by whom he had Margaret (married to Richard, Viscount Longueville), and a son,

Simon White, who married, in 1760, Frances Jane, daughter of Richard Hedges-Eyre, of Mount Hedges. He predeceased his father, and left, amongst other issue :—

Richard, who succeeded to the estates upon the death of his grandfather. He was born August 6th, 1767. On the 31st of March, 1797, he was raised to the peerage of Ireland, as baron of Bantry, in appreciation of the valuable services which he rendered in opposing the French in their attempt at landing in Bantry Bay. On the 29th of December, 1800, he was advanced to the viscountcy of Bantry; and on the 22nd January, 1816, he was created Viscount Berehaven and Earl of Bantry. He married, in November, 1799, Margaret Anne, daughter of William, first Earl of Listowel; by whom he had :— Richard, the late earl; William Henry, who assumed the surname and arms of Hedges; Simon, an officer in the army; Robert Hedges, and Maria. Upon the death of the first earl, in 1851, his eldest son,

Richard, the second earl, succeeded. He was born in 1800. In 1830 he married Mary, third daughter of William, Marquis of Thomond. She died in 1853. His lordship, who was a representative peer, died in July, 1868, and was succeeded by

William Henry, the present earl.

CARRIGBUIE.

About five miles south-west of Bantry is the pretty little village of

Carrigbuie. It is agreeably situated at the head of Dunmanus Bay—one of the great inlets from the Atlantic—and in a district where copper barytes, flags, and slate of superior quality, are to be found in abundance. The copper-mines in this locality are favourably known. The "south band," which runs along the coast from Mizen-head to Roaringwater, has already produced copper-ore worth a hundred thousand pounds. The Bandon barytes mine has rewarded the energy and perseverance of a Liverpool company with a yield of several thousands of tons. Flag quarries, which overhang the sea, produce flags of a fine buff colour, and are represented as capable of being worked to great advantage; and the slate veins of Sea-lodge and Rossmore, already traced to a length of two miles, are found to have an average width of ninety feet. These are also worked by an English company, who have a ready market for their produce in France, as well as in many parts of England and Scotland. "After a careful and minute search of the Carrigbuie estates of the Earl of Bandon, we find," say Messrs. Thomas and Son, two eminent mining engineers, who have been for a long time acquainted with that country, "that there are no less than thirteen ploughlands that contain minerals, offering every inducement to the capitalist to develop them."*

Carrigbuie—that is, the yellow rock—lies in a well-sheltered vale, through which flows a noisy stream, which empties itself into the bay here. Previous to the expiration of the lease by which Carrigbuie was held under the Earls of Bandon, it consisted of but a few thatched cabins, which are described as being both filthy and miserable. These have now disappeared; and a great improvement has taken place in its appearance, as well as in its prospects, since it has come into Lord Bandon's hands. The mud cabins have been replaced by rows of clean and substantial houses. Good-sized shops display tempting wares in their windows and on their shelves. A post-office delivers and dispatches the inhabitants' letters. A dispensary is furnished with every requirement for the sick; and a hospitable hotel, with its well-supplied table and its comfortable accommodation, helps to persuade the traveller that he is at home.

Durrus Church is but a short distance from Carrigbuie. It was

---

* Vide Descriptive reports on the mines, minerals, flag, and slate quarries on the estate of the Earl of Bandon in the south-west of the county of Cork, printed at the *Mining Journal* office, Fleet Street, London, 1865.

built about the year 1793, on the site of a chapel-of-ease, which was used for divine service before the breaking out of the great rebellion in 1641. After the suppression of that memorable rising it does not appear to have been used again; as in little more than sixty years afterwards, although its walls (which were built of large square stones, imbedded in clay mortar) were standing, its roof was gone.

Most of the lands of Durrus and Kilchohane were forfeited by the Irish proprietors in 1641. In the reigns of William the Third and Queen Anne, the principal landed proprietors in this immense district were Judge Bernard, Lord Anglesea, Colonel Freke, Lord Cork, Mr. Hull, Mr. Hutchins, and Major Eyre.

ROSSCARBERY.

Rosscarbery—anciently Ross-Alithra—(the wood of the pilgrims) and Ross Lehir, is situated in the west division of East Carbery. Upon the conquest of Ireland by the English, the fee of the county of Cork was conferred by Henry the Second on Robert Fitz-Stephen and Miles de Cogan, and they bestowed the town and all the lands of Ross (save those belonging to the bishop) upon Adam de Roche; and subsequently a charter of incorporation, by which many privileges were secured to "Ross Lehir," was granted to it by King John. Like a great many cathedral towns, the cathedral or abbey, or some religious house, was first erected, and then a town nestled around its walls. Such was the origin of Rosscarbery.

"St. Faghna or Fachnan," says Dr. Hanmer, in his *Chronicles of Ireland*, published in 1571, "lived in the time of Finbarry, and founded a monastery upon the sea, in the south part of Ireland, where he became abbot; the which seat grew to be a city, wherein a cathedral church was builded and patronized by Faghna. This town—of old called Rossai Lithry, but now Roskarbry—hath been walled about by a lady of that country; but now, according to the fruits of war among the Carties, O'Driscales, and other septs, scarce can the old foundations be seen. There hath been there of old a great University, whereto resorted all the south-west part of Ireland, for learning's sake. St. Brendan, bishop of Kerry, read publicly the liberal sciences in that school."

Farther (of Faghna or Faghnanus), mine author recordeth :—"That he being a wise and good man, by mishap, fell blind; and, with many prayers and salt tears, desired of God restitution of his sight, for the good of his convent and the students brought up under him. A voice he heard :—'Go, get some of the breast-milk of Broanus, the artificer's wife ; wash thine eyes therewith, and thou shalt see.' He went to a prophetess called Yta (St. Yta, an abbotess) to learn how to come by this woman, and it fell out that this woman was her sister. He found her out, washed his eyes, and recovered his sight. Whether it be true or no," says the doctor, "I know not ; I report it as I find it."

Archbishop Usher gives an extract from the *Life of St. Mocoemey,* which speaks highly of the renowned school at Ross-Alithra ; and states that a city sprung up there owing to the great influx of students from all parts.

In the reign of Henry the Eight, Ross O'Carbery was part of the country of McCarthy-Reagh. Towards the close of Elizabeth's reign, "Florence McCarthy, notwithstanding the infinite favours and bounties which he had received from her Majesty—being wholly Spainiolized—had possessed the minds of those in Carbery and Desmond with a strange opinion of his worthiness ; and having combined with Tyrone and other rebels at his late being in Munster, did show himself in open action against her Majesty. Whereupon the commissioners—Sir William St. Leger and Sir H. Power—sent Captain Flower and Captain Bostock into Carbery, with twelve hundred foot and one hundred horse, to make prosecution against the rebels of those parts."

In their way to Ross, the English, we are told, not only spoiled the country, but they contrived to lay hold of the heads of thirty-seven notorious rebels, besides others of lesser note.

In the beginning of September, 1600, the garrison of Kinsale marched to Rosscarbery, "upon hope of doing service thereabout ;" but they were disappointed—probably they were unable to catch anything they could do service upon. However, it would never do for them to return from such a long march as empty as they set out. Accordingly, they pushed on to Leap, and from thence made a sudden descent upon Kilcoe. Here they were rewarded for all their toil by a prize of three hundred cows. Driving these home before them, they returned to Kinsale without losing either a man or a beast. On another occasion, the whole country from Kinsale to Ross was so utterly wasted, that there was neither horn or corn, or even a house left there to shelter a rebel ; and from Ross to Bantry the country was similarly spoiled.

In 1642, Florence McCarthy, of Benduffe, Black O'Cullane, and others, after plundering the town of Ross, besieged Captain Arthur Freke and his heroic little garrison in Rathbarry Castle. Notwithstanding the valiant defence made by Freke and his warders, victory would eventually decide against them—owing to the want of food, as well as to the overwhelming numbers which prowled round and round the castle walls, like famishing wolves round a sheep-fold—had not the Bandon militia and Lord Forbes's regiment of Scotch come to their assistance, and conveyed them safely to Bandon.

During the siege—which lasted thirty-five weeks—the Irish used the cathedral of Ross as a shambles; and within its precincts they used to slaughter the cows and sheep which they took from the Protestant inhabitants.

It was at Ross the last act in the drama of the great rebellion was performed; when the town was surrendered to the English, and a peace concluded between General Ludlow on the side of the Parliament, and Lord Muskerry on behalf of the Kilkenny Confederation, on the 22nd of June, 1652.

A great deal of the lands forfeited in the parish of Rathbarry and the neighbourhood, and which had belonged to the O'Heas and the Barrys,* were granted to William Penn, Phillip Percival, and the Duke of York; but the town itself was conferred by Cromwell (April 12th, 1653) upon Captain Robert Gookin, "he having laid out £600 in fortifying the abbey, and in buildings intended for the English inhabitants, and to strengthen the place."

Upon an inquiry in 1654, a report was made, from which it appears that all these improvements cost no less than £2,143 9s.; and, in consideration of this, Gookin was granted Abbey-Mahon and twenty-six ploughlands adjoining.

Edward Synge, bishop of Cork, obtained a patent, dated July 1st, 1675, for three fairs to be held here annually—one on the 15th of August, one on the 8th of September, and on the 8th of December; also two weekly markets—one on Wednesday, and one on Saturday.

In James the Second's time Ross was garrisoned by some Irish troops, under General McCarthy; and so well posted were they, that an English

---

* James and John Barry were seized of the fee of Rathbarry Castle in the time of Charles the First, as appears by an inquisition taken at Bandon-Bridge in A.D. 1627.

force sent to reduce them considered it too hazardous an undertaking, and marched elsewhere.

It is stated that the first Christians in Ireland were the Corcailaidia, who are said to have been believers in Christ before the arrival of St. Patrick. From them sprung Liedania (the mother of St. Kierman, who was born in the Island of Cape Clear, A.D. 352). From the Corcailaidia also, and from King Macconius, was Mongach (the hairy); and St. Fachnan was the son of Mongach.

There is also an old legend about St. Fachnan or Faghna, who is the patron saint of Ross, which says that he used to pray daily on the side of a hill, half a mile to the east of Ross; but that one day he left his prayer-book behind him. The following night turned out to be very wet; nevertheless, not a drop of rain touched the holy book, as the angels—knowing what was coming—hurried down and built a chapel over it to protect it.

St. Faghna was succeeded by

Saint Finchad, who was a pupil of St. Finbarr's. He was followed by twenty-four bishops, not one of the names of whom have been preserved. Then came

Dongal Mac Folact, the twenty-seventh bishop. He, as well as the previous twenty-six, were all of the same line, a circumstance which gave rise to the following lines :—

> " Hail, happy Ross ! that could produce thrice nine—
> All mitred sages of Liedanias line.
> From Fachnan, crowned with everlasting praise,
> Down to the date of Dongal's pious days."

Benedict was bishop in 1172, and sat about eighteen years.

Maurice, who followed, died in 1196.

Daniel, consecrated at Rome by Pope Celestin the Third. He produced letters purporting to be written by the Irish bishops, asserting that he was elected to the vacant See, and thus imposed on his Holiness. Two other monks also went from Ross to the Pope, pretending that they were elected. The great Vicar, not knowing which of them to believe, entrusted the examination of the pretensions of the three candidates to the archbishop of Cashel and bishop of Killaloe. They reported in favour of Florence, one of the two monks, and they confirmed him in the See. Shortly after Pope Celestin died, and Innocent the Third occupied the Papal chair. Daniel again went to Rome; and told Innocent that the reason he was deprived of his mitre, was because he did not give the King of Cork money; and that the King—one of the McCarthys—was vexed with him, and ordered his dean not to obey him. That the dean readily complied with his Majesty's instructions, because he had a pique against him, for not conferring the archdeaconry upon his son—an infant. He also charged the dean with stealing the holy oil.' But he severely punished him for this—he excommunicated him; but even this severe chastisement does not appear to have done him any good, for shortly after he stole the church books.*

Florence, who died A.D. 1222.

Robert (*alias* Richard) was bishop in 1225.

Malechias (who held lands from the chapter of Cloyne; these he equally divided between his two sons, John and Lawrence).

Florence (*alias* Fineen O'Clogheena) resigned the bishopric in 1252.

Maurice (chaunter of Cloyne) succeeded. He died in 1269.

Walter O'Micthain succeeded, and died in 1274.

Peter O'Hullecan succeeded, and died in 1290.

Laurence was his successor. He died in 1309.

Matthew O'Finn succeeded. This active prelate recovered several of the lands belonging to the See, which had been unjustly usurped by Thomas Barrett and Phillip de Carew.

Laurence O'Holdecan succeeded. He died in 1335.

Dennis succeeded. He died in 1377. The See was vacant for some time after this; and the *custos* was fined a hundred marks for not appearing when summoned to attend and account at the Parliament held at Castle-Dermot.

Bernard O'Connor succeeded Dennis.

Stephen Browne was bishop in 1402. He had the temporalties restored to him on the 6th of May, 1402, having removed all clauses in the Pope's bull prejudicial to the rights of the crown.

Matthew died in 1418.

Walter Formay died in 1424.

Cornelius Mac Elchade was bishop in 1426.

Timothy sat in 1488.

Odo or Hugh succeeded in 1489.

Edmund de Courcey followed in 1494, and died in 1518.

John Imurily followed in 1519, and died same year.

---

* See Dr. Brady's *Records.*

Bonaventure (a Spaniard) was bishop in 1523.

Dermot Mac Donnell followed in 1544. He died in 1552.

Thomas O'Herlihy sat in 1561, and resigned in 1570. He assisted at the Council of Trent with two other Irish bishops, namely,—Donat, of Raphoe, and Eugene, of Achonry. O'Sullivan, an Irish historian, says that this prelate was detained for some time a prisoner in England; but that he was at length discharged, as the authorities considered him half a fool. He resigned in 1570, and died in 1579. He was buried in Kilcrea Abbey.

William Lyon succeeded in 1582. He died in 1617. From Lyon's time the See of Ross was united to that of Cork.

The cathedral,* which has always been used as a parish church, was rebuilt in 1612. It was considered a handsome structure, in the English style, and had a square tower. It was in a vault in this building—which was taken down and again rebuilt some years ago—that Mrs. Goodman (wife of the Rev. Richard Goodman, vicar of Bally-modan) was buried; and concerning whom it is related, that the sexton, being anxious to make his own of a ring which was on one of her fingers, entered the tomb at night, and in his efforts to possess himself of the coveted jewel, awoke her out of the state of catalepsy she was in.

In the vicinity of Rosscarbery is Rathbarry Castle (now Castle Freke),† the residence of George Patrick Evans-Freke, Baron Carbery. The family represented by Lord Carbery claim descent from Elystan Glodrydd, prince of Fferlys.‡

---

* In the year 1747 some underground passages and chambers were discovered near the cathedral. They are represented as being similar to those found near Kinneigh Church, which was a cathedral at one time.

† There were several coins found here some years ago bearing the names of Edmund and Athelstane, or Adelstone. These are supposed to have been brought to Ireland by Aulaf, who took refuge here after his defeat by Athelstone in A.D. 934.

‡ It is related of one of this family, that being in England on one occasion, he was conversing with some acquaintances on the antiquity on their respective families. One derived descent from a gentleman who perilled his life and his fortune for Charles the First; another travelled back to the era of the rival roses; another farther still, to the days of the great Norman invader; and another to that remote period when that almost fabulous hero, Prince Arthur and his knights sat at their round-table. But our Cambrio-Hibernian surpassed them all; he traced himself up to some one, with a name unpronounceable by civilized tongues, who ruled over a territory in Wales hundreds of years before Prince Arthur's great grandmother showed her first tooth. "Ah! Oh: indeed! I shouldn't wonder"—remarks one of those whom he addressed, and who naturally felt indignant at finding he was but a mere sapling alongside the gigantic oak of the Evanses—"if some ancestors of

In the reign of Elizabeth this branch of the Evanses possessed such wealth and influence that they were able to return eight members to sit in the English Parliament. Two brothers—John and Robert Evans—came over and settled in Ireland in the sixteenth century. John was ancestor of the Lords Carbery, and Robert of the Evanses of Bay-mount, county Dublin.

John, who was living in Limerick in 1628, was the grandfather of

The Right Hon. George Evans, of Bulgaden Hall, county Limerick, barrister-at-law. He was a zealous promoter of the revolution; and after the accession of William he was made a member of that monarch's Privy Council. He represented Charleville, in the county of Cork. In 1617 he married Mary, daughter of John Eyre, of Eyre Court, and had, with other issue,

George, his heir, who was advanced to the peerage, May 9th, 1715, in the dignity of Baron Carbery, of Carbery, county Cork, with remainder (default his own) to the male issue of his father. He was member for the county of Limerick in the Irish Parliament. Was governor, constable, and keeper of the castle and fort of Limerick, and a member of the Privy Council. So well pleased was Queen Anne with his services that she presented him in person with a valuable emerald ring, which is still an heir-loom in the family. He also sat in the British Parliament as representative for Westbury, in Wiltshire. He married, in 1703, Anne, daughter and co-heir of William Stafford, of Blatherwick, in Northampton, and had

George, his successor, of whom presently.

John, of Bulgaden Hall, who, in 1741, married Grace, only daughter of Sir Ralph Freke, Bart., of Castle-Freke, county Cork, and sole heiress of her brother, Sir John Redmond Freke, M.P., by whom he had five sons and four daughters; among whom were:—George Evans, who married Miss Stamer, and died issueless; and John Evans, who assumed the additional surname of Freke, and was created a baronet in 1768. He (Evans-Freke, baronet) married, in 1764, Elizabeth, daughter of Arthur, Earl of Arran, and, dying in 1777, left John—sixth Baron

---

your's were in the ark with Noah at the flood." "There were none of them there, sir!" replied Mr. Evans, sternly. Then drawing himself up to his full height, and making a low bow:—"I beg to acquaint you, sir," continued he, "that, upon that memorable occasion, my people were on board their own yacht; and, when sailing past the ark, Noah took off his hat to them, and said how delighted he was to find his old friends, the Evanses, were all right!"

27

Carbery—his successor. George, of Bulgaden Hall, married the widow of the fourth Lord Carbery. Percy, who married, in 1797, Dorothea, daughter of the Rev. Dr. Harvey, of Kyle, county Wexford, and left issue:—George Patrick, the present peer; Percy Augustus, lieutenant-colonel, died in 1847; Fenton John, late captain in the 2nd Life Guards. He married, in 1851, Catherine Felicia, eldest daughter of Thomas, Earl of Longford, and has a daughter, Georgiana Louisa. William Charles, married, in 1840, Sophia, third daughter of Phillip, Earl of Harborough, and widow of Sir Thomas Whitecote. Jane Grace Dorothea, married, in 1843, the Hon. and Rev. Charles B. Bernard, present bishop of Tuam—second son of James, Earl of Bandon—and has issue.

George—the second baron—succeeded upon the death of his father in 1759. He married, in 1732, Frances, daughter of Richard, Viscount Fitz-William, by whom he had :—George, his eldest son and successor; John, who became fifth baron; and Frances Anne. He was succeeded upon his death in 1759 by his eldest son,

George—the third baron. He married, firstly, in 1760, Juliana, daughter of Baptist, Earl of Gainsborough, by whom he had an only daughter, married to Hartopp Wigby, of Dalby House, Leicestershire. His lordship married, secondly, Elizabeth, daughter of Christopher Horton, of Catton Hall, county Derby, and had an only son, George, who, upon his death in 1783, succeeded him.

George—the fourth baron—represented Rutlandshire in the English Parliament. He married Susan, only daughter and heiress of Colonel Henry Watson; and died without issue in 1804. His widow married George Evans, uncle of the present peer. He was succeeded by his uncle, John, the second son of the second baron.

John—the fifth baron. He married, in 1759, Emma, daughter of the very Rev. William Crowe, Dean of Clonfert, by whom he had issue—a son, who predeceased him, and three daughters. He died in 1807, and was succeeded by his second cousin, Sir John Evans Freke, who became

John—the sixth baron. He married, in 1783, Catherine Charlotte, third daughter of Arthur, Earl of Arran; and dying without issue in 1845, was succeeded by his nephew,

George Patrick—the seventh baron. His lordship married, in 1852, Harriet Maria Catherine, only daughter of Edmund William Shuldham, lieutenant-general E.I.C.S., of Dunmanway, and has issue, Georgiana Dorothea Harriet.

MACROOM.

Macroom (that is the plain of Crom) was formerly spelt Macromp. Smith says the town takes its name from an old crooked tree which stood there at one time, and under the branches of which travellers used to rest themselves.

After Druidism disappeared, the bards (who were next in importance to the first Order of the Pagan priesthood) retained most of the privileges they had previously possessed; and for centuries after the introduction of Christianity they contrived to hold their assemblies here on the plain of Crom.

The town, which was probably coeval with the castle, had some new blood poured into it, when Cormac McCarthy,* in the reign of James the First, induced the Hardings, Kents, Goolds, Fields, and other English families to settle there.

In 1641, Donough, Lord Muskerry, who lived in Macroom Castle, was one of the most prominent leaders in the great rebellion; and upon its suppression in 1652, the town, castle, and the vast territorial estates of that nobleman, were forfeited. Upon the accession of Charles the Second, however, they were restored, and enjoyed by his descendants until the reign of William the Third, when they were again forfeited† for the active part taken by Donough, the fourth Earl of Clancarthy in the cause of James the Second.

At the great auction of forfeited estates held in Dublin in 1703, the greater portion of the Clancarthy property underwent the hammer; and on the 23rd of June in that year the Hollow Sword Blades Company purchased 55,000 acres of this estate,—including "the town of Macroom, Tubbernacool Park, Warren Park, and the Orchard; Wholehehane's tenements, several houses, cabins, shops, gardens, parts of gardens, three closes, the fairs, markets, mills, and the mile-end called Magheren; Pidgeon-house Park, Slevine; the house wherein are held the manor courts of Macroom, the guard-house in Macroom, and the market-house; together with the manor and seigniory of Macroom, the master-

---

* He died in 1616, after being chief of the great house of McCarthy-More for thirty-three years.

† About the year 1750 these estates were valued in £150,000 per annum; in 1796, in £200,000; and they would let at the present day for probably half-a-million sterling annually.

ship of the same, the conservatorship of the river Leigh (Lee), and the fishings therein, the manor of Kilcrea, and the manor of Blarney, &c."

The governor and company for making hollow sword blades in England did not retain their purchases very long, and they parted with many of their newly-acquired lands, and the town of Macroom, with its manor and seigniory, the conservatorship of the river Lee, the manors of Kilcrea and Blarney, &c., to Judge Bernard, ancestor of the Earls of Bandon.

In addition to the fairs which were held in Macroom when he became the owner, the judge obtained a patent, dated September 3rd, 1712, for holding four more, namely, on the 1st of May, on July 1st, September 1st, and on the 1st of November; and two markets, one to be held on Wednesday, and one on Saturday (weekly).

About half a mile to the north-west of Macroom is a chalybeate spring, the waters of which are said to contain medicinal qualities similar to those of Leamington.

Macroom Castle is of early date. Some say it was erected by the Carews; others, by the Daltons; and others, by the O'Flyns. O'Flyn's Castle, by which it is known in Irish, giving some stability to the assertion of the latter. It was enlarged by Teige McCarthy, who died there in 1565. In 1602, its then owner—Cormac Mac Dermot Carthy (Lord Muskerry)—who was suspected of hostile designs against the government, was detained prisoner in Cork. During his incarceration, Sir Charles Wilmot laid siege to the castle, but he was unable even to gain any advantage from which he could ultimately hope to make himself its possessor. Weary of his ill-success, he determined to abandon the enterprize altogether, and had made up his mind to strike his tents and march next day for Cork. Fortune, however, which had frowned on him heretofore, seemed now determined to atone to him for her previous neglect; and that fortress, upon whose battlements he never expected to plant the red flag of England, fell into his hands without striking a blow.

It appears that the castle warders being sadly in want of fresh provisions, did exactly what any respectable housekeeper would do in our own day under similar circumstances, they killed a pig. As no one, even in those rude times, could think of eating the meat with the bristles on, they resolved on getting rid of them as well as the difficulties of their situation would allow. Water, they had none—at least none to spare; and going down to the Sullane, although it almost washed the very walls of the garrison in which they stood, and bringing up a supply, was out of the question, as Wilmot's men kept strict ward on the river. What is to be done? As they cannot get water to scald the hair off, why not use some of the straw and fern upon which they sleep, and singe it off? Happy thought! The dead porker is raised on end, he is surrounded with the combustibles just mentioned, a light is applied, and the martyr to their anxiety for fresh meat is circled with flames. It may be that the McCarthys were revelling in the prospect of a feast on roast pork; or they may have shaken their heads, and said, laughingly, if they could but lay hold of Wilmot just then, however highly he may think of his social position, they would soon convince him that they thought a burning pig company good enough for him. They would seem, at all events, to have been making merry in some way, and not to mind what they were about, as they suffered some of the lighted straw to fall on the thatched roof of a cabin which lay against the wall of the bawn outside. The roof instantly blazed up, and the flash bounding through an open window, seized on a loft of tallow and other ignitibles. Thus vigorously sustained, the giant blaze, whirling and roaring as it rushed along, filled every apartment, and soon the whole stronghold was lapped in flames.

The McCarthys were terrified. Obeying their first impulse, they fled into the bawn; but they did not remain long there, as the gushes of hot, suffocating smoke, and the flakes of fire from the great conflagration now girting them almost on every side, compelled them to open a sally-port, and endeavour to escape. In this effort many did escape, but about fifty were overtaken and killed.

When the besiegers entered, the fury of the flames had well nigh spent itself, and they, having the command of the river, speedily extinguished what remained. Then hastily effecting some indispensible repairs, Sir Charles laid in a supply of provisions, barracked a company of foot there, and set out for Cork.

In 1650 Lord Broghill, who was dispatched from Clonmel by Cromwell, attacked the Titular bishop of Ross in the park—to which place the garrison retreated to join their main body after setting the castle on fire.

The Irish were defeated. Numbers of them were killed, and several were taken prisoners. Amongst whom were the high-sheriff of the county of Kerry and the bishop himself.   The former was speedily disposed of—he was shot on the spot; but the bishop was hanged the next day at Carrigadrohid.*

When General Ireton (Cromwell's son-in-law) was made lord-president of Munster, he sent some troops from Kilkenny, who burned not only the castle but the town in addition.

The year after the battle of the Boyne the English garrison in the castle were hard pressed by a body of Irish in the service of James; but on learning that Major Kirk and three hundred dragoons were marching against them, they raised the siege and made off.   The castle, which consists of a vast quadrangular mass of masonry, overhangs the river Sullane, and commanded a ford which was formerly there.

---

* For particulars see page 156.

CHAPTER XX.

" NO. 84, OR THE ANTIENT BOYNE"—JOHN WESLEY'S FIRST VISIT TO BANDON—THE
LINEN MANUFACTURE—OUR OLD WATCHMEN—OLD BANDON BRIDGE SWEPT AWAY—
HOW THEY WOO'ED A HUNDRED YEARS AGO.

THE first Masonic lodge was established in Bandon. It is styled "No. 84, or the Antient Boyne." Although, 1738. as we have just stated, it is numbered eighty-four, we must by no means infer that there are eighty-three lodges now in existence that were established before it; the fact being that it is the oldest fraternity in the kingdom, with a few exceptions. Whilst so assiduous were the members in the performance of their various masonic duties, and so well did they appreciate each others friendship and society, that—saving the 27th of December, 1796, when the French fleet lay in Bantry Bay, and when a French army was hourly expected in Bandon—there is not a single recorded instance of the non-observance of a festival.

The warrant constituting the lodge, appointing officers, &c., was issued by the Grand Lodge, and was signed by the Earl of Tyrone, grand-master of Ireland, and Cornelius Callaghan, D.G.M. The first lodge was opened on the 12th of June, 1738, in a room in the house of Mr. Thomas Bourk, when the following were present :—

Matthew Adderly, Esq., master.	Mr. Thomas Wheeler.
Mr. John Friar, deputy master.	Mr. Thomas Bourk.
Richard Screech, senior warden.	Mr. William Norwood.
Robert Morris, junior warden.	Mr. Robert Simmons.
Rev. John Friar.	Mr. John Donnellan.

After entering into a subscription to pay for the warrant and other necessaries, they made arrangements for duly celebrating the festival of

St. John. During the next fifteen years the undermentioned were duly
initiated :—

Bernard, Arthur.	Harman, Thomas.	Minnear, William.
Bennett, Thomas.	Honner, Robert.	McCarthy, Charles.
Cotter, Edward.	Hammett, Richard.	Rugg, Henry.
Ellis, Peter.	Jarvis, Samuel.	Tottenham, Cliffe.
Gillman, Stephen.	Laone, John.	Travers, John Moore.

Sixteen years after they first met, a member was guilty of some conduct
unbecoming a Christian and a mason. It came to the ears of the lodge,
and they were determined that no stain should rest on the escutcheon
of their fair fame. Accordingly "an emergency" was called, and the
erring brother was expelled forthwith; and, adds Moore Travers, the
secretary, "there was not a member of this society present would vote
in favour of him."

In 1768 a bye-law was passed, "That upon the death of any
member, the brethren shall apply to the friends of deceased to know
if their attendance at the funeral will be agreeable; if so, then
every member shall, at. his own expense, furnish himself with a band
scarf, gloves, and aprons bound with black riband, and attend the
funeral with the jewels, &c." There are a number of resolutions on
the books from time to time, directing that sums of money be given to
various poor brethren.

In 1779 a lodge held in Kinsale had the presumption to call themselves "The Boyne Lodge." The original Boyners would'nt stand this;
they considered it an unwarrantable invasion on their exclusive right
to "the Boyne;" and they memorialized the Grand Lodge that the Kinsale
pretenders "should no longer assume that name, it only belonging to
this lodge."

In 1790 a resolution was passed, to the effect "that no more than one
bottle of wine, or a pint of rum in punch, shall be allowed each
brother every lodge-day before the bill is called for and settled, except
on the festivals."

On the 24th of June, 1793, the members walked in procession to
church; and on their return to their lodge-rooms, they unanimously agreed
to a vote of thanks in favour of the Rev. William Gorman, their "chaplain, "for the very excellent and learned sermon preached by him on
the occasion." They also thanked Lieutenant-Colonel Jacques, of the
—— Regiment of Foot, "a worthy brother, for his very politely
granting the band of his regiment for their lodge on this day."

On the 24th of March, 1814, the brethren marched in possession, with Lodges 167 and 413, from the market-house in the South Main Street to Irishtown, to witness the laying of the foundation-stone of the School of Industry for Females, by Catherine Henrietta, Countess of Bandon.

Tuesday, the 29th of May, 1838, was the centenary anniversary of the foundation of "The Antient Boyne."

"This rare and interesting event," says Dr. William Belcher, the secretary, "was celebrated on the above day, by the brethren of 84 assembling at their lodge-rooms, Williams's Inn, at ten a.m.; where they were joined by the officers and deputations from the following lodges of Cork, Clonakilty, and Castle-Townsend:—Nos. 1, 3, 8, 27, 67, 71, 95, 156, 385; and the deputy provincial grand-master, the senior and junior grand-wardens of Munster. The brethren, attired in ancient masonic costume, marched to Ballymodan Church, where a charity-sermon was preached by the Rev. James Gollock, the provincial grand-chaplain of Munster, in aid of the funds of the Cork Masonic Orphan Asylum. . . . . Ninety-six brethren sat down to dinner at six o'clock p.m., including twenty-nine brethren of 84. The evening was spent in the utmost harmony and brotherly love, and every brother present appeared highly gratified with the proceedings of the day. The officers of the lodge present on this occasion were:—

Francis B. Hingston, W.M.	Robert T. Belcher, S.D.
Adderly, Beamish, S.W.	James Hamilton, J.D.
Franklin, Baldwin, J.W.	William Belcher, sec. and tres.

Richard Bailie, senior tyler.
Hugh Douglass, junior tyler."

Among the names on the muster-rolls of this venerable fraternity are the following:—

Bandon, Francis, Earl of.	Duntze, Sir John.
Boothby, Colonel.	Garibaldi, General.
Butler, Hon. James (son of the Earl of Ormond).	Hall, Col., Devon Militia.
Bushe, Charles Kendal.	Hindle, Capt., 6th Dragoon Guards.
Blonden, Capt. 18th Light Dragoons.	Kinsale, John, Baron of.
Blake, Lieut. Colonel, Galway Militia.	King, Col., Sligo Militia.
Cox, Rev. Sir Michael.	Moore, Sir Emanuel.
Cane, Capt. 12th Lt. Dragoons.	Quintin, Capt., 10th Hussars.
Cunningham, Hon. John.	Williamson, Major, Light Dragoons.
Coote, Lieut.-Genl. Sir Eyre.	Warren, Sir Augustus.
De Courcy, Hon. William.	Younghusband, Capt., 7th Dragoon Guards.
Dyson, Capt. 3rd Drageon Guards.	Westmeath, George, Earl of.

There were also a great many French officers admitted, who were prisoners in Bandon in 1746 and 1747, as :—

Comes, Jean Baptiste.	Du Roche, Francois.	Kersabie, Chevalier.
Cottin, Pierre.	Fostain, Louis.	Florence, Pierre.
Du Portas, Jean, M.D.	Guzeau, Louis.	Du Roche, Francois.

Although the collars worn by this lodge are of orange velvet, yet they have no political significancy whatsoever, as the orange was adopted by them sixty years before the existence of the Orange Society; and so well aware were the Roman Catholic brethren of this fact, that when a deputation—consisting of two Protestants and two Roman Catholics —was sent to Cork by "84" some years ago, the Roman Catholics refused to wear any other colours than those of their lodge.

It appears that the deputation, being duly announced, presented themselves for admission; but were peremptorily refused on the grounds that they wore party emblems. They protested against this assertion, urging that orange was the colour worn by their lodge ever since its foundation; but it was of no avail, in they should not come until they were properly habited. Finding all remonstrance useless, the two Protestants uncollared, and prepared to comply; but the Roman Catholics would not hear of it; they turned furiously on their brother deputies, and upbraided them in the most emphatic language, taunting them with deserting their colours, and exciting the feelings of the antient Boyners to such a pitch, that they flung from them the loathed blue, and, returning to their first love, they put on their orange collars, and indignantly left the room.

Some amusing stories are told in connection with old "84." An inquisitive fellow, who said he caught the tyler asleep one night on his post, averred that he peeped through the keyhole, and saw the brethren inside walking in procession round a big black jug; whilst a skeleton sat under each light, and played "The Boyne Water" upon a skull with a pair of cross-bones. Another, who alleged he looked through a crevice in the floor overhead, stated that each of the members used to go three times to the corner of the lodge-room, where a voice used to speak to them out of a coffin; and to a married man would say :— "Fear God, honour the King, and be a good husband and father;" and to a single man, after lecturing him a great deal, it used always conclude by telling him above all things never to marry a Papist. The ordeal of the poker has had at all times great terrors for the uninitiated.

Some years ago, a gentleman, whom we shall call Mr. B——, was ballotted for, and accepted as a candidate for masonic honours. He was duly noticed to be present at the Devonshire Arms on a certain day for initiation, and he attended. As he ascended the staircase, ominous knocks and the mutterings of distant thunder caught his ear, and by no means helped to allay the fears which had possessed him during the greater part of the previous week. Arriving on the landing, he gently asked the tyler may he go in ; but the redoubtable Dick Baylie would not even allow him to put his nose inside the scarlet curtain which hung some feet in front of the lodge-door. Even the dress the tyler wore appeared in harmony with the sanguinary and mysterious deeds that were said to have been often perpetrated within. A huge red cloak covered him to the very toes; the large sleeves, which hung below his hands, terminated in cuffs of orange velvet, on each of which was a representation of a skull and cross-bones in lustrous black ; the blue collar had on it moons and stars of bright yellow ; and candlesticks, compasses, and other cabalistic symbols of the craft, nearly covered it with odd-looking devices. On his head was a gigantic cocked-hat, which would almost have served him for a boat, it was so large. This was surmounted with blue and red feathers; and in his hand was a flaming falchion.

"Keep off !" said the terrible Dick, as the bewildered candidate moved forward a step or two, "or before you can say *domine salvum fac*, I'll run you through the gullet !"

Mr. B——, not caring to encounter so fierce-looking an opponent, went down stairs, and after strolling about for a little time, he sauntered into the kitchen. A roaring fire was down at the time, and the covers which lay on the various cooking utensils kept up a perpetual trotting-match with one another, as if to see which of them would be on the floor first ; but the monstrous poker—more than half of which was thrust in between the bars, and which already looked soft and white with the glow of intense heat—fixed his attention at once.

"Ah ! well, Johanna," said the victim, addressing the cook in an assumed indifferent tone, "what do you want that big poker for ?"

"Faith, sir," replied the latter, looking very thoughtful, "I'm afraid I'll get into a scrape about that same poker !"

"Why so ?"

"Because, by some mistake, their own was taken up to the farm, and put as a prop under the loft where the master keeps the oats for the horses, and I suspect they'll never be satisfied with this piece of wire!" looking contemptuously at the great poker.

"And who is it that—that—that wants such a thing at all?" falteringly inquired poor B——.

"Why, the freemasons, sir, to be sure! The doctor* ran down to me while ago and told me to be quick, as they were going to make a mason immediately; and many is the one I reddened for them before; but I suppose they'll kill me entirely now!"

"And why wouldn't that poker do—do—them?"

"Yerra! is it that knitting-needle? Whisht! by gor, here they are!" as a door was heard to bang-to upstairs.

Pressing his hat on his forehead, the applicant for masonic honours shot out of the kitchen like a flash of lightning; and fleeing through the open door, he bounded down the limestone steps, and ran for his life.

"Come back!" roared the cook; "Hould him!" cried the boots; "Catch him!" shouted the waiter; but away he sped faster than before.

When the fellows who lounged outside on the steps, and who, to do them justice, were never averse to a bit of fun, got an inkling of what occurred, they gave tongue with a vengeance, and some of them even gave chase; but they might as well try and overtake a telegraphic message on its way to its destination along the wires. The affrighted candidate was soon out of sight; and, from that day to the present, no one has ever seen him in this locality.

Masonry has been much on the increase of late years. Men are more anxious than heretofore to congregate where they can enjoy one another's friendship and society irrespective of creed and party; and where they can spend their evenings more profitably than in taxing their ingenuity to discover a religious or a political grievance.

Another excellent department of masonry is that which is devoted to charity. Out of their abundance there are but few who do not give cheerfully to a fund, out of which a brother less fortunate than themselves can be assisted to get on his legs again, and again, and again, to fight the great battle of life; and, should he fall in the struggle, a

---

* The late Dr. O——n.

fraternal hand will tend his orphans until they are ready to enter the great conflict, and battle for themselves.

So long as freemasons adhere to the divine precept which teaches peace and good-will among men—and it has been their guiding-star ever since their venerable institution had a beginning—so long may they continue to smile at those tissue-paper thunderbolts which occasionally illumine the darkness of our daily press.

1739. This was known as the year of the great frost, which was so intense in this vicinity, that potatoes are said to have been found frozen in the middle of large balls of woollen thread. All the rivers in this neighbourhood were frozen over; whilst such was the severity of the frost in Cork, that the Lee was not only sheeted over with ice, but the ice was found to be strong enough to support shows, and booths, and tents. In consequence of the great severity of the weather, provisions became very scarce, and wheat brought as high as forty-two shillings the kilderkin.

1748. The Methodists first visited Cork in 1748. We have been favoured with an original letter written by one of their hearers at this time, in reply to an unjustifiable attack made upon them by a clergyman of the Establishment. The letter goes on to say, "I would ask any gentleman what fault he can find with the doctrine of those Methodists? Do they not preach, with the utmost zeal and ardency, the word of God according to the dictates of revealed religion? And what visible inducements have they for undergoing the troublesome fatigues of preaching—for quitting their native homes and families, but the happiness of their fellow-creatures. If we are to believe their words, they want none of our gold or silver, but all they desire is to rouse us from the lethargy under which we have, for a long time, unthinkingly laboured. On the other hand, those gentlemen who write and speak against them for putting them in mind of their duty, care not how the shadow is, so they have the bone; and, when they are inducted, will not do any one individual act relative to their duty without payment, and to a man verify the old proverb, 'No penny, no pater noster.' What benefit can the immortal part of us receive or expect from a set of people who must be hired for showing us the road to heaven? Must not everybody, who thinks at all, imagine that the benefits resulting to our souls by preaching the methods lately prescribed and laid down to us without gratuity, fee, or reward, will be greater than those laid down at the price of a great part of our worldly substance? For my part, I cannot find any fault with these Methodists; but what I would desire would be, that the lazy, imperious shepherds would mind their flocks, so that we may have no need of procuring gratis what we ought to get from those who are too well paid for the little they do."

A regular post was first established, this year, between Cork and Skibbereen. The unfortunate postman, who was not only obliged to walk the entire way, but to carry the mail-bags in addition, was paid only the miserable sum of six pounds per annum—a little over two shillings a week. In some years later, the biped was displaced by a quadruped, which was bestrode by one William Leary, and to whom the custody of his Majesty's royal mails was entrusted.

John Wesley paid his first visit to Bandon. He put up at 1749. the residence of Mr. Hawes, a very respectable man, who occupied a house near the middle of the northern side of the South Main Street. In his journal he writes:—" I rode over to Bandon, a town which is entirely inhabited by Protestants. I preached at seven, in the middle of the main street. Here was by far the largest congregation, both morning and evening, of any I had seen in Ireland." Under date June 2, he continues:—" In the evening a gentlewoman informed me that Dr. B. had averred to her, and many others, that both John and Charles Wesley had been expelled the University of Oxford long ago; that there was not a Methodist left in Dublin or any town in Ireland, but Cork and Bandon, all the rest having been rooted out by order of the government; that neither were there any Methodists left in England; *that it was all Jesuitism at the bottom.* Alas, for poor Dr. B.! God be merciful unto him a sinner!" In about twelve months after this, Wesley visited Bandon again, of which he writes:—"God gave us great peace at Bandon, notwithstanding the unwearied labour, both public and private, of good Dr. B. (Dr. Browne, rector of Kilbrogan) to stir up the people. I began preaching in the Main Street, at the usual hour, but to more than twice the usual congregation. After I had spoken about a quarter of an hour, a clergyman, who had planted himself near me, with a very large stick in his hand, according to agreement, opened the scene—indeed, his friends assured me he was drunk, or he would not have done so; but, before he had uttered many words, two or three resolute women, by main strength, pulled him into a house, and, after expostulating a little, sent him away through the garden; but here he fell violently on her that conducted him—not in anger, but in love, such as it was—so that she was constrained to repel force by force, and cuff him soundly, before he would let her go.   The next champion that appeared was one Mr. M., a young gentleman of the town; he was attended by two others, with pistols in their hands; but his triumph, too, was short.   The third came on with greater fury, but he was encountered by a butcher of the town—Jim Moxley—who used him as he would an ox, bestowing one or two hearty blows upon his head.   This cooled his courage, especially as none took his part."

It is rather singular that the very pulpit from which old Browne used to fulminate his anathemas against his fellow Christians, the Wesleyans, was the very one used by them in the services in connection with the laying of the foundation-stone of the present Methodist chapel.

At the August Assizes following (1749), the persecuting spirit which had pursued the Wesleyans in various parts of the county and city of Cork, was embodied by the Grand Jury in a presentment as slanderous as it was lying and malignant.   It is as follows:—" We find and present Charles Wesley to be a person of ill-fame, a vagabond, and a common disturber of his Majesty's peace; and we pray he may be transported."   They also presented a similar request against eight Wesleyan ministers, who had previously visited Cork.

Despite those persecutions, not only here but throughout Great Britain, the Wesleyans flourished.   At all times they have shown regard for the Church of England, and they allow her clergy even still to baptize their new-born infants, to perform the marriage ceremony when they seek to enter the marriage state, and then, when they have passed through the last scene of all, to bury them.

The admirers of Wesley consider themselves Church of England people; but Church of England people of that stamp who have worshipped within her walls before many of her clergy and laity became infected with a passion for ceremonies and baubles.   They look upon themselves as possessing that pure and healthy Protestantism which the church enjoyed before Archbishop Laud endeavoured to seduce her from the Faith of the Reformation, and lead her to Rome.

An anecdote is still told here of Dr. Browne, the rector of Kilbrogan; and who, amongst other matters, was accused, as we have seen, by Wesley, of "making love, such as it was."   In those days, however extensive a place morality may have occupied in a homily or a discourse, practical morality was not the fashion with the clergy as it is now. It is said that a married lady left her liege lord, and that the doctor—perhaps, purely out of politeness—escorted the fair matron to her retreat. Be that as it may, an action-at-law was brought against him, and the injured husband recovered a thousand pounds damages.

The doctor determined to turn over a new leaf after this. He saw the error of his ways, and he made up his mind to atone for his misdeeds by devoting himself anew to the all-important duties of his calling. Meeting Captain Savage, the provost, one Sunday morning :—

"Well, captain," said he, "how is it that I never see you in church ?"

"Well, really I don't know," said Savage.

"Don't know !" said Browne, who felt irritated at being treated so lukewarmly by our chief-magistrate. "Do you know anything? Come, now, could you tell me how many commandments there are ?"

"How many commandments there are ?" said the provost, repeating the question and looking thoughtfully on the ground, then moving his lips as if repeating them, and counting on his fingers at the same time, "there are nine, doctor," said he, appearing quite pleased at being able to answer this great theological crux.

"Well, I always thought," said the rector, rising to his full height, and looking quite triumphant with the easy victory he had gained over our great civic dignitary, "that there were ten !"

"And so there were, too," said Savage, submissively ; then looking up innocently in his interrogator's face, "but you know you broke one of them, and we have only nine ever since."

The doctor suddenly recollected he had an appointment elsewhere, and left abruptly.

1749. About this time great efforts were made to introduce the linen manufacture into Bandon. Although the manufacture of linen was not as extensively entered upon as its promoters would wish, yet what did leave our looms was so highly valued, that one of our townsmen, John Starkey, was one of the few in Ireland who received a prize of fifty pounds ; and Jonathan Tanner, another townsman, not only received another prize of fifty pounds, but also an additional sum of forty pounds, on the grounds " that he had distinguished himself as a useful manufacturer in that part of the kingdom."*

The principal article of our local trade at this period was camlet,

* Vide the *Gentlemen's and Citizens' Almanack*, for A.D. 1751.

which was a coarse cloth, made of woollen thread, and dyed a bright colour. It generally found a market in Portugal and the West Indies, and was shipped in small casks about the size of butter firkins. Butter was also forwarded by the same shippers, to the same markets, and always commanded a high quotation. Towards the close of the last century, and the beginning of this, the camlet manufacture again revived, but in the course of a few years it again left us, never, we fear, to return.

The population of our town must have been by this year very considerable, as it contained no less than a thousand men amongst the manufacturing classes capable of bearing arms. Many of these used to parade in full regimentals, consisting of a red coat, faced with black, knee-breeches, &c.

About this time watchmen were first appointed here. Their duty was to cry the hours at night, and to keep strict watch and ward from sunset to sunrise. Although they walked the streets after the sun went down, they did not give the regular cry until within an hour of midnight. Then they began :—" A-pa-st e-le-ven oh-o-'clock !"

> " Maids in your smocks, look at your locks ;
> Put out your fire and candlelight ;
> And so good ni-i-i-ght, good ni-i-i-ght !"

The injunction to the unmarried ladies, who were presumed to be in a state of semi-nudity, to look to their locks, was a regular double entendre, and one which we are surprised to find the gravity of our forefathers and foremothers permitted to continue so long. It meant, that not only should they see that their doors were all duly secured, but that they should inspect their silken tresses before they sought the solace of Morpheus. In addition to calling the hours, they called the direction of the wind also :—" Wind from the Nau-au-aurth !" &c. ; but if it blew south-west, or showed indications of rain from any point, they used to add, " and we-ll sure-ly have the ra-in before maur-ning !" There was one old fellow, however, who was totally unacquainted with even the four cardinal points, and instead of saying wind from the north or south, he would say :—" Wind blowing up Sea-ly's Lane !" or down, as the case may be. If the wind was from the east or west, he'd be obliged to go on another tack. If from the east, he would say :—" Wind blowing a-gen me as I walks to Tom Laone's cor-ner !" If from the west :—" Wind straight into my face as I goes up to where Bill Anstis lived before he went to Ameri-ky-ky-ky !"

28

The townspeople got so accustomed to those announcements, that, as if by common consent, they fixed on a word or a term in each cry, and at once knew the course of the wind. Thus :—when they would hear " up," they knew the wind was northerly, and " down," southerly ; " Tom Laone" told them that the wind was from the east, and " Bill Anstis," that it was from the west.

1754.   The first meat shambles was erected here. It was built at the northern end of the bridge (western side), and contained twenty-two stalls. These were in great demand by the butchers, who paid one pound annually for each stall, and occupied them on the opening day in the following order :—

1. William Moxley.
2. Timothy Keneash.
3. James Harris and Will Tomson.
4. Richard Morgan.
5. Christopher Lisson.
6. James Moxley.
7. James Moxley, junr.
8. Denis Murray.
9. Michael Hurley.
10. Thomas Wholehane.
11. John Burchill.
12. Cornelius Rickard.
13. John Reen.
14. William Searls.
15. Timothy Murphy.
16. William Moxley.
17. John Searls.
18. Cornelius Forehane & Son.
19. Stephen Moxley.
20. Robert Searls.
21. John Lisson.
22. Edward Drake.

1761.   A new Parliament assembled in Dublin this year. The members for Bandon were William Conner and Thomas Adderly.

1762.   Alice Cambridge, the well-known Wesleyan minister, was born in Bandon on the first day of this year. Her father was a member of the Established Church, and was a regular attendant ; and her mother, who was even still more regardful of her religious duties, was a Presbyterian ; but Alice, in making her choice, selected that system which appeared to her to combine the excellencies of both the previous ones, and the faults of neither—she was a Methodist.

Miss Cambridge was a woman of great energy and perseverance. Nothing daunted her. Although a preacher in petticoats was in her day almost as great a novelty as in our own, and though she knew her congregation often contained those who came to jeer and not to pray, nevertheless, she stood up in the pulpit unabashed, gave the little cap which she wore on the back of her head a twist, tightened her apron-strings about her waist, and entered becomingly on her discourse. She died in 1829, having enjoyed a long life, in which she did a great deal of good and no harm.

Upon the proclamation of war between England and Spain, in the beginning of this year, a lot of the disaffected in this kingdom banded themselves together, and under various names—as Fairies, Redboys, Whiteboys, Levellers, &c.—they traversed the country, principally between sunset and sunrise, attacking the houses of peaceable inhabitants, and doing serious injury to life and property. Their avowed object was to level the fences recently constructed round waste lands or commons in various parts of Ireland, and which lands, they alleged, belonged to the poor; but their real object was to co-operate with Spain, and, if possible, restore the Pretender. Many of them were taken prisoners; and in the pockets of several were found military commissions, lists of the the names of many of their confederates, and the following ballad :—

" Come cheer up, my lads, for your glory is near!
Away with all doubt, and away with all fear !
To freedom we call you—a Stuart shall reign—
Usurpation shall vanish—accept aid from Spain. ·
    Chorus.—Right royal is our prince, right royal our men!
        In the cause we are ready—steady, boys, steady !—
        We'll fight till we die, or restore him again.

" No longer we'll wait for assistance from France,
Nor again shall they lead us a wandering dance;
For Spain, on whose word we may surely depend,
Has the power and will our rights to defend.
    Chorus.

" The offspring of Brunswick or Strelitz—poor lords !—
Shall never usurp or command our brave swords.
For the sword shall again be adorned by a king,
Of whose great ancestors our Druids shall sing.
    Chorus.

" Come cheer up, my lads, for the time it draws near
When the land of all whelps and true-blues shall be clear;
When Prince Charles as king, my boys, toasted shall be,
And our bondage reversed into grand liberty.
    Chorus.

" No blue-livered whelp, or Cromwellian black boor,
In grandeur shall ride, or in splendour shall move.
Of their titles we'll strip 'em, and enslave 'em, my boys.
Their sorrows we'll heighten, and retrieve our own joys.
    Chorus.

The loyalist party here had a poetaster, too; and he replied in a song of similar style and metre, and well known in this neighbourhood at that time :—

" Come cheer up, my lads—dear Protestant boys!
Let's support well our rights, our religion, and laws;
In spite of the power of the hard-hearted crew,
Who their hands in our blood would most gladly imbue.

  Chorus.—The Protestant cause now calls for our aid.
    To defend it be ready—now's the time to be **steady**—
    We'll conquer or die ere slaves we are made.

"They say they'll enslave us—Oh, subjects most rare!
More savage in nature than India's wild bear.
The aid that must come is expected from Spain;
For which they may hope and long wish for in vain.

  Chorus.

" Their treason they speak 'gainst our gracious, good King;
And malice they vent on his great noble kin
Of Brunswick and Strelitz, of mighty descent;
For which they in time will most sadly relent. ∗

  Chorus.

" Their Prince Charles, they say, on the throne they will fix;
But can they forget the great year forty-six.
Then let rebels dare not think him to bring in,
For we'll die before a Papist be king.

  Chorus.

" My Protestant boys, the time is now come,
When we should be ready at the beat of the drum,
To support our good King, and the old English cause—
So famed for its rights, its religion, its laws.

  Chorus.

In another loyalist ballad which was very popular here, **Prince Charlie** is spoken of with great acrimony. Speaking of **King George**, it says :—

  "And in his stead, to place upon the throne
  A vagabond, whose parents are unknown:
  Pretender to three kingdoms not his own."

" An epitaph for the Levellers (commonly called the **Whiteboys**") shows the bitter feelings entertained by the loyalists for **those free-booters** :—

  "Now judgment passed by the great God of Heaven—
  Die, die, you must, in numbers odd and even.
  You purchase shrouds, Great George provides the rope,
  In spite of France, the Spaniards, and the Pope.

∗ " When they are going to be hanged," is the remark made in a foot-note of the old MS. copy which was kindly lent to us.

" In heaps within this hole, you lie together,
 Rebellious crew—you birds all of a feather.
 Secure them, devil ; let your bolts be tight ;
 Loose them by day, but guard them well by night.

" Poor Satan thinks, perhaps, their number few ;
 But hundreds of them shall the same steps pursue,
 Since living is the Light-horse and the Blue.

" They're fixed with you for evermore to dwell.
 All that I fear—not big enough is hell."*

1765. Scarce was this year a fortnight old when a great flood swept away old Bandon bridge. It appears that a large tree having fallen into the river at the park, was rolled down by the angry waters, and having, unfortunately, got across one of the main archways of the bridge, it lay there. It was not very long in its new position, when a rick of hay floated out of the kitchen-garden belonging to a widow woman named Barry—who lived in a house on the site of the premises occupied by the late Miss Anne Williams—and sidling into the huge stream, was stopped in its downward course by the tree. The tree and the hay-rick were speedily supplemented by a host of other impedimenta, including bundles of faggots, branches of trees, straw-stacks, &c.

The current being now greatly obstructed, back-water was the result ; the vast volume of which was every instant on the increase. The old boundaries can restrain it no longer. Quickly reaching to their utmost height, it overtops them, and pouring down, the foaming waters rudely force every obstacle out of the course of their onward sweep, and soon a great portion of the town lies under water. Meanwhile the old bridge firmly holds its ground ; but after a little time it begins to tremble ; a little later, and it shakes ; later still, and a fissure appears ; and another, and another, and then a huge rent announces its impending doom. And now, as if conscious that its work was done—that its inevitable fate was at hand—it lowers its old historic front, and dropping slowly and silently into the grave of angry waters that are impatiently awaiting it below, it disappears ; and in a few short minutes there was not a stone left to record where it stood.

The bridge was in excellent repair when this casuality overtook it.

---

* We know of no species of composition more calculated to give one a correct idea of the feelings possessed by the contending parties than the popular ballads of the times. They are written when the blood is up, and they express in unmistake-able language what the writers thought and felt at the time.

It was only the year before the old pavement was ripped up, as appears by an account furnished the corporation by John Harris; in which he charges six and sixpence for cash paid Daniel Dineen, Darby Dogane, Matthew Sullivan, and Teige Downey, three days each, for ripping up the pavement of the bridge.

This great inundation which occurred on the 15th January made a breach in Innoshannon bridge, which the Bandon corporation hastened to repair at their own expense, "so as to make a communication for carriages to and from the said town of Bandon, to Cork and other places." The bill for these repairs contain the following items:—

	£	s.	d.
Robert Browne, five days at 18d.		7	6
Robert Browne's boy, five days at 16d.		6	8
James Callahan, five days at 18d.		7	6
Daniel Carthy, five days at 18d.		7	6
Twenty-six labourers, at 6d.		13	0
Robert Hailes and horse, three days, 1s. 1d.		3	3
Denis Connel and horse, five days, 1s. 1d.		5	5
James Hickey and horse, three days, 1s. 1d.		3	3
Two quarrymen, a day each at 10d.		1	8
Quayage for timber, four tons at 6d.		2	0
Bringing the timber to the bridge		1	6
My attendance five days at 2s. 2d.		10	10

(Signed) WILLIAM MARTIN.

Week ending May 11th, 1765.

The flood not only destroyed Bandon bridge, but it caused a great deal of suffering and distress in the town. To relieve this, a public meeting was held at the South Market-house, in the month of February, under the presidency of Jonathan Tanner, the provost, at which it was resolved that:—

"Whereas, by the great inundation on the 15th of January last a great part of the town of Bandon was overflowed, by which many of the inhabitants were great sufferers, and some so much distressed as to be under the necessity of accepting some public benevolence. We, therefore, in order to relieve such of them as are in greatest want of our assistance, do agree that the sum of sixty-one pounds eight and sixpence shall be immediately borrowed from James Bernard, Esq., who proposed to lend said sum; and accordingly do pay the same to Jonathan Tanner, Esq., provost of said borough, to be by him given to the following persons, agreeable to the sums therein annexed."

Another resolution providing a boat for the river also passed:—

"And, whereas the bridge on the river Bandon was by the said inundation carried away, and it is thought necessary a proper boat should be provided to carry on communication from the north to the south-side of the town. We do, therefore, agree and order that any sum not exceeding twenty pounds shall be expended in procuring a boat and other necessaries for conveying passengers over said river."

1766.   Upon the death of Mr. Conner, Francis Bernard, of Castle-Bernard (familiarly known as Squire Bernard), and who had a seat in Parliament more than forty years before, having been representative for Clonakilty in 1725, was elected in his place.

1768.   An immense fall of snow, which continued for several days. In many places it was six feet in depth. An old newspaper records the case of a gentleman who was riding from Bandon to Cork, and so firmly did his horse get embedded in the snow, that spades and shovels were had recourse to in order to dig him out. Francis Bernard and Thomas Adderly elected to represent the town in Parliament.

1770.   Block wheels were first introduced into this neighbourhood. They were composed of solid blocks of timber, about three feet and a-half in diameter, and from six to eight inches in thickness, and were heavily bound all round the edge with iron. A carpenter named William Hennessy was said to be the first to bring them into notice here; and so slowly did our public take to them, that at the Red Strand, near Clonakilty—now famous as the daily resort of hundreds of sand-carts—only three wheeled vehicles made their appearance there during the entire year.

1773.   The new bridge over the river, in place of the one carried away, was completed and opened for traffic. The delay was owing to the largeness of the sum required, and the imperfect state of the Grand Jury laws, which rendered it a matter of great difficulty to procure the necessary funds. The sum required, however, was at length forthcoming, partly in assistance from the county, but principally from private subscriptions; and the bridge was formally thrown open to the public this year.

On a mural tablet in the battlement over the centre arch, and facing the roadway, is the following inscription :—

> "TANDEM EMERGO,
> SUB AUSPICIIS,
> JOHANNIS TRAVERS,*
> PRÆPOSITI ANNO DOM,
> 1773."

During the interval that intervened between the destruction of the old and the completion of the new, intercommunication was kept between both sides of the town by the ferry-boat, for the procuring of which, as

---

* It was Mr. John Travers, who was provost in 1769, 1771, 1773, and, lastly, in 1775, who laid the foundation stone.

we have previously stated, funds were voted by the corporation. In ordinary week days this mode of conveyance was safe enough, but on market-days it was dangerous, owing not alone to the crowded state of the boat, but to the state of the boatman, one Tade Callaghan (Boskeen).

It happened that on one market-day in particular, the boat was passing over more than usually depressed, while Tade, who was quite the other, being more than usually elevated, roughly laid hold of the oars; and scarcely had they arrived mid-way, when by some mischance he upset the boat and passengers, and all were tumbled into the water. The river happened at this time to be much swollen after a prolonged fall of rain, and some of those who were thrown in never reached the banks alive. Amongst those who perished was the inebriated charm of the Bandon river—poor Tade Callaghan himself.

Abductions were very prevalent about this time. Many a fellow, when he took a fancy to a girl in those days, showed the warmth of his affection for her by stuffing a pocket-handkerchief, or an old stocking, or perhaps the torn-off sleeve of his shirt, half-way down his Dulcinea's throat, to stifle her cries; or knocking down her father; or, it may be, fracturing her brother's skull in his efforts to make her his own. They did not understand the amenities and courtesies of civilized life in the country parts round here at this rude period. A rustic lover never thought of " seeking an introduction ;" or even if he did become acquainted with his intended, he never took the trouble to try and create a favourable impression on her mind concerning him, by saying a few nice little things to her, as he strolled with her along the *boreen*, or gently pressing her soft hand as he bid her good-night, or endeavouring to look as if he would die of a broken heart if she did not throw him a smile or two, so as to enable him to survive until he would see her again. He could not be charged with any of those puerilities. When he became enamoured, 'twas the might of Hercules* he called to his aid, and not the blandishments of Cupid.

On one occasion one of those pastoral youths tumbled head and ears into love at first sight. Now, if some charming little creature threw a

---

* An advertisement appeared in one of our county papers about this period, in reference to an abduction case in our own neighbourhood, in which a reward of twenty guineas was offered for the apprehension of Daniel McNamara, of Enniskeane, distiller, and a similar sum for the apprehension of one Daniel Horrigan, a Popish priest, who married him to a young lady of thirteen years of age, " forcibly and against her will " carried away from her paternal roof.

coy glance at him over the top of a fan, to fan the spark of admiration, which glimmers with more or less intensity in the breast of every lord of the creation for the fair sex, into a blaze; or did she utter a pretty sentiment or two, or even say a kind word to him, one would not be much surprised to see the flames of love bursting through the combustible soul of a young man of two-and-twenty.   But no, gentle reader; when this refined rural first saw Bessie; when his heart for the first time beat quick, and then, as if ashamed of itself for being so foolish, suddenly almost came to a stand-still; when he felt a kind of creamy, sugary sensation flushing all over him—she, industrious, sensible young woman as she was, had one end of a sugawn in her bronzed fist, whilst the other end was carefully secured to one of the hind legs of a pig, which she was endeavouring to sell to the best advantage at Bandon fair. · Poor Bumkin looked, and he loved; and then of course he made up his mind that the loved one should be his wife.   Accordingly he collected a lot of his friends, and on the second night after he. stormed his charmer's abode.

The old man (her father) hearing a lot of voices shouting to Bessie to get up and dress herself, put his head out of the window and asked what they wanted?

"We want your daughter, Bessie," cried the storming party, "and we must have her!"

"You shan't!" says old paterfamilias, as he shut down the window, and bolted it.

"Let us in this instant, or we'll burn the house!" said the outsiders; but there was no answer.   "We'll burn it to the ground!" again shouted they; but there was still no answer, and all within was as silent as the grave.   Then they began battering at the door with their whip-handles, but there was no reply.

After some little consultation among themselves, two or three of the strongest of the party came forward, and putting their shoulders to the back-door, they forced it in; and rushing up-stairs, headed by the intended husband—who had previously ascertained the room in which his intended wife slept—they entered Bessie's apartment; and rolling her up in the bedclothes, and wrapping a huge frieze cloak round her, they brought her away.

The poor girl, who heard everything that passed since the storming party surrounded the house, was so overcome with fright that she could make no resistance. She sobbed a little at first, but in such a low tone that she could scarcely be heard; and then knowing that nothing could turn these cruel men from their purpose, she remained silent altogether, contenting herself merely with hiding her bashful young face from the gaze of those who surrounded her.

She was quickly lifted into a cart, which was ready for the purpose, and away they drove as fast as they could, escorted by the storming-party on horse-back. On they went at a gallop. Not a syllable was spoken—they did not even whisper to one another—as those who had been guilty of such a gross outrage were hurrying to get away from the scene of their guilt with as much celerity as possible. Bessie, too, was as quiet as a mouse. Notwithstanding that she sighed occasionally, and exhibited other signs of suppressed feelings, she was calm and collected. On they sped, and on, until miles lay between the terrified daughter and her disconsolate parents.

And now the day was beginning to break. Bright beams of light shooting up from the east, and stretching across the cold morning sky, were fast dispelling the darkness. For some time previously the swain, who began to look upon his fair prisoner as now undoubtedly his, made up his mind that he ought to get a kiss—one at the very least—to console him for all he had gone through for her sake. If she would but allow him to take one—even ever, ever so small a one—he would feel well satisfied for the risk he ran of having a foreign body, like a charge of duck-shot, or a musket-bullet or two, impelled through the axis of his alimentary canal, by a discharge of a blunderbuss by her incensed father; or of being sent to rusticate among the flora at Botany Bay for the period of his natural life, by the judge of assize; or, worse still, of being battered into a pancake at the next fair, by her indignant cousins.

Bessie resisted with all her might.

"Yerra! wouldn't his own colleen do that for him, after all he went through for her?" But not a word did his own colleen permit to pass her lips. He must get it. "Bad luck to me!" says he, "if I'll be fit to look at for a month of Sundays, if I don't get—if it was only the least bit of a taste of a kiss. By gor! I'll die dead entirely, entirely, if I——" Forcing her hands and the hood of her cloak from her face, he looked; and, lo! it wasn't Bessie was there at all, *it was her mother!*

"Holy Mary!" yelled the distracted man, as with one bound he sprang out of the cart upon the road, "for blooming Bessie to be changed into—'twas the fairies did it!" "Holy Mary!" roared he again, as he caught sight of Bessie's mother, who now sat bolt upright in the cart, nightcap and all, and nodded familiarly at him—as much as to say, how are you, Johnny; then dragging his hat down on his forehead, he took to his heels, and made off across the country.

It appears that when the old lady heard the stormers crying out for her daughter, a thought flashed across her mind; and instantly going to Bessie's room, she made that young lady go up to her father's bed, whilst she took possession of her's—previously taking the precaution of hiding the candle least it should be lighted, and the imposture discovered.

When the escort saw their leader make off, they naturally thought they were pursued; and putting spurs to their chargers, they all endeavoured to save themselves by a precipitate flight. Meanwhile, materfamilias, seeing the coast was clear, leisurely turned the horse's head round, and steered for home; where she duly arrived, bringing the horse and cart with her, as trophies of her ingenuity, and the possession of which she retained unchallenged—the owner being afraid to demand them.

The unhappy lover was ashamed to show himself. He kept lurking about the neighbourhood for some time, and then reached Cork. From Cork he went to Liverpool; and from that city he set sail for America. And, we may safely assume, that much as he chafed under the bad treatment he received from Bessie and her mother, he kept his opinion of their conduct to himself; and that when he did make up his mind to take a colleen in the new world, he did not do things in the take-it-for-granted style he did in old Ireland.

CHAPTER XXI.

THE MAC CARTHY DUVES—THE BANDON YEOMANRY—THE HAZLITTS—OUR VOLUN-
TEERS AT BALLINCOLLIG—TRADE COMBINATIONS PREVALENT—STRIKES FLOOD—
THE COAL-YARD—ANECDOTES.

TWO of the Mac Carthy Duves (pronounced *Dhooves*) were hanged, in the April of this year, on the Gallows Hill in Bandon. There were three brothers, all of whom were leaders in the famous band which bore their name. Originally they were labourers to a farmer at Rockfort, near Innoshannon, where they were born, and where they lived until their numerous crimes left them no house and scarce a resting-place to hide in. The three were noted for their uncommon daring and effrontery; but the worst of the entire lot, as well as the cleverest, was the notorious Donogh. We are told that he even outwitted a celebrated highwayman of his day, and that on his own especial territory—Kilworth Mountain. It is related that a gentleman in this neighbourhood was robbed by the well-known desperado on his return with the rents of some property of his in that district. Being naturally afraid to venture there again, unless under the protection of a sufficiently strong escort— an opportunity which seldom presented itself—he was obliged to trust to the chapter of accidents, and let the matter lie. Some short time before this, he had the good fortune to do good service to the famous Donogh; but whether, by so doing, he conferred a favour upon society, or perpetrated a gross injustice upon it, is a subject we will not stop to discuss. One thing, however, is certain, that, were it not for his zealous interference, it would have been literally all up with Donogh. Being anxious to do something for so great a personal favour, Donogh went to him, and volunteered not only to go down single-handed, but to bring up every stiver of the money safe and sound. The gentleman, nothing loth, boldly entrusted him, and gave him a letter to his agent; and, early upon the next morning, Donogh was mounted and far upon the road to Kilworth. He had not travelled over more than half of that bleak moor, when a well mounted man overtook him, and, with a "God save you!" reined in his horse to the jog-trot pace of Duve. After a few civil remarks, the stranger inquired what brought him to such a dreary place, surmising that it must be something very important. Donogh unhesitatingly told the truth—that he was sent for a considerable sum of money, adding that he expected to be back there by the day after the morrow. Soon after, his new acquaintance struck into a by-path, giving Donogh a half-crown piece to drink his health, and warning him, above all things, to take care of his money.

In due time, our traveller arrived at his destination, presented his letter, got the money, and, having rested both himself and his horse, again started off on his way home. Having arrived in Kilworth, he was soon joined by his former companion, who, after bidding him the top of the morning, asked if he got the money. Duve mildly replied in the affirmative.

"Come then," said he, "out with every blessed cross of it this minute!" roaring into his astonished ears the name of the dreaded freebooter.

The poor country boy was all aghast. He began to clasp his hands, and to cry, and he implored the " dacent gintleman" not to take his money away; but the highwayman was inexorable—his heart could not be softened. He swore out a tremendous oath, and the terrified pursebearer dropped the money-bag.

"Wisha, sir!" said he after a pause, getting off his horse, and brightening up as if a thought suddenly struck him, " I wish you'd drive a bullet through my hat," at the same time putting his *caubeen* upon the ground, "in order to make the master think I made a terrible hard fight of it entirely."

Donogh's late opponent was highly amused at the design; and, having procured what he wanted, readily consented to oblige the poor simpleton; and, dismounting, speedily accomplished the desired object.

"Drive another through this, yer honour," says Duve, holding out the cape of his coat. Again he complied. " And another through this," holding up one of his ample skirts.

"Oh! I have fired off both my pistols," quoth he, walking towards his horse, which had strayed away a little distance in quest of a mouthful of fresh grass.

Quick as lightning, Donogh rushed between them, and, presenting a large horse-pistol at his head, swore by the —— that, if he did not deliver up every mortal rap in his possession, he would blow him to pieces that very instant, shouting out in a voice of thunder, "For here's the master of your master! here's Donogh Duve!"

The other had often heard of Duve before; and knowing there would be no use in trifling with such a powerful opponent, who, in addition to being armed, was physically his superior, he therefore acted like any sensible man would have done under the circumstances, and disgorged to order. He first laid down his pistols, then his ball-cartridge, Donogh's money-bag, and his own purse containing fourteen guineas; next followed three watches and a few trinkets. Having turned his pockets inside out, and rid himself of everything worth taking, he was ordered to march off some paces to the rear, and turn his back. In the interim, Duve, who had safely secured all the valuables, coolly mounted Brennan's charger; then riding up to him, and stooping over the pommel of the saddle, he told his outwitted antagonist in a confidential whisper, that whenever he met a poor simpleton again, not to forget Donogh Duve.

The immediate cause of the arrest of the Duves, and their subsequent execution, was an attack upon the house of a man named Holland, who lived as dairyman and caretaker to Mr. Alcock, of Roughgrove, and resided in the old residence, which, at that time, occupied the present site of Roughgrove House.

Holland had returned from Cork late in the evening, after disposing of some butter, and brought with him, amongst other things, a heavy iron bar—in those days used for shoeing block-wheels. About one in the morning, he was awoke out of a sound sleep by the smashing in of the front door; and, before he could well arouse his dormant senses and seize on the iron bar just mentioned, two of the daring burglars rushed up stairs. The staircase was very narrow, and led from the landing into his room by a very sharp angle. It was mainly owing to this, and the circumstance that only one person could pass up at the time, that rendered Holland's position so advantageous. The first to come up was a man named McCarthy, from the neighbouring townland of Shinagh, and

behind him was Daniel Duve with a loaded blunderbuss. Holland was
at the top of the stairs, and threatened Mac Carthy if he dared to
approach another inch. The latter's reply was a bound forward, and,
with one blow, Holland struck him dead. He then rushed down, holding the dead man in his arms, and pressing him upon Duve, who was
thus forced to retreat foot by foot without being able to get a shot at
his opponent. When he had reached the last step of the stairs, Holland,
putting forth all his strength, made a violent rush at him, still pushing
on the corpse. He upset Duve, and instantly throwing himself upon
him, after a fierce struggle, he tore the blunderbuss from his grasp.
Duve again seized it, and, after a fight still more fierce and prolonged,
Holland was again victorious, Meanwhile, some of the gang, who had
been left outside to watch, came in, and furtively carried away Mac
Carthy's body. Upon their return, they found that not only was Dan
a prisoner, but that his powerful antagonist had received assistance.
Again they retreated, but this time with the loss of another of their
number—the second brother, Michael Duve. He was bravely seized
upon by the servant-girl, and held until her master and the servant-boy
came to her help. They then secured their prisoners by spancelling
their arms and legs, and twisting ropes about them in such a way,
that for them to effect their liberation was impossible. Then barricading the doors and windows as well as circumstances would admit, with
beating hearts they anxiously awaited the morning dawn. So cautious
did they deem it necessary to be, that they were afraid to light a splinter
of bog-wood, or even to blow a sod of turf, lest the light would betray
them. Nay, they did not venture to speak even in a whisper, in dread
lest the voice should become a guide to the armed gang assembled outside, and a fatal discharge from a blunderbuss terminate all further
solicitude. Several times stones were thrown at the doors and windows,
sometimes at a distance, but at other times so close that it was evident
there were but a few feet between the assailants and Holland and his
trembling companions. On one occasion (and it was the only one), a
fellow attempted to climb in through a window ; but here the iron bar
again came into requisition, and it descended with such force within an
inch of the intruder's skull, that he instantly jumped to the ground,
and was not imprudent enough to repeat the experiment. All this time,
the Duves were singing away merrily, probably to let their friends outside know their exact position. These evidently understood them, and,

by whistling and coughing, endeavoured to keep them in courage. Time rolled heavily away, every minute they thought now was as long as an hour at another time. "Will it ever be day?" thought Holland, as he anxiously peered through the diamond-paned window-glass, and looked out upon the black massed clouds that lay before him. Again he looked out, and again; but the prospect was as uncheering and the darkness as impenetrable as ever. At length, a pale blue flash flared in the eastern sky. The cock gave out a lusty crow. Again Holland looked out, and, lo! the morrow had come. Shortly after, a neighbouring farmer knocked at the door, and asked if any thing was wrong, stating that his dogs were barking all through the night, and he thought there must be mischief somewhere. He was told in a few words, and directed to wake up the neighbours. These soon began to drop in, armed with pikes, reaping-hooks, and whatever offensive weapons they could conveniently lay hands on. Finding that all hopes of a rescue were now at an end, Michael Duve burst into fits of crying, and asked God to forgive him for his numerous offences; but Dan preserved a sulky silence, broken but once, when calling to one of those that surrounded him. He addressed him by his Christian name, and asked for a *shough* of the pipe—a request that was instantly complied with. In a few hours later, a sergeant's guard arrived; and the Duves, being delivered up to them, they were handcuffed, and marched into Bandon.

Meanwhile, news of the capture of the famous Duves had spread far and near. It ran from ploughland to ploughland, from parish to parish. The peasantry of one district no sooner told it to those of another, than, throwing down their mattocks and grephanes, they flocked in crowds to Bandon. The whole flat of Barry's Walk, extending from where the Convent of the Order of the Presentation now stands, a full mile and a half along the old Macroom Road, was black with people; but there was one place in that swaying mass of humanity where the thick crowd was thickest, and where the murmur of voices was the loudest. In the middle of this thick crowd, a small space was with difficulty preserved; and in the centre of this was a little old woman, with a white kerchief tied round her head, and her figure enveloped in a frieze cloak of ample dimensions. This little old woman was the mother of the Duves, and, when the unfortunate men arrived before where she was standing, she went upon her knees to give her boys her blessing; but tho salutation she received was a terrible one.

" Oh, damn you ! you old ——— !" cried Dan, " it was you were the cause of all !"*

At the ensuing Spring Assizes they were both tried, as was also their eldest brother, Donogh, who had been arrested in a house on the lands of Geara, in the parish of Kilmeen, to which place he and some others had forcibly carried off a young woman named Taylor, with the intention of marrying her to one of his comrades.

The Rev. Emanuel Moore, having heard of the outrage, collected some of his neighbours, and, accompanied by his brothers, followed in hot pursuit, and came up with them in the house just mentioned. Having knocked several times at the door without receiving any answer, they were preparing to burst it in, when it was at length partially opened by an old woman, who, thrusting out her head, asked what they did want.   They soon told her; but she stoutly denied that there was any one within.   This, however, did not satisfy Mr. Moore. He resolved to judge for himself, and announced his intention of making a search.   Accordingly, pushing past the old woman, he gained admittance; but, finding the inside was all in darkness, he groped his way to the fire-place, and taking up a sod of turf, he began to blow it in order to procure a light.

Duve, who had been in the loft overhead, and who was an anxious listener to all that had passed, had previously descended a few steps of the stairs, where he sat down, and quietly awaited the turn of events; but finding that the place was about being searched, and that he must necessarily be made a prisoner, with a poor chance of escaping the halter, or fight his way through his assailants, boldly resolved on the latter.

He afterwards declared he had no intention that time of shedding blood; his object being to escape, and to use his arms only for that purpose if necessary; but, when the glowing turf-sod revealed the features of his untiring foe, he could not resist the tempting opportunity.   He raised his blunderbuss to his shoulder, took deliberate aim, and Mr. Moore fell mortally wounded upon the hearthstone; then, jumping down, he daringly rushed for the door; but here he was met by the guard outside, and, after a desperate resistance, he was finally disarmed and secured.

---

* It is stated, that when her sons were children, one of them stole a halfpennyworth of brogue-nails, which he brought to his mother; and she, to encourage him, gave him a penny, and sent him back for more.

For this murder he was arraigned; but the judge directed the jury to acquit him, it being found that Mr. Moore had no warrant for his arrest. He was, however, immediately put upon his trial for having stolen the blunderbuss with which he committed the fatal deed; and, this being satisfactorily proved, he was found guilty of the felony, and sentenced to death, as were also his two brothers, who had been convicted of the burglary at Roughgrove.

It was ordered, in addition, that the executions should take place in the towns nearest to where the offences had been committed. Accordingly, when the three unfortunate men arrived in Bandon, Michael and Dan were detained there; but Donogh was sent on strongly escorted to Clonakilty. When the escort arrived at a cross-road adjoining that town, then and still known as Fac's Bridge, they found that every preparation had been made by the local authorities for carrying out the dread sentence of the law, and also that numbers of persons from the country as well as from the town had assembled to feast their eyes upon one of the most notorious criminals of the day, and to see if that reckless daring which tracked his career through this world would cower as he approached the next. He soon took his place on the drop; the rope was adjusted; and, after nodding and smiling to some of his old friends whom he recognized in the crowd, the bolt was about being drawn, when he sought, as a last request, to be allowed to say a few words. This was assented to; and, stepping a pace or two to the front, "Good people," said he, with a comic expression of countenance, which provoked roars of merriment from those who had come to see him die, "all I have to say is, that the best thing for you to light a pipe with is the faded stalk of a potato!" Then, turning with the same humorous leer to the executioner, he told him to go on.

This apparent disregard for his impending doom might in some measure be accounted for by the fact that he wore an iron collar round his neck, with strong projecting hooks; so that when the drop would fall, the rope would glide up, and, being caught by them, would be prevented from pressing fatally on the jugular—a contrivance that was made for him by a smith named Lane, from Ballinacurra, in this neighbourhood. But this did not avail him; for Hastings Moore—a brother of the murdered man, and one of those who assisted in his capture at Geara—was watching his every move from the foot of the scaffold, and perceiving that his neckerchief was unusually large, or, as some assert, having received private information; he ordered the hangman to lay bare his neck; and, lo! the imposture was discovered. The collar was speedily removed. Again the rope was adjusted. And, casting a vengeful glance at his insatiable enemy, "O Moore!" quoth the wretched man, "may the curse of the unfortunate and the worst of bad luck attend ye, and all belonging to yees, for ever and ever!" And, with those direful maledictions upon his lips, he passed into eternity.

His two brothers, Michael and Dan, as we have said, were detained in Bandon; and when the time appointed for their execution drew near, endless droves of the country people—many of whom were on foot all the previous night—kept streaming in from every village and cabin for miles around. Each successive arrival adding itself to the already swollen mass, soon filled up the area in front of the guard-house in which the condemned lay, and, flowing over, occupied every thorough-fare and passage in the neighbourhood. The houses at the opposite side, and those from which even a distant view could be obtained, had their doors, windows, and very chimney-tops alive with the townspeople, all burning with the same consuming curiosity which, at an early hour on that morning, drew the peasantry in thousands from their beds.

The huge mob waited and waited noiselessly. There was scarce a whisper to disturb the monotony of that gigantic silence. At length, the large hand of the clock, which had been tediously toiling round and round the big black dial-plate, approached the appointed hour. A body of foot, who had taken up their position close to the prison-windows, where they grounded arms and stood at ease, were now ordered, "Attention!" and "Fix bayonets!" The dragoons, who sat listlessly upon their horses, rode sharply to the front; then, drawing swords, they wheeled to the right, and halted in rear of the infantry. The excitement became vehement. The enormous crowd, waving to and fro, carried people by hundreds off their feet. Many were in danger of their lives; and several received injuries so serious, that they carried the marks of them to their graves. But, nevertheless, every eye was still fixed upon the doorway from whence the Duves were to come forth.

They had not long to wait. In a few minutes, the two miserable men, heavily ironed and handcuffed to each other, were led out and marched into the centre of the escort. Their appearance was the signal for a tremendous shout, which was caught up and echoed and re-echoed even by those who were so far distant as to be scarcely able to distinguish

29—2

the glittering accoutrements of the soldiery. All through the streets, and up to Gallows Hill, the shouting continued; the hoarse roar of voices rolled from one end of that vast assemblage to the other.

It could not have been a shout of sympathy, for no honest men could sympathize with those whose hearts were hardened, and whose hands were stained with crime; nor could it have been one of exultation, for how could thousands exult over the choking of two wretched beings? No: it was an outburst of a feeling generated by circumstances, and not an impulse of nature. It forbade them setting the captives at liberty; for they shuddered at the thought of their being again free. It showed them the expediency of punishing by death those who had well deserved their doom; but yet those Duves had for years despised the laws and derided the authorities—hence the feeling which lifted Mick into a brave man and Dan into a hero.

The preparations for the last scene were simple, and were soon completed. It was then inquired of them if they wished to say anything. To this, Mick answered that he could not deny the justice of his sentence; and, after some few remarks to the same purpose, he concluded by imploring the prayers of all those present in behalf of his soul. But when Dan, who was scarcely less criminal than his brother Donogh, was asked what he had to say, "Och! the divil a bit!" he replied, " only I wish to J—— the job was over, as I don't want to be standing here in the cowld!"

After hanging a considerable time, the bodies were cut down, and stretched upon the ground. A few scores of the curious still hovered about the spot. As time passed on, those thinned to units; and in a few hours, of that immense concourse which deafened the overhanging skies with their cheers, and thronged in multitudes around their scaffolds, there was not even one left to scatter a handful of straw over their corpses, or even to shade their livid faces from the light. The evening closed in, and there was no one would own them. At last, Mr. George Kingston, who was the owner of a timber-yard in the vicinity, and who had often good reason to complain of the frequent robberies committed on his premises after nightfall, had them removed, and buried within his concerns; trusting that even in death their very ashes would prove a safeguard against the ill-disposed. The timber-yard is now the site of that agreeable suburban retreat known as Kingston's Buildings, and which upon two sides enclose an ornamental shrubbery, in the western portion of which, and within a few feet of where groups of little children are continually engaged in play, repose the peaceful dust of the once notorious and dreaded Duves.

1775. The corporation being anxious to encourage an efficient schoolmaster to settle in the town in place of the Rev. George Wood, who was unable to perform the duties of principal, owing to the bad state of his health, granted the sum of twenty pounds annually, to be paid to the new head-master, "over and above the sum appointed by the late Earl of Cork. In consideration, said master shall instruct four boys appointed by the provost and burgesses of said corporation."

The first Earl of Cork, who died at Youghal in 1643, provided for the erection of a free school in Bandon, and then bequeathed the sum of twenty pounds annually towards the payment of the master; which sum was doubled in 1812, by the Duke of Devonshire.

The first schoolmaster, about whom we have been enabled to collect any particulars, was the Rev. Thomas Mills—Mills who obtained deacon's orders in Kilbrogan Church, in March, 1700, obtained a sizarship in Trinity College, Dublin, in 1694. He remained head-master until his death, in 1720. He was succeeded by the Rev. John Fryer, who was licensed to the curacy of Ballymodan in 1720, previous to which he was *hypodidasculus* of Bandon school, on the nomination of Mills. The Rev. George Wood, who was head-master in 1775, and who, as we have above stated, was obliged to resign owing to his infirmities, was ordained deacon in 1742; in which year he probably replaced Fryer. In 1761 Wood was curate of Kilbrogan; and in 1764 he obtained the rectory of Garryroe, upon the death of the Rev. William Meade. In 1748 he married Jane Beamish, of Kilmalooda. He died in 1792.*

---

* His eldest son, Thomas, inherited most of his effects. He had also a son, George [whose son, George, an officer in the 82nd Regiment, was the author of *A Subaltern Officer*], and two daughters—Mary, married to John Teulon, and Elizabeth, married to James White.

John Teulon had by his wife:—John, of whom presently; Charles, lieutenant-colonel 28th Regiment, fought at the Peninsula and at Waterloo, where his regiment suffered severely; Peter, lieutenant-colonel 12th Madras Native Infantry, was commandant at Delhi; George, lieutenant-colonel her Majesty's 35th Regiment; Thomas, A.B., Dublin, died in France; Lewis, died young; Richard, M.D.; Maria, married John Beamish, M.D.; Frances, died unmarried.

John married Catherine Morris, daughter of George Beamish, of Clohine, and had issue:—George B. Teulon, J.P.; Charles Peter, B.L.; Thomas, major 35th Regiment; Catherine Maria.

Pierre Teulon—progenitor of this branch—fled to England upon the revocation of the Edict of Nantes, accompanied by his brother, Antoine (ancestor of Seymour Teulon, of Tenchley Park, Surrey). Their elder brother remained behind, and inherited the family property at Mount-Pelier, Languedoc, and from him is descended

The Rev. Mark West obtained the head-mastership upon Wood's resignation. West was a scholar of Trinity College, Dublin, in 1770. In 1774 he was licensed to the curacy of Desertmore, Knockavilly, and Brinny, for performing the duties of which he received fifty pounds per annum. In 1778 he was curate of Ballymodan; and from 1782, until his death in 1787, he was prebendary of Currograngemore.

Mr. St. Leger Chinnery succeeded West; and upon his death, in 1786, Mr. Michael Kiely succeeded.

The Rev. William Sullivan obtained the mastership in 1808, upon the death of Kiely. Mr. Sullivan obtained deacon's orders in 1798. From 1818 to 1836 he was prebendary of Templebryan; and from 1825 to 1836 (when he died) he was rector of Kilnagross.

· The Rev. Dr. John Brown succeeded Sullivan in the spring of 1826. He obtained first scholarship in 1819, and shortly after was admitted to deacon's orders. He resigned in 1842, on being appointed principal of Kilkenny College, and was succeeded by his brother, Dr. Stephen Browne. Dr. Stephen obtained the second scholarship in 1826, Bishop Law's mathematical premium in 1830, and honours in each of his undergraduate years.

1776. William Brabazon Ponsonby, and Lodge Morris, elected to represented Bandon in the new Parliament.

1777. The Bandon Boyne (corps of yeomanry), which consisted of but one company, was enrolled. Their uniform was a blue coat, edged with buff, yellow buttons, buff waistcoat and small clothes, and gold epaulets. In 1782, amongst other officers, were ensigns John Laone and —— Wright, surgeon Richard Laone, and secretary Bernard Blake.

1778. The Bandon cavalry were enrolled. They wore a dark olive-green jacket, half lapelled, cuffs and collar of crimson velvet, and epaulets of silver; furniture—white cloth, hosing, and holster-caps, embroidered; device—"B. C.," harp and crown. The officers in 1782 were:—

Colonel	. . . . . .	Sampson Stawell.
Major	. . . . . .	John Moore Travers.

Pierre Emil Teulon, president of Ministers under the late King Louis Phillipe. Pierre, who married Miss Jacobs (a Dutch lady), came to this country from England, and settled in Cork. He had two sons—John and Peter. John married Sarah Bruce, of this county; by whom he had John, who married Mary Wood, as mentioned previously.

Captains }	. . . . .	Robert Waterhouse.
		Simon T. Davies.
Cornet	. . . . .	Charles Bernard.
Chaplain .	. . . .	Rev. Charles Hewitt.

The Bandon Independents were also enrolled this year. Their strength was the same as that of the Boyne—one company. Their uniform consisted of a scarlet coat faced with black, yellow buttons, and gold epaulets. In 1782 the officers were :—

Colonel	. . . . . .	Francis Bernard.
Captain	. . . . .	Robert Sealy.
Lieutenant	. . . .	Thomas Child.
Ensign	. . . . .	John Travers.
Adjutant	. . . . .	George Kingston.
Surgeon	. . . . .	Richard Laone.
Secretary	. . . .	Richard Needham.

The Rev. Mr. Hazlitt was Presbyterian minister at Bandon for some years.

" His theological views," says a writer, " were those of that kind which is called the English Puritan school. Being bound to no creed, they used the Scriptures with great freedom ; and as many of that school became first indifferent to some popular theological opinions, and finally Unitarians, so Mr. Hazlitt was more anxious about moral than doctrinal teachings."

The same authority also furnishes us with some of the pranks played off by some of the military officers stationed here at this time, from which we extract the following :—

" Amongst the English visitants who were sent to this country to irritate it by bad conduct, was a regiment of cavalry, the officers of which were a set of giddy coxcombs, who amused themselves by mischievously annoying the mere Irish, and perhaps with as cruel an ignorance, but as little individual malice, as schoolboys. Our aborigines wore large cloth cloaks with hoods to them. The women, coming into Bandon from the neighbourhood to buy milk, had, on their way to the milk-market, to pass the mess-room, where the officers idled some of their time. The mess-room was at the White Hart Inn, in the centre of the town, and conveniently placed for a war upon the women natives. They had in the room a sufficient store of sods of turf; and the sport was to throw at each woman as she passed by. The cream of the joke was, if the earthen jug or pitcher fell broken on the street, and the poor woman's purchase of milk ran about, the military hero got great applause for his good aim, and his merit was deemed as high as what he won at 'blind hookey.' This excitement, however, lost novelty and interest, and the military sent over to reconcile the Irishry discovered one of higher zest. Bandon did not then enjoy public shedded-in meat-markets; and the meat was exposed for sale in the streets, and on the 'big bridge.' The sport-seeking heroes noticed this facility for fun; and, seeing a poor Papist eyeing the beef on a Friday or a fast-day, they compelled him to turn up the knees of his breeches, kneel down on his knees in the street, and eat a bit of raw beef at the point, and from the point of the sword."

The house in which the Rev. Mr. Hazlitt lived was in Gallows-hill Street, near where the mill-stream crosses the roadway, and it adjoined the cross lane leading north to the Castle Road. Every trace of this house is now completely gone. Mr. Hazlitt had several sons, amongst whom were—Hazlitt, the biographer of the first Napoleon, and a celebrated critic; also John and William, his brothers, who became afterwards men of artistic and literary fame. John was a painter, and some of his works were highly approved of by connoisseurs. William was a writer of ability; and Hazlitt's *Round Table*—two duodecimoes of light but useful essays—read well even to those who love the masterly style of the *Spectator*. These two brothers—for the painter could handle the pen with the same facility as the brush—were active contributors to the *London Examiner* of their day; and it is stated that that publication was entirely indebted to the two Hazlitts for the high intellectual style and independent bearing which, at that time, rendered it so popular and attractive.

Mr. Hazlitt took a great interest in the war that was raging between England and her American colonies. He altogether sided with the latter, and he openly expressed his desire that they should succeed. This brought upon him the reproaches of his fellow-townsmen; and whenever they would see him in the streets, they used to cry out to beware of the black rebel.

To some of the members of his congregation, too, his advocacy of American notions was not agreeable. One Sunday morning he was more than usually vehement in advocating the right of our Transatlantic cousins to govern themselves, when up started one of his hearers, and hurriedly pulling his plug of tobacco out of his mouth—" I didn't come hear to listen to treason !" said he, addressing the preacher; then taking up his hat and cane, he indignantly walked out.

Hazlitt was succeeded by the Rev. Mr. King—a quaint and somewhat singular personage, but with a rich stratum of humour cropping out on the surface. We are told that, whilst staying with a friend (the late Richard Dowden Richard) at Sunday's Well, in Cork, he pointed over to the imposing palatial residence of the Lord Bishop of Cork, Cloyne, and Ross. "Look, Richard," said he to him, "look at the fisherman's hut!" Mr. King was succeeded by the Rev. William Hunter, the clergyman now in charge. The congregation is not at present large, owing to the decadence of the woollen and linen manufacture, and the extensive emigration consequent thereon.*

1780. The woollen trade again revived, and flourished vigorously for about thirty years, during which time there was a very extensive business carried on, and an immensity of employment afforded. Some idea of its extent may be surmised from the fact that, at this period, there were no less than eighteen hundred looms employed in one department of the trade alone. The principal manufacturers and exporters were the Messrs. Dowden, Wheeler, Biggs, Quinlan, Popham, and Sealy.† A considerable portion of the product of the Bandon looms was disposed of in Dublin, in Limerick, and even as near home as Cork.

In the latter city, the principal agent was an old Puritanical oddity, that kept a shop near the Exchange, and was familiarly known as "Ould Dowden." So strict was this old gentleman in his habits, and so cautious in his replies to the various interrogatories put to him during the course of a long business-life, that he was scarcely ever known to venture out into the world of words beyond yea or nay. He attended his place of worship with scrupulous punctuality; and whether he was in good health, or on the point of death, or whether the sun was shining, or whether it was pouring "cats and dogs," it made no difference with "Ould Dowden"—he was the first man to enter the Prince's Street Presbyterian meeting-house, and the last to leave it. From all these circumstances put together, it was thought that, if he ever did curse anybody, the execrated party must necessarily wither up like a blasted potato-stalk; so that "the curse of ould Dowden down atop of ye!" became an anathema by no means calculated to add to the personal comfort of the anathematized.

* The old Bible, published in 1610 by Robert Barker, of London, and used in "the meeting-house" for over a century and a quarter, was presented, in 1695, to the congregation of English Presbyterians—Puritans—worshipping there, by Mrs. Anne Jackson, with the following inscription :—"This Bible was given by Mrs. Anne Jackson to the church of Christ gathered in and about Bandon, and soe to continue by succession." It is probable that Mrs. Jackson was the wife of James Jackson, who was provost in 1702.

† There was an old ballad, very popular at this time, beginning with :—
"The Dowdens, and Wheelers, and Pophams, a score,
All weavers and dyers—a terrible bore."

The volunteers of this county were reviewed at Ballincollig by the Earl of Charlemont. They formed a select and well disciplined body, amounting to thirty-five thousand men. The Bandon companies mustered strong on the occasion,* and were mainly composed of very tall and heavy men; the man on the extreme right of the first rank being close on six feet five inches in height, and in weight exceeding twenty stone. Their splendid appearance, and the precision with which they executed the various military manœuvres, drew strong expressions of admiration from the general officers present. They also earned the approbation of an old apple-woman—a native of the town—who could not restrain her exultation. "Yerra, well done entirely," said she, "my fine black Protestants from Bandon!" The Bandonians were amongst the first to arrive on the field, and marched to their position to a tune not likely to infuse much military ardour into their ranks, the drums and fifes playing, "Oh! what a Rasping Beau your Daddy was!"

Although the Bandonians, collectively, were thought highly of, yet there was among them a corps which did not share in the fair fame of the others. Amongst them was a body known as the Bandon Independents. Most of the men of this force were said to be leavened with the principles which became notorious the year after in the volunteers of 1782. Their disapproval of the then existing state of things was referred to in a ballad as follows:—

1781.

---

* This event was celebrated in a song, a few verses of which we subjoin:—

> " And have you seen the grand review ?
> And have you seen the grand review ?
> And have you seen the grand review ?
>   On Ballincollig's plains ?
>
> " And have you seen the Boyne True Blue ?
> And have you seen the Boyne True Blue ?
> And have you seen the Boyne True Blue —
>   The Bandon Volunteers ?
>
> " And every man stood six feet two,
> And every man stood six feet two,
> And every man stood six feet two—
>   The Bandon Fusiliers.
>
> " Hearts of oak, and clad in blue
> Faced with orange, were the Boyne so true ;
> Oh ! such Britons no one ever knew
>   As the real True Blues of Bandon !
>
> " And, when rebellion rose in the land,
> England always could command
> The loyal and devoted band
>   That lived in the town of Bandon."

" The Bandon Independents, too,
  'Dependents, too, 'dependents, too ;
The Bandon Independents, too,
      Were all reviewed that day.

" Says the general to his aide-de-camp :—
  ' Pray, Colonel Barry, send them home ;
  They don't deserve a fife or drum !
Let pipes before them play,
      Let pipes before them play !' "

1783.   Francis Bernard, of Castle Bernard, (subsequently Earl of Bandon) and Lodge Morris, elected to represent Bandon.

1784.   The old Bandon Quarter Sessions book contains various entries which show how our forefathers encouraged trade in those days. Amongst others, is a charge preferred against Cornelius Mahony, " that he, on the 18th of December, did, in the suburbs of Bandon, buy two hundred weight of butter, valued three pounds, which was designed for the markets of Bandon ; and being market-day, did forestall and buy up same."

Manure does not appear to be worth much at this period, as appears by another entry under date March 22nd, 1785 ; which states that Darby Kealeher and several others, were indicted for going upon the lands of Ballylanglay, and carting and carrying away one hundred and fifty loads of dung, valued in 12s. 6d. [a penny a load], the goods of Charles Martin.

It contains also a copy of an indictment against Thomas Starkey, William Starkey, and another, for contemptuously entering the parish church of Desertserges, and maliciously disquieting and disturbing the congregation during divine service ; and that they did, in addition, assault William Bottimore, the clerk.

We are unable to say what could have induced the Starkeys to enter a place of worship during divine service, and conduct themselves as is represented. Perhaps they were some of those old-fashioned Bandonians who would become as wicked, on being shown a table-cover with a cross on it, as a bull would on being shown a piece of red cloth. We suspect there must have been something atrocious in their eyes, however, or they would never have acted so contemptuously as they did. When a man shows his contempt, it must be for something he contemns. It may have been that the rector got suddenly infected with a rage for candlesticks and holy-water, or he may have propounded doctrines from

the pulpit to which their Puritan ears were unaccustomed. Be that as
it may, their conduct was unpardonable. If they did not like the proceedings in Desert Church, they should not have gone there. And what
right had they to maltreat poor dearly-beloved Roger, for doing, perhaps,
only what he was ordered?

1785.   A great row happened this year. It seems that one of
the 5th Dragoons, passing over the bridge, met a countryman,
and taking a fancy to his stick, tried to wrest it from him; and would
probably have succeeded, had not the countryman's companion come
to his assistance, and knocked the soldier down. A well-known
mischief-maker named Joan Cunningham, who happened to be present,
immediately ran off, and told some of the troopers, whom she met in
Irishtown, what had occurred. These instantly hastened to their comrade's help. The townspeople sided with the countryman, and a regular
battle took place. In a short time, all the troops in the barracks turned
out, armed with swords, and attacked indiscriminately every civilian;
but the country people were the especial objects of their vengeance.
Of these, forty-two were wounded, several severely injured, and two
killed.

The Rev. Robert Swindells—a celebrated Wesleyan minister—visited
Bandon. He was about preaching in the open piece of ground in front
of the present Saving's Bank, when down came some of the officers of
the gallant 5th Dragoons, bringing with them several trumpeters for
the purpose of preventing his being heard. Swindells well knew their
object, and, by a humourous contrivance, turned the laugh completely
against them. He commenced the service by giving out the well-known
Wesleyan hymn, "Blow ye the trumpets! blow!" He only gave
out the first line, and then stopped. Upon this the trumpeters blew
away, much to the amusement of the congregation, and the confusion
of the officers, who felt quite disconcerted to find that their men should
take such an instrumental and prominent part in the service, and that,
too, at the bidding of the very man whom they had come to blow down.
So indignant were they at being out-generalled by the simple Wesleyan,
that they ordered their men back instantly to barracks; and, slipping
away one by one, they left Mr. Swindells in undisputed possession of
the field.

1786.   Unlawful assemblies and trade combinations were rife at this
period. Indeed so much so, that our corporation felt it their

duty to express themselves strongly on these matters, as appears by a resolution dated June 7th, in this year; in which they state that they will give every assistance in their power to suppress all unlawful assemblies and combinations, and bring the authors and all persons in any way concerned therein, or in aiding or abetting the same, to justice.

The audacity of some of those who took part in those unlawful assemblies may be surmised from the circumstance that, upon one occasion, our chief magistrate was assaulted in the execution of his duty by a leader among them—one John·Davis—"in contempt of the law and in open defiance thereof;" and, as if "that most daring outrage and insult" was not enough to canonize Davis in the eyes of the mob, he absolutely had the effrontery to rush on the provost's rod, and break it in two. So indignant were the respectable townspeople at this wanton injury and display of contempt for the authority of their chief magistrate, that they called a public meeting, and collected subscriptions for the purpose of having the offenders speedily brought to justice.

1787. John Wesley again visited Bandon, and remarked of some of the inhabitants, "that, though they were very well dressed, they were very badly conducted." ·Whilst preaching in the open air, in front of where the court house now stands, his old opponents, the trumpeters, made their appearance, and began to play away as usual. Wesley was an old tactician by this time, and quietly lay upon his oars until they were done. Again he endeavored to preach, and again they trumpeted away; but, getting weary of this perpetual blowing, they rested themselves, and Wesley, taking advantage of the intermission, was eagerly addressing an attentive audience, when up rode Colonel Walpole, shouting out to the trumpeters with the voice of a Stentor, "Blow! Blow! Blast and blow ye! why don't you blow?"

1789. On the 17th of January, there was a great flood known as "Strike's flood." A very heavy fall of rain began on the previous day, which continued incessantly throughout the night. The rain dissolved the snow which had covered the ground for several days, and the town was visited with an inundation which even exceeded that of "65," when old Bandon bridge was carried away. So high did the water rise, and with such rapidity, that many people could only escape out of their houses by breaking through the roofs. Some notion of its depth in the lower parts of the town may be conjectured from the measurement of the water at Weir Street, which at one time reached a height of four feet and a-half. It went away as suddenly as it came; and, however it may have damaged property, there was only one life lost—that of a blacksmith named Strike, whose forge was on the site occupied by the late Mr. William Hart's establishment.

The flood, having entered Strike's smithy, began rolling the movables to and fro; upon which some one jestingly remarked to him "to see to his anvil, as it was beginning to float!" Hearing this, he jumped off the hob, with the intention of shutting the door, and preventing its exit; but, by some mismanagement, instead of keeping within, he got outside, and having "a drop taken," he lost his footing and fell. At this time, there was no wall or fence of any kind where Burlington Quay now stands. It was an open space, with a slope continuous to the river. Poor Strike was swept down the declivity, until he was carried into the main channel; here the fierce waters hurried him along, and so rapid was their progress, that no trace of the body could afterwards be discovered.

The centenary anniversary. of the Black Monday insurrection was kept on the 25th of February as a great holiday. All the shops were closed; the bells rung out a merry peal, in commemoration of that great event; and the provost, free-burgesses, and common council, duly robed, attended divine service, accompanied by most of the inhabitants; after which a procession was formed, which walked through the streets, carrying the flags of the old Bandon militia, and other interesting relics of bygone days.

The first Methodist chapel was built in Bandon. It was erected on a plot of waste ground, in front of the church gate at Kilbrogan, and adjoining the present fish-market. Previous to this, the Wesleyans worshipped in the large room of a house which, with others, possessed the site now occupied by the bridewell. The chapel was opened on Thursday, the 3rd of May, by John Wesley, on which occasion he preached a very impressive sermon, from the text, "To the Jew first, and to the Gentile." Our informant—an old lady only a few years deceased, and to whose excellent memory we are indebted for many interesting facts contained in these pages—was present on the occasion, and assured us she was even then old enough to be on the look-out for a husband. She treasured up every minute particular connected with the interesting ceremony, and, after the lapse of seventy-two years, was able to describe the very dresses worn by many of those present on the occasion.* This was Mr. Wesley's last visit to Bandon. During this time, as well as on a previous occasion, he was the guest of the late Mr. Thomas Bennett, of Shannon Street; who used to relate, that upon Wesley's entering the parlour, Mungo, who had been *sunning* himself on the hearth-rug before the fire, got up and violently barked at the venerable apostle. The host was distracted, and seizing his gold-headed cane, made several ineffectual attempts to demolish the canine miscreant; but Wesley stopped him, and patting him familiarly on the shoulder, "Never mind, Tom," said he, "never mind! there is many a dog in the human family that barks, intent more on making a noise than on doing an injury."

1790.   At the new Parliament assembled in Dublin, B. Chinnery, Esq., was returned for Bandon.

1791.   Several of the flour-mills, both in town and country, were much injured this year by a large mob. This did not result from any scarcity or want of provisions, but from the fact of the bolting millers, as they were called, beginning now for the first time to buy up large quantities of wheat. The townspeople considered this an interference with their established usage, having up to this time been accustomed to buy their weekly supply of raw grain direct from the farmer in pecks, half-pecks, or bushels, according to their requirements. They used then to take it to the manor mill, where it was ground and prepared for consumption. The farmers, of course, were glad to meet with a purchaser who took their entire lot, and paid as much for it as they could get from the small buyer by retailing it. Consequently, they gave the former the preference. This stirred up the working-classes. They first attacked the mill belonging to Mr. Jacob Biggs; then they went to Kilbrittain, and attacked Mr. Stawell's; from thence they proceeded to Mr. Pratt's, of Shannon Vale; then to Balliniscarthy, and to several others.

---

* There is an old lady still alive, and living here, who received the sacrament no less than three times from the hands of John Wesley. The great age she must have now attained to will be evident to the reader, when we remind him that Wesley was born the year after the death of William the Third—that is one hundred and sixty years ago. But there is even here a more singular instance still of a long stretch into the past—our old and much-respected fellow-townsman, the Rev. T. Waugh, often conversed with one who was old enough to remember the siege of London-derry; and who used to relate, with all the freshness and vividness of a recent impression, many interesting facts connected with that ever-memorable struggle. We doubt if the whole world can furnish another instance of so close a connection between our day and any event so long since recorded in history.

1790.   April 19th—Lodge Morris, Esq., of the city of Dublin, and Broderick Chinnery, Esq., of Anne's Grove, elected to represent the town in Parliament.

1792.   On the 13th of December in this year the coal-yard for the benefit of the Bandon poor was established.

At an assembly of the provost and free-burgesses, &c., on December 13th, it was agreed to take into consideration the very high price of firing, and the distressed state of many of the poor inhabitants of Bandon and the suburbs thereof, on account of the scarcity of firing, which is likely to continue; and to consider the best means of keeping so necessary an article at moderate price.

"We, the provost and free-burgesses of said borough, having considered the same, do think that the only and best means of doing so, is by creating and establishing a coal-yard; and for that purpose do consult and agree to permit and suffer a sufficient part of Gallows Hill belonging to the provost and free-burgesses, and our successors for the time being, to be taken in, and enclose at such part of said Gallows Hill as the provost and any three or four burgesses of said borough shall think most convenient and proper for the purpose of erecting said coal-yard; and that the same, when erected, shall be under the management and direction of the provost and free-burgesses for the time being. And that the provost, from time to time, shall make such rules and regulations, and nominate and appoint such person or persons, as may be necessary to regulate and superintend the same; provided that at the making of such rules and regulations, no less than three of the free-burgesses shall be present with the provost, and shall consent thereto. And this we, the said provost and free-burgesses, do for the good of said borough; and do hereby give our consent and grant to, and ensure to and for their uses and purposes aforesaid, against us and our successors, provosts and free-burgesses of said borough, for ever. Witness our hands.

The provost and free-burgesses, pursuant to the above, have appointed Robert Travers, Esq., Thomas Biggs, Esq., Armiger Sealy, Esq., Francis Fielding, Richard Donovan, William Banfield, Thomas Weldon, James Sweeney, George Allman, gents., and John Campbell, Esq., to be overseers of the coal-yard, and to raise subscriptions for carrying the same into effect.

> SAMPSON JERVOIS.
> J. STAWELL.
> FRANCIS BERNARD.
> AUGUSTUS WARREN.
> THOMAS BIGGS.
> THOMAS BERNARD.
> SAMUEL BEAMISH.
> ROBERT TRAVERS."

1793.   On the 18th of November, Colonel Bernard (afterwards Earl of Bandon) obtained permission to raise and organize a body of infantry—the old force, enrolled in 1777 and 1778, having been disbanded for some years. This body was divided into three corps—the Boyne, the Union, and the True Blues.   The Boyne wore scarlet coats, faced with blue, and trimmed with gold lace, and upon their breastplates an equestrian statue of William the Third crossing the Boyne.   The Union, too, had scarlet coats; but their trimmings were laced with silver, and their facings were of black velvet.   The True Blues, also, had coats of scarlet, braided with silver lace.   Each company had three officers—a captain, lieutenant, and ensign.   Those of the Boyne were:—

Captain	Robert Travers.
Lieutenant	Joshua Cooper.
Ensign	John Laone.

THE UNION.

Captain	George Kingston.
Lieutenant	Isaac Dowden.
Ensign	Thomas Dowden.

THE TRUE BLUES.

Captain	Anthony Connell.
Lieutenant	William Jenkins.
Ensign	Allen Evanson.

These companies being entirely composed of volunteers, there was very little difference in the social scale between the officers and men; the full private of one year being a full-blown captain in the next, and *vice versa*.   The Boyne company, which was first called out in 1777, was a recognized embodiment of the Bandon volunteers, the original members of which we have seen taking part in the decisive engagement between William and James more than a century before.   As vacancies would occur in the ranks of those that smelt powder on that memorable occasion, they were filled up by the sons of those that were there; as time rolled past, by the grandsons; then great-grandsons; when these could not be had, then by undoubted sympathizers.   Thus was the body kept up; and, now that yeomanry corps and Irish volunteers are things of the past, yet this old fraternity still clings together, with its outward appearance, indeed, changed—an orange ribbon being substituted for a scarlet coat, and an orange lodge doing duty as a barrack-room; but the old spirit still lives.   There is the same uncompromising hatred of Pope and Popery that raged in the bosoms of those that plunged into the water with their brethren of Londonderry; and their repugnance for receiving brass money at its impressed value, and their horror of wooden shoes, are as great as ever.

There are a great many anecdotes still told here about the old Protestant inhabitants and their intense aversion to the Papacy. Many of these are very amusing, but others are positively ludicrous. We are told that the grandfather of the late Mr. ———— was a very well-intentioned, simple-minded man, who used to say his prayers not only every morning and evening, but even in the middle of the day, whenever he could conveniently do so. Yet it was notorious of him, that, in repeating the Lord's Prayer (which he never failed to do in his supplications), whenever he came to "As we forgive them that trespass against us," he would always put in as a contingency, " provided they weren't Papists ;" the simple-minded man telling the Great Creator that he would be afraid of his life to ask forgiveness for any of them, for if Sally (his wife) heard it, she'd throw boiling water on him.

Even yet, not many years since, one of those old-fashioned Protestants happened to be summoned to give evidence in a case at the Cork Assizes. He was cross-examined by the late Mr. George Bennett, who, amongst other questions, asked him what religion he was of.

"Yerra, Bill !" quoth the witness, turning to a friend who had accompanied him from Bandon, "does you hear that ?"

Bill did hear it, and indignantly told the learned counsel he must be a very ignorant fellow that would not know a Bandon Protestant by looking in his face.

Nothing daunted by Bill's rebuff, counsel persevered :—" How do you know you're a Protestant ?"

" How do I know I'm a Protestant ?" said he, repeating the words in a contemptuous and mimicking tone, " O holy Moses ! for a learned man to ask such a question as that !"

" Yes, sir : I again repeat it ;" but this time it was observed that the worthy advocate's voice betrayed no inconsiderable share of irritation, " How do you know you're a Protestant ?"

" 'Cause I ates mate of a Friday, and hates a Papist !" was the surly reply.

Bandon Protestantism was believed to be the *ne plus ultra* of orthodoxy; and even the Roman Catholic inhabitants, whether from hearing so much about it, or being brought so often in contact with its professors, we know not, but certain it is that they absolutely became tinged with it themselves, and used to institute favourable comparisons between themselves and the Protestants of the neighbouring towns. " A Bandon

Papist is better than either a Cork or a Kinsale Protestant any day !" is an aphorism, the truth of which is so self-evident, that it has never yet been called in question.

The Bandon militia, after a respite of nearly a century, were called to arms this year.

CHAPTER XXII.

THE BANDON MILITIA, OR SOUTH-CORK LIGHT INFANTRY.

THE history of the South Cork regiment is so entwined with the history of Bandon and the Bandonians during that eventful period which began with the furious outbreak on the 23rd of October, 1641, and terminated with the great revolution which displaced a dynasty which had occupied the throne of England for generations, and firmly established another in its stead, that it is no easy matter to separate them. The history of the South Cork is a portion of the military history of Bandon during the momentous interval mentioned previously ; and the military history of Bandon includes all that of the South Cork during the same time, in addition to many other heroic achievements of her chivalrous sons in this locality during the same period and anterior to it. To produce a history of the South Cork or Bandon militia, apart from the various social and political events from which it originated, and rendered its maintenance indispensable for the protection of live and property, saving those which are barely necessary—to show under what circumstances the regiment was called out, and why its services were no longer requisite —is the object of the following pages.

This distinguished corps was enrolled when the great rebellion had broken out, and when hundreds of settlers, outlaying in the surrounding country, had fled in consternation to Bandon—the only walled-in town to the west or to the south of Cork. At that unhappy period, the demon of destruction stalked unchecked through the land.* In every

---

* So little were the authorities prepared for this outbreak, that, when the rebellion broke out, there were in the entire province of Munster but four hundred foot and seventy-two horse,—namely, the lord-president's, Lord Baltinglasse's, Captain Phillip Venman's, and Captain Price's. The horse consisted of the lord-president's sixty arbineers, and Captain Peasley's twelve.

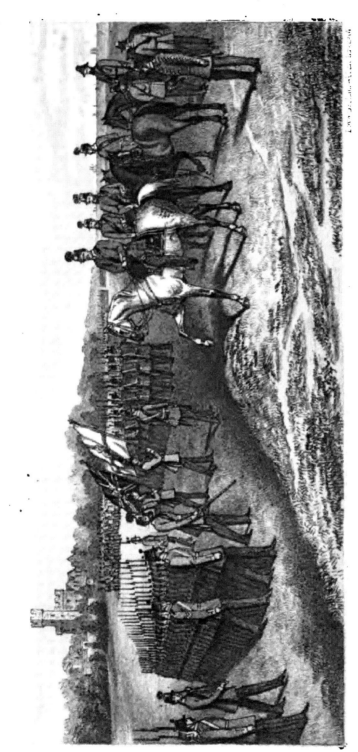

A MOVABLE AMBULANCE DEPOT OF THE HASPITAL CORPS ON A WINTER FIELD DAY AT ALDERSHOT.

direction one could see farm-houses in flames, cattle being driven away or wantonly destroyed, and murders committed in the broad glare of open day. The gates of the town were ever opening and shutting. At one time it was a terrified creature who knocked frantically for admission —at another time it was a band of refugees, bemoaning the loss of all the industry of their lives, who begged an entrance. Great numbers were soon collected; the women and children were helpless, but the men, used to labour, and accustomed to the use of arms, were eager to be led against those by whose hands they had been such terrible sufferers.

Efforts were quickly made to stay this onrush of incendiarism and slaughter. Volunteers were called for in Bandon, and two hundred men stepped into the ranks. But it was subsequently found, that with the work before them—now hourly accumulating—two hundred men were insufficient. More volunteers were called for; and before the first day of the summer of the succeeding year the Bandon militia mustered four hundred rank and file. There were many others, too, ready to obey the call; but as four hundred were the utmost the town could pay or equip, they were compelled to seek employment for their military services elsewhere.

This force was divided into four companies; each company consisting of a captain, lieutenant, ensign, and one hundred men. This was the first military body which the English colonists, who had come over in Elizabeth's reign, had raised upon a permanent footing,* westwards or southwards of the city of Cork, solely for the performance of active military duties; and its present representative is known amongst us as the South Cork Light Infantry Regiment of Militia. At various times it had various names. At first it was " The Valiant Bandonians ;" then " The Bandon Militia ;" then, towards the close of the great rebellion, when the fame of its exploits had spread far and wide, it was known as " The Fire-Eaters ;" then, as " The Bandon Militia " again, and by this name it appears towards the end of the seventeenth century and

---

* There was a town militia ever since the town was built, composed of horsemen and footmen, furnished by the military tenures. These were called out annually for inspection; and so numerous had they become nearly twenty years before, that, on the visit of the commissioners in 1622, there were paraded before them sixty-six horse and five hundred and sixty-four foot—exclusive of officers, sergeants, and drummers. Even many years before this, this young corps saw service; when in the reign of Elizabeth, under Captain Taffe, it lapped its first blood on the upper banks of the Bandon river, on which occasion the Pope's apostolic vicar and many of his followers were slain.

the beginning of the eighteenth, when it was under arms for several years.

From the date of its enrollment, up to A.D. 1854—a period of over two hundred years—it was the only force regimented in the west or south of the county, or that even marched outside of the county from all this country to take part in a siege, or in a battle, or join in any of the other sanguinary necessities of war. The other militia forces formerly existing in the south and west being merely isolated companies, raised under pressing circumstances by some gentleman of influence in his locality—such as Captain Freke, of Rathbarry, who raised a company of foot amongst the English residents of Ross and its neighbourhood in 1641, and again in 1666, when the French were daily expected to land in Kinsale or Bantry; also Colonel Townsend, who raised a similar force out of like material. Captain Gooking, also, and Colonel Arnopp, Colonel Gifford, and others. But these companies were merely for the defence of the localities in which they were raised, and they rarely marched any distance from home.

When the war broke out between England and France in 1793,[*] this old system was given up. The militia were no longer called upon to fight against their own countrymen in civil war, but against a foreign nation—one of whose numerous armies, filled with an enthusiastic soldiery, and led by able and experienced officers, was expected to make a descent upon our shores. It would, therefore, never do for a country gentleman, who knew no more about military tactics than the pack of hounds who yelped at his horse's heels, to be called upon to measure strategy with a Dumouriœ or a Kellerman; or could it be expected that gaping rustics, fresh from the potato-garden or the cow-stall, would stand fire with the French battalions, who, but a short time before, had forced back the Prussians at Valmy, and swept the Austrians from the heights of Jemappes.

---

[*] The militia regiments were for the first time numbered in 1793; on which occasion the South Cork bore the number thirty-two. Presuming that the city regiments, which are the oldest, were numbered first, one for each county, and omitting one which may have been suppressed for disloyalty or some other cause, this would make the South Cork the oldest county regiment in Ireland, and which it is believed to be—a belief based, to some extent, upon the fact that, when the rebellion broke out, the city regiments had enough, and more than enough, to do to defend themselves. But Bandon being unassailed, it was the first that was enabled to send out its large and well-organized force to assist its neighbours, and join in military enterprises far from home. The regiment at the other side of the county corresponding with ours—now known as the North Cork Rifles—on the numbering above mentioned, was numbered 34.

The authorities were aware of this; and when the new levies were raised, they were drilled, armed, and equipped as troops of the line. They were called out in 1793; and, as Bandon militia was too local a 'term to apply to a regiment now to be recruited in all the south and west of the county, and, moreover, as the test of the religious professions of the recruits—a test which does not appear to have been even once over-looked for a period of upwards of one hundred and fifty years—was now deemed unnecessary, it was considered judicious to begin a new era with a new name; hence the Bandon militia, which typified the old era, was replaced by the South Cork, which typifies the new.

We are enabled to give the names of many, if not all, of those who at any time held commissions in the regiment during the first eight years of its existence, as:—

Aderly, Captain Thomas,	Gwinn, Daniel,
Aderly, George,	Harrisson, Thomas,
Baldwin, Walter,	Holcombe, Captain William,
Bernard, Francis,	Hooper, Captain George,
Beamish, Thomas,	Jefford, Captain Sir John,
Beamish, Francis,	Kinalmeaky, Lord Lewis,
Bennett, Captain Thomas,	Langton, Lieutenant John,
Bennett, George,	Newce, or Nuce, Lieut. Edmund,
Berry, Lieutenant,	Nicholet, Charles,
Bird, Captain Walter,	Poole, Captain John,
Brayly, Captain John,	Shannon, Lord Francis,
Dunkin, Ensign Thomas,	Turner, Major Henry,
Dodgin, Ensign Thomas,	Wade, Bryan,
Dixon, James,	Watkins, Captain John,
Elwell, James,	Woodhouse, Captain Sir Michael,
Elwell, Joseph,	Woodroffe, Holmstead,
Fuller, Cornet William,	Woodroffe, Jerediah,
Fleming, John,	Woodroffe, Clement,
Gookin, Captain Robert,	Woodroffe, Samuel.*
Grove, Captain John,	

The names of all these are mentioned in some authentic records relating to the period beginning with the breaking out of the great rebellion, and ending with the passing of the Act of Settlement and Explanation, excepting that of Lieutenant Berry, who, probably for the active part he took in the revolt of the Bandonians from under the King's rule, had his services ignored.

---

* We have given the rank of the officers in the above list as we have found it. Although the rank of the others is not given, yet they were commissioned officers, and as such are on the roll of 1649 officers; and most of them were rewarded with grants of lands and sums of money for their military services. For particulars concerning officers, see end of this chapter.

A great many had lands granted to them in lieu of their arrears of pay, whilst others had their arrears charged upon certain estates, vested in trustees for their liquidation. Amongst the former, were Thomas Aderly, who obtained the lands of Drounkeen, Corranure, Classafree, and half the townland of Ballinlanglay,* forfeited by Daniel McCarthy-More; also Francis Bernard,† who was granted part of the lands of Knockane—Ideene, previously a portion of the estate of Charles McCarthy-Reagh. And amongst the latter, were Captain John Watkins,‡ for the sum of £2,164 17s. 1d.; Captain Thomas Bennett, for £1,099 14s. 6d.; Ellinor‖ (wife of Captain Holcombe), for £769 5s. 7d.; Lieutenant Edmund Nuce, for £240 14s. 4d.; and Anne Dunkin, for arrears due to Ensign Thomas Dunkin, amounting to £245 6s. 2d. These amounts were charged on grants made to Randal Clayton, registrar, or chief clerk of the commissioners, to whom were assigned valuable estates in trust, for the payment of certain monies due to others similarly circumstanced to those whose names we have just mentioned.

During the time the regiment belonged to the town, it undertook to pay it the sum of forty pounds a week in hard cash; and, in addition, it expended a further sum of a hundred and twenty pounds in providing it with gunpowder and other necessaries. The officers appear to have served gratuitously; but the privates, in addition to their pay, were billetted upon the inhabitants. When, however, the regiment was placed under government control, a captain was entitled to receive five shillings a day, and a lieutenant two shillings and sixpence.

The exact date at which the volunteers passed into the King's service does not appear; but, presuming this to have taken place when commissions were sent down by the Lord-Lieutenant for the Bandon troop

---

* When a regiment was disembodied, the officers got grants of land as near to the place where the regiment was broken up as the forfeitures in the hands of the authorities would permit. The object of this was to have them all conveniently at hand in case their services should be required again.

† Francis Bernard, junr., of Castle-Mahon, father of Judge Bernard. It is interesting to note that it is a lineal descendant of this gentleman—the Hon. Colonel Bernard—who at present commands this old corps.

‡ It is probable that the large sum due to Watkins was made up of money advanced by him for the payment of his company, as well as arrears of pay due to himself.

‖ Ellinor, wife of Captain William Holcombe, was daughter of Francis Bernard, senior, of Castle-Mahon, by his wife, Alice Freke. She was sister to Francis Bernard, junior, a brother officer of her husband's. She died, leaving three daughters surviving—namely, Mary, Elizabeth, and Alice.

of horse and foot, our soldiers must have being doing duty as part of the regular army towards the close of August, 1642.*

With great difficulty the townspeople struggled to maintain their little army. The demands on their resources were very great, and the resources themselves were very small. They were no longer producers. The industry and skill which had enabled them to sit at a plenteous board, and which had lined their purses with the broad gold pieces of Holland and Spain, were no longer of any avail. They could not even count on a supply of food for any length of time, as the sheep and cattle which the country colonist had brought with him within the walls, and which he had succeeded in rescuing from the wanton destruction of his flocks and herds, were being consumed at every meal; and the corn-stacks, which he had torn from the blazing haggart, were being doled out to crowds of famishing people. Under these circumstances, it is no wonder that the pay of the soldiers should drop into arrear, and that the soldiers themselves should be " apt to complain of their governor, Lord Kinalmeaky, for whom it is in a matter impossible to keep so great a number of men in want, and with all in good appetite and affection towards him, for it is not his carriage, but the want of money, that displeaseth them."†

Lord Inchiquin, in one of his letters to Lord Cork, also speaks of the distress of the Bandon garrison at the close of 1642; and also of that of the townspeople. "The garrison of Bandon," writes he, "hath also been greatly distressed, and the soldiers famished, if the town hath not advanced a matter of three-score pounds to their relief; and now I find that the town is no-less necessitous than the soldiers."

Notwithstanding all the difficulties that lay heaped around them, still they were ever ready for the fray, and longed for the time when they should confront the enemy in the open field. They had not very long to wait. Scarcely had they got through their rudimentary drill, and knew how to handle their musketoon and pike, when the spring

---

* So far back as the 25th of the previous February, Lord Cork urged upon the government the necessity of taking some of the new levies into its pay. " My younger sons, Lords Kinalmeaky and Boghill," says his lordship, " are in a worse condition [*i.e.*—than Lord Dungarvan], for although each of them have one hundred horse, which I have hitherto paid, I am forced now to make it my humble suit to your lordship to move the lord-lieutenant that they may be taken into his Majesty's pay, for the horses and men are very good, well seasoned, and acquainted with the service." One of the two troops mentioned here is the troop of horse belonging to the Bandon militia.

† See Lord Cork's letter to the Speaker of the House of Commons.

began; and scarcely had the first shade of green peeped through the brown hill sides, when McCarthy-Reagh—a powerful chieftain, who lived in Kilbrittain Castle—came to Bandon, and having loudly declared that he would fight for the English, he induced Lord Kinalmeaky (the governor of the town) to furnish him with a good supply of arms.

We are unable to say whether his loud profession of loyalty was merely a pretence in order to procure arms, or that he was induced upon his return home to follow the example of his great kinsman, McCarthy-More. Be that as it may, he distributed among his kern and gallow-glasses the arms he got from Kinalmeaky; and putting himself at their head, marched the very next day to attack the astounded Bandonians. He approached to within about a mile of the town walls; then facing to the north-west, with the town on his right, he advanced as far as Knockegarane, which is about half a mile south of the Bandon river, with the intention of being joined by the Hurleys and O'Downeys, who dwelt on the river's upper banks. Here he threw up a strong earth-work, with a deep fosse in front of it, and lay there for several days, in-active and undecided as to what he should do. He, whose ancestors had often fought side by side with the English, must have heard of their prowess, and of the success that almost invariably attended them. Should he require any proof that this prowess had not degenerated, or that success did not still glitter in the track of " the stranger," he had but to look at the last great outbreak in our county, and then cast his eyes on the forfeited lands and castles of Cnogher O'Mahony,* and on the hundreds of thousands of acres wrested from Gerald, the Red Earl of Desmond.

Meanwhile, "the valiant Bandonians" hourly expected the onslaught; as it was not made during the day, it surely must be at night; as it was not made during the night, it surely must be on the morrow, and so on—disappointment followed on disappointment. As the mountain would not go to Mahommed, Mahommed must go to the mountain.

Towards the close of the month of February, 1642, the four companies of foot assembled for morning parade as usual, but it was observed that their troop of horse,† which consisted of sixty well-mounted men, was now paraded with them for the first time. There was something ominous

---

* Cnogher O'Mahony lived at Castle-Mahon—now Castle-Bernard—a residence of the O'Mahonys, only a few miles distant from Kilbrittain.

† The troop of horse which formed part of the regiment was no expense to the town, as the officers and men supported themselves.

in this. The men sniffed the coming struggle, and were in high glee.
News that on that day they were to measure their strength with the
McCarthys had sped along from rank and file to rank and file; and,
being caught up by the spectators, was soon carried to every house on
both sides of the river. The townspeople heard it exultingly, and
flocking to the parade in crowds, they shook the soldiers by the hand,
and clapped them encouragingly on the back. A group of matrons,
too, came forth on that portentous morning, and occupied a place from
whence a good view of the troops could be obtained; and with big tears
silently trickling over many a sorrowful face, they took a fond lingering
look at the ranks in which were many a husband, a son, a son-in-law;
then following the example of their leader, with one accord they all
knelt on the ground—"Thy will be done on earth," cried they, "as it
is done in heaven!"

After a careful inspection, a few rounds of ball-cartridge were served
out to each man from the scanty supply of ammunition in store. They
were then ordered to load. This was the signal for a prolonged cheer,
in which soldier and civilian joined lustily together; then followed
another; then another in quick succession upon another, announced that
the day of retribution had begun.

Everything being now ready, the order was given to march. Instantly
West-gate swung wide upon its hinges, to welcome them out with its
open portals. The horse marched out first, under their captain, Lord
Kinalmeaky, then followed the foot, in close column.* The former
proceeded up what is now known as the Castle-road, and then through
the woods of Castle-Mahon, intending to get between the enemy and
the river, and then wheeling to the left, fall on his rear, whilst the
foot attacked in front and in flank. The latter passed up through
Ballycloghane, then made straight for the Kilbrittain road; gaining which,
they pushed forward vigorously for the rebel lines. They had not moved
very far, when they were observed by one of McCarthy's outposts.
Tha na Sassanig a teachd ! (the Sassenachs are coming) screamed he,

---

* Although this was the first enterprise of any note they were engaged in, yet
they did more than learn their drill prior to this, as some weeks before a detachment
marched out of the town, and five or six miles along the road to Clonakilty, probably
to bring in some of the outlaying colonists. Neither were these marchings-out
unattended with danger. A small body went out on one occasion "to fetch a prey,"
when they were pounced upon by Sir Robert O'Shaughnessy's troop of horse from
Timoleague, and one of their number—namely, Private John Phipps—was taken
prisoner and put to death. This was, probably, the first man in the regiment who
was slain by the enemy.

and ran for his life. The cry was taken up by the chain of sentinels; and *Tha na Sassanig a teachd!* echoed from mouth to mouth, until it reached the main body.

When the McCarthys heard of the approach of the Bandonians, they eft their camp, and were standing in a field gazing at them as they were hurrying down Filedearg hill. Meanwhile, Captain Watkins, who was detached with the light company for the purpose of attacking in flank, stole unperceived along the morass through which runs the new mail coach-road to Clonakilty, and lay alongside the northern ditch of the very field in which the enemy stood gaping at the handful of men who were boldly wending their way up to fight him. Here he had orders to wait until the attack commenced in front; but he found it impossible to restrain the ardour of his men—any one of whom, in all probability, considered himself just as well fitted for command as his captain, and who could not be persuaded that it was good generalship to have such a splendid chance at the enemy, and yet do nothing. What could Watkins do but give in? He gave the word to fire, and sixteen of the enemy lay dead.

The McCarthys were terror-stricken. On their flank were those who had just fired a fatal volley into their ranks. The cavalry were already visible in their rear, and were hurrying up in full gallop, and between them and their own country were the Bandon men, making towards them as fast as they could. To get back to the sheltering walls of Kilbrittain was to them now a matter of life and death; but this was no easy matter, as an almost impassible bog lay at the foot of the hill, save in that part where the road lay, and that was in their enemies possession. Nevertheless, they take chance, and rushing down one hill, they rush up the other. In this desperate enterprise many were shot down, and many overtaken and piked. Indeed, so great were the numbers slain, that the little river which runs under the old chapel-bridge was discoloured with blood, and the very hill itself from that day forth bore a new name, and as Filedearg, or the Red Cliff, it is still pointed to as the scene of a great slaughter on that eventful day in February, 1642.

This was called the battle of Knockegerane,* and was the first

* Cox speaks of the sixteen killed by Captain Watkins's company, and says the Irish then fled. Another account says the Irish had a hundred and five slain, of whom five were gentlemen of note, and great numbers wounded. Tradition is positive as to the large number slain. Happening to mention to an intelligent

occasion in which the regiment inflicted a loss in killed and wounded upon the enemy.* For several weeks after this they were doomed to inactivity. It was during this interval that McCarthy-Reagh sought to procure an exchange of prisoners.

Although, as we have said, it was a period of inactivity for the entire regiment, yet detachments occasionally marched out into the surrounding country, to escort in some of the settlers, to convoy provisions, and to make prisoners when they could conveniently do so. On one of these excursions they captured one Daniel O'Garson. McCarthy sent a message to Lord Kinalmeaky by a female prisoner named Deane, offering to restore a servant-man named Andy Bartram for a friend of his in safe custody in Bandon, and tendering Deane herself in exchange for an Irishwoman. This proposal was refused. He then offered Bartram for O'Garson. This was also refused. Whereupon he became so annoyed, that he had poor Andy brought out of his prison, and hanged forthwith.

Anxious as the regiment was to materially assist those who cried to them with outstretched arms for help, what could they do ? They could not attack the enemy, or batter down his castles, without cannon and powder and shot; and they had not even one of the former, and very little of the latter. At length, on the evening of the 6th of April, the troop of horse, after a hard fight with the Roches and the McCarthys, who lay in ambush near Shippool Castle, arrived from Kinsale, bringing with them four hundred muskets, fifty swords, five new colours—one for each foot company, and one for the troop of horse—two hundred belts, two drums, lead, matches, and six barrels of gunpowder.

---

farmer who lives on the spot, that one writer speaks of but sixteen killed. "Why," said he, "I found more than that number of graves in the corner of that field!" pointing to a place that only adjoined the tomb-field (so called from being the field where they were nearly all buried). Without having as correct data on this subject as we would wish, the traditional estimate of the number killed does not appear improbable, when we bear in mind that the affrighted McCarthys had no other means of getting home but by running up to the very muzzles of their enemies muskets.

* Tradition says, that when the enemy fled, an Irishwoman who belonged to them bolted into a pig-stye, and there concealed herself under the straw. After some time she began to think that the worst had passed. At all events, to make sure, she cautiously put her head outside the stye door, in order to convince herself by ocular demonstration whether her conjectures were well or ill-founded. But scarcely had she done so, when her eye caught that of a Bandon soldier who was hurrying by. "Ugh!" groaned she, as she hastily withdrew and burrowed under the straw deeper than before, "musha, but 'tis now I'm gone in earnest!" The soldier did see her, but she was so ugly and so dirty—in fact, so unlike the fair and blooming country-women of our day—that he took no further notice, but passed on, thinking she was a pig.

It appears that the Kinsale troop of horse, who had escorted them about half-way to Bandon, apprehending no danger, thought they need go no farther. Accordingly they wheeled round, and marched back for their quarters; and the Bandon troop, without suspecting anything, rode leisurely on their way. But the enemy had his eye on their every move. The thick woods which at that time overspread the country effectually concealed them from observation, and they awaited their unsuspicious foe whilst he walked into their lair. With the bound of a tiger, and the roar of some king of the forest, they leaped upon the road, and the little band of warriors were surrounded with a thick cordon of infuriated men. But their strength arose with the dangers that faced them. Drawing close together, they presented a live wall, which the enemy could neither scale or penetrate. Round and round surged the inimical sea; each angry wave dashed madly against the human rock, and then toppled back upon its successor, dark with blood. The right arm that wielded the trusty steel was not idle, and the voice of the arquebus, as it bellowed through the surrounding woods, sent death-message after death-message into the crowded ranks of the Irish. The Kinsale troop hearing the shout with which the Bandon troopers were welcomed to their expected doom, reined up. Then they stood awhile to listen, and then hearing shot after shot, they surmised that their Bandon fellow-soldiers must be in peril. Accordingly, putting spurs to their horses, they rode hard to their relief; and arriving at full gallop, they soon turned the scale. Then joining together, they both fell mercilessly on their opponents, and speedily forced them into the adjoining woods, where they fled, but with the lost of eighty of their number, who lay dead upon the road. This engagement took place about a mile to the east of Shippool; and the McCarthys and the Roches who engaged in the attack formed portions of the garrisons in the adjoining castles of Carriganass, Poulnalonge, and Kilgobban, aided by some kern from the neighbourhood.

These were no times for letting the grass grow under their feet. If they wished to save their country from utter ruin, they must be up as well as awake. On every side they were encircled by a hostile people, and a string of hostile garrisons encompassed them. Teige O'Conner, in Downdanial, and Patrick Roche, in Poulnalonge, intercepted communications between Bandon and the east; Daniel McCarthy-Reagh, in Kilbrittain, and Sir Robert O'Shaughnessy, in Timoleague, did the

same in the south; Randal Oge Hurley, in Ballinacorriga, and Teige
O'Downy, in Dunmanway, severed all intercourse between Bandon and
the west; and Owen McSwiney, in Masshaneglass, and Lord Muskerry,
in Macroom, acted similarly in the north.

On the 20th of April, the regiment marched out to attack Downdanial.
The horse was under Lord Kinalmeaky, and the foot was commanded by
Captain Aderly.* Teige O'Conner made a resolute defence, and succeeded in killing three of his assailants—namely, Coleman, Moaks, and
Wood—and in holding his ground for some time; but being hotly pressed,
and expecting no quarter,† he fled, leaving his fortress uninjured in the
enemy's hands, and made all haste for Poulnalonge. But the Bandon
men hurried after in close pursuit, and coming up with him near Roche's
Castle, he faced about. The Roches had by this time joined him; and
massing their troops together, resolved to withstand the onslaught of the
Bandonians. A fierce struggle ensued; but at length the chiefs gave
way, and fled in confusion, leaving a hundred of their dead upon
the ground, and a considerable share of booty. O'Conner escaped
across the hills to the lands of Barna, where he quickly entrenched
himself; and Roche made for his castle walls as fast as his legs could
carry him.

After a fortnight spent in refitting and recruiting, they were again on
the march on the 4th of May. This time their destination was Shippool
wood, where it was arranged they should receive assistance from Kinsale.
The promised succour was forthcoming, and consisted, amongst the rest,
of a large gun, and probably some gunners. Carriganass Castle lay

---

* Captain Thomas Aderly, of Innoshannon, obtained a grant of the lands previously
mentioned. His name is recorded in the inrollments of certificates to adventurers
and soldiers; also on the roll of 1649 officers. And in the reign of James the
Second, in consequence of the part he took in the revolution, he was placed on the
" List of persons who have notoriously joined in the rebellion and invasion of
this kingdom, and are hereby adjudged traitors, convicted and attainted of high-
treason, and shall suffer such pains of death, &c."—Vide Proclamation of James the
Second, 1689.

† Teige O'Conner could not expect much mercy. Some time before, five votaries
of the rod and line were amusing themselves fishing on that even yet favourite
resort of anglers—the banks of the Bandon river, adjoining Downdaniel Castle.
Whilst thus engaged, and not dreaming of receiving any hurt—particularly from
those whom they had never injured—they were suddenly seized upon by some of
the garrison, and carried within the castle walls. Here they were soon made short
work of—four of them were hanged on the spot; the other, named John Unletter,
offered ten pounds to spare his life. This was agreed upon, and some of O'Conner's
men went home with him to get the money. But on ascertaining where it was kept,
they took all that was there, amounting to £35, and then they hanged him also,
probably with as little remorse as they did his companions.—Vide MSS., Trinity
College.

on the opposite side of the river, and Dermot McCarthy and a numerous garrison held it for the Irish and his chieftain, McCarthy-Reagh. Being summoned to submit to the King's authority, and place his fortress in English hands, Dermot stoutly refused. Upon this the gun was brought to bear, and the cannonade was about to begin, when McCarthy hung out a white flag, intimating his desire to surrender. A boat put off immediately to arrange the terms, and had got near half-way across, when the besieged suddenly opened fire on her, killing two of the passengers, and sinking the boat herself. But they were not content with even-this barbarous outrage on the laws of war, for, amid jeers and derision, they continued the fusillade, severely wounding three or four of the poor creatures who were madly struggling in the water to reach the shore, from whence they had but a few moments before shoved off in high spirits.

Witnessing this act of diabolical treachery, the Bandon men panted to be avenged. The big gun was silent no longer. It was rapidly discharged, and nearly every discharge told. At one time it was a lot of stones from one of the towers that came rumbling down the front wall. At another time it was a portion of the battlement that fell to the ground, with a loud crash. At one time a shot passed through to the inside; and then again one of the coignes showed unmistakable signs of detaching itself from the continuous masonry. Meanwhile, most of the foot, under Lord Kinalmeaky in person, secretly ascended the hill from which the gun still threw its ponderous shot, and descending on the other side, marched westwards, keeping the ground now occupied by Shippool demesne between them and the Roches at Poulnalonge, until they arrived at Coolmoreen ford. Here they easily crossed over —it being low water at the time; and having cautiously proceeded towards Carriganass, they possessed themselves of the wooded heights in the rear, and the eastern and western approaches, unperceived. A signal was then made to their comrades on the opposite bank to man their boats. This being accomplished, and the great gun still whirling its destructive missiles at the now fissured and crumbling castle walls, they slowly and silently closed in.

For some time before, McCarthy and his men had been obliged to withdraw from the inside, it being dangerous to remain there any longer, as stones and *debris* were falling about their ears in all directions; and they had sought for safety on the outside, where they all stood huddled up together under the southern wall, screened from the shot of the enemy, and awaiting in trepidation the arrival of his boats. Another signal! and out flared a murderous discharge of musketry from the wall of exasperated men that circled them. Then bounding from their coverts, with loud yells of triumph and revenge, they sprang upon the foe. The work of death was but the work of a few minutes. The terrified McCarthys fell to the earth in scores; several had their brains beaten out with a clubbed musket, many were shot and sabred, and others had their skeans buried to the haft in their vitals. The ground they had stood upon was soon slippery and red with their blood. At first the blood began to dribble lazily over a shelving rock, on its way to the great outlet that flowed on the other side of the building. Then the red track became a stream; and then rushing past all obstacles, the current poured into the river, darkening its fair waters for a long way in its course to Kinsale. Their retributive vengeance was terrible, and extended itself even to those who had any signs of life remaining. These they quickly dispatched, after which a large hole was dug, many of the bodies were flung in, and luxuriant crops in the vegetable-garden at Rock Castle, it is said, even yet outline their bloody grave.

News of the terrible punishment inflicted on the garrison at Carriganass soon reached Dermod-ni-Glack, at Kilgobban, another of McCarthy-Reagh's fortresses; and so disheartened were the warders by the apprehension of a similar fate,* that long before the Bandon soldiery could reach them, they had abandoned the castle, and made off as fast as they could.

The next day Shippool was peremptorily ordered to strike its flag, and submit. The Roches naturally shared in the consternation which the massacre on the opposite bank the day before had spread far and wide throughout the country, and they probably thought that, under certain circumstance, discretion was the better part of valour. At all

---

* The garrison at Kilgobban were notorious plunderers. On one occasion some of them broke into a gentleman's house near Ballinadee, and, amongst other articles, carried away a signet ring which had been used to seal a document still in the possession of that gentleman's descendants. Some years ago a poor man was wandering one morning through the castle ruins, and, happening to look up, observed a piece of mortar falling from one of the upper windows. Looking closer, he thought he perceived the corner of a small box peeping through the masonry from whence the mortar had just fallen. He lost no time in climbing to the spot, and returned home greatly pleased with his good fortune. Among the treasure-trove discovered by him was the very signet ring taken from the residence of the gentleman above referred to, more than two centuries before.

events, they did not await the planting of the big gun. Indeed, scarce had the echoes of the summoning clarion died away in the woods, when Roche hauled down his colours and gave up his castle.

After this the regiment took a little rest, and was not again on active duty until the 29th of May. On that day, under the command of Lord Kinalmeaky, they marched to Coolmaine Castle,* and demanded its surrender. It does not appear to have made any resolute defence. It may have been that its governor was terrified by the fate of Dermod McCarthy ; or he may have thought it useless to protract a contest with those for whom victory seemed ever to declare ; and, therefore, perhaps after a plausible show of resistance, he submitted. And now only one castle† in all his broad lands remained to McCarthy-Reagh. But this was the principal one, as well as his favourite residence, and had been the residence of his ancestors ever since one of them dispossessed the De Courceys hundreds of years before. The castle was large, and was surrounded by a strong wall, upon which were a half a dozen turrets strategically placed for defence. It seems almost unaccountable that a vigorous stand was not made here. Was this old fortalice of the McCarthys, whose walls were hallowed by the expiring breath of many a proud scion of that old race, to pass into the sacrilegious hands of " the stranger" without a struggle ? Was he, whose ancestors wore the royal purple‡ long ere Strongbow placed his ambitious foot on these shores, to be driven on the world—houseless, hopeless, and a beggar— without a desperate and bloody encounter to save the lands and the

---

* Coolmaine Castle, at present the marine residence of the Hon. H. B. Bernard, the colonel of this very regiment. After the seizure of Coolmaine from the McCarthys, it was granted by Cromwell to Colonel John Jephson, in whose possession it remained until the restoration, when it was taken from him and given to the Duke of York (afterwards James the Second). Upon James's arrival in Ireland, Coolmaine, and other estates in the possession of the McCarthys prior to the great rebellion, were conferred by him on Donough McCarthy, Earl of Clancarthy. Lord Clancarthy did did not retain Coolmaine long, having forfeited it, together with all his other castles and estates, by his adherence to King James. After remaining the property of the crown for some years, it was sold at the great auction of forfeited estates and bought by the Hollow Sword Blades Company, on the 23rd of June, 1703, and, by purchase from them it again became the property of the Jephsons, by one of whom it was sold some years ago.

† Kilbrittain Castle at the breaking out of the rebellion was in the possession of Thomas Fitzmaurice, Esq., who was married to McCarthy-Reagh's mother, and to which lady the castle belonged as part of her jointure. McCarthy, however, marched against it with a company of foot, and dispossessed Fitzmaurice by force.

‡ When Strongbow arrived in Ireland the McCarthys were on the throne of Cork—a kingdom which at one time embraced all this county, a good portion of Kerry, and the western part of the county of Waterford.

home of his fathers? Was the prestige of his race—a prestige which had become inseparable from this historic pile, and which generation after generation of those who had long preceded him had built up, and looked upon with affection and pride—to be dashed to the ground, to be trodden under foot, without one arm being raised in its defence?

Tradition, as well as history, is silent concerning many particulars of its surrender. Enough, however, remains to satisfy us that the warders made no resistance; and we know that McCarthy was not there, he being at that time in the rebel encampment at Killavarrig wood. And though this place is only distant from Kilbrittain a few miles, he does not appear to have been aware of what was going on.*

Bryan McSwiney was the name of the commander to whom Kilbrittain was entrusted; and he may have considered himself unprepared to resist a vigorous onslaught; or it might have been that its defenders, finding themselves unaided by the large force at Killivarrig, thought themselves abandoned by them. The garrison, however, did march out; but whether they capitulated, or surrendered unconditionally, we are unable to say.

When intelligence reached Killivarrig on the morrow that Kilbrittain was also in the hands of those from whom McCarthy could expect no favour, he was greatly incensed. An eye-witness, who was a soldier in the rebel camp at the time, tells us its effect upon him. "He seemed much displeased," said he, "and went a little apart from his company, and sat him down under a bush a pretty space of time, and no man, in regard of his discontent, spoke anything to him."

Having entirely cleared their communications with Kinsale and the sea-coast to the south, and having dismantled some of the castles which they took, and placed garrisons in others, they were ready to march elsewhere. At this time Inchiquin, who was wearied with complaints of want of provisions from every garrison under his command, thought the best thing he could do was to collect all the available troops in them, and lead them against the enemy. His enterprise was a hazardous one; for a hungry man is neither in good condition, nor in good humour, to fight. But a fight under any circumstances almost must be an

---

* Another account says he was aware of it, and that he marched as far as Timoleague bridge on his way to its relief, and there heard of its seizure by the English. This statement, however, does not appear until many years after Kilbrittain was taken, and is irreconcilable with the evidence furnished to the commissioners by an eye-witness a few months after the event occurred.

advantage to him.   If he beat the enemy, he may capture a good store of provisions for his winter quarters; and if he was beaten himself, he would have the less mouths to feed, and consequently the more to give those that remained.   With two thousand foot and four hundred horse, he boldly took the field; and overtaking the Irish near Liscarroll, he attacked them.   The Irish army consisted of seven thousand foot and five hundred horse.   Their foot was divided into three divisions, of two two thousand three hundred men each.   The division on their right lay near an earthwork which they had thrown up and manned; and on the brow of the hill, a little to their right again, stood their horse, massed into one column.   Their left lay near Liscarroll Castle, and adjoined another earthwork, within which was their artillery.   Between their two wings was their centre, composed mainly of pikemen.

Inchiquin endeavoured to draw away the cavalry which protected the right division, and to do so he advanced against them with a strong party of his own horse.   The enemy threw out skirmishers to meet him, and lined the hedges with their best musketeers.   It was at this time that Lord Kinalmeaky, riding at the head of the Bandon troop, was shot in the neck, and killed on the spot.

The Irish horse could not be coaxed from their position—not even to follow in pursuit—so the English were obliged to retire without effecting their purpose.   Again Inchiquin advanced on the right wing, and this time with his entire army.   His horse began the fight, but they were soon a confused mass, owing to the front rank, when they delivered their fire, wheeling to the right and left, and trotting back to the rear to reload.   This movement was misunderstood by the rear-rank men, who thought when they saw their comrades in the front retire, they saw them retreat; and thus the whole body got into disorder.   The enemy saw that now was his time, and pushing forward his right, he fell on the English infantry, under Colonel Myn.   Myn stood his ground like a man; not only did he resist the attack, but he attacked them in return, and forced them to fall back.   Emboldened by this unlooked for success, Inchiquin's horse take courage and charge.   The Irish horse withstand the shock.   They do not give way an inch, and afford no prospect of a triumphal onslaught by the enemy.   But foremost in the ranks of the English horse are the Bandon troop; and they have sworn to rescue the body of their dead commander, and to avenge his fall.   Stubbornly they press against the Irish front, and the Irish front as stubbornly resists them. Again they rush desperately at the human wall before them, and again, and again; but they retire, leaving the wall unbroken. At length the Irish squadrons are growing weary of the protracted struggle. They are beginning to look disheartened. Hope is paling on their banners. Already the timid are striving to free themselves from the ranks. The ranks are widening, and the tie that bound them together is now thinned to a thread. Retiring a short distance, the English troopers re-adjust their arms and rest their horses. After a little they advance at a walk. Soon they warm into a trot. Then they break into a gallop; and gathering strength and speed at every pace, and amid the thunder of sounding hoofs, the jingling of accoutrements, and the vengeful exclamations of angry men, they swoop down, and bursting on the affrighted column, they shiver it to pieces. A panic seizes the foot, who lately fell back before Myn, and throwing down their arms, they run for their lives. Meanwhile, Sir Charles Vavasor, at the head of six hundred foot,[*] marched against the Irish left, and pushing through them, scaled the parapet of the redoubt, and carried it. The cannon were captured, and the enemy, who do not appear to have struck a blow for their defence, escaped to a neighbouring bog. The Irish centre finding itself now at the mercy of Vavasor's guns, and seeing both its flanks unprotected, left its position in dismay, and followed the left. If Inchiquin—who had been in pursuit of the Irish horse, and who, in returning, unfortunately mistook some of his own foot for the enemy's, and retreated before them—had been up in time, the Irish would have been entirely destroyed. As it was, they lost some of their artillery, some barrels of gunpowder, twenty-six colours, three hundred muskets, and seven hundred men killed. Save in one instance, there was not a prisoner made—no quarter being the cry raised in the English ranks when Kinalmeaky fell.

His lordship's body, and also his charger, were rescued from the Irish horse by his own troop, led on by his youngest brother, Mr. Francis Boyle—afterwards Lord Shannon—on the occasion of the prolonged contest mentioned previously. The body was borne from the field by his faithful troopers; and with slow and measured tread, and with arms reversed, they followed the remains of their young hero to the grave.[†]

---

[*] Tradition states that the Bandon foot served that day under Vavasor.

[†] He was buried with great military pomp in the southern transept of St. Mary's, Youghal. Kinalmeaky had assigned to him by his father—the first Earl of Cork—part of Gill-Abbey, the manor of Kinalmeaky, the lands of Kilbeg and Kilbrogan,

Inchiquin obtained great glory by this victory, but no provisions. Starvation stared him in the face as much as ever. He could do no more, and, therefore, with great reluctance, he was compelled to send back his handful of men to the garrisons from which he had only just drawn them. The next month, Lord Forbes, with his regiment of Scotch, landed in Kinsale, and marched to Bandon.

It was now the middle of October, and important military projects must be abandoned until next spring. But, before they shut themselves up in winter quarters, they resolve to make an effort to relieve, if not to bring away with them altogether, Captain Arthur Freke and the stubborn warders of Rathbarry Castle.

For upwards of thirty-five weeks Rathbarry was effectually blocked up. John Barry, of Dundeedy, Teige O'Hea, of Kilgarriff, Daniel O'Donovan, of Karigleaky, Richard O'Donovan his brother, Daniel Ffinin McCarthy, of Rosscarbery, William Barry, Thomas Mahown, of Rathbarry, and the eldest son of Florence McCarthy, of Benduffe, all uniting their forces, marched against it at the head of several hundred men, and closely beset it. They were not content with drawing a cordon of troops round it, so as to prevent all egress and ingress, but they lay down before it, and besieged it in a regular manner. They threw up earthworks to screen themselves from the shot of the garrison, and they pushed their parallels so close to the besieged, that the latter could hear them talking in the trenches. Putting his head for a second or two above the parapet, a fellow would cry out :—" Ah, you Parliament rogues !" " You rebels !" sounded strangely from the mouth of another fellow, who never had a loyal aspiration in his life ; and " Ye dogs !" displayed the intense hatred entertained by the insurgents for those who strove to uphold the supremacy of England.

The store of provisions laid up by Freke, in anticipation of a siege, was now exhausted. Since the 21st of the previous April the inmates of the castle had nothing to drink save the stagnant waters in the castle ditch, and from the middle of July they were in want of bread. The supply of food, if rationed only to those who carried arms, would have held out a much longer time ; but there were many women and children who found an asylum within the walls, and to put them out, was to hand them over to the sword, or to famine. But the owner of

---

the manor of Coolfadda, the town of Bandon-Bridge and Ballymodan, and lands in the barony of Carbery.

Rathbarry was not the man to ferry those helpless creatures to the other side of the moat, and leave them there to await the slow process of death by hunger, or the more expeditious one of the pike or the skean. He resolved to share with them his last morsel of food; and should that fate, which hung by a thin thread above their heads, fall upon them, better that they should perish in one massacre rather than that he should be accessory to their death.

Such a man was not to be left to die without a vigorous effort to save him. 'Twas true that the march was a long one, and through a country where "great O'Donovan," Teige O'Dounce, Black O'Cullane, and others, had stripped the English settlers of everything they possessed; and, adding sacrilege to their other crimes, had actually turned the Protestant cathedral of Ross into a shambles, for the slaughter of cows and sheep. On the 18th of October, a strong detachment from the Bandon garrison marched for Clonakilty. Lord Forbes led on his own regiment in person, and the three companies of the Bandon foot were under their old commander, Sir Charles Vavasor. Upon their arrival at Clonakilty, a small detachment, consisting of two companies of Forbes' foot, under Captain Weldon, and one company of the Bandon foot, under Captain Grove, remained in charge of the town, whilst the rest marched to Rathbarry. But scarcely were they well beyond hearing distance, when up rose a large body of the insurgents, who had been lying concealed in the neighbourhood; and rushing on the detachment, strove to annihilate them. Grove urged on Weldon to endeavour to rejoin their main body—not yet very far distant—but he refused. He thought his two companies of Scotch Presbyterians an over-match for any quantity of the "meer Irish," but he was mistaken. Bravely contending with overwhelming numbers, he was himself soon killed, and his two companies of Scots cut to pieces. But Grove and his valiant Bandonians were more fortunate. For a full mile along the road they fought hand to hand with the enemy, until they reached an old Danish fort on the way to Ross. Here they heroically held their ground against all odds, until Forbes and Vavasor returned, bringing with them Captain Freke and the brave defenders of Rathbarry.* Uniting their forces, they

---

* Whilst the Irish lay encamped round Rathbarry, they seized an English soldier named Christopher Rossgill, who was killed with a pike by one James Lumbart; Thomas Tantully, a Rosscarbery man, they hanged; and Christopher Crosse and John Gilbert (two of Captain Freke's servants) they put to death, within sight of the castle walls.—See MSS. in Trinity College.

closed with the foe near the island of Inchidonny, and fell on them without mercy. The rebels were badly circumstanced for a retreat. On one side of them were Forbes and Vavasor, and on the other side was the island. If they could only reach the latter their lives were safe. But between them and it swept a strong ebb tide. What was to be done ? The avenging steel of the Scotch and Bandon soldiers rang in their ears, and they must decide quickly. Before them was deep water rolling out to sea, with swift current, and behind them was a maddened soldiery, thirsting for their blood. They did not hesitate. Plunging in one and all, they strove to reach the opposite shore. Several were successful in the attempt, but hundreds were unsuccessful. Counting those that perished in the water, and those that fell by the sword, the enemy on that day lost upwards of six hundred men.

Returning to Clonakilty, their arrival was most opportune. A lot of the Protestant inhabitants of the town, consisting of some men and many women and children, had been seized by the rebels, and imprisoned in the market-house ; and it was their intention to have made one common bonfire of the market-house and its inmates, when they had been as successful with Forbes and Vavasor as they had been with the two companies of Scots under Weldon. Throwing open the market-house gates, the relieving force took the terrified inmates with them ; and after a day full of exciting events, and a long tiresome march, they arrived, footsore and weary, at Bandon.

These rapid successes surpassed the most sanguine expectations, even of those who expected great things from them. They were nearly always victorious. Success generally awaited their summons to the hostile fortress to surrender. Victory crowned their efforts in the siege, and they were among the conquerors in every pitched battle, and in every skirmish in which they were engaged. The fame of their exploits sped across the channel, and crossing the threshold of the Commons assembled at Westminster, induced that august assembly to notice " their remarkable services."

In the spring of next year (1643), Sir Charles Vavasor quitted his appointment at Bandon ; and matters being very quiet in the surrounding country, it is likely he took the Bandon regiment with him, as we have no account of their proceedings at this side of Cork until 1645. In that year the detachment in garrison at Baltimore, under the command of Captain Bennett and his brother George, renounced their allegiance to Charles the First, in disgust at the alliance made between him and the Irish whom they had been previously fighting against. Whether the rest of the regiment followed their example, or whether they did not, does not appear. It would seem, however, that their sympathies were strong in the same direction, as there is no record of their being again quartered in the western side of the county until after Cromwell's arrival. Indeed, so apprehensive was the Royalist lord-president of Munster that the very people who supplied the rank and file of the Bandon regiment would themselves declare for the Parliament, that he ordered a troop of horse into the town, together with some Irish foot and Colonel Courtnay's force (consisting of five hundred men), for the purpose of disarming them; and, notwithstanding that the intended disarmment did actually take place, and the hopes of a successful attack by unarmed and undisciplined townsmen upon well-armed and trained soldiers must have now diminished to a shadow, yet even this could not induce them to forego their intention of pronouncing in favour of Cromwell and the Parliament, and then seizing the garrison, rid their town of rebel and Royalist, now banded together in the same cause.

The attempt, which was made about the 16th of November, 1649, was under the guidance, and for the most part under the leadership, of officers of the regiment then in Bandon—perhaps on leave, or who had made their way into the town to assist in the enterprize—as Major Turner, Captain Brayly, Captain Robert Gookin, Lieutenant Berry, Lieutenant Langton, Ensign Dunkin, Ensign Gwinn, and Cornet William Fuller, and a few corporals belonging to the regiment. The movement was not attended with the success anticipated. Captain Brayly, accompanied by Lieutenant Berry and some civilians, over-powered the guard at west-gate; but the other gates not being attacked simultaneously, as was intended, the enemy was on the alert, and saved them.

Brayly did not enjoy his victory long. Two hundred of Courtnay's men, under the command of Major Harden, besieged him; and after some firing, he was forced to yield up the guard-house, and surrender himself and his lieutenant as prisoners of war.

In about three weeks after this, another attempt was made, and with more success. Two houses near the sallyport at the northern side of the town were seized and fortified; and thus having possessed themselves of a very small portion of the town, they considered they had a right to dictate to those who held all the rest. Accordingly, Mr. John Smith (the provost), Major Turner, Captain Gookin, and some of the townsmen,* waited on Governor Courtnay, and plainly told him, " that it was vain for him to oppose, as they were resolved to deliver up the town to Lord Broghill;" also, that if he did not submit, they would seize the sentinels on the postern gate, and let Broghill in.

Courtnay was terrified. The audacity of the Bandonians over-awed him. "He desired them not to deliver him up before he had some hours to make conditions for himself and party." His request was acceded to, and at the expiration of the allotted time he gave up.

When Courtnay's soldiers marched out, it is probable that the Bandon soldiers marched in; and had accompanied Broghill, whom they served under for a long time previously, to the walls of the town, to aid him if necessary in forcing his way in, and expelling the obnoxious Royalists.

Some days prior to Christmas-day Cromwell arrived in Bandon from Kinsale, with Lord Broghill, Major-General Ireton, Sir William Fenton, and many others. After reviewing the garrison, which consisted of the Bandon militia and Colonel Ewer's regiment of foot, he is said to have ordered the former to the front; and there, in the presence of their fellow-townsmen, their fellow-soldiers, and the crowds who had flocked in from the country to feast their eyes upon that great man, whose name was now on every tongue, he thanked them on behalf of the Parliament, for their great services to the cause of England. It was on this occasion the Bandon militia were first called " The Fire-Eaters"†—a name said to have been conferred on them by no less a personage than Oliver Cromwell; and by which name they were known long after peace and prosperity had returned and overspread our country with happiness and abundance; and long after the last survivor of the corps—mayhap some venerable old soldier, who sat all day in the summer sun, and cowered in the chimney-corner all through the long winter—had passed away, the townspeople and their children, and their children's children, grew taller when they spoke of the old " Fire-Eaters " of old Bandon-Bridge.

---

* The Carte MSS. mentions the names of several of the Bandon civilians who took a prominent part in the revolt; as Abraham Savage, John Jackson, Jonathan Bennett, John Smith (the provost), Richard Shute, Richard Sealy, Richard Nobbs, James and Henry Rice, William Bull, Francis Hill, Jonah Butler.

† This term was subsequently applied to other forces who distinguished themselves in the south of Ireland, as well as to the Bandon militia.

PARTICULARS CONCERNING OFFICERS.

Aderly, Thomas, given previously.

Aderly, George, brother of Thomas. On the list of 1649 officers;* also in the inrollment of certificates to adventurers and soldiers.

Baldwin, Walter, junr., son of Walter Baldwin, of Granahoonick. Mentioned in the report addressed to the Court of Claims. Under the Act of Settlement, he obtained part of the lands of Knocknough and Kilbolane. Walter Baldwin (the elder) was the son of Herbert, and grandson of Henry, the eldest of three brothers who settled here towards the close of Elizabeth's reign. This Henry was the son of Henry, ranger of woods and forests in Shropshire, who married Elinor Herbert, daughter of Sir Edward Herbert, of Red Castle, who was the second son of the first Lord Pembroke, by Lady Anne, daughter of Lord Parr, of Kendall, and sister of Lady Catherine Parr, surviving queen of Henry the Eighth. Walter Baldwin was succeeded by his son Henry, who married Miss Field, niece of Colonel Beecher, of Sherkin. He was succeeded by his son Henry (who married Elizabeth, daughter of Dive Downes, bishop of Cork), by his third wife, Elizabeth, daughter of Thomas Beecher, of Sherkin, and relict of Captain Townsend. Henry had two sons:—Henry, progenitor of the Baldwins of Mount Pleasant, and William, B.L., progenitor of the Baldwins of Lisarda; the former married Miss Warren, sister of Sir Robert Warren, and the latter Miss French, daughter of Alderman French, of Cork. William of Lisarda, who was a very eminent barrister, was succeeded by his son Henry, who married Miss Morris, of Dunkettle, and was high-sheriff of the county in 1777. He died, leaving, amongst other issue, William, who married Mary Kirby, daughter of Franklin Kirby, of Bamborough Grange, Yorkshire. He was also high-sheriff of the county in 1813. He died in 1838, leaving numerous issue.†

Bernard, Francis, given previously.

Beamish, Francis, ancestor of the Beamishes of Kilmalooda. Mentioned in the inrollment of certificates to adventurers and soldiers. He obtained, under Act of Settlement, part of lands of Maulbracke, previously belonging to Donough Oge Murphy, and several gneeves of Kilmalooda, late the property of Daniel McCarthy-More; jointly with Captain Freke, Cahavalder, part of Knockeagh, three parcels of Cahirconwey, and part of Rosemore; and, jointly with Lieut. Langton, part of Capuebohy, Ballinloghly, and Ballryry. He married Katherine, sister of his brother officer, Francis Bernard;

---

* The list of officers who served prior to June, 1649.

† The Baldwins claim descent from Baudwin (or Baldwin) bras de fer, a French nobleman attached to the court of Charles the Bold, by whom he was created Earl of Flanders. He married Judith, Charles's daughter, and great grand-daughter of Charlemange. She was the widow of Ethelwolf, King of England, and stepmother of Alfred the Great.

and by her had two children—Francis and Alice. He deposed
to losses caused by the rebellion before the commissioners at
Bandon.

Beamish, Thomas, also appears in the enrollment of certificates to
adventurers and soldiers; and in the Act of Settlement, for portion
of the lands of Kilmalooda, and, jointly with Thomas Francke,
the north-side of Altagmore, containing two hundred and thirty-
eight acres. Mr. Beamish was provost of Bandon in 1655, 1665,
and 1675.

Bennett, Captain Thomas (governor of Baltimore Castle, ancestor of
the Bennetts of Bandon, and of Bennett's Grove, Clonakilty), was
second son of Thomas Bennett, of Bandon; which Thomas is
believed to have been the eldest son of a younger brother of
Thomas Bennett, of Clapcot, the father of Thomas Bennett, who
was high-sheriff of London in 1694, and lord mayor upon the
accession of James the First (1603), upon which occasion he was
created a baronet. During the latter part of the reign of Queen
Elizabeth, the colony of Bandon-Bridge was established by Phane,
son of Alderman Henry Beecher, of London. Beecher was accompanied to his "new plantation" by the sons of some of the members
of the London corporation, as well as by younger sons of families
from various parts of England. These together founded the
original colony; and amongst them was Thomas Bennett. He
died prior to 1632, and three of his sons—Jonathan, Thomas, and
George—were appointed "executors to their father dying intestate." His second son, the governor of Baltimore, was, as we have
said, Thomas Bennett. He was an active member of the Bandon
corporation, of which he was elected a burgess, June 12th, 1632,
in room of Stephen Skipwith, one of the first twelve elected. In
1637, having removed to Baltimore, he resigned his burgesship,
to the regret of the corporation, as follows:—"Whereas Thomas
Bennett, one of the free-burgesses of this borough, has removed
himself out of said corporation; and it is now declared in forth
and so forth that, in respect of his residence, he cannot be any
way of assistance to the provost and free-burgesses of this corporation, and he having desired that he might be deprived of the said
office of free-burgess of this borough, we regret his having so
desired as aforesaid."—(Vide Corporation Records.) The year
before (1636) he obtained from Walter Coppinger the castle, town,
and lands of Baltimore, and part of the lands of Tullough, as
appears by an indenture bearing date June 30th, 1636, in which
"Walterius Coppinger," demised to him "castr' vill' et terr' de
Downeshed als Baltimore, an messuag' et tribus carrucat' terr' de
Tullough in com' pred'," &c. Governor Bennett was strongly
attached to the Parliament, and took an early opportunity of
declaring in its favour. "Baltimore Castle, well-mounted with
ordnance, was in the hands and under the command of Thomas
Bennett, a Parliamentarian."—(Vide Carte MSS., Oxford.) Notwithstanding his avowed hostility to the Royalist party after they
became united with the Irish, yet his services in the cause of England

were of too prominent a character to be passed over unrequited; accordingly his name was inserted in the savings under the Act of Settlement for the full amount of his claims, (*i.e.* £1,099 14s. 6d.) He is also mentioned in the list of 1649 officers. He died, leaving, with other male issue, Thomas, his successor, and a daughter, Frances, who married Sir Richard Hull, a justice of Court of Common Pleas (*temp.* Charles the Second); by whom she had a son, William, who inherited the manor of Lemcon and other considerable possessions, and a daughter, who married her cousin Moore, of the family of Sir E. Moore, baronet, of Rosscarbery. Thomas, his successor, married a Miss Wood, of Baltimore, by whom he had two sons:—Thomas, who inherited the family estates, and resided at Ringrove (*alias* Bennett's Grove), Clonakilty; and William, who settled in Bandon, where he married (December 27th, 1715,) Dorothy Whelply, by whom he had, with other issue—Thomas, who married Mary, daughter of Captain Smith, and sister of the Rev. William Elliott Mars Smith, of Easingwold, Yorkshire, and died in 1808, leaving numerous issue.

Bennett, George, settled in Cork, is on the list of 1649 officers.

Berry, Lieutenant Edward. Name not mentioned on any official list. Was made free of the Bandon corporation in 1637. In 1654 he lived at Garrimore, barony of Ibane.

Brayly, Captain John, is on the list of 1649 officers, and in the inrollment of certificates to adventurers and soldiers. Under the Act of Settlement, he obtained small portions of the lands of Killgleny, Ballyroe, Drumskellope, Skeagh East, and Ballycotten, the latter late the property of McCarthy Reagh—in all two hundred and eight acres—barony East Carbery.

Bird, Captain Walter, mentioned on list of 1649 officers.

Dunkin, Ensign Thomas. Was provost of Bandon in 1654. Is on the list of 1649 officers. His widow, Anne Dunkin, obtained the sum of £245 6s. 2d., under the savings under the Act of Settlement.

Dodgin, Ensign Thomas. Was dispoiled of £200 worth of goods by Donough McDaniel Carthy, of Lishane, and his Irish tenants. Is on the list of 1649 officers, inrollment of certificates to adventurers and soldiers, report addressed to Court of Claims, and, jointly with Theophilus Carey, he obtained portion of the lands of Raheroone, Farranmareen, Gortlegher, Ballyolane, Knocknecoole, Derry, and Lisscheagh—in all eight hundred and twelve acres— late the property of Daniel McFinin Carthy.

Dixon, James, in report addressed to Court of Claims, inrollment of certificates, &c. Under the Act of Settlement he procured the lands of Ardacrow and Killalo (three hundred and seventy-six acres), late the property of Charles McCarthy-Reagh. Mr. Dixon was provost of Bandon in 1673, also in 1683, 1694, and in 1710. A portion of Ardacrow (one hundred and sixteen acres) was conferred on James the Second, but at the revolution it was forfeited, and sold to the Hollow Sword Blades Company.

Elwell, James, on list of 1649 officers. He was made free of the

Bandon corporation in 1635.   He deposed before the commissioners to losses in cattle and money, by reason of the rebellion.

Elwell, Joseph, on list of 1649 officers.

Fleming, John, quarter-master, on list of 1649 officers, also inrollment of certificates, &c.   Before the commissioners at Bandon, he deposed to losing, by reason of the rebellion, the sum of £1,107.

Fuller, Cornet William, was son of William Fuller, treasurer of the Bandon corporation in 1636, and grandson of Ralph Fuller (one of the original colonists of Bandon), who married Elizabeth, youngest daughter of John Ware, by his wife, Mary, eldest sister of Sir Hugh Owen, of Orielton, Pembrokshire.   John Ware was elder brother of Sir James Ware, the historian.   From Cornet Fuller descended George, who married Mary Unkles; and had, with other male issue, Ralph, William, Thomas, and George.   William (his second son) married Jane, daughter of William Orange Clarke,* by Rachel Daunt, cousin-german to Captain William Daunt, of Kilcaskan; and by her had, with other issue, William, in holy orders, died unmarried; Joseph, married Mary Williams; Mary, married Joseph Bennett; Eliza, died young.

Gookin, Captain Robert, was grandson of Sir Vincent Gookin, who married a daughter of Sir Thomas Crooke.   Captain Gookin, described by Lord Orrery as "a man of good brains," was a devoted Parliamentarian.   Indeed, so identified was he with the acts and aspirations of that great body, that he, together with Colonel William Pigott, Captain St. John Brodrick, and Colonel Richard Townsend, were represented as four spies sent over by Cromwell to give him intelligence of passing events in Ireland.   He applied to the Court of Claims for compensation for his services, but his name does not appear on the list of certificates.   He was made a member of the Bandon corporation in 1666, in which year he is supposed to have died at his residence in Courtmasberry.   He married Hester Hodder, and by her had a son, Robert, who was the father of Major Gookin, whose son, Robert, was accidentally killed at Castle-Bernard in 1760.   Although Captain Gookin was refused a certificate by the Court of Claims, yet his services were not overlooked by Cromwell, who, on the 12th of April, 1653, granted him Abbey Ross, in West Carbery.   In 1654 a report was made that the fort which he had built at Abbey Ross (alias Rosscarbery), the fortifying of the abbey, and the erection of buildings for the English inhabitants, had cost him £2,143, instead of £600; and, in consideration of the extra sum which he expended, Abbey-Mahon was bestowed on him, and the adjoining nineteen ploughlands, and subsequently seven ploughlands more.   At the restoration, Gookin, who knew he was a marked man, passed his grants to Lord Orrery, at that time a devoted Royalist, and from

---

* Mr. Clarke's father was a military officer, and came to Ireland in the same ship with William the Third.   His wife accompanied him; and on the voyage she gave birth to a son—the above-named William Orange Clarke.   He was called William Orange in compliment to William of Orange, the illustrious prince under whom Captain Clarke served at the Boyne, at Limerick, and elsewhere.

him he took a lease of them for a hundred years. This lease expired on the second of March, 1760, since which period the lands have been possessed by the Shannon family, descendants of Lord Orrery.

Grove, Captain John, subsequently a major, is mentioned in a memorial forwarded to Charles the Second, complaining that he and some other officers had served the King prior to 1649, " and have not since received any reward under the usurper, but, on the contrary, are suffering." His services and sufferings, however, were not overlooked by the restored government, for under the savings to the Act of Settlement he received £612 10s. 0d. ; and under the Act itself, the lands of Drinagh West, Kilursin, and Bally-hymock, in barony of Orrery and Kilmore ; Keatingstown, Bally-nemongroe, Ballytotsy, Ballytrasna, Kilburnie, barony of Fermoy, and Ballymacmurragh, in barony of Duhallow—in all two thousand four hundred and nine acres.

Gwinn, Ensign Daniel, is on the list of 1649 officers.

Harrison, Thomas, appears in report addressed to Court of Claims, in inrollment of certificates, &c. ; and in the Act of Settlement, for lands of Knockahawly and Bealegooly—in all one thousand and thirty-nine acres—barony of Kinalea. He married Grace, daughter of Matthias Anstis, and widow of Mr. Townsend. In his will he bequeathed the sum of ten pounds per annum for ever to the poor of Bandon.

Holcombe, Captain William, on the list of 1649 officers ; also in savings under Act of Settlement, for the sum of £769 5s. 7d. ; and under the Act itself, for the lands Colenapishey, part of Knocknacappul, Clonguas, Ballinvotane—in all nine hundred and seventy-seven acres—barony East Carbery. Captain Holcombe married Ellinor, daughter of Francis Bernard, of Castle-Mahon, and by her had four daughters :—Jane, married William Sweete ; Eliza, married John Johnson ; Mary and Alice.

Hooper, George, on the list of 1649 officers.

Jefford, Captain John (afterwards Colonel Sir John), commanded his company at the battle of Knockegerane. Is on the list of 1649 officers. Lieutenant John Jefford (probably a son of his), was married to Mrs. Catherine Bernard, at Ballymodan Church, on the 15th of October, 1703.

Kinalmeaky, Lord Lewis, given before.

Langton, Lieutenant John, obtained a certificate in the Court of Claims ; and under the Act of Settlement was granted part of the lands of Capuebohy, Ballinloghly, Ballryry, Curran, Banemore, and Farren-larren, barony of Carbery. Lieutenant Langton married a daughter of Francis Bernard, of Castle-Mahon, and by her had three sons and three daughters, viz. :—John, Thomas, William, Elizabeth, Abigail, and Alice. In his depositions before the commissioners at Bandon, he is described as of the parish of Kilbrogan, and his losses, by reason of the rebellion, he represents as amounting to £474 ; independent of the loss of his house, and £300 due to him, which he never expected to get.

Nuce, or Newce, Lieutenant Edmund, was probably the son or grandson of Sir William Newce, our first provost. Obtained £240 14s. 4d. under savings under the Act of Settlement.

Nicholet, Charles, son of Rev. Charles Nicholet, of Ballymodan, appears in inrollment of certificates, and under the Act of Settlement for part of lands of Farlaghaus and Lisnebrinny—total, three hundred and ninty-eight acres—barony Carbery East.

Poole, Captain John, ancestor of the Pooles of Mayfield, was the son of Thomas Poole, who purchased the Mayfield estate in 1628, from the Aderly's. This Thomas and his brother Samuel were both younger sons of Sir Henry Poole, who was high-sheriff of Gloucestershire in 1571. Captain Poole is on the list of 1649 officers, the inrollment of certificates, &c. Under the savings of the Act of Settlement he obtained the sum of £93 19s. 7½d.; and under the Act itself, one hundred and eighty-five acres of the lands of Raheroon. He married Mary, daughter of Francis Bernard, of Castle-Mahon, by whom he had a son, Francis, and two daughters, Mary and Jane.

Shannon, Lord Francis, youngest son of first Earl of Cork. Upon the death of his brother, Lord Kinalmeaky, at Liscarroll, Lord Dungarvan obtained the Bandon troop of horse, and Lord Shannon a company in the Bandon foot. He appears on the list of 1649 officers, inrollment of certificates, &c. Under the Act of Settlement he obtained the lands of Aghamarty and Attenfranky—total, eight hundred and fifty-seven acres—barony Kerricurrihy; and under the savings to the Act of Settlement, for £120 4s. 5d.

Turner, Major Henry, was provost of Bandon in 1627. Although his name is on the list of 1649 officers, inrollment of certificates, &c.; and although he lost £774, and £500 per annum by reason of the rebellion; yet so obnoxious was he to the government of Charles the Second, that they never gave him a grant of a foot of ground, or paid him a shilling of his arrears of pay.

Wade, Bryan, appears in reports addressed to Court of Claims, inrollment of certificates, &c., and in Act of Settlement, for lands of Phealc (four hundred and eighty-five acres), late the estate of Owen McDonough Carthy, parish Ballymoney. Colonel Wade was provost of Bandon in 1698, in which year he died.

Watkins, Captain John, was son of Lieutenant Daniel Watkins. He was made a freeman of the Bandon corporation in 1652, and was provost of Bandon in 1672, 1681, and 1682. Is on the list of 1649 officers, inrollment of certificates, &c., and in savings to Act of Settlement, for £2,164 17s. 3d.

Woodhouse, Captain Sir Michael, on list of 1649 officers.

Woodroffe, Holmstead, and his three brothers, probably sons of John Woodroffe, provost of Bandon in 1642. His name appears in reports addressed to Court of Claims, inrollment of certificates, &c., and under Act of Settlement, for part of lands of Tullilane and Knocknemartelagh—total, two hundred and sixteen acres— late the estate of Charles McCarthy Reagh, parish Ballymodan.

Woodroffe, Jedediah, appears in reports addressed to Court of Claims, inrollment of certificates, &c.; and in Act of Settlement, for part of Tullilane East—total, two hundred and sixty-two acres—parish Ballymodan.

Woodroffe, Clement, provost of Bandon in 1650 and 1662. Name in reports addressed to Court of Claims, and inrollment of certificates, &c.

Woodroffe, Samuel, appears in reports addressed to Court of Claims, inrollment of certificates of adventurers and soldiers; and under Act of Settlement for lands of Carragarriffe, part of Carren and Drometiclough West—total, one thousand one hundred and thirty-six acres—late the estate of Teige O'Crowly, barony East Carbery.

CHAPTER XXIII.

THE BANDON MILITIA, OR SOUTH CORK LIGHT INFANTRY.

N the 26th of September, 1651, it was officially announced that the rebels were subdued, and the rebellion appeased and ended. There being no further necessity for the services of the regiment, they were disbanded, but the services of the troop of horse were retained; and this troop was one of the four in the province of Munster when England declared war with France and Holland in 1663. In that year the Bandon militia were again under arms, and ready for active service. A foreign invasion was looked upon at this time as a certainty. The hostile fleets of the French and Dutch were hourly expected to make a descent upon our southern shores. At one time it was at Bantry Bay they were to land; at another time it was at Kinsale; and then, in hot haste, an express reached the lord-president that sixteen sail of great ships came from the seaward, and were then actually in Dunworly Bay,* where they could easily land their munitions of war undisturbed, and where their troops could form and reach Clonakilty, Bandon, and Kinsale, in less than a day's march. But it was not with a foreign foe alone they had to contend. All the country, south of the Lee, was entrusted to them and some companies of militia raised by some gentlemen in the west of the

---

* This proved to be the squadron under the command of Sir Sydney Smith, who was on his way to Kinsale. It consisted, amongst others, of the Plymouth, Advice. Tiger, Pearl, Ruby, Sweepstakes. Elias, two ketches, two fire-ships, an East India prize, &c. So excited was the lord-president on receipt of this startling piece of intelligence, that in one hour after he heard it, he was on his way to Kinsale as fast as his horse could carry him.

county; and they received orders to answer all alarms from the sea, and towards Kinsale, as well as to keep in good order those turbulent people in the west, of whom Lord Orrery writes :—"There are not such a pack of rogues in all Ireland as those in the west." "The worst sort of people," &c.

In the document sent to Bandon calling out the Bandon regiment, "the worst sort of people" are also referred to, the regiment having got instructions "to seize the several loose and idle persons who, having nothing of their own to subsist by, do labour to live upon the honesty of others ; and that they may have the more opportunity to do it, will go about spreading false reports and seditious rumours."

Speaking in anticipation of the Bandon regiment, Orrery says :— "They will be four hundred good men, all English, and Protestants." Again, speaking of them, he says :—"That the four hundred militia of the town, and two of those three troops I begged of your grace for the province, if garrisoned there, would make it considerable there, and a great countenance to that country."

It would appear that the horse could not be spared for this purpose, for we find that, when the regiment was under arms, it consisted of only three companies of foot; the fourth company being mounted,* in order to strengthen the cavalry—an arm of the service then in high favour.

The war did not last long, and peace was duly proclaimed. As there was no invasion, the ill-affected people in the Carberies did not deem it prudent, on their own account, to arise and measure swords with those† whose heroism was still fresh in their memories ; and everything having again relapsed into tranquility, the halbert was replaced by the wood-man's axe, and the reaping-hook and the grephane were back once more in the hands of those who lately shouldered the musket and wielded the sword.

After the fate of James the Second and his followers was decided at the Boyne, great numbers of stragglers from the Jacobite army sought to make their way back to the west of this county, from which they had not long since set out. This was by no means a difficult task, as all the country through which they had to pass, from Dublin to Cape Clear, -

* They were armed with carbines, and the front rank were supplied with back-plate, breast-plate, and a helmet—in those days called a pot.

† Speaking of the militia at this time, Smith says they were undoubtedly as well officered as any militia since their time, most of the commanders having served in the civil wars.

was in friendly hands, save Bandon alone—the inhabitants of which town, in little more than a fortnight after the successful battle fought near Drogheda, boldly proclaimed William and Mary as King and Queen of England and Ireland, heedless of all consequences.

The stragglers were members of an ill-disciplined, disorderly militia, who were hastily brought together and muskets being placed in their hands for the first time, they were marched northward by O'Driscoll, McCarthy, O'Donovan, and other chieftains—some of whose selves, and many of whose fathers, ever since the days of Cromwell, were on the run, with a price set on their heads. Such were the men who were to lead them to fight with English and Anglo-Irish regiments, under Lanier and Ormond, under Mitchelburne and Wolseley; and with the French Huguenots, the Danes, and the Dutch, under Caillemot, under Wirtemberg, and under Schomberg.

Although they were no longer soldiers, yet they liked the soldiers rations; which consisted, for the most part, of fat oxen and fat sheep which they had plundered from the Protestant colonists, and upon which they had been living ever since they travelled two day's march from their native bogs and mountains; and those they were unwilling to exchange for the goat's flesh and sour milk of western Carbery.

To stay their wholesale robberies, and to rid this locality of themselves, the Bandon militia were again called out for active service, and soon our immediate neighbourhood was cleared of those pests. From the material our soldiers had to contend with at this time, a pitched battle, or even a good fight, was not to be expected. Nothing but skirmishing at the utmost was to be looked for from a body, whose highest aspiration was to steal a flock of sheep, and who thought themselves victorious when they set fire to a settler's thatch, or houghed his cattle.

The Bandon militia scarcely ever fought together as a regiment. It was split up into detachments, and each detachment fought away for the common weal, more in obedience to their natural instincts, or to circumstances that suddenly stood before them, than to any orders received from head-quarters, or the carrying out of some preconceived plan of campaign.

On the 20th of January, 1691, a little party, composed of twenty of the Bandon troop (subsequently known as the East Carbery horse), and eighteen rank and file from one of the foot companies under Lieutenant

Arthur Bernard,* ventured into O'Driscoll's country. This was about
as great a feat in that day as if a similar number of British soldiers
should, in our day, hazard a march into the country possessed by armed
and hostile Caffres, or venture in among the towering mountains and
dark defiles where the warlike Maories stand at bay. The Bandonians
were fortunate as usual. Although one hundred and twenty of O'Donovan's picked men attacked them, they were not only repulsed but
beaten back ; and Bernard and his detachment returned in safety to the

---

* Lieutenant Arthur Bernard, progenitor of the Bernards of Palace-Anne, was
the only brother of Judge Bernard (ancestor of the Earls of Bandon), and youngest
son of Francis, who served many years in the regiment during the great rebellion.
He was born at Castle-Mahon, Bandon, in A.D. 1666, and was married on the 23rd
of December, 1695, "at the castle of Lismore, in the great dining-room, about
eight of the clock on Sunday night," to Anne Power (or Le Poer), of Mount
Eglantine, county Waterford. In 1714 he built the splendid family residence—now
almost a ruin—and called it Palace-Anne, in compliment to Anne, his wife. In
1697, Mr. Bernard was high-sheriff of the county ; and again in 1706. In 1715 he
was elected to represent Bandon in the Irish Parliament, but declined to serve.
In 1718 he was provost of Bandon, on which occasion he gave all the emoluments
of his office to a fund then being raised for the repayment of a sum borrowed to
pay a portion of the fine imposed on the Bandonians by General McCarthy in
1688-9. Mr. Bernard was attainted by King James, and his name appears in the
in the list of "Persons who have notoriously joined in the rebellion and invasion of
this kingdom, and are hereby adjudged traitors, convicted and attainted of high-
treason, and shall suffer death." He was succeeded by his eldest son, Roger
Bernard, provost of Bandon in 1737, and again in 1751 ; who was succeeded by his
only child, Roger. The latter was high sheriff of the county of Cork in 1767, and
died young. Upon his decease the estates passed to his uncle, Arthur Bernard, who
married his cousin, Mary Aderly, great grand-daughter of the lord chief-justice, Sir
Matthew Hale. This Arthur was provost of Bandon in 1745, 1755, 1762, 1772,
1780, 1784, 1786, 1788, and in 1790 ; and died at an advanced age, in 1793. He was
succeeded by his son, Thomas Bernard, who married Harriet, daughter of —— Lucas;
and dying in 1795, issueless, left his estates to Arthur Beamish—the second son of his
sister, Elizabeth, who married Richard Beamish, of Raheroon—thereby disentailing
his brother, Arthur (a captain in the 84th regiment). Arthur had a sister, who
married Captain Jocelyn—one of the Roden family. She accompanied her husband
to America, and was close at hand during the memorable battle at Bunker's
Hill, June 17th, 1775. Previous to her husband marching to the attack, she
obtained a promise from him that, should he survive unhurt, he would return
to her at once when the engagement was over. Not having done so, she boldly
went in quest of him. Many a corpse she turned over, and enquired of
many a poor wounded soldier wearing the familiar facings of her husband's
corps if they could give any tidings of him, but they could not. At last
she came to where the dead lay unusually thick, and there, almost in the
centre of the ghastly group, was the object of her search. He was lying on the
ground, and beside him was his faithful servant, both dead. Catching him up in
her arms, as well as she could, she moved with him some little distance away, and
having washed him and powdered his hair, she garbed him in the full dress which
he often wore on a happier occasion ; then wrapping him up in a pair of blankets,
she scraped out a grave with her own hands, laid the body therein, and having
" smoothed down his lonely pillow," she took the first ship for home. Arthur
married Margaret, daughter of John Warren, of Castle-Warren, niece of Sir Robert
Warren, of Warren's Grove, and by her had eight children. Of whom Francis, the
eldest, was a captain in the 84th Regiment (his three brothers, Arthur, William, and
John, were successively majors in the same corps—a corps which was for many

civilized world, after killing some of the enemy, and bringing with them five hundred sheep, thirteen horses, and fifty cows.

On the 11th of April, Enniskeane was attacked by Brigadier O'Carroll, at the head of McTommies regiment, McCarthy's regiment, and two others. The little garrison, which was composed of a detachment of Sir David Collier's regiment, consisted of Ensigns Lindsay and Daniel, and forty-four rank and file. After fighting some time in the streets, they were obliged to retreat into a house. Here they maintained themselves manfully; but faggots being procured and piled around the walls of the dwelling wherein they were, they would all soon be consumed in one great funeral pyre, had not Major Wade, with ten rank and file of the Bandon regiment, arrived to their assistance. Notwithstanding that fifteen hundred armed and infuriated soldiery, in addition to many civilians equally inimical, surrounded Lindsay's little band, and although six hundred yards lay between the outside of the rebel lines and the house they were in, nevertheless, the Bandon men entered the hostile cordon, and forced their way through the enemy up to the very door. Scarcely had they succeeded in this hazardous attempt—indeed, before the Irish could well recover from the surprise* occasioned by this daring exploit—when Major Ogilby, of Coy's dragoons, gallopped up, and falling on them, he soon routed them. Then following quick in pursuit, he slew seventy-two of them, and scattered the rest.

On the 15th of May, the O'Donovans were again attacked by a portion of the Bandon regiment, when Captain Hugh O'Donovan and six of his men fell into their hands. About the same time a small force, consisting of a lieutenant and eight men, whilst on night patrol, had their attention attracted by the glare of a fire in one of the neighbouring woods. Creeping up noiselessly to where the light proceeded

---

years known in the service as the Bernard's regiment). Captain Francis married, firstly, his cousin-german, Jane, daughter of Richard Beamish, of Raheroon, and had four children:—Arthur, a lieutenant in the 26th Regiment, died in India: Richard, died young; Elizabeth, married her cousin, William Austen; and Mary. And secondly, Marie-Anne Eveline, daughter of George Breton, of Dublin, by whom he had, with other issue, who died young:—William, lieutenant and adjutant of the 81st Regiment, killed in the battle of Ferozeshah, December 22nd, 1845. The day before he had three horses shot under him. So conspicuous were this officer's services, that a special pension was granted by the War Office to his mother. Margaret, who married and settled in Northumberland; Emma; Francis Arthur, died at sea; Frederick Robinson, served in the 31st Regiment, and also in the 56th, married Miss Heffernon, of Cecilstown House; Goderich; and Eveline Aderly.

* It is said the Irish thought these were but the advanced guard of a large body.

from, they came upon a body of forty rapparees, who were sitting round the blazing faggots and enjoying their supper. Although the enemy were five to one, they resolved to attack them. Raising their muskets to the shoulder, they silently awaited orders; and at the word "fire!" four of the rapparees fell dead. The rest, terrified at the sudden onslaught, ran in all directions; and owing to the darkness of the night they were able to escape, leaving, however, twenty horses, some sheep and some cattle, to reward the victors.

On the 1st of May, Sir Richard Cox was appointed governor of the city and county of Cork; and on the 4th he arrived from Dublin to enter on his duties. One of his first acts was to increase the strength of the three militia regiments of the county and city to nine companies each,—namely, the Bandon militia, the city of Cork militia, and the regiment probably at present represented by the North Cork Rifles. He also augmented the cavalry to thirty-six troops, which he divided into six regiments of six troops each. One of these was the East Carbery or Bandon horse, and was chiefly recruited in Bandon and the towns and country adjoining, and from similar material to that of the original troop which behaved so gallantly at Liscarroll. Cox was not satisfied with merely recruiting and organizing his forces—he sketched out a plan of campaign; and it was by his orders Enniskeane was fortified the month after he became governor, and garrisoned by a strong body of the Bandon militia.

This force kept the adjoining country in good order—indeed, one of its detachments penetrated to the neighbourhood of Bantry, where it succeeded in killing close on a hundred of the rapparees, and retracing its steps with a large booty. In less than a fortnight after this the company under Colonel Moore.scoured the country all round Bandon, and killed sixty more of the rapparees. Detachments from head-quarters were always on foot, and were always endeavouring, with more or less success, to rid the country of those desperadoes who would not turn to and earn an honest livelihood for themselves, but would prevent those who strove to do so. The detachment under Captain Nash, in particular, committed such havoc among them, that numerous stories still circulate by our country fire-sides of the summary process by which Shane Dearg used to render it impossible for any of those who fell into his power to interfere any further with the privileges or properties of their fellow-subjects, and which has obtained for him a notoriety which, after the lapse of nearly two centuries, is even yet found to possess a fresh and vigorous vitality.

When the rapparees had been hunted down, and when the Irish gentry to whom the disaffected looked for sympathy and support had transferred themselves and their available assets to foreign lands—not to procure a temporary residence there, but to live and die outside the sway of the Saxon—the country enjoyed a profound calm, undisturbed by a menacing outcry, for nearly a century. Throughout this long night's rest, the services of the Bandon militia were not required. At length a pale flickering light started from among the smouldering political combustibles of France. It soon spread out into flames; then burst into a conflagration; and then, mounting high into the skies with loud and angry roar, flung its broad red glare upon the trembling soil of neighbouring nations. Principalities, kingdoms, empires, rang with the clash of arms. It was but natural that the people of our own favoured isles, who had been enjoying for many generations the civil and religious liberty which the French nation were now madly struggling to attain, should sympathize with them in their efforts, and they did so. But when liberty was supplanted by license; when to be free meant to be free to rob one's fellows; and when doctrines were being preached and practised which aimed at uprooting the very foundation-stones of society, England united with Austria, with Prussia, and with other continental powers, in an effort to stamp out the revolutionary fires which were fast overspreading Europe, and joined those governments in a declaration of war against France.

The French Directory accepted the challenge; and among the schemes they devised for crippling the English enemy was the invasion of Ireland. To meet the difficulty, as well as to suppress the spirit of disaffection now exhibiting itself all over this country, our executive called out the militia. The Bandon regiment (now for the first time called the South Cork) was amongst the number. Throughout the long interval that passed by since it last grounded arms, it would seem that the colonels were regularly nominated as a death vacancy, or a resignation, would occur; and when the bugle summoned the regiment to fall in for the first time within three generations, the colonel was Sir John Cox. He kept his head-quarters at Dunmanway, in which town a great many of the men were now raised, as also in Bantry and Bandon.

Shortly after it was recruited it was marched to Doneraile, where it was armed and disciplined under the eye of its new colonel, Lord Doneraile.* Here they remained only two months, when they got the route for Youghal, where they wintered and staid until the following spring, when they marched for Limerick and Ballyshannon. They staid here, going through the ordinary routine of garrison duty, and occasionally sending out detachments to some of the neighbouring towns, until the latter end of 1796, when a mounted orderly reached head-quarters in great haste, conveying an order for the regiment to set off at once for Cork. This was in the month of December, and the French fleet was daily expected in Bantry Bay. There was no time to be lost. Accordingly the colonel ordered the men to get ready; and, in order to dispense with as much impedimenta as possible, he directed that the cues then worn by them, in common with the rest of the British army, should be cut off, so that no time should be lost in stiffening and powdering those useless appendages. The "assembly" being sounded, the men fell in, and at the word "March!" they turned their backs upon their comfortable quarters, and on a bleak winter's morning took the road for their destination.

It was a long and tedious journey. For eight-and-forty consecutive hours they were never off their feet. They had no time for sleep, or even to dry the wet clothing which clung round their half numbed limbs—nay, there was not even a halt called, unless to snatch a hurried meal, so eagerly were they pressed forward. Day was succeeded by night, and night again by day, and still they were on the march, treading their way through a country, covered deep with snow as far as ever the eye could reach, and over roads, where they sank above their ankles at every step. There was no cheering song during that long dismal route, nor scarce was a word exchanged, save when some poor fellow fell in a faint, disarranging for a moment the succeeding rank and file; at which time some soldier may be heard asking his comrade, in a low, hoarse whisper—"Who is it?" Throughout those two weary days and nights the snow fell for many hours, then a cutting wind prevailed for many more, and then it snowed again. On the second night, just as they were passing the boundary wall of a gentleman's

---

* St. Leger Aldworth, Viscount Doneraile, sat in Parliament for the borough of Doneraile in 1749. Upon succeeding to the estates of his maternal ancestors (the St. Legers) he assumed their surname and arms. He was raised to the peerage, July 2nd, 1776, as Baron Doneraile, of Doneraile; and was created Viscount Doneraile in 1785. He married Mary, eldest daughter of Redmond Barry, of Ballycloughe, and died in 1797, leaving numerous issue.

domain, a little after midnight, the moon, stepping from behind a dark cloud, stood forth in the cold sky, illuminating the chilling scene beneath her with a flood of brilliant light. But it came unlooked for, and was unwelcome to men whose minds were weakened by fatigue, and who, among the shadows of the trees that lay across their path, saw spectral arms outstretched to embrace them; and by the bright silvery light which streamed through the trees themselves, they beheld hideous demons sitting cross-legged in the leafless branches, and beckoning them to come. The hardships they passed through on this terrible occasion were the theme of many a barrack fire-side for many a year afterwards, and a South Cork man who made that memorable march was looked upon by younger soldiers with mingled feelings of admiration and awe.

The morning after their arrival they were paraded for the inspection of General Johnson, whose red-tape eye quickly detected the absence of the all-important cue. Turning to Lord Doneraile, who rode by his side:—"Where's their powder?" gruffly enquired he.

"By G—d! general," said the colonel, "'tis in their pouches; and 'tis there it ought to be in such times as these!"

Johnson quietly took the rebuff, and made no farther enquiries on that subject.

From Cork they were moved to Mammoor camp—about three miles to the west of Bandon—where they remained until the departure of the French fleet from Bantry Bay. They then proceeded to Blarris, in the county of Limerick, and from thence to Wexford, where they lay during the battle of Vinegar Hill, in which affair their light company was under fire. Its casualties, however, were very small, consisting of only two wounded—one of those was a man named Murphy, familiarly known amongst his comrades as Arigadeen. This poor fellow was believed to have been killed, having received a bullet through the cheek, which felled him to the ground, where he lay motionless, and, so far as appearances went, would never "ram down cartridge" or "fix bayonets" again; and, indeed, there is little doubt that the blood from his wound would have choked him eventually, had not Tom Ahearn, the bugler of his company—a wild scamp of a fellow, whom the fear of the black hole, or even of the triangle itself, would not deter whenever he felt inclined for a spree, or any sort of innocent recreation—heard of poor Murphy's mishap.

Smoking his pipe that evening by a camp fire, Tom suddenly remembered that Arigadeen had a watch; and thinking the matter over, he came to the illegal but natural conclusion that Arigadeen being dead, the watch had no owner. Heirs-at-law, and such subtile fictions of the long robe, he had never heard of; and even if he did, it does not seem that he was at that time prepared to recognize them. Be that as it may, Ahearn was determined to have an article so useful to him as a time-keeper. Accordingly, when all was quiet, he strolled over the field in quest of Murphy. He found him after some little time, and putting his fingers into his fob, he was in the act of pulling out the watch with the intention of fobbing it himself, when Murphy awoke; and suddenly sitting up, he shook his fist menacingly in the bugler's face. Almost any one would have taken to their legs under such circumstances, but Tom was not afraid of any man—dead, alive, or on horseback.

"Arn't you dead?" said he, looking complacently at his quondam fellow-soldier.

"No, I ain't!" gurgled out the indignant Murphy.

"Will you say the devil kill the liars after that?" says Tom, who was beginning to think the watch might not be his after all.

"Ov coorse I will!" replied the wounded man. Then, after an effort or two, he succeeded in removing some of the clotted blood that impeded his utterance. "I'm no more dead than you are, Tom Ahearn!" says poor Murphy, "I'm only kilt; and shure if you're not a heathen entirely, entirely, you won't lave me here all night!"

Tom's heart softened at last, and taking poor Arigadeen upon his back, he carried him safely into camp. Under the skilful treatment of the surgeon, Murphy soon came round, and was enabled to serve several years after in the regiment, where he was always known as a steady and well-conducted man.

From Wexford they marched to the Curragh of Kildare, where they lay under canvas for a short time. Their next destination was Galway, where they remained for the winter. Early next spring they set out for Kinsale, to which place they leisurely proceeded by easy marches.

The rebellion being now virtually over, the services of the regiment were needed no longer. Accordingly their arms were stored, and the South Cork, consisting at that time of six hundred and fifty bayonets, were disembodied.

They did not remain long in retirement when they were again called

to arms, and fell into line in the old barrack-yard in Kinsale, after an
interval of only eleven months.

In 1803, being in a high state of efficiency, they left Kinsale in the
April of that year for Mallow, where they recruited to their full
strength. They were only two months here when they got the route
for Waterford, where they remained until 1805. In that year they
were stationed in the county of Roscommon, with head-quarters at
Boyle. They staid here but twelve months, when they moved to
Mayo (1806), detaching from where the regiment lay, at Castlebar.
One detachment, which consisted of Captain Newman's company, was
quartered at Ballina, and to this town the head-quarters shortly after
removed. Detachments were also sent out from Ballina. One of these
was at Westport; another at Crossmolina, on the western extremity of
Lough Conn; another at Eskerough, and elsewhere.

About this time, a body of men known as the Threshers, or Carders,
kept all Mayo in terror. Their hostility to tithe-corn, and their running
off with it and thrashing it for their own benefit, earned for them the
sobriquet by which they were universally known. They committed
great injury not only on the property of Protestant clergymen, but also
on that of those who sympathized with them, and whose exertions in
their behalf caused the Threshers to look on them as their avowed
enemies. There was no ascertaining who the perpetrators were.
Fellows who spent all night wrecking the revenues of the parson
looked the very incarnation of innocence in the morning, and would
speak of the devastators with as much virtuous indignation as if they
were tithe-owners themselves. They had no word in their mouths too
bad for them—they were ruffians; they were blackguards; they were
thieves; and if they only knew who they were, they'd soon bring the
sojers upon 'em. But as they did not know them, their friendly
sentiments were valueless in staying the transgressions or informing the
authorities who the transgressors were.

At last it was likely that the mystery would remain a mystery no
longer, and that the midnight doings of the Threshers would soon be
submitted to the broad glare of mid-day. A man who went by the
name of Murty the Thresher, and who was long suspected of being
one of their most active partizans, had turned informer, and gave the
authorities such intelligence as led to the arrest of several of his former
accomplices. These were seized, and lay in the County Gaol awaiting

their trial at the next Assizes. Murty was the principal witness against them, and was, of course, a marked man. So well was he aware of this himself, that he left the country where he had been residing all his life, and went to live in Ballina; and for better security still, put up at the very next door to the barracks occupied by the South Cork. He had lived in the country, as we have said, where he had a snug farm, a few miles from the town; but as he had given up all notion of ever living there again, he let it be known that he would dispose of his interest in it, as he intended to emigrate when the trial in which he was concerned was over.

Early one Sunday morning, a respectable old farmer called to see him. His story was soon told. He had a family of grown-up sons; and as one of these could be well married if he could get him possession of a good farm, he would close with him for the one he had to sell at once, if they could agree. As this was the very thing for the old man, Murty put a good stiff price on it; and after a reasonable time spent in endeavouring to reduce the sum demanded, Murty and the old man struck a bargain. As the purchaser wanted to get possession at once, Murty must come home along with him that very moment to his house, distant only three or four miles, until he'd get the purchase-money. Murty went with him, and they passed along the road very agreeably together. "A dry bargain isn't lucky," said the old farmer, entering the door of his house, and ushering in his guest. Accordingly he opened a cupboard, and placed a bottle of whiskey and glasses upon the table. "Come Murty, my bochill," said he, filling up his glass at the same time, "drink success to this day's work." Murty did so, and the old man drank to the same. Then they had together another glass apiece, during which they talked over the merits of the farm; and then another. Then followed a song; and so pleasantly did the time fly by, that Murty did not mind it passing; but not so his wife, who remained at home. She grew very uneasy at his protracted stay; and seeing no signs of his returning, she went straight to the farmer's house where he was. She urged him to return with her at once; but some plausible excuses were made by the old man, and by some means or other she was also delayed. It was not very long, however, until the door opened, and a man roped all over with sugawns, and accompanied by two other, entered with a hatchet on his shoulder. The wife instantly knew what was intended, and with a fierce courage and determination which women sometimes display under circumstances where men are unnerved and undecided, she sprang upon the intended assassin, and tore the straw ropes from his face. Murty screeched through sheer terror, and jumping up from the table, rushed for the door; through which he would have escaped, had not one of the farmer's sons caught him by the skirts of the coat, and pulled him back, causing him to fall upon one knee; and in this attitude he was when the man with the hatchet reached him, and, raising his formidable weapon, with one terrific blow upon the forehead he killed him on the spot.

The detachment of the regiment which lay at Crossmolina marched out and brought in the body, and also the farmer's son who caught poor Murty by the coat, the old farmer himself, the assassin, and his two accomplices; and the next morning a strong guard escorted them heavily ironed to Castlebar. Amongst the precautions taken to ensure their safe arrival at their destination, was that of cutting the string by which they tightened the waistband of their breeches round their loins, in order that if any of them attempted to run away the breeches would fall about their heels and prevent them.

Poor Murty was terribly mutilated. In addition to his skull being broken in, it was found that there were no less than twenty-seven stabs of some sharp instrument on his unfortunate corpse. Most of these had the appearance of being made with French bayonets—probably by some of the very weapons distributed among the peasantry by Humbert when he landed a few years before at Killalla.

At the trial, Murty's widow swore positively to the man with the hatchet, also to the farmer's son who pulled down her husband. She also swore to the presence of the old man, and the two accomplices. The jury returned with a verdict of guilty against them all, and the judge sentenced them to be hanged. A strong division of the regiment surrounded the place of execution, which was at that time known as the artillery ground. A long ladder was placed horizontally, having each end resting in the fork of a tree. The prisoners were then brought up in carts, and placed under what was to serve as the fatal beam; and the ropes being secured round their necks and fastened to the ladder overhead, the carts were rolled away, and the five bodies as they swung to and fro in the cold morning air testified to the supremacy of the law.

From Ballina, where the regiment gave a large number of volunteers to the 15th and 41st of the line, they proceeded to Limerick. They did not remain long there, owing to a bad feeling being entertained by the citizens, towards them, in consequence of a sentry belonging to the regiment, who was placed on a pump, having bayonetted a civilian who insisted on drawing water from it in spite of him. Accordingly they set out in the spring of 1808, and marched to Clonmel.

The following is a list of the officers who served with the regiment at this time :—

Colonel Lord Viscount Doneraile.*	Lieutenant McCarthy.
Lieut.-Colonel Redmond Barry.†	,, Morris.
Major A Hill.	,, Townsend.
,, Langton.	Ensign Kilner Barry.
Captain Browne.	,, Bruce.
,, Atkins.	,, Carey.
,, Cooker.	,, Daunt.
,, Crone.	,, Foot.
,, Godsell.	,, Harris.
,, Newman.	,, Lindsay.
Lieutenant Francis Heard.	,, Nash.
,, E. Hungerford.	Adjutant Bagley.
,, T. Hungerford.	Assistant-Surgeon Chomley.
,, Langley.	Quarter-Master Lieut. Lucas.
,, Lloyd.	

As several of the men were suffering from ophthalmia, the regiment got the route for the Curragh ; but had only reached Athy when a countermand overtook them, and they were ordered to Wicklow, where they remained all the summer, detaching to Arklow, Hacketstown, Tinahely, the Seven Churches ; and in the autumn of the same year they went to Dublin, where they wintered and staid until April, 1809, in which month they arrived in Kerry. Their head-quarters were at Killarney, and detachments were sent to Tralee, Castle-Island, Kenmare, and Millstreet. Here they remained some time, and then proceeded to Boyle, county Roscommon, in 1810, where Colonel Barry died of fever. Again they returned to Limerick ; and while in quarters in that garrison, in 1811, they furnished many volunteers to the 31st Regiment. From Limerick they got the route for Galway,

---

* Upon the death of Lord Doneraile, Lord Riversdale, who married his daughter, Charlotte Theodosia, was appointed colonel. William Tonson, Baron Riversdale, of Rathcormac, was born in 1775, and died in April, 1848.

† Colonel Barry was succeeded in the lieut.-colonelcy by Hayes St. Leger, Viscount Doneraile ; and, upon the death of Lord Riversdale, to the full colonelcy. He was born in 1786, and in 1816 he married Charlotte Esther, second daughter of Francis, Earl of Bandon. He died in 1854, and was succeeded by the present colonel.

where they were stationed at Tuam, and subsequently at Loughrea; and it was whilst at the latter place they volunteered to serve in any part of the United Kingdom. In 1812 they marched to Athlone; and after giving a great number of volunteers to the 62nd, they left in 1813, and marched direct to the Cove of Cork. Here transports awaited them; and after a rough passage they landed at Plymouth, and proceeded direct to Brighton. Whilst occupying those fashionable quarters, they were officially inspected by the Duke of Clarence (afterwards William the Fourth); and so pleased was his Royal Highness with their soldierly bearing, and the precision with which they executed the various military manœuvres they were put through, that he publicly avowed they were by far the best Irish regiment he had ever seen; and to stamp his appreciation of their efficiency with an enduring mark of his approval, he had them changed from an ordinary regiment into one of light infantry; and from that time forward, Light Infantry has been added to the South Cork—the name, we need scarcely say, by which this old corps is at present known. From Brighton they went in cantonments at Lewes, and remained there until the following December, when they got the route for Plymouth. They were three weeks on this march, and both officers and men suffered severely from the frost and snow. They were but a few months here when they were ordered to Dartmouth, where many French and American prisoners were confined; and they remained there until peace was proclaimed on the 30th of May, 1814.* Back again to Plymouth, and across St. George's Channel to the Cove of Cork, where they arrived in September, 1814; and on the 14th of the following month—that is October, 1814—they were disembodied in Cork barracks.

The staff proceeded to take up its quarters at Rathcormac. It consisted of Captain Bagley (the adjutant), Captain Gregg (paymaster), Walter Evans (quarter-master), forty sergeants, twenty corporals, twenty buglers, a sergeant-major, a bugle-major, a quarter-master sergeant, &c.—ninety-three men in all, exclusive of the officers whose names we have just mentioned.

---

* So indignant were the French prisoners at Dartmouth at Napoleon being sent to Elba, and a Bourbon again mounting the throne of France, that they seized an unfortunate dog upon one occasion, and, before the eyes of some officers of the regiment who happened to be present, they secured a royal cockade between his ears, and tricking him out in the Bourbon colours, they hunted him round the prison; and then placing a rope round his neck, they hanged him with every sign of ignominy and contempt.

In May, 1815—just seven months after they had got the "dismiss" in Cork barracks—the regiment was again assembled at Fermoy, and they were then for the first time clothed and equipped as light infantry, the authorities not having permitted the new uniform to issue until the one previously in use was worn out; and as the latter continued good for the residue of the time the regiment was embodied, they had no opportunity of donning the new regimentals until now. From Fermoy they marched to Clonmel, and from thence to Carlow, where they remained hard at drill until they were ordered back to Fermoy. Here they were again disembodied on St. Patrick's-day, 1816. The staff removed to the quarters from whence it had issued but just ten months before, and here it reposed, free from all the exciting scenes and dangers of a soldier's life, for eight and thirty years.

During this long interval the old adjutant died; the old paymaster died; and the doctor and the quarter-master, too, discharged that great obligation which we must all fulfill; and of the ninety-three sergeants, corporals, and buglers, who marched out of Fermoy barracks in 1816, there were only three left to obey the bugle call in 1854.

On the 28th of March in that year, the war trumpet, whose thrilling notes had not been heard in the United Kingdom for more than the third of a century, again made the welkin ring with the call to arms, and England proclaimed war with Russia. The summons was ardently responded to. Young soldiers volunteered for immediate service, and wished they had been old enough to take a part in the great battle which has immortalized the plains of Waterloo; and old soldiers—even those who had suffered in the disastrous Walcheren expedition, and who had endured fearful hardships in the retreat to Corunna—tendered their services, too, and wished they were young once more, that they may fight their battles over again. Again the drums and fifes resound through our streets; the recruiting sergeant, with his drawn sword and many-coloured ribands streaming from his shako, invites the younger portion of his male audience to step forward like men, and take the shilling in the name of the Queen. A military ardour seizes on the public mind, and recruits in dozens join the ranks.

The 1st of February, 1855, was a memorable day in the annals of the South Cork. On that day the old stand of colours, which had remained unseen for many a weary year, again stood erect, and waved proudly in the breeze. On that day the few survivors of the old corps

33

looked thoughtfully on their young fellow-soldiers, and on the busy scene before them, as their minds strayed back to old associations and the comrades of a former age; and on that day the regiment assembled for embodiment within the very walls where the regiment was originally enrolled upwards of two hundred and twelve years before. Two hundred and four men answered to their names on the day of embodiment, and the following are the names of those who bore commissions in the regiment at that time :—

Colonel Hon. H. B. Bernard.
Lieut.-Colonel H. Wallis.
Major Hon. H. Freke.
Captain P. Somerville.
   ,,   Hewitt Poole.
   ,,   Robert Heard.
   ,,   George Bowles.
   ,,   E. A. Shuldham.
   ,,   R. T. Rye.
   ,,   A. L. Newman.
   ,,   William Johnson.
   ,,   Sir J. L. Cotter.
   ,,   H. D. J. Gaynor.
Lieutenant W. Ryder.
   ,,   William Bowles.
   ,,   J. R. Wheeler.
   ,,   M. C. Wall.
   ,,   F. D. Cornwall.
   ,,   Godfrey Baldwin.

Lieutenant S. S. Tresilian.
   ,,   J. H. Cole.
   ,,   R. White.
   ,,   Frank Heard.
Ensign Chambro Baldwin.
   ,,   Robert Holmes.
   ,,   C. Deane.
   ,,   W. P. Hosford.
   ,,   S. Hawkes.
   ,,   W. H. Bird.
   ,,   R. Agar.
   ,,   J. H. Markham.
Adjutant Captain A. H. Lucas, late 45th Regiment.
Surgeon John G. Gregg.
Quarter-master D. Cummins.
Paymaster T. D. Perry, late captain 81st Regiment.

After remaining some time in Bandon, the regiment marched to Kinsale, where they received their new colours in July; and then, some months after, proceeded to Cork. They were only a few months there when they got the route for Limerick, in which garrison, after the delay of only one week, they received orders for Dublin. On their arrival in our metropolis, they were quartered in the Palatine Square Royal Barracks; and throughout this kingdom there was no regiment more admired for its steadiness and discipline, than the gallant South Cork.

On the 30th of March, 1856, a treaty of peace was signed between Russia on one side, and England and her allies on the other; and in a few months afterwards the regiment arrived in Cork barracks, where they were disembodied on the 12th of August, 1856.

During the eighteen months they were out, they gave upwards of two hundred recruits to the line, and the following officers :—Lieutenant

John R. Wheeler, to the 1st Foot; Lieutenant F. D. Cornwall, to the 62nd Foot; and Ensign Hawkes, to the 37th.

Upon the disembodiment, the staff, which consisted of the adjutant, the quarter-master, twenty-seven sergeants, and ten buglers, were quartered where the regiment first drew its breath; where it first smelt powder and saw blood; where it received the thanks of the most memorable Parliament in the long list of memorable Parliaments of Great Britain; where the greatest general the world has ever seen since the era of the great Cæsar, complimented them; and where her sons, comprising, as they did, its officers and rank and file, for more than the first sixty years of its existence, covered themselves with a glory which will endure as long as heroism will be admired.

CHAPTER XXIV.

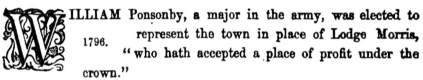

ILLIAM Ponsonby, a major in the army, was elected to
represent the town in place of Lodge Morris,
"who hath accepted a place of profit under the
crown."

1796.

On the 21st of October the Bandon corps of yeomanry cavalry
were called out. Lord Bandon was appointed captain, Robert Hedges,
lieutenant, and Arthur Beamish Bernard, cornet. It was unanimously
resolved by the corps, that they would serve without pay, and,
in addition, provide their own clothing; but that they would accept
accoutrements and arms from the government. The Rev. Ambrose
Hickey was their chaplain, Richard Laone, surgeon, Edward Cotter,
junr., secretary; Timothy Deasy, junr., Henry Bowen Browne, and
and John Hawkes, sergeants; and Thomas Browne, Samuel Hawkes,
John Sweete, and William Popham, corporals.

The foundation-stone of the Roman Catholic chapel on Gallow's
Hill was laid on the 28th of April. The ground was given gratuitously
by the Earl of Bandon, who, in addition, subscribed liberally towards
its erection, as also did many of the Protestant inhabitants. When the
rebellions were over, and when many of those who were possessed of a
feverish anxiety for revolt and bloodshed had left the country, or had
turned to peaceful pursuits, the necessity for maintaining the Penal
Laws in their rigour—laws which the English colonists had been compelled to enact in their self-defence, in order to save themselves from

being not only overwhelmed, but exterminated by the Irish enemy—had gradually become less and less. The Roman Catholics saw this, and soon their places of worship began to arise again.

The first chapel within whose walls the people in this neighbourhood used to assemble was at Kilhassen,* where a site was given them by Mr. Poole, of Mayfield. In this remote place, which is several miles to the west of Bandon, a small building, thirty feet long by twelve broad, was raised, and covered with straw. The materials of which this edifice was constructed were of the rudest kind; the stones being for the most part taken out of ditches, and collected off fields, and out of dykes; and the rafters were pine trees, roughly shaped, to support the thevauns or laths upon which rested the thatch. Even the altar was nothing more than a pile of undressed stones put together by unskilful hands, and bedded in clay mortar. An addition of fifteen feet by twelve was made to the eastern side of this building by Father Daniel Quinlan, but he was unable to roof it. Consequently, when the wind blew from the east, the congregation were exposed to its biting effects. To avoid this, he built an altar on the western side of the western gable, so that when his people were unable to worship at the eastern side they could at the western.

The distance of Kilhassen from Bandon rendered it desirable that the Roman Catholic place of worship should be nearer the town. Accordingly, Father Dan Neville—one of Quinlan's successors—obtained a piece of ground from Mr. Travers, of Roundhill, where he erected a spacious building, around which grew the hamlet now known as the Old Chapel. This structure stood in a field near the mill at the north side of the road. The last priest who was appointed to this chapel was Father Shinnick; and he continued to celebrate mass in it until the completion of the new chapel at Gallow's Hill. During the erection of the latter, several of the most respectable and influential of our Protestant townsmen took a warm interest in it. Amongst the rest, the Rev. Henry Hewett, the Protestant vicar of the parish, who acted as treasurer to a fund collected from among his own congregation in aid of the building. This chapel, in course of time, being found too limited for the comfortable accommodation of the congregation, the foundation-stone of a spacious and

---

* So thickly overgrown with trees was this locality so late as 1750, that, it is said, a man could pass from Butler's Cross to the Bandon river without touching his foot to the ground.

elegant structure was laid on the 17th of March, 1858. It is dedicated to St. Patrick, and although not perfectly finished, divine service has been performed in it for some years.

The French fleet arrived in Bantry Bay towards the close of December. A letter written by a Bandon man to his brother, in a few weeks afterwards, gives us an opportunity of seeing matters as they then were—or, at least, as they then presented themselves to one who was there, and saw them at that eventful period. After alluding to the journey of a friend and himself from Limerick, he says:—" When we came to Bandon, there was nothing there but the appearance of war and hunger. I could not get as much bread in town as would do me for my breakfast. Bread was so scarce that the bakers were obliged by the provost to bake on Christmas-day, to supply the wants of the great number of soldiers that were in the town; and which were daily increasing, for they were coming from all parts of the kingdom, with artillery and cannon continually rolling in. The churches, meeting-house, and preaching-house, were filled with soldiers. The chapel was formed into a horse-barrack, so that our town was dressed in all the horrors of war. All the little towns and country were thronged with militia. Expresses hourly arriving from Bantry." Again :— "Many of the moneyed people here took their flight from Cork and Dublin, to embark for England. Lord Bandon sent off his family with all his valuable effects. The ladies and married people are greatly in dread. Many of them had their money at interest, and those that had it would not own to have a shilling, so that they were tortured by double fears. Thus were the holidays spent in Bandon, and for seven days after, until the Lord arose a mighty wind that drove them from the bay, and damaged their shipping, so that they could never muster after."

1797.   Broderick Chinnery, of Anne's Grove, county Cork, and the Hon. William O'Callaghan, of Shanbally, were elected to represent Bandon in the last Parliament that was to be held in Dublin.

Private Dominick Giligan, Roscommon militia, and Corporal Drumgold, Westmeath militia, were tried by court-martial at Bandon, on the 10th of July in this year (1797); and Corporal McAuliffe, and William Larracy (both of the Second Fencible Dragoons), on the 20th of July, also at Bandon; " for beginning, exciting, causing, or joining in a mutiny or sedition in the corps to which they belong, by having taken unlawful, mutinous, or seditious oaths, or being instrumental in their being taken; as also for being present at a mutiny or sedition, or intended mutiny or sedition, and not using their utmost endeavours to suppress the same; or coming to the knowledge of a mutiny, or intended mutiny, and not, without delay, giving information thereof to their commanding officer."

From the evidence given by John Daly, it appears that Giligan was the agent of the United Irishmen at the camp at Mammoor. He also swore that another soldier, named MacDonald, told him " that they put a coal of fire to the wagon-stores, which was found and put out by a dragoon who had stables near it; and that they were waiting for a letter from Fermoy camp, and when they received that, they would place the cannon on the 30th Regiment's barracks to keep them in, as they could not depend on them."

Patrick Dangan, of the Galway Light Infantry, deposed :—" After going up stairs, Giligan asked him if he had a mind to know more of the secret; when he took out a paper and began to read, and swore him to be true to the French Republic, and take the life of any man that would attempt to discover."

Henry Curren, private, Second Fencible Dragoons, deposed :—" That about three months before, Corporal McAuliffe and John Purcell, of the same regiment, took him up Cork-road, and told witness, if he would do as they desired, he would never want a friend, a shilling, or a drink while a brother could give it to him. That McAuliffe sent Purcell for Larracy, who asked them what news? They said good news; and then Larracy said he always thought witness a sober, settled fellow, and believed he (the witness) would become a brother. That Denis Callaghan, the slater, coming up, asked if witness was a brother. He was told that he meant to become one. Callaghan then shook hands with him, and then took him inside a ditch, where he swore him to keep secret what he should see or hear. They all then went to Murphy's public-house; and after getting some liquor, Callaghan read the articles—which were to be true to a brother, and never to see one of them want so long as he would have twopence-halfpenny, and that he was to join the French when they'd come. At the bottom of the paper were two hearts and a tree, apparently done with silk. Callaghan said he got them from a Mr. O'Connor, in the west, and that the tree denoted liberty. They then showed him signs with the hand, of love and liberty; McAuliffe and Larracy often repeating them to him; and Callaghan taught him a catechism by which he'd know a brother. They all told him that they intended to rise about the 1st of July, to seize the cannon and the camp, to murder the officers and all who would not join them; and that even if the French did not come, they thought they would be able to march through the kingdom themselves."

It was principally upon the evidence of a man named Riely that Corporal Drumgold was convicted.

'In addition to the evidence we have just given in reference to the prisoners, there was other evidence given concerning them and their accomplices, from which we extract that of John Hargrove, who deposed :—" That, about a month before, he was walking by the river, near Mammoor camp, when he was called by seven or eight men of the Meath, county Limerick, Wexford, and Waterford; when he was told by one of them—a man named Allen—that they intended writing to the North and other parts of the kingdom, to inform them that they would go on with their intentions on the 1st of July; and then to have the kingdom on fire on both ends, and in the middle; and then, with what friends Mr. O'Brien, near Bandon, could send them, and what friends they had in the camp (about four hundred), that they intended first taking the cannon, and then the bell-tents, with the small arms (which they would give the country-people that would be sent by Mr. O'Brien), and then put General Coote to death, and as many officers as they could, and then retreat to Bandon, and take possession of the battery, and keep it, if possible, until the French would land.*

The prisoners were found guilty, and sentenced to be shot. The day after they received their sentence, they were brought in two carriages from the camp of Mammoor, through Bandon, and down to a field midway between Bandon and Innoshannon. Giligan and Drumgold were accompanied by Father Haly; and McAuliffe and Larracy, of the Second Fencible Dragoons, by Father Shinnick. All the troops in Bandon and at Mammoor camp were drawn up, so as to form the three sides of a square, the fourth being reserved as the place of execution. The unhappy men being brought forward, their sentence was again read to them, after which they were pinioned and placed kneeling upon their coffins. The firing party having moved forward,

* See appendix to report from the select committee of the House of Commons, 1798.

they were ordered to make ready. At the word "present!" the men levelled their pieces at the accused, and kept them poised in that position, awaiting the next order. The suspense for a few seconds was agonizing, and then the suppressed feelings, unable to bear the strain on them any longer, gave way, and one simultaneous "Oh!" burst from the thousands of spectators who had assembled to witness this sad scene. "Fire!" and the loud report which ran along the green hill side told its own story. When the smoke had cleared away, it was found that Giligan, McAuliffe, and Larracy, were shot dead, but that Drumgold was untouched. Upon this, the provost-sergeant leisurely marched up to him, and placing the muzzle of his pistol against his right temple, deliberately blew out his brains. The four bodies were then coffined, and buried in the graveyard of Innoshannon.

For a long time afterwards—indeed up to a few years since—four large mounds of stone marked the place of execution; but the utilitarian spirit of the age has removed even these, and the last time we saw this *place de greve*, a good crop of turnips concealed beneath their luxuriant leaves all traces of an event, the like of which we hope this locality will long be a stranger to.

According to some patriotic poetaster, who has committed this affair to verse, and whose lucubrations we now give, they were innocent— that is, according to an interpretation often given to that term in this country, however guilty they may have been, they ought not to be punished; and their lives were taken away by traitors, who falsely swore. Nevertheless, he honestly tells us, that General Coote offered to pardon them "if they'd make discovery." But that they instantly refused, and told him to his teeth that they would prove constant; and, besides, that they were united, and that they hoped to be rewarded for it hereafter.*

"Assist me all ye muses, and give me no excuses,
    Concerning these few verses, I mean for to relate,
  On the laws of extirpations, and bribed perjurations,
    Which caused great desolations in this country of late.

"To make a just inspection, it would hazard no reflection,
    To treat on that horrid action, done at the camp Mammoor—
  By the laws of General Coote, I dare not tell the truth
    Of this perpetual murder, would be treason, I am sure.

---

* This is what is called a treasonable song, and is never sung unless the doors are closed, and a watch kept, lest some myrmidon of the law should be eavesdropping, and get the singer and his auditory into trouble.

"There's McAuliffe, Larracy, and the noble brave Drumgold,
    Giligan, we learn, is the subject of my theme;
To the time of all duration, and to its consummation,
    With grief and great vexation, I moralize on their fame.

"No heroes could be braver, they were lads of good behaviour,
    Until Curran, Reily, and Daly swore their lives away;
For the sake of golden ore, the traitors falsely swore,
    And left them in their gore at Innoshannon that day.

"Bandon may remember, these heroes once in splendour,
    In all their pomp and grandeur, a-glittering from afar;
Light infantry advancing, and cavalry a-prancing,
    And shining armour glancing, all in the pomp of war.

"The hills and dales were crowded, and all parts beshrouded,
    The streets were strongly guarded, most shocking for to see;
Drums and trumpets rattle, as of veterans going to battle,
    And these heroes to be slaughtered for the sake of liberty.

"The appointed ground they arrived at, their lives to be deprived of,
    Then off their garments stripped, and from them flung away;
Their arms being unbounded, with numerous bands surrounded,
    And the trumpets loudly sounded, their valour to display.

"They held a consultation, to find out the combination,
    And in an exultation the general he did say:—
'By me you'll be remembered, and your guilt you'll not be charged with,
    And, besides, you'll be pardoned, if you make discovery.'

"They stood awhile amused, their senses being confused,
    And instantly refused, and made him this reply:—
'We know the laws which arm, and your threat don't us alarm;
    Our souls you cannot harm—we have but once to die.

"'Although we are young and tender, to you we won't surrender,
    But like Hibernia's defender, most constant we will prove;
And, besides, we are united, and of death we're not affrighted,
    And we hope we'll be requited by He who rules above.'

"There is the noble Father Haly, attended the infantry,
    And the noble Vicar Shinnick, the cavalry did attend.
Placed in a hollow square, well guarded front and rear,
    The guards did prepare to cause their fatal end.

"The peace, boys, it will restore throughout the Irish shore;
    We'll be present here no more—we'll die for liberty.
The guns they were presented, and their gentle breasts were entered—
    Thousands of souls lamented to see such cruelty.

"To see those lovely four, a-weltering in their gore,
    And their breeches all dyed o'er with this barbarity.
To the coffins they were hurried; to Innoshannon carried;
    And instantly were buried—a dreadful sight to see!"

On the 19th of June, the Westmeath regiment of militia, consisting of upwards of seven hundred men, under the command of Colonel Sir Hugh O'Reilly, marched from Clonakilty, where they had been some time quartered, for Bandon. When they had reached within a short distance of Balliniscarthy, several hundreds of the insurgents, armed chiefly with pikes, hastened to meet them. Sir Hugh called a halt, formed his men, and gave the word to load. The order they obeyed, and rammed down cartridges in due form, but *without the balls*: these they bit off, and dropped upon the road. The rebels still pressing on, the section on the right of the column was ordered to fire; but the harmless discharge only produced merriment. Anticipating little injury after this friendly reception, the insurgents now boldly came up. Some of them shook the soldiery by the hand, and familiarly addressed them by name. More of them slapped them on the back, and swore the day was their own. Others bestrode the cannon; and one huge fellow, named Teige-an-Astna, more audacious than his fellows, actually walked up, and seized the colonel's charger by the bridle. But a sergeant, who was in the ranks, and one of the few who had loaded with ball, stepped a pace or two to the front, and, levelling his piece at Teige, shot him dead; but he did not live long to congratulate himself upon his loyalty, for his rear-rank man, taking aim, discharged his musket through his back, and he fell in agony upon the ground. There were a few rank and file scattered throughout the ranks of the same way of thinking as poor Cummins; and now they began to grow uneasy for their lives, and well they might. Some of their comrades, with whom they had never once interchanged an angry word, now pushed intentionally against them; others spat in their faces, and in a short time, in all probability, they would have shared the sergeant's fate, had not a strong company of the Caithness Legion, under Major Jones, opportunely made its appearance.

This little force had been sent out to reconnoitre, and to keep the Westmeath in check, information as to the premeditated disloyalty of that corps having been received in Bandon the night before. Their unexpected arrival produced a magical effect upon the disaffected. The most turbulent amongst them became instantly silent. They fell into the ranks without even waiting for the word of command; and, when ordered to march, they set forward with alacrity. Meanwhile the Caithness continued to advance, and having got between the rear of the Westmeath and the enemy's front, they faced to the latter; then, suddenly opening out their ranks, they discharged their two field-pieces at them with much effect. Accompanying this with a volley of musketry, they soon sent them scampering off to the hills.

The bodies of the two men were taken in a cart to Clonakilty. That of Teige-an-Astna was ignominiously flung into a pool of water in the Strand, called Crab Hole; but the remains of Sergeant Cummins were buried with full military honours in the graveyard attached to the parish church of the town.

The following humorous extract from a letter, dated Bandon, July 10th, shows that the new century opened out with the old state of things :—

1800.

"The loyalty of this town never appeared more conspicuously than on the glorious 1st of July. The windows were decked out with green boughs, variegated with flowers and orange lilies, and appeared at a distance as so many hanging gardens; while the mind was awfully impressed with the sight of those royal culprits, King James and Queen Mary, who were hanged, shot at, and consigned to the flames, as they ought to be. The spectators beheld, with pleasing astonishment, King William placed on a spire of one of the churches, majestically moving in the air, riding over a salmon, painted orange colour, and with purple fins. The battle of the books was nothing to the real battle that took place between the caps. In the beginning, the country-women, who were accustomed to pluck sheep, had by far the advantage, when a reinforcement coming down to the Orange girls, victory was soon decided in their favour, when caps, ribbons, and hair were plentifully distributed about."

We ought not to be surprised that many Roman Catholics, who believe in that unchristian dogma of their communion, which pronounces inevitable damnation against all those who are not members of the Papal church, should entertain inimical feelings towards their Protestant fellow-subjects; but these feelings are mildness itself, when compared to the hostility—in fact, the dire hatred—entertained by them towards those who have renounced their faith and become Protestants. They won't believe, or they affect not to believe, in the sincerity of their conversion—"it was for lucre they turned." In addition to the repugnance with which they see the number of the faithful diminishing, in their case, there is another reason. When one of them becomes a member of the Reformed church, in their eyes, he ceases to be a Celt, and becomes a Saxon. Instead of being one of the oppressed, he is now among the oppressors. Instead of howling with his quondam fellows after that which belongs to others, he will be expected to tell them that they ought to work vigorously and create something for themselves; and, henceforward, his interests and his aspirations will be wholly Saxonized. Hence, a man when he became a Protestant never had a day's luck. If his pig took the meazles, or his cow shortened in her milk, or his horse wanted shoes, it would be :—" Yerra! how could he have luck, and to turn !"

In addition to the reasons assigned by Protestants for conversions to their faith, such as the study of the scriptures, &c., the following is the strangest we have met with yet, and is assigned as the reason why the H——s became Protestants.

Old H——, said our informant, was a strong farmer, who scraped together a considerable sum of money by dint of hard industry, and he kept it together by dint of not spending it. His wife was also very saving, and was the very counterpart of old H—— himself. They had only one child—a son—a smart, intelligent fellow, who scarcely ever entered the neighbouring town without bringing home a book of some sort with him, and with the contents of which he made himself familiar. This annoyed the old people, who thought that a book was all very well in its way, and that it was a nice thing on a Sunday, when one had nothing to do, to be turning over the leaves, and be looking at the pictures; but to be wasting week-days in reading it, was a thing not to be listened to. Pat, his father, would often say to him, " 'twould be fitter for you to go out and see if the cows eat all their hay, or to bruise a kitch of furze for the horse, or to throw a handful of bran into the trough to the pigs, than to be idling your day in larning larning." " I never saw much good come of books," would chime in his old mother; " and it must be bad larnin' is in the books you read, Pat a gilliah, when they'd make you go walking about the fields of a Sunday, instead of going to prayers."

In due time the old man died, and young Pat became the owner of a well-stocked farm, and a good round sum in hard cash. A short time after the funeral, Father Dan, the parish priest, went to condole with the old woman, and to ask the son when he was going to have masses said for the repose of his poor father's soul.*

---

* Cardinal Mazarin was asked one time how many masses it would take to save a soul? "As many snow-balls as it would take to heat an oven," was the significant reply.

"If I thought they'd do him any good," said the son, "I wouldn't begrudge him dozens of them; but as I don't believe they would, I won't pay for any."

"Oh, that will do!" said Father Dan, walking off in a huff, and muttering something which Pat could not make out.

Pat thought no more about the matter, but went on as usual, save that he looked after the farm much more carefully than he used previous to his father's death, now that the duty of doing so solely devolved upon him; and when his farming work was over, he spent the rest of his time either by his own fire-side, in his favourite pastime, reading, or he strolled over to some neighbouring farmer's house, where a well-to-do young bachelor was by no means an unwelcome guest among the unmarried girls. He was returning from a visit of this kind one night, when a frightful apparition stood before him. It had the head and horns of a bull; the body was also that of a bull, whom it resembled in almost every particular, save that it stood on two legs instead of four.

"In God's name!" said Pat, "who are you?" as the the bull sauntered out of the dike near the ditch, and walked leisurely to the middle of the road.

"Boo! boo! boo!" said the ghost, "I'm your poor father's sowl!"

"Yerra! then are you?" said Pat, as a strong suspicion of an attempt to play him a trick entered his mind.

"I am!" said the spirit; "the poor sowl that you wouldn't lose a farthing by to get out of purgatory!"

"Yerra! I thought," said Pat, "that 'twas only wicked people went there?"

"Every one goes there," said the ghost.

"By gor! thin, if that's the case," says Pat, "a fellow might as well take his whack out of this world while he's in it, as he must put in an appearance at limbo, whether he's good or bad. At all events," continued he, "I'll speak to Father Dan, and if he does them for nothing——"

"Oh!" interposed the spirit, "wouldn't you lose a penny by me, after all the money I left you?"

"But," says Pat, "if the masses are said, what is it to you whether the priest did them for nothing, or was paid for them?"

"Ah, Pat," said his father, emphatically, and shaking his head in a knowing manner, "that wouldn't do at all. They wouldn't give. a trawneen for a mass in the other world unless 'twas paid for!"

"And how do the Protestants manage, father?" says Pat; "sure there's never a mass at all at all said for one of them."

"Boo! boo! boo! the heretics, the heretics!" said his father.

"By gor! 'tis they're the lucky heretics," says Pat; "'tis they get all the crame, and the skim-milk is for the faithful. Yerra! if you see a grand carriage rowlin over the big bridge, drawn by grand grey horses, and every baste of them striking his hoof agen the ground—by gor! as if he was a king—ax who owns them, and you'll find 'tis a Protestant; or if you see a great house, with a window in it for every week in the year, and hundreds of trees—that you'd think grew big on purpose to plaze them—all round it, to keep the cowld from it, ax who owns it, and 'tis sure to be a Protestant. Ax yourself who did you pay rint to, and who all your neighbours and friends pay rint to, and you'll find 'tis a Protestant; and sure God wouldn't be always rewarding thim if they were wrong—eh, father?"

"Boo! boo! boo!" again, said his father, "that's in this world," says he; "boo! boo! boo!" and he was very vexed.

"But, by gor! there twice as well off in the next," said Pat; "and signs on, who ever heard of one of thim turning back and standing on the public road of a cowld night, begging to have some one pay for masses for his poor sowl—eh, father?"

"Boo! boo! boo! boo! I suppose I may be off now!" said the ghost.

"Be off! is it?" said Pat. "Yerra! shure you wouldn't think of going all the way back again, without stepping up and having a shawn-a-mone with my poor mother, and she so fond of you? The devil from me, father!" said he, "but you wouldn't know yourself at all, if you were to hear her talking about you. 'Oh! wisha, 'twas he was the dacent, honest man, entirely, entirely,' she'd say, and she swaying hither and over upon the little stooleen, up by the fire, as if she was going to Ameriky in a row-boat, 'and may the heavens be his bed this night!' little thinking, father, that you put heaven out of your head altogether; and that you thought you'd be doing mighty well if you hadn't to put up with a shake down in limbo."

"I won't go!" said the ghost.

"Excuse me for contradicting you, father," said the son, "but you must!"

" But I say I won't !" said the ghost, and he boo'd awfully.

" Walk up before me there at once !" said Pat, taking the bull with a whack of the whip across the calves of his legs, that made him screech for all the world like a Christian. " Walk up this very instant, or I'll soon persuade you that the pains of purgatory arn't fit to hold a candle to the licking I'll give you ! Walk up !",said he, as he struck him three or four times about the region of the tail, just to show him he was not joking at all.

" Well, let me off this time, Pat, alleah," coaxingly said the ghost, " and I'll never trouble you again."

" No, father, up you must go !" said the son, and he gave him a very rough push. He then drove him before him like a pig on his way to the slaughter-house, until he got him safe and sound inside his own kitchen, where the servant-boy sat waiting up for him ; then rousing up the whole house, he told them all that his father's ghost had come to see them.

Meanwhile the ghost got into a dark corner, with his face to the wall, and he would not say a word. " He never asked after the old woman ; or if the potatoes were getting black ; or if pork was riz ; or how was corn. No ! bad luck to the word he'd say at all, at all !" said Pat ; " there wasn't even a boo out of him, and I to tell him that there was my mother to the 'fore, and to tell her what he had to say about the masses."

At last, seizing the bull by the horns, and giving his skin a sharp tug or two in the front, he pulled the hide off his poor father's spirit, and before them stood　*　　*　　*

H—— went openly to church on the following Sunday, and on the the roll of the clergy of the church of England the name of more than one of his descendants may be seen ; and those that bear it have never been accused of a want of knowledge of the holy scriptures, or a lack of zeal in the performance of the duties of their sacred calling.

On the 30th of July, Sir Broderick Chinnery, of the city
1802.　of Bath, was elected to represent Bandon in the new Parliament to be held at Westminster, on the 31st of August.

Additional accommodation for two thousand men was taken
1803.　this year in Bandon. Cornwall's brewery, Bigg's mills, Dowden and Wheeler's stores, Kingston's buildings—in fact, nearly all the large concerns in the town—were rented by the authorities.

All the shop-windows in Bandon up to this year were unglazed. They consisted merely of a timber frame-work, in which two or three shelves were placed; these were equi-distant from one another, and were parallel to the pavement. Samples of the various wares to be had inside were piled upon them, with the intent that their alluring aspect would attract customers. Now, for the first time, a townsman, who lived at least half a century ahead of his fellows, introduced a glass window. The old people, who had as much respect for novelty as the devil is said to have for holy water, crowded round it, and showered sarcasm on the unfortunate innovator, unsparingly.

"Haw! Yerra, Bill, I suppose the shop that was there before you wasn't good enough for you! Wisha, dhe vora dheerig!"

"Well, by jingo!" says another, "the dust won't be able to get on Dolly's purty face, any how!"

"I suppose he'll turn Papist next!" soberly remarked a third.

"I am afraid, friend William, thou hast done a dangerous thing!" said Tommy Weldon—an old Quaker, who was recognized as the sense-carrier of the community for the previous forty years. "William," continued the old man, "if thy door happeneth to get closed, won't thou and thy household be smothered?"

This never struck bewildered Bill before. He never saw his danger until now. He became terrified, and looked as ghastly as if a pan of charcoal was on the floor smouldering away his last moments, as tranquilly as if he had selected that method of gliding from this world to the next. "You're right, sir!" said the panic-stricken man, as he demolished the panes in the lower sash with as much vehemence and indignation as if he had just discovered a plot to take his life.

Many of our peasantry are proud of running up their pedigree to some famous Protestant in "the ould times;" and the worse he would appear to us now-a-days, the better they would like him, and the prouder they are of him. A short time since, we overtook a poor man returning from mass; and, in the course of conversation, he mentioned his name. We remarked that it was the name of a very old Protestant family that formerly lived in Bandon. "Why," said he, "my grand-father was a Protestant; and he was none of your wake-tay or staggering-bob Protestants either, but a fine, rale ould illigant black bull. Oh!" continued he, "he was so fine and black in himself, that he wouldn't say, 'God save all here!' if there was a Papist present."

34

The "old black bull" was generally a member of that rigid and uncompromising sect of religionists, the Presbyterians. Socially, he was as playful as a kitten, and as harmless as an old horse; but he was a man of strong prejudices, and so honest was he in the advocacy of what he thought right, that he flung toleration, respect for his opponent's convictions, and other results of an advanced civilization, to the winds. John Knox he looked upon as a hero, as well as an apostle. Of the high Episcopalians, he thought, "The least said, the soonest mended." "The high church," he used to say, "is on the high road to Rome." In his eyes, there was scarcely a difference between the Prelacy and the Papacy. The clergy of both churches wore vestments, and claimed power to absolve penitent people from their sins; the confessions were the same, one merely repeating in Latin what the other repeated in English; the baptismal service was the same, even to marking the newly initiated members of the church with the sign of the cross; and the intolerant and persecuting spirit which always characterized the one was not wanting in the other. Concerning the latter, he could never forget that, in the reign of the second Charles, several thousands of the best men of the nonconformists were flung into prison, with nothing more laid to their charge than that of refusing to adopt the tenets and ritual of the Church of England. But, great as was his aversion to the Prelacy, it was exceeded by his horror of Popery. His Puritanical abhorrence of the latter had been transmitted to him through generations. Indeed, it was often the only legacy his fathers had to bequeath. With it spiritually he had nothing to do. He knew well that the humble Roman Catholic, who told his beads upon his knees, had the same right to think that he had, and was as sincere in his devotion as he was himself. It was against the political Papacy that the strongest feelings of his nature were directed—his very instinct recoiled from it—he could never be prevailed upon to give it credit even for good intentions. When he looked at those who exercised such peremptory powers in religious matters, carry the same spirit which produced them into temporal affairs; and when he saw those under their sway, who ventured to express an opinion not sanctioned by them, reproved by the thumb-screw, and their arguments silenced by the Inquisition—he did not believe them when they shouted for liberty of conscience. But his dislike to the Papacy by no means extended itself to its professors. His ear was ever open to the wail of woe, regardless from whence it came; and his hand was out-stretched with charity, without heeding whether the applicant looked for divine truth among the unadorned worship-houses of the noncon-formists, or amidst the gorgeous colonnades of Rome. He was ever foremost to help a poor neighbour; and, should death enter the humble cabin and remove its provider, amongst the readiest to step forward, catch the little orphan by the hand, and share with him the comforts of his own home, was the "old black bull."

There are some specimens of the *taurus antiquus niger* still in being. Not long since, we happened to be present when a friend of ours, who sought the representation of his native town upon principles more in vogue than those previously advocated, called upon one of those.

"Well, Dick, my old boy," quoth the candidate for senatorial honours, "I know you'll stand to an old neighbour and an old friend."

Dick raised his eyes, and observing a Roman Catholic gentleman, who formed one of the deputation, surlily growled out, "I don't like your company."

Upon this, we all addressed Richard blandly, some reminding him of interesting incidents connected with their mutual childhood; others told him humorous little anecdotes, and spoke as softly, and handled him as gently, as a young mother would her firstborn babe. In course of time, we thought we made some impression upon his obdurate heart; and even one or two of the most sanguine amongst us fancied we could discern a faint streak or two of a smile flitting about his upper lip. Again our chief led the attack :—

"Well, Dick? Ah! I knew I could always count upon your vote and interest."

Dick, thus challenged, again raised his head, and ran his eyes over the Protestant portion of us fairly enough; but when they alighted on the admirer of the triple tiara, oh, the scowl! 'twas as black and deep as a thunder-cloud, and every bit as dangerous. He hissed like a cobra de capella, made a rush for his hammer, and we—why we ran, of course. Would you blame us?

The Bandon Protestants may fairly be divided into three classes—the positive, the comparative, and the superlative; or fair, brown, and black. Of these, the positive or fair Protestant is a rational being, and may be classed with the Liberal Conservatives or moderate Whigs of our own day; the second think, that when Victor Emanuel holds his court at the Vatican, and the Pope reduced to the position of a big parish priest upon small dues, things may mend; but as for the superlative or black Protestant, the following anecdote will help to illustrate the nature of his undying hatred at all times, and in a place where it is to be hoped none of our readers will ever be found, to Popery and everything connected with it.

A good many years ago, there lived here one Dick C.———. Dick was one of the superlatives, and he hated Pope and Popery with as much, if not more, intensity than he did Satan himself, and his fell domains. Notwithstanding all his virtues—and he had many—Dick had one vice. Who is there that has not his weak point? He was not a teetotaller, so far as abstaining from intoxicating liquors was concerned. On the contrary, he was often teetotally the other way, and used indulge in what was known in those days as a rookawn. On one of these occasions—whether it was in order to obtain proper ventilation when he was asleep, or that his *locus standi* glided from under his feet and left him there, or that his powers of locomotion had come to a stand-still, we do not pretend to say—at all events, he was found by an acquaintance lying in the channel outside his door, and as blind as a bat. Another acquaintance of his coming up shortly after, the two held a consultation, and they struck upon a plan for terrifying the discomforted Bacchanalian who lay snoring at their feet into sobriety for the unexpired term of his sub-lunary demise. Raising him up, they carried him between them into an adjoining outhouse, and stripping him to his shirt and stockings, they wrapped him up in a sheet. To a short rope, which they hung round his neck, they tied a rosary, which they borrowed from an old woman who kept an apple-stall in a gateway at the opposite side of the street; then laying him on some boards on the floor, they placed a wisp of straw and some shavings under his head, to serve him for a pillow. One of those who helped him in then went away; but the other, who sometimes went rookawning himself, and who suggested the plot, remained behind. In course of time, Dick awoke, and feeling queer, and everything on every side of him appearing strange and odd, he hurriedly sat up, and eagerly asked, " Where am I ?"

"In hell," said a ghastly figure in a deep sonorous tone.

"Ah, that's a bad job," said poor Dick, scratching his head : " a very, very bad job indeed." His eye suddenly rested on the obnoxious beads which were dangling against his orthodox breast-bone, and which had escaped his notice until now. " Oh, good God," said he, nervously catching the rosary between his forefinger and thumb, and holding it up to the light so as to make sure of what it was, then letting it go as if it was a rattlesnake, and wiping his fingers in his shroud as if to rub off the slime. " Oh, good God," he continued, " to go to hell is bad enough, and, I suppose, I deserved it; but, oh, Father of mercy, to die a Papist ! !"

Then appalled by the magnitude of his punishment, he buried his face in his hands, and sobbed aloud in the agony of his soul. The ghost could hold out no longer; throwing aside his winding-sheet, he ran over to the unfortunate sinner, and slapping him with his open hand between the shoulders, swore out he was true-blue to the backbone. He then explained the entire of the contrivance to him; and when he had handed Dick his clothes, and when the latter had put them on, the two worthies adjourned to an hostelry in the neighbourhood, and there, over many a refreshing cup, they sung the " Boyne Water," and drank over and over again to the glorious, pious, and immortal memory of the great and good King William, who, amongst a crowd of other evils, saved us from brass money, Popery, and wooden shoes.

The old Bandonians were most indignant when they were called Irish, and indeed there was a broad line of demarcation between them and the Irish Celt. They spoke in a different tongue—they professed a different religion. In the eyes of the Bandon man, the Irishman was an idolater. In the eyes of the Irishman, the Bandon man was a heretic. Their instincts, their prejudices, their aspirations, were as widely apart as the poles. Up to about a century and a half since, the two nationalities in Ireland were recognized as such by every writer of the day. There was the English as opposed to the Irish; the Englishry in contradistinction to the Irishry; the British colonists, and not " the meer Irish;" the plantees and the Cromwellians, in contrariety to the natives and the old Irish.

It is seldom that the inhabitants of a nation superior in strength and civilization adopt the habits and customs of the inferior people whom they have conquered or settled amongst, much more assume their name—the Greeks, for instance, who colonized Marseilles never called themselves Gauls. Bearing in mind that Bandon was founded by Englishmen—many of whom were accustomed to all the comforts and pleasantries of London life; and that they established their colony in a wild barbarous country, where wolves roamed about unmolested, and where humankind was represented by a few half-nude barbarians, who strayed in there from the territory of some Carbery chieftain; but principally by some marauding woodkern, who instinctively made their own of all they could lay their hands upon, and then escaped to the swamps and woods of Kinalmeaky, to save themselves from the skean or the rope.

Bearing all this in mind, their distaste can be accounted for. They greatly prided themselves upon " being bred and born in Bandon." One who first opened his eyes within the walls of the ancient and loyal borough, trod the earth with as lordly an air, as if he was lineally descended. from one of those iron-plated barons who came over with William of Normandy, or could claim half a county as his estate.

A good many years ago, a poor fellow, who was obliged to leave Bandon owing to want of employment, made his way to London, where he resided a long time fighting for his daily bread in the great battle of life. At length he lay on a dying bed. A clergyman was sent for, who lost no time in coming to his bedside, and administering those religious consolations which help to smooth the rugged road leading . from this world to the next. Lingering awhile in the humble chamber, the clergyman, who was an Irishman, said, in reply to an observation of the sick man :—

" I perceive you're an Irishman, like myself."

" I'm no Irishman," said the dying man.

The divine was amazed. Even the very accent in which he asserted he was no Irishman was redolent of the Emerald Isle.

" And what country are you from ? Are you from France ?—are you from Russia ?"

" No," interrupted the old man, " I'm from Bandon."

" And isn't Bandon in Ireland ?" said the clergyman ; "and, therefore, are you not an Irishman ?"

" Tell me, sir," said the old Bandonian, whose " no surrender" spirit swelled against the taunt: " tell me, sir," said he, as he struggled to raise himself in the bed—for he was weak, and the shadow of the outstretched hand of the grim King of Terrors was already upon him— " wer'nt the Israelites four hundred years in Egypt ?"

" They were," mildly replied the divine.

" And were they Egyptians ?"

The knowledge of some of our old townsmen was limited to the town itself. Either they did not care to trouble themselves about what lay outside the walls, or they may have thought that when they knew what was inside of them they knew what was quite sufficient for any ordinary man. A poor soldier was mortally wounded at the siege of Cicudad Rodrigo. On being removed to the temporary hospital, he enquired for a Bandon gentleman—an officer in a regiment quartered near him. The officer came to see his fellow-townsman as soon as he could; and, among other questions, asked him what part of Bandon he was born in.

"I was born on the other side,"* was the odd reply.

Those born in the suburbs were not looked upon with near the same favour as those fortunate fellows who were born in the town itself.

"Ar'nt you an old Bandonian?" we enquired one day of an old man.

"No sir," replied the old man, with a melancholy air, "I was born at Gallow's Hill."

---

* That is the northern side of the town.

CHAPTER XXV.

THE FIRST ROMAN CATHOLIC WHO VENTURED TO LIVE IN ONE OF OUR PRINCIPAL STREETS—JACK, THE JOBBER—NOBODY DID IT—THE BATTLE OF THE CROSS—THE DUNMANWAY BOY AND THE GAUGER—MAD MARY AND THE TOBACCO—THE SUPERVISOR AND THE POTHEEN—COMPLETE LIST OF OUR CHIEF MAGISTRATES— OUR MANOR COURTS.

THE Right Hon. Courtney Boyle (Tory), captain Royal Navy, elected to represent the town, in lieu of Sir Broderick Chinnery.

1806.

1807. May 15th.—Right Hon. Henry Boyle (Tory)— commonly called Lord Viscount Boyle—was elected to represent Bandon; and, on the 3rd of the following August, the Right Hon. George Tierney (Whig), of London, and of Wimbledon, in Surrey, succeeded Lord Boyle—he having become Earl of Shannon upon the death of his father, Richard, the second earl.

It was about this time that the first Roman Catholic shopkeeper ventured to reside in any of our principal streets. For several years previously some Roman Catholics had crept into the town, but they were content with the humblest habitations within the walls, and in the most out of the way places. The name of this adventurous pioneer was Paddy Gaffney. He was a resolute sort of fellow, and a very good-tempered fellow at the same time; but he was as ugly as if he was made to order. Notwithstanding his lack of personal attractions, he was a light-hearted soul. Smile after smile was constantly in pursuit of one another over his pugnacious physiognomy. Pat kept a pie-shop, in which he sold pies, and what, by a long stretch of charity, was known as mutton-broth. The pies were made of flour and water, and were just ovened enough to stiffen them. Around their outer edge was a battlement of indurated dough, and in the centre was a thin pellicle of the same material, and under this slender covering was, or ought to have been, some meat. But nobody could tell what it was. Some said it was sole-leather, which Paddy cut off a pair of worn-out brogues, and boiled. Others, that it was Bible covers, cut into pieces, and fried ; but the generally received opinion was that it was bog-wood, warmed in a pot of cabbage-water, into which was flung a crubeen or two, to give it a meaty flavour. As for the mutton-broth—even Gaffney had not the audacity to assert it was ever in contact with mutton, or even under the same roof with it. It was composed of boiling-water, heaps of salt, and a dust of pepper. The first morning that he took down his shutters and invited the public to enter his refectory, it became known that a Papist had come to live in the street.

"Yaw! where are you going, Sammy?" says one old fellow to another, who was trudging past his door on his way up to Paddy's.

"Be dad, Johnny, up to see de live Papish dat's cum to live near the Patey-market!"

"Lawks, man! a live Papish?"

"A live Papish?" chimed in another old neighbour, with wonder spreading in his eyes. "Yaw! Dick," calling out to another friend who had just put his head out of the window, " sure you never he-ard sich news! sure dere's a live Papish here!"

" Is it de French is come agen to Bantry Bay?" eagerly enquired an old woman, who, on perceiving the earnest manner of the old people, thought something really awful had occurred.

"No, Betsey, it ain't! but 'tis what's a great dale worse—dere's a live Papish come to live in the street!"

"By dis and by dat!" said another old townsman, who heard all that passed, " de end of the world can't be far off now."

Young men, as well as old men, took part in the consultation, and after a little talk on the subject, they all went up to see Paddy.

"What de divil brought de likes ov ye in here at all, at all?" said the principal spokesman, striking the end of his stick upon the ground, and looking wickedly at the owner of the pie-shop.

"Wisha! gintlemen," said Pad, who well knew they would not like him the less for giving them a lift in the social scale, "I don't wonder at your axing the question! Yerra! how can I help it, whin I hadn't the good luck to be born a Bandon Protestant. Sure the next best thing to that was to go and live among thim, and in course of time, by reading good books, and pitching the Pope to the divil, I may, with God's help, become one myself! Tisn't every one," continued he, "has the luck that ye's have, gintlemen!"

"Well, he ain't a bad Papish, any how!" said one of the deputation.

"Well, I think 'tis wrong to be blaming the poor man," said another. "Sure 'tis hard to censure him for his parents being idolaters, and he not born at de time."

"And isn't my daughter, that's married to Bill Forbus, a Protestant?" said Paddy. "Faix, she is so!" said he; "and that's the girl that would eat mate of a Friday for you, and make herself as hoarse as a beetle on the 1st of July, singing "The Protestant Boys," and "Croppies lie down!"

Here several interposed, and said they knew this to be a fact.

"And you may ax Tom Sloane," said he, "if he didn't see me drink the glorious memory on the day King William (God rest his sowl in glory, said Pad, reverentially taking off his hat at the same time), bate the Papists; and, by gor! 'twas a murderin sin he didn't kill them all, for then all the people that came into the world since would be Protestants; and then, sure, I'd be as good as any of ye's, gintlemen!" said Paddy.

"Do you go to the mass-house?" said Sammy, who wasn't easily imposed on.

"Very seldom!" said Paddy.

"Will you promise never to darken the durrens of the door of it again?"

"I will, and welcome!" said Pad.

'Twas impossible to say any more to such an obliging poor fellow as this; so they all withdrew; and we must do Gaffney the justice to say he faithfully kept his word. His knowledge of human nature saved him. Indeed, the thorough knowledge of ordinary humanity possessed by some of our countrymen, and their intimate acquaintance with all the windings and the workings of the human heart, prove them to be possessed of perceptive powers of a high order. And not only do they possess the knowledge we have just mentioned, but they know full well how to turn it to account. If a man had a prejudice or a passion; if he aspired to be a patriot, or was a sensible man; if he was rich or poor; an old Whig, or a Fenian; one of those shrewd pieces of humanity could see what was written on his very back-bone, before he would be able to utter half-a-dozen sentences, and would shape his conversation accordingly. "Poor!" he would say to a poor man: "Yerra! why wouldn't we be poor; sure the big fellows have all that's going amongst themselves." Should he be talking to a big fellow, however, he would base their poverty upon different grounds:—"No wonder for us to be poor, your honour, when we frighten the capital from coming into the country that would give us all employment, and frighten those among us who have anything from laying it out, by threatening to take it away from them when the 'Mericans come, and keeping it ourselves."

Not long ago there lived in an adjoining parish one whom we will call Jack, the jobber. Although Jack was a cute, crafty, calculating fellow, yet he could not be looked upon in the light of a *rara avis*, or a small prodigy, as dozens of his species are to be met with in both sexes in the transactions of every-day life. He was simply a member of that classification of the genus *homo*, known as "a fine boy," but nothing more. Our friend Jack could not be said to have received a liberal education—in fact, he did not receive any at all. Neverthless, he knew a one pound note very well, but he could scarcely recognise the difference between a three pound note and a five, or a ten. He knew they were not ones, and, therefore, unless very much pressed for time, he was very particular in paying them out. We ought to have said long ago, that Jack was by profession a buyer and seller of pigs, and there were few, if any, that ever entered Bandon fair knew better what they were about in the pig line than the self-same Jack.

"What do you want for that little creature?" he'd say, looking disparagingly at a broad-backed Berkshire, whose sides quivered with flesh, feeling her across the loins with his outstretched hand at the same time. "What are you axing me for her?"

"Three pound ten."

"Wisha, I believe you're only making game of us this fine morning, Mr.——, addressing the owner, who may be a turf-begrimed, bog-trotting biped from the wilds of West Carbery. Jack used to treat all those whom he had hopes of knocking a bargain out of with studied civility. "No, but what are you axing in earnest, Mr.——," talking softly into his ear. "Here!" he would cry out, as if suddenly over-powered by a gush of profuse generosity—"Here! hould your hand!" slapping a big penny into it at the same time, "will you take two pounds for her?"

" No !"

" Will you take the other five shillings for her ?" giving the penny another slap into his horny palm.

" No !"

" Will you take the other half-crown ?"

" No !"

" What do you want for the pig ?"

" Three pounds."

" By gor, you may as well ax me three hundred. Is it three pounds for that poor, thin, wake little spaddareen ? Bad luck to the man in the whole fair, Mr.——, I'd give two pound five to for the like's of her but yourself."

" Why, you offered me two pounds seven and sixpence just now."

" Well, by dad, if I did, although I'm but a poor man, I'll never brake my word ;" and Jack goes to mark her, as if 'twas all settled at last, but the seller prevents him, who then comes down another five shillings, and offers to take two pounds fifteen.

Jack, who now perceives that the owner is losing courage, goes close up to him, and tells him in a confidential whisper, that he wonders a dacent, respectable farmer like him wouldn't ax some knowing man the value of his pig before he put a price on her. " Well, what do you ax me now ?"

" Two pound twelve and sixpence."

Here a bystander, on receiving a look from Jack, steps in, and enquires how much between them.

" Only a crown-piece," says Jack, " but it's too high entirely."

" Oh, d——n it ! tear the five shillings between ye's," says the disinterested looker-on.

" By gor, I couldn't !" says Jack, " she's too dear already."

The countryman demurs too.

" Well, wo'nt you take the two, seven, six," says Jack, buttoning up his coat to go away.

" Ah, d——n it !" tear the five shillings, as I told ye's before."

" By gor, I'll never break your word," says Jack, who thought that was the least compliment he could pay the bystander for the trouble he took in the matter.

" Wisha, you may have her," says the owner ; and Jack puts three clips of a scissors on her panting flank, and she's his for two pounds ten.

"You got her for the value, Jack," observes a fellow-trader in passing by.

"Wisha, no Daney!" remarks Jack, endeavouring to look as if he was taken in; "if she brings her own money, she'll be doing a dale."

We previously stated that Jack was not able to read; and that, although he knew a one pound note very well, the others bothered him. He bought a pig one day from a friend—a neighbour of his own—and in paying him he unfortunately gave him a three pound note instead of a one. Something told him at the time that he was making a fool of himself, but he couldn't tell how, and he hadn't leisure just then to think about it.

After he eat his supper that night, he threw himself upon the settle, and putting his hand over his eyes, he indulged in mental arithmetic. He added together all the moneys he paid for all the pigs he bought. He knew how much money his wife gave him that morning, and he ought to have so much left. He then counted his cash, and found he was two pounds short. It then occurred to him that it was when he felt a little queer about himself he paid the wrong money, and that was the very time when he was just after paying Tade ——— for his pig. The next morning, after breakfast, he lit his pipe, and sauntered up fine and leisurely to Tade's habitation.

"God save all here!" says Jack, as he pushed open the half-hatch, and walked into the middle of the floor. "Well, Tade," says he, addressing the master of the house, before he had time to open his mouth, "that was a nate little pig, entirely, I got from you yesterday."

"You may say that!" says Tade; "only she was good, Jack, you wouldn't get her!"

"Well! see what it is to have a friend, ma'am!" says Jack, smiling, as he turned towards Tade's old wife, Peggy, who was busy flapping the corner of her apron before a sod of turf, more with the intent of thinking what she ought to say, for she knew well what Jack was about, than of making a good fire.

"Wisha, that's true for you, al-leah!" says she.

After some more rounds of cautious sparring, in which neither party was able to gain any advantage over the other, Jack resolved to close with his opponent.

"I came up to you for that trifle of change!" says he, taking off his hat, and scratching his head; yawning at the same time, as if he looked upon the handing out of the cash as a mere matter of course.

"What change?" says Tade, looking innocently in his face.

"Yeah! don't be joking a poor man!" says Jack; "sure, when I was paying you yesterday, I gave you two pounds extra; and if you want the loan of it for a month or two longer, sure you may have it, and welcome, and more besides;" it just having occurred to him, that by lending him a couple more, he may get an I.O.U. for the entire.

"Och! the devil a penny you lent me; nor I didn't ask it from you!" replied the other. "You gave me the two pound fifteen for my little pig; and if I sold her to any one else, I'd get three pounds for her!"

"Ah! then you would!" says Peggy, as the idea of counter irritation suggested itself to her as a means of getting rid of Jack, who was a very close-fisted fellow. "You could, then," says she, "and three pounds five, too; and if Jack has the spirit of a man dealing with him, he'll give us our ten shillings this minute. Indeed, faix," continued she, "I suppose that's what brought him up!" winking to the old man at the same time, as much as to say, dwell on that note, and he'll soon vanish.

Old Tade took the hint at once.

"Oh! bad luck to the step you'll budge out of this, Jack!" says he, "until you give us the remainder of our money!" going towards the door at the same time, to shut it.

"Leave me out!" says Jack.

"Not 'till you pay us our honest ten shillings!" says Peggy, running over to her husband's assistance, with the tongs.

"Are you going to rob and murder me?" says Jack.

"Give us our ten shillings!" roared Peggy.

"Ah! you'll do!" said Jack, as he stood in the middle of the road, after struggling through the door, which the old couple had half closed upon him. "You'll do, by good looking after!"

"Faith! then, we'd want somebody to look after us when we'd be dealing with the like of you, and not to have us imposed upon the way we were!" replied the old woman.

Jack went straight off to Father ———, and told him all that happened; and that very night the priest made it his business to see Tade and his wife on the subject. But they solemnly assured him that all they got from Jack was the two pounds fifteen.

Years rolled on, and in course of time Tade lay on his dying bed. He now began to feel uneasy, and he sent for the priest to help him to make up his accounts for the next world ; and among other items which he considered himself not entitled to take credit for, was Jack's two pounds. Calling in Peggy to his bed-side, he told her in the presence of his reverence to pay Jack, and she faithfully promised she would.

After poor Tade was decently and respectably buried, and a blanket of green sods wrapped fine and comfortably round his grave, the way the frost or the wet could not get at him, Jack, who had been told of what happened, walked up and asked Peggy for his two pounds.

"Wisha! didn't ye get that out of your head yet?" says the old termagant, whom the intervening years only improved for the worse.

"No!" says Jack. "You know you have it, and that poor Tade—God rest his sowl—told you to give it to me!"

"He didn't!" says Peggy.

"Say the devil take the liars!" says Jack, "and I'll leave it with you!"

"Wisha! now I wonder at you, after all," says Peggy, "to be axing an ould creature like me to be larning cursing in the end of her days. Sure, I have sins enough of my own to answer for, without being after blaspheming to plaze Jack, the jobber. Here, be off out of my house," says she, "you tempter. I think it must be the devil himself that sent you here!"

Jack made his exit once more.

What was to be done now? She had no shame in her. She did not care twopence for priest or minister, or for any one living. Could the dead persuade her to give it up, thought Jack, as he lay awake in his bed a few nights after.

Since Tade died, Peggy had no one living with her but a woman as old and as feeble as herself. They used to go early to bed; and for additional comfort and warmth, they removed their bed close to the fireplace. Jack became aware of this, and of the fact that there were only the two old people residing in the house, which was a detached one, being distant from the nearest habitation by some hundreds of yards. Climbing up to the top of the chimney, just as the great town clock had announced midnight, Jack threw some gravel down into the fire-place, so as to awaken the sleepers ; then putting his mouth down to the opening of the flue :—" I can't rest in my grave till you give Jack, the jobber, his money!" says he, in a deep sepulchral tone. He then got quickly down again, and went home.

He had some idea that Peggy would be down with him early next morning with the money, but he was mistaken. He did not catch a glimpse of her for the whole day.

He went up again next night, and announced his uneasiness about the non-payment of the money, through the same channel, and in the same words; but the next day Peggy was as obdurate and as invisible as ever. But now for the third and last effort. This was to be the great night. If he was to succeed at all, it must be now.

" I can't rest in my grave till you give Jack, the jobber, his money," said he in a voice more supplicating than ever; but not a stir out of Peggy.

After an interval of a few minutes, " Oh, Mike don't!" said he, as if addressing the spectre of Peggy's brother—a fine, stalwart fellow, who was killed about forty years before in a faction fight. " Oh, Mike, don't!" said he imploringly, " sure she's the wife of my buzzom after all." " Wisha, don't Kitty," says he again, as if beseeching her favourite sister—a young unmarried woman, who died many years ago, and who was then supposed to be armed with a red-hot spit, with which she was going to run Peggy through the gizzard—Jack used to say she had no heart—" Don't, Kitty, machree," says he, in a soft, seducing tone, " who knows but she may be a Christian yet!"

After another pause, during which Peggy showed no signs of relenting :—" Well, will this contint ye's?" addressing all the family ghosts, who had become furious at Peggy's cruelty to her husband; " if she doesn't give it up to-morrow, you can all do as you like with her to-morrow night!" Then throwing some burning sulphur down the chimney, he went home.

Peggy was now fairly circumvented at last. She was as pale as she could be, and almost frightened out of her life. The smell of the sulphur, which in due time pervaded every cranny in her domicile, excited surmises about her future abode, which rendered her very uncomfortable. Nevertheless, she strove to persuade herself that it was because Jack's money had no blessing attending it, and not that she did anything wrong by making her own of what did not belong to her, that made the ghost's so much vexed about it.

" Yerra! milia, murther!" says she, as she was dressing herself next morning, "mus'n't his money be awful bad entirely, when my own relations and friends would come all the way from the next world to kill me for leaving a farthing of it inside the four walls of my house. By gor! I'll throw it out into the road this minute if he doesn't take it! Bad manners to me, if I'd allow a copper of his to cross the threshold of my door again, if I was to get the whole ploughland for it—that's what I wouldn't."

Jack had hardly the shutters of his little shop down next morning, when Peggy walked into him.

"Here, John," says she, "here's the two pounds you lent Tade long ago; and there's neither luck nor grace attending it, or anything belonging to you!"

"Thank ye, ma'am," says Jack, counting the money and putting it securely into his breeches pocket: "Thank ye, ma'am! Wisha! I hope," continued he, "that ye slept well last night, ma'am, after we all went away?"

"After all who went away?" says Peggy, as a suspicion of a foul trick struck her for the first time.

"Why, your brother Mike, ma'am, and I, and your sister Kitty!" says Jack, putting his hands on his two sides, and roaring out laughing. "Well, by all that's lovely, Peggy," says he, "you're done clean at last!"

Peggy gave him one look; and then, mortified and chagrined to the very back-bone, she made the best of her way to her bed, and before the New Year's day she was lying peaceably alongside poor Tade.

1809.   It was customary for the Bandon volunteers, which consisted of the three companies previously mentioned, to meet often for the purpose of inspection and ball-practice. Information as to the appointed time was usually given by a printed cirular, a copy of one of which we annex:—

"BANDON UNION.

"SIR,—You are requested to parade next Monday, at eleven o'clock, in full uniform, arms, &c., to fire at a target.

"GEORGE KINGSTON,
"To Mr. ———."   Captain.

July was their favourite month for parading, and the anniversary of the battle of the Boyne was their favourite day. Throughout the entire of this month, every man used to turn out with a flower (generally an orange lily) in the muzzle of his musket, just as the patriotic troops still do in Italy, Germany, and other places.   On the 6th of July, in this year, Colonel Auriel, the commandant, issued an order for a full-dress parade.   The corps assembled in their usual places.   The Boyne "fell in" in the open space where the meat-shambles now stand; the True-Blues took open order in front of the court-house; and the Union opposite the house now occupied as the Provincial Bank.   Riding up, in company with Lord Bandon and several other officers, to the Boyne, the commandant made a vigorous speech, in which he specially denounced political badges, and finally concluded by ordering the men of that corps to take out the lily or lay down their arms.   The men un-hesitatingly adopted the latter alternative, and down went the arms with a crash that sent ramrods and broken bayonets ringing about in every direction.   Auriel and his party then rode down to the True-Blues, where the previous order was repeated, and down went brown Bess without a murmur.   But he was more successful with the Union, several of the men retaining the musket and removing the obnoxious lily.   The same day, the three corps were formally disbanded.

Whether Colonel Auriel had received instructions from the Executive to seek a pretext for disbanding these volunteers, we know not; but certain it is, that no government would sanction some of the language used by him on that day.   He told them, that the wearing of the lily was an act of cowardice; and that, although they had that badge of loyalty in their caps, he made no doubt but they may have the United Irishmen's oath in their pockets.

The policy of wearing badges of any sort has long since grown into disfavour; and we doubt if there ever was any need of symbolizing one's attachment to the institutions of his country, by wearing either a flower or a ribbon.   As to the latter statement, that he "made no doubt but they may have the United Irishmen's oath in their pockets," this could only have been uttered with the view of causing excessive irritation; for well he must have known, that there was no body of men in the British empire more devotedly attached to the crown and constitution of Great Britain than the yeomanry of Bandon; and their amazement could have been only surpassed by their indignation, when they found that any power occupying the place of Cromwell or of William III. could entertain any doubt as to their loyalty.   It must have sounded strangely in their ears to hear the term "cowardice" applied to the descendants of those who never knew what it was to retreat in the terrible times of 1641, and of those who, when they were surrounded by the disciplined regiments of Clancarthy in 1689, and when destruction threatened their town, and death themselves, yet they quailed not. 'Twas unmanly—'twas unjust—'twas unsoldierly—yea, it was cowardly, to daub this slanderous lie upon such men; upon men, too,. who would at any time have thought the welfare of our cherished institutions cheaply purchased by the sacrifice of their lives.

1810. This year, the woollen trade, which had been reeling for some time under the effects of repeated strikes, at length fell down altogether. For years before, the workmen had entered into trade combinations, and used to meet regularly in a large field to the south-west of Messrs. Fitzgerald's distillery, where everyone who could invent a grievance or picture an injury was eagerly listened to; but the palm of patriotism was reserved for him who could force up wages to the last endurable degree, so that the artizans divided all the profits between them, and left the manufacturer nothing to reserve for a protested bill, an uprise in the raw material, or any of the other contingencies to which trade is liable.

At first, the masters strove hard against all this; but what could they do? Then they became irritable, sulky, and finally indifferent. Whilst the trade was thus dragging along with just sufficient life in its paralyzed limbs to keep moving, a very large order had been received by Thomas Bigg, best known as "Governor Biggs." The weavers heard of the order. They called a special meeting, and they struck, of course. Mr. Biggs was a sensible, practical man, and one greatly interested in the prosperity of his native town; and, fearing matters might terminate badly, he sent for the workmen, and, producing the contract, showed them the impossibility of being able to increase their wages by an additional farthing. He also drew their attention to a clause in the agreement, liberating him from the fulfilment of his obligations in case of a strike. But it did not avail. They should have what they demanded. "Well," said he, "there are the carts still laden with the balls of thread which they have brought out from Cork, and there they shall remain until Monday morning. Meanwhile, turn the matter well over in your minds; for, by that time, I must have your final decision." In the interim, he called the manufacturers together; and they, after a short consultation, decided on closing their

establishments if the weavers persevered. The trade was to them un-
remunerative; they were sick of it; and they did not regret that
matters had now come to an issue.

On the Monday morning, the workmen came, and brought with them
the old story—they should get the required advance. The "governor"
was a very determined man. He ordered the horses to be put to;
crack went the whips; away rolled the carts, and with them departed,
we fear, for ever the once staple article of our old trade, and the basis
of our commercial prosperity for over two hundred years. A deputation
called on him that evening to say they would reconsider their decision;
but he told them *it was too late*. They came again next morning, and
said they would work for the old wages. Again they came, and they
offered to take twenty-five per cent off even these. Before one o'clock
they had resolved to sacrifice another large slice. *But it was too late.*
A day of apprehension and of want slowly trailed its weary hours over
them. Early on the morrow of the next day they came. "Give us
what you like," they cried; "but, oh! save us from starving." *It
was too late.* The fact was, Mr. Biggs had thrown up the contract by
the Monday's post, and, even if desirous of recalling it, it was now
impossible. *It was too late.*

Then commenced an exodus, the like of which, considering the extent
of our population, we have scarce seen paralleled even in history, and
which has left us, after an interval of fifty years, with not one-half the
number of inhabitants the town contained in this year. Family circles
—indeed, we are told, entire communities—fled to Manchester, Leeds,
London, and even to Paris. Crowds crossed the broad Atlantic; and
many passed away to unknown lands, and have not left even a trace of
their whereabouts. Those that could not make away were employed on
the relief-works; many of the hilly roads in our neighbourhood being
then cut down, as Barrett's Hill, Lovell's Hill, &c. Lodgings were
unlet; houses were unoccupied; whole streets were deserted; and many
and many a green meadow, now roamed over by an "Ayrshire" or a
"Durham," was then the site of a clean, orderly row of white cottages;
and the solemn stillness of the country now reigns where the unvarying
click-clack of the shuttle and the weaver's merry song once held undisputed sway.

Several spirited attempts were subsequently made by Messrs. George
Allman, Richard Wheeler, and James Scott, to introduce the cotton

trade. The first-named gentleman erected extensive concerns for that purpose, being one hundred and thirty-four feet in length, thirty-four in width, and fifty in height. They contained five floors, all underlaid with sheet-iron. They also contained ten thousand spinning spindles, with all the necessary machinery for turning out three thousand pounds' weight per week of manufactured cotton. We are unable to say whether it was owing to the distance to which the raw material, when landed, was obliged to be carted inland, and, when manufactured, carted back again for shipment, or to what other cause; but certain it is, that this attempt soon languished and died out, and the large premises, after being idle for a number of years, were eventually hired out as an auxiliary workhouse.

The manufacture of corduroys was tried here, too, and, with varying success, held its ground for a number of years; but, in the end, it, too, perished. The linen manufacture (principally tickings) continued here for about a century and a quarter; but it also sickened, and followed in the wake of the others, but not, however, without leaving some trace of its existence behind, and for which we are solely indebted to the perseverance of one individual, who, amongst the multifarious pursuits of an extensive commerce, has yet found leisure to keep alive a few lingering mementoes of the old Bandon loom.

1812.   Honorable Richard Boyle Bernard (Tory)—second son of Francis, Earl of Bandon—elected to represent the town in Parliament.

1815.   William Sturgess Bourne (Tory), Testwood, Southampton, elected in room of Hon. R. B. Bernard, who resigned.

1818.   Augustus William James Clifford (Whig), elected to represent the town.

The Rev. Verney Lovatt resigned the rectory of Kilbrogan. He was the only brother of Sir Jonathan Lovatt, and was his natural heir; but he lost the ancestral estate, and all Sir Jonathan's chattels in addition, by his love of fun and humour. It appears the old baronet was an irritable and eccentric specimen of the genus *Homo*, but Verney was the very opposite. He was as comical as the other was testy. One day Verney got behind Sir Jonathan's chair, and was revenging himself by making hideous faces at him, and by sundry movements of his legs and arms was intimating what he thought ought to be done to him, when old Growly suddenly turned round, and caught him in the act·

He never forgave him. All his property—including the Liscombe estate, which Richard de Lovatt, one of his ancestors, obtained from William the Conqueror, besides all his personal effects—he bequeathed to a distant relative, and did not leave his only brother even an angry shilling.

Whilst he was rector of Kilbrogan, it was customary with Mr. Lovatt to dispense the parochial charities weekly, and the recipients of them he used to recognize, not by the names conferred upon them when a few of their friends undertook serious responsibilities on their behalf, but by some accomplishment, or blemish, or peculiarity that they were noted for. A poor woman who sold him a lame duck for a whole one was Mrs. Duckey, and her daughter was the little duck; another, who had an oblique vision, was Squinty; Honey was the dulcet appellation he had for one whose sweet tongue often poured copious blessings on his rectorial head; and the Wasp was a peevish creature, that would fight with the shadow of her own dyspeptic countenance.

The doctor was a great humorist. Nevertheless, under the guise of pleasantry and merriment, he could administer a rebuke that would not soon be forgotten. Passing hurriedly through his hall one night in the dark, he knocked against a poor man who was waiting to see him.

"Who's that?" said the divine, as he recoiled off the unfortunate fellow's ribs with such force as to fall in a most unclerical position on the floor.

"Nobody, your reverence!" was the timid reply.

"Nobody," repeated the rector, rising rapidly to his feet; "well, thank goodness, I have you at last!" laying a firm hold of the intruder by the collar of his coat, and calling loudly to the servants to hasten to him at once, and bring lights. They rushed towards him, snatching up a lamp or a candle, or any other kind of light they could lay their hands upon, thinking something serious must have occurred; and their fears were more than half realized, when they beheld their master looking determinedly at a strange man who stood trembling in his grasp. Gathering them about him, he addressed his prisoner :—

"Well, Nobody," said he, "you're the very fellow I have been looking for these thirty years. There is not a dish broken in the kitchen, or a bottle of wine finished in the pantry, or a joint of cold meat, or a book, or a blanket, that has been stolen out of my dwelling, ever since I became a housekeeper, but it was you that did it."

The unhappy captive most energetically protested that he was never inside the walls of his reverence's habitation before, and that he never touched anything belonging to him since he was born.

"Monstrous! Absurd! Impossible!" roared the doctor. "Thirty successive cooks—thirty successive housemaids—thirty successive butlers, whenever I asked what became of this, or who carried away that, have told me over and over again that it was Nobody took it." Turning to those whom he had summoned around him, "if after all the censure this fellow has brought upon you," said he, "and all the suspicions that he has caused to be laid on your shoulders, I ask you, don't you agree with me in thinking that hanging is a good deal too good for him?"

Although he put the question to them three or four times, there was no reply. Those whom he addressed sheepishly held down their heads, and did not utter a syllable. Having obtained from the prisoner his name and where he lived, he then directed his domestics that they should look closely at the man's face; for that the very next time anything would be missed, they should go off in a body to Nobody's house, seize him neck and heels, drag him before a magistrate, and follow the matter up until he was either gibbetted or transported. After they all retired, he gave the terrified individual, whom he had held in duresse for the previous half-hour, a five-shilling piece, and asked him what was there he could do for him.

1820. Honorable James Bernard (Tory)—commonly called Lord Viscount Bernard—elected to represent Bandon.

1821. What is known here as the battle of the Cross, took place this year, on the 2nd of July. The first having fallen on a Sunday, the customary procession on the anniversary of the battle of the Boyne was deferred until next day. Having assembled on Monday, at the open space in front of Ballymodan Church, the members of three Orange lodges marched in procession to Kilbrogan Church, carrying appropriate banners. Every man in the procession wore an orange collar and sash, and an orange lily in the front of his hat. The numerous friends who surrounded them also wore orange lilies and roses in honour of the day. Upon their arrival in Kilbrogan, an excellent sermon was preached for them by the Rev. William Sullivan, on "Fear God, honour the King;" after which the procession formed again, and they marched down through the North Main Street, over the bridge, through the South Main Street, and up through the Castle Road, until they reached the western entrance of Castle-Bernard. Here they halted, and one of them—a man named Sam Hosford—who had charge of the piece of ordnance which accompanied the procession, loaded it. They then fired three rounds from it, and from the few small arms they had with them, in compliment to Lord Bandon, who was a great favourite with the townspeople; and then concluded with three tremendous cheers, in which the bystanders joined with all their might.

Upon their return, when they got to the Cross lane, news was brought them that if they attempted to march through it, and through Gallow's Hill Street, a mob would prevent them by force. This alone was sufficient to induce the majority of those present to go there at all hazards. Accordingly, two out of the three lodges, consisting of one hundred and twelve men, marching two abreast, advanced leisurely up the hill; and descending at the Gallow's Hill Street side, they were met by a mob, variously estimated at from two hundred to five hundred people, headed by two men named Galivan and Hurly, both of whom were armed with muskets. When they approached the mill stream at the bottom of the hill, volley after volley of stones were poured into their ranks. This they patiently withstood for about ten minutes, but seeing that their forbearance only excited the mob to more stones, Hosford, the volunteer gunner, aided by one McDaniel, again loaded the old gun, and fired. The contents fled high over their heads, and were all scattered among the tops of the trees surrounding Mr. Jervois's residence on the opposite side of the road and stream. Seeing there was no casualty, the rioters became emboldened, and the stone-throwing increased in violence. The gun was loaded again, and in the absence of canister or grape, the cannoniers were obliged to substitute gravel, buttons, and even a penknife. At this discharge—which was aided by shots from small arms—a woman named Crowly was killed, and several were wounded, amongst whom was a man named Shea, who died on the next day. This was enough. When the mob became convinced that the Orangemen were in earnest, they broke up and made for their several homes as fast as they could.

The following members of the Protestant party, namely:—Edward Appleby, George Dineen, Patrick Coghlan, John Searles, James Sealy, Bat Malony, Samuel Hosford, Joshua Donovan, Robert Warner, and James

Malony, were tried at the ensuing Cork Assizes; but the jury having declared " that there was no use whatsoever in their remaining together, as there was not the slightest possibility they could ever agree," they were discharged, and the traversers were liberated on their own recognizances.

Great distress prevailed in Bandon this year. Subscription 1822. lists were opened, and a committee was appointed to provide employment for the poor. In order to induce those who could afford it to give employment, the committee paid fourpence out of the eightpence daily paid to labourers, " provided the work to be performed was an extra work, and such as would not be undertaken except for the purpose of giving employment to the poor." From the various returns sent into the committee, it seems that at one time there were no less than two thousand one hundred and thirty-four persons in receipt of charitable assistance.

Illicit distillation at this period was in the zenith of its career. The revenue suffered heavily from it; and the honest manufacturer, who paid heavy duties, was unable to compete with those who paid none. The excise authorities were everywhere on the alert. They determined to suppress it at all hazards; and with that object in view, they placed some of their smartest officers in the districts where they believed the traffic in illicit whiskey and tobacco was greatest.

Mr. H———, a very energetic supervisor, was at that time stationed in a certain town in the west riding of this county, and he made great havoc among the smugglers and their aiders and abettors. It was next to impossible to throw dust in his eyes, or to seduce him from the track of a bale of tobacco, or a keg of potheen. But at last he was fairly befooled and outwitted, and that, too, by a bare-legged bog-trotter from the wilds of Dunmanway.

Mr. H——— was riding along the road one day, when he met a young countryman, who looked the very picture of innocence and simplicity—in fact, the latter was the most prominent of the two in his unmistakably honest face. This ingenious youth was coming to the close of his journey, with a horse laden with two panniers piled with turf (a frequent contrivance for conveying smuggled whiskey in those days); and when Mr. H——— saw the suspicious panniers, he reined up his horse, and prepared to dismount.

" What have you there?" shouted he, in a loud and authorative voice.

"Potheen," your honour, unhesitatingly answered the unreflecting gorsoon, touching his hat respectfully at the same time.

"And who is it for, my good lad?" blandly asked his interrogator, who all at once became very civil at the prospect of an easy prey.

"For one Mrs. H——," mentioning Mr. H's own wife.

"Who sent it?"

"Mr. ——," replied ignoramus, giving him the name of one of the most active still-hunting magistrates in the part of the country he came from, and, moreover, a particular friend of the supervisor himself.

"Oh! very well," hurriedly said Mr. H——, "that will do. Here," said he, taking a key out of his pocket, "give that to Mrs. H——, and tell her she is to give you your breakfast, and a shilling for your trouble!"

"Wisha! long may your honour live!" quoth the poor boy, as he took off his caubeen and put it under his arm, so impressed was he with the magnanimity of Mr. H——; then showering blessings on him and all belonging to him, he resumed his journey.

In due time he reached the town, and safely deposited his whiskey at the public-house for which it was intended. He then coolly walked up to Mr. H——'s residence, knocked at the hall door, and asked to see the mistress. When she came out, he showed her the key Mr. H—— gave him, and told her that he was to get his breakfast and—not a shilling, as Mr. H—— told him—but half-a-crown.

Mrs. H—— thought this somewhat strange, although she had received similar messages before. Nevertheless, that undoubtedly was Mr. H——'s key; and the guileless youth who handed it to her described his dress minutely, when interrogated on that point by Mrs. H——. She accordingly placed a good meal before him, and during its progress, asked him what was it that made the supervisor so fond of him?

"Wisha! by gor, my lady," says he, "I suppose it was because I tould him where he'd find a still at full work!"

This satisfied her at once, and she gave him the half-crown. Before he left the house he borrowed another from her, telling her ladyship she could stop it out of what was coming to him from the master.

On his way home, with more silver in his pocket than ever he had owned before in his life, he met Mr. H—— returning.

"Well, my boy, did Mrs. H—— give you your breakfast?"

"Ah! thin, she did, your honour, and a good one, too!"

"Did she give you the shilling as well?"

"Wisha! I don't care about it!" said the incarnation of simplicity, as if endeavouring to evade the question, out of delicacy for Mr. H———'s feelings. "Sure a shilling isn't much here or there!"

"Oh! tut, tut!" petulantly said H———, who knew his wife was very close-fisted in money matters, "here's the shilling for you!"

After interchanging a few more words, they both parted the best of friends; the country boy pouring good wishes on his honour's head until he was out of sight as well as out of hearing, then laying his clealpeen on the ribs of his bony garron, he made off to his mud cabin as fast as he could lay legs to ground.

When the supervisor reached home, and heard how he had been done out of a profitable seizure—how his wife as well as himself had been swindled out of a breakfast and their hard cash, by a half-witted-looking creature from among the briars and big stones of Dunmanway—their chagrin may be imagined; but we would not undertake the task of even endeavouring to describe it. Of one thing, nevertheless, we are morally certain, and that is, that however reluctant Mrs. H——— was to be tricked out of her money by the unsophisticated cherub from the mountains, her ladyship made no effort to stop it out of what was coming to him from the master.

Smuggled tobacco was not so easily disposed of as smuggled whiskey. When one got some of the former, he often had great difficulty in getting it manufactured, and often incurred great risk in passing along the roads to some place where he could get it spun, or could sell it in the leaf. A farmer, who lived not very far from Ballineen, and who became possessed of some bales of this undutiful article, was anxious to get rid of it, but found it no easy matter to do so. At last he hit upon a plan, the ingenuity of which, and the fertility of the resources of those engaged in carrying it out, are demonstrated by its thorough success—in fact, the contrivance was more successful than the plotters intended; and, to a great extent, they atoned for the great evil they did, by the great improvement they effected in the religious persuasions of some of their neighbours.

Emptying a feather-bed of its contents, he filled it with leaf tobacco. Then throwing a quilt or two over it, he tied his daughter—a fine, healthy, strong young woman—upon it, and set out for Rosscarbery.

Mary received orders from her father to pretend she was mad, hoping by this means to keep off any people who may ask for a lift in the cart, or who may be anxious to have a chat with her. When about half-way to their destination, they met two Protestant farmers, who were neighbours of their's, and who consequently knew Mary well.

" Why ! what's the matter with Mary ?" said one; who, on seeing her nearly covered with ropes, and her hair all tumbled about her face, thought there must be something wrong with her.

" Ah ! ow ! whaw ! whew !" said Mary ; who, on seeing them approaching her along the road, put a piece of soap into her mouth, and it was now in a profuse lather. " Ah ! ow ! ah ! ow ! whoo ! whaw ! whoo !" says she, as the froth ran lavishly from her lips.

" What ails you, Mary ?" said he, putting his hand on the side of the cart.

Her reply was a snap at his head ; and if she succeeded in placing her incisors on his cranium, it would not be hazarding too much to say he would have carried the mark of them to his grave.

" She's mad entirely !" said her poor distressed father, pulling him away from her, " and I'm taking her to Father John, to see if he could do anything for her—the creature !"

" Did you try a doctor ?" enquired the other man, who was so absorbed in pity for poor Mary, that up to that moment he had not uttered a word.

Meanwhile the unfortunate lunatic was howling piteously.

" Well, we won't delay you any longer !" said his two neighbours, as they gave their horses a crack of the whip, and resumed their journey.

The Ballineen man got safe to Rosscarbery, disposed of his goods satisfactorily, and came home.

It happened that one of those who met him in the morning was standing at the door of the forge as he passed by, and he ran out and enquired anxiously about Mary.

" Oh ! she's as well as ever she was in her life, thank God !" said the exultant parent. " There she is, and ask herself !"

" Father John ! may the heavens be his bed !" said the grateful girl to the crowd that was now gathering about her, " cured me in a minute !"

After delaying some little time, the father and daughter went home, in all likelihood rejoicing in the success of their trick, and, perhaps, laughing at the credulity of their friends and neighbours.

The two Protestant farmers were so impressed with the visible proof of the great superhuman accomplishments of Father John, and the lamentable lack of any power to do a similar act of kindness in any of their own clergy, that they became Roman Catholics; and each of them, it is said, has a son living, and working vigorously among the priesthood of that great Christian community.

The illicit whiskey, which was manufactured in large quantities among the Dunmanway mountains, was not only disposed of in the neighbouring towns, where it met a ready sale, and was a great favourite with all classes, but also in the great country highways.

Not many years ago, on the old road leading from Bandon to Dunmanway, there lived an old man named Teige-na-Phillia (Teige of the Poets). He kept a public-house, in which he sold porter and potheen; and his tap was much frequented by carriers and travellers on their way to and from Cork. In due time Teige died, full of years; and, if report be true, full of money also—most of which he is said to have made by selling whiskey, which, from the moment it dripped out of the worm until it tumbled down the consumer's throat, never had the misfortune to reflect the spoil-sport physiognomy of a gauger. Well, after poor Teige had shuffled off his mortal coil, and lay on the flat of his back in old Kilbarry churchyard, his widow carried on the establishment as well as ever; and was even more daring than the defunct Teige, as she publicly sold the potheen in the shop, whereas Teige used generally disseminate it down in the kitchen, or outside in the stable; or if he had much company, and was pushed for space—there being a funeral, or it being "fair-day" in Bandon or Dunmanway—he used to ventilate a half-gallon or two of it in the pig-stye, or in the fowl-house.

An Englishman, fresh from the other side of St. George's Channel, was the newly-appointed supervisor of the district in which Teige's widow openly disposed of her non-tax-paying commodity; and intelligence of her doings soon reached his acute ears. He was determined to catch her. He would teach the old sinner a lesson which she would not forget for the rest of her days; and he would show the illicit whiskey-sellers that they need expect no mercy from him.

Starting one morning from the town where he was stationed, he took a young excise-officer from an intervening station with him—more in the capacity of a witness than of anything else, as he was resolved to monopolize to himself the entire glory of catching Koith-More, and of causing such a penalty to be inflicted upon that old defrauder of the revenue, as would compel her to disgorge no small share of her illicit gains. Getting out of his gig, he walked into Mrs. Teige's hostelry, and boldly knocked with the end of his whip on the counter.

"What's wanting?" says the old widow, putting her head inside the little shop-door from the kitchen, where she was sitting before the fire, darning an old stocking.

"Haw! I want two glasses of potheen whiskey, please!" said the Anglo-Saxon, in an accent that smacked strongly of the land of roast beef and plum-pudding.

"Is it potheen, yer honour? By the hokey!" said the old lady, who knew well who the Englishman was, and who knew what he was then up to just as well as he did himself. "By the hokey!" says she, "there wasn't a pint of it within the four walls of this house those forty years; but I have some of Cornwall's crame, that I got in last night, and a quart of it would do you more good than if you were drinking the best of potheen for a month of Sundays!"

"Haw! but its potheen I want, and I won't have anything else!"

"By gor! thin, yer honour!" replied she, "if you were to give me Lord Bandon's castle to live in, and his grate, big illegant park for a praty-garden, bad cess to the sup I could give you!"

"Oh! come, come, I must have it!" said the supervisor, who was beginning to get angry.

The old woman seeing she could not get rid of them, began to get alarmed, and dreaded lest they would search the house.

"Well, gentlemen," said she, "go down in the room ablow there, and I'll try and get some for you!"

They readily complied; the Englishman giving his assistant a knowing wink, as they pulled a stool a-piece to sit down upon, as much as to say, I knew I'd catch her.

They had scarcely turned their backs upon Mrs. Teige, when she adroitly removed a gallon jar of the coveted liquid which she had under the counter all the time, and sent a boy with it as hard as he could run, to empty its contents into the Bandon river, which was only distant a field from the house. When she thought he was well out of the range of detection, she went up stairs, where she made a great noise in opening and shutting a box, and then returned with a little mug. Meanwhile, the supervisor and the young officer with him had come up from the little tap-room, and were standing outside the counter. Excusing herself for keeping them so long, she placed two glasses on a tray, and laid them before them. She filled the glass nearest the supervisor first, thinking he would be the first to drink, but he handed it to his companion. She then filled the other, telling him at the same time, that in order to get the entire good of it, he should drink it down in one swallow. He did as she directed, and emptied the glass in a gulph. The young man who drank first, suspected something was wrong the very moment he caught the flavour of the villanous compound on his palate; but he turned his back, and held his handkerchief to his face until the supervisor (who was no favourite with the youngsters) should get his supply safely down. When he perceived this, he got rid of his doze (which he had kept in his mouth) as fast as he could, crying out that he was poisoned.

"Gracious God! and so am I!" exclaimed the unhappy Englishman, and began retching violently. "Oh! what will become of my poor wife and my helpless young family?" muttered he, as the cold perspiration ran in torrents down his pale face. "Oh! you wretched woman, you'll have my life to answer for!"

"Oh! you wretched man!" cried the wicked old woman, "sure, if you haven't mine to answer for, it ain't your fault. Potheen, you want, alleah! Bad luck to your impudence, and you have a deal of it daling with you! So, Cornwall's crame wasn't good enough for the like of ye's! Wisha! dha voora dheerig!"

"Send for a clergyman!" faintly asked the supervisor, who really believed he was dying.

"Do!" said the old woman, with a nod to the servant girl, "bring him a parson; a priest wouldn't have time to hear half his confession before he'd die, he has such a big rowl of sins to answer for, God help him!"

"Oh, God have mercy on me!" says the sick man, after a prolonged attack of empty straining.

"Wisha! I don't think he will!" says Job's comforter. "I'm told he'd have nothing to say to the likes of ye's at all!"

Addressing his young companion, he asked him to get him some water, which he contrived to do, and was about handing it to him, when Mrs. Teige again spoke.

"Maybe ye'd like another drop of potheen in it, acushla!" said the old wretch, as she lifted the fatal jug and placed it before him.

After another protracted effort to discharge his stomach, in which some of the bystanders, who had now increased to half-a-dozen, really thought he would throw up his very ribs, he recovered sufficiently to be able to make his way to a magistrate, to whom he detailed particulars of the attempt made upon his life by old Teige-na-Phillia's widow.

The justice had her sent for immediately; and when brought before him, he asked her why she tried to murder the supervisor and his companion?

"I did not, yer honour!" smilingly replied Mrs. Teige, with a reverential courtesy. "They wouldn't be off until I'd give them a drop of potheen, and so I did, to plaze them!" She then told his worship, in an audible whisper, what it really was that she served them with.

When the supervisor found that, at all events, his life was not in danger, he took the matter good-humouredly enough; but shortly after he went back to the sister country, and has never been seen here since.

1826.   June 17th.—Hon. John William Ponsonby (Whig)—best known as Lord Viscount Duncannon—elected to represent the town. Having been also elected for county Kilkenny, he resigned the representation of Bandon; and the vacancy thus created was filled on the 19th of December, by the election of the Right Hon. John Russell (Whig), of Woburn Abbey, Bedfordshire.

1830.   August 7th.—Hon. James Bernard (Tory)—commonly called Lord Viscount Bernard—elected to represent the town.

1831.   January 6th.—Hon. Francis Bernard (Tory)—Lord Viscount Bernard—of Connaught Place, London, and of Castle-Bernard, Ireland, elected in room of his father, James, who succeeded to the earldom of Bandon upon the death of the first earl, on the 30th of November, 1830. Lord Bernard was the youngest member in the House of Commons, having obtained his seat the third day after he became of age.

May 7th.—Lord Bernard returned to sit for Bandon in the new Parliament to assemble on the 14th of June.

July 22nd.—Sir Augustus William Clifford (Whig), knight, captain Royal Navy, Eaton Square, London, in room of Lord Bernard, who accepted the stewardship of the Chiltern Hundreds. This election, which, like many previous ones, was held in Mr. Doherty's office, was sharply contested. Sir A. Clifford was proposed by the Hon. William Smith Bernard, and seconded by John Leslie, Esq. Hon. William Lowther (Tory)—Lord Viscount Lowther—was proposed by the Rev. Somers Payne, and seconded by the Rev. Robert Meade. On a poll, there were :—

For Clifford.	For Lowther.
John Swete, provost.	Rev. Robert Meade.
Hon. and Rev. Richard Boyle Bernard.	Benjamin Swete.
	Rev. Somers Payne.
Hon. William Smith Bernard.	William Holland Kingston.
John Leslie.	

The votes being equal, the provost gave his casting vote, as returning officer, in favour of Clifford.*

1832. This year took place the first election under the Reform Bill. It was held at the court-house, on Thursday, the 13th of December; John Swete, Esq., the provost, presiding. The candidates were :—Hon. William Smith Bernard (Tory), and Jacob Biggs, Esq. (Whig). The former was proposed by Jonathan Clark, M.D., and seconded by Robert Tresilian Belcher. James Clugston Allman proposed Mr. Biggs, and he was seconded by Michael Patrick England. The polling, which continued for three days, was concluded on Saturday, the 15th; when it was found that there were for Captain Bernard, one hundred and thirty-three votes, and for Mr. Biggs, one hundred.

1835. Joseph Devonshire Jackson (Tory). Sergeant Jackson was proposed by the Rev. Somers Payne, and seconded by Joseph Thomas Wheeler. James Redmond Barry (Whig), proposed by Edward O'Brien, seconded by Henry Heazle. The provost, Francis B. Sweeney, presided. At the close of the poll, there appeared for Mr. Jackson, one hundred and eleven, and for Mr. Barry, seventy-nine.

1837. June the 27th.—Alexandrina Victoria proclaimed " Queen of the United Kingdom of Great Britain and Ireland," in the ancient and loyal borough of Bandon-Bridge, at the places following :— First, at the West-gate; second, Market-house; third, Irishtown-

---

* Although this was the Duke of Devonshire's turn to nominate a member for the town, in accordance with an arrangement made with the Earl of Bandon, yet the burgesses who supported Lord Lowther objected to be bound by it on this occasion; they having sworn to preserve, as far as in them lay, the rights and privileges of the corporation, did not think they could consistently vote in favour of one who avowed he would destroy them.

36

bridge; fourth, north side of the great bridge; fifth, Kilbrogan-cross; sixth, Shambles; seventh, Court-house.

ORDER OF PROCESSION.

A detachment of the 78th Infantry.   Highlanders.
Police.   Parish Constables, with staves.
Gentlemen.   Revenue Officers.
Magistrates of the County.
Sergeants-at-Mace.
Town Clerk.
Provost.
Commanding-Officer.   Francis Percy, Sub-Inspector of Police.
Free-Burgesses.   Common Councilmen.   Freemen.
Gentlemen of the Town.
Police.
Detachment of the 78th Infantry.

August the 1st.—At the general election, consequent upon the accession of the Queen, Joseph D. Jackson (Tory), was proposed by Hon. William Smith Bernard, and seconded by Abraham Lane; and William George Cavendish (Whig), was proposed by the Rev. Armiger Sealy, and seconded by Michael Galway. Mr. Jackson obtained one hundred and thirty-three votes, and Mr. Cavendish, eighty-one.

September the 29th.—The Hon. William Smith Bernard entered on the office of provost. He was the last of a long line of provosts, as the old charter became extinct upon the expiration of his official year, on the 29th of September, 1841.

1840.

The following is a complete list of our chief magistrates, including the first who took his seat in the reign of James the First, down to and and including the last, when the office ceased, in the reign of Queen Victoria:—

William Newce	. . 1613.	Richard Tickner	. . 1620.
Henri Beecher	. . . 1614.	Randall Fenton†	. . 1621.
Richard Crofte	. . . 1615.	Anthony Skipwith	. 1622.
Thomas Adderley*.	. 1616.	Eban Woodrooffe	. . 1623.
Edward Beecher	. . 1617.	Nicholas Blacknall	. 1624.
William Newce	. . 1618.	Anthony Skipwith	. 1625.
Thomas Taylor.	. . 1619.	Thomas Dickenson	. 1626.

* For the sake of simplicity, we have called the largest portion of the year in which the provost served as his year of office, although, in reality, he entered on his duties the year before. For instance, Thomas Adderley, whom we have placed opposite 1616, entered on his office, September 29th, 1615; but as he served three times as long in 1616 as he did in 1615, we have placed the former after his name. We have applied the same rule to all the others.

† We have given the spelling as we found it.

Henry Turner	. . .	1627.	George House . . .	1677.
John Lake	. . . .	1628.	Richard Cox . . .	1678.
William Brooke	. .	1629.	John Poole	1679.
Christopher Skipwith	.	1630.	William Chartres . .	1680.
Edward Dunkin	. .	1631.	John Watkins . . .	1681.
Thomas Atkinson	. .	1632.	John Watkins . . .	1682.
William Newce	. .	1633.	James Dixon . . .	1683.
Thomas Taylor	. . .	1634.	Christopher Greenway	1684.
Richard Tickner	. .	1635.	Christopher Greenway	1685.
Randal Fenton	. . .	1636.	Thomas Polden . . .	1686.
Thomas Dickenson	.	1637.	Daniel Beamish . .	1687.
Henry Turner	. . .	1638.	Teige Carty (*temp.* Jas. 2.)	1688.
William Brooke	. .	1639.	Teige Carty	1689.
George Fenton	. . .	1640.	Robert Casey . . .	1690.
Anthony Skipwith	.	1641.	John Nash	1691.
John Woodroffe	. .	1642.	Saul Bruce	1692.
Daniel Howard	. .	1643.	George House . . .	1693.
John Landon	. .	1644.	James Dixon . . .	1694.
Jeffery Sale	. . . .	1645.	Christopher Greenway	1695.
Robert Bathurst	. .	1646.	Isaac Browne . . .	1696.
Abraham Savage	. .	1647.	William Lapp . . .	1697.
William Brooke	. .	1648.	George Symmes . .	1698.
John Smith	. . .	1649.	James Martin . . .	1699.
Clement Woodroffe	.	1650.	Thomas Polden . . .	1700.
Michael Bull	. . .	1651.	Thomas Polden . . .	1701.
William Wright	. .	1652.	James Jackson . . .	1702.
William Wright	. .	1653.	John Nash	1703.
Thomas Dunkin	. .	1654.	Richard Willoe . . .	1704.
Thomas Beamish	. .	1655.	Thomas Shorten . .	1705.
John Jackson	. . .	1656.	Daniel Conner . . .	1706.
Samuel Browne	. .	1657.	Saul Bruce	1707.
Nathaniel Cleare	. .	1658.	Richard Cox . . .	1708.
Abraham Savage	. .	1659.	William Lapp . . .	1709.
John Landon	. . .	1660.	James Dixon . . .	1710.
Jeffery Sale	. . . .	1661.	John Nash	1711.
Clement Woodroffe	.	1662.	Saul Bruce	1712.
William Wright	. .	1663.	James Martin . . .	1713.
John Jackson	. . .	1664.	George House . . .	1714.
Thomas Beamish	. .	1665.	Jonathan Tanner . .	1715.
John Browne	. . .	1666.	James Jackson . . .	1716.
John Browne	. . .	1667.	John Jones	1717.
Matthew Percival	. .	1668.	Arthur Bernard . .	1718.
John Poole	. . .	1669.	John Travers . . .	1719.
William Chartres	. .	1670.	William Bull . . .	1720.
William Chartres	. .	1671.	James Martin . . .	1721.
John Watkins	. . .	1672.	Daniel Conner . . .	1722.
James Dixon	. . .	1673.	John Nash	1723.
William Wright	. .	1674.	John Nash	1724.
Thomas Beamish	. .	1675.	Saul Bruce	1725.
Samuel Browne	. .	1676.	Jonathan Tanner . .	1726.

John Lapp	1727.	Francis Travers		1777.
William Lapp	1728.	Isaac Hewett		1778.
John Jones	1729.	William Conner		1779.
James Jackson	1730.	Arthur Bernard		1780.
James Jackson	1731.	John Travers		1781.
Ralph Clear	1732.	Isaac Hewett		1782.
Honble. Henry Boyle	1733.	Robert Sealy		1783.
James Martin	1734.	Arthur Bernard		1784.
Daniel Conner	1735.	William Conner		1785.
Matthew Adderley	1736.	Arthur Bernard		1786.
Roger Bernard	1737.	Thomas Biggs		1787.
Robert Sealy	1738.	Arthur Bernard.		1788.
John Stammers	1739.	Thomas Biggs		1789.
John Stammers	1740.	Arthur Bernard		1790.
William Conner	1741.	Thomas Biggs		1791.
Jonathan Tanner	1742.	Samuel Beamish		1792.
Daniel Conner	1743.	Sampson Jervois		1793.
Ralph Clear	1744.	Samuel Beamish		1794.
Arthur Bernard	1745.	Sampson Jervois		1795.
Matthew Adderley	1746.	Samuel Beamish		1796.
Ralph Clear	1747.	Sampson Jervois		1797.
Daniel Conner	1748.	Samuel Beamish		1798.
Edward Martin	1749.	Sampson Jervois		1799.
Daniel Conner	1750.	Samuel Beamish		1800.
Roger Bernard	1751.	Sampson Jervois		1801.
Jonathan Tanner	1752.	Samuel Beamish		1802.
George Sealy	1753.	Sampson Jervois		1803.
John Stammers	1754.	Samuel Beamish		1804.
Arthur Bernard	1755.	John Campbell		1805.
John Stammers	1756.	Samuel Beamish		1806.
Jonathan Alleyn	1757.	Joseph Jervois		1807.
Francis Travers	1758.	Samuel Beamish		1808.
Richard Savage	1759.	Joseph Jervois		1809.
Jonathan Tanner	1760.	Samuel Beamish		1810.
George Sealy	1761.	Joseph Jervois		1811.
Arthur Bernard	1762.	Samuel Beamish		1812.
Charles Bernard	1763.	Joseph Jervois		1813.
James Bernard	1764.	Thomas Meade		1814.
Jonathan Tanner	1765.	Samuel Beamish		1815.
George Sealy	1766.	Joseph Jervois		1816.
George Conner	1767.	Samuel Beamish		1817.
James Bernard	1768.	Joseph Jervois		1818.
John Travers	1769.	Samuel Beamish		1819.
Isaac Hewett	1770.	Joseph Jervois		1820.
John Travers	1771.	Samuel Beamish		1821.
Arthur Bernard	1772.	Joseph Jervois		1822.
John Travers	1773.	Samuel Beamish		1823.
Richard Savage	1774.	Hon. W. Smith Bernard	1824.
John Travers	1775.	John Swete		1825.
James Bernard	1776.	Hon. W. Smith Bernard	1826.

John Swete . . . . 1827.	Francis B. Sweeney . 1835.
Hon. W. Smith Bernard 1828.	Hon. W. Smith Bernard 1836.
John Swete . . . . 1829.	Robert Tresilian Belcher 1837.
Hon. W. Smith Bernard 1830.	John Wheeler, junr. . 1838.
John Swete . . . . 1831.	Edward Doherty . . 1839.
Hon. W. Smith Bernard 1832.	Somers Payne . . . 1840.
John Swete . . . . 1833.	Hon. W. Smith Bernard 1841.
John Wheeler, junr. . 1834.	

The Manor Courts were at this time in full operation. We had three of them connected with Bandon. The court for the manor of Castle-Mahon was of late years held at the sign of the "Admiral"—a public house at the Old Chapel. The owner of this hostelry, where entertainment was provided for man and horse, was one Jerry Sullivan—an old salt, who spent most of his life on board ship, and who, in his early days, had served under Lord Nelson. Jerry gloried in the great naval hero; and to show his respect for the memory of his old commander, he had his portrait painted in full uniform, and placed on his sign-board. The late Mr. William Lovell was for many years the seneschal of this manor. Upon his decease, Mr. Edward Doherty was appointed.

Mr. John Baldwin was seneschal of the Coolfadda Manor, and held his court at Mallowgatton; and Mr. John Cotter was seneschal of the Manor of Ballymodan, and held his court at the sign of the "Fortune of War," in Shannon Street. By far the most important of these Manors was Castle-Mahon. The patent, dated July 8th (10th of James the First), confers many privileges upon Henrie Beecher, Esq., his heirs and assigns. After reciting the rights, &c., bestowed on his father, Phane Beecher, Esq., deceased, in the grant bestowed on him " of the halfendale of the countrie Kylnallmechie," all of which are re-affirmed to Henry Beecher, the seigniory is created a manor, and entitled the Manor of Castle-Mahowne; and Beecher, his heirs, assigns, &c., have granted to him and them " full and absolute power, by fine, feoffment, or any other lawful means, to give and grant to any loyal subject of us, our heirs, &c., (said subject not being meer Irish), any portion of the said seigniory." Power was given to patentee to hold a Court Leet, at or near Castle-Mahon, twice every year. The seneschal, to be appointed by Beecher, his heirs, assigns, &c., " was to have full power, authority, and jurisdiction, to enquire of all and singular felonies, trespasses, deceipts, nuisances, and all other crimes, offences, matters whatsoever, which shall be committed, perpetrated, done, or shall happen in, and within the said seigniory." The same authority was also conferred that was exercised in any other Court Leet. "And furthermore, the said patentee was empowered to keep one court in the nature of a Court Baron, to be holden from three weeks to three weeks, before the seneschal; and he shall have full power, &c., in said court, to hold pleas of all manner of debts, covenants, trespasses, accounts, causes, contracts, matters whatsoever, in which debts and damages do not exceed forty shillings correct money of England. Patentee, his heirs, assigns, also entitled to all waifs, estraies, deodands, the goods and chattels of felons, fugitives, and all persons condemned as outlaws. He had, in addition, the right to appoint the clerk of the market in the town newly erected, called Bandon-Bridge, situate in the said seigniory, or in any other town which shall hereafter be made a market-town, within the halfendale or cantred of the said countrie of Kynallmechie; and the power of licensing, or permitting any person, or persons, to exercise the trade, craft, or ministerie of butcher, baker, brewer, or merchant; or which shall sell, or cause to be sold, any aqua-vitæ, wyne, ale, or beere within the town of Bandon-Bridge."

For a long time these courts were much availed of. In fact, up to the beginning of the present century; all the law business of the country, criminal as well as civil, of which these courts took cognizance, passed through them; but since then they have gradually fallen into disuse, and, as a consequence, some of the seneschals grew careless and in-different, more or less, to that decorum which should be preserved in a court of justice.

Some amusing stories are still told of the seneschals who dispensed justice—we were going to say who dispensed with it—within a radius of twenty miles from our town. The courts of late years were usually held in some public-house, and the jury was generally composed of twelve men from the neighbourhood. Sometimes the jury did not con-tain more than half that number, and, for a few years before the courts were swept away, his worship had often to charge only three. It was customary—indeed it had almost grown into a matter of right in some of our local courts—for the party in whose favour the verdict was given, to stand the judge, and that great palladium of our liberties, the jury, two gallons of porter—that is, a pint for his lordship, one for each of the jury, one for the summons-server, and one a-piece for the two bailiffs. The consequence was, that when they had adjudicated upon a good many cases, or when the jury was a small one, they were hardly able to see, much more to walk home.   More than once, when after a long day's work, and whilst under the influence of the black nectar, the judge has been known to offer to fight the entire jury, individually and collectively ; and it was no uncommon thing to hear one of the bailiffs offering to bet " a half-gallon" with his lordship on the solution of some point of law.   If a 'fellow was too poor to stand the necessary malt—for instance, if the defendant non-suited the plaintiff, and had not a penny to pay for his night's lodging—he was dismissed with a kind of moral kick, and told that if ever he was caught there again, he would pay for it.   It happened on one occasion that the defendant, who was a strong, comfortable farmer, got a verdict in his favour by the jury.   They demanded their customary fee, but he was a close-fisted, hard-hearted fellow, and they could not squeeze a drop out of him.   They forthwith appealed to his lordship, and he directed the defendant to call for the porter at once ; but the defendant refused point-blank to do any such thing.

"Well, we'll try the case over again, boys !" said the judge ; but even that hint would not do.

Upon this the jury were ordered to sit again ; and the fellow's ingratitude, and everything bad that was ever heard of him since he was able to peel a potato, was duly laid before them.

When the judge's charge was completed, the jury consulted together, and having apparently agreed, were asked in the usual way :—" How say you, gentlemen of the jury ?"

The foreman replied that they were unanimous in finding a verdict of wilful murder against the accused.

Whereupon the judge addressed the prisoner in a solemn and im-pressive tone.   He pointed out to him the ignominious fate which must sooner or later overtake those who do not behave with justice and honour to their fellow-men ; and he concluded by sentencing the un-fortunate man to be hanged from the iron bar that supported the sign-board of a neighbouring public-house ; adding, that after the execution the body should be cut down, and buried at an adjoining cross-road.

Seeing the turn events were taking, the comfortable farmer began to grow very uncomfortable ; and fearing that something serious might really befall him, called for the required two gallons, and then for two gallons more, to damp the indignation of those who had just consigned him to the gibbet.

The jury were not prohibited from the use of the dudeen during their labours, and were allowed to cross-examine the witnesses as they liked.

"So, you lent him five shillings? By gor! I don't believe you!" one of them would say, "for I know you hadn't it of your own, and there's no one would lend it to you!"

"Yerra! give the poor man time!" would cry another. "Sure you didn't think he was going to keep the money in his pocket until you plaze to ask him for it?"

"Take and pay the woman at once!" another would say. "'Tis a shame for the like of ye—a dacent-looking man—to be walking about with the few pence belonging to that poor creature in your pocket!"

Even the public took part in these trials. Addressing one of the jurors, Mick would shout out—one of the great unwashed, who, by standing on the tips of his toes, would succeed in catching an occasional glimpse of the court inside—"Don't mind a word he says" (referring to the witness), "as there isn't a man, woman, or child in the street would bleeve a word from him!"

"Swear!" would cry another of the *magni illoti;* "by gor! he'd swear a hole through the bottom of a brass skillet, and he looking as innocent as a new-born baby all the time!"

The courts were not favourites with the well-to-do classes. However it may fare with the poor man, the rich man had often good reason to complain. Consequently, when their fate was placed in the scales, he did not stand up in their behalf.

1841.   Joseph Devonshire Jackson (Tory), returned to represent the town. No opposition.

1847.   August 2nd.—Lord Bernard (Tory), proposed by John Wheeler, J.P., seconded by Franklin Baldwin. No contest.

1852.   July 9th.—Lord Bernard (Tory), proposed by John Wheeler, J.P., seconded by William C. Sullivan. No contest.

1857.   February 11th—Captain Hon. William Smith Bernard (Tory), proposed by William C. Sullivan, seconded by Richard Tresilian. William Shaw (Whig), proposed by Richard L. Allman, seconded by John Heron. At the conclusion of the poll, there were found recorded for Captain Bernard, one hundred and one votes, and for Mr. Shaw, sixty-seven.

March 31st.—Captain Hon. William Smith Bernard (Tory), proposed by William C. Sullivan, seconded by Richard Tresilian. No contest.

1859. May 2nd.—Colonel Hon. William Smith Bernard, (Tory), proposed by William C. Sullivan, seconded by Richard Tresilian. No contest.

1863. February 24th.—Colonel Hon. Henry Boyle Bernard (Tory), proposed by Henry Unkles, seconded by Richard Tresilian. Thomas Kingston Sullivan (Whig), proposed by Henry B. Ormston, M.D., seconded by John Heron. For Colonel Bernard there were one hundred and twenty-four votes, and for Mr. Sullivan, eighty.

1865. Wednesday, July 12th.—Colonel Hon. Henry Boyle Bernard (Tory), proposed by Captain Wheeler, seconded by Richard Tresilian. William Shaw (Whig), proposed by Richard L. Allman, seconded by William C. Sullivan. For Colonel Bernard, one hundred and eleven votes, and for Mr. Shaw, one hundred and six.

1868. November 20th.—Hon. Colonel Bernard was proposed by John Wheeler, seconded by Henry Unkles. William Shaw proposed by Richard Allman, seconded by William C. Sullivan. This was the first election for a member of Parliament for the town under the new Reform Bill, by means of which occupiers of tenements rated at £4 per annum were entitled to vote.

For Hon. Colonel Bernard (Conservative) . . 137*
William Shaw (Whig) 141

---

* The following extract is taken from a letter to a newspaper, which appeared at the time, and gives interesting particulars concerning the religious professions of the electors, how they voted, &c. :—

"Of the 294 names on the electoral list, 177 were those of Protestants, and 117 of Roman Catholics.

Of the latter, dead 1	Of the former, dead 0
Absent from home 3	Absent from home 1
Voted for Mr. Shaw 113	Voted for Colonel Bernard . . . 137
Remained neutral 0	Remained neutral 12
Protestants voted for Mr. Shaw . 28	Roman Catholics voted for Colonel Bernard 0

Of the Protestants who voted, there were :—

FOR MR. SHAW.		FOR COLONEL BERNARD.	
Episcopalians 9	Episcopalians 91
Wesleyans 8	Wesleyans 35
Presbyterians 6	Presbyterians 5
Unitarians 4	Plymouth Brethren 5
Independents 1	Unitarians 1

Of the twelve who remained neutral, there were :—
Episcopalians 7
Wesleyans 5

If the Hon. Colonel Bernard, who is enumerated among the Episcopalian neutrals, followed the example of Mr. Shaw, and voted for himself, the majority against him would have been three, and not four, as at present."

INDEX.

APPENDIX.

THE BERNARDS OF PALACE-ANNE.

THE GOODMANS.

THE BERNARDS OF PALACE-ANNE.*

WHEN the traveller from Bandon to Dunmanway arrives about midway on his journey, he finds the road on both sides lined with tall elms and stately oaks, whose large limbs entwining over head, form the dark arcade through which he passes. About a hundred yards from the road, and at the foot of a low chain of hills, is, or rather was, the residence of the Bernards of Palace-Anne. That the mansion still stands it is true; but where are its hunting parties? Where is "Ould Teige na Mourna"—the old huntsman, whose winding horn, ringing through the echoing woods, and swelling over hill and dale, goaded the kennel into an uproar, and brought the scarlet coats in swift trot to the door? Where are its pastimes, its hospitalities, its glories? The grand and venerable roof, that sheltered rank and beauty in its palmy days, now affords a questionable shelter to a dairyman and his humble assistants. The Rakes' hall, where the worthy host used to entertain his brother-sportsmen on the morning or the evening of the chase, and where many a bracket or a spike-hole still speaks of the trophies of the field, is now a turnip-shed. The horse-pond is still there, and supplies water for the cows and for dairy purposes; but the fish-ponds have run dry, the parterres have become obliterated, and the gardens entirely possessed by weeds.

The house itself was erected about a century and a-half ago, and was built of red brick, brought chiefly from Bristol. The principal front consists of a centre and two wings. The centre rises into three ornamental gables, in the old French style, and each wing terminates in a gable nearly similar in size and shape to those of the centre. There are numerous windows, and their long and even still white sashes and shutters, contrasting with the warm colouring of the bricks and the deep green of the trees, tell us of the dignity and independence of those who once paced its lordly halls.

Early in last summer, accompanied by a friend, we visited this venerable pile. The great entrance gate was barred up with loose stones; however, we contrived to gain admission through the rear. Ascending a flight of limestone steps, we found ourselves on the broad terrace

---

* "The Bernards of Palace-Anne," and "The Goodmans," were originally intended for another publication; but, at the suggestion of some friends, who think that, as they mention personages and events referred to in our preceding pages, this is the proper place for them, we have inserted them here.

extending the entire length of the front, and overlooking where the shrubberies and flower gardens formerly occupied the ground intervening between it and the mail-coach road. We knocked repeatedly at the hall door, and our only response was the echo within. Descending by the way we came up, we went round to the back, and easily entered by one of the many doorways in the basement. We were soon in a long, vaulted corridor, which communicated with the apartments above, by either two or three staircases. Of these only one remained, and even this it was difficult to mount, owing to some of the lower steps being wanting. We wandered through many of the rooms, and saw nothing but ruin. The demon of desolation seems to have laid his hand on them, and marked them as his own. In some the painted ceilings were broken, and large patches of plaster lay strewn around; in others the flooring was ripped up, and the fire-grates and chimney-pieces were ruthlessly torn from their berths; and in more than one we observed the door hanging by a single hinge, as if unwilling to sever the last tie that bound it to its old home. Passing through the wainscoted hall, the grand staircase lay before us; and it required but little effort of the imagination to crowd its broad steps with the inhabitants of former days—with courtly dames and damosels passing down to the supper or the dining-room, attended by gallants in gold-laced coats, or carrying on a flippant flirtation with that gay young fellow, whose powdered peruke and ruffles, or whose jewel-handled rapier, silk hose, and broad silver shoe-buckles, proclaim him one of the fashionable bucks of the day. Retracing our steps, we could not help musing over that proverb which says: "Man proposes, but God disposes."

Sir Theophilus, "a valiant knyghte," was one of the band of adventurers that landed at Pevensey with William of Normandy. He had a son, Sir Dorbred, who was the first to assume the surname of Bernard, and whose descendants eventually settled at Acorn Bank, in Westmoreland, one of whom, Robert Fitz-Bernard, accompanied Henry the Second to Ireland in 1172; and such was the high opinion entertained of him by that monarch, that, upon his departure for England, he entrusted Fitz-Bernard with the sole governorship of Wexford and Waterford.

Sir Henry Bernard, a lineal descendant of Sir Dorbred's, lived at the old family seat in Westmoreland, and married Anne, daughter of Sir John Dawson, a neighbouring knight, by whom he had four sons—Robert, William, Francis, and Charles. Of these, Francis, his third son, came to Ireland (temp. Queen Elizabeth), and permanently settled in the newly-planted colony of Bandon-Bridge. He died, leaving, besides two daughters, a son, Francis, whose son Francis married Mary Freke, daughter of Captain Arthur Freke, of Rathbarry Castle, (ancestor of Lord Carbery,) and granddaughter of Sir Percy Smith, by Mary Boyle, sister of Richard, first Earl of Cork. By this lady he had two sons, Francis and Arthur, both born at Castle-Mahon.

Francis, his eldest son, (born in 1663,) devoted himself to the study of the law, and soon attained to eminence. In 1713 he was selected to fill the office of solicitor-general; and was shortly after raised to the

Bench as one of Her Majesty's judges of the Court of Common Pleas. For many years he sat for his native town of Bandon in the Irish Parliament, where he was well known and appreciated as an active and painstaking representative. He was ancestor of the Earls of Bandon. His brother Arthur (born 1666) was progenitor of the Bernards of Palace-Anne.

Arthur took a very active part in the eventful times in which he lived. When the Bandonians heard that Lord Clancarthy was approaching with a body of foot, to aid the force already in possession of their town to disarm them, several of them met, and resolved to imitate their heroic brethren of Londonderry, by shutting their gates in the teeth of the advancing foe. But they were not content to rest even satisfied with this, for, falling upon O'Neill's garrison at cock-crow on a Monday morning, they stripped them of all their arms and accoutrements, and then turned them outside the walls. This was called the "Black Monday Insurrection," and its similitude to a like proceeding in the North has earned for Bandon a name by which it is still known and honoured—that of "the Southern Derry."

Mr. Bernard took a foremost part in this outbreak, and was one of "the leaders of the late revolt" demanded of the inhabitants by Major-General McCarthy upon his laying siege to the town, and concerning whom they made that reply which has travelled to every region to which the fame of "the ancient and loyal borough" has extended, and which will survive as long as the historic associations connected with it will endure: "That they had no objection to treat about delivering the town into his hands upon honourable terms; but as for giving up their leaders, their answer was—'No surrender!'" Owing to the interference of their fellow-townsman, Dr. Brady—who, in conjunction with Nahum Tate, composed the version of the Psalms now in daily use in our churches—McCarthy was induced to let the Bandon people off very easy. But James the Second was not so soft-hearted. When that monarch landed at Kinsale, and became aware of all the circumstances connected with "the late revolt," he did not allow the capitulation to stand between him and his vengeance. He directed that indictments for high-treason should be prepared against the leaders on the spot, and ordered his chief-justice, who was then presiding at the Cork Spring Assizes, to have them put upon their trial at once. McCarthy, however, urgently protested against this, and, taking advantage of James's departure for Dublin, he forced Nugent to postpone the case until the next assizes. In the interim the battle of the Boyne was fought, and the conquered having changed places with the conquerors, the prisoners were never after called upon to plead.

Mr. Bernard filled the office of high-sheriff of the county in 1697, and again in 1706; he was also colonel of the East Carbery Horse—a volunteer regiment of Light Dragoons, to which the State was at that time indebted for many valuable services. On the 22nd of December, 1695, according to a quaint old family M.S., he was married "at about eight of the clock on Sunday night, at the great dining-room at the castle of Lismore," to Anne, daughter and co-heiress of Roger Power (or Le Poer), of Mount Eglantine, Co. Waterford, by whom he had issue, four sons[*] and eleven daughters, all baptized and christened in due order. In the long list of their godfathers and godmothers, we find the names of Colonel Congreve, Judge Bernard, Mrs. Ludlow, Alderman Knapp, Mrs. Hedges, Sir Ralph Freke, Nancy Barrett, Mat. Adderley, Aunt Cook, Brigadier-General George Freke, Sir Richard Cox, Lady Pyne, Lord Ikerrim, &c., &c. At his decease he was succeeded by his eldest son, Roger Bernard, who was succeeded by his only child, Roger Bernard.

The latter was principally brought up in England, where he graduated as B.A. of Cambridge. Upon his attaining to the inheritance, he indulged in all the vices and follies of the day. He kept a house open to everyone that could sing a good song or tell a good story. His mahogany was fringed by the jolliest fellows the country could produce; and it used to be said, and probably with much truth, that scarcely anyone was known to walk away from his table—*they were carried.* "Mick, your Master is down;" or, "Jerry, yours is tottering;" or, "Tady, Mr. So-and-so fell, after his fourth bottle," was an ordinary intimation from the butler to one or other of the servant-men, who sat smoking round the kitchen fire, to go to the Rakes' hall, and take his master to bed. Sometimes this feat was accomplished by dragging the master the entire way on the broad of his back; but, when assistance was at hand, the usual plan adopted was for one man to put his head between his legs, and for two others to put their shoulders under his, and in this way to carry him upstairs, as if he were a sack of wheat. His own man then pulled off his boots, loosened his cravat, put the washing-stand basin under his nose, and left him to grunt and snore until the hounds and hunting-horn woke him up next day.

Roger was a great steeplechaser, and was the best man in the three kingdoms to manage a wicked horse, or to stick to the pigskin under any circumstances. Whilst in England on one occasion, he was at a racecourse where a lady of high rank had a horse to run. The vicious beast a few weeks before had killed his groom, and, even on that very morning, had thrown his jockey with such force as to render him incapable of moving. The news spread that the favourite would not run. His backers were in a panic, as no one could be got to mount him. The intelligence soon reached our hero. This was just the kind of adventure to his liking. Quickly making his way through the crowd, he desired the horse to be led out. This was accordingly done; and, catching him boldly by the bridle, he jumped into the saddle. In vain the ill-tempered brute tried to pitch him over his head, then off

* His youngest son, Captain George Bernard,—known in England as the handsome Irishman,—married Mary, daughter of Sir William Codrington, and cousin-german to Sir Edward Codrington, the hero of Navarino. By her he had a son, George, who was usher of the Black Rod to the Duke of Rutland, when Lord Lieutenant of Ireland. He was also usher to the Knights of St. Patrick. Two battalions of the 84th Regiment were raised by him, for which service he was promoted to the rank of colonel. He subsequently became a lieutenant-general, and died in 1817, leaving a daughter, married to Captain Arthur Beamish, who assumed the name of Bernard in addition. By her Captain B. Bernard had an only child, Mary Isabella, so called after her godmother, the Duchess of Rutland, (Mary Isabella, youngest daughter of Charles, fourth Duke of Beaufort,) who was married, in 1847, to John Bowen, Esq., junior, of Oak-grove, Co. Cork.

his back; he then tried to bite him, and, as a last resource, lay down, and absolutely endeavoured to roll over him. But he at last had found his master: he was kicked and licked into good behaviour; and, when the start was made, away he went at a pace that speedily brought him to the winning-post, leaving all his competitors behind him—distanced and chagrined.

"Claim what you wish, Mr. Bernard," cried the fair owner, in a fit of exultation, "and it shall be granted."

Taking off his hat, and making a low bow: "Then, my lady, I claim the honour of kissing your ladyship's hand."

It was instantly extended, and, with this poor requital, he felt amply compensated for the repeated risk he ran of being killed.

He died young, but not until he had left charges upon the estate from which it was only freed by the hammer.

Arthur, his father's second brother, was his successor. He married his cousin, Mary Adderley, great-granddaughter of the Lord Chief-Justice Sir Matthew Hale. For many years he was provost of Bandon, and died at a good old age, in 1793.

He was succeeded by his eldest son, Thomas Bernard, who married a Miss Lucas, but had no issue; and whose brother Arthur, a captain in the 84th Regiment, married Margaret Warren, of Castle-Warren. This lady, after the birth of her infant son, Francis, paid a visit to the old family seat, taking the baby with her. The child was a remarkably fine one, and the mother was proud of it. Taking the little cherub from the nurse, and holding him up in her arms:

"Tom," said she, "look at the future owner of Palace-Anne."

"He shall never own a sod of it," growled he; and he kept his word.

Sending into Bandon for his solicitor, he levied fines and suffered recoveries, and made his will, by which he bequeathed all he possessed to Arthur Beamish, second son of his sister Elizabeth, who was the wife of Richard Beamish, of Raheroon; and so bent was he on disinheriting the lawful heir, that he died soon after, "lest," as a fair correspondent of ours suggests, "he should by any means be induced to change his mind."

A few years before he (Arthur Beamish) became possessed of the estate, and whilst yet a very young man, his career was near being abruptly brought to a close, as he had the misfortune to get into a quarrel, and exchange shots, with one of the most successful duellists of the day.

There was a gentleman named Henley living at Innoshannon, who had permission from Mr. Adderley, the owner of that estate, to shoot over it. Mr. Beamish subsequently obtained a similar favour for a friend of his, afterwards known as Captain Jack Sealy. Henley vowed revenge, and openly declared that the first opportunity he had of insulting Beamish he would do so. An occasion soon presented itself in a house where he called to pay a visit, and, walking up to him, he looked contemptuously in his face, and told him he was no gentleman.

"You're a liar!" replied Beamish, and instantly felled him to the ground.

In those halcyon days an appeal to the King's Bench was unfashionable. Should the plaintiff feel himself aggrieved by the defendant, he resorted to a summary process, about which the only thing wrong was, that the innocent man had just the same chance of being murdered as the guilty one. Indeed, we may truly venture to affirm that he often had a greater; for it was by no means uncommon for a professed shot to roam about the country, or swagger through our streets, seeking for a *casus belli*, and then bring his deadly skill to bear upon one with whom he had purposely picked a quarrel.

"Name your friend!" roared Henley, jumping to his feet in a rage.

"Captain Tonson, sir. Yours?"

"Mr. Spread."

The seconds met that evening, and it was arranged that the affair should come off early on the following day.

As we have said, Beamish was a very young man, and had never pulled a trigger on such an occasion in his life. Henley, who was a member of the notorious Hell-fire Club, was, on the contrary, an old hand, and had already stretched his fourth man.

The news went everywhere. Everyone that heard it reckoned Beamish a gone man. "Before to-morrow's sun will reach the meridian, he'll be a gone man," said one. "You might as well bring him before a sergeant's guard, and let them shoot him decently," said another. There was no man in his senses would give more than twelve hours' purchase for his life.

The place appointed for the meeting was at Killanethig, about three and a-half miles south of Bandon. Both men were on the sod well up to time. It was observed that the younger one looked cool and collected, but thoughtful. His friend had great hopes of him.

"Keep cool, Arthur, my boy," said he; "keep cool; and if you don't let the daylight into his bread-bag, I'm not Jake Tonson!"

The elder displayed the most perfect *nonchalance*, occasionally whistling snatches of a popular air, or making some indifferent remark to those around him. When his second began walking the paces:

"Make them long," said he, "as it may give this spirited young chap a chance."

"I don't want any chance," cried his opponent in an angry tone. "Do you hold one end of a handkerchief, and I'll hold the other, and let us blaze away."

"Oh, no, my young friend," replied Henley, with a ceremonious bow, "that would be murder;" adding, in a low tone, "a little bleeding will bring him to reason."

Tonson, after loading the pistols, gave one to each of the combatants; then handing the powder-flask to Beamish, who carelessly put it into his breast-pocket, he retired. Having taken their places, at the word "present!" both slowly raised the armed hand, with the right arm extended, until it almost formed a right angle with the body, and remained motionless as statues. Upon the signal being given to fire, they discharged their weapons simultaneously. The spectators, rushing in before the smoke had yet rolled away, found Beamish erect—his adversary's bullet struck the powder-flask, and, glancing off obliquely, did no harm. But Henley was down. The ball entered the lower abdomen, tearing the flesh, and making an ugly laceration, from which the blood flowed copiously. To the crowd that gathered round him :

" I have nothing to say, gentlemen," said he, " only that everything was fairly conducted, and I wish that no proceedings should be taken." Then, after a pause, turning to his second, who was assisting in endeavouring to stay the red stream that still poured through the wound : " Spread," said he, in an earnest tone, " avenge me."

He was removed shortly after to the house of a farmer named Mason, who lived in the vicinity of the village of Ballinadee, where he was carefully attended to ; but, notwithstanding all that the skill of his medical advisers could do for him, he sank gradually, and before twelve that night he was dead.

When his uncle died, Mr. Beamish—whom we shall now call Captain Bernard—returned from the West Indies, where his regiment was stationed, and arriving in Cork on the top of a coach, went into the coach-office to warm himself by the fire. A gentleman who was sitting before it looked up at him, and immediately placed his leg on the grate at the side at which he was. Not pretending to notice the affront, he passed round to the other side ; but the sitter instantly put his leg up there also.

" Oh, if you want to keep all the fire to yourself, sir," said Bernard, " I'll give you enough of it," catching him by the collar at the same time, and forcing him into a sitting posture on the fire, where he held him until he roared with pain. Still gripping him by the collar, he pulled out his card and handed it to him.

" Now, Mr. Spread, you knew me before, and you know where to find me now."

Spread, whose feelings may be imagined with greater facility than described, rushed upstairs to his room, where, we may presume, he thought over the injury he received and the remedy suggested, and came to the conclusion that, in this case, discretion was the better part of valour. At all events, he held his tongue, and there was no more about it.

Captain Bernard was a very active county magistrate, and was more than once thanked by the Government for his exertions in the Whiteboy business of 1821 and '22. At that time bands of men, many of whom were armed, used to roam over the rural districts in his neighbourhood, attacking the houses of the gentry for arms, and enforcing their demands for " powder money" from the farmers.

The Palace-Anne Corps of Yeomanry, with their gallant leader at their head, were scarcely ever off their legs. On one occasion, whilst " on patrol," they overtook a gang, who were on their way to assault the house of a gentleman living a few miles distant. Being ordered to " halt!" they broke and fled.

" Halt !" again roared the captain. " In the King's name, halt, or I'll fire !"

But they ran even faster than before.

Putting his rifle to his shoulder, he took dead aim, and down tumbled one of the marauders. . It was found that the wounded man—who, by the way, is still alive and in good health—was absolutely *his own carpenter*, and from whom he on that very evening received the keys of the stable-yard, and to whom he at the same time handed a strong tumbler of Irish whiskey-punch, mixed by his own hand.

All the estates were sold within the last fifteen years, excepting Palace-Anne house and domain, in which Captain Bernard had only a life interest, and which he held from the creditors as a tenant from year to year until his death.

He died in 1854, and was succeeded by his brother, Captain Bernard Beamish, the present owner, who has also but a life interest in the house and domain ; but even these he does not enjoy, owing to his being unfortunately involved in his brother Arthur's affairs, and they are now in Chancery. The heir to the fame, and to the wreck of the fortunes, of the Bernards of Palace-Anne, is a young man, who, when last heard of, was working for his daily bread in one of the Western States of America; and whose only brother, Richard, and the husband of his sister Elizabeth, were both killed in the battle of Antietam, whilst serving in the ranks of one of the Federal regiments as private soldiers.

THE GOODMANS.

WELL authenticated instances of suspended animation are to be met with. A late president of the Royal Medical and Chirurgical Society knew a case where the patient, saving some short intervals, continued in a state of insensibility for two or three weeks ; and he records the case of a female who was so unmistakeably defunct that she was laid in her coffin, and the cover was about being laid on, when a bystander noticed a profuse sweat suddenly break out over her face and hands, and thus her life was preserved.

Dr. Gooch mentions the case of another female who fell into catalepsy. Her eyes were wide open ; she was thin, pallid, and the very picture of a corpse ; and although he placed his mouth alternately to either ear and called loudly, she did not hear a word—she did not even move, or show more signs of animation than a statue.

Bonet states that a soldier who deserted from his regiment, upon being overtaken and captured, became so overpowered by sheer terror as to become perfectly unconscious. Whatever position his body was placed in, there it would remain, and for upwards of twenty days the unfortunate man neither ate nor drank, or showed by the performance of other duties essential to vitality that he was even alive.

Catalepsy is to be met with still. A short time since a messenger called at the residence of a surgeon in this neighbourhood, and left directions that he should call at a certain number in a certain street, and see a young woman who was dangerously ill. Upon his return from the country, where he was when the message was delivered, he immediately set out, and entering the sick-chamber, approached the bedside of his new patient.

"You're too late now, doctor," said an old woman who sat at the head of the bed, rocking herself to and fro in an agony of grief; "you're too late—she died about half-an-hour ago."

And to all appearance she was dead. There she lay, stiff and motionless. The *rigor mortis* had set in, and there was that calm, composed silent look, which told that the spirit which shone in those lustreless eyes; which glowed in those chill, damp cheeks; which circled in innocent smiles round those stiffened lips, had fled from its earthly tenement for ever. Influenced more by the force of habit than of anything else, he mechanically took hold of her hand and placed his fingers where the pulse was, and then let it go; but, to his horror, there it stood pointing towards him. He then lifted one of her legs, and there it remained outstretched also. He now became convinced that this was a case of catalepsy, and resorted to active remedial measures at once. Nevertheless, the young woman exhibited no signs of consciousness for over eight-and-twenty hours, at the end of which time she began to come round, and in a day or two was able to walk.

So far back as the reign of Queen Anne, a very interesting case of prolonged catalepsy, or trance, as it was then called, occurred in Bandon, and so strange and exciting were many of the incidents connected with it, that it still holds a foremost place among the stories and traditions of our town and neighbourhood.

The Reverend Thomas Goodman, precentor of Ross, died in 1681, leaving seven sons, namely—Richard, Thomas, Charles, James, John, William, and Synge; and two daughters—Susannah and Mary. Richard and Thomas, his two eldest sons, following the footsteps of their father, entered the church. Richard, who was born in 1657, became one of the vicars-choral of Cork in 1682, and the next year his brother Thomas obtained a similar appointment. They do not appear, however, to have performed their duties with even ordinary attention, for scarce had Thomas Goodman been twelve months in office, when he, as well as his brother, were admonished to be more diligent, and to attend on every Sunday and holiday in the cathedral. A graver charge still was brought against Richard, who was accused of marrying a couple without either banns or license. In 1687 Richard was licensed to the curacy of St. Michael's, and in 1692 he succeeded the Reverend Paul Duclos as vicar of Ballymodan, Bandon, where he resided until he died, in 1737. His brother Thomas also obtained a curacy in 1687, and, from 1695 until 1731, he was one of the four vicars-choral of Ross. In the latter year he died; and in his will, dated the year previously, he desired to be buried in the cathedral church of Ross if he should die there.

The Reverend Richard Goodman, vicar of Ballymodan, was a married man, and, as before stated, resided in the parish. He lived in a respectable residence,—one befitting his social position,—and the site of which is now occupied by Shannon Lodge. His wife's christian

38

name was Hannah, and, from all that has reached us about her, she appears to have been a good-tempered, amiable woman, and was one with whom Mr. Goodman spent a long and happy life. Sickness at last visited the vicarage, and Mrs. Goodman fell ill. She became worse and worse. All that medical skill, and kindness, and attention could do was unavailing. She gradually sank until she died.

The sad news soon spread everywhere, and was everywhere received with regret. The well-to-do parishioners bemoaned the loss of an agreeable companion, and the poor parishioners the loss of a generous benefactor.

In two or three mornings after the occurrence of the melancholy event just referred to, groups of mourners might be seen collected about the front door. Shortly after, the bier was brought out, and on it lay the shrouded form of the vicar's wife. Taking their places in silence behind the sorrowing husband and immediate relatives of the deceased, they formed part of the mournful procession that set out on its long and tedious journey to Ross. By-and-bye one knot of sorrowers turned off at one cross-road; another moved off at the next; others stood and let the funeral pass, and then turned back. Their example was followed by another, then another and another, until at length, of those who left the vicarage in the morning, there were but few in attendance at mid-day. It was late in the evening when the funeral arrived at Ross-carbery cathedral, and the remains of the deceased lady were, with due formality, laid in the family vault of the Goodmans.

By some means or other, the sexton became aware that the deceased had a valuable diamond ring on the little finger, and thinking, probably, that as it could not any longer be of use to her, and may be of some benefit to him, he might as well become its possessor. Accordingly, early on the next morning he got up, and removing the flags which had been only temporarily placed over the mouth of the tomb until they could be properly secured the ensuing day, he was soon by the side of the corpse, endeavouring to make his own of the coveted trinket. He pulled hard. He was under no apprehension of hurting a dead body, and diamonds were rare ornaments upon those whom he consigned to dust and ashes. He tried again and again; but the ring would not stir; the unyielding flesh seemed to record its silent protest against the sacrilege. He did not come there, however, to be balked by a dead finger. As the ring would not come off the finger, he determined the finger should come off itself, and, grasping it tightly, he tried by twisting to dismember it. The body moves! He starts, and instantly drops the hand. Oh, 'twas only a motion communicated to the corpse by lifting the arm. Raising it again, he endeavours to force back the finger so as to snap it off at the joint. With a long yawn, the dead woman flings aside the grave-clothes and sits bolt upright.

"Where am I?" cried she, struggling to open her closed eyelids.

The impious thief takes to his heels, leaving his lantern behind him, and flies for his life.

In a short time Mrs. Goodman realized her strange position, and wrapping her shroud around her as well as she could, and taking the grave-digger's lantern in her hand, she hurried out of the ghastly chamber.

The church door stood conveniently open—the affrighted sexton not even waiting to close it in his flight—and crossing over to the residence of the Reverend Thomas Goodman, her husband's brother, which was just outside the church-yard, she knocked at the door. In a few minutes a head appeared out of the window, and asked:

"Who's there?"

She told who she was.

The head quickly vanished, and in a short time there was a light in every room, and the terrified inmates were dressing themselves as fast as they could. Descending in a body, some of the most courageous amongst them tremblingly undid the door fastenings, and before them stood Mrs. Goodman. Some screamed; others drew back in horror, lest the grave-clothes should touch them; even the most resolute shook in every limb.

"Don't be afraid," said she, "I'm not dead;" telling them at the same time all the particulars connected with the strange occurrence that she was acquainted with.

Being somewhat reassured, they brought her in, placed her in a warm bed, gave her a warm drink, and made her as comfortable as they could. After an hour or so she fell into a sound sleep, from which she did not awake until near midday, her brother-in-law and his servant-man keeping watch by her bedside, not yet entirely persuaded but that she who lay before them was a spirit, and that her new kindred would come and claim her at cock-crow. She awoke greatly refreshed, and after putting on suitable clothing, she came downstairs, and eat what, under the circumstances, was considered a hearty breakfast; after which she walked about the village, dined with the family at their usual hour, and in due time after supper retired for the night, and got out of bed on the following morning so fresh and strong that she resolved to set out for home. She travelled slowly, as the effects of her recent illness had not disappeared, and she did not arrive in Bandon until the homely townspeople were beginning to close their shutters and make preparations for the evening meal. Leaving her horse outside the gate, she walked into the little flower-garden in front of her husband's home. Brushing past many an old floral acquaintance, whose drooping head seemed to mourn her loss, she looked in through the little parlour window; and, as she looked closer, she perceived the familiar form of one to whom she was devotedly attached, sitting listlessly before the fire; his head was resting on his hand, and he seemed melancholy and forsaken. She tapped at the glass.

"Who can that be? 'Twas so like —— "

She taps again, and then, hurrying across, knocks at the door.

"Surely that was her knock!" Oh, God, thought he, do the dead ever ——

Trembling in every limb, and sweating at every pore, he drew back the bolt, and the dead wife was in her husband's arms.[*]

She soon explained all. Both felicitated themselves over and over

---

[*] Mr. and Mrs. Goodman were fond of relating every particular connected with this strange event.

again upon their miraculous good fortune, and, in the exuberance of
their joy, they not only forgave the sacrilegious sexton, but they absolutely drank his health.

She lived some years after, and had a son, who died at a good old
age, towards the close of last century, in Innoshannon; and such a
dissolute and dissipated fellow was he, that he was known, not as
Goodman, but as "Badman;" and there are those still living who
knew and conversed with "Badman," in his old age. A lady of our
acquaintance often saw and spoke to him. She says he used to
wear a frilled shirt and knee-breeches, and was fond of displaying a
pair of large silver buckles in his shoes. Another lady had a perfect
recollection of sitting upon his knee when a child, and of his telling
her that he was the man who was born after his mother was buried.
Before old Goodman left this world—we hope for a better—he had
spent all he had inherited from his parents, and died in poverty, leaving
a son, who had to subsist by the labour of his hands.

This man also married, and died, leaving a son, who served a part of
his time to a shoemaker in Bandon; but, before his apprenticeship was
half completed, he lent an attentive ear to the seductive wiles of a
recruiting sergeant, and, when last we heard of him, he was a private
in the Grenadier Company of Her Majesty's Sixty—— Regiment of
Foot.*

* We are aware that stories similar in some respects to what we have just detailed
are told in connection with other places. Of their truth or falsehood we know
nothing—perhaps they were all founded upon this; but that the circumstances
we have mentioned above occurred as narrated, we, as well as others who have
interested themselves in collecting all the particulars of this extraordinary case,
implicitly believe.

CORK:—Printed by FRANCIS GUY, 70, Patrick Street.

CPSIA information can be obtained at www.ICGtesting.com
Printed in the USA
245336LV00002B/68/P